INTRODUCTION TO
REGIONAL SCIENCE

WALTER ISARD
University of Pennsylvania

Prentice-Hall, Inc. Englewood Cliffs, New Jersey

Library of Congress Cataloging in Publication Data

Isard, Walter.
    Introduction to regional science.

    Includes bibliographical references.
    1. Regional planning.   I. Title.
HT391.I83   309.2'5   74-22031
ISBN 0-13-493841-0

Printed in the United States of America

10 9 8 7 6 5 4 3 2 1

Prentice-Hall International, Inc., *London*
Prentice-Hall of Australia, Pty. Ltd., *Sydney*
Prentice-Hall of Canada, Ltd., *Toronto*
Prentice-Hall of Japan, Inc., *Tokyo*
Prentice-Hall of India Private Ltd., *New Delhi*

Contents

Chapter One
INTRODUCTION AND OVERVIEW   1

What Is Regional Science?.   Relation of Regional Science to Other Fields:
What Is Different About Regional Science?.   Definition of Regional Science.
The Who of Regional Science.   The When and Where of Regional Science.
The How of Regional Science: An Overview of This Book.

List of Tables

List of Figures

Preface

This book is an introduction to the new field of Regional Science. It is designed primarily for a half-year course. However, it may be combined with other readings to serve as a text for a full-year course. All the materials and analyses are developed from scratch, so that the book can be appropriately used in freshman courses as well as courses at the sophomore and other levels. Because regional science is a new field, this book draws much material from traditional social science fields and is therefore multidisciplinary in character.

The book is written primarily for curious students in diverse fields interested in the exciting and challenging problems which regional science attacks. These cover local unemployment, growing discrepancies in per capita incomes among people in the regions of a nation and the world, the related aspects of social injustice, urban problems, problems of sparking economic development, conflict management, and environmental pollution, to name just a few. Because regional science is new and offers fresh and positive approaches, it cannot be characterized as dismal, as some of its sister social sciences have been and continue to be. I have tried in this introduction particularly to point out the places at which regional science is not only relevant but also promises to mount more effective attacks upon our current day problems.

This introduction to Regional Science is obviously aimed to serve as a text for the increasing number of students entering the field of Regional Science. It is also aimed at the large number of students who go into economics, planning and urban studies, and geography. It is clear now, given the overwhelming number and intensity of society's problems, that these students must become acquainted with the basic principles of regional science if they are to be effective in their careers—although it is equally clear that too many of the older generation in these fields have not awakened to this fact. In the case of students in geography, this text combined with readings from economic and other areas of geography should be very effective for a principles of regional science course. Similarly, this text combined with readings from the area of planning analysis and theory should be very effective for a principles of regional science course in planning and urban studies departments. Finally, in economics departments especially in the many universities which are sensitive to the problems of their cities and regions, introductory courses in economics, or regional economics, or regional science can use this book as a text when coupled with supplementary readings. I have tried to cover, in the main text and appendices to chapters 5, 6 and 10, all the necessary micro-economics which I consider essential for such introductory courses at these universities, leaving out the refinements of tradi- tional economic texts which too frequently bog down the eager student searching for relevance.

While the book was written to serve as a text for introductory courses in regional science, geography, economics, urban studies and planning, it can serve two other important uses. First, the book should be of considerable interest to the intelligent layman, concerned public official and forward-looking business- man whose education has not encompassed this new approach to the under- standing of some of our age-old problems of depressed regions and poverty, resource conflicts, urban degradation and the like. While regional science can and hopefully will lead to more effective attacks on these and other social problems, it certainly cannot do worse than economics, sociology, political sci- ence and other sister disciplines as they struggle, too often ineffectively, with these problems. The socially sensitive layman, public official, or businessman will want to read this book to broaden and deepen his base for the under- standing of these problems. He of course should be selective in his reading, omitting in the typical case such technical materials as those in the Appendices and in chapters 7, 14 and 15, as well as elementary materials, such as those on price determination in chapter 4 with which he may be familiar.

Second, where the conservative character of a university precludes the intro- duction of courses in the principles of regional science or drastic revision of existing introductory courses, many chapters of the book can be used for supple- mentary reading purposes. For example, suppose an urban or regional economics course at a conservative institution like Harvard or Yale were to use E. M. Hoover's basic work on *An Introduction to Regional Economics* as a text, Then the materials covered in chapters 9 to 18 of the present book could be effectively used as supplementary readings, since none of the materials in these chapters are in Hoover, except some in chapters 15 and 16; and in chapters 15 and 16 the basic meat—namely the linear programming approach—is not, nor is the emphasis on world regional development problems and world social welfare.

This book represents a first attempt at an introduction to regional science. The author had no past experience to draw upon, neither his nor that of others who might have attempted such a text. Therefore, it is highly likely that not all relevant materials have been included and that not all topics have been properly weighted. The author has tried to set down what he thinks are the most important topics, problems and analytical aspects of concern to regional science. Inevitably, the experience with this text book will point up desirable changes in subsequent introductory texts.

I would like to thank the Free Press (Macmillan and Co.) for permission to use Table 3.6 of my book, *Ecologic-Economic Analysis for Regional Development*; the Yale University Press for permission to use materials on page 118 and a revision of Figure 35 from *Economics of Location* by August Lösch (translated by William Woglom); the editors of *Economic Geography* to use Table 9 on page 257 of my article (with John Cumberland), "New England as a Possible Location for an Integrated Iron and Steel Works," Vol. XXVI (October, 1950); the University of Chicago Press for permission to use data on page 205 in my article, "Some Locational Factors in the Iron and Steel Industry Since the Early Nineteenth Century," *Journal of Political Economy,* Vol. LVI, June 1948; the M.I.T. Press for permission to use a redesigned figure of the Dacron A Program on page 87, to reproduce Tables, in whole or part, on pages 40–49, 90–91 and 207, and to reproduce pages 30–31 in my *Industrial Complex Analysis and Regional Development* written with E. Schooler and T. Vietorisz; the M.I.T. Press for permission to reproduce Tables on pages 207-208 and 214 from my book with Thomas Langford, *Regional Input-Output Study;* the M.I.T. Press for permission to use large parts of pages 415-19, slight modifications of Figures 4 and 5 on pages 511 and 514 respectively, and to reproduce the Table on page 395 in my book, *Methods of Regional Analysis: An Introduction to Regional Science;* the M.I.T. Press for permission to reproduce extensive materials from Chapter 4 in my book, *General Theory: Social, Political, Economic and Regional,* written with Tony E. Smith and others, and which was based on previous work with Thomas A. Reiner.

I have gained much from conversations with my associate Robert C. Douglas on historical matters, and have drawn heavily upon work of my colleague Thomas A. Reiner on the Puerto Rican experience. I have also been able to make important improvements to the manuscript on the basis of both critical and constructive comments from the reviewers Douglas Amedeo, William Beyers, Emelio Cassetti, Gerald Goldstein, and Edwin S. Mills. I am, of course, fully responsible for all statements and viewpoints.

Robbieburr Berger was of invaluable assistance in editing the final drafts of the chapters and helping me achieve whatever lucidity they have.

For efficient typing I am indebted to Joanne Moore, Rita Raymond, and particularly Rebecca Weiss, who handled the difficult task of preparing the final manuscript. Others who were helpful in diverse ways were Henry Berliner, Colin Gannon, Jerene Good, Eileen Heron, John Parr and Frank Robinson.

Finally, I am most grateful to my wife and my children for their patience and encouragement in the writing of this book and to all my students (some of whom I like to think of as my children) who have helped me study and learn about regional science.

Introduction and
Overview

WHAT IS REGIONAL SCIENCE?

Regional science is, at the time of this writing, the newest of the social sciences. Its emergence means that there are many new and old problems that have not been adequately treated by traditional social sciences. In introducing regional science and the new theories, concepts, and techniques concerned with it, many rich and fruitful areas of research will hopefully become evident. But first it is necessary to define this new discipline.

Regional science, obviously, is about *regions*. But a region is not merely an arbitrarily demarcated area; rather, it is an area that is meaningful because of one or more problems associated with it which we as regional scientists want to examine and help solve.

For example, an area described solely as being between 70 and 80 degrees longitude and 50 and 60 degrees latitude is meaningless to the regional scientist. However, it may be very meaningful to the civil engineer or natural scientist; these boundary lines may have significance in his work. In contrast, the description of the region defined around New York City by contiguous minor civil divisions having population densities of at least 150 persons per square mile is very important to the regional scientist. It contains or has associated with it many, if not all, of the social problems connected with urban life. To the civil engineer concerned with surveying or to the geologist fascinated with rock formations, this particular region may have little, if any, significance.

Of course, there are regions that have significance for both regional scientists and natural scientists. For example, when environmental problems are attacked, a river basin region such as the Delaware River system has relevance to the regional scientist, hydrologist, marine biologist, and others.

Areas that are meaningful to the regional scientist can vary greatly in size. They may be small communities or towns concerned with finding a new industrial activity to solve their unemployment problems, like Fall River, Massachusetts, or Lowell, New Hampshire, which became ghost towns in the Twenties because textile plants moved to the South in order to exploit its cheaper labor. Or they may be of greater dimensions—like the Tokyo region, where the problem is to control environmental pollution. The region may even be a subcontinental area such as South Asia, where the problem is to eliminate both grinding poverty and excessive population growth.

Regional science is also about *science.* That is, it involves study which uses scientific methods and procedures. A purely scientific study might entail a lifetime spent merely collecting and processing information pertaining to one or more meaningful areas. But this type of activity is not central to regional science, because a regional scientist likes to ask as well: Why are things as they are? And he likes to follow up this query with some hypothesis or theory to be tested, or a policy proposal relating to one or more *social* problems of his region of study. A scientific study also might involve a lifetime spent at trying to solve a technical mathematical problem thus far unsolved. Such a problem might be an analytical method for determining the point of minimum transportation cost when the market for a good exists at a location some distance from the location of two raw materials. But this purely analytical activity does not have a sufficient social problem dimension to be classified as central to regional science.

Although regional science is concerned with social problems, however, it typically does not extend much into the area of policy formulation and determination. A regional scientist is not an *activist* planner who sees the critical nature of today's problems and judges that he cannot wait longer than three months to study the problem and then start to attack it. The typical regional scientist wants to surround himself with research assistants and a computer for a long time in order to collect all the relevant information about the problem, analyze it carefully, try out some hypotheses, and finally reach some conclusions and perhaps recommendations. His findings are then passed on to key decision-makers. But, as with the economist and social scientist, this last stage may never be reached—because good hypotheses may not have been found which stand up under testing, and because the critical social problems may have changed while the study was being conducted.

In brief, regional science as a discipline concerns the careful and patient study of social problems with regional or spatial dimensions, employing diverse combinations of analytical and empirical research.

RELATION OF REGIONAL SCIENCE TO OTHER FIELDS: WHAT IS DIFFERENT ABOUT REGIONAL SCIENCE?

Regional science can also be defined by being contrasted with other social sciences. In doing so, we bear in mind that the regional scientist's region or system of regions represents to him living organisms containing numerous and diverse behaving units—political, economic, social, and cultural—whose interdependent behavior is conditioned by psychological, institutional, and other factors. He focuses on a location or a system of locations, an urban area or a system of urban areas, a transportation route or a network of transportation routes, a resource use or a system of resource uses, all of which are part of his meaningful space or region, or system of meaningful spaces or regions.

His central concerns are quite different from those of an *economist*, who at most gives peripheral attention to space and is instead primarily concerned with investment, employment, trade, balance of payments, prices, wages, interest rates, taxes, and similar dimensions of a system. The economist looks at the behavior of business enterprises, consumers, and financial and governmental institutions most frequently from a national standpoint and often from the standpoint of the international system. Unlike the economist, the regional scientist is concerned with all these topics and others only when they relate to locations, local areas, cities, and regions. He asks how the spatial setting and dimensions significantly affect the behavior of enterprises, consumers, and institutions. But like the economist, the regional scientist does pursue analysis with mathematics and models based on mathematics, and uses extensive sets of data to operate his models and test hypotheses.

The major concerns of *geography* are with the arrangement of things on the face of the earth, and with the associations of things that give character to particular places. This field has pioneered and continues to develop the use of maps (cartography) and other descriptive devices, and the concept of a region. Data-based studies of the significance of similarities and differences among places, and of the way things change at these places (that is, spatial processes in an historic setting) are central to geography. Recently, a small number of geographers interested in theory have started to look into the causes of things in a multifaceted manner more characteristic of regional scientists and economists, though still within the framework of phenomena that can be mapped and data that can be observed. But by and large, and almost by definition, pure spatial theory is removed from the central focus of geography. Thus regional science, while overlapping in a healthy manner with geography in terms of topics that are studied, does effectively complement it by adding a deep analytical thrust into locational, regional, and spatial problems and the behavior of the numerous decision-making units involved.

In *political science*, as in economics, the elements of space and the physical environment are secondary considerations. Political science focuses on the study of man's organization in diverse political bodies. Specifically, it is concerned with both the manner in which institutions of government might ideally operate and be interrelated and their actual operation and the efficiency with which they provide services. Balance of power (both within a nation and internationally), as it relates to the ways in which men control decisions and exert pressures in order to achieve their objectives, is another concern. Finally, political science deals with functions of governments—the enactment of legislation and regulations, the administration of programs, the judicial process, and the legal and constitutional restrictions on governmental power and actions. Thus, the core issues and areas of political science are quite apart from those of regional science. Yet, as we shall see, the regional scientist must be quite informed on how the political system operates and how legislation and administration can be influenced to assist in the realization of regional development goals.

Sociology studies man and his interaction with and adaptation to the physical and social environment. Its central focus, however, relates to those interactions and adaptations embodied in group processes such as family life, administrator-employee-patient relations in a hospital, or leader-follower connections in a teen-age gang. It studies the diverse roles individuals perform as members of groups, and the ways in which customs, traditions, norms, and values are established to guide the behavior of individuals within groups and their behavior with respect to members of other groups. Also, the central tendencies and qualities of groups, as well as the linkages of different groups, are examined in order to understand the way new institutions emerge and become legitimized, consensus is reached, and status is defined. It looks at power and dominance, coercion and reciprocity, the group's ability to take collective action toward goals, sanctions of deviant behavior, the allocation of the organization's resources, and other related phenomena. As in economics and political science, the physical environment and the spatial setting are peripheral to sociology's concerns. However, the importance of understanding how targets, goals, and values are set by the different social groups in different regions is critical to the regional scientist. Also critical is the knowledge of how institutions can be changed, how people can be educated to perceive regional problems more explicitly and accurately, how they can be influenced to realize their common goals or to resolve their conflicts, and how group attitudes can be changed.

Anthropology, too, has placed considerable weight on the mutual interactions of the environment and man. Physical anthropology is concerned with the biological features of human beings and with the physical environment within which they exist. Cultural anthropology, looking at the past, has tried to reconstruct extinct societies and cultures, and to identify the geographic spread of peoples and cultures throughout the world. In terms of the present, it has tried to examine the language, belief systems, and other traits and patterns of existing societies and their component groups, particularly as they shape and are shaped by individual behavior. Yet on the whole, anthropology has been concerned with historical rather than intensive current analysis, and with description and explanation of the similarities and differences among human ethnic groups. A basic technique has been field study by observation and participation, as well as verbal interviews of groups. So its emphasis tends to be qualitative rather than quantitative. Also, perhaps because it seeks to understand the totality of man—and must thereby interrelate materials from the entire range of the social sciences and many physical sciences—it does not and in the future is not likely to attack the interdependent economic, social, and political structures of a regional body with the depth, both in empirical and theoretical analysis, for which we strive. Nor is it able to develop policy models for attacking social problems, as regional science must do.

DEFINITION OF REGIONAL SCIENCE

With this background, we can set down a variety of definitions of regional science.

1. Regional science is the study of a meaningful region (or system of regions) as a dynamic organism.

2. Regional science is the synthesized (integrated) analysis of the political, economic, sociological, cultural, and psychological factors affecting the development of a meaningful region or system of regions.

3. Regional science is the comprehensive study of a meaningful region or system of regions in all its key economic, political, social, cultural, and psychological aspects.

4. Regional science is the study of the space-time development of society and its people in all their social, economic, political, and psychological dimensions.

5. Regional science is the study of the diverse organizational and institutional structures of society as they govern the behavior and spatial distribution of population and economic activity.

6. Regional science is the study of all kinds of spatial processes over time as they pertain to people's habitation of the various parts of the world.

7. Regional science is the analytical study of the development over time of meaningful spaces, such as, for example, urban areas, regions, districts, river basins, and subcontinental masses.

8. Regional science aims to identify and expose simple, basic principles of spatial organization—principles that govern equilibrium and organizational structure and relate to efficiency, equity, and social welfare.

9. Regional science studies systems of places, locations, cities, urban regions, and world regions; and patterns of human settlements, industry and economic activity, jobs, income generation and receipts, and resource use, all in the setting of the physical environment.

10. Regional science is a synthesis of the art of planning and management with the science of spatial systems.

11. Regional science is the study of spatial conflicts among behaving units and the methods for analyzing and resolving these conflicts.

12. Regional science is the systematic study of the time-space patterns of systems and the ways in which social problems associated with these patterns can be effectively attacked and resolved.

13. Regional science is the study of the joint interaction of social, political, and economic behaving units and the physical environment within meaningful regions and systems of regions.

It is clear from the diversity of definitions that no single one can be considered the best or most complete. Each researcher and student will need to develop or synthesize his own definition after having read this book and other studies.

THE WHO OF REGIONAL SCIENCE

A field like regional science is often defined by what regional scientists do. Where have they come from? How did they become involved?

Because regional science developed as a field because other social sciences neglected important analytical approaches to urban-regional problems, and because it covers an uncultivated area intermediate between the cores and boundaries of several disciplines, it is to be expected that it would be populated and invaded by concerned people from all the bordering fields. Thus we have in the regional science field geographers who find it worthwhile to develop pure theory with extensive use of mathematics and to engage in the construction of large-scale models with considerable analytical content and employing extensive sets of data. We have in our group economists who have become concerned in more than a trifling manner with urban and regional problems and who want to dig into them with more than the tools that economics provides. We have in our midst planners who recognize the shortcomings of their many hastily constructed plans and actions, and who want to root their proposals in more solid ground. We also have architects who want to develop physical designs that are more consistent with the behavioral patterns and demands of people within specific areas. We have engineers who want to design projects and systems of facilities more in line with the needs of people and institutions as they are clustered in urban and regional areas. We have sociologists who want to go beyond the narrow traditional confines of group analysis, and bring into their thinking important economic factors as they interplay in urban-regional complexes. We have political scientists who want to go beyond analyses of political group behavior and the system and bring into their framework important urban-regional economic factors. We have psychologists interested in both individual and mass behavior within urban and regional settings. We have anthropologists who find it fascinating and relevant to introduce abstract theorizing in their thinking about cultures in the different territorial areas in both advanced and backward parts of the world. We have lawyers who have become concerned in a deep, humanistic sense with social justice, particularly for the poor in urban and rural slums, and who seek ways to reinterpret and change the law to preclude human deprivation.

In short, we are a melting pot of numerous social scientists, natural scientists, "pure" scientists, and professionals who want to be hard at work on critical social problems.

THE WHEN AND WHERE OF REGIONAL SCIENCE.

Regional science had its beginnings in the late 1940s, when there was dissatisfaction with the low level of regional economic analysis and a strong urge to upgrade it. Concerned regional economists often convened at the annual meetings of the American Economics Association. Gradually, their analyses improved in quality and relevance with regard to social problems. Interested scholars from planning and geography soon joined in the discussions. Then came sociologists, political scientists, engineers, and lawyers. In time, they outnumbered the pure regional economists. Accordingly, in 1954 the Regional Science Association was formed and held its first independent meetings; since then annual meetings have taken place. With the growth of interest in other parts of the world, it became desirable and feasible in 1961 to institute annual European meetings, and most recently biennial meetings covering the vast Pacific Region. At the same time, various sections of the Regional Science Association have been formed: the French section, the Scandinavian (later Nordic) section, the Japanese section, the British section, the Hungarian section, the German section, the Italian section, the Argentine section, and most recently (1973) the Israeli and the Multilingual Northwest Europe sections. In North America there are four sections: the Western, the Midcontinent, the Southern, and the Northeastern. As of 1974, there are about twenty serials (journals) in the field, several Ph.D. programs, and several study series of books and monographs devoted to the subject supported by established publishing houses. In short, regional science now has all the accoutrements of a well-established social science field. It also has the distinct advantage of having only a handful or so of its active members and leaders in their fifties, more in their forties, and thousands in their thirties and twenties; the last have been subject to rigorous scientific analysis and creative imaginative thought in their training and are likely to keep the field high up among the most active and fruitful scientific disciplines.

THE HOW OF REGIONAL SCIENCE: AN OVERVIEW OF THIS BOOK

The *how* of regional science really involves an overview of this book. So let us summarize each chapter in turn.

In Chapter 2, we discuss what we want to know about the city and region. What are its interesting and critical features? On which of its problems do we wish to concentrate? These questions determine the kinds of data we want to collect. For example, most people are interested in jobs. So we want to know what kinds of jobs are currently offered, how they are related to different kinds of economic activities, and what are the prospects for more or fewer jobs of different types.

Chapter 3 is also concerned with the kinds of things we want to know about regions. We want to know about differences in per capita incomes between developed and underdeveloped regions and between ghetto and nonghetto areas. We want to know about differences in educational levels of inhabitants and in resources with which they are able to work. We are interested in the spatial distributions of population and resources, and the kinds of problems associated with these distributions. We are also interested in the travel patterns of different kinds of people, particularly their journey-to-work patterns, for this tells us, for instance, about who works where, and the forms of discrimination that are practiced. We also want to know the extent to which the people who make the basic decisions are aware and sensitive to the problems of a region.

Having found out what we are interested in and what are the relevant kinds of data we need, we begin analysis in Chapter 4. We must examine the way in which prices and wages are determined. Unless we know how these prices and wages are set, we cannot explain why differences in prices and wages in regions exist. Nor can we explain why, as a result, industries like to locate in some regions and not in others; and therefore provide jobs in some regions and not in others. But it is not enough to determine how prices and wages are set. We must go beyond this and determine the cost of operating different kinds of establishments—whether private, such as oil refineries, or public, such as hospitals. Here we must understand the forces that determine these costs. Then we can contrast these costs with revenues or with estimated social benefits to judge whether or not to locate an enterprise or facility in a region or to expand or contract an existing one. The analysis of cost factors is taken up in Chapter 5.

Having analyzed prices and costs, we move on in Chapter 6 to compare different regions and subareas in terms of their potential for attracting industry.

Here we must do comparative cost analysis. We see how favorable labor cost, energy cost, and transport locations attract industries and unfavorable ones repel them. But on further examination we find that the calculation of the full costs and benefits is difficult. There are benefits and costs in an enterprise's operations which depend on how many other industries are at a location, or how big an urban area it is located in. For example, in larger urban areas, there may be better schools and lower fuel costs than in smaller areas. At the same time, there may be higher rents and more traffic congestion. Thus, we find that there are many complex linkages (industrial, commerical, and others) that must be examined. This we do in Chapter 7, using input-output tables, with reference to planning regional development and new towns.

Because jobs in many subareas and regions are dependent upon export trade, we must examine the trade and other economic interconnections between subareas in metropolitan regions, the regions within a nation, or diverse parts of the world. We want to know when and why trade takes place. At the same time, because colonies are often a source of raw materials and because trade with them is often controlled by a few related enterprises, we wish to know to what extent monopolistic exploitation has been present and is responsible for the underdevelopment of many of these colonies. We also want to study human migration from one region to another, and find out why this phenomenon has not eliminated per capita income differences. We want to know something about goods and people movements within metropolitan regions, particularly as they relate to pollution and the problem of environmental management. Finally, we want to examine the causes of capital flows and impediments to the flow of ideas and knowledge among different regions. All these areas of analysis are considered in Chapter 8.

It is not enough to analyze relevant information on prices and costs, on the benefits and disadvantages of an urban location, and on economic gains from trade in order to project or determine whether or not a key decision will be made. This is so because there is much uncertainty in the world around us. An investor making a decision has to ask: What is the probability that the next year will see a depression, a recession, or an upswing in economic conditions? In seeking answers to such questions, we find that the attitude of a decision maker plays a key role. If he is a conservative banker and interested only in sure things, any small likelihood that analysts might assign to a depression state of affairs will keep him from making any new investment. Not so for the optimist who finds the world benevolent. Likewise, the policy taken by a key political leader—given the probability that he associates with the breakdown in the international monetary system, or with new local wars, or with a change in the party in office—is influenced by his attitude and willingness to bear risk. Because we often want to influence the decision to be taken by a key figure, we must dig into the attitude variable, as we do in Chapter 9.

But social problems are often much more complex. They exist because the goals and actions of one interest group are different from those of another. That is, conflicts exist. We are all too familiar with the conflicts between in-groups (majority groups) and out-groups (minority groups). If we are going to do something about social problems, we must know the causes of conflicts. We are concerned not only with the easily discernible conflicts—like those between the whites and blacks in U.S. society, or Protestants and Catholics of Northern Ireland—but also the conflict between the individual and society. For example, we have conflicts when each individual of a large population takes an action which by itself has a negligible influence upon social welfare, but where all the individual actions taken together have a major negative influence on social welfare. We find this to be particularly relevant for explaining slum areas and environmental degradation. Having studied the causes of conflict in Chapter 10, we then ask: What kind of guiding principles and cooperative procedures can be evolved to help manage and resolve conflicts? This we do in Chapter 11.

Now, up to Chapter 11 we talk about behaving units—a small firm, or an individual, or an industrial entrepreneur, or a political leader—who may have complex personalities but who are, relatively speaking, simple units. In contrast, all around us stand a number of complex organizations—ITT (International Telephone & Telegraph), GM (General Motors), GE (General Electric), Mitshubishi, Unilever and other multinational corporations, as well as huge national corporations whose decisions have major implications for social and individual welfare. To understand their decisions we must probe still more deeply. We must ask why these organizations exist, when and where they exist, and how they have grown and changed. What kinds of personalities are involved in them? Again, we often want to have this information not only to understand their behavior but also to influence it in directions we consider desirable.

Of course one of the big organizations in society is government itself, with which is associated the *public sector*. Like ITT and multinationals, this organization has been growing very rapidly. In Chapter 13, we look at its various functions and why they exist. We know that there has been a tremendous growth of governmental organizations of all sorts—from the local governments to state, metropolitan, national, and world units. In large part this growth has been in response to the need to provide various social welfare programs and to reduce social injustice. But why should the public sector be involved? Further, how large should the public sector be at the local, regional, national, and world level? Where is it going?

It has become increasingly evident that a major function of the public sector is to manage the environment. We know that we cannot leave this problem up to individuals or business enterprises acting in their own narrow self-interest. We need to spell out, in terms of a system of environmental regions, the specifics of the environmental problem and the conflict that exists between economic growth and maintaining environmental quality. We need to integrate these specifics into our thinking, as we begin to do in Chapter 14.

Against the background of Chapter 14, we can better probe the problem of regional development, economic and noneconomic, as it is related to social welfare. We need to view it in terms of the limited resources available for use. We need to evaluate different alternatives for employing these resources. We also need to be sharper in anticipating some of the basic problems that come from development. Conflicts arise in identifying the particular path of development that should be pursued because regions and nations differ over basic values to govern decision making. Should the institution of private property prevail along with freedom of economic enterprise and of the individual to pursue his own self interest? Conflicts arise among regions and nations over basic goals to pursue.

Should they seek per capita income equalization, land reform, the maximization of gross national product, or some combination of these? Conflicts also arise over specific programs to achieve goals. Should there be major construction of low-income housing, or new transport routes, or more educational facilities? Often these conflicts occur in decision-making situations wherein political leaders from different regions form coalitions. The conflict resolution problem and the possible cooperative procedures proposed for use must embody this additional consideration.

On a number of occasions the analyst or planner is faced with making a decision concerning investments for the development of a region. Obviously she uses the best data, theories, and techniques she has at her disposal, and does the best she can. Surely she can expect that new problems, which she was not able to foresee, will emerge with development. This point comes up clearly in Chapter 17. There we examine Puerto Rico as an actual experience in development. The author and his associates were involved in it, and they developed an industrial complex approach to identify new economic opportunities for the region. We describe what went on, what we had hoped for, and what resulted. We point out the number of new problems (social, economic, and political) that did emerge with successful economic development. We state the lessons learned for use by the next generation of development planners.

Finally, in Chapter 18 we look at the world situation. We observe our limited capacity to handle the major environmental problems that will emerge and the major unrest that will be associated with discrepancies among regions in per capita incomes, which have been constantly increasing and which we expect to increase still further. We look at some of the benefits and costs of a new world organization in terms of managing and coordinating development in the several world regions—economic, political, and social. Its possible tasks and functions are examined, and in particular its taxing and income redistribution powers with respect to development programs are considered.

Against the background of this overview, we turn to the main text. We hope in this *Introduction to Regional Science* to be able to achieve a rounded inquiry into the subject and to point up effectively the numerous social problems that a scholar trained in regional science can fruitfully attack.

Chapter

2

The City and Region: Some Description

INTRODUCTION

As indicated in Chapter 1, a true regional scientist is concerned with acquiring knowledge. First, he wants to satisfy his curiosity and eagerness to understand phenomena; second, he wants to attack social problems. Hence, although he may want to study the city and region abstractly and as an intellectual pursuit, he should also seek to obtain knowledge that leads to wiser policies helping to mitigate urban and regional problems. It necessarily follows that before a scholar or practitioner can do anything about a pressing social problem, he should know at least something about his subject matter. It is foolish to prescribe policy for a city or region when one does not have some knowledge about the key properties or characteristics of that city or region. Hence, in this chapter we want to say something about possible relevant properties of a city or region, and how we can efficiently use data that we may accumulate about these properties.

Let us begin with some definition, however crude, of the city or region. Any definition is dependent on the particular problem with which we are concerned. We may define an area in terms of a political unit such as the city of Philadelphia, the metropolitan region of Philadelphia, or the state of Pennsylvania—that is, in terms of definite boundaries of the political unit. Or, if our problem is to attack transportation congestion in the Philadelphia region, we must look beyond political boundaries and concentrate on sites from which goods are shipped (factories, warehouses, terminals) and sites to which they are shipped (shops, institutions, houses, processing points). For this problem we must pay great attention to the places (primarily residences of population) from which different kinds of personal trips (by auto, rail, mass transit, airplane) originate, and the places (sites of employment, entertainment, religious worship, etc.) at which they terminate. The current economic battles between the suburbs and central cities over who should bear the financial responsibilities for various city services, such as the maintenance of streets and police protection, remind us vividly that transportation patterns, the demand for transportation facilities, and the consumption of their services do not follow political boundaries. Nor do the spread of crime, disease, air and water pollutants, and urban tension and insecurity. Consequently, when we dig into an urban problem, we often confront the prior research problem of identifying the proper geographic area for study and the collection of data. We must confront this problem even for exceedingly complex situations such as environmental management. Here, for example, watersheds seem to have little or no relation to the highly variable (volatile) airsheds that crisscross watersheds in all sorts of ways. Yet the way we manage airsheds greatly influences the quality of water to which we are exposed, and vice versa. Hence, watersheds, airsheds, and other elements of the environment must be jointly managed, and to do so requires that a nation like the United States be divided into regions.

For the moment, assume that the region of study for a particular problem has been prescribed for us, or can be easily determined. Or suppose it is delineated because of a deadline that existed as of one minute ago, which forced us to immediately define our regions. We know that when we face difficult social problems we cannot afford the luxury of spending an unlimited amount of time collecting data, running models, and speculating about what the most appropriate region or set of regions should be. In dealing with such problems as transportation regulation, educational subsidization, assistance to urban areas in their poverty programs, and flood and other emergency relief administration, at some point the Secretary of Transportation, or the Secretary of Health, Education and Welfare, or even we must make a decision. And we must live with that decision (usually uncomfortably) for some years to come. So assume that in our role as right-hand man to some cabinet secretary, we have met the deadline date and have defined our regions. To hedge against criticism, we may say that the set of regions we have identified represents the best we can do at the moment, given the pressures of the time; and that we intend to look at this question again later (when we have more time) and do a better job. We should note that in practice, that "later" rarely comes; once we begin with a set of regions we find that diverse inflexibilities crop up and accumulate over time. It becomes increasingly difficult to change that set. We are usually "stuck" with that which we began.

RELEVANT PROPERTIES OF CITIES AND REGIONS

Suppose one of the regions that has been sliced out is the eight-county Philadelphia Standard Metropolitan Statistical Area (SMSA). What do we want to know about it? Incidentally, many analysts will object to asking this question so soon. How can you start collecting information for a regional study when you have not discussed the *concept* of a city or region? You are putting the cart before the horse.

However, we must recognize that we have a circle of interdependence, of cause and effect—a chicken and egg problem. Our concept of a meaningful region, as we have already suggested, depends upon the particular social problem with which we are concerned. This in turn depends upon aspects and features of social and individual living which we consider important. We might argue that we cannot properly define the concept of a region (which involves a theory) until we have decided on those aspects of social and individual living that are of primary concern. In this case, we cut the circle of interdependence at the point where we begin with facts, the relevant aspects or properties of social and individual living as we see them. Of course, it is equally valid to cut the circle at the concept of a region, a theoretical notion, which has come down to us from the many good studies of the past, and examine problems for geographic areas that conform to this concept (inherited theory). We choose not to do so. We choose to let our perception of the facts help determine our theory of what is a region. Thus when we must present data on regions, we generally do so for a given administrative region, such as the Philadelphia SMSA. In some cases, we let the facts prescribe new regions, when existing areas are inadequately defined for the problem.

In order to learn about relevant properties of cities and regions, it is an orthodox procedure to consult standard works and encyclopedias. We might go, for example, to standard geography, sociology, economics, political science texts, the *Encyclopedia Brittanica,* the *International Encyclopedia of the Social Sciences,* etc. But we already know that these standard works are biased in the direction of perpetuating the old and accepted ways of thinking, which may or may not have proved to be workable in the eighteenth and nineteenth centuries and the pro World War II era. As standard sources, they have the objective, which is quite appropriate, of preserving their ways of thinking, their methods and tools, and their views on relevant properties of cities and regions. However, our world has changed radically since the pre–World War II era. Many of us seriously question the validity of our traditional approaches and social science disciplines. Thus, it seems highly desirable to avoid, if possible, *thought* pollution by tradition—which so easily and often influences us. To avoid this bias, I have sought information from my students, particularly college freshmen and high school seniors, who have had less time to be exposed to biases through the usual socialization and education processes (though they too are not free of bias). I have asked them to put down what they consider to be the key properties of cities and regions. To see if other key properties should be added, I have then consulted standard works and my own store of knowledge and experience (reflecting, of course, the biases of the highly ethnically and racially discriminating society of pre–World War II, during which I received my basic training). Hopefully, having two different sources of information will provide a more balanced base.

In response to questioning, my students have invariably placed at the head of the list properties with reference to diverse social phenomena, and at the bottom physical properties like geographic position (latitude and longitude), temperature, rainfall, soil characteristics, and mineral resources—data that were considered fundamental and of first priority in urban-regional study in previous generations. Their response explains the shock of a professor of geography who found that 95 percent of the students in his class did not know where Kuwait is. Rather than considering its geographic location of primary importance, the students were more interested in knowing who gets what and how much in Kuwait.

Who controls? How many are economically, politically and otherwise subjugated? Who is happy?

To come back home, consider the youth who sees close at hand the tremendous amount of poverty, crime, and other dysfunctional aspects of U.S. society—and paradoxically the emotional misery, insecurity and spiritual deprivation of affluence. When a professor of geography points out to him the tremendously abundant mineral resource endowment of the United States, his reaction might be: "So what!" To him, this blessing of rich mineral resources is of second or third-order importance, if not irrelevant. However, as the analyses in subsequent chapters will indicate there is indeed a critically important link between mineral resources and the state of affairs that he perceives.

A set of properties which students frequently cite as the most important for a city or region relates to its population. What is its ethnic background, racial composition, size distribution by families, income distribution by households, age-sex structure, and educational level (for example, the percent who have finished college, secondary school, and primary school)? Here the population censuses and other governmental publications provide very useful information. Other data, such as ownership of durable goods, the concentration of wealth among a population, and crime rates can also be significant for study and are often available.

Additionally, students want to know something about the physical structures in the city or region. What is its stock of housing, by size and type of unit, by age, and by rent class? Here the census of housing may be helpful. They want to know something about the industrial structure of the city, its kinds of industry, and the different types of jobs available. Here industrial directories and censuses of employment may be useful. They wish to know something about its schools, cultural facilities and traditions, transportation network, sewerage systems, commercial establishments, and vacant areas. Here data collected by planning authorities and other groups may be useful.

Students also assign considerable significance to unemployment rates, number on welfare, prospects for growth of industry and employment for the unskilled, the stability (cyclical) of the city's or region's economy, and its vulnerability to cutbacks in military expenditures. What is the likelihood that a city may become an old-industry town with high rates of unemployment? This type of information they consider critical, particularly for societies in which only a small fraction of the population may be considered affluent. In most of the urban and rural populations of the world, poverty barely permits people to survive, let alone live in a reasonably satisfactory way.

One can go on unendingly and list the properties that students have suggested as pertinent. But, as already suggested, topography, soil, vegetation, climate, hydrology, and so forth are far down on their list, and employment, job prospects, and physical well-being are high.

JOBS AND ADEQUATE INCOME

Hence, let us begin our urban and regional analysis by focusing upon jobs, employment, and income—current and in prospect. Such a beginning is appropriate at least for the U.S. society, in which economic factors play a dominant role in determining not only the available amount of food, clothing, shelter, and general health but also the social, political, and religious status ascribed to the different population elements.

We are all aware of the significance of the Rockefeller millions for Nelson Rockefeller's political position, or the Kennedy millions for the political success of the Kennedy clan. We are also aware of how the social status of the Vanderbilts, Astors, Drexels, and Biddles has been closely linked to their wealth. So, although emerging values may suggest that the tie between dollars on the one hand and political power, social status, and even religious prestige on the other should and may be considerably weakened in future decades, this is yet to be realized and factually observed. It seems safe to predict that even for those who possess small amounts of income and wealth, contributions to religious causes will account for much of the c-rectitude and c-respect[1] received from religious institutions. Contributions to political parties, however modest, will still be exchanged for c-power (political influence); and the vote or right to exercise political power will still be traded for dollars in "behind-the-scene" markets.

Let us take a hard look at jobs and unemployment, and prospects. Here we have good data, provided by the Bureau of Labor Statistics and other government agencies. We can record total jobs or total unemployment in a city. We can break down these jobs by broad divisions of industries, such as agriculture, manufacturing, construction, service trades, and government. Next, for each broad division, we can subdivide into jobs by type of industry: aircraft, textiles, iron and steel, chemicals, furniture, aluminum, and so forth. We can even obtain employment by segments of industries. For example, employment in the aircraft industry can be broken down into employment in helicopter, military airplane, and commerical aircraft production. Moreover, we can often break down jobs by skilled, unskilled, and professional class, and by specific occupations. So we have a wealth of data on jobs and employment. But we want to make the data talk; and to do so we need to link these and other data systematically in order to help in the analysis.

To illustrate what we mean by making the data talk, let us pose some questions of basic interest to various social scientists and students. Suppose we wish to investigate the impact of a cutback in military expenditures. We may be Marxists who claim that military expenditures are required in a capitalist economy to avoid unemployment. Or we may be politicians seeking votes and therefore concerned with the possibility of shifting funds spent on aircraft carriers to programs for providing housing, transportation, and education for our constituency. We may be Quaker idealists concerned with eliminating all forms of military expenditures and devoting resources to improving the lot of mankind. Or we may be any of a host of other kinds of people. In any case, if we are interested in a region such as the Philadelphia SMSA, it is not sufficient for analysis to obtain data just on employment at the Philadelphia Navy Yard, the Frankford Arsenal in Northeast Philadelphia, and other plants producing military items. Clearly the income that Navy Yard employees receive is largely spent in the

---

[1]The terms c-rectitude and c-respect are Isard inventions. They stand for non-economic commodities (*c* being an abbreviation for the word commodity), which are defined in Isard et al., *General Theory: Social, Political, Economic and Regional* (Cambridge: MIT Press, 1969), pp. 565–86.

city. Therefore any decrease in the number of Navy Yard employees and thus their income adversely affects the volume of sales and the numbers employed in retail stores in the Philadelphia region. Clearly, too, the Navy Yard buys many goods from Philadelphia firms. Any cutback in Navy Yard expenditures will lead to cutbacks in purchases from Philadelphia firms, and perhaps to cutbacks of employment in these firms, etc. So we must consider more than the direct impact of cutbacks. We must consider as well the indirect impacts not only of the sort described but also of a more subtle nature, such as the cutbacks in orders from Philadelphia firms by retail shops whose sales have fallen because lower wages were paid out by the Navy Yard subsequent to the Navy Yard cutbacks. Clearly then, we want to get data on all kinds of linkages between different economic units, between households and retailers, and in general between all kinds of buyers (demanders) and sellers (suppliers) in our city or region. It is extremely important to have these data reflecting all the interdependencies of economic activities before we start to advance our particular panacea or pet theory for managing the local economy.

THE INPUT-OUTPUT TABLE: A CHECKERBOARD DESCRIPTION OF A REGION'S ECONOMY

When we begin to study the problems of the Philadelphia region, we are somewhat more fortunate than scholars in most other metropolitan regions. We have much more extensive data on linkages in Philadelphia. We have available a rather elaborate checkerboard table of the Philadelphia economy, which in the technical jargon of economists is called an input-output table. This table has 496 rows and 496 columns and was developed from the data obtained from interviewing thousands of firms and other economic and government units and from diverse published sources. In essence, it provides us with a fine, detailed snapshot of the Philadelphia economy. It also proves useful, as we shall show later, for providing insights into critical dimensions of social problems.

Now what is the idea behind a checkerboard table? To begin to answer this question we might ask: What would be an ideal form of census of economic activity? First, we want data on employment in each firm (or industry) and on total output, physical and dollar value. Then, we want data on each firm's expenditures—that is, on the purchases of each type of good—where the data tells us the firm from which each item was purchased. We also want data on the products each firm sold to every other firm and to each government unit, household, and exporter. With such data, we can build a nice checkerboard table.

But as soon as we start setting up the table we find ourselves overwhelmed by the sheer quantity of data we have. There are thousands of firms in the Philadelphia region. In 1959, there were 43,393 in the retail trade sector alone. Hence, we need to aggregate the data. That is, we need to condense the amount of data we have by adding and averaging. A typical way to aggregate data is to set down a classification of industries (or sectors) and assign each firm to an industry. Thus, Gimbels would be assigned to the department store subsector of the retail trade sector, U.S. Steel Corporation would be assigned to the iron and steel sector, the Girard Bank to the financial sector, the University of Pennsylvania to the education sector, and so forth. In this way we can aggregate the data by firms to get data by sectors or industries. Now this, of course, raises the question of how to get an appropriate set or classification of sectors suitable to the problems we wish to attack. We do not wish here to enter into a discussion of this and many other related problems. However we must state that what is a suitable classification too often depends on the pet theory of the investigator and how he perceives what is important in social problems.

For the moment, let us examine a classification of sectors that has been developed by the U.S. Department of Commerce—namely, the Standard Industrial Classification (SIC). This set has been found to be fairly acceptable for input-output studies, although it clearly reflects all the biases of the Establishment. Now if we use that classification of sectors we can get a notion of what the Philadelphia economy looks like, at least to the Establishment. For example, we present in Table 2.1 a condensed snapshot of the Philadelphia economy in 1968 for forty-two different sectors. (For the moment, ignore the last six rows and the last two columns). We list by rows the sectors or industries into which the economy can be broken down. We also list these sectors in the same order along the columns. For example, the first sector is agriculture, forestry, and fisheries, the second is food products, the third is textile products, the fourth is apparel, and so forth. The 42 by 42 table that corresponds to these sectors is our checkerboard, and is called the structural matrix.

In the households sector, row 41, we include all families, whether one-person or many-person, whether low-income, middle-income, or high-income, whether black or white, and so on. At a later time we may wish to break this sector into its basic parts, and to consider each part as a sector in its own right.

The last sector is labeled "unallocated." Let us be frank. No matter how good a census one takes, no matter how complete a survey one conducts, no matter how fine a classification of sectors one develops, there will always be discrepancies and errors. There is no such thing as a perfect input-output table. There is no such thing as a perfect set of data when many behaving units (individuals and organizations) are involved. We therefore need to have both a row and a column in which to put fictitious numbers to achieve consistency and to eliminate discrepancy. Thus we talk of the fictitious or dummy sector—the unallocated sector. Each cell of the unallocated row indicates the extent to which we have not been able to account for all the inputs that go into the production of the corresponding sector at the head of the column. Each cell in the unallocated column indicates the extent to which we have not been able to account for the allocation among all consumers of the total output of the sector corresponding to the row of that cell.

Already, we have discussed some of the data that could go into the table; namely the average number of jobs per year by industry (sector). We could put these data in the households row of the table so that for each column the recorded item would state the average number of jobs that are provided by the industry at the head of the column; or we could state the data in terms of average number of man-hours of labor used by each industry. Now, for the Soviet Union or a socialist economy which sets up its tables in terms of physical units of commodities (tons, pounds, ton-miles, etc.) and services (man-hours etc.), these data might be satisfactory. But for the United States, the federal government (Washington) has found it more useful to list the wages and salaries (and other income) that

Table 2.1 Philadelphia Region Input-Output Flows Table, 1968
(Based on 1959 Coefficients Partly Updated to 1968, and 1968 Sector Outputs in Millions of 1968 Dollars)

PURCHASING SECTOR columns:
1. Agriculture, Fisheries
2. Food Processing & Kindred Prod.
3. Textile Mill Prod.
4. Apparel
5. Lumber & Wood Prod.
6. Furniture & Fixtures
7. Paper & Allied Prod.
8. Printing & Publishing
9. Chemicals & Chemical Prod.
10. Petroleum Refining & Prod.
11. Rubber & Misc. Plastic Prod.
12. Leather & Leather Prod.
13. Stone, Clay, & Glass Prod.
14. Primary Metals
15. Fabricated Metal Prod.
16. Machinery (excl. Electric)
17. Electric Machinery
18. Motor Vehicles
19. Misc. Manufacturing
20. Prof. & Scientific Equip.

PRODUCING SECTOR	1	2	3	4	5	6	7	8	9	10	11	12	13	14	15	16	17	18	19	20
1. Agriculture, Fisheries	61	382	20	1	*	–	–	–	*	–	28	*	*	*	–	–	–	–	10	–
2. Food Processing & Kindred Prod.	14	668	*	*	–	–	1	–	20	1	–	6	*	–	–	11	–	–	8	–
3. Textile Mill Prod.	*	*	166	248	–	2	2	1	12	–	13	1	1	*	*	*	1	*	2	2
4. Apparel	*	*	–	40	–	–	*	–	*	–	–	–	1	–	–	*	–	–	*	–
5. Lumber & Wood Prod.	1	1	*	*	19	9	*	*	*	–	*	*	2	2	4	3	2	9	17	*
6. Furniture & Fixtures	–	--	–	–	*	4	–	–	–	–	–	–	–	–	–	*	27	2	–	*
7. Paper & Allied Prod.	*	106	5	7	3	4	205	157	36	16	6	*	7	1	12	3	15	3	11	4
8. Printing & Publishing	*	10	*	1	1	*	2	46	16	2	1	*	1	1	1	6	4	11	2	1
9. Chemicals & Chemical Prod.	3	12	16	1	2	4	21	11	351	59	51	1	10	10	25	3	11	4	19	6
10. Petroleum Refining & Prod.	7	10	3	1	*	*	5	1	34	119	1	*	6	23	4	8	2	2	2	1
11. Rubber & Misc. Plastic Prod.	*	*	*	1	*	2	11	*	3	1	3	*	1	*	8	5	15	10	3	2
12. Leather & Leather Prod.	--	–	*	1	–	*	–	*	–	–	*	5	–	–	–	*	–	–	*	*
13. Stone, Clay, & Glass Prod.	*	17	2	–	1	1	–	–	19	7	*	–	39	23	3	4	19	4	15	2
14. Primary Metals	–	*	*	*	*	25	1	4	3	7	3	*	7	186	266	253	105	168	17	29
15. Fabricated Metal Prod.	1	46	*	1	7	9	*	1	16	53	*		4	2	15	67	42	41	5	7
16. Machinery (excl. Electric)	1	*	*	*	*	*	*	7	2	*	1	*	*	20	6	82	17	92	8	7
17. Electric Machinery	–	*	–	–	1	–	*	–	*	–	–	–	*	*	*	78	317	38	2	27
18. Motor Vehicles	*	*	–	–	–	–	–	*	–	3	–	–	–	–	–	–	1	1	100	–
19. Misc. Manufacturing	*	*	–	4	6	*	*	*	2	–	–	*	1	–	–	–	*	*	4	2
20. Professional & Scientific Equip.	–	*	–	–	–	–	*	–	2	–	–	–	–	–	2	2	6	4	*	10
21. Coal, Gas & Electric Power	1	18	5	4	1	2	12	4	28	31	4	*	7	24	8	12	10	7	3	2
22. Transportation	–	*	–	–	–	–	–	*	–	–	–	–	–	–	–	*	–	–	–	–
23. Wholesale Trade	–	–	1	–	*	–	*	–	3	–	*	–	*	30	3	*	–	–	–	–
24. Retail Trade (excl. Eating Places)	–	–	–	–	–	–	–	–	–	–	–	–	–	–	–	–	–	–	–	–
25. Communications	1	7	2	3	*	1	2	11	8	3	2	*	1	5	4	8	6	4	2	2
26. Finance & Insurance	1	16	6	8	1	1	6	7	19	15	3	*	4	12	7	9	6	4	3	2
27. Real Estate & Rentals	*	1	*	1	*	*	*	1	1	*	*	*	*	*	*	1	1	*	*	*
28. Business Serv. (incl. Advertising)	2	68	7	9	*	2	8	35	135	38	11	1	5	13	10	15	25	15	6	4
29. Hotel, Personal, & Repair Serv.	1	2	2	3	*	*	1	1	1	–	1	*	1	2	1	2	2	*	1	*
30. Automobile Repair	*	13	*	*	1	*	1	*	2	2	*	*	1	1	1	1	*	*	*	*
31. Private Household Serv.	–	–	–	–	–	–	–	–	–	–	–	–	–	–	–	–	–	–	–	–
32. Amusement & Recreational Serv.	–	–	*	*	*	*	*	*	*	*	–	*	*	*	*	*	*	*	*	*
33. Eating & Drinking Places	–	–	–	–	–	–	–	–	–	–	–	–	–	–	–	–	–	–	–	–
34. Misc. Industries	*	*	–	–	–	–	–	–	*	8	–	–	14	1	*	*	–	–	1	–
35. Nonprofit Orgs.	*	*	–	–	–	–	*	–	–	–	–	–	–	–	–	*	–	–	–	–
36. Construction	2	11	*	1	*	*	3	3	2	3	*	*	*	9	1	3	2	2	1	*
37. Research & Development	–	*	*	–	–	–	*	–	3	1	–	–	*	1	*	2	*	1	*	*
38. Medical, Health, & Hospital Serv.	*	–	–	–	–	–	–	–	–	–	–	–	–	–	–	–	–	–	–	–
39. Elem., Sec., & Higher Educ.	*	–	–	–	–	–	–	–	–	–	–	–	–	–	–	–	–	–	–	–
40. Local Gov't.	3	41	10	14	1	3	11	10	25	25	15	*	5	17	12	18	29	16	4	5
41. Private Households	36	409	139	249	14	47	162	284	309	148	123	11	97	293	276	502	455	403	92	143
42. Unallocated	1	432	94	193	9	45	116	81	444	72	49	6	81	237	141	142	204	88	51	32
43. Imports (Noncompetitive)	4	155	56	14	1	3	72	19	138	735	101	*	20	215	9	22	45	10	9	7
44. Gov't Taxes—Fed. & State	4	49	12	12	1	3	29	40	108	63	19	1	11	91	22	52	50	42	8	15
45. Profits & Dividends	41	38	8	9	1	2	25	23	68	60	14	*	10	79	21	40	42	41	8	11
46. Capital Allowance	15	56	15	7	1	4	23	17	91	181	12	1	15	41	18	37	32	15	8	6
47. Scrap & Misc. Charges	–	14	9	5	*	1	18	8	30	12	5	*	3	74	11	13	20	11	3	4
Total	202	2585	583	838	67	176	740	776	1935	1663	468	35	354	1413	890	1394	1514	1148	322	331

*Less than $500,000. Figures have been rounded to nearest million. **Final Demand covers government (except local), capital formation, and gross exports.

21. Coal, Gas, & Electric Power	22. Transportation	23. Wholesale Trade	24. Retail Trade (excl. Eating)	25. Communications	26. Finance & Insurance	27. Real Estate & Rentals	28. Business Serv. (incl. Advertising)	29. Hotel, Personal, & Repair Serv.	30. Automobile Repair	31. Private Household Serv.	32. Amusement & Recreation Serv.	33. Eating & Drinking Places	34. Misc. Industries	35. Nonprofit Orgs.	36. Construction	37. Research & Development	38. Medical, Health, & Hosp. Serv.	39. Elem., Sec., & Higher Educ.	40. Local Gov't.	41. Private Households	42. Unallocated	43. Final Demand** Less Imports	44. Total
14	*	–	*	*	*	–	–	*	–	–	*	–	–	1	1	*	2	3	*	179	–	−500	202
*	1	*	2	*	*	–	–	*	–	–	–	–	–	6	–	*	15	13	3	1281	–	545	2586
*	*	63	*	*	–	–	*	6	*	−1	*	–	–	–	*	–	2	*	*	91	–	− 30	583
*	*	*	*	*	*	–	*	9	*	*	*	*	–	*	–	–	1	*	2	243	–	542	838
2	1	1	*	–	–	–	–	*	–	–	–	–	*	*	66	*	–	2	*	38	–	−112	67
*	*	–	*	1	1	–	–	1	–	–	–	–	–	*	10	1	*	4	1	53	–	71	176
–	*	22	26	*	*	–	1	7	*	–	*	4	–	1	4	*	–	1	*	21	*	52	740
2	3	20	18	12	26	2	113	3	1	–	2	1	*	10	4	1	2	12	2	44	*	392	776
3	1	3	*	*	*	–	1	11	2	–	*	1	1	3	30	1	17	2	3	136	–	1100	1935
29	50	8	18	2	*	2	2	6	1	–	*	6	2	7	18	*	11	3	8	186	–	1075	1663
*	8	*	1	*	*	–	1	3	7	–	*	–	*	–	*	*	1	*	*	14	–	368	468
–	*	–	–	–	–	–	*	*	*	–	*	–	–	–	–	–	–	–	*	58	–	− 29	35
*	*	*	*	*	–	–	*	2	3	–	–	1	–	–	138	*	1	2	3	19	–	29	354
16	2	*	–	*	*	–	*	*	–	–	–	–	*	–	56	*	–	*	2	2	–	261	1413
5	1	51	1	*	*	–	*	1	3	–	–	*	*	*	80	*	*	2	2	12	–	414	890
4	10	–	2	6	15	1	12	2	3	–	–	*	*	*	34	2	*	4	5	9	–	1042	1394
38	*	–	–	1	–	–	*	13	4	–	–	–	–	*	58	3	1	1	6	54	–	872	1514
3	7	–	1	*	*	–	*	*	29	–	*	–	–	–	–	–	*	1	4	255	–	743	1148
*	*	1	1	1	–	–	6	11	*	–	2	*	–	3	2	*	1	2	1	128	*	144	322
3	*	–	*	*	–	–	3	7	*	–	1	–	–	*	3	2	26	4	1	6	–	249	331
8	7	18	48	5	6	2	6	10	4	–	1	14	1	7	2	*	3	23	10	232	*	− 14	574
13	141	*	4	1	1	–	–	–	*	2	–	–	–	*	–	*	1	*	1	119	*	944	1227
–	*	–	–	–	–	–	–	–	–	–	–	–	–	–	–	–	*	–	*	437	*	1287	1761
–	–	–	–	–	–	–	–	–	–	–	–	–	–	–	–	–	–	–	–	1627	–	570	2197
2	8	37	25	5	17	2	84	3	1	–	1	2	*	2	5	*	4	5	2	135	–	178	590
36	44	63	78	11	142	5	6	8	5	–	3	12	1	4	37	*	10	48	24	395	*	1806	2868
*	1	6	7	1	25	*	1	2	1	–	1	1	*	*	*	*	1	3	*	353	–	− 267	142
5	6	78	123	11	49	4	9	10	3	–	4	6	2	3	56	*	11	3	7	*	*	−234	565
*	*	5	5	1	*	1	3	15	–	–	–	5	*	*	–	*	1	*	*	522	–	− 75	504
1	42	17	18	1	9	*	3	5	3	–	–	*	*	1	9	–	2	*	1	69	–	− 8	197
–	–	–	–	–	–	–	–	–	–	–	–	–	–	–	–	–	–	–	–	129	–	− 85	44
–	1	2	2	9	1	*	1	–	–	–	35	*	*	1	–	*	2	3	*	62	–	30	149
*	1	–	–	*	–	–	–	–	–	–	–	–	–	*	–	–	–	*	*	303	–	43	347
–	*	–	–	–	–	–	–	–	–	–	–	–	–	*	14	–	–	–	1	*	–	6	45
*	*	*	–	*	13	1	*	*	*	–	*	–	–	50	–	*	4	*	3	163	–	146	380
12	35	16	14	18	14	12	*	1	3	–	3	5	*	20	518	2	18	6	6	1	*	1239	1986
*	1	–	–	*	–	–	–	–	–	–	–	–	–	–	–	–	1	*	1	–	–	42	53
*	*	–	–	*	4	–	*	*	*	–	*	–	–	8	–	–	39	12	7	400	–	273	743
–	–	–	–	*	–	–	*	*	*	–	*	–	–	106	–	–	1	21	227	137	*	458	950
27	38	11	38	35	62	5	7	11	4	–	4	9	1	3	29	*	7	*	7	208	–	−172	598
148	578	786	866	202	1141	82	143	161	44	42	38	140	13	115	561	25	255	649	240	–	–	−326	10,035
26	79	250	651	35	612	1	27	131	59	*	30	97	16	22	104	7	9	40	4	120	–		
81	19	98	107	10	334	5	22	25	8	–	7	16	1	2	4	1	15	42	3	54	–		
47	40	40	20	88	130	9	17	4	1	–	2	4	1	1	35	1	11	3	3	1740	–		
17	15	107	38	53	207	2	20	10	*	–	3	4	1	–	52	3	231	–	–	–	–		
27	69	44	76	67	23	2	31	23	8	–	10	15	5	–	45	3	20	–	–	–	–		
3	15	13	7	13	36	2	5	2	*	*	*	1	*	5	12	1	17	34	9	–	–		
574	1227	1761	2197	590	2868	142	565	504	197	44	149	347	45	380	1986	53	743	950	598	10,035	*		

correspond to the jobs provided and man-hours used. So we record along the households row the dollar value of the labor inputs, by industry, which the households sector provides. For those who prefer data on jobs and to have these jobs broken down by types in the different industries, we list in Table 2.2 such a disaggregation for four specific (4-digit SIC) industries. It shows, for every 10,000 employees in an industry, the number employed in selected occupational categories. We can do this for every other sector and see the distribution of jobs among the sectors of the Philadelphia economy.

For any industry, say food products, we want to know more than what its labor inputs are, or how much it paid out in wages and salaries for these inputs. We want to know what its other inputs are: Inputs of agricultural products, chemicals, power, steel, transportation, etc. And we want a record of them, as we have in Table 2.1. Specifically, going down column 2 of Table 2.1, we note that the food products industry in the Philadelphia region purchased for use as inputs $382 million of products from the agriculture sector, $668 million of products from itself (that is, factories in the food products sector purchased a considerable amount of goods from each other), $1 million from the lumber and wood products sector, $106 million from the paper and allied products sector, and finally, $409 million of labor services from the households sector. Note that $432 million of input purchases could not be assigned to any sector, and so are recorded in the unallocated sector (42). Thus, column 2 gives the total set of inputs purchased for use by the food products sector. If we add to these dollar costs the costs of its imports of goods of the kind that the Philadelphia region does not produce—that is, non-competitive imports (in row 43); federal and state taxes (in row 44); profits, dividends, and interest which are purchases of managerial and capital inputs (in row 45); funds set aside for later use to replace machinery being used up in production—that is, capital allowance and depreciation (in row 46); and finally scrap and miscellaneous costs (in row 47), we account for the distribution of all the revenues received by the food products sector. Its total costs are listed in the last (totals) row.

Similarly, when we go down column 3 we observe for the textile mill products sector the set of inputs it used (purchases it made) in order to produce goods. It purchased $20 million of inputs from the agriculture, forestry, and fisheries sector, $166 million from itself (that is, textile mill plants buying from textile mill plants), and going to row 41, $139 million of labor services from households.

Likewise, each other column lists the set of inputs into the sector at the head of the column. Thus Table 2.1 can be said to relate to inputs and input structures. However, note that the last two columns of the table do not strictly refer to production activity. Column 43 refers to final demand less imports. Final demand covers the demands of state and federal civilian government, federal military activities, the capital formation (investment) sector, and the export sector. It records the goods consumed by these sectors. From this final demand we subtract gross imports of the kinds of goods that Philadelphia does produce (that is, competitive imports). The last column records the total output of each sector.

We have an alternative way of interpreting Table 2.1. We know that what one industry purchases as inputs from a second industry is also the sales of the second industry to the first. So while the figure, $382 million, in the first cell of the second column represents an input of product of the agriculture, forestry, and fisheries sector to the food products industry, it also represents a sale of the product

Table 2.2   Employment by Occupation, per 10,000 Employees (1968)*

Selected Occupational Categories	Industry Employing			
	Meat-Packing Plants SIC 2011	*Set-Up Paperboard Boxes SIC 2652*	*Sheet-Metal Work SIC 3444*	*Shipbuilding and Repairing SIC 3731*
110 Aeronautical Engineers	- - -	- - -	21	5
•	•	•	•	•
•	•	•	•	•
•	•	•	•	•
114 Industrial Engineers	24	45	94	50
115 Mechanical Engineers	12	55	192	186
•	•	•	•	•
•	•	•	•	•
•	•	•	•	•
205 Office Managers	3	2	3	1
•	•	•	•	•
•	•	•	•	•
•	•	•	•	•
301 Sales Agents and Brokers	185	134	94	17
•	•	•	•	•
•	•	•	•	•
•	•	•	•	•
403 Bookkeepers	66	26	30	11
404 Cashiers	5	2	4	4
•	•	•	•	•
•	•	•	••	•
•	•	•	•	•
534 Job and Die Setters	7	14	102	124
535 Machinists	23	44	337	410
536 Machinist Apprentices	15	- - -	- - -	- - -
•	•	•	•	•
•	•	•	•	•
•	•	•	•	•
612 Truck Drivers	450	237	106	53
613 Delivery Men	188	34	7	8
•	•	•	•	•
•	•	•	•	•
699 Operatives, NEC	5044	4799	502	275
•	•	•	•	•
•	•	•	•	•
742 Guards & Watchmen	6	26	49	75
•	•	•	•	•
•	•	•	•	•
•	•	•	•	•
810 Construction Workers	73	85	20	92
•	•	•	•	•
•	•	•	•	•
816 Warehousemen and Stock Handlers	20	13	61	14
•	•	•	•	•
•	•	•	•	•
819 Laborers, NEC	245	152	126	167

Based on Philadelphia and Baltimore data, Regional Science Research Institute.

of the agriculture, forestry, and fisheries sector to the food products sector.
Likewise for every other item along the first row. Each item is a sale of the out-

put of the agriculture sector to the industry at the head of the column, and at the same time an input (purchase) by the industry at the head of the column from the agriculture sector.

Thus, the third item in the first row represents $20 million of sales of agriculture products to the textile mill products sector; the fourth, $1 million of sales to the apparel sector; and the forty-first, $179 million directly to the households sector.

Similarly, we can observe the distribution of sales of the output for every other sector such as iron and steel, transportation, etc. In sum, the rows give us a comprehensive picture of how the *output* of every sector is distributed among purchasers and users. This comprehensive picture by rows complements the comprehensive picture of *inputs* for each industry given by the set of columns. Hence, it is reasonable to characterize this checkerboard as an *input-output* table.

Well, suppose we have all these data available for our use, as we do in the Philadelphia region. So what? How do we make them talk? Because this chapter concentrates on how to depict or describe a city or region and not on analysis, it would not be appropriate to dig down into this question at this point. But we can give a preview of how we may try to answer this question.

USEFULNESS OF THE INPUT-OUTPUT TABLE FOR ATTACKING SOCIAL AND ENVIRONMENTAL PROBLEMS

Suppose in 1968 you had asked, as the author did: What is the impact of the Vietnam War, and in particular, its costs and burden? What are the things we are giving up? The price we are paying? There are many ways to begin to answer the question. However, you might have noted that in the Philadelphia region there is the Naval Shipyard. If there had not been a war, its operations would not have been swollen; in fact, they would have been at least 20 percent smaller. The level of annual expenditures would have been $165.8 million instead of $206 million, the actual level of expenditures for fiscal year 1968. The reduction in expenditures of $40.2 million would have been distributed over the products of many sectors. If we were to look down the column for sector 9137 headed Philadelphia Naval Shipyard in the huge Philadelphia input-output table, we could trace in detail the amounts by which diverse purchases would have been smaller. Broadly speaking, purchases of machinery (except electric machinery) would have been smaller by $6.4 million, of electric machinery by $2.4 million, of primary metals by $4.4 million, of food products by $1.6 million, of utilities including electric power by $2.9 million, and so forth. Finally, the value of labor inputs and services purchased from the households sector would have been smaller by $15.7 million; and about 1,700 fewer workers would have been employed.

Now, at first look one might react by saying that the Philadelphia economy would have been worse off. Its industries would have been selling less goods, and there would have been additional unemployment of 1,700 people. This kind of "first look," and "no-digging-below-the-surface" reasoning is often used by politicians to justify continued war expenditures. But a more careful look reveals that this is not the case for the Philadelphia region. Because of the Vietnam War, the federally sponsored housing program had to cut back its targets. Educational and public welfare programs were not set in motion at the levels that would have been justified. Less hospital construction was subsidized, and less medical research sponsored. In short, resources were used up in the increased Navy Yard activity that would have been available for other programs.

In particular, the $40.2 million could have been spent on sorely needed low-income housing construction, and on elementary, secondary, and higher education. If appropriate federal and local policies had been pursued, these activities could have fruitfully employed another 1,700 workers and paid out in wages and salaries a sum of $15.7 million, so that consumer demand would have been maintained. Thus, the adverse effects on the sales of consumer good industries and wholesale and retail firms could have been avoided. Machinery and steel products suited for housing and school construction and for housing and school repair, maintenance, and operation could have been produced instead of the machinery for the Navy Yard. In short, all the resources could have been very effectively used. The Philadelphia region might have been better off.

In a later chapter we will go into this question at greater depth. The point that we wish to establish is the usefulness of input-output data for attacking socially significant problems. Programs of all sorts require resources, and we need to have detailed tables such as input-output tables to provide at least some of the information on resource requirements that is essential for sound social planning.

Before closing this chapter, there are several other important points to make. First, keep in mind that the checkerboard table describes with numbers a system that is operating. The system is the Philadelphia region economic system. We may want to tinker with the system. But before we do so, we will need to understand more precisely (and with the aid of some shorthand notation such as algebra) how that system interconnects and links its parts. So we must poke our nose into system analysis, sooner or later. We will begin to do so in Chapter 7.

Second, note that the biases of the Establishment have been overtaking us. I have been presenting you with an input-output table describing the operations of a system. Note, however, that it refers to the operations of an *economic* system. But why the economic system? The reply is that this is the only system for which we have comprehensive and systematic data. But why? Because to collect and process data is very costly, so the collection and processing of data can only be undertaken when problems are sufficiently crucial to justify the cost. What problems have been sufficiently crucial? The answer is obvious for a society whose decision-making elite has been traditionally "money-mad"—*economic problems* are most important. And so we have a lot of economic data which we are able to organize to study the problems of the economic system—especially those which interfere with its growth (the ideal of real estate promoters), and with the maximization and/or maintenance of abundant profits (the interest of executives of corporations like General Motors and ITT). We also have a huge amount of data on related factors such as unemployment (a concern of both socially motivated political leaders and those motivated to win votes). But note that we are in a rut, or dilemma, however you wish to look at it. Because we have data on our economic system, we are better able to analyze it and attack its problems. Consequently, many analysts who throw up their hands in despair because of lack of data when trying to attack our *noneconomic problems* are easily induced to study and attack economic problems. As a result, the non-economic problems, such as an equitable distribution of society's output and wealth, health, education, and social stability are much less successfully attacked. So, we get farther behind than ever with them. We must break this cycle in which, because of good data on the economic system, the best analysts study it and in turn demand more data on that system. This leads to still more concentrated study of it and still more demands for data on it. On the other hand, few and not nearly as capable analysts study noneconomic systems; thus relatively little de-mand for data on them is generated. This in turn induces relatively few to study these systems. Now although I say this and will try to make some sugges-tions about how to break this cycle, keep in mind throughout this book that we are indeed caught in it. In one sense we are trapped in a quicksand of accumulated knowledge.

Now, how to break this cycle? One way, obviously, is to accumulate more—much more—information on noneconomic systems. We need much more data than a census currently gives us on the different sectors—political parties, lobbies, other interest groups—of our political system. More data is needed on other sec-tors of our social system—religious organizations and groups, social clubs and groups, nonprofit research organizations, and so forth. And right now we need a hell of a lot more data on our ecological system. Here, we can be specific and to the point.

Air pollution, water pollution, solid-waste pollution, noise pollution, visual pollution, etc. are all too well known to even require identification as critical prob-lem areas of the socioecologic system. We are not able to probe much into these areas because we have failed to accumulate relevant data. What data do we need?

One set of data is obvious. If the federal government has been collecting information on the output of steel from a steel plant over the years through the census, why has it not yet started to collect the data on its SO_2 (sulphur dioxide), particulates and other air-pollutant outputs, and on its BOD (biological oxygen demand), COD (chemical oxygen demand), and other water-pollutant outputs? One answer is that in a society in which a profit-maximizing economic elite has exercised a dominant influence, these are outputs to be forgotten about as long as the masses and their representatives and noneconomic social leaders allow—for they have negative prices. You cannot sell these outputs on the market. Rather, it costs to get rid of them. So forget them as long as you can. And this is exactly what the census reflects.

Now, because of the failure of our leaders and ourselves to have recognized the onslaught of serious environmental problems despite many warnings, we are caught unprepared. We sorely need data and we don't have them. We sorely need valid models for making the little data we have talk. We don't have them.

Exactly what kinds of data do we need? One set is clear. We want data on the output of air pollutants, water pollutants, noise pollution, and solid wastes. Specifically, we want a systematic classification of different types of pollutants such as that in Table 2.3.

Further, we want similar disaggregated data collected and reported by the cen-sus on solid wastes, noise, and other pollutants by firms and for the different processes of production they employ.

Table 2.3   A Commodity Code for Air Pollutants

Air Pollution Commodity Code	Air Pollutant
.	.
.	.
.	.
1121	Sulphur Dioxide, SO_2
1122	Sulphur Trioxide, SO_3
.	.
.	.
.	.
1210	Carbon Monoxide, CO
1211	Carbon Dixoide, CO_2
1220	Aromatics
1230	Hydrocarbons
.	.
.	.
.	.
1310	Nitrogen Oxides, NO_x
.	.
.	.
.	.
3000	Particulates

Water Pollution Commodity Code	Water Pollutant
.	.
.	.
.	.
1031	Biological Oxygen Demand, BOD 5-day
1032	Ultimate Oxygen Demand, UOD
1033	Chemical Oxygen Demand, COD
.	.
.	.
.	.
1041	Suspended Solids
1042	Settleable Solids
1047	Turbidity
1048	Color
.	.
.	.
.	.
1057	Alkalinity

Table 2.4   Selected Pollutants: Tons Per Year Per Employee, New York State, 1971

Pollutant	•••	Chemicals SIC 28	Petroleum Refining SIC 29	Rubber & Misc. Plastics SIC 30	Leather and Leather Prod. SIC 31	Stone, Clay, and Glass SIC 32	Primary Metals SIC 33	•••
SO_2		0.269	5.198	0.000	0.000	0.472	0.549	
Particu- lates		3.552	378.405	0.369	0.016	7.310	15.461	

Once these data are available, we can organize them for effective use. One way is to develop them in checkerboard input-output fashion. This allows us to add additional rows to the input-output table which describes the economic system, each additional row referring to an ecologic commodity. The SO_2 and particulates rows might be developed directly from the data in the corresponding rows of Table 2.4. For a more complete listing of pollutant coefficients by typical column (sector) of an input-output table, see Tables 14.3 and 14.6 relating to petroleum refining (SIC 2911) and leather tanning and finishing (SIC 3111), respectively.

With data such as those in Table 2.4 we can see how direct expansion or contraction of the steel industry, petroleum refining, and every other sector adds to or decreases the amount of pollutants generated. Thus we can see the direct impact of the different economic sectors on the ecologic system. We see that with a complete set of data we can examine systematically the direct impact of economic growth. Later we will examine indirect impacts as well.

But we want more. Economic activities dump upon the ecologic system diverse outputs as suggested above. These outputs unfortunately affect not only our own biological (physical) processes but also all other processes external to us as human beings. To evaluate these effects we need to understand biological processes themselves (especially those relating to the physical health of a human being). As we shall point out in Chapter 14, we will need to organize systematically knowledge in many scientific areas if we are to properly regulate the quality of the environment.

CLOSING REMARKS

In closing, we again point out that before attacking social problems and formulating policies, we should know something about our region. We have suggested some relevant properties of cities and regions.

We have focused specifically on jobs, the data we need for study, and how to organize these data to make them talk. The input-output table is useful here for giving us a picture of a region's economy and the interdependencies of its sectors. It is also useful for showing the possible effects of alternative policies and programs, as we indicated in terms of Vietnam War expenditures. We will return to this in Chapter 7.

Finally, we mentioned the data we would like to have for attacking environmental problems. As we will point up in Chapter 14, we want to know the linkages between the economic and ecologic systems in order to trace the direct and indirect impacts of changes in either one.

APPENDIX TO CHAPTER 2. An Input-Output Questionnaire

In introductory textbooks it is quite common to talk about surveys of different sorts and the diverse kinds of questions asked—this is particularly true when input-output analysis is reviewed. But rarely is the questionnaire itself presented to satisfy the curiosity of that student who wants to see the full set of specific questions asked, or to give a student a feel for the survey process. Accordingly, in this appendix we present one of the questionnaires used in the Philadelphia region input-output study, including instructions on filling it out. A full discussion of the construction of the questionnaire is contained in W. Isard and T. W. Langford, *Regional Input-Output Study* (Cambridge: M.I.T. Press, 1971). Because we were greatly concerned at the time the study was initiated with the impact of the Vietnam War, we included a set of questions relating to sales to defense-related agencies. At other times, other specific concerns would suggest other special kinds of questions.

ECONOMIC DATA: WHARTON SCHOOL PHILADELPHIA REGION STUDY–CONFIDENTIAL

Please complete this questionnaire and mail to

    Professor Walter Isard
    Department of Regional Science
    The Wharton School
    University of Pennsylvania
    Philadelphia, Pennsylvania   19174

If any questions arise with regard to specific items in this questionnaire, please call

    Professor Gerald J. Karaska
    University of Pennsylvania
    Philadelphia

Information is requested for *Calendar year 1959*. If it is not possible to provide data for 1959, please do so for the nearest year after 1959. Specify here the year used, if not 1959. If your records are arranged by fiscal year, you may use the fiscal year; simply indicate if used.

Please report information (data) only for the plant listed below.

The Philadelphia region includes the following counties: In Pennsylvania, Bucks, Chester, Delaware, Montgomery, Philadelphia; in New Jersey, Burlington, Camden, Gloucester.

    1. Name of establishment

    2. Address of establishment

    3. Respondent's name

    4. Respondent's position

    5. Average employment*

    6. Total wages and salaries (payroll)*

*See attached supplementary information sheet for particulars regarding these items.

7. Materials Used in Production*

Type of Material (Specify in Detail)	Total Costs	Indicate if Transportation is included in Total Costs*	Origin of Shipments	
			Percent in Philadelphia Region	Percent outside Phila. Region. If possible breakdown by state or other geographical area
Example: Steel casting— 200 tons	$100,000	Transport cost included	25%	75%
a.				
b.				
c.				
d.				
e.				
f.				
g.				
h.				
i.				
j.				
k.				

*See attached supplementary information sheet for particulars regarding these items.

8. Sales (Value of Shipments)*

Type of Product (Specify in Detail)	Sales Value of Shipments	Indicate if Transportation is included in Sales Value	House-holds (Direct)	Retail Outlets	Whole-salers	Sales To:	
						Other Manuf. Firms	
						Phila. Region Percent	Outside Phila. Region Percent
Example: Tractors— 225 units	$1,000,000	transport costs not included		20%	30%	25%	25%
a.							
b.							
c.							
d.							
e.							
f.							
g.							
h.							
i.							
j.							
k.							

*See attached supplementary information sheet for particulars regarding these items.

9. Products Shipped to Other Manufacturing Firms Outside Philadelphia Region (Continued from Table 8)

Type of Product (Same as in Table 8)	Sales To Other Manufacturing Firms—Outside Philadelphia Region	
	Purchasing Industry—group*	Value
Example: a. Tractors	#5—Coal Mining #37—Construction and mining machinery	$ 50,000 $200,000
a. b. c. d.		

See attached list of industry groups

10. Expenditures on Power and Energy
   a. coal
   b. gas
   c. oil
   d. electricity

11. All Other Current Operating Expenses—Exclude all investment expenditures. (Note—payroll, material inputs, power and energy expenditures also excluded.)

Sales to Defense-Related Agencies*

1. What percentage of your sales in fiscal 1960 (July 1960 to June 30, 1961) went directly to defense-related agencies; i.e., direct sales as part of a *prime* government contract?

2. If you are a prime contractor, what percentage of the prime contracts was subcontracted to another firm?

3. What percentage of your sales in fiscal 1960 went indirectly to defense-related agencies; i.e., sales going to another firm and which could be designated as a *subcontract* on a prime defense contract?

4. For subcontract sales, please indicate the percentage of their distribution by geographic area:

	Subcontracts from Your Prime Contracts	Subcontracts from Another Firm's Prime Contracts
a. Philadelphia Metropolitan Area**		
b. rest of Pennsylvania		
c. rest of New Jersey		
d. California		
e. Massachusetts		
f. Connecticut		
g. Texas		
h. List other states		

Dept. of Army, Dept. of Navy, Dept. of Air Force, Dept. of Defense, National Aeronautics and Space Administration.

**Counties of Philadelphia, Bucks, Montgomery, Delaware, Chester, Camden, Gloucester, Burlington.*

We have attempted to keep the accompanying questionnaire simple and short, and to ask for figures that would be readily available in business records. Most definitions of sales and purchase items conform to those used by the U.S. Bureau of the Census and are likely to have been calculated for previous census returns.

Notes on specific questions from first list:

Question 5—*Average employment.* This is the census definition. If you have to calculate a figure it should be the average of employments during March, May, August, and November of the year used. Please include wage and salary employees in this figure.

Question 6—*Wages and salaries (payroll).* This should be the definition used for federal withholding tax calculation. It includes all compensation such as commissions, bonuses, vacation pay, etc. before deductions of taxes and other similar items.

Question 7—*Materials used in production.* Costs should be the amounts paid (after discounts and including freight charges) for materials and components actually put into production during the year. If you pick up items in your own trucks or otherwise cannot include freight charges, please indicate in the right-hand column. Note that components purchased through contracts or subcontracts *should be included.*

Question 8—*Sales (value of shipments).* Sales should be after discounts and allowances, f.o.b. plant, and excluding excise taxes and freight charges. (If freight charges cannot be excluded, or if you deliver in your own trucks, please indicate so in the extreme right-hand column.)

Question 11—*All other operating expenses.* This should include rents, taxes, insurance, warehousing, telephone and telegraph, office supplies, advertising, and any other business services. It should *exclude* all capital (investment) expenditures and, desirably, depreciation allowances.

Question 9—The purchasing industries may be classified by SIC number or by the following industry groups if you choose not to list companies:

Sector
1. Livestock and products
2. All other agricultural products
3. Forestry and fishery products
4. Agricultural, forestry, & fishery services
5. Coal mining
6. Food and kindred products
7. Tobacco manufacturing
8. Broad & narrow fabrics, yarn & thread mills
9. Miscellaneous textile goods, including floor coverings
10. Apparel
11. Miscellaneous fabricated textile products
12. Lumber & products, except wooden containers
13. Wooden containers
14. Household furniture
15. Other furniture and fixtures
16. Paper and allied products, except paperboard containers and boxes
17. Paperboard containers and boxes
18. Printing and publishing
19. Chemicals
    a) Mining
    b) Manufacturing

20. Plastics and synthetics
21. Drugs and toilet preparations
22. Paint and allied products
23. Petroleum and related products
   a) Mining
   b) Manufacturing
24. Rubber & miscellaneous plastic products
25. Industrial leather
26. Other leather products
27. Glass and glass products
28. Stone and clay and their products
   a) Mining
   b) Manufacturing
29. Iron and Steel
   a) Mining
   b) Manufacturing
30. Nonferrous metals
   a) Mining
   b) Manufacturing
31. Metal cans, shipping barrels, drums, kegs, and pails
32. Heating, plumbing, and fabricated structural metal products
33. Screw machine products, stampings and bolts, nuts, etc.
34. Other fabricated metal products
35. Engines and turbines
36. Farm machinery and equipment
37. Construction and mining machinery and equipment
38. Materials handling equipment
39. Special and general industry machinery and equipment
   a) Metalworking machinery & equipment
   b) Special industry machinery & equipment
   c) General industrial machinery & equipment
   d) Miscellaneous machinery
40. Office, computing & accounting machines
41. Service industry machines
42. Electric transmission and distribution equipment and other industrial apparatus
43. Household appliances
44. Electric lighting & wiring equipment
45. Communications equipment
46. Electronic components and accessories
47. Miscellaneous electrical machinery, equipment, and supplies
48. Motor vehicles and equipment
49. Aircraft and parts
50. Other transportation equipment
51. Professional, scientific & controlling instruments & supplies, including watches and clocks
52. Optical and photographic equipment
53. Miscellaneous manufacturing
54. Ordnance
55. Gas & electric power & water service
56. Transportation (and warehousing)
57. Trade (including eating & drinking places)

Chapter

3

Spatial Distributions, Regional Differences and Social Problems

INTRODUCTION

Chapter 2 approaches interdependence in a very oversimplified and unrealistic manner. By and large it assumes that all people, activities, and resources are concentrated at a single point in geographic space. In short, it posits a single-point economy. But we know that physical space is all around us. We know that distances have to be covered in living, and that people and organizations spread or distribute themselves over space in order to function. This omnipresence of physical space is the setting for a number of problems that have emerged in the cities and regions of the United States.

For example, you can recognize that low-income, low-skill populations tend to be concentrated in certain areas of the city, some of which are designated as ghettos and slums. In contrast, high-income, highly educated professional populations tend to be concentrated in high-quality residential areas of the urban regions of the U.S. Rarely do the two groups mix in this society, though this is not always true in other societies.

Moreover, the quality of facilities such as housing, street maintenance, school systems, parks, and libraries varies among areas of the city. Lower quality is usually associated with the low-income areas; higher quality with the high-income areas. Similarly, we find high unemployment rates in the low-income areas, and low unemployment rates in the high-income areas.

Major problems arise because of these differences. One problem that is associated with these differences is crime and violence. Neighborhood deterioration, nonmaintenance of housing, and social and family disruption are others. Inadequate public facilities and fiscal bankruptcy of cities are also problems. Traffic congestion, rats, and the spread of disease are still others.

It is reasonable to ask why the particular spatial distributions regarding these differences have evolved. Moreover, our concern with the welfare of people and, in particular, with the welfare of people of all income, ethnic, and religious groups, motivates us to ask to what extent the differences in welfare are caused by, and in turn cause, these spatial distributions and differences. We would like to have some understanding of why differences arise so that we can change them, particularly if we think that change can improve the welfare of all or a large number of groups.

On further study, we see that major differences among groups of population are not associated just with the different areas of the city or metropolitan region. They are also associated with particular states of the U.S.A. Compare California with Mississippi, New York with Arkansas, Connecticut with Alabama. Why the differences? Are they caused by variations in the resources of these states— in coal, iron ore, and soil—or by the educational levels of the populations as measured by the percent of literacy, or the percent who complete college? Or do differences in the income levels and economic wealth of the population of these states lead to differences in educational levels and in efficiency with which agricultural and other resources are exploited? Or are both sets of causes and effects at work?

We can go beyond states and think of nations of the world. The United States is a political region. Why is its population on average so much better off than the population of Peru? Why is the population of Israel so much healthier and better trained than that of Egypt? Why is the population of Japan so far ahead of that of the Philippines? How does one explain the stark differences between the starving millions of Calcutta and the fabulously affluent of Athens? Again, one can state that differences in resource endowment lead to differences in income and social-political-cultural organization. But also one can attribute differences in the use of resources and income generation to differences in religious institutions, political organizations, and social structure. It is necessary to do analysis, spatial and nonspatial, in order to understand the forces at play.

But why stop here? There are differences between populations in southeastern Florida and northwestern Florida—that is, within any one state. There are differences within counties or provinces or by concentric mile zones around cities, or by direction from the center of a city. And so forth.

Another kind of spatial difference that is becoming increasingly important is the difference among sites and subareas in the quality of the environment. The quality of the environment in large industrial concentrations such as the Philadelphia region is very low compared to the quality of the environment in Montana. Offhand, we can explain this. But when we tackle the problem of making policy recommendations for environmental management, it becomes important to understand how different kinds of policies can affect these spatial differences. We must be able to distinguish between factors that will have little impact and those that will have major impact. To do this we are forced to consider the spatial setting and spatial analysis.

There is yet another kind of problem associated with space. All of the forces or factors we have hitherto mentioned concern people and things in *place*—that is, houses in different subareas, schools in different neighborhoods, population in different districts, and soil in different subregions. But we well recognize that people and things *move*. People journey to work, school, shopping centers, and cultural sites. Goods that are produced generally must flow to other places to be consumed, either by people or production processes. Hence, we have problems that are generated by people and goods flowing. They are transportation problems, and are not simple ones that can be attacked independently of other problems. Because of the use of automobiles and trucks, and their emissions of hydrocarbons and carbon monoxide, transportation contributes greatly to the air-pollution problem. Hence, the environmental management problem is directly linked to the transportation problem. Also, in many areas the mental health problem is highly sensitive to levels of tension. In turn, tension levels are associated with transportation congestion and the features of a movement system. Thus, the mental health problem is interrelated with and may even be considered part of the transportation problem. Jobs and residences of workers are not next door to each other. Typically they are spatially separated, and sometimes the job problem in one region cannot be licked until the transportation problem linking one region to another is successfully tackled.

In short, we are going to find that there are many interesting and diverse problems associated with the factor of physical space. Sometimes they are only simply linked; at other times they are linked in a complex way.

We have made clear the presence and importance of physical space in our existence and some of the numerous problems it generates. We wish to attack these problems. But once again we need to size them up. We need data that pertain to their relevant aspects.

DISCREPANCIES BETWEEN DEVELOPED AND UNDERDEVELOPED REGIONS

Suppose we consider the problem of economic development. More specifically, take two regions, the state of Mississippi and the eight-county Philadelphia metropolitan area. We know there are great differences between these two regions. What are these differences? One way to depict them is through the regional input-output tables we have. One exists for the Philadelphia region for the year 1959. Another exists for the state of Mississippi for 1961. The two years 1959 and 1961 are close enough to allow us to make comparisons.

First consider income per capita. For the Philadelphia region in 1960, with a population of 4.4 million, it was approximately $2500. For the state of Mississippi in 1960, with a population of 2.2 million, it was $1168. (In 1957, it was $992). This is a major difference.

From a comparison of the input-output tables for these two regions, we note that this major difference is associated with the different industrial structures of the regions. The agriculture sector dominates the Mississippi region. This sector is relatively insignificant for the Philadelphia region. We know that for the type of low-mechanized technology prevailing in Mississippi agriculture, the earnings per gainfully employed person must have been much lower than for such a person in the Philadelphia region.   But we are not able to put together good, reliable data to substantiate this point.   In the food and kindred products sector, we observe from our input-output tables that earnings in the Philadelphia region were approximately $4400 per person employed in 1959 compared to approximately $3500 in Mississippi.   In textile mills, earnings were approximately $3500 in the Philadelphia region compared to about $3300 in Mississippi.   Food products and textiles are sectors that are low-paying and that are prevalent in both regions to a significant extent.   But now let us consider the high-paying industries.   Consider the machinery sector.   In Mississippi in 1958 there were 3,900 jobs in electrical machinery products.   In the Philadelphia region, with twice the population, there were at least twelve times as many jobs in this sector.   Further, in these jobs, the average earnings per worker were approximately $5500 in the Philadelphia region in 1959, but only about $4000 in Mississippi.

Other industries that are high-paying and present in the Philadelphia region are space-age research and development activities.   They are not present, at least to any noticeable extent, in Mississippi.   Some industries, like the service trades, are present in both regions, but again in the Philadelphia region they pay much higher wages.

Now these are the kinds of differences one typically finds between developed and underdeveloped regions.   In general, the underdeveloped region pays lower wages and salaries in the same occupation and sector and generates less local income per unit of output.   Moreover, the less-developed region usually has a much larger percentage of its labor force in the low wage-paying sectors, and little specialization and activity in the high wage-paying sectors.

Further, the pattern of the flow of goods from one sector to another within these regions differs greatly.   In the Philadelphia region, one notes the large flows of electrical machinery and other products and services of high wage-paying sectors to many sectors within the region. In Mississippi these flows are relatively small, certainly on a per capita basis.   In general, in the developed region there is a large local demand and market for the products of high wage-paying sectors. In the underdeveloped region, this demand is low.

Why do these differences exist?   There are numerous, complicated reasons, many being rooted and complexly entrenched in the cultural system.   And it takes many years of study to appreciate and be able to attack the problem comprehensively.   Still, at our introductory level much can be said.

First, there is the matter of resources.   In the Philadelphia region there exists much capital in the form of plant and equipment employed per worker; in the Mississippi region, little.   In the Philadelphia region there exists a relatively highly educated and skilled population.   In the Mississippi region, there is a low-skilled, low-educated population.   Thus, we expect the typical worker in the Philadelphia region to earn much higher wages than his counterpart in Mississippi who has much less capital to work with and is less skilled.

What can we do about this inequity?   Again we shall not attempt analysis in this chapter.   Rather we shall point up the analysis that is needed and the data that is required to back it up.

When we point to the problem of major discrepancy in per capita income between the Mississippi and Philadelphia regions, or between an underdeveloped and a developed region in general, a typical proposal put forth to solve this problem is to bring more and better jobs to the lower-paid workers. Specifically, build more plants with the most modern equipment in Mississippi. Set up training schools to develop within the Mississippi labor force the basic skills required by these plants. Then pay the Mississippi workers the higher salaries they need and would merit.

But the problem is not so simple. Frequently this kind of attack has failed; certainly it has failed more often than it has succeeded, the reasons being both simple and complex. The complexity of the problem is partly seen when some social planners state: No, we should not bring the jobs to the workers! We should bring the workers to the jobs. We should train the workers in Mississippi and give them jobs in Philadelphia. But here, too, major problems would arise. New housing would need to be provided in Philadelphia. New schools would need to be constructed. New community and other facilities would need to be built. New jobs and increased industrial activity would mean more emissions of air, water, solid waste, and noise pollutants. Further, shifting labor to a new environment could disrupt the social community in both the old and new locations and could lead to asocial behavior, as has happened so often in the past. Thus, many different kinds of costs could arise.

The problem is still more difficult than suggested. Who is going to make the investments in plant and equipment? If the federal government were to start operating steel plants in Mississippi, there would be widespread outcries of socialism and communism. It would be an improper incursion of the federal government on the sacred rights of the business community. The federal government would be in competition with private enterprise, and this is unacceptable in an unplanned, semicapitalistic society such as the United States. In short, pending major changes in the social-political-economic system, the federal, state, and local governments are precluded from engaging in many high wage-paying economic activities in Mississippi. Only private business can. But as we all know, private business is rarely motivated in any private way by considerations of social welfare and justice. Private business will look at Mississippi in a very hard-nosed manner. It will ask: If we invest capital in a high wage-paying plant and equipment in Mississippi, can we obtain any greater profits, or at the minimum can we do as well in Mississippi as in any other region? That is, for the markets we plan to serve, can we produce and distribute the goods to those markets from a plant in Mississippi at no higher cost, and hopefully at a lower cost, than elsewhere?

Now this is a much more analytical question. If private enterprise is to locate in Mississippi and bring high-paying jobs there, it must be because of lower costs in Mississippi, or because there are certain tax advantages or local, state, and federal subsidies which fully offset higher costs of operations in Mississippi. Then and only then can decision makers in the private sectors justify investments in Mississippi. Accordingly then, if we are to examine this approach to the solution of the problem, we must do comparative cost studies. We will need to calculate costs in Mississippi and other locations, and compare them. We will need to consider prices of different raw materials, labor, and other inputs that must be paid at different locations. But then we will need to ask first how prices are determined. This we will do in the next chapter.

The second approach mentioned for removing discrepancy in per capita income is to train labor in Mississippi and encourage it to migrate to Philadelphia and other major metropolitan regions. The incentive for migration would be the higher pay obtainable in a job elsewhere once the migrant worker has acquired the requisite skills. But why do jobs pay a higher wage in Philadelphia than in Mississippi? To answer this question we have to ask how wages, the price of labor, are determined in any economic system—another question to be examined in the next chapter.

Before we leave this particular case of the Philadelphia region versus Mississippi, we should point up another matter. We have indicated that one reason for the large output of high wage-paying industry in the Philadelphia region is the large local demand for the products of these industries in the Philadelphia region. The local demand for these products in the Mississippi region is small. This point suggests that we should look at nonlocal demand as well as local demand. Therefore, for each region we want data on the places and industries outside the region to which the region exports its goods. Export markets may be just as important as local markets in the sense that both may offer potentialities for possible investment and growth in employment. With this consideration in mind, while constructing the Philadelphia input-output table, we asked each firm to specify the places and industries outside the region to which it sold.

Exports are one side of a coin; imports are the other. In economic development work, we must be equally interested in knowing from which places and industries the firms inside our region import. We want this information for two reasons. First, if our region is a nation and has a different currency than other regions from which it imports (for example, if we are Egypt and importing from the Soviet Union), the imports must be paid for in the currencies of the other regions. Thus we must constantly know whether we can earn sufficient foreign exchange, such as rubles, through our exports to pay for our imports; and whether our balance-of-payments position is favorable or unfavorable. Limited foreign exchange can act as a serious brake on growth and development of new industries. However, we want knowledge of imports from other regions for a second reason. We would like to examine whether or not some of the goods being imported can be replaced by identical or similar goods produced by new plants in our own region. Of course, we need to engage in comparative cost analysis to determine whether or not it is economically sensible to replace imports by locally produced goods.

DISCREPANCIES BETWEEN GHETTO AND NONGHETTO AREAS IN THE METROPOLITAN REGIONS

Our interests as regional scientists go beyond comparisons of the Philadelphia region and the state of Mississippi, or Egypt and the Soviet Union, or Africa and Europe. We often need to probe within regions, and particularly metropolitan regions, to attack problems with important spatial dimensions. Currently in the United States our greatest social problems are associated with per capita income discrepancies among the subareas of metropolitan regions, and with major differences in available opportunities among the residents of the ghettos, slums, and poverty-striken subareas, the grey areas, and the more wealthy suburbs. Once again we can exploit input-output tables effectively to describe differences. For example, we can construct a checkerboard table for the black ghetto of North Philadelphia, and one for the white elite of Montgomery County (largely Main-Line Philadelphians). If we were to do so, again we would see some of the basic differences that we noted when we compared the Philadelphia region with Mississippi. We would find that the economic sectors in North Philadelphia provide jobs which, on the whole, require relatively little skill. The firms in these sectors in North Philadelphia use little modern plant and equipment. Investment per worker is small. Management capability is low. In contrast, if we look elsewhere, such as in the central business district and especially the industrial districts, the jobs provided require a much higher level of skill and are associated with a much higher investment of capital and level of managerial ability. Moreover, many of the factories in North Philadelphia are in older industries and are using older, if not obsolete, technology. Few new activities and plants are present.

Even in service sectors, which are common to both North Philadelphia and other subareas, less modern equipment is used and lower wages paid in North Philadelphia.

On the commodity export side, North Philadelphia ships out goods of relatively low value, such as food products and paper and paperboard products. In contrast, for other subareas containing industrial activity, exports consist of much higher-valued commodities, such as computers and specialized machinery.

Because we are examining intrametropolitan structures, the distances between subareas are not great. They are much less than the distances between the census regions of the United States. Accordingly, it is economically feasible within the metropolitan region for a subarea to export on a large scale the labor services of its residents. This export occurs when its residents journey to other subareas to work. But this journey-to-work pattern, or export of labor services, is different among subareas. The residents of a typical suburban area encounter few obstacles in their search for employment in other subareas. Although they tend to move in concentrated fashion to the central business district where a large fraction of a metropolis' jobs are situated, these residents can also move easily to other subareas. This point is clearly seen in data on their movements. In contrast, the journey-to-work pattern (export of labor services) is quite different for North Philadelphia. It, too, shows a concentrated flow toward the central business district and other subareas where heavy industrial plants and jobs of relatively low status exist. But the access of its residents to jobs in other subareas in the Philadelphia region is much more restricted; this is evidenced in the absence of certain links in the pattern of movement of its residents. In particular, the movement to certain suburbs consists solely of movement of female domestic workers, another low-paying activity. In short, the exports of labor services from North Philadelphia to certain subareas consists primarily of the low-pay type, and movements of male breadwinners does not appear.

For the Mississippi region, it was suggested that jobs might be brought to the residents in order to help eliminate per capita income discrepancies. One can propose the same policy for North Philadelphia. But such a policy has little chance for success if it is based upon decisions of private investors who reside elsewhere. Such investors are reluctant to go into this area and other ghettos. There are risks of destruction of property and higher insurance costs. There are major difficulties in getting skilled labor and administrators residing in other subareas to come to the slums to work because of the risk of personal violence and mugging.

The alternative of training the residents of a ghetto area and upgrading their skills so that they can compete more effectively for high-paying jobs in other subareas is more feasible. However, there is a third possibility. It is to subsidize private investments by residents of slum and ghetto areas in plant and equipment to be located in these areas. The problem of obtaining necessary skilled labor still must be faced, though. This practice of subsidization by federal, state, and local governments in low-income subareas does not run counter to the capitalistic tradition. It is politically feasible. But there still remains the hotly debated question as to whether there exists among the residents of slum and ghetto areas sufficient entrepreneurial capability and drive to mount a major economic development program. It is the same question that is raised when we consider development for the state of Mississippi or for the many underdeveloped regions of the world, such as Africa, Latin America, Asia, and even parts of Europe.

JOURNEY-TO-WORK AND OTHER TRAVEL PATTERNS IN THE METROPOLITAN REGION: THE GRAVITY MODEL

Another very interesting set of spatial phenomena relates to journey-to-work patterns, or commuting fields. This set falls under the general class of spatial phenomena involving movement and communication over space. Further, we will find that for reasons we do not know, there exists a standard general pattern for many diverse and important communications and movements, at least within the context of the society of the United States. To provide some rationale for the standard pattern to be set forth, we need to do a little "theorizing."

Suppose we take a metropolitan region. For the moment let me tell you nothing about this region except that it has a population of size P. Further, let us subdivide this region into subareas a, b, ..., z, as in Figure 3.1, where the populations are P_a, P_b, ..., P_z, respectively. We know that $P_a + P_b + ... + P_z = P$. The characteristics of the population and other features are the same in all subareas. Now consider an individual whom we will designate i. Suppose he lives in subarea a and on the average takes 100 trips per month within his metropolitan region. Without knowing any more, what is your best guess as to how this individual distributes his trips among the several subareas (including trips that end at a place in his own subarea)?

I have been asking this question of students in my classes for over twenty-five years. I have received many kinds of answers, but the answer that most frequently occurs is this: Individual i will distribute his trips among the various subareas, including his own, in proportion to the percent of population in these subareas. That is, if 10 percent of the population resides in subarea b, then ten trips, or 10 percent of his total trips, will terminate in subarea b. If 6 percent of the population resides in subarea c, then six of his trips, or 6 percent of his trips, will terminate in subarea c; and so forth. Now proceeding from individual i in subregion a to the entire population P_a in subregion a, we may consider the distribution of the total number of trips generated by this population—the

Figure 3.1   The Subareas of a Hypothetical Metropolitan Region

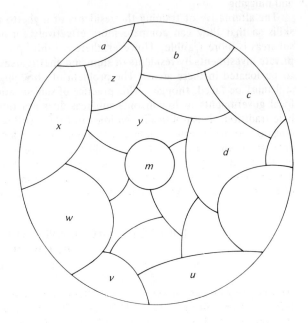

total will be $100P_a$ if individual i is an average person. Then according to our theory, we can expect that $10P_a$ or 10 percent of the total number of trips will terminate in subarea b, $6P_a$ or 6 percent in subarea c, etc. In short, if we let $T^{a \to b}$ represent a prediction of the total number of trips from a to b and recognize P_b/P as the percent of the total population of the metropolitan region which resides in subarea b, then we need to multiply the total number of trips that residents of subarea a take—namely $100P_a$ by this percentage to obtain the number of trips which our theory predicts. That is,

$$T^{a \to b} = \frac{P_b}{P} (100P_a)$$

Or, generally speaking, if we let j represent any possible originating subarea and k represent any possible terminating subarea, we have

$$T^{j \to k} = \frac{P_k}{P} (100P_j) \qquad j, k = a, b, ..., z \qquad 3.1$$

You know as well as I do that a good theory should be able to stand up against the facts. In our case, the predicted number of trips should correspond to the actual numbers of trips. In the major metropolitan regions in the United States there have been many surveys of the origins and destinations of trips. In their simplest form, these surveys ask drivers to state the point where they began their trip and the point where they intend to terminate. Suppose, as in Figure 3.2, we measure numbers of actual trips along the horizontal axis and predicted number of trips along the vertical. Then for the pair of subareas, *a* and *b*, we can plot a point on the figure which indicates both the actual number of trips originating in *a* and terminating in *b* and the theoretical number predicted by formula of Equation 3.1. Now, if our theory is good, the actual and predicted numbers should be the same, or approximately so. The point should fall on or close to the straight line in Figure 3.2 which begins at the origin and cuts the *x*-axis at a 45° angle. And so too with every other pair of subareas, *a* and *c, a* and *d, ..., a* and *z; b* and *c, b* and *d, ..., b* and *z; c* and *d, ..., c* and *z*; and finally *y* and *z*.

Figure 3.2   Theoretical and Actual Numbers of Trips

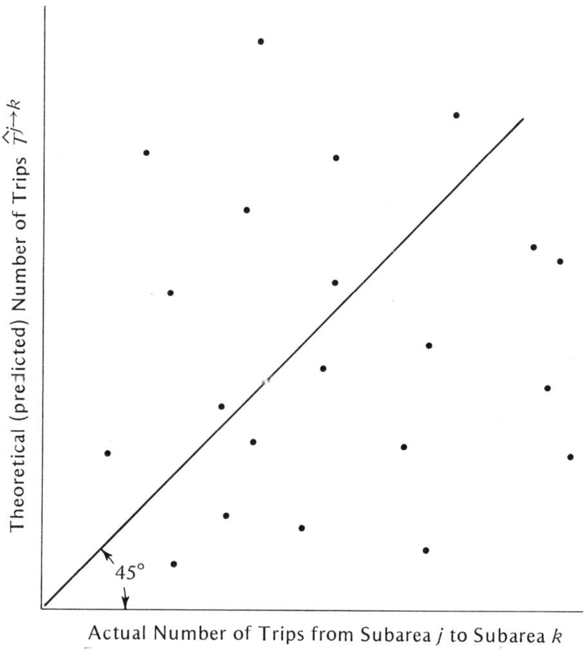

Actual Number of Trips from Subarea *j* to Subarea *k*

When we actually observe the plot of points, we find that the points do not fall on the straight line from the origin; rather, they are scattered all over the figure. Clearly, the theory is a bad theory.

At this point I ask my students for reactions. Some suggest starting over again. Most do not. Most continue to consider numbers of population in the terminating region to be an important factor. They respond by saying that we have not considered all factors. And then usually several, independently and almost simultaneously, state that we must also consider distance or transportation cost between subareas, or the time it takes to go from one subarea to another. After additional thought they speculate that the greater the intervening distance (or transport cost or travel time), the smaller the number of trips from one subarea to another; and the less the intervening distance (or cost or time), the greater the number of trips. Further, they frequently say that we should divide the right-hand side of Equation 3.1 by distance, $d^{j \to k}$, and then multiply by some constant C so as to end up with the right number of total trips. That is, they suggest

$$T^{j \to k} = C \frac{100 P_j P_k}{P d^{j \to k}} \qquad\qquad 3.2$$

This new formula represents a somewhat more sophisticated theory. It involves two independent variables, population and distance, rather than one. Again we must test. So in Figure 3.3 we plot a point for each pair of subareas, giving the actual observed number of trips between them and the predicted as given by Equation 3.2. This time when we look at the plot we are surprised at the great improvement that results; the fit of the data to the 45° line is much better. In fact, for some metropolitan areas the fit is remarkably good—as good as one can find in most social science studies.

Figure 3.3   Theoretical and Actual Numbers
of Trips with Distance as a Variable

Theoretical (predicted) Number of Trips $\widehat{T}^{j \to k}$

45°

Actual Number of Trips from Subarea j to Subarea k

So we have a relationship which seems to hold for the distribution of trips among subareas in a metropolitan region. It is a crude one. It considers only two variables. We suspect that it can be substantially improved by introducing still more variables, as we will do shortly.

Bear in mind that this type of relationship has been found to be valid not only for intrametropolitan transportation but also for railroad, airplane, and bus trips

between pairs of cities; for movement of commodities such as that by rail express; for communications phenomena such as number of telephone calls and
telegrams between pairs of cities; and for many other kinds of goods, people, and
idea movements such as the spread of rumors, newspaper circulation, the search
for marriage mates, and the diffusion of innovations.

Already some readers may have noted an interesting parallel. If instead of
transportation flows between any two subareas, j and k, we consider interaction, which in general may refer to any type of transportation or communication flow, and which we designate by I_{jk}, and if we recognize that P is a constant
and introduce a new constant $G = C \dfrac{100}{P}$, we can simplify Equation 3.2 to read

$$I_{jk} = \frac{GP_jP_k}{d_{jk}} \qquad\qquad 3.3$$

where d_{jk} = distance between j and k.

Those of you who have studied physics in high school recognize that Equation 3.3 is a potential energy definition, especially if we recognize that P_j and P_k
are masses for which we may substitute the symbols m_j and m_k, respectively.
And furthermore, if we square the d_{jk} in the denominator and drop the subscripts so that we refer to any two masses in general, we have

$$F = G\frac{m_jm_k}{d^2} \qquad\qquad 3.4$$

which is the formula for the gravitational force, F, that each mass exerts on the
other. Because of this parallel, we have called the "model" associated with the
formula of Equation 3.3, the *gravity model*. As with gravity phenomena in
physics, we are not able to explain the journey-to-work and related spatial
interaction phenomena in the social world. We can only speculate on the "why"
of them. But as with the massive space exploration efforts of the United States
and the Soviet Union, we are able to employ the gravity model, as modified by
refinements to take into account relativistic and other effects, to provide a
basic guideline for operational and practical planning programs.

All this is very vague. We want to ask: Is the gravity model a useful tool?
Let us examine a specific study to illustrate how this formula can provide a useful reference pattern. Suppose we examine the rather deep-seated and disruptive
conflict between the French-speaking and Flemish-speaking populations in Belgium. A study has been conducted to determine how important the difference
in language is in communications and consequently in decision-making in the
Belgium society. A team of scholars of the Netherlands Institute of Economics
analyzed a survey of telephone calls in Belgium. They observed the number of
telephone calls among French-speaking subareas—that is, where one French-
speaking subarea was a point of origin and another the point of termination.
They found that the predicted number of telephone calls among the French-
speaking subareas that are at different distances from each other was roughly
consistent with Equation 3.3. They did the same for telephone calls among
Flemish-speaking areas. Again, Equation 3.3 held up well as a predictive device.

However, when they examined the data for telephone calls where an origin was a French-speaking area and the termination a Flemish-speaking area, or the reverse, they found that Equation 3.3 was not a good predictor. But they noted that if one multiplies the distance variable by the factor 2.8, the formula of Equation 3.3 once again works well. In short, their finding was that the difference in language effectively increased physical distance by a factor of 2.8. Thus, they got hold of one handle on the conflict problem arising from cultural difference.

Now Belgium is rather removed from those of us in the United States. Not only is it thousands of miles away, but there are few of us who are socially close to the people of Belgium—that is, have friends and relatives there. Hence, we are not emotionally involved in the major internal conflict in Belgium, and we can look at this specific application of a gravity formula objectively and accordingly judge its usefulness. In fact, the best way to examine the usefulness of a tool, technique, or methodology for analyzing one's own problems is to see how well it holds up in the analysis of a problem in which one is not emotionally involved. Then the analyst or policy maker is in a better position to attack his own problem with that tool, technique, or methodology and to know its virtues and limitations for his particular situation.

Suppose we now consider the use of the gravity model for a major conflict in the United States,—the one that arises from color difference. What is the significance of color difference? Can we examine this question in a way similar to that in which language difference was examined in the case of Belgium? Suppose we were to analyze the number of telephone calls among subareas—say telephone calls with reference to job opportunities in different subareas. Or suppose we were to examine trips for all purposes from white to white subareas, from black to white subareas, from white to black, and from black to black. It is indeed very likely that we would find that the number of trips from black residential areas to white, and from white to black, were much less than the number of trips recorded from white to white subareas and from black to black, especially when we omit journey-to-work trips. Perhaps the sharpest discrepancy would emerge with regard to trips in connection with search for new housing. We do not need to assemble the data here to know that the effective distance between a black and white subarea would be much greater than between a black and a black or a white and a white. However, it would indeed be interesting to obtain data in order to observe whether the factor by which we multiply distance to take into account the effect of different color is increasing, staying constant, or decreasing with time.

Aside from problems of conflict, there are a number of interesting ways in which the gravity model can be fruitfully used, especially for planning purposes. Take the typical problem of examining the impact of a new transportation facility—say a superhighway. We anticipate by how much the highway might cut the time and other costs of movement between a pair of major metropolitan regions. We thus can expect that the volume of traffic between these regions will increase. But by how much? If we can approximate the change in effective distance, d_{jk}, between these two metropolitan regions, j and k, then we can substitute the new for the old value of effective distance in the formula of Equation 3.3 to obtain a first estimate of the new level of interaction. This estimate is, of course, crude and must be employed with considerable caution and circumspection by any planning agency, as we shall detail in later chapters.

Some thoughtful persons may not be satisfied with the simple formulation of Equation 3.3. They may argue that in addition to numbers of population and distance, other variables are present. Doesn't the income of a family play an important role in determining the number of trips it takes, or packages it sends by railway express, or telephone calls it makes? Doesn't the level of education within a family also affect the number of letters it writes or its number of airplane trips or long-distance telephone calls? If so, then doesn't it follow that cities with populations having high income and education generate more airplane trips, railway express shipments, letters, telephone calls, telegrams, and other communication than cities with populations having low income and education? Shouldn't we expect that the volume of diverse interactions between a pair of wealthy cities will be much greater than that between a pair of poor cities?

These are appropriate questions. If the analyst is convinced that income, level of education, and other factors are relevant, he can introduce them in a number of appropriate ways. For example, instead of using simple population numbers, $P_a, P_b, ..., P_z$, in the different subareas, he may weight these numbers by per capita incomes $\overline{w}_a, \overline{w}_b, ..., \overline{w}_z$, respectively to obtain $\overline{w}_a P_a, \overline{w}_b P_b, ..., \overline{w}_z P_z$, as his relevant variables. Or if he wishes to take into account education levels, he may weight population numbers by number of years of education per capita, $\hat{w}_a, \hat{w}_b, ..., \hat{w}_z$, to obtain as his relevant variables $\hat{w}_a P_a, \hat{w}_b P_b, ..., \hat{w}_z P_z$. Or, on the basis of income, education, and other factors, he may develop a composite index with values of $w_a, w_b, ..., w_z$ with which to weight the respective populations. Accordingly, then, our formula for interaction, I_{jk}, between any two subareas j and k, becomes

$$I_{jk} = \frac{G(w_j P_j)(w_k P_k)}{d_{jk}} \qquad 3.5$$

Still other refinements of the formula of Equation 3.5 are discussed in the appendix of this chapter.

PROBLEMS FROM ABSENTEE OWNERSHIP AND DECISION-MAKING AT A DISTANCE

Still other social problems are related to spatial separations. An example is absentee ownership, and the making of decisions outside an affected region. Historically, the early stages of the amassing of wealth and the building up of fortunes take place in a local area based upon some local operation. Witness, for example, the wealth of the New England merchants based upon shipping and later industrialists based upon textiles, or the wealth of the Texan billionaires based on local oil deposits, or the wealth of Carnegie and others based on local steel production. But with time, as fortunes based on local activities develop and as local activities become linked to the New York money market and the interdependent economic system, the wealthy often move elsewhere (as with the railroad barons), or invest their fortunes elsewhere (as with New Englanders), or sell their local assets to others outside the region (as with steel magnates). Colonialism is a fine example of investment of fortunes in other regions obviously sparked by the search for profits. And so we run up against the problem of having constructed in underdeveloped regions plants and facilities whose owners reside elsewhere. Not only are the profits of their operations too often drained out of the region (colony), but the social apathy and low local visibility of absentee owners frequently lead to important decisions that do not properly take into account impacts on the local human, social-cultural environment, and local sensitivities. These decisions, then, are often poor decisions both from the standpoint of owner's profits and local welfare. Moreover, not only are these decisions poor, but frequently because excessive profits are drained from the local economy, little attention is given to the economy's needs. Local resentment builds up, the probability of revolution increases, and the perceived risks of investment mount. This, in turn, deters development as well as generating local economic instability and insecurity.

Within the United States we see a somewhat related phenomena in our metropolitan regions. Historically, cities were small in the beginning. Although the wealthy or political and religious elite who made decisions on the use of fortunes and on public investments did not typically reside in low-income areas, they were nevertheless close enough to the scene to have high local visibility. In time, as cities grew, the decision makers tended to take up residence farther from the center, thus tending to lose some of their local visibility. And with the advent of the twentieth century and the phenomenon of "invasion and succession" wherein classes of lesser wealth and prestige have continuously invaded the residential areas of the elite and pushed them out to the next zone, the elite have come to reside in suburban areas and to possess little visibility of local conditions, except those in the central business district. Accordingly we might expect, as has actually transpired, that decisions made by the elite have been less and less sensitive to the needs of the masses within the political boundaries of the city. For example, the elite, in their carefully guarded environments, have been able to avoid the undesirable features of city living, such as traffic congestion, noise, and exposure to crime and dirt. When making decisions to invest more in industry or when promoting the growth of the city in order to reap gains from their own real estate holdings, they have asked only infrequently, if at all, if perhaps the cities were growing too big. Even today, because they can escape much of the air, water, solid-waste, noise, and visual pollution, and exposure to crime, their decisions that relate either directly or indirectly to urban growth do not properly take into account the rapidly mounting social costs of growth. These costs are largely borne by those who have little if any choice other than to reside within the less desirable areas of cities.

Moreover, almost all of these decision makers and elite are not constantly aware, as they would be if they were exercising their responsibilities properly, of the changing conditions in elementary and secondary schools, of the gradual deterioration of neighborhoods and public facilities such as libraries and playgrounds, of the gradual increase in crime and insecurity, and of the gradual decay of social structure and cohesiveness. They become aware of these undesirable changes only after much change has transpired, when typically it is too late to do anything about it, or only at excessive dollar costs.

Conversely, a sensitive decision-making elite with high local visibility responds more rapidly to the need for increased property and other taxes to provide adequate education and public facilities. They can change the tax structures of central cities before they have become obsolete and impossible to reform.

The problem is even more complex than it appears from this description. Only after a considerable time lag does the decision-making elite become aware of the major contributions that the central city affords its members. When the elite lived within the city boundaries and favored a road system to facilitate people and goods movement within the city, they effected policies to provide adequate taxes for the construction and maintenance of a road system. When the higher-income groups moved out to the suburbs, it was still taken for granted that the central city should add to and maintain such a road system. This view was taken even though the elite were no longer paying property taxes on their residences to central cities. When a similar view is taken with respect to other services a central city provides to nonresidents who work in the city, a fiscally unsound situation develops. The persistence of this view in part accounts for the fact that many major central cities like Boston and Philadelphia tend to be close to bankruptcy.

These views, moreover, have led nonresident decision-makers to allocate funds for investment and operation of central city facilities in an inequitable manner. The facilities they need (and to whose deterioration they are sensitive) have found more generous support than facilities such as schools, libraries, and playgrounds, to whose deterioration they are less sensitive. But inadequate facilities for the local population have only intensified the problems of poverty and crime. These problems are doubly intensified when the decision-making elite continues in its unrestricted drive to promote growth of the metropolitan region and to make decisions that lead to a large influx of low-skill, low-educated migrants who come to reside in the ghettos and cause still further overcrowding of already inadequate schools and other public facilities.

CONCLUDING REMARKS

In this chapter we have seen the different ways in which *space* must enter our thinking. Different regions and subregions exhibit startling discrepancies in terms of their economic structures, per capita incomes, and employment opportunities. When we gather data on social problems, we frequently make comparisons between regions. Thus, we want to look at regional (and subregional) differences and the forces that have given rise to them, and ask what can be done about them.

We also looked at flows over space, particularly travel patterns and population movements. In this area, we have examined a simple gravity model to explore some of the regularities we have observed. This model also provides an introduction to the type of analytical thinking we will need to conduct in later chapters.

Finally, we looked at the impact of spatial separation, especially with reference to the location of key decisions regarding an affected region. This is a matter of great importance for underdeveloped regions. We shall examine this factor at greater depth in later chapters, where we shall develop our spatial analysis in a more systematic fashion than is provided by the sampling of spatial questions raised in this chapter.

48

APPENDIX TO CHAPTER 3. *Further Discussion of the Gravity Model*

As indicated in the text, there are many ways in which an analyst might refine the crude gravity model for use in a study of a particular type of communication-transportation phenomenon. We have already indicated in the text that the simplified formula

$$I_{jk} = \frac{GP_jP_k}{d_{jk}} \qquad (3A.1)$$

can be appropriately modified to consider income, level of education, and other factors one may wish to introduce. An appropriate index can be developed by which to weight population in order to use the adjusted Equation 3.5, which is

$$I_{jk} = \frac{G(w_jP_j)\,(w_kP_k)}{d_{jk}} \qquad (3A.2)$$

In addition to weighting population, the analyst may wish to effect other revisions. We have already noted that the distance variable in Equation 3.3 is raised to the first power to suggest a potential energy type of relationship between two masses, while it is raised to the second power in Equation 3.4 to suggest a gravitational-type force exerted by one mass upon the other. We are not able to provide a rationale for choosing one formulation rather than the other, for we still cannot explain gravitational phenomena, physical or social. But then, if we cannot choose between the exponent of 1 or 2, why choose at all? Why not let the actual data determine which of the two is the more relevant? Better yet, why not consider the exponent a variable to be determined by the data on people's travel and communications behavior? Actually, this point of view has been adopted by a number of transportation analysts, and some, therefore, employ the revised equation

$$I_{jk} = \frac{Gm_jm_k}{d_{jk}^b} \qquad (3A.3)$$

where $m_j = w_jP_j$; $m_k = w_kP_k$; and b is the variable power to which the distance variable is raised.

To see more clearly the relevance of this approach let us rewrite Equation 3A.3 in terms of logarithms. We obtain

$$\log I_{jk} = \log Gm_jm_k - b \log d_{jk} \qquad (3A.4)$$

or

$$\log \frac{I_{jk}}{m_jm_k} = \log G - b \log d_{jk} \qquad (3A.5)$$

Now to make explicit the impact of distance, we plot on Figure 3A.1 the data for our pairs of subareas which we have plotted on Figure 3.3. On Figure 3A.1 we measure along the horizontal the logarithm of distance in miles (that is,

Figure 3A.1   The Influence of Distance on Interaction

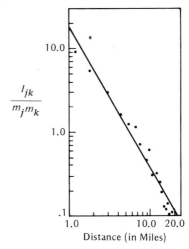

Source: Walter Isard, *Methods of Regional Analysis* (Cambridge: M.I.T. Press, 1960), p. 511.

log d_{jk}) and along the vertical the logarithm of the ratio of actual interaction I_{jk} between two subareas j and k to the product of the weighted masses of these subareas (that is, $I_{jk}/m_j m_k$). Note how clearcut is the "falling-off" or attenuating effect of distance. According to some transportation analysts, the slope of the straight line which best fits the data is the exponent b to which the distance variable should be raised, and the intercept value of the straight line is then log G. Further, some of these analysts also advance the hypothesis that the effect of distance varies with the type of trip undertaken. They would fit straight lines on double log scale to the data on different kinds of trips. They might obtain a figure such as Figure 3A.2. Here we observe a high value of b for school trips, indicating their high sensitivity to the distance variable; and a lower value of b for social recreation trips, indicating their lower sensitivity to the distance variable.

Still other variations of the gravity model have been suggested. In one, the form of the function of Equation 3.2 is replaced by

$$I_{jk} = aP_j P_k - bd_{jk} \tag{3A.6}$$

or simply

$$I_{jk} = k - bd_{jk} \tag{3A.7}$$

Both these equations capture an attenuating influence of distance. In yet other variations, the population variables P_j and P_k are raised to powers, say α and β, respectively, so as to yield

$$I_{jk} = \frac{G w_j P_j^\alpha w_k P_k^\beta}{d_{jk}^b} \tag{3A.8}$$

Moreover, certain sociologists have suggested that often it is not physical distance that serves as the barrier to interchange, but rather the number of intervening opportunities. This variable would then substitute for d_{jk}^b in Equation 3A.3.

50

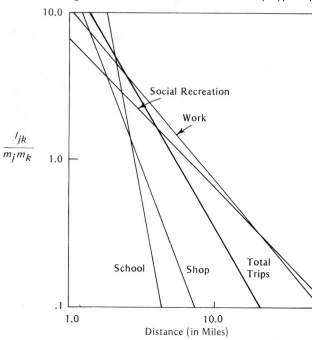

Figure 3A.2   The Influence of Distance by Type Trip

Source: Walter Isard, *Methods of Regional Analysis* (Cambridge: M.I.T. Press, 1960), p. 514.

Still other social scientists might consider time distance, or social distance, or psychological distance, or political distance, or transport cost distance as relevant for a particular type of interaction rather than physical distance. Some would use a constant, G_{jk}, specific to each pair of subareas in order to reflect the particular complementarities of each pair rather than the same constant G; and some would use Gross Subarea Product, or Capital Stock, or some other magnitude as a measure of mass.

These and numerous other interesting variations have been discussed elsewhere. (For example, see Isard, *Methods of Regional Analysis*, Chapter 11.)

Chapter

4

The Market System: Its Workings

INTRODUCTION

We have examined the data of an input-output table. In the United States system, the input-output table usually records *dollar* value of inputs or purchases and *dollar* value of outputs or sales. It does not refer to physical magnitudes, such as tons of coal or gallons of oil, as do input-output tables in Eastern European countries. Each number in a cell in a United States input-output table thus represents a physical quantity times a *price*, where we define price to be a dollar value per physical unit. Now the physical quantities of inputs and outputs are obtainable from engineers who know production processes, or from persons experienced in the operation of a plant. For example, if we are producing a standard type of steel, we pretty much know how many tons of ore, coal, and limestone are required per ton of steel. When we multiply each of these physical quantities by the relevant price, we obtain dollars' worth of ore, coal, and limestone inputs which correspond to ore, coal, and limestone purchases (in dollar value). When we multiply the ton of steel by its price, we have its corresponding dollar value as output.

But from where do these prices come? They certainly do not fall out of heaven; nor are they prescribed by any dictatorial price control board. Rather, they reflect directly and indirectly the desires of many individuals who want to consume goods and who are also motivated to make profits and income in order to consume goods (or amass wealth). Nor are prices, which in a sense are simply cultural symbols, trivial magnitudes. They are highly significant symbols. We need to understand the forces that determine prices, not only to be able to construct relevant input-output tables and employ them effectively but also to formulate fruitful development policy. We have already noted that sound development policy requires the identification of profitable opportunities for private investments, which are needed to create new jobs and new demands for the output of existing or possibly new producers. But to identify these profitable opportunities we need to compare the profit potential of an operation in one region or location with that in another. To make this comparison we need to determine prices at which inputs and raw materials can be bought by plants producing at different locations, and the prices at which these plants can sell their output in different markets.

THE DEMAND SCHEDULE AND THE DEMAND CURVE

Let us begin with a situation that may be familiar to a young female in the United States (and that is becoming increasingly familiar to the male). If she has just finished school and is searching for a job, she may open the *Philadelphia Inquirer* to the classified ads section. There she may see a number of ads for Girl Fridays, and may consider such a job. Why are these companies advertising for Girl Fridays and offering a salary of around $100 per week (as of 1972)?[1]

If you are a businessman, you may find that it is very useful to have in your office a capable, alert, quick young lady with some typing skill and some knowledge of bookkeeping. She can save you the constant annoyance of answering telephone calls, writing standard letters, adding numbers, and so forth. To you, one such young lady may be worth $100 per week. So at a wage of $100 a week you have a demand for one such employee, and you accordingly find yourself advertising in the *Philadelphia Inquirer*. If the going wage for Girl Fridays were to increase to $110 per week you might feel that such an employee would be an unwarranted luxury and that you should do the jobs that a Girl Friday might do. On the other hand, if the going rate for a Girl Friday fell to $65 per week, you might find it desirable to have two such persons around. They could relieve you of so much routine that you could begin to tap some new markets for your product or service.

Consider a second businessman, in somewhat the same business situation as the first. Suppose, however, that he is a grumbling old man with little patience and ability at typing. He is much more annoyed than the first by having to do routine tasks. The presence of a Girl Friday in his office would improve his disposition greatly and reduce his morning's misery, especially after a bad night's sleep. We then would expect that the maximum wage he would be willing to offer would be higher, say $125 per week; further, he might be willing to hire two Girl Fridays if the going wage were to fall to $80 per week.

Take a third businessman. He may be willing to employ two Girl Fridays at a wage not exceeding $110 per week, only one if the wage exceeds $110 but is not greater than $130, and none if it exceeds $130. If the wage were to fall to $70 per week, he would want to employ three.

[1]We use the situation in year 1972 since many of our figures are derived from 1972 data.

So the demand factor goes. If we now consider the 100,000 or so business enterprises in the Philadelphia region, we can see that there is a very large demand for Girl Fridays. If we add all these demands together, as we do in Table 4.1, we obtain a totals column that may be viewed as a *demand schedule*. The demand schedule records the total number of Girl Fridays demanded at different weekly wages. At the high wage of $140 per week, there would be few firms in the Philadelphia region that would want to employ a Girl Friday. The number demanded would total 1,600. At the lower wage of $135, more firms would be interested in Girl Fridays; the total number demanded would be 3,000. And so on. At the bargain wage of $80, the number demanded would rise to 26,000; and at the excessively low wage of $75, the number demanded would increase to 30,000.

It is convenient to summarize the information in the totals column of Table 4.1—that is, the information of a demand schedule—by use of a *demand curve*.

Table 4.1   Demand Schedule for Girl Fridays

Weekly Wage	Demand of Business Firm							Total
	#1	#2	#3	•	•	•	n	
•	•	•	•	•	•	•	•	•
•	•	•	•	•	•	•	•	•
•	•	•	•	•	•	•	•	•
$140	0	0	0	•	•	•	0	1,600
135	0	0	0	•	•	•	1	3,000
130	0	0	1	•	•	•	1	4,600
125	0	1	1	•	•	•	1	5,700
120	0	1	1	•	•	•	1	8,000
115	0	1	1	•	•	•	2	9,400
110	0	1	2	•	•	•	2	11,000
105	1	1	2	•	•	•	2	12,800
100	1	1	2	•	•	•	2	15,000
95	1	1	2	•	•	•	2	17,400
90	1	1	2	•	•	•	2	20,000
85	1	1	2	•	•	•	2	22,800
80	1	2	2	•	•	•	2	26,000
75	1	2	2	•	•	•	3	30,000
•	•	•	•	•	•	•	•	•
•	•	•	•	•	•	•	•	•
•	•	•	•	•	•	•	•	•

To do so we plot the data of the demand schedule in a figure such as Figure 4.1, where we measure weekly wage (price) along the vertical axis and total number demanded along the horizontal. Point A on Figure 4.1 indicates that at a weekly wage of $140, the total number demanded is 1,600, as indicated by the top figure in the totals column of Table 4.1. Point B on Figure 4.1 indicates that at a a weekly wage of $135, the total number demanded is 3,000, as indicated by the second figure in the totals column of Table 4.1. And so forth. Clearly the DD curve of Figure 4.1 closely approximates the data in the totals column of Table 4.1 and can be used in place of the data to facilitate analysis.

THE SUPPLY SCHEDULE AND THE SUPPLY CURVE

The eagerness of business firms to hire Girl Fridays is only one side of the picture. The other side is the eagerness of females to be Girl Fridays (or males to be Boy Fridays). Currently, those who most qualify as Girl Fridays are the young females who come out of college and high school each year looking for jobs. Each such person considers the pros and cons of this type of work. If the weekly wage is $100, one young lady might very well choose to pursue this occupation, given the variety of tasks entailed and bearing in mind the opportunity to rub shoulders with diverse personalities. She may make this choice, particularly if she can find no other employment at least as interesting but paying her more—or if some higher-paying job that she finds is more routine and in a less pleasant setting. This other employment might be in a factory that is not air-conditioned, or be located in a section of town that is "unsafe" or that does not have the kaleidoscopic stimuli that some central business districts provide. So she offers her services at the weekly wage of $100. Even if the wage rate were as low as $95, she might still offer her services. However, if the wage rate were to fall to $90, she would not accept a job as a Girl Friday. She might choose not to be "exploited" and thus take a less interesting but better paying job. Or, if financial matters are of secondary importance to her, she might choose to stay at home and be involved in diverse tasks.

Figure 4.1   Demand and Supply Curves

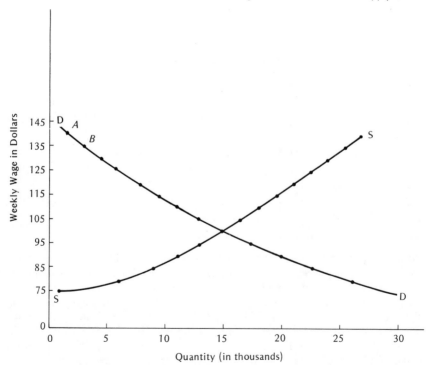

Consider a second female. She may come from a poor family and have a pressing need for a job. Her employment alternatives may be the same as those of the first. However, because of her greater need for work, she is more eager than the first to work at any given wage. She may, for example, be willing to work for as low as $85 per week, but no lower.

A third might be willing to work at $100 but no lower; a fourth at $105; a fifth at $115; a sixth at nothing less than $150. And so forth. Moreover, if the weekly wage were as high as $110, some young females, currently employed at boring, routine typing jobs, might consider giving up these jobs to take on the more interesting Girl Friday occupation. And clearly, if the wage rate for Girl Fridays were to increase still more, more young females might decide that it was not worthwhile staying at home; some might even decide to quit college and go to work.

Just as we set up a table to derive a demand schedule, so can we derive a *supply schedule*. We simply list along the left-hand tab various possible weekly wages. In each column we indicate whether or not a particular young female is willing to offer her services at each possible weekly wage. If she is, we put down the number "1"; if not, we put down the number "0". When we add the numbers (ones and zeros) by row, we obtain a totals column. This totals column may be defined as a supply schedule, which lists for each weekly wage the total number of females who would offer their services as Girl Fridays. At the high weekly wage of $140, the number would be 26,700; at $135, 25,400; at $130, 23,900; at the very low weekly wage of $80, 6,000; and at $75, only 1,000.

In short, this is how we develop a supply schedule for Girl Fridays for the Philadelphia region. We plot the data of this supply schedule on Figure 4.1. We approximate these data by drawing a curve, the SS curve, through them, which we designate the *supply curve*.

Table 4.2   Supply Schedule for Girl Fridays

Weekly Wage	Supply by Young Female								Total
	#1	#2	#3	#4	#5	#6	• •	n	
•	•	•	•	•	•	•	• • •		•
•	•	•	•	•	•	•	• • •		•
•	•	•	•	•	•	•	• • •		•
$140	1	1	1	1	1	0	• •	1	26,700
135	1	1	1	1	1	0	• •	0	25,400
130	1	1	1	1	1	0	• •	0	23,900
125	1	1	1	1	1	0	• •	0	22,500
120	1	1	1	1	1	0	• •	0	21,000
115	1	1	1	1	1	0	• •	0	19,400
110	1	1	1	1	0	0	• •	0	18,000
105	1	1	1	1	0	0	• •	0	16,200
100	1	1	1	0	0	0	• •	0	15,000
95	1	1	0	0	0	0	• •	0	13,000
90	0	1	0	0	0	0	• •	0	11,000
85	0	1	0	0	0	0	• •	0	9,000
80	0	0	0	0	0	0	• •	0	6,000
75	0	0	0	0	0	0	• •	0	1,000
•	•	•	•	•	•	•	• • •		•
•	•	•	•	•	•	•	• • •		•
•	•	•	•	•	•	•	• • •		•

THE DETERMINATION OF WAGES AND PRICES
IN A COMPETITIVE MARKET

Having derived and plotted both the demand and supply schedules and having developed for each a curve, we may now specifically ask: How is the weekly wage of a Girl Friday set?

To begin, suppose the wage were $85. At such a wage, businessmen would want to hire 22,800 Girl Fridays (see Table 4.1), but only 9,000 young females would offer their services (see Table 4.2). There would be a major discrepancy between what was demanded and what was supplied. This is clear from Figure 4.1 by comparing the quantity offered, as given by the SS supply curve at $85, and the quantity demanded, as given by the DD demand curve at $85. At most, only 9,000 businessmen will be satisfied and able to hire Girl Fridays. Now from Table 4.1 and the demand curve of Figure 4.1, we know that many more businessmen want to hire a Girl Friday, even at a wage as high as $90 (the number demanded at that wage is 20,000). So if some of these businessmen were not among the lucky ones who hired one or more Girl Fridays at $85, they would start raising the wage to $90. Consequently some Girl Fridays would shift from a job paying $85 to one paying $90. Moreover, some young females who would not work at $85 would come on the market and accept a $90 weekly wage. Because of the highly competitive market for Girl Fridays, businessmen who started hiring Girl Fridays at the wage of $85 would pretty soon have to raise the wage to $90 to hold onto their Girl Fridays.

The process does not stop here. We observe from the demand schedule that at $90 the number of Girl Fridays demanded is 20,000, but the supply schedule indicates that only 11,000 young females would take such a job—again a major discrepancy, but a discrepancy that is significantly less than the one at the wage of $85 (see Figure 4.1). Clearly, only some of the businessmen wanting Girl Fridays will be successful in obtaining one or more of them to work. Once again, we find that some unhappy businessmen, not lucky enough to hire a Girl Friday, would be willing to pay more than $90. They may be willing to pay $95, and so would offer the higher wage. As a consequence, some Girl Fridays would shift away from jobs paying $90 to jobs paying $95. Another group of young females who were not willing to work at $90 would come on the market at $95. Businessmen who were previously able to hire at $90 would find that they must raise their weekly wage to $95. But at $95 the number demanded still exceeds supply, as can be seen from Figure 4.1 and from the schedules of Tables 4.1 and 4.2. Those businessmen who still do not have as many Girl Fridays as they desire and who are willing to hire at $98 or $100 will bid up the price. New young females come onto the market. Others will shift to the higher-paying business firms. So the wage rate creeps up to $98. At $98, Figure 4.1 shows that the number demanded still exceeds supply. Consequently, we can expect the wage rate to continue to rise—it will do so until the wage rate reaches $100.

At the weekly wage of $100, a new situation develops. We see that at that wage the demand and supply curves of Figure 4.1 intersect. That is, they have a point in common, referring to the same price and quantity. This can be verified from the data of Tables 4.1 and 4.2. At the wage of $100, 15,000 Girl Fridays are demanded, and 15,000 young females offer their services for hire. *Demand equals supply*. If demand equals supply, it signifies that all the businessmen who want to hire one or more Girl Fridays at $100 are able to do so. There are no unhappy ones among them, and so no businessman has an incentive to bid up the wage rate. There is nothing to gain by doing so. Also, at $100 all the young females who want a job as a Girl Friday are able to find one. So there are no unhappy ones among them—as would be the case if some could not find a job. This means that there is no incentive for young females to "bid down" or under-cut the price. Let us see why.

Suppose we had begun our analysis with a weekly wage that was well above $100—say $115. Such a wage rate for a Girl Friday is fairly attractive (1972). Accordingly, at this wage 19,400 young females seek Girl Friday jobs. But businessmen only demand 9,400 Girl Fridays at this wage—a major discrepancy reflecting excess supply. Approximately 10,000 of the young females would be unsuccessful at finding a job. Now, as noted above, there would be among these unsuccessful young females a large number who would be willing to work at a wage of $110. Some of them would offer their services at this lower wage in order to get a job. They might take a job away from a female who is paid $115, or they may be able to get a job from a businessman who is willing to pay only $110. In time the news will get around that some businessmen who cannot or will not pay $115 are getting Girl Fridays at $110, and that others have replaced a young female paid $115 with one whom they pay only $110. Other business-men try to get away with paying only $110 and find they can. Before long, the going wage for Girl Fridays has fallen to $110.

At the wage of $110, the number of females who would want a job would be 18,000. But only 11,000 jobs would be available, even after taking into account the new demands of businessmen who can afford to pay only $110 and of businessmen who will hire an additional Girl Friday if the wage is as low as $110. Again, supply significantly exceeds demand. The forces that tend to decrease the wage rate continue to operate. Wages keep declining until the rate of $100 is reached. At $100, supply comes to equal demand. We find no Girl Fridays who are willing to work at $100 or less who do not have a job. Therefore they have no inclination to offer their services at a lower wage. The only Girl Fridays who do not have a job are those who want more than $100 before they are will-ing to work. They too have no inclination to undercut the $100 wage. Hence the decrease in the wage rate will stop at $100.

This discussion illustrates how a competitive market works. The outcome is the establishment of a price, which equates supply and demand—this is defined as the *equilibrium price*. Note that the actual wage paid a particular young female at a particular point of time does not necessarily need to correspond to the equilibrium wage in an unchanging market situation. Her actual wage can fluctuate around the equilibrium wage for various reasons—including mispercep-tions, lack of information, and irrationalities. For example, an inexperienced or naive female may accept a Girl Friday job at $95 from some businessman trying to cut corners. Sooner or later, however, she will learn that she can earn $100 at a job similar to the one she holds. If she is rational, she will change jobs and the price for her services, as with others like her, will equal the equilibrium price.

In the case of the market for Girl Fridays there are many demanders and many suppliers. No one demander can be in a monopoly position and influence price in any way. Each businessman takes the going market wage as given, and out of self-interest demands that number of Girl Fridays which is consistent with a plan to maximize his profits. Similarly, no one female has any monopsonistic influence—that is, control of the quantity of females seeking jobs so as to influence price. The demanders for Girl Fridays are unorganized. So are the females who come on the market and offer their services. Hence, we have an excellent example of a situation that may be characterized as *pure competition*—a situation relevant for a large fraction of our population. Behaving units are free to enter or leave the market, whether they are businessmen (who are free to place an ad in the local newspaper) or young females who are also free to do so. There are no restrictions to entry and exit in this market.

CHANGE IN EQUILIBRIUM WAGES AND PRICES

Having obtained the equilibrium price, we next ask how it can change. What accounts for the increases in the equilibrium wage for Girl Fridays that have taken place in the past? What accounts for the decreases that we can observe? To explain such changes, we must keep in mind that the intersection of the supply schedule and the demand schedule determines the equilibrium price. Hence, the equilibrium price can change only if the supply schedule changes, or the demand schedule changes, or both. That is, the price changes only if the eagerness of young females to sell their labor services at different prices changes, or the eagerness of firms to buy these services at different prices changes, or both.

Let us be specific. Suppose that the general economic conditions of a nation deteriorate. Hard times come. Fewer jobs are available for college graduates in their field of specialization, whether it be economics, music, history, government, literature, chemistry, biology, or design. Because of fewer opportunities in these fields, there will be a smaller fraction of the graduating class of young females who can find jobs in them at the going wage rates. Consequently, there will be a larger fraction available for employment in other nonspecialized jobs, such as Girl Fridays, at each of the wages that might prevail. At the wage rate of $80, 8,000 rather than 6,000 young females might want to hire out as Girl Fridays; at a wage of $90, 15,000 instead of 11,000; at $95, 17,000 instead of 13,000; at $100, 19,000 instead of 15,000. And so forth.

Hence, we may consider that the supply schedule for Girl Fridays has shifted down and to the right. We approximate the shifted schedule by the dashed curve on Figure 4.2. Observe that the old equilibrium wage of $100 is no longer relevant. At the wage of $100, the demand for Girl Fridays is still 15,000. However, the supply of Girl Fridays in this new situation is 19,000. Hence, at a weekly wage of $100, supply well exceeds demand. Accordingly, we can expect that many of those young females who are unable to find a job at $100 per week will underbid the existing wage rate and offer their services for less. Through this competitive process, the weekly wage rate will fall and continue to fall until supply equals demand. From Figure 4.2 we see that equality will be realized at the price of $95, where the old demand curve intersects the new dashed supply curve. At any lower price, excess demand exists, which will drive the wage up to the new equilibrium level. At any higher price, excess supply exists, which will drive the wage rate down.

The above analysis assumes that the demand schedule for Girl Fridays does not change. Suppose it, too, changes. Suppose that national conditions have deteriorated and many of the small business firms are less eager to hire Girl

Fridays. In view of less profitable conditions and smaller markets, the first businessman we discussed might no longer be able to pay as much as $100 per week. At this wage, he might feel that the gains do not offset the costs. The highest wage he might be willing to pay is now $90; and the wage rate would have to fall to $60 per week for him to hire two Girl Fridays to work in his office. Or reconsider the second businessman. He might be able to employ one Girl Friday if the wage rate were not more than $110 (instead of $125) and two Girl Fridays if the wage rate were not more than $65 (instead of $80).

Figure 4.2   Shifts in Demand and Supply Curves

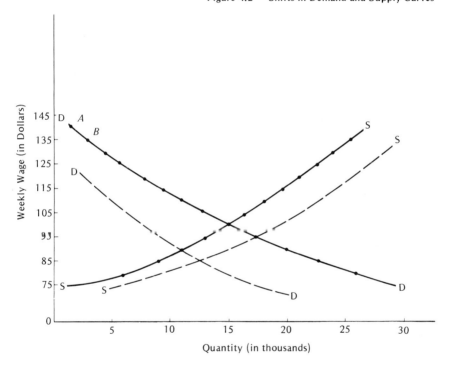

Similarly with other businessmen. In the new situation, the number of Girl Fridays demanded is less for every wage that we might consider. In sum, we have a new demand schedule as represented by the dashed demand curve of Figure 4.2. In effect, the demand curve has shifted down and to the left.

We proceed as before to determine the equilibrium price in the new situation. We consider the relevant demand and supply schedules and their respective curves, which are the dashed curves in Figure 4.2. We see that at the equilibrium price for the first situation discussed, namely $100, demand and supply are no longer equal. Hence, the price of $100 is not an equilibrium price in the new situation. We also see that at the equilibrium price for the second situation discussed, namely $95, supply and demand are not equal. At the price of $95, conditions of excess supply exist. Accordingly, the wage rate will fall and continue to fall until it reaches $85, a wage that yields an equality of supply and demand as indicated by the intersection of the dashed curves on Figure 4.2.

This discussion pertains to conditions in which the supply curve has shifted down and to the right and the demand curve down and to the left. But we can also imagine other conditions. Suppose there is a sudden upsurge in federal government programs to accelerate scientific development. Many new job opportunities for research assistants are created, which can be filled by college graduates. The alternatives for any young college graduate are increased, and it is likely that fewer may choose to hire out as Girl or Boy Fridays. The supply curve thus shifts up and to the left. Or such a shift might occur because of a new trend in which young females once again find it highly desirable to marry and immediately raise a family.

Or, to again illustrate the opposite condition, discrimination against blacks may continue to decrease and more young black females may be able to enter the Girl Friday market and thus increase the available supply at every wage.

The demand schedule may also shift up and to the right. Business conditions may improve, and at the same time many firms may find it profitable to use modern office equipment—equipment to which the old-time businessman is less able to adapt than a younger person. (For example, an old-timer can change a ribbon in a manual typewriter with little difficulty, but is apt to be totally incompetent when it comes to putting a new carbon ribbon in the latest IBM). Hence, his need for and eagerness to hire Girl Fridays increases. Or suppose he starts taking more vacations and longer weekends, in keeping with trends in a society becoming more and more affluent. All these factors then lead to a shift of the demand curve up and to the right, which together with any accompanying shift of the supply curve will once again lead to a new equilibrium wage. We must, of course, realize that because of random disturbances (small, short-lived factors), at any one point in time the equilibrium price may not be in effect. The actual price may be somewhat above or below it. But sooner or later forces will be set in operation, tending to move the actual price toward the equilibrium price and to keep the actual price from being too different from the equilibrium price.

Thus, if we pick up the *Philadelphia Inquirer* today and note that there are want ads for Girl Fridays with wage offers at and around the figure of $100, with $100 being the figure used most frequently, we can pretty much conclude that $100 is the equilibrium price (or very close to it) for a *standard* Girl Friday.

We may now wish to generalize. Not only is the equilibrium weekly price (wage) of Girl Fridays determined in the way we have discussed, but so also are the prices of a number of other commodities such as wheat, chickens, butter, shoes, and shirts. In their consumption and production, conditions of pure competition are met. For example, consider the determination of the equilibrium price of wheat. There are many sellers—the numerous farmers who produce wheat—none of whom is big enough to exert any control over the price of wheat. There are many demanders—the many enterprises that buy wheat to produce diverse wheat products—none of which is big enough to influence prices. There is freedom of entry into the market. Any person can decide to become a farmer and produce wheat, or any farmer not now producing wheat can consider doing so. There is also freedom of exit from the market. No farmer is required by law or other edict to produce wheat and only wheat. No firm is required to buy wheat and only wheat.

In markets in which pure competition prevails, changes in equilibrium prices for commodities occur in the same way as changes in the wage for Girl Fridays.

That is, changes occur because changes transpire in underlying forces governing the eagerness of behaving units to buy and sell at different prices, as depicted by the demand and supply schedules and curves. For the interested reader, we present the more technical aspects of demand and supply curves in a few appendices, after the basic materials have been covered. In the appendix to Chapter 10 we indicate how the demand curve is derived both for the individual consumer (nonindustrial) and the aggregate of consumers. In the appendix to Chapter 6 we indicate how the demand curve for a factor of production or an intermediate commodity (one that is used in production) is derived for the industrial firm and the aggregate of firms. All these demands when added yield the demand curve for a factor or the output of an industry. Finally, in the appendix to Chapter 5 we indicate how the supply curve of a commodity is derived for an industrial firm and industry.

IMPERFECT COMPETITION
AND MARKET INADEQUACIES

In reality, conditions of pure competition often do not obtain. All kinds of imperfections in the competitive system are present. Consequently, the simple results we obtained in the previous sections are not realized. Most markets do not work in the simple ways discussed. Natural harmony, as Adam Smith imagined it, does not prevail.

Let us consider the various imperfections in the competitive system. At one extreme is the monopolist, who is the only producer of a commodity for which there is no effective substitute. If there is no governmental regulation, he has complete control over the price to be charged for the good. We shall discuss this in detail in Chapter 8. We shall see that when he maximizes his profits, he charges a price higher than would ordinarily exist under conditions of pure competition. Further, he produces a smaller amount of goods and in general uses resources inefficiently from the standpoint of social welfare.

At the other extreme is the imperfectly competitive situation, in which there is a multitude of small firms. Each produces a good which, though very similar to the goods produced by many other firms, is still unique. This may be because of some style factor, because of its particular location or retail operation, or because of some minor patent held by the firm. In short, each product is somewhat differentiated from all others. In this sense, each firm has some monopoly power and within a narrow range can control the prices of its product. In this situation again, prices tend to be too high, outputs too small, and resources inefficiently used when compared with what would exist under pure competition.

In between the two extremes are situations in which there are two, three, or relatively few producers, as in the steel industry, or a fair number of producers—ten, fifteen, or twenty—as in the petroleum refinery industry. These situations are often called oligopolies. They do not yield the ideal results of pure competition either. Consequently, in Chapter 13 we shall specifically discuss the need for public regulation of monopoly with the welfare of society in mind, and what we say also pertains at least in part to oligopolies and other imperfectly competitive situations. We shall do so keeping in mind the diverse aspects of exploitation, colonialism, and other related phenomena presented in Chapter 8.

The discussion in the previous section oversimplifies the workings of the market in other important respects. The market for a Girl Friday is one where the qualified labor has the ability to understand an advertisement and also has access to information, because a newspaper costs so little. Unfortunately, information about many other markets is either not available to qualified persons, cannot be understood or perceived by such persons, or both. In Chapter 8 we shall, for example, consider the typical poor white in Appalachia and the poor black in Mississippi. He may be very qualified for certain kinds of jobs in a major metropolitan region like New York City or Philadelphia; but there may not exist an information service in Appalachia or Mississippi to let him know that jobs exist. Further, if a source of information does exist in Appalachia or Mississippi, the employee may not be able to read and understand the information that is available. Or even if he does understand it he may not be able to perceive New York City or Philadelphia as a meaningful place to work.

These are serious obstacles to the working of the market in a more efficient manner. In Chapter 13, we indicate that one of the roles of the public sector is to supply the right kind of information at the right places, thereby decreasing the costs of searching for a job. A related role is to provide the right kind of training so that the information can be effectively communicated to prospective employees. Nonetheless, attitude and other psychological variables may continue to intervene and interfere in the well-intentioned actions of concerned public officials.

Markets also do not operate as ideally as depicted in the previous sections because many barriers exist with regard to both entry and exit. We know too well the widespread discrimination against many racial and ethnic groups—blacks, Puerto Ricans, Indians, etc.—that have existed and continue to exist. We know there are widespread obstacles set up to entry of females in many job markets. And despite the many efforts of the public sector to lower or remove such obstacles, they will continue to persist for many decades, if not centuries. This again reflects the limited capabilities of mankind.

Finally, we shall point up in Chapter 13 that there are many important goods and services that are or should be produced but that cannot be marketed. These are called nonmarketable goods and services. They include such items as national defense and public education and those things which enhance the quality of the environment.

Some Basic Elements of Cost Analysis and Profit Maximization

INTRODUCTION

In the previous chapter we viewed supply as reflecting the *eagerness* of sellers to offer their goods and services for sale at different prices, and demand as reflecting the eagerness of buyers to purchase goods and services at different prices. We now wish to examine some of the forces underlying such eagerness. Why are business firms (big and small), public bodies, and other institutions eager to buy certain goods and services and produce other goods and services for sale. Or. put in another way, how do they decide on the level of their output and the level of their input?

We begin to answer some of these questions in this chapter. In subsequent chapters we will develop the analysis further, and also examine what lies behind the eagerness of individuals, such as the young females in the previous chapter, to supply services for hire and otherwise buy and sell goods.

COST CURVES FOR A SIMPLE OPERATION

To begin, let us consider a simple firm that is motivated to maximize profits. It purchases inputs and produces goods for sale. For the moment, assume that the amount of goods it can sell in a market is given, and that the firm is too small to affect prices in the market. Hence, the sales revenues of this firm, which are derived by multiplying the number of units it sells by the market price, are also given. Because profits are given by the difference between sales revenues and total costs of inputs, and because the firm takes its sales revenues as given, to maximize profits the firm must minimize total costs.

Consider total costs. For our purposes, we need to look at only two different types of costs, although in more sophisticated analysis we should look at more. One type of cost is *fixed costs*. *Fixed costs* are the costs that a firm must bear regardless of its level or scale of output—for example, whether it produces 10 units of output or 100 units. These costs comprise annual rent for a factory building, annual salary of a manager, insurance, fixed charges and depreciation on equipment, and similar items. In Figure 5.1, where we measure total output along the horizontal axis and dollar costs along the vertical, total fixed costs can be represented by the straight horizontal line FF.

The second type of cost is *variable costs*. *Variable costs* do depend on the scale of output. The cost of iron ore, for example, is a variable cost to an integrated steel works. If the works doubles its output of pig iron, its requirement for iron ore will roughly double. The cost of labor for operating machines in a textile factory is a variable cost; labor costs must increase as the number of machines operated increases. In general, variable costs include costs of raw materials, fuel for processing, production labor, transportation, office supplies, and similar items. In Figure 5.1, we plot the variable cost curve VV, which rises as output increases. For convenience we plot it as a straight line from the origin.

Figure 5.1   Total Fixed Costs, Total Variable Costs, and Total Costs

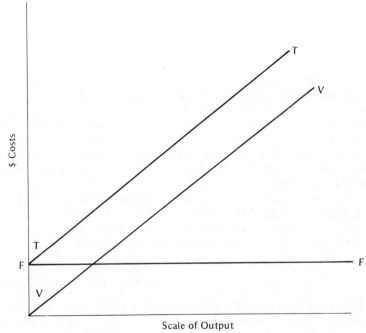

Scale of Output

Between the two extremes of strictly fixed and variable costs are other categories of costs. We know that if output were to fall to very low levels, a firm might sublet part of its plant and thus reduce its net rent costs. Its rent in this situation would not be a pure fixed cost. Its manager might also be able to find part-time employment elsewhere. In that case, managerial costs could be reduced to some extent, and would not be a pure fixed cost. In contrast, the costs of certain materials may not be strictly variable costs. For example, certain items can be purchased only by the dozen. Therefore, the costs for these items are fixed insofar as we might require less than a dozen. So we see that analysis based on a classification of strictly fixed and variable costs must be qualified. Nonetheless, several important points can be made.

When both fixed and variable costs of a firm are determined, we can sum them to obtain its total costs. In Figure 5.1 we plot the *TT* line, which depicts total costs for each level of output. We see that the *TT* line is the sum of the *FF* line and the *VV* line.

In a similar way, we may consider the operation of a government-type unit, say a public health unit. This unit operates a facility to provide certain basic medical services, free of charge, to all citizens in the community. Here, typical fixed costs are the annual depreciation charges, insurance, and interest on building and equipment. Typical variable costs are costs of medical supplies and wages for nurses and clerical help. This unit, too, has a fixed cost curve, a variable cost curve, and a total cost curve like the ones in Figure 5.1.

In addition to depicting costs with a figure, we may wish to set down the cost data in a table, such as Table 5.1. We record along the left-hand tab different

Figure 5.2   Average (Unit) Costs: Fixed, Variable, and Total

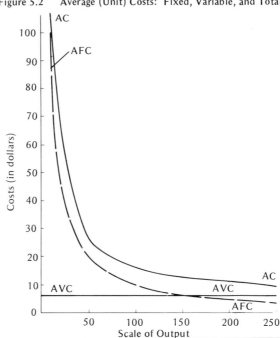

levels of output, and list by column the different kinds of costs. The first column records *fixed costs*, which are the same for all levels of outputs. The second column records *variable costs,* which increase with increased output. The third column records *total costs.* Because we are also interested in the costs per unit of output, we add three more columns to Table 5.1. The fourth column records *fixed costs per unit output*, which we designate as *average fixed costs*, AFC. Note that they decline from $100 to $4 as we go down the column because we are spreading a fixed amount among more and more units of output. The fifth column records *variable costs per unit of output*, also called average variable costs, AVC, which are $6 per unit. In this particular example they do not decline but stay the same per unit of output. However, in general they may either rise or fall or both, provided that total variable costs increase as total output increases. The sixth column records *total costs per unit output,* also called *average cost*, AC. These are the sum of fixed costs per unit output and variable costs per unit output; that is, AC = AFC + AVC. They fall from $106 to $10 with increase in output.

We can plot these data on Figure 5.2 and obtain relevant cost curves. Observe that the AFC curve, the curve of fixed costs per unit output is a rectangular

Table 5.1   Annual Costs of Operation: A Textile Plant

Level of Output (units)	Total Fixed Costs (1)	Total Variable Costs (2)	Total Costs (3)	AFC: Average Fixed Costs (4)	AVC: Average Variable Costs (5)	AC: Average Total Cost (6)
.						
.						
.	.	.	.	.	.	.
10	1,000	60	1,060	100	6	106
.						
.	.	. .	.	.	.	.
.						
50	1,000	300	1,300	20	6	26
.						
.	.	.	.	.	.	.
100	1,000	600	1,600	10	6	16
.						
.						
.	.	.	.	.	.	.
150	1,000	900	1,900	6.67	6	12.67
151	1,000	906	1,906	6.62	6	12.62
152	1,000	912	1,912	6.58	6	12.58
153	1,000	918	1,918	6.54	6	12.54
154	1,000	924	1,924	6.49	6	12.49
155	1,000	930	1,930	6.45	6	12.45
.						
.						
.	.	.	.	.	.	.
200	1,000	1,200	2,200	5	6	11
.						
.	.	.	.	.	.	.
250	1,000	1,500	2,500	4	6	10

hyperbola. It shows fixed costs per unit falling off significantly as output increases. Also observe the AVC curve, the curve of variable costs per unit output. It is a horizontal line. It shows that in this particular example, variable costs per unit remain constant. Typically, they will increase, decrease, or both as output increases, but not by nearly as much as fixed costs per unit fall. Finally, we see that total costs per unit, the AC curve, fall significantly, reflecting the rapid fall in fixed costs per unit output.

SCALE ECONOMIES AND DISECONOMIES

The curves of Figure 5.2, especially the curve of average fixed costs, illustrate an important principle. Because certain charges are fixed, the average total costs (total costs per unit) that a firm must meet or that a public health unit must justify in the operation of its facility fall with an increase in output or services rendered. This means that the firm can make greater profits per unit if it produces more output, provided the amount of output it markets does not influence prices (as in pure competition). It realizes these greater profits because it realizes "scale economies"; that is, economies that can be obtained through increasing the scale of operation. The same is true with the public health unit. The larger the population that uses its facilities or that it serves, the lower average costs will be. Thus we see that, everything else being the same, a city of larger size is in a position to offer services at lower average costs than a city of smaller size. But, as we shall soon see, this is true only up to a point.

We note that scale economies are quite prevalent in the fields of both private and public enterprise. Most modern industries attain lowest average costs at large scales of operation. An integrated iron and steel works achieves lowest average costs when it operates at full capacity and produces at least ten million tons of steel annually. Likewise an electric power plant, an oil refinery, or a deep coal mine operation operates at lowest average costs when its scale is very large. Many important functions provided by a city, region, or central government are also subject to scale economies. These functions range from cultural activities such as a symphony or national park to basic services in providing law and order (such as police and fire protection), highway maintenance, and water and sewage disposal.

Although scale economies are a major factor in unit cost analysis, it is important not to exaggerate the role they play. First, fixed costs vary greatly among different types of firms, government units, and social organizations. They are huge when considering a symphony of the quality of the Philadelphia Orchestra; they are small when considering a symphony of a local community such as Lansdowne, a suburb in the Philadelphia region. In food retail organizations, fixed costs are very large in the operation of a supermarket, but much smaller in the operation of a corner grocery store. In education, fixed costs are small in running a country school house, but large in operating a highly specialized system of senior high, junior high, and many elementary schools. Despite major differences among firms, governments, and other units in the size of fixed costs, it does not follow that the quality of the food, retail, or educational services they provide increases with size of the unit. It may decrease or stay the same.

Second, as the scale increases, certain diseconomies develop. Administration becomes unwieldy, bureaucracy develops, and workers get in each other's way. Moreover, environmental costs may appear when an industry or region or population cluster becomes so large that its pollution emissions exceed the natural capacity of the environment to absorb them.

The presence of diseconomies is often reflected in increases in specific variable costs per unit. For example, more and more management services per unit of output may be required as operations expand, more and more inputs of administrative personnel per unit of output may be needed in running an educational system, and more and more paperwork and secretarial services may be required to reach a decision.

Or, while raw material costs per unit may decrease up to a point because of economies in buying raw materials in volume (say in carload lots), these costs may then rise. Beyond a certain scale the demand may exceed the supply capacity of a nearby source of that raw material. It may become necessary to tap a more distant and more expensive source, or a source able to provide only a lower quality of the raw material.

Moreover, the production of some of the direct inputs used may itself be subject to scale economies or diseconomies. For example, there are scale economies in transportation and in the production of electric power. Hence, if a business firm's demand for these inputs goes up, it may be able to obtain them at lower and lower rates as its demand increases, but only to a point. Beyond that, rates or supply prices may rise, reflecting scale diseconomies in the provision of these inputs.

Figure 5.3   Falling and Rising Average Costs and Average Variable Costs

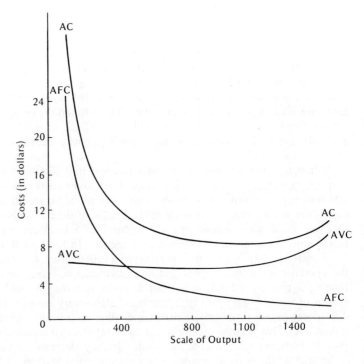

In the case of hospitals, we easily see that as the scale of operation becomes excessive, average variable costs rise because of bureaucracy and the difficulty in transportation and circulation—both within the hospital and to and from it.

Given that average variable costs turn up after a certain scale is reached, as indicated by the AVC curve of Figure 5.3, it also becomes clear that sooner or later (in the case of Figure 5.3, very soon) average variable costs may rise so sharply that they offset the gains from falling average fixed costs. In Figure 5.3, this situation is depicted after a scale of 1,100 is reached. Thus, there are economic limits to increases in scale, and we find these limits in both private and public enterprises. A company can become too big for efficient operation—as the United States Steel Corporation. A metropolitan region can become too big also, such as the New York metropolitan area. In later chapters we will discuss further the question of "efficient" size.

MAXIMIZING PROFITS AND CONTRIBUTIONS TO PUBLIC WELFARE

Total Cost and Revenue Analysis

Many real-life decisions concern setting up a new firm or facility, or undertaking an entirely new project. A person may be deciding whether or not to construct a hospital with free medical services, or an integrated iron and steel works, or a new pizza outlet. For such decisions, the investigator draws up charts and tables similar to the ones in this chapter. He gets some notion of how unit costs vary with level of output. He gets some notion of prices at the market, if he is producing an economic good, and how his output might affect these prices, if at all. He also estimates the number of his sales; that is, the size of his market. Given this knowledge, he constructs a scale of plant that will maximize his profits, or contributions to the public welfare.

To be more specific, consider Figure 5.4. There, based on the data behind Figure 5.3, we have put down the total cost curve, specifying for a manufacturing operation the total costs for each level of output. We have also put down the total revenue curve, specifying the total revenues for each volume of sales when a fixed market price obtains. In this particular case, the price is taken to be constant and given, so the total revenue curve is a straight line, increasing with increase in sales.

Now profits are given by the difference between total revenues and costs. They can be determined at each level of output by subtracting the value given by the total cost curve from the value given by the total revenue curve. Doing so for each level of output yields a profit curve such as that in Figure 5.4. In the case of this figure, profits are negative at low outputs (because of high average fixed unit costs), positive at modest outputs, and reach a maximum at the output of 1200. Profits then fall and become negative again when average variable unit costs rise sufficiently to cause total costs to exceed total revenues.

In the case of a public body, rather than facing a fixed price such as $2 per commodity or service, it might judge that the value of each service is equivalent to $2. That is, if the cost does not exceed $2, it is worth providing a free medical service. In that case, the total revenue curve can be viewed as a total equivalent value curve where each unit provided is priced at $2. In the case of public bodies, as we shall discuss later (in Chapter 13), there may not be any motivation for holding output to the level where the spread between the total revenue and the total cost curves is maximized, as is the case for a private enterprise motivated to maximize profits.

Figure 5.4   Total Revenue, Total Cost, and Total Profit Curves

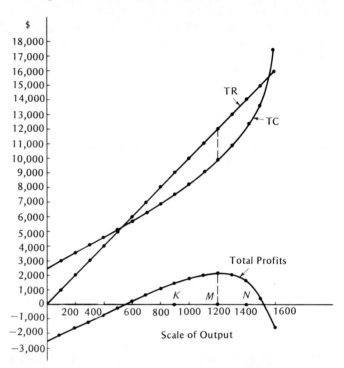

Marginal Analysis

The above type of total revenue and total cost analysis can be quite satisfactory in the planning stage when we consider the construction and operation of a new plant or facility. Before making commitments, the investor wishes to be sure that over the life of the plant or facility the total revenues or gains that accrue will equal if not exceed the total costs that will be incurred. However, there is another class of significant decisions which are of a different character. We may designate them "incremental-type" decisions. The decision maker is frequently involved in the operation of an *existing* plant or facility. Current conditions are usually different, often drastically different, from the conditions that were anticipated when the initial decision to construct a plant or facility was reached. Hence, the problem now is to make the right decision, given the plant and facility as it now is and considering current and anticipated future economic, political, and social conditions. The decision may involve small, incremental-type or marginal changes, as well as big changes, in the level and nature of operation of the plant and facility. Accordingly, it is frequently desirable to extend the use of the total revenue and cost curves with emphasis on changes in them with change in output.

Let us consider marginal changes, such as expanding or contracting output of at most 5 or 10 percent. When we make decisions relating to such changes, many costs are already fixed. If we contract the output of a plant, we still incur the same annual fixed charges on plant and equipment. However, we may wish to contract the output because the plant, although currently reaping positive profits, could make still greater profits if such a contraction were to take place. This possibility would exist if the costs (strictly variable) incurred in producing the last few units of current output exceed the revenues obtainable from their sale. More precisely speaking, we can make greater profits by not producing the last unit of current output if the cost of producing that last unit, which we now designate *marginal cost*, exceeds the additional revenue accruing from its sale, which we now designate *marginal revenue*.

Figure 5.5   Marginal Cost, Marginal Revenue, Average Cost, and
Average Revenue Curves

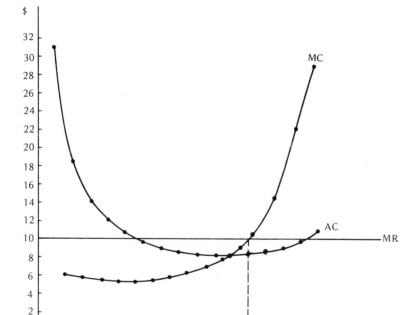

In Figure 5.5 we plot a marginal cost curve, labeled MC. For every level of output, this curve indicates the increase in total costs when an additional unit is produced. It can be obtained from the total cost curve, and in fact is the slope of the total cost curve.[1] We can also obtain the marginal cost curve from the

[1]For those who understand calculus, we define total cost (TC) as the sum of (1) fixed costs (F) which are constant and (2) variable costs, which we have seen are a function of output (x); that is, variable costs are stated as $f(x)$. Then marginal cost is $\dfrac{d\,\mathrm{TC}}{dx} = f'(x)$, and is the change in total variable costs. This change at any level of output x represents the slope of both the total variable cost curve and the total cost curve.

Table 5.2   Costs and Revenues in Operation

Level of Output	Fixed Costs (1)	Variable Costs (2)	Total Costs (3)	Average Costs (4)	Marginal Costs (5)	Total Revenue (6)	Marginal Revenue (7)	Profits (8)
100	$2500	$ 610	$ 3,110	$31.10	$ 5.90	$ 1,000	$10	−$2110
200	2500	1,200	3,700	18.50	5.70	2,000	10	− 1700
300	2500	1,770	4,270	14.23	5.50	3,000	10	− 1270
400	2500	2,320	4,820	12.05	5.30	4,000	10	− 820
500	2500	2,850	5,350	10.70	5.10	5,000	10	− 350
600	2500	3,360	5,860	9.77	5.30	6,000	10	140
700	2500	3,880	6,380	9.11	5.60	7,000	10	620
800	2500	4,440	6,940	8.68	6.30	8,000	10	1060
900	2500	5,070	7,570	8.41	7.00	9,000	10	1430
1000	2500	5,770	8,270	8.27	7.70	10,000	10	1730
1100	2500	6,540	9,040	8.22	8.70	11,000	10	1960
1200	2500	7,410	9,910	8.26	10.40	12,000	10	2090
1300	2500	8,450	10,950	8.42	14.50	13,000	10	2050
1400	2500	9,900	12,400	8.86	22.00	14,000	10	1600
1500	2500	12,100	14,600	9.07	29.00	15,000	10	400
1600	2500	15,000	17,500	10.94		16,000	10	− 1500

data contained in Table 5.2. There we list the cost data for our manufacturing operation. As in Table 5.1, for every level of output we list fixed costs, variable costs, total costs, and average costs, respectively, in the first four columns. In column 5, we calculate marginal costs. Specifically, we take the difference in total costs for two successive levels of output and divide it by the difference in the levels of output. This gives an approximate marginal cost of production within those two levels. For example, the difference in the total costs of producing 200 units and 100 units is $590. We divide the $590 by 100 units, which is the difference in the two levels of output, to obtain the figure of $5.90. This approximates marginal cost. Note that in column 5 of Table 5.2, we place the $5.90 figure in the interval between the two rows corresponding to the two levels of output, 100 and 200. These approximations to marginal costs are then plotted in Figure 5.5. They are connected by a smooth curve, which we have designated the marginal cost or MC curve.

It is also useful to plot the data in column 4 of Table 5.2 on average costs, thereby deriving the average cost curve in Figure 5.5. Note that in the figure, the marginal cost curve goes through the minimum point of the average cost curve. This is to be expected. Whenever the marginal cost of producing an additional unit is less than the average cost, we pull down the average by producing another unit. Whenever the marginal cost of producing an additional unit exceeds the average cost, we raise the average by producing another unit. It is only when the marginal cost of producing an additional unit is exactly equal to the average cost that we do not change the average by producing another unit. Hence, when marginal cost equals average cost, which is the case when the two curves intersect in Figure 5.5, then the average cost curve should be horizontal at the intersection point. Further, by the above reasoning, it should fall before that point and rise after that point if the marginal cost curve is as indicated in Figure 5.5. Thus, the intersection point must be a minimum point on the average cost curve.

We now wish to compare costs with revenues. Therefore, in column 6 of Table 5.2 we list for every level of output the total revenue that will be received if all output is sold at a price which is given—that is, when pure competition prevails. We take the price to be $10 per unit. Then from column 6 we can compute the marginal revenues of column 7. To calculate marginal revenue for any two successive levels of output, we take the difference in total revenues associated with these two levels and divide it by the difference in the amount of production corresponding to these two levels. Here, we always obtain a marginal revenue of $10. Marginal revenue is constant in this particular case because price remains unchanged. Thus, the additional revenue from producing an additional unit must always equal the price received from selling that unit. Because marginal revenue is constant and equal to the prevailing price, we can construct the marginal revenue or MR curve in Figure 5.5 as a straight horizontal line at the $10 level.

Now, consider the marginal cost and marginal revenue curves of Figure 5.5. If we are producing an output less than *OM*, say *OK*, we can see that it pays to increase output. By doing so, profits will increase because additional revenues will exceed additional costs. This situation will persist when output is somewhat greater than *K*, and will continue until output reaches the level of *OM*. At that level, marginal cost equals marginal revenue, and no additional profits can be obtained. This result also follows from an examination of Figure 5.4. At output level *OK* in that figure, profits are positive but not at their maximum. Profits increase with additional output, and continue to increase until a level *OM* is reached. There, total profits reach their maximum.

We can also reach this conclusion by considering initially a level of output of *ON*. At that level, marginal cost exceeds marginal revenue (see Figure 5.5). It pays not to produce the last unit that was produced. So also with the next to the last unit. This situation holds until we contract output to the level *OM*. At that level, marginal cost no longer exceeds marginal revenue; in fact, they are equal. So it does not pay to contract output any more. This analysis can also be carried out by an examination of the total profits curve of Figure 5.4. There we see that total profits, although positive, are not at a maximum when the level of output is *ON*. Total profits increase as we contract output until the output level *OM* is reached. We discuss this type of marginal analysis further in the appendix to this chapter. There we find that it provides the basic tool for deriving the supply curve for the industry.

The above analysis has been in terms of an increase or decrease of output of a single unit. Frequently, however, the question concerns changes in output not of one unit, but by amounts corresponding to 5 percent, 10 percent, or 15 percent of output. But clearly the reasoning of the above paragraphs is the type that must be pursued when decision-making is in terms of any increment or decrement. The investigator considers the additional revenues from any given increment as against the additional costs of that increment. If the revenues exceed the costs, the investigator should consider a still larger increment. If the excess of revenues over costs is still greater for the larger increment—that is, if it increases—the investigator should consider still larger increments until he reaches a point where the surplus no longer increases and, in fact, starts to decrease. That point defines the additional increment of output which may be the most desirable. In similar fashion, we can determine the size of the decrement or contraction that should take place, if in fact it is desirable to contract.

To sum up, incremental decision-making is often very relevant, and complements other types of decision-making with regard to whole new plants and facilities to be constructed. Of course, real life is not so simple, and there are refinements to the analysis which a sophisticated analyst must introduce. Some of these, particularly those relating to production decisions and cost minimization, are discussed in the appendix to Chapter 6. For our purposes, however, we have covered some of the basic groundwork required to understand the conditions under which goods and services will be supplied by a private or governmental decision-making unit.

APPENDIX TO CHAPTER 5. Derivation of the Industry Supply Curve of a Commodity

The analysis associated with Figure 5.5 allows us to develop the aggregate supply of a commodity by the firms of an industry. Suppose we consider the many firms in an industry and order them according to their efficiency.

More specifically, we list as no. 1 that firm whose average cost curve reaches the lowest of the minimums of all firms' average cost curves. We list as no. 2 that firm whose average cost curve reaches the minimum that is the next lowest. We list as no. 3 that firm whose average cost curve reaches a minimum that is third lowest. And so forth. These firms are depicted graphically at the left in Figure 5A.1. For the moment, let us confine our attention to their AC curves only.

Consider firm 1, whose average cost curve reaches the lowest minimum of all. If that firm is to avoid operating at a loss, the price it receives for the commodity must be at least as high as the minimum average cost that it can achieve. Otherwise, its average cost will always exceed price, whatever it might produce. Further, because this firm's average cost curve has the lowest minimum of all the firms' average cost curves, it follows that no other firm will be willing to produce if the price is below this minimum.

In Figure 5A.2, we have blown up the average and marginal cost curves for firm 1. For any price, say p_0, which is below the minimum of its average cost curve, neither this firm nor any other is willing to supply the commodity. That is, the supply is zero. As price gradually increases from the level p_0, the supply of the commodity offered by any firm continues to be zero until price rises to the level of p_1. At the price p_1, the most efficient firm, firm 1, can just meet average cost if it produces a quantity q_1. That is, producing a quantity q_1 allows that firm to achieve its minimum average cost. Hence, at the price p_1, the quantity q_1 will be supplied.

Now let price rise a little more to p'. Firm 1 will be able to make surplus profits. Because it is interested in maximizing its profits, it will produce (supply) that quantity of good, namely q', at which its marginal cost equals price (which is its marginal revenue). If price rises still further to p'', then firm 1 will increase its output (supply) to q'' at which output its marginal cost again equals price. Finally, let the price rise to p'''. Then firm 1 will increase its output (supply) to q''', where its marginal cost once more equals price. In short, we can conclude that as long as price equals or exceeds the minimum of the firm's average cost curve, it will supply goods at that quantity at which marginal cost equals price. That quantity is always measured by the horizontal stretch from the given price to the marginal cost curve. Thus, the marginal cost curve charts out the different quantities of the good which firm 1 will produce and supply at different prices above price p_1. We can see that the supply curve of firm 1 consists of two parts. The first part is given by the horizontal stretch AE, indicating that at all prices below p_1 the supply is zero. At p_1, which is the price equal to the minimum point of its average cost curve, it is willing to supply quantity AE. At this quantity, price equals both average cost and marginal cost.

The second part of the firm's supply curve consists of that segment of its marginal cost curve which lies above and to the right of point E (the minimum of its average cost curve). As we have just noted, this defines the different quantities of the good that firm 1 will produce and supply at different prices above the minimum of its average cost curve. We have indicated this part and the first part of the firm's supply curve by a bold line in the first diagram at the extreme left of Figure 5A.1.

Now consider how other firms respond as price rises. We know that at a price equal to p_1 or less, the supplies they offer will be zero. At these prices, none of them can meet average cost, no matter what they produce. Let price increase from p_1. The supplies still remain zero, until the price rises to the level of p_2. At p_2, the second most efficient firm can just meet its lowest average cost if it produces a quantity BF. This point also corresponds to a point on its marginal cost curve. Hence, it will supply quantity BF. And as price continues to rise, the second firm, too, will produce more, and the amount it

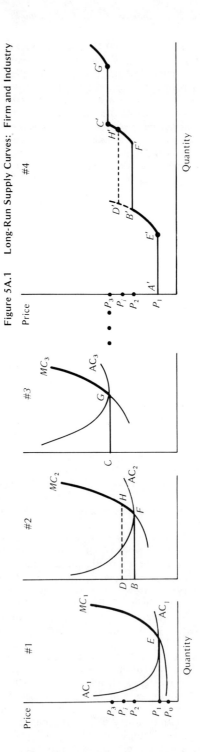

Figure 5A.1   Long-Run Supply Curves: Firm and Industry

Figure 5A.2   Long-Run Supply Curve of Firm 1

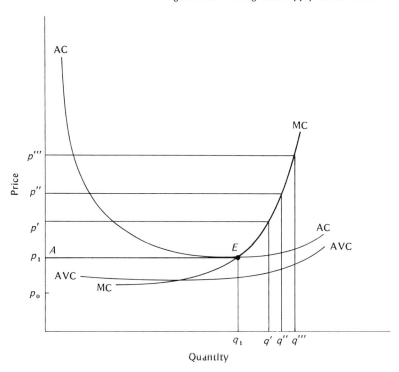

Quantity

will produce at any of these higher prices will be charted out by its marginal cost curve. Thus, for firm 2, its supply curve (outlined in bold) also consists of two parts. The first part is BF, a horizontal stretch at that level of price which just equals the minimum point of its average cost curve. The second part consists of that segment of its marginal cost curve which lies above and to the right of point F.

Now let price continue to rise above p_2. Firms 1 and 2 continue to increase the quantities they supply, but no other firm produces until price rises to the level of p_3. At the level of p_3, price just equals the minimum of the average cost curve of the third most efficient firm, and it supplies CG. And from our discussion we know that its supply curve (in bold outline) will consist of two parts: the stretch CG and the segment of its marginal cost curve above and to the right of point G. As price continues to rise above p_3, firms 1, 2, and 3 continue to increase their supplies. Also, if price continues to rise, other firms will begin to supply goods once price reaches the level of the minimum point of their average cost curves.

Now, an industry supply curve is simply the *sum* of the quantities that all firms in the industry will supply at different prices. So at any given price we derive the industry supply curve by simple addition. Let us see how with the use of the diagram at the extreme right of Figure 5A.1. There we show that at any price below p_1, the supply is zero; no firm is willing to produce. At price p_1, firm 1 starts to supply, and as price rises above p_1 but does not reach level p_2, only firm 1 supplies the good. So the industry supply curve is simply the supply curve for firm 1, as the figure depicts. However, once price reaches the level of p_2, firm 2 begins to supply goods. At that price, it produces BF amount of

78

goods. This amount of goods must be added to what firm 1 produces at that price. It is indicated by adding on the stretch $B'F'$ $(= BF)$ in the diagram at the extreme right of Figure 5A.1. Now, as price rises above p_2, both firm 1 and firm 2 are supplying goods. The amount that firm 1 supplies is indicated by the dashed curve on the diagram. We need to add onto this dashed curve the amount that firm 2 produces at any given price above p_2. For example, at price p_i, firm 2 supplies DH goods. So on the diagram at the extreme right, at the price level p_i we add the horizontal stretch $D'H'$ $(= DH)$ beginning at the relevant point of the dashed line (which is firm 1's marginal cost curve and hence defines its supply). We obtain the point H', which represents the *sum* of supplies made available by both firms 1 and 2. In a similar way, we obtain for any other price between p_1 and p_2 the sum of the supplies made available by both firms 1 and 2. This allows us to define the segment of the industry supply curve $F'C'$ for that range of prices.

Now, what happens when price reaches p_3? At that price level, the sum of the supplies from firms 1 and 2 is given by point C'. But also, at that price firm 3 begins operations and is willing to supply CG amount of goods. Then we must add the amount $C'G'$ $(= CG)$ to what firms 1 and 2 supply to obtain the total supply of all firms operating in the industry. This total supply at price p_3 is indicated by point G' on the diagram at the extreme right. And as price rises above p_3, we must add to the supply that firm 1 makes available the supplies that both firms 2 and 3 make available. In this manner, we obtain the stretch of the industry supply curve which lies to the right and above G'.

It should now be clear how the industry supply curve is derived as an addition of the supply curves of all operating firms in the industry. On the diagram at the extreme right of Figure 5A.1, the industry supply curve that is derived is kinky. This is because we have looked at only a few firms, and have made the average cost curves significantly different in order to make the graphic presentation clear. When there are many firms in a highly competitive industry, we can expect any two firms next to each other (in the ordering of firms according to efficiency) to have average cost curves whose minimums differ less. Hence, we can expect the derived industry supply curve to approach more closely the smooth ones of Chapter 4, which are convenient to use.

In the long run, a firm must meet all its costs, both fixed and variable. However, in the short run, a firm that has incurred fixed costs cannot avoid them by closing down. In that case, what is important to the firm if it cannot make profits is to meet at least its variable costs, and then as much of its fixed costs as it can. So in the short run, a firm that has already incurred fixed costs will start to produce (supply) a commodity once the price rises to the level of the minimum of its average variable cost curve. To derive what we call the short-run industry supply curve, we order firms in terms of the minimum of their average variable cost curves. The first firm, whose average variable cost curve has the lowest minimum of all, will start supplying a commodity when price rises to the level of that minimum. (Note in Figure 5A.2 that the firm's marginal cost curve passes through this minimum point.) Then as price rises still further, the firm will increase its output (supply) until its marginal cost equals price. Thus, as in the derivation of the long-run industry supply curve, the firm's supply curve is defined in two parts. The first part consists of a horizontal stretch from the vertical axis to the minimum point on its average variable cost curve. The second part consists of the segment of its marginal cost curve which lies to the right and above this minimum point.

As price rises, it soon reaches the minimum of the average variable cost curve of firm 2, and that firm starts producing; and then the minimum of the average variable cost curve of firm 3, and that firm starts producing. And so on. Thus, we derive the short-run industry supply curve in the exact manner as the long-run industry supply curve, except that we pay attention to the average variable cost curve rather than the average cost curve.

Of course, in the very, very short run, when the period of time is a minute, an hour, or a morning, it may not be possible to change the total amount of a good brought by suppliers to the market during that time period. For example, it may not be possible to increase the amount of tomatoes available for sale during a morning hour even though its price has doubled. In that situation, supply is fixed regardless of price, and the industry supply curve can be characterized by a straight vertical line as in Figure 5A.3.

Figure 5A.3   The Very Short-Run Industry Supply Curve

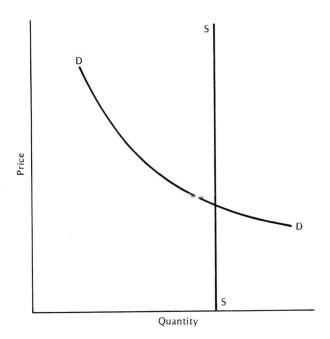

Comparative Costs and Industrial Location

In the previous chapter we obtained some idea of the forces that determine the prices at which goods are bought and sold at different markets. In later chapters we will discuss how, through trade, the price of a good in one market is related to the price of that good in all other markets. We will also discuss in greater detail and sophistication the interplay of a larger variety of forces in determining prices. But we now have enough background to proceed to discuss some fundamental questions of growth and development.

We have already seen that whether we are talking about a leader (or concerned individual) in the ghetto, a declining area such as the coalfields of West Virginia, a low-income region such as Southern Italy, a low-income state such as Mississippi, or an underdeveloped nation such as India, one basic question that must be asked is: What new industries can be brought to this area to provide more jobs, reduce unemployment, and create new income opportunities? Even in growing and prosperous regions such as Texas and Philadelphia, this kind of question is constantly on the minds of political and economic leaders.

Although this question is truly basic, we must still bear in mind that growth and development can occur without the introduction of new industries. We do see ghetto areas effectively attacking their poverty problems, depressed regions pulling themselves up by their bootstraps, and low-income states, provinces, and nations moving ahead on their own steam. They do so by supplying themselves with most, if not all, of the increases in demand for products—increases that come from normal population growth and growth in per capita income generated by gradual rise in the productivity of the labor force.

THE COMPARATIVE COST APPROACH

To get at the heart of the first question, concerning the potential for new industries, we must examine costs in considerable detail. Previously, we discussed business firms in general and their motivation to hire Girl Fridays. Let us now consider a specific kind of economic activity, one that may hire one or more Girl Fridays, but more importantly one that employs a large labor force to produce some textile fiber, such as nylon. We then ask whether this textile activity might be attracted to our specific ghetto area, depressed region, or low-income state. If wage rates for textile labor were the same in all regions, the problem would be a simple one. The textile activity should locate and build its plant at a site central to its market—say a site in Philadelphia or New York City. In choosing such a location, the textile plant would probably minimize overall transportation costs and would certainly minimize transport costs on the finished product. But for an economic activity such as textiles, costs other than transportation do differ from region to region. Wage rates do vary significantly among regions and subareas. So do rates for power, taxes, costs of fuel, and many other items. Hence, we must consider differences in the costs of these items as well as differences in the transportation costs of raw materials and finished products.

Differences in the costs of operations can arise not only from differences in the prices that must be paid for labor, power, fuel, and other items but also because of variations among different areas in the production process or technique used. In one area it might pay to use old machinery and an extremely large amount of labor that is low-paid and low-educated but has some skill at textile work. In another region, where the employees are expensive because they are well-educated and accustomed to a fairly high standard of living, it might be more economical to use much more advanced and more costly equipment and less labor. For the moment, let us avoid this issue by assuming that wherever a given textile activity is located, it will use the most modern plant and equipment, regardless of the quality of labor required and the surrounding physical and cultural environment. (We find that this is often the case with regard to new types of textile products.) In such a situation, the analysis is simplified. From an experienced engineer who is an expert on textile operations, we obtain information on the requirements of labor by type, power to run the machinery, fuel for space heating, and various raw materials and other items. In textile operations, we usually expect a large amount of relatively untrained labor (with little engineering knowledge) to be required.

With these technical data on input requirements, we ask whether a new textile activity can be profitably introduced into the region (subarea) of our concern. Generally speaking, we do not wish to bring in such an activity if it will go bankrupt after a year's operation, thereby causing fresh unemployment and generally disrupting the local economy. Rather, we want an activity that will find it profitable to operate over the long run and that can be competitive with other plants at other locations. That is, we want to introduce a new plant that has a sound cost advantage in the long run.

Suppose our region or subarea is one in which the wage rate is high for the type of labor predominantly required. Suppose also it has little or no advantage with respect to the purchase of other inputs and raw materials, and access to market. Then clearly this textile operation is not for us. On the other hand, suppose the wage rate for the type of labor required is much lower in our area than in others, and is likely to remain lower for many years. (Our area may have a high birthrate and the population may not be prone to migrate, because of lack of motivation and cultural ties.) Then this type of operation may have considerable appeal.

Entrepreneurs can be most easily induced to locate a new enterprise in an area when the area's advantages are presented in dollars-and-cents terms rather than in vague and general statements. Further, the dollars-and-cents data must be presented in a simple form so that a vice-president in charge of location can quickly understand them; and they must be backed up with full information on how they were derived so that the engineers of an interested company can check them out. Specifically, we must present carefully developed data comparing labor, transportation, power, and other costs in our area with the same costs at other locations. These locations should include those currently producing the textile good in question and those eligible for textile production in the future because of distinct advantages they may possess. A comparison is facilitated by recording the relevant data in a table such as Table 6.1. In this table we list along the left-hand tab our area N, existing textile locations A, B,..., F, and potential locations M, ..., Z. For each of these locations we record in the first column estimated labor costs per unit of product, say 100 pounds of nylon. These labor costs are obtained by procuring information on wage rates per man-hour that are paid for textile labor at each of these locations and then multiplying the relevant wage rate by the number of man-hours required to produce a unit of product.

In the second column we list the power costs that would be incurred per unit product at the different locations. Again we derive these costs by multiplying the kilowatt-hour costs at each location by the number of kilowatt hours which the expert engineer states are required per unit product.

In the third column we list estimated fuel costs for space heating. In the fourth column we list estimated costs of raw materials. Here we would multiply the delivered price of a raw material at a new or existing location by the quantity of raw material required per unit product. However, because the different locations might obtain their raw materials from different sources (one might secure its cotton from Texas, another from Alabama), the differences in raw material costs may reflect both differences in the price of the raw material at the several sources and differences in the transport cost from the source to the existing or potential location.

In still another column we list transportation costs on finished products to the market. And so forth. Finally, in the next to last column, we list the taxes that might be incurred at each of the several locations.

With such a table we can now make comparisons between our area, region N, and any other region. We can add up the costs expected at any one location to

Table 6.1   Locationally Significant Costs Per 100 Pounds Nylon at Selected Locations

Location (Region)	Labor (1)	Electric Power (2)	Fuel (3)	Raw Mate- rial (4)	Fin- ished Product Transport (5)	· · · ·	Taxes (n)	Total of Selected Costs
A	$6.00	$3.00	$2.00	$9.00	$10.00		$5.00	$35.00+
B	6.00	3.50	2.00	7.00	8.00	· · · ·	5.00	31.50+
C	4.00	3.00	2.00	6.00	8.00		6.00	29.00+
D	3.00	3.00	2.00	7.00	8.00		6.00	29.00+
E	6.00	2.50	1.50	5.00	7.00	· · · ·	3.00	25.00+
F	7.00	2.50	1.50	5.00	9.00		4.00	29.00+
·	·	·	·	·	·		·	·
·	·	·	·	·	·		·	·
·	·	·	·	·	·		·	·
M	6.00	3.00	2.00	8.00	6.00		3.00	28.00+
N	8.00	2.00	2.00	8.00	6.00	· · · ·	4.00	30.00+
·	·	·	·	·	·		·	·
·	·	·	·	·	·		·	·
·	·	·	·	·	·		·	·
Z	5.00	3.00	2.00	9.00	8.00		6.00	33.00+

obtain a corresponding total costs figure in the totals (last) column of the table. Now, if we had listed by column every single cost item expected in the projected textile operation, the last column would record total costs (actual or estimated) of operation at each location. However, if there are certain costs that are standard and the same for all the locations, it is not necessary to record them for comparative purposes. For example, if the entrepreneur does his advertising through a Madison Avenue agency in New York City, the costs for advertising would be the same regardless of his firm's location. Hence, listing advertising costs does not help to identify the best location; the data would only clutter up the table. In fact, in order to facilitate our analysis and understanding of the basic forces at play, it is best to list only those items which *vary significantly* among different locations. This we do. Thus, the totals column in the table is the total of just those costs which vary significantly among locations.

For a given market, it is obvious that that location is best which has the lowest total for items whose costs vary significantly among locations. If our area, region N, happens to be the best location, and further, if we check out our estimates and computations with knowledgeable businessmen, engineers, and investment analysts who also have some sense for historical trends, then we have a solid basis for promoting a textile activity in our area. If our area is not among those few with lowest costs, and hence is not the best location, then we should discard textile activity from our consideration and move on to the study of other economic activities.

The strategy of considering other economic activities can be developed with reference to some of the data already assembled in Table 6.1. If our location cannot compete primarily because of higher labor costs, then it is clear that our location is probably not good for all kinds of textile or other activities which require that same type of labor. We can then look down other columns of Table 6.1. Suppose we look down the column relating to electric power costs, and we note that there is a significant relative (not necessarily absolute) difference between the power costs at our location and most others. Suppose closer examination reveals that at each location the same number of kilowatt hours is required per unit of product. But the power rate in our area is the lowest of all—and, in fact, is 20 percent lower than the power rate at the location with the next lowest rate. This finding suggests that we ought to seek those types of economic activity which can take maximum advantage of our cheaper power, and thus may have the best chance of finding a sound economic base. Such types are likely to include those economic activities which require much power to produce a unit of product—for example, the aluminum and electroprocess industries. Hence, we should consider constructing tables for the aluminum and other electric process industries to see whether our location is the best or one of the best for one or more of these activities.

Accordingly, we construct Table 6.2, wherein we develop some data that relate to the aluminum industry. Unfortunately, it turns out that, although our location, location N, has an advantage over most locations in terms of power costs, it does not have such an advantage over locations like C', having cheap hydropower or cheap coal which can be efficiently burned to produce low-cost power. Against these locations, which we must explicitly consider in Table 6.2, our location would not be able to hold its own in the competition.

We need to probe in still other directions. Suppose we look down another column of Table 6.1, say the column on local and state taxes. Suppose we observe a major difference. Our local and state taxes are lower than those in most other locations, particularly locations outside the state. (Federal taxes are likely to be the same for all locations.) We might immediately jump to the conclusion that here is a decided advantage for us, and that we should try to attract those industries which are "footloose" but sensitive to tax rates. These

Table 6.2   Locationally Significant Costs Per Pound Aluminum at Selected Locations

Location (Region)	Electric Power	Transport of Raw Materials	Transport of Finished Products	· · · · · ·	Total of Selected Costs
A'	6.3¢	2.0 ¢	1.5 ¢		9.8 ¢
B'	5.4	2.5	2.0	· · · · · ·	9.9
C'	1.8	2.0	2.0		5.8
.	.	.	.		.
.	.	.	.		.
.	.	.	.		.
M'	5.4	2.5	1.5		9.4
N	4.5	2.0	1.5	· · · · · ·	8.0
.	.	.	.		.
.	.	.	.		.
.	.	.	.		.
Z'	6.3	3.0	1.0		10.3

industries would include those for which labor, power, transportation, and other costs do not differ much among locations because labor is highly unionized, because sources of raw materials are close to all locations, or because transportation costs on finished products are insignificant. We would have an advantage in attracting this type of activity, because it can take advantage of our lower tax rates.

We must be cautious, however. We have already indicated the undesirability of having an industry come to a town because of a temporary, short-run advantage and then close down as soon as this advantage disappears. Such situations can cause unemployment and disrupt the local economy. Hence, if our tax advantage is transitory, we should be wary of new industries that cannot point to other features of our location that are on the "plus" side for them.

On the other hand, our tax advantage may be of a long-run character. It may reflect the fact that our location is a town in a rural economy where the costs of police, fire, and many other services are low because fewer of these services are required than in other locations (such as major metropolitan regions). Also, welfare costs at our location may be very low. We know that if a worker in New York City becomes unemployed, he still must pay exorbitantly high rent for housing and high prices for food. If he becomes unemployed in our location, which is also relatively unattractive to migrants, he can return to the farm from which he came, or go live with relatives who work on a farm and there find relatively cheap housing and food. Or he can eke out an existence through subsistence farming. In short, the community will need to provide him with relatively little welfare assistance. If our tax advantage is of a long-run nature, then we have a basis for attracting a modest amount of new industry oriented to the favorable local and state tax structure.

However, our location may not be a cheap labor location. It may not be a cheap power location. It may not have long-run tax advantages. Then we must examine other columns; for example, the column on the costs of transporting finished products to the market. If we do not find a major advantage here for our location N, or in any other column in this table or one that we might construct, then we must conclude that it has slim possibilities for attracting new industries. Our best hope for development lies in the steady internal growth of economic activities currently operating at our location, growth that gradually increases the number and productivity of those employed and involves a population "taking in each other's wash."

Or, our findings may suggest that we (if we are the political decision makers or planners) ought to plan an orderly phasing out of our town (region). This would involve a transition period in which our population is gradually relocated to other places that can provide low-cost living conditions, a healthy and esthetically pleasing environment, and an infrastructure attractive to both firms and people—and do so within a setting that is consistent with a good quality of life.

But suppose that in looking down the column on transport costs of finished products, we do find a major advantage for our location, at least compared with several others. This finding would suggest that for some of the same reasons that our access to markets for finished textile products is good, our access to markets in general is good—particularly to markets that consume large amounts of food products, building materials, and other basic consumption goods demanded by the population. We might then do comparative cost studies for other types of industries which require less labor than textiles, thus putting us at less of a disadvantage relative to locations having very cheap labor. Suppose we consider the food-processing industry and concentrate on that market to which our location has the best access, say the market of the nearest metropolitan region. Suppose we consider producing standard food products such as cold cuts, bologna and hot dogs, canned chicken, ham spreads, and cheese spreads. Suppose we do a comparative cost study and develop the data as in Table 6.3. Suppose we find that our location is the best location in terms of locationally significant cost factors. We thus reach the end of this phase of our search and now have some idea of the new kinds of industries we might promote.

In sum, we find that one fruitful approach in searching for new employment opportunities for our location is through comparative cost analysis. We now wish to turn to the other approaches.

ELEMENTS OF LOCATION THEORY

We have presented one way—a dollars-and-cents way—of approaching the question of what new industries to bring to our area. It is a type of approach that has greatest appeal to the businessman who must undertake the investment. From the standpoint of a researcher in a planning commission or development agency, it is not necessarily the most efficient. We can arrive at some findings on the potential for new industries much more rapidly if we are able to employ effectively certain principles that can be derived from location theory. We will try to develop some of these principles in this section. Then in Chapters 15 and 17 we can illustrate how these principles, together with the dollars-and-cents approach, can be effectively focused on development problems.

The Effect of Ubiquities

Let us begin with a highly simplified case. Take the question of the location of a Coca-Cola works or other simple plant that produces beverages, soft drinks, and the like. Let the process be highly mechanized, requiring little labor. Assume also that relatively little power and fuel are required. The main items of cost, then, are the Coca-Cola extract, the container, perhaps some sugar and other chemical items, the transportation cost of the raw materials and the finished product, and water if it must be purified. Suppose we imagine the market to be a point, such as point M on Figure 6.1, and the source of the extract another point, such as point A on Figure 6.1. Suppose also that we can represent the transport link connecting these two points by the straight line on Figure 6.1. The question then is: Where should we locate a Coca-Cola plant? At the market? At the source of the extract? Or at some intermediate point such as J, which is on the transportation route linking the market to the raw material source.

To keep the analysis as simple as possible, imagine that we are in a region where an abundant water supply is available at all locations at small or negligible cost. (This, of course, is no longer the case for many regions in the United States and other industrialized nations.) Also assume that the delivery price of containers, sugar, and other chemicals to the plant will vary only negligibly for the locations

Table 6.3   Meat Products Production: Selected Costs Per Unit for Market X

Location (Region)	Labor	Taxes	. . . . . .	Transport Cost on Finished Product	Total of Selected Costs
			Costs of		
A"	$ 8.00	$5.00		$6.00	$19.00+
B"	10.00	5.00	. . . . . .	7.00	22.00+
C"	11.00	6.00		5.00	22.00+
•	•	•		•	•
•	•	•		•	•
•	•	•		•	•
•	•	•		•	•
M"	6.00	6.00		9.00	21.00+
N	10.00	5.00	. . . . . .	2.00	17.00+
•	•	•		•	•
•	•	•		•	•
•	•	•		•	•
•	•	•		•	•
Z"	9.00	6.00		5.00	20.00+

we consider. If we locate the plant at point *A*, the source of the extract, we avoid transportation costs on the extract and incur to-the-market transport cost on the finished product, the bottle (or can) of Coca-Cola. If we locate the plant at the intermediate point *J*, we must transport the extract from *A* to *J*, and the bottle of Coca-Cola from *J* to the market *M*. If we locate the plant at the market, we only need to transport the extract from the source *A* to the market *M*.

Figure 6.1   A Line Location Problem

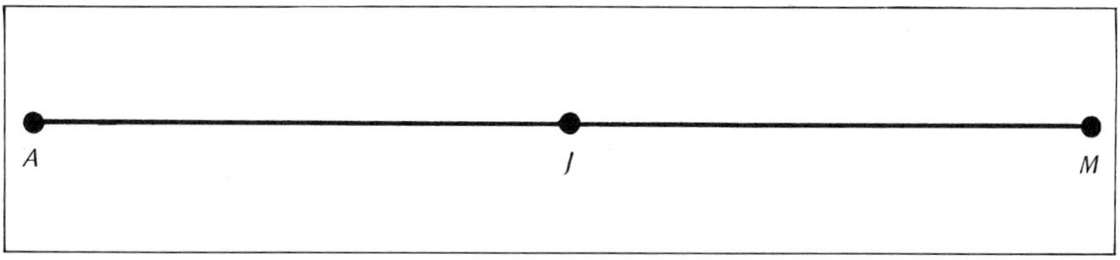

We can see that it is most economical to locate at the market. The cost of transporting the amount of extract required for a bottle of Coca-Cola is much lower than the cost of transporting the bottle of Coca-Cola itself. Therefore, transportation costs for a plant operating at point *M* would be much less than those for one operating at point *A*. Similarly, it is cheaper to transport the extract from *A* to *M* than to transport the extract from *A* to *J* and the bottle of Coca-Cola from J to M. Accordingly, M incurs lower transportation costs than J. M is the point of minimum transport cost. If the transport cost difference dominates all other cost differences (such as those for labor, power, fuel, and taxes), as we assume to be the case, then the optimal location is at the market, the point of minimum transport cost.

This simple illustration of a Coca-Cola plant can be generalized to some extent. Suppose there is a *localized* raw material—that is, a raw material that is available at only one or a relatively few sources (such as the extract in the Coca-Cola case). Suppose that in the production process we add to this raw material other *ubiquitous* materials—that is, materials that are generally available at or close by all sites (such as water, air, and limestone). When ubiquities are incorporated in a finished product, they add their weight (in whole or part) to the weight of the localized raw material, making the finished product heavier than the raw material. Therefore, the transportation cost of the finished product tends to be higher than that of the localized raw material. Because it is wise to avoid transporting the heavier item—the finished product—the best location is at the market. Put another way, if into the finished product there is incorporated an ubiquity that is available everywhere, why transport that part of the finished product? Why not avoid transporting it by locating the plant at the market and securing the ubiquitous material from the source that is right at hand? We conclude: *ubiquities tend to pull location to the market*.

The Effect of Weight Loss

We can use our simple line case to illustrate another important location principle. Suppose we want to manufacture a product like aluminum. Its production requires large amounts of electric power. We find that cost differentials on power are by far the most important ones when we do comparative cost studies for possible production points. Therefore, we must locate the aluminum operation at cheap power sites such as the Pacific Northwest, the Ohio Valley, the Niagara Falls area, and the Tennessee Valley. In producing aluminum, we also need the raw material aluminum oxide, which is called alumina. Further, we need two tons of bauxite to produce one ton of alumina, as well as crushing machinery, and fuel and labor to run that machinery. Suppose for the moment that labor is unionized so that there are no labor cost differentials in producing alumina from bauxite, and suppose also that too little fuel is used to really make a difference among locations.

Now, the market for alumina corresponds to the locations of aluminum plants in the Pacific Northwest, the Ohio Valley, the Niagara Falls area, and the Tennessee Valley. The sources of bauxite are Jamaica and other Caribbean locations, or the Gulf Coast (because in the past, the United States government and producers have on several occasions decided that they cannot afford to locate outside U.S. borders any facilities needed for a strategic industry such as the aluminum industry). Imagine that the bauxite site is point A in Figure 6.1, which might be Mobile, Alabama, on the Gulf Coast. Let an existing aluminum production site be M, say in the Pacific Northwest. Also let the straight line of Figure 6.1

represent the transport link connecting A and M, say the link that is least costly from a transportation standpoint. Where should we locate the alumina plant? At A, J, or M? If we locate at M, we need to transport two tons of bauxite from A to M to provide one ton of alumina to the aluminum works at M. If we locate at J, we need to transport two tons of bauxite from A to J and one ton of alumina from J to M. If we locate at A, we need to transport only the one ton of alumina from A to M. Clearly, if a ton of alumina and bauxite incur the same transport cost, and both require the same amount of handling and care, it is most economical to locate at A. By doing so we need to transport only one ton rather than two tons (the whole distance or part of the distance) in order to deliver one ton of alumina to the aluminum works at M.

Note that this case involves a production process in which the basic raw material, bauxite, loses weight as it is converted into an intermediate product, alumina—that is, two tons of bauxite become one ton of alumina. The bauxite can then be designated a *weight-losing* raw material. When a single weight-losing raw material is involved in production and when this raw material is localized at one or a few sources, it is most economical to locate the plant at the source of that raw material, everything else being the same. For why transport *unnecessary* weight, namely the impurities in the bauxite?

We thus may generalize. When production processes involve raw materials that are weight-losing, the locational attractiveness of the raw material site is enhanced. Or, *weight-losing processes increase the locational pull of the source of the weight-losing raw material.*

The Effect of Transport Costs Less than Proportional to Distance

We now proceed to a third principle, which relates to the effect of transport rates on the location of an activity. We have discussed scale economies in the previous chapter. Scale economies typically characterize transport operations in industrialized or industrializing regions. A railroad terminal involves a large initial investment, and consequently there are large fixed costs (interest, depreciation, insurance) to be met each year. Likewise, there are large initial investment costs and large annual fixed charges to be met for highway and port terminal facilities.

When a ton of goods is shipped from a terminal to any other location, it is subject to a *terminal* charge, required to meet unit costs of the terminal (covering both fixed and variable unit costs), and a *line-haul* charge, required to meet the costs of hauling the ton along the railroad line, highway route, or water route. The terminal charge is levied for each use of the terminal—that is, for each shipment—whether the shipment involves moving one ton a distance of 10 miles or a 100 miles. We record the terminal charge in the first column of Table 6.4. The second charge, the line-haul charge, usually increases with distance of shipment, but perhaps less than proportionately with distance. This charge is associated with the costs of maintaining the rail tracks or highway and the labor and fuel costs of operating a train, truck, or ship. We have recorded a proportionate line-haul charge in column 2 of Table 6.4. Adding columns 1 and 2 yield column 3,

Distance of Shipment (miles)	Terminal Charge (1)	Line-Haul Charge (2)	Total Charge (3)	Charge or Rate per Ton-Mile (4)
5	$3.00	$ .50	$3.50	$0.70
10	3.00	1.00	4.00	0.40
15	3.00	1.50	4.50	0.30
20	3.00	2.00	5.00	0.25
25	3.00	2.50	5.50	0.22
30	3.00	3.00	6.00	0.20
35	3.00	3.50	6.50	0.186
40	3.00	4.00	7.00	0.175
45	3.00	4.50	7.50	0.167
50	3.00	5.00	8.00	0.16
.	.	.	.	.
.	.	.	.	.
.	.	.	.	.
95	3.00	9.50	12.50	0.131+
100	3.00	10.00	13.00	0.130
.	.	.	.	.
.	.	.	.	.
.	.	.	.	.
195	3.00	19.50	22.50	0.115+
200	3.00	20.00	23.00	0.115

Table 6.4   Transport Rates Per Ton Mile

the total charge for each shipping distance. If we divide the total charge for each distance by the distance, we obtain the charge per mile for shipping a ton—or in brief, the charge per ton-mile. This charge is listed in column 4. It falls with distance of shipment, reflecting of course the spreading of the fixed terminal costs among more units (ton-miles) as the distance of shipment increases.

In reality, then, transport rates are less than proportional to distance, signifying that it is cheaper per ton-mile to transport goods over long distances. This point is of major significance for industrial location. For example, take a line case where we assume that 100 miles separate the raw material source and the market. Further assume that one ton of raw material is required per ton of product (there is no weight loss and no use of an ubiquity). Then clearly it would be desirable to locate either at the raw material source or at the market. To locate at an intermediate point, say the halfway point *J*, would involve one 50-mile trip for the ton of raw material and another 50-mile trip for the ton of finished product. Because the rate per ton-mile is higher for a 50-mile stretch than for a 100-mile stretch, as recorded in Table 6.4, it is more economical to locate at the raw material source or the market, realizing the savings from the significantly lower rate for a single 100-mile shipment.

Generalizing, *the transport rates of actuality, which are less than proportional to distance in most industrialized or industrializing regions, increase the locational pull of the market or source of raw material.* Such rates tend to discourage industrial location at intermediate points, everything else being the same.

The Effect of Loading and Unloading Costs

In transportation there are other large costs which are independent of the distance of movement. These are the costs of loading and unloading. They have always been significant and are more significant than ever today.

Clearly, if loading and unloading costs are large, a profit-maximizing producer wishes to minimize the amount of loading and unloading, everything else being the same. Suppose we locate a plant at an intermediate point and decide to transport a raw material, coal, there. We would need to load the coal from the mine onto a coal car, unload the coal at the intermediate factory site, take the finished product and load it onto another freight car, and finally unload the freight car at the wholesale warehouse, which we take to be the market. Now, if the plant were located right next to the warehouse, we would only need to load the coal onto a coal car, transport the coal to the plant, unload the coal car, and finally carry the finished product from the plant to the warehouse. If we choose the latter alternative, and if carrying the finished product from the plant to the warehouse next door involves approximately the same effort and costs as carrying that product from a railroad car siding into the warehouse, then by locating the plant next to the warehouse we avoid the costs of loading the finished product onto a freight car. If such costs are not trivial, they represent a disadvantage of locating at an intermediate point. Hence, we reach the principle: *Loading and unloading costs generally increase the attraction of raw material sources and markets, and decrease that of intermediate sites.*

At this point an acute observer might ask: How is it that a city like Cleveland has developed as a steel center when it is intermediate between the Great Lakes Mesabi ore deposits and major Eastern seaboard markets like New York City? The answer lies in the fact that Cleveland is a break point—that is, a point at which there occurs a break in the transportation system, in this case between water and rail modes. The actual transport costs for a shipment from the upper Great Lakes to New York are not based upon a single rate quoted by a single carrier for the total distance between the raw material source and the market. Rather, they involve a water transport rate applied to the distance shipped over water, plus a rail transport rate applied to the distance shipped by rail, plus a cost for unloading the ore from an ore carrier onto a rail car at Cleveland, plus a cost for unloading the ore from a rail car into a production plant at the market. To this of course must be added a cost (equivalent to an unloading) of carrying the steel from the plant to the warehouse. Now, if Cleveland is a steel production point, the ore on the water carrier at Cleveland can be unloaded at the production plant. Then the finished product at Cleveland needs to be loaded onto the rail car. Finally the steel needs to be unloaded from the rail car at the warehouse. Under such circumstances an intermediate point like Cleveland is not at a disadvantage relative to an end point. The number of loadings and unloadings is the same. Further, if Cleveland has some advantage with regard to labor or some other cost item, or for other reasons is a convenient location, then we might expect some production activity at Cleveland. Historically, many great cities have developed at breaks in the transport system—for example, ports like London, Tokyo, Antwerp, Calcutta, and San Francisco; and rail hubs like Chicago, St. Louis, and

Kansas City, where one rail line comes to an end and another begins. Or currently, in the air age, there are cities like Pittsburgh, a break in the network of primary and secondary airways. Pittsburgh is a major stop on the transcontinental trunk system and at the same time a central location for commuter-type operations for a host of cities in the region, each of which does not generate sufficient traffic to qualify as a stop on the main line.

Location Analysis for More Complex Situations: The Iron and Steel Case

Up to this point, we have developed location principles in the context of the "line" case, with a single source for one major raw material. But often more than one major raw material is involved, each having a single source. The classic case is iron and steel production. This case is classic because (1) it has been relevant for over 200 years, since the advent of the Industrial Revolution and (2) it relates to an industry that has been the backbone of economic, social, political, and military power in the modern world, at least up to World War II. So even if ten years from now the iron and steel industry is completely replaced by other industries producing substitute metal and other materials, what we have to say is still important. Economic historians clearly associate economic, social, and political power in the late eighteenth, nineteenth, and early twentieth centuries with iron and steel production capability.

In the iron and steel industries there are three major raw materials—coal, iron ore, and limestone. Limestone, however, is more or less a ubiquity, available everywhere in sufficient quantity and at only small differences in cost among relevant locations. So sophisticated analysis that takes into account the cost of limestone rarely differs from the findings of studies that exclude limestone from consideration. Accordingly, we can pose the problem with the use of a triangle often called the *locational triangle*. In Figure 6.2, we represent the source of the ore by point O, the source of coal by point C, and the finished product market by point M. Connecting the three points by straight lines, we have the locational triangle of Figure 6.2.

If ore is the only source of iron, and if its iron content ranges from 50 percent down to 33 1/3 percent (or from 55 percent down to 35 percent if we allow for some wastage) approximately 2 to 3 tons of it are required to produce 1 ton of pig iron. If coal is both the source of fuel and the reducing agent that takes up the oxygen in the iron ore, all of it is lost in the form of carbon monoxide, carbon dioxide, ash, gases, and heat. The gases can, of course, be caught and used for fuel, but by and large coal loses close to 100 percent of its weight in the processing operation.

These considerations suggest that because of the weight loss, the production of iron and steel ought to be located at the source of a raw material. But which one—ore or coal? There is no problem when the sources of iron and coal coincide or are close by each other, as was the case in the Cleveland-Durham area of England. When the Durham coal and Cleveland ore sources were used after the 1850s, at which time approximately 3 to 4 tons of coal and 2 to 3 tons of ore were required per ton of pig iron, the blast furnaces were indeed located in the districts containing ore and coal, away from any major market in Great Britain, such as London.

Figure 6.2   Three Forces Pulling at the Equilibrium Point *P**

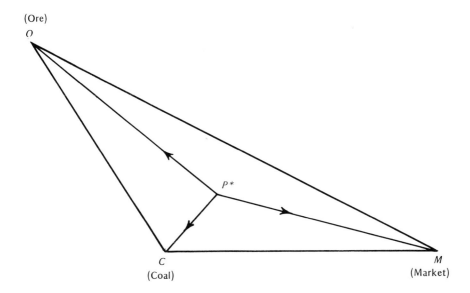

But if the locational triangle is that of Figure 6.2, it is not obvious where the location of the steel works should be. We need additional knowledge. For example, we need information relating to the amount of each raw material required, distances to potential plants and markets, and transportation rates. With this, we can first work out the problem conceptually. We start by assuming that transport costs are strictly proportional to distance and weight, and that transport rates per ton-mile are the same whether we are transporting a raw material or a finished product. (We recognize, of course, that this is a far cry from reality.) The problem becomes one of finding the equilibrium of three forces acting on a point, point *P** of Figure 6.2, where each force is directed to a specific corner of the locational triangle. One force is the pull toward the coal source, represented by the savings in transport costs of coal by moving closer to the source. Another force is the pull toward the ore source, represented by the savings in transport costs of ore by moving toward that source. The third force is the pull toward the market point, represented by the savings in transport costs of the finished product by moving closer to the market. If, then, there exists a point *P** within the locational triangle that minimizes total transport cost, it will be the point at which these forces are in equilibrium. If the point of minimum transport costs does not lie within the locational triangle, then it can be demonstrated that it lies at one of the three corners.

We can find the point of minimum transport cost by geometric construction or by using a high-speed computer with programs for finding the optimal location *P**. But often we can find this point simply by using common sense and recognizing that transportation rates fall off with distance, that additional loading and unloading costs must be considered, that the transport rates on finished products are much higher than those on coal or iron ore, and that the rates on coal and ore also differ.

Let us start with the beginnings of the modern iron and steel industry, when pig iron was the primary output. Take the situation in 1780 in Great Britain. To produce one ton of pig iron, 8 to 10 tons of coal and 2 to 3 tons of ore were required. Clearly the tonnage of coal exceeded the combined tonnage of iron ore and the finished product. Coal was the dominant raw material, and so we could predict and find that the location was at the coal site.

The location of the iron industry stayed at or close to the coal site for a long while. But with time came technological advance. This advance was primarily reflected in smaller and smaller requirements of fuel per ton of finished product. (After all, one cannot change the iron content of the ore with which we are endowed; weight loss per ton of ore remains pretty much the same today as 200 years ago.) See Table 6.5 for relevant data on the decline in coal requirements per ton of pig iron. If we look at a locational figure, such as that of Figure 6.2, we can see that the decline has resulted in the force pulling toward the coal source being considerably weakened.

But to understand the locational strategy of iron and steel industries, we must recognize that other forces have been operating. Ever since the late nineteenth century, the steel industry has found it economical to use scrap as a substitute for pig iron in the production of steel. During the nineteenth century, the accumulated stock of steel in structures had reached such a level that it was economical to collect scrap from the iron and steel structures which were torn down, and to use this scrap as a substitute for pig iron. Thus, we note that in the production of steel, the percentage of pig iron in the charge (pig iron and scrap combined) fell from 62.8 percent in 1909 to 48.1 percent in 1938, whereas the scrap percentage

Table 6.5   Consumption of Coal Per Ton of Pig Iron Produced, 1750–1938

Year	Great Britain (Tons)	United States (Tons)
1750............................	8-10*	· · ·
1788............................	7*	· · ·
1798............................	6*	· · ·
1801............................	5*	· · ·
1840............................	3.5-4*	· · ·
1869............................	3*	· · ·
1879............................	2.19	2.10
1889............................	2.01	1.85
1899............................	2.02	1.72
1909............................	2.04	1.62
1919............................	2.14	1.53
1929............................	1.91	1.31
1938............................	1.67	1.27

*Rough data from diverse sources which are not strictly comparable. Source: W. Isard, "Some Locational Factors in the Iron and Steel Industry Since the early Nineteenth Century," Journal of Political Economy LVI (June 1948), 205.

rose from 35.7 percent to 51.3 percent in the same time period. Because scrap accumulates at sites that have been markets for long periods of time, the increased use of it tends to increase the pull of established markets, for if you do not locate at such a market, you must transport the scrap from the long-established market point to the production point. At the same time, its increased use means that less pig iron, and thus less coal and ore, is required per ton of steel.

In short, technological advance, the substitution of scrap for pig iron, and finally the much higher transport charges on steel than on coal and ore, have meant that the forces pulling P^*, the point of minimum transport cost, to both O (the ore site) and C (the coal site) have been considerably weakened. The force pulling P^* to M (the market) has been considerably strengthened. In fact, these forces had changed so much by 1938 that the force pulling toward the market clearly exceeded the sum of the forces pulling toward the ore and the coal sites, and hence the market in most situations was the point of minimum transport costs. This analysis did allow us to predict and of course explain why, in the early 1950s, the United States Steel Corporation constructed its Fairless Steel Works in the Greater Philadelphia–New York Region, specifically in Morristown, New Jersey, just outside of Trenton. This location, among those locations having the necessary bedrock conditions and port facilities, was the closest to the New York market.

Now, this type of analysis, based on a location triangle and the notion of an equilibrium of forces, may be considered too abstract by some and certainly would not be convincing to many businessmen who want the argument in dollars-and-cents terms. This can be done easily. In Table 6.6, we present the data that

Table 6.6   Transportation Costs on Ore and Coal Required per Net Ton of Steel and on Finished Product for Selected Actual and Hypothetical Producing Locations Serving New York City*

| Location | Transportation Costs | | | |
	Ore	Coal	Finished Product	Total
Fall River (Labrador ore)	$4.56	$6.01	$10.40	$20.97
(Venezuela ore)	3.68	5.63	10.40	19.71
New London (Labrador ore)	4.56	5.79	8.80	19.15
(Venezuela ore)	3.68	5.42	8.80	17.90
Pittsburgh (Mesabi ore)	5.55	1.56	12.40	19.51
Cleveland (Mesabi ore)	3.16	3.85	14.00	21.01
Sparrows Point (Venezuela ore)	3.68	4.26	8.40	16.34
Buffalo (Mesabi ore)	3.16	4.27	11.60	19.03
Bethlehem (Mesabi ore)	5.56	5.06	5.80	16.42
Trenton (Venezuela ore)	3.68	4.65	4.80	13.13

*Source: W. Isard and J. H. Cumberland, "New England as a Possible Location for an Integrated Iron and Steel Works," Economic Geography 26 (October 1950), 257.

were worked up in a 1950 study with reference to the feasibility of a major integrated iron and steel works in the Greater Philadelphia–New York region, and before any decision had been reached on a Fairless Steel Works location. The locations noted covered *actual* production locations such as Pittsburgh, Cleveland, Sparrows Point (Baltimore), Buffalo, and Bethlehem and new *hypothetical* locations such as Fall River, New London, and Trenton. For serving the

New York City market, the Trenton (Fairless Steel site) had a major advantage. Compared with Pittsburgh, whose historical dominance in the iron and steel trades was based on excellent nearby coal deposits, the finished product transport cost advantage that Trenton has relative to Pittsburgh in being close to the New York market far outweighs its disadvantage in being far from the coal site.

In general, we may conclude that for other parts of the world as well, coal and ore sites have lost much if not all of their attraction for iron and steel, and markets have gained considerably. In many situations, they have become dominant. And all this has had important implications for the power politics of the last half of the nineteenth and the first half of the twentieth century. Of course now, as military and thus political power in the international arena are becoming less oriented to heavy hardware (tanks, cannons, and warships) based on steel, and more oriented to nuclear and electronic weapons based on scientific research capability and know-how, the study of the locational strategy of iron and steel industry becomes less significant for understanding international power politics.

CHEAP LABOR LOCATIONS

Thus far we have concentrated on transportation costs. In more advanced courses we spell out in much greater detail the direct and indirect impacts of transportation costs and of their changes. Here, however, we must move along and consider other location factors as they affect, in both theory and practice, industrial location and regional development. Clearly, at this point, we want to ask: How is it that development has taken place in locations or regions having a great disadvantage with respect to transportation?

We have already partly answered this question in an earlier section of this chapter in which we presented different tables for comparative cost analysis. Recall Table 6.1, which records labor, electric power, fuel, transport, and other cost differentials among locations. We saw that a region might have a disadvantage with respect to transportation costs but have a more than compensating advantage with respect to labor costs. It might then be able to attract a textile-type operation. Or a region might have such a great advantage with respect to power costs that this would outweigh its cumulative disadvantage on all other counts. The region might then be able to attract an electroprocess activity, where profitability is highly sensitive to power cost differentials.

Attraction of cheap labor or power sites, or sites with other advantages, can be depicted graphically. Suppose we construct a locational triangle relevant for a particular industry, such as Figure 6.3. Suppose we locate the point P^*, which is the point of minimum transportation costs—the optimal transport point. Suppose it is an intermediate point. Now, we might identify around P^* all those locations for which production would involve *total* transportation costs (of raw materials and product) which would be $1 greater per unit product than if production were at P^*. The locations are not efficient locations. Nonetheless, out of curiosity let us connect them. Suppose we obtain the first circular-type curve that courses around P^* in Figure 6.3. We might then try to find a set of locations that would be still more inefficient, in the sense that each of these would involve transportation costs $2 greater than if production were at P^*. We connect these points and obtain the $2 circular-type line. We do likewise for other points and

Figure 6.3   A Case of a Cheap Labor Location

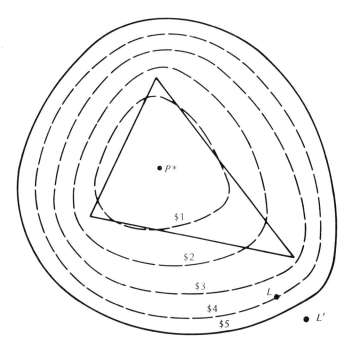

construct the $3, the $4, and other lines. For any point on any one of these lines, the dollar figure associated with the line shows the additional transport costs per unit product of raw materials and finished product that would be incurred if production were at that point rather than at *P**. The set of lines as a whole refers to inefficient points and illustrates that the degree of inefficiency with respect to transportation cost increases with distance from *P**. Of course, this increase in inefficiency is not of the same intensity in all directions—that is why we obtain the distorted circular lines in Figure 6.3. These lines are similar to contour lines that we find on weather maps. They might be designated *isolines*, for each line is a locus of points, all of which have the same additional transportation costs or the same degree of inefficiency when compared to *P**. Because later we shall employ other kinds of isolines, we call these isolines *isodapanes*, consistent with the accepted convention. (Isodapane comes from the Greek, *iso* meaning equal and *dapane* meaning cost.)

Suppose we are examining the development potential of a location that has cheap labor and from which, because of strong local ties and a closely knit stable culture, there has been little out-migration in the past. Suppose we have in mind the particular process for which the location situation in Figure 6.3 is relevant. Can we induce the plant to move away from *P** and to locate at our cheap labor point? We calculate the advantage of our location. Suppose there would be a savings of $5 in labor costs per unit output if the plant operated at our cheap labor location. We then examine the set of isodapanes and identify the $5 one—that is, the one connecting all points that would incur $5 additional transportation costs if the plant located at any of them rather than at $P*$. We designate this $5 isodapane as the *critical isodapane* for this particular situation. It is critical in the sense that if our cheap labor location lies within it (that is, is on an isodapane connecting points involving less additional transportation costs), then we can attract the industry to our point.

For example, if in Figure 6.3 our cheap labor location is L, we see that it can attract the activity. The $5 savings it offers in labor costs per unit are only partly offset by the additional transport costs it incurs—which are $4 per unit, because L lies on the $4 isodapane. It therefore offers a net gain of $1 per ton relative to the optimal transport point $P*$. If, however, the cheap labor location lies outside the $5 critical isodapane, say at L', then the additional transport costs would be greater than $5 and would more than offset the savings in labor costs. It would not be economic to shift the location from $P*$ to L'.

CHEAP POWER AND OTHER LOCATION FACTORS

In similar manner we can examine the pull of cheap power locations, cheap tax locations, and other locations having specific advantages. For example, in Figure 6.4 we denote a cheap power location by the letter R. Location at R would

Figure 6.4   A Case of a Cheap Power Location

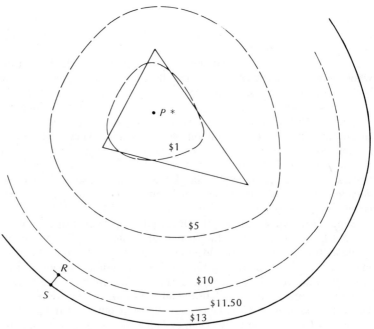

involve a savings of $13 per ton in power costs while incurring additional transport costs of $11.50 per ton. The location, then, lies within the critical isodapane by a "transport cost distance" of $1.50. This transport cost distance is represented by the line segment *RS* separating the $11.50 and $13 isodapanes in Figure 6.4.

Let us consider still another kind of industry, say one that is sensitive to taxes. Suppose there happens to be an enclave populated by a culture, such as. the Amish, with quite distinct attitudes toward work and play and government involvement in affairs. Suppose the tax levels in the enclave, the shaded area in Figure 6.5, are very low. We can then consider any point in this area as a cheap tax point. The tax savings per unit at each of these points would be $7. But all the points in the enclave lie outside the critical isodapane. Hence, the industry would not be deviated to any of them.

Before bringing this chapter to a close let us examine a few more complicated cases. First, suppose there are two or more cheap labor locations, such as *L* and *L'* in Figure 6.5. Let the savings in labor costs per ton product be the same for both locations, namely $7. Hence, the critical isodapane is the same for both, namely the solid $7 line. We observe that point *L'* lies farthest within this critical isodapane. It incurs fewer additional transportation costs and thus obtains the greater net savings per ton. It wins out in the competition.

In the situation depicted in Figure 6.5, we introduce another location, a cheap power location *R*. The savings in power costs per ton product that can be achieved at this location are $10. Hence, the relevant critical isodapane is the dashed line

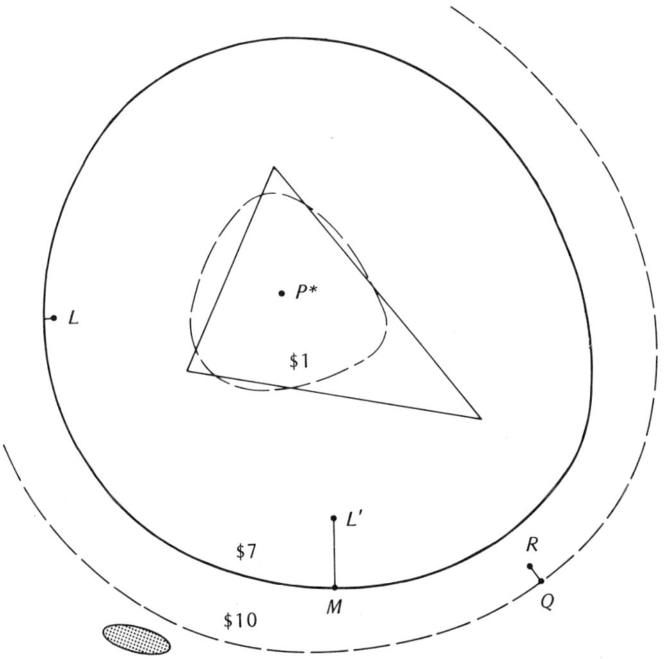

Figure 6.5   A Case Involving Cheap Tax, Cheap Labor, and Cheap Power Sites

in the figure. The cheap power location R lies within this critical isodapane; thus there would be a net savings per ton product if the activity were located at R rather than at P^*. But we have already noted that there would be a net savings if the activity were located at L' rather than at P^*. Hence, we must ask: Which location achieves the greater net savings, the cheap power location R or the cheap labor location L'? The answer can be readily seen from Figure 6.5. By comparing the two lines segments $L'M$ and RQ, which represent transport cost distances, we observe that the location L' lies farther within its critical isodapane than does the location R. Hence, a greater net savings is achieved at L'.

The analysis can be further developed to take into account cheap tax locations, cheap interest rate locations, and so forth. We can also consider the possibility of utilizing substitute sources of raw materials (replacement deposits) when we consider production locations other than P^*. Such sources might generate additional savings. For example, a cheap labor or tax location might utilize a source of coal that is closer to it than the coal source that would be used by the location P^*; by doing so, it can cut down on the additional transport costs. Moreover, still greater savings might be achieved at a cheap labor location by substituting cheap labor for more expensive power and capital—that is, by changing to a production process that uses relatively more cheap labor and thus exploits this resource more effectively. (This possibility will be discussed in the appendix to this chapter.) These savings will be in addition to those achieved by the labor cost differential itself. Further, we can deepen the analysis in comparing a cheap labor location and the transport optimal point P^* by introducing other advantages and disadvantages of these two locations relative to each other—that is, other cost differentials such as power and taxes. Such analysis may be found in more advanced textbooks on location theory.

APPENDIX TO CHAPTER 6.   Factor Substitution and Production Theory

In the text of this chapter, we have indicated that at a cheap labor location or a cheap power location, or other location having a factor whose price is particularly low, the cheap factor is substituted for other factors. We now want to develop the reasons for this substitution. While doing so, we will also present some production theory, which will be useful for understanding the operations of a typical firm.

Think of a textile operation at a potential location. Assume that the manager has decided to produce 1,000 and only 1,000 units of the textile product. His best estimate is that he can sell this amount at a price of $16, which is expected to prevail at the market. He goes to his engineers and asks them to tell him the ways in which he can produce these 1,000 units. His two chief inputs are labor and the services of capital. So for the moment, let us concentrate on these two. We define a unit of labor as a *man-hour* of work by an average laborer who operates a piece of machinery with average efficiency. An extremely efficient worker who produces in one hour twice the output of the average worker in effect furnishes two man-hours of labor for every hour he works. We define a unit of services of capital as a *machine-hour*—that is, as an hour's use of a standard or representative piece of machinery, say one that costs $10,000. Hence, a piece of machinery that costs $20,000 is viewed as providing two machine-hours of capital services when it is operated for an hour.

In Figure 6A.1, we have constructed a curve which we call an *isoquant*. It summarizes the information the manager receives from his engineers on the various combinations of labor and capital services that can be used to produce 1,000 units. Point *H* represents one combination that can be used, namely 3,250 units of labor and 5,000 units of capital service. Point *G* indicates another combination: 2,000 units of labor and 8,000 units of capital services. Point *J* indicates still another: 7,000 units of labor and 2,400 units of capital services. And so forth.[1]

But which of these combinations is the best for producing the 1,000 units? Obviously the one that involves the lowest cost. We can calculate the cost of each of these combinations as follows. Take the price of a unit of labor to be $2 and the cost of a unit of capital services to be $2.50. Hence, the *H* combination involves a cost of 3250 X $2.00 plus 5000 X $2.50, or in total $19,000; this figure is put alongside point *H*. The *G* combination involves a total cost of $24,000; and the *J* combination involves a total cost of $20,000. Of these three

---

[1] Note that the isoquant, in general, has a particular shape and curvature. First, it is negatively sloping. This is to be expected. This simply means that if one wants to use less of one factor, say labor, in producing a fixed amount of goods, he must use more of capital. For if not, one could keep on decreasing the amount of labor one used, save on costs, and still have the same output—a nonsensical result for any operation that is designed by engineers to be efficient.

Second, the isoquant has a particular shape, called *convex to the origin*. This is also meaningful. To show why, consider the combination represented by point *V*. Here much labor is employed, and little capital. One might argue that there is, relatively speaking, an abundance of man-hours and a dearth of machine-hours. Further, one might argue that we could expect, relatively speaking, a large gain in output if we were to increase the use of capital by a small amount, and a small loss in output if we were to decrease the use of labor. So we have a situation where, in producing 1,000 units of output, a small amount of capital, say the amount represented by the horizontal stretch *AB* in Figure 6A.1, can take the place of a much larger amount of labor, say the amount represented by the vertical stretch *AC* in the same figure. Now, if we increase capital by another small dose of the same size, we can expect another large gain in output, but not as much as from the first dose, because we start off with a larger amount of capital. Further, if we decrease the use of labor by the same small amount as before, we can expect a small loss in output. But it is a greater loss than in the first situation, because we are starting off with a smaller amount of labor. So now in producing the same 1,000 units of output, the same small dose of capital, say the amount *DE*(=*AB*), still takes the place of a large amount of labor, say *DB*, but not of as large an amount as before. That is, *DB* < *AC*.

Carrying through this argument for a third, fourth, and further doses suggests that in each situation the same dose of capital takes the place of smaller and smaller amounts of labor. Finally, in the vicinity of point *G*, where we now have an abundance of machine-hours, relatively speaking, and a dearth of man-hours, another dose of capital can take the place of only a very small amount of labor. Thus, we have what may be called a decreasing rate of substitution of capital for labor as we increase our use of capital, given that we produce 1,000 and only 1,000 units of output.

In parallel fashion, we can start from point *G* and consider adding to the combination represented by that point a series of equal doses of labor, each depictable by the same small vertical stretch. The reader can demonstrate for himself that the first dose substitutes for a lot of capital, the second for somewhat less, the third for still less, and so forth, until we come to point *V*, where another dose of labor substitutes for very little capital. Hence, along the isoquant there is a decreasing rate of substitution of labor for capital as we increase the quantity of labor that we use.

Figure 6A.1   An Isoquant, Isocost Lines, and the Optimal Combination of Factors

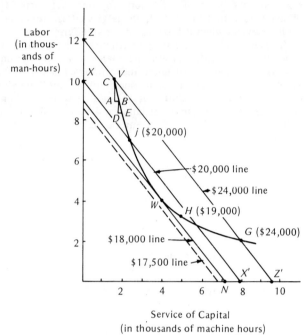

Service of Capital
(in thousands of machine hours)

combinations, combination H incurs the lowest cost, and thus seems best. But maybe there is still another combination corresponding to a point on the isoquant which costs still less. How can we find out about this?

One simple way is to draw what we call *isocost* lines. An isocost line is a line that is the locus of all points representing combinations of labor and capital inputs that incur the same total cost. So, if we look at the combination represented by point G, we see that it costs $24,000. Another combination that costs $24,000 is the one given by point Z, namely 12,000 units of labor and zero units of capital services. Still another combination that costs $24,000 is given by point Z' namely zero units of labor and 9,600 units of capital services. Now if we connect points Z and Z' by a straight line, it will pass through point G and all other combinations that incur a total cost of $24,000, such as point V, a combination of 10,000 units of labor and 1,600 units of capital services.

We immediately see that we can do better than using the combination represented by point G or point V, both of which would allow us to produce 1,000 units of product. We can, for example, produce 1,000 units with combination J, incurring a total cost of only $20,000. ($J$ lies on the $20,000 isocost line, as do points X and X' and all others representing combinations whose total cost is $20,000.) Again, we observe that there are points on the isoquant which involve a total cost of less than $20,000. For example, point H lies on a $19,000 isocost line. But we see that we can do even better. That is, we see that we can go onto lower and lower isocost lines until we reach the isocost line, the $18,000 line, that is just tangent to our isoquant. The point of tangency, W, represents a combination that can be used to produce 1,000 units of product. It also lies on a lower isocost line than any other point on the isoquant curve. Therefore, it involves the lowest cost of all points on the isoquant curve, and represents the best factor combination for the given situation. Note that if we try for a combination that lies on a still lower isocost line, say $17,500 (the dashed line in Figure 6A.1), we can find no point on that line which also lies on the isoquant. That is, there is no point on that line which can produce the 1,000 units of products that are specified. So from a production standpoint, we must consider as infeasible all the combinations that lie on the $17,500 and any other isocost line less than $18,000. We must discard them from consideration.

By this time, the sharp student may have noticed that even if the firm is using its best combination of labor and capital inputs, given by point W, its cost for these two inputs, namely $18,000, exceeds the $16,000 of revenue from selling the 1,000 units of product at $16 per unit. Hence, the manager would not choose to locate at a site where the prices of labor and capital are $2 and $2.50, respectively. He may be motivated, then, to look for a cheap labor location.

Now, suppose the manager finds a cheap labor location, and considers locating there. Suppose that at this location the cost of a man-hour of labor is one-half of what it is at the first location (The first location might be one that minimizes transportation costs.) Because labor is half as costly, we are able to obtain the services of more labor and more capital for any given amount we have to spend on them. To show this, examine Figure 6A.2 on which we construct the same isoquant as Figure 6A.1. Here we take the price of a man-hour of labor to be one-half that in the first location, namely $1. This would be similar to a change in the price of labor at the first location. The price of a machine-hour of capital services is the same, namely $2.50.

Now, for $18,000 we can obtain 18,000 units of labor and zero units of capital services, as given by point M, or zero units of labor and 7,200 units of capital as given by point N, or any combination represented by a point on the straight line MN. For comparison we dash in the old $18,000 line from Figure 6A.1. Except for point N, every point on the new line corresponds to both more capital and labor than the corresponding point on the old line along a straight line from the origin.

Now, if we have a new $18,000 isocost line because of the lower price at the cheap labor location, we also have a new $17,000 isocost line and a new $16,000 isocost line and other new isocost lines. Also, we have a new point of tangency, Q, of the isoquant line with an isocost line. Q represents that combination which can produce 1,000 units at the lowest cost, because it lies on the lowest isocost line, a $13,000 line, that has a point in common with the isoquant. Compare point Q with point W, which represented the best combination at the non-cheap labor location and which involved a total cost of $18,000. First, we see that the total cost of producing the 1,000 units has decreased to $13,000 at the cheap labor location. Moreover, at this location we use more labor and less capital to produce the 1,000 units. In effect, we substitute labor for capital, and are better off because total cost has fallen by $5,000.

If the price of labor at the cheap labor location were to fall, say to $.70 per man-hour, we can see that the $18,000 line would start from point N but slope still more steeply. Likewise all the other isocost lines would begin from the same point on the horizontal axis but slope still more steeply. As a consequence, the new point of tangency, R, of the isoquant line with a new isocost line would involve still less total cost, and would involve the use of still more labor and less capital. That is, there would be still more substitution of labor for capital.

With Figure 6A.2, we can illustrate what we mean by the statement in the text that at a cheap labor location there would be additional gains achievable from substitution of the cheap labor for capital. If the same amounts of labor and capital were used at the cheap labor location as at the optimal transport cost point—that is, if we continued to use the combination represented by W—total cost would fall from $18,000 to $14,000 at the cheap labor location. (At point W, we use 4,000 units of both labor and capital which, at the prices of $1 and $2.50, respectively, yield a total cost of $14,000.) But point W is not a lowest cost combination for the cheap labor location. We obtain the lowest cost combination by shifting from point W to point Q. By substituting cheap labor for capital, we move from a $14,000 isocost line to a $13,000 isocost line, an additional savings of $1,000.

Figure 6A.2   Effect of a Labor Price Change on Optimal Combination of Factors

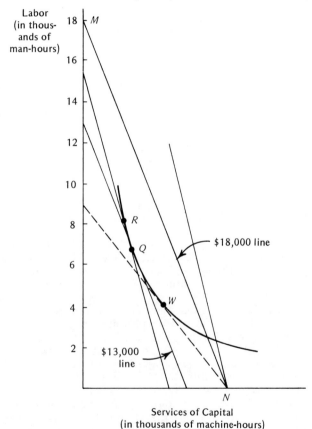

Services of Capital
(in thousands of machine-hours)

The above discussion also allows us to derive a demand curve for labor when we hold output, and also the prices of capital and all other inputs, constant. From Figure 6A.2 we see how the quantity of labor demanded (used) will increase as its price decreases. In fact, we can plot the three quantities of labor as given by points W, Q, and R, corresponding to the three prices $2, $1, and $.70, respectively. We do so in Figure 6A.3. Plotting other quantities that we can obtain from Figure 6A.2 for still other prices of labor, and connecting all such points on Figure 6A.3 with a curve, we obtain the demand curve of the firm for labor. If we add to this demand curve the demand curves of all other firms in the industry, we then obtain the industry demand curve for labor. This curve corresponds to the demand curve for Girl Fridays in Chapter 4. However, it is more continuous because in any textile factory many more laborers are employed than are Girl Fridays in an office; so that each textile firm's demand curve for textile labor is more continuous.

Figure 6A.3   The Firm's Demand Curve for Labor

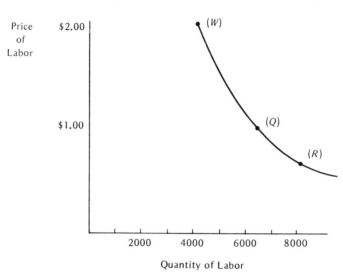

Quantity of Labor

In similar fashion, we can derive the demand curve of a firm or industry for any factor of production. In general, the quantity demanded increases as price decreases, so that the demand curve is negatively sloping as in Figures 6A.3, 4.1, and 4.2.

We can proceed further. Let the level of output change. In Figure 6A.4, we construct isoquants corresponding to the production of 500, 1,000, 1,500 and 2,000 units of product. For the initial set of prices, namely $2 per man-hour and $2.50 per unit of capital services, we indicate in Figure 6A.4 the point of tangency of each isoquant with an isocost line. We connect these points of tangencies with a curve, giving us the lowest cost combination of labor and capital for each level of output. This curve represents the expansion path of the firm for the given prices. Of course, the expansion path will be different for the firm at the cheap labor location because of different prices there. We have indicated this by the dashed curve on Figure 6A.4.

For the moment, let us return to our initial situation, the noncheap labor location. Let us say that the local government has decided to provide an incentive to the firm to locate there by paying for half of the capital services.

Figure 6A.4   A Set of Isoquants and the Expansion Path

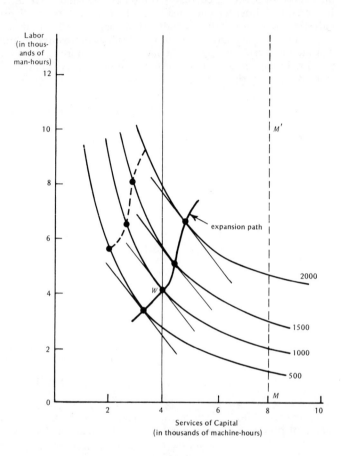

In addition to factor substitution, we are interested in the production function which relates the use of a single factor like labor to the output of textiles, when all other factors are held constant. This relationship can be seen by drawing a straight vertical line in Figure 6A.4 at a level of input of capital which is relevant. In Figure 6A.4, we construct the vertical line at 4,000 units of capital. Then, if we go up the vertical line we see for each amount of labor input, as measured along the vertical, the amount of textiles produced, as given by the isoquant which cuts the vertical line at that level of labor input. In Figure 6A.5 we can plot this output (measured along the vertical) for each amount of labor input (now measured along the horizontal). For example, from Figure 6A.4 we know that on the vertical line representing 4,000 units of capital, point W corresponds to an input of 4,000 units of labor and an output of 1,000 units, because the 1,000 isoquant line cuts the vertical line at W. We plot the 4,000 units of labor and 1,000 units of output as point T in Figure 6A.5. From Figure 6A.4, we see that the point where the 1500 isoquant cuts the vertical line corresponds to an input of 5,700 units of labor. So we plot 5,700 units of labor and 1,500 units of output as point T' in Figure 6A.5. Also in Figure 6A.4, the point where the 500 isoquant line cuts the vertical line corresponds to an input of 2,800 units of labor. We plot 2,800 units of labor and 500 units of output as point T'' in Figure 6A.5.

Figure 6A.5   A Total Product Curve: Total Product For Different Levels of Labor Input

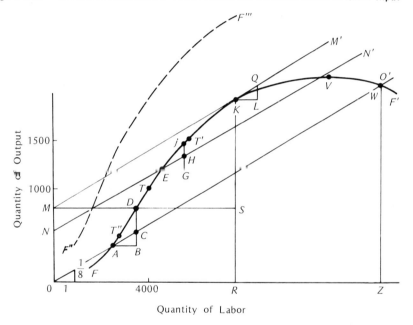

Quantity of Labor

In this manner we can obtain for each level of output the corresponding input of labor. When we plot enough of these points in Figure 6A.5 and connect them with a curve, we obtain the FF′ curve, which we designate the total product curve. For a given level of input of capital services, it specifies the output that can be obtained for different levels of labor input. Of course, if we had started off with more units of capital, as indicated by the dashed vertical line in Figure 6A.4, we would obtain another total product curve, the dashed curve F″F‴ in Figure 6A.5. Because we have more capital available, the output for any given amount of labor exceeds the output given by the curve FF′. And if we had started off with still more capital we would obtain still another total product curve. This one would lie still further above FF′, because for each level of labor input we would be employing a still greater amount of capital and thus would obtain a still greater amount of output. In this manner, we can derive a family of total product curves, one for each level of capital input we wish to consider.

Obviously, we now have another question to answer. We see from the total product curve FF' the different amounts of product obtainable for different amounts of labor input. But which amount of labor do we choose to use? The obvious answer is: The one that is most profitable. Which will it be? We can begin to find the the answer in this way. A firm interested in maximizing profits says to itself: If the cost of another unit of labor is less than the additional revenue obtained from the additional product which it yields, it pays to increase the quantity of labor. Moreover, it will pay to keep on increasing the quantity of labor until we reach a point where this no longer holds—that is, when the cost of an additional unit of labor is equal to the additional revenue. And we do not go beyond this point when the cost of an additional unit of labor exceeds the additional revenue. Now, what is the additional amount of product that we need in order to pay for each additional unit of labor that we might use? We know that the price of labor is given to the firm and remains constant no matter how much labor it uses. We also know that the price of the firm's output is given, and is constant no matter how much it produces. So, if the price of labor is $2, and if the price of the finished product is $16, then clearly we need one-eighth of a unit of product to pay for each unit of labor that may be employed. Now, we could indicate this on Figure 6A.5 by a little triangle at the origin which would have as its vertical one-eighth of a unit of product and as its horizontal one unit of labor. If we were to do this, however, the triangle would be so small (because we measure quantities in thousands along both axes) that we would not be able to see it. Instead, we construct a small triangle whose base corresponds to 1,000 units of labor and whose altitude corresponds to 125 units of product. This indicates that we need one-eighth of 1,000 units of product to pay for 1,000 units of labor. The situation depicted by this triangle is especially realistic for the firm that employs or fires labor not in terms of a single man-hour but in terms of 1,000 man-hours (equivalent to one man working for a period of half a year, or six men working for a period of one month). The slope of this triangle will serve as our reference slope in depicting that 125 units of product are required to pay for 1,000 units of labor (or one-eighth of a unit of product is required to pay for one unit of labor), no matter how much labor the firm uses or how much output it produces.

We have constructed a number of lines in the figure with this same slope, namely OO', NN', and MM'. Take the lowest of these lines, the one constructed from the origin. It intersects the total product curve FF' at point A. At A, we mark off 1,000 additional units of labor—the horizontal stretch AB—and observe that we have to go up 125 units of product—the vertical stretch BC—to reach the straight line OO' that comes from the origin. As we indicated, this represents the amount of additional product required to meet the cost of the additional 1,000 units of labor depicted by AB. But note that if we go up from point B to point D on the production curve FF', we see that the additional thousand units of labor yields BD additional product—much more than the 125 units required to pay for the labor. So it pays to use an additional 1,000 units of labor at this point.

Now consider the line NN'. It intersects the total product curve FF' at point E. If at point E we employ an additional 1,000 units of labor—as given by the horizontal stretch EG—we need 125 units of product—as given by the vertical stretch GH—to meet its cost. But notice that this additional 1,000 units of labor will yield the additional product *GJ*, as indicated by the total product curve FF′. It is much more than the 125 units required to pay for it. So we employ an additional 1,000 units of labor. And we continue to employ additional 1,000 units of labor so long as the slope of one of the straight lines is less than the slope of the total product curve at the point at which that straight line intersects the total product curve.

Finally, we come to the point of tangency, point *K*, of a straight line with the total product curve FF′. At this point, we observe that an additional 1,000 units of labor—as measured by the horizontal stretch *KL*—produces somewhat less than 125 units of additional product. (The vertical stretch *LQ* corresponds to 125 units of product.) This tells us that at the level of labor use and production represented by point *K*, it no longer pays to employ an additional 1,000 units of labor. And if we could enlarge the area around point *K* by 1,000, we would see that it would not pay to hire even one more man-hour. Further, because the slope of the total product curve beyond point *K* continues to fall off, it is not going to be profitable to employ an additional 1,000 units or even one unit of labor at any level of labor input greater than *OR*.

How can we prove that the level of labor use represented by point *K* is *best*— that is, maximizes the profits for the firm, given the initial amount of input of capital services that we assume? The answer is easy. The straight line that goes through point K starts from the vertical axis at point *M*. If we draw a large right triangle *MSK*, we know that the cost of *MS* amount of labor is *SK* amount of product, which corresponds to one-eighth of a unit of product per unit of labor. The total output produced by *MS* amount of labor is given by the vertical line *RK*. So the total amount of product left after paying for labor is *RS*, which is also equal to *OM* on the vertical axis. This represents a surplus product. Now, we observe that of all the straight lines which have in common a point with the total product curve FF′ (that is, either intersect it or are tangent to it), the one that intersects the vertical axis at the highest point is the straight line that is tangent to the total product curve. That is, it gives the largest surplus product. We see, for example, that the line *NN′* intersects the vertical axis at *N* and so generates a surplus product of only *ON* if we were to produce with the labor input corresponding to point *E*. Also, line *OO′* intersects the vertical axis at the zero point, and so generates a zero surplus product if we were to produce with a labor input corresponding to point *A*. So we see that of all the lines that have a point in common with the total produce curve *FF′*, the one that is tangent to it cuts the vertical axis at the highest point. The point of tangency therefore defines the most profitable amount of labor to employ.

At this point, the student might well state: You have identified the best amount of labor to be used in a situation in which you have held the input of capital services constant. But we know that the amount of this input can vary. Therefore, might there be a still more profitable output for some different amount of capital inputs? The answer is that there may well be. To see whether or not this is the case, we first need to recall that corresponding to each level of capital inputs that we may assume, there is a particular total product curve. (For example, the dashed total product curve of Figure 6A.5 corresponds to the input of capital services given by the dashed vertical line *MM′* in Figure 6A.4.) For each of these, we determine the most profitable labor input and the surplus product corresponding to it. Once this is done, it becomes necessary to deduct from the maximum surplus product, corresponding to each total product curve, the amount of product required to pay for the capital inputs being employed. The amount of this deduction will be different for the several total product curves because they use different amount of capital inputs. When these deductions are made, we have an adjusted (or net) surplus product associated with each of the total product curves. We compare them, and choose that total product curve that has associated with it the largest adjusted surplus product (and thus profits for the firm). The optimal combination of labor and capital inputs is then defined by that amount of capital inputs associated with this total product curve and that amount of labor input which generates the largest surplus for this total product curve.

Finally, it is useful to develop one more set of curves. In connection with Figure 6A.5 we have been considering the additional product from an additional 1,000 units of labor for several levels of labor input. Or, if we enlarge Figure 6A.5 1,000 times, we can consider the additional product from an additional unit of labor. We may call this additional product the *marginal product*. We would like to have a curve, a marginal product curve, that specifies the additional product obtainable from an additional unit of labor at all levels of labor input. We have constructed such a curve in Figure 6A.6, where we measure marginal product along the vertical and the level of labor input along the horizontal. At any level of labor input, the marginal product (as measured by the vertical coordinate of the marginal product curve) is equal to the slope of the total product curve FF' of Figure 6A.5 corresponding to that labor input. We should note that the marginal product curve reaches its maximum at the level of labor input corresponding to the point where the total product curve FF' has its steepest slope. Also, the marginal product curve falls to zero when the total product curve reaches its maximum (corresponding to a zero slope) at point V.[2]

We also find it useful to graph an *average product curve*. For each level of labor input, this is obtained by reading from the total product curve the total quantity produced at that level and dividing by that level. For example, in Figure 6A.5 we produce a total product of ZW for a level of labor input of OZ. Dividing ZW by OZ gives the average product—that is, product per labor unit—at that level of labor input, which also corresponds to the slope of the hypotenuse of the right triangle OZW. This is indicated by point α on the average product curve of Figure 6A.6. Or, the average product for OR amount of labor is given by dividing RK by OR. We see that this average product is higher than the average product for a level of labor input of OZ, because the slope of the hypotenuse (if we were to draw the right triangle ORK) is greater than the corresponding slope of the right triangle OZW. Point β on the average product curve of Figure 6A.6 indicates the average product for the labor input OR.

Note that the marginal product curve intersects the average product curve at the latter's maximum point. This is consistent with the reasoning we developed in the text of Chapter 5. As long as a marginal curve is above its corresponding

---

[2] If we were to multiply the marginal product corresponding to any level of labor input by the price of the product (which is $16 in our situation) we would obtain a *marginal revenue curve* from the marginal product curve. In plotting the marginal revenue curve we would measure marginal revenue in dollars along the vertical axis. Moreover, if we were to mark off the price of labor, which is $2 in our situation, along the vertical axis, and draw a horizontal line from this point, we would have the marginal cost curve of labor. The marginal cost of labor in our situation is constant, because the firm must always pay the same price for each unit of labor, no matter how much it hires. The point at which this marginal cost curve of labor cuts its marginal revenue curve indicates the best labor input (given that capital inputs are 4,000)— and will correspond to the level of labor input for which the marginal product of labor is one-eighth of a unit ($2 worth of product).

Figure 6A.6   Marginal and Average Product Curves

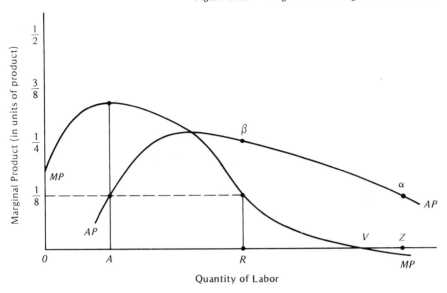

average curve, it raises the average. Whenever a marginal curve is below the corresponding average curve, it lowers the average. And the average curve stays unchanged when the marginal curve is just equal to the average—that is, when the marginal curve intersects the average curve. Thus at the intersection the average curve must reach either a maximum or minimum. In our case it is a maximum.

The Base, Economic Structure, and Development of a City or Region

INTRODUCTION

In this chapter, we wish to take the next step in deepening our understanding of the forces that lead to the formation and growth of urban and regional economies. In the previous chapter, we used comparative cost analysis to see how diverse forces (in the sense of potential cost savings) pull a particular activity to any given location. In doing so, we examined the operation of each activity as an isolated event. We made no reference to the simultaneous operation of all other activities. We ignored the effects of the operation of our particular activity on other operations and vice versa. More specifically, we assumed that the market for our particular activity was given. But from where did the market come? Also, we assumed for our particular activity that power costs, labor costs, and taxes were given at different locations, and that transportation rates had been predetermined. But from where did these costs and rates come?

Such questions as these involve deeper analysis. They require that we explicitly recognize the interdependence of activities. The existence of a market at any given point or geographic area depends on the presence of behaving units who use or consume a product. The prevailing labor costs at any location reflect the existing wage rate. This wage rate, in turn, reflects the forces of demand and supply operating at that location. The demand for labor is an aggregate of the potential demand of our particular activity and the demands of all activities at a given location. The supply of labor is an aggregate of the supply curves of all behaving units at that location supplying labor. It is the interaction of this demand and supply that determines the price of labor, the wage rate, at the location. Hence, we must study this interaction. This means that we must study why other activities are or might be at a given location, as well as the complex interdependence of economic activities through their demand and supply schedules. In this chapter we will look at mutual interdependence in two different ways. One way will be in terms of agglomeration economies and diseconomies. The other will be in terms of the interrelated input-output structures of different activities. We will of course give particular attention to *basic* industries; that is, industries whose operations have extensive impact upon all other activities in a region.

AGGLOMERATION AND DEGLOMERATION ECONOMIES

An understanding of the development of cities and regions cannot be acquired without a full appreciation of the forces of agglomeration and deglomeration that are at play. These forces lead to *the concentration and deconcentration or dispersion of industrial and other activity*. They help explain the existence and perpetuation of huge masses such as Tokyo, New York City, London, Peking, Calcutta, and Rio de Janeiro, to cite only a few. Such forces can be grouped into three categories:

Scale Economies. As already indicated, there may be *economies in the internal production of a given facility as its scale of operation increases*. Very large annual fixed costs, resulting from a large investment in plant and equipment, make it desirable to utilize the plant and equipment at a large scale in order to spread annual fixed costs over many units. Lower unit costs result. A firm is better able to meet the competition of other firms, can make greater profits, or both. A nonprofit facility can provide services at a lower cost to the taxpayer.

We have already suggested that we cannot have things like a planetarium or a fully equipped modern surgical facility or a stock exchange for every small village or town. All these facilities involve large initial investments of capital and need to be operated at a large scale to avoid excessively high unit costs of operation. Hence, they can be justified only at locations serving large populations (having a large market). The larger the population, the lower the unit costs of the product or service. Thus we conclude that the existence of scale economies internal to a facility tend to give an advantage to larger rather than smaller concentrations of population, industries, and other activities.

Localization Economies. A second type of force leading to industrial concentration is that associated with *economies accruing to all the firms in a single industry at a single location*. They are due to the increase in *total* output of that industry at that location.

To illustrate, take the operation of a textile factory. Suppose we consider a case of an underdeveloped region, where it is feasible to establish small modern factories that do not require excessive capital investment and that can operate without specialized and highly skilled labor. We know that machinery occasionally breaks down and that it is necessary to have a repair facility close at hand. Any one textile factory might use the services of this facility a few times per year, say four or five; but when that factory does need repair service, it needs it right away. Hence, the repair facility should be nearby. However, unit costs of repair services will be very high if the facility is used by only one textile factory four or five times a year and lies idle the rest of the time. The facility's total annual costs (including its fixed charges) will be spread out among only a few uses. On the other hand, if there is a cluster of ten different textile factories, each having quick and easy access to the repair facility, then the facility can be used much more fully, say as often as forty or fifty times per year. Its annual fixed charges will be spread among more uses. It will be able to establish a much lower rate for the use of its repair service and still make an adequate profit. True, it may turn out that the machines in more than one plant break down at the same time. It may then be necessary for the facility to incur additional variable costs because of overtime work and for the textile plants to accept some delay in service; but these additional costs and delays would not be excessive and in general would not occur so often as to constitute a major disadvantage. In short, then, by being clustered, textile plants can utilize more effectively the services of a repair facility and thus can expect significantly lower costs for repair. This constitutes a localization economy.

Consider another item, such as electric power. Many of us have observed that, in general, power companies are large in size. If we were to take the time to study the costs of their operation, we would find out that up to a very large scale of operation, the cost per kilowatt-hour falls with increase in output. Ten small-to modest-size textile factories could probably obtain significantly lower power costs if they banded together and operated a power plant than if each operated its own small-scale power plant independently in some isolated small town, or bought power from a small community power facility.

Moreover, these ten textile factories might find that they could obtain their raw materials at lower costs if they coordinated their purchases through a single broker, so that he could buy raw materials in large volume and pass on to the factories a large part of the discounts and savings that come from lower transport rates with volume shipments. Or consider the problem of curtailing pollution emissions and waste treatment. If textile plants were to develop a common facility to process their wastes and emissions, they could gain from sharing in the lower costs of processing.

In sum, these and many other considerations of a like nature provide the basis for the existence of important localization economies. Such economies tend to lead to the clustering and concentration of plants in a given industry or sector within a confined geographic area, and to the rise and growth of cities.

Diagrammatically, we can depict the effect of localization economies with the use of Figure 7.1. In this figure we have constructed three locational triangles, one relevant to each of the three plants. Ignoring localization economies, we may imagine that plants a, b, c, would locate respectively at $P_a{}^*$, $P_b{}^*$, and $P_c{}^*$, their optimal transport points. However, plants a, b, and c would reap localization economies of $7, $5, and $6, respectively, if they could all agree to locate at some common site. Accordingly, we identify the $7 isodapane line for plant a (which is its critical isodapane), the $5 isodapane line for plant b (its critical isodapane), and the $6 isodapane line for plant c (its critical isodapane). Now, if we were to propose a common location at point Z in Figure 7.1 we see that it would

Figure 7.1   The Area of Potential Agglomeration Sites Owing to Localization Economies

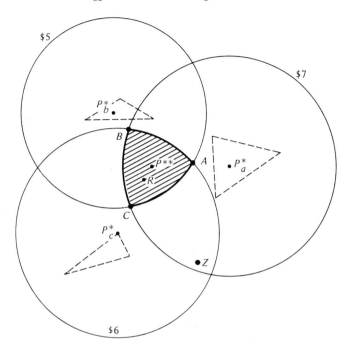

lie within *a*'s critical isodapane and thus lead to a gain for *a*, and within *c*'s critical isodapane and thus lead to a gain for *c*. However, *Z* lies well outside *b*'s critical isodapane (the $5 line), and thus would lead to a loss for *b*. Therefore, unless side payments or some other kinds of gains were offered to *b*, *b* would not agree to locate at the common site *Z*. If localization economies cannot be reaped unless all three plants locate at a common site, then we may conclude that point *Z* does not qualify as a common site.

However, consider point *R*. We observe that *R* does lie within the critical isodapane of all three producers *a*, *b*, and *c*. It qualifies as an agglomeration site. So do all other points in the shaded area of Figure 7.1. We therefore designate this the *area of potential agglomeration*.

At this juncture we may ask which of the sites in the shaded area will be chosen. If the objective were to minimize total transport and production costs for the three plants together—as might be the case in a socialist or planned society—then we could locate the best site *P*** which achieves this objective. However, in a capitalistic system, and even in many noncapitalistic systems, each producer is primarily interested in his own gains and at best only secondarily in the gains of others. Each producer is interested in that site in the shaded area which lies farthest within his own critical isodapane, which is the location involving the lowest additional transportation cost for him. Thus producer *a* votes for *A* as a site of agglomeration, *b* votes for *B*, and *c* votes for *C*. Immediately a conflict arises, which needs to be resolved if localization economies are to be reaped. This conflict is typical of many situations in real life, and we shall examine the possibilities for its resolution in Chapters 11 and 16. In some cases, we shall note that the conflict has been resolved and a common site chosen by agreement. In other cases, the conflict may be resolved only after long years of struggle, or perhaps not at all.

Also, we note that still other sites may qualify as agglomeration sites. This possibility becomes important when large relocation costs are involved. If there are large relocation costs, why have three relocations? Why not seek a solution whereby only two relocation costs are incurred, which would be the case if, say, P_b* were chosen as the agglomeration site and if b could give a and c sufficiently large side payments. These, together with the localization economies realized, would make it profitable for a and c to relocate at P_b*. But how large should these side payments be? Naturally, b would like them to be as small as possible, while a and c would each like his own side payment to be as large as possible. Once again conflict arises. How should the three producers share the surplus or "pie"? To answer this question, we will want to examine several kinds of interesting and relevant negotiation processes and cooperative procedures.

Urbanization Economies. Urbanization economies are a third type of agglomeration factor. They are available to all firms in all industries. *They are associated with the increase in the total size (in terms of population, industrial output, income, and wealth) of a location for all activities taken together.* They relate to the mass of not one industry or sector, but to an aggregate of industries and sectors. To be specific, take an activity that is highly dependent upon creative management and skilled labor. In this regard, there are risks to being located in a small urban area. Your manager might suddenly quit for any one of a thousand different reasons. Your restless chief engineer might pull up stakes and accept an unusual, exciting job in exotic Malaysia. In a small area, it will be much more difficult to find a replacement.

A second urbanization economy is associated with the increase in the diversity and specialization of goods and services accompanying the increase in size of an urban area. A huge metropolitan region like New York City can provide more specialized knowledge and know-how to a business establishment needing assistance than a smaller urban area can. It can support a technical library having a complete collection of relevant engineering and other kinds of technical journals. It can support one or more engineering, law, business administration, and scientific faculties within a university structure. It has many specialized repair facilities—a facility that specializes in Ford trucks, another in General Motors vehicles, a third in Volkswagens, and so forth. It can provide many household goods and services not available elsewhere, and can offer other goods of high quality. This enables a firm to attract outstanding management and technical personnel more easily and at lower salary scales. The number and diversity of governmental units—federal, state, and local—and of cultural, social, and other noneconomic organizations also grow with an increase in urban mass.

On the other hand, associated with increased size in the urban area are many diseconomies. They become increasingly difficult to counteract as the urban mass grows. We know too well how traffic congestion mounts with increase in size; greater and greater loss of time in travel results, as well as more and more psychic discomfort, strain, and general discontent. Many social scientists hypothesize that impersonality within the community, crime rates, and social anxiety also increase with urban growth. More recently, we have noted how air, water, solid waste, sonic and visual pollution seem to increase significantly with an increase in urban mass.

In terms of dollars and cents, we observe the general relationship between rise in rent and size of metropolitan region. Likewise with the cost of living, partly reflecting the region's need to go farther and farther afield and incur greater and greater transport costs in procuring its food supplies. So the money wages that private and nonprivate enterprises pay must rise, as well as the prices of many other inputs.

In sum, we see numerous urbanization diseconomies, or put otherwise, deglomeration economies, cropping up as we examine larger and larger urbanized regions. These set limits to urban size and growth. They offset the desirability of different sizes of urban masses as potential locations for industry and other activities. Together with scale, localization and urbanization economies, urbanization diseconomies act to condition the size and composition of the diverse economic and noneconomic activities of a city and region.

INTERINDUSTRY STRUCTURE AND INDIRECT EFFECTS OF GROWTH

A second, entirely different approach to the understanding of the structure and function of a city can be obtained by approximating the complex interdependence and linkages of its economic and other activities through a linear system. In Chapter 2 we laid the base for using a linear system for this purpose. There we described or depicted the city statistically with an input-output table (see Table 2.1). We set down in comprehensive and systematic fashion the different industries or sectors of an urban region. We listed the sectors by columns, and listed them in the same order by rows. We then put numbers in the cells of the table. The numbers in any column represent the inputs of the various commodities into the sector at the head of the column. For example, the number $61 million (more strictly speaking, $60,603,300) in the first row of the first column represents the input of agriculture products (the sector corresponding to the first row) into the agriculture industry (the sector at the head of the first column) of the Philadelphia region for the year 1968. The number $14 million (actually $13,543,700) in the second row of the first column represents the input of food products (the sector corresponding to the second row) into the agriculture sector. The number $1 million (actually $769,900) in the fifth row of the first column represents the input of the lumber products sector into the agriculture industry. Thus, considering the table by columns, we see the complete set of inputs for each and every activity of the Philadelphia region.

The table also provides basic information when its rows are studied. Each row shows, for the corresponding industry or sector, how its total output is distributed among the diverse purchasers of this output. Put another way, the row gives the allocation of this total output to all those in the economic and social system who use and consume it. For example, if we study the second row pertaining to the distribution of the total output of the food products industry of the Philadelphia region in the year 1968 among its consumers (including industrial and institutional users as well as households), we observe the following. The first figure in the row, namely $14 million, represents the sale of the food products sector to the agriculture sector, the industry listed at the head of the first column. The second item refers to the sale of $668 million of food products to the food products industry itself, the sector listed at the head of the second column. This sale is not unexpected, because certain kinds of plants in the food industry purchase food products from other plants in the industry for further processing. For example, a cheese-spread manufacturer may purchase his basic input of cheese from a cheese manufacturer.

The ninth item in the second row represents $20 million of sales of food products to the chemical and chemical products sector, the sector listed at the head of the ninth column. The twelfth item of the second row represents $6 million of sales of food products to the leather and leather products sector, the sector listed at the head of the twelfth column.

Continuing in this manner along the second row, we see how the total output of the food products sector is distributed or allocated to all sectors, including itself. Note also that this distribution corresponds to the dollar sales of the food products sector to all other sectors. If we add the sales along the row, we obtain total sales which, after taking into account inventory changes, correspond to total output.

When we study each row in this manner, and then all the rows together, we obtain a comprehensive, detailed view of how the diverse sectors of an urban region are linked via the distribution of their total outputs.

Table 2.1 represents one kind of input-output table, namely a *flows* table. Such a table shows the dollar flows from one sector to another. It enables us to understand how changes in the level of output of one sector *directly* affect the level of output of other sectors. For example, suppose the output of the iron and steel sector were to double because a huge new integrated iron and steel works complex was put into operation in the Philadelphia region. If we were asked for a quick answer to the question: How would the steel sector's purchases from other sectors be affected? we would say that these purchases would be roughly doubled. Specifically, going down column 14, which corresponds to the iron and steel sector, we might expect its purchases of output from the chemical and chemical products sector to be not $10 million but twice that amount, namely, $20 million. We might expect its purchases from the stone, clay, and glass products industry to be not $23 million but twice that amount, namely, $46 million. And so forth. Finally we might expect the wages and salaries paid out to the households sector to be not $293 million but twice that amount, namely, $586 million. In this manner, we get a quick answer to the question concerning the direct effect of a doubling of the output of the iron and steel industry.

Our analysis, however, cannot stop here. We must look into the *indirect* effects. We already know that a good fraction of the additional purchases of the steel sector will come from plants producing in the Philadelphia region. For example, a large fraction of the inputs of the food products sector will come from factories in the region. However, to produce these additional food products to be used as inputs by the steel sectors, the factories will require additional inputs of raw materials, labor, power, and other items, some of which will also come from Philadelphia producers and households. Moreover, doubling the output of the steel sector will lead to an increase in wages and salaries paid to labor. This will mean that there will be some households in the Philadelphia region with income to spend where previously there was no income, and that there will be other households with larger incomes to spend. Then, retail and other kinds of sales will rise, more labor will be employed in retail stores, and more power will be consumed by them. In turn, output levels of other sectors will increase, and on and on. In short, there will be many rounds of indirect effects, which can be substantial.

At this point, can we increase the power of the techniques of analysis at our disposal in order to yield estimates of what these indirect effects are likely to be? Specifically, can we use input-output techniques for this purpose?

Note that we are dealing with a very important question. In a study that was made some time before the Fairless Integrated Iron and Steel Works was put in operation in the Philadelphia region, the following was estimated:

1. The direct employment in the steel plant, when its output reached 3 million tons annually, would be 11,666.
2. The direct employment in the steel fabricating and similar industries that could be expected to agglomerate around the steel plant to take advantage of being close to a steel mill (saving transport costs on obtaining raw materials) and at the same time in the heart of a major consumer market (saving transport costs on shipping finished products to the market) was estimated to be 77,014.
3. The total direct employment in the Philadelphia region generated by the need to produce, in the region, some of the new required inputs of the integrated steel works and the steel fabricators agglomerating around it was estimated to be approximately 19,000—a first-round expansion effect.
4. The total employment in the Philadelphia region generated by the need to produce, in the region, the new required inputs to realize the first-round expansion was estimated to be approximately 26,000—a second-round expansion effect.

And so forth. All told, it was estimated that corresponding to the employment in the iron and steel works of 11,666 was the employment of 77,014 in steel fabricating and 70,089 in the subsequent rounds of indirect effects, a multiplier effect (in terms of employment) of close to 13. Thus we see that these indirect effects are significant. And although we cannot go back historically and determine whether or not the iron and steel works did have this impact—simultaneously other new basic industries such as oil refineries, petrochemicals, and electronics were expanding in the Philadelphia region—we are fairly certain that the new Fairless Iron and Steel Works has had at least as large an effect, direct and indirect, as estimated.

THE CONSTRUCTION OF AN INPUT-OUTPUT COEFFICIENTS TABLE

We have now presented data indicating the importance of understanding and estimating indirect effects, and have suggested that the input-output technique is useful in this regard. But what specifically is the rationale for its use in this connection?

Suppose you are a steel fabricator. In particular, suppose you manufacture refrigerators. Suppose also that with the general expansion of basic activities in your region, the income of its households goes up by 50 percent. You estimate that the demand for new refrigerators will also go up by 50 percent. Then, if you make the decision to produce 50 percent more refrigerators, you are likely to increase your purchase of steel by 50 percent, your purchase of chemical refrigerant by 50 percent, and so forth. You know that you currently produce 1,000 refrigerators a year, each of which costs $300. That is, your annual sales are $300,000. Each refrigerator requires $30 worth of steel as an input. Thus, your total annual purchases of steel amount to $30,000. If you now plan to increase your output by 50 percent, you estimate sales of $450,000 and steel purchases of $45,000. By noticing the relative magnitude of these figures, you may have already determined that for every $1 of output you need 10 cents worth of steel; so if you produce a refrigerator that sells for $300, you need 300 times 10 cents worth of steel (or $30 worth of steel, as we said above). Hence, once you have estimated your total dollar output of refrigerators you simply multiply 10 cents by the total output to determine the amount of your steel purchases. Of course, 10 cents represent $0.10 dollars and for reasons we explain later, $0.10 can be viewed as a constant coefficient.

Now consider the chemical refrigerant required for each refrigerator that costs $300. This refrigerant costs $6 per refrigerator. Hence, we can say that for every dollar's worth of refrigerator that we produce, we require 2 cents worth of refrigerant—or, per $1 output of refrigerators we require $0.02 of refrigerant. Thus, we take the $0.02 as another constant coefficient. In like manner we determine the cents worth of every other input required per $1 output of refrigerators. When expressed in dollars worth of inputs per dollar output this gives a set of coefficients.

Let us return to Table 2.1 and examine column 15, fabricated metal products, which includes refrigerators. We know from going across row 15, which refers to the fabricated metal products sector, that its total output was $890 million in the Philadelphia region in 1968. If we now take this total dollar figure and divide it into each of the dollar figures in column 15 of Table 2.1, we obtain the set of coefficients listed in column 15 of Table 7.1. These coefficients tell the dollars' worth of each input required per $1 output of the fabricated metal products sector.

Just as we have calculated the constant coefficients for the fabricated metal products sector, we can calculate constant coefficients for every other sector of a region. We can set these down in table form to obtain a table of constant coefficients, often called *constant production* coefficients. For any column, they tell us the dollars' worth of each of the diverse inputs that needs to be used in the production of one dollar of product of the sector at the head of the column.[1]

In making these calculations, we are assuming two things. First, in using a linear system, as we do, we assume that the pounds of steel required to produce a refrigerator do not change no matter how many refrigerators we produce. Second, we assume that prices remain constant during our period of analysis. Then, if prices are constant—for example, if the price of steel does not change—then when

[1] We obviously do not calculate these coefficients for the column 43 (final demand less imports) because that column does not represent a production sector, and also lies outside the structural matrix, the 42 by 42 table. However, it is useful to calculate coefficients for rows 43 through 47 for they provide useful information on accounting charges. Also, this leads to column sums adding to one.

we divide the dollars' worth of steel input per dollar output of fabricated metal products by the price of a pound of steel, we obtain the pounds of steel required to produce one dollar's worth of fabricated metal products. Also, if the price of a typical fabricated metal product, say a refrigerator, stays constant at $300, then if we multiply the pounds of steel needed to produce $1 of refrigerators by 300, we obtain the pounds of steel required to produce one refrigerator.

In this sense the pounds of steel required per refrigerator represents a *technical production coefficient*—technical in the sense of reflecting the physical input-output magnitudes of a given technology or of the given technological process used.[2] Also, in this sense the constant production coefficients in any column of Table 7.1 may be considered to be constant technical production coefficients when prices of the diverse inputs and outputs are assumed constant.

We have already indicated in Chapter 2 that in the United States, and in general in capitalistic systems, we set up input-output flows tables in terms of dollar purchases when we go down each column and dollar sales when we go across each row. Thus, when we use input-output tables our flows are in dollars, and our constant production coefficients are in dollars' worth of input per dollar of output. In socialist societies, and in general in planned societies where there is much less reliance on the market to allocate goods and services among household consumers and other users, it has been found convenient to construct input-output tables in terms of physical units. Thus, if we were to go down the column of a flows table, we would see the physical amounts of each input required to produce the total number of units of the product of the sector at the head of the column. For example, if in the Leningrad region, 10,000 units of a typical fabricated metals product like refrigerators were produced in 1968, we would see how many pounds of steel, pounds of chemicals, electric power, man-hours of labor, etc. were used in the production of those 10,000 units. Moreover, if we

---

[2] The curious student who has read the technical materials in the appendix to Chapter 6 may ask how the constant technical production coefficients are related to the production theory presented there. The answer is obvious. The total product curve of Figure 6A.5 simply becomes a straight line radiating from the origin, whose slope is the constant technical production coefficient. For example, if the coefficient is 10 pounds of steel per refrigerator we have as our total product curve:

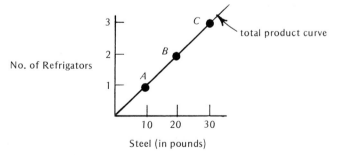

Moreover, the input-output linear production system requires that if we consider any other input, say the chemical refrigerant, twice as much of that input must correspond to production at point *B* than at point *A*, and three times as much to production at point *C* than at point *A*. And so forth. Further, the isoquants of Figure 6A.4 reduce to a series of points along a straight line radiating from the origin. No factor substitution is possible.

Table 7.1 Philadelphia Region Input-Output Coefficients Table for 1968
(Based on 1959 Coefficients Partly Updated to 1968)

PURCHASING SECTOR (columns):
1. Agriculture, Fisheries
2. Food Processing / Kindred Prod.
3. Textile Mill Prod.
4. Apparel
5. Lumber & Wood Prod.
6. Furniture & Fixtures
7. Paper & Allied Prod.
8. Printing & Publishing
9. Chemicals & Chemical Prod.
10. Petroleum Refining & Prod.
11. Rubber & Misc. Plastic Prod.
12. Leather & Leather Prod.
13. Stone, Clay & Glass Prod.
14. Primary Metals
15. Fabricated Metal Prod.
16. Machinery (excl. Electric)
17. Electric Machinery
18. Motor Vehicles

PRODUCING	1	2	3	4	5	6	7	8	9	10	11	12	13	14	15	16	17	18
1. Agriculture, Fisheries	.301	.148	.034	.001	.003	—	—	—	*	—	.061	*	*	*	—	—	—	—
2. Food Processing & Kindred Prod.	.067	.258	*	*	—	—	.001	—	.010	*	—	.158	*	—	—	*	—	—
3. Textile Mill Prod.	.001	*	.285	.296	—	.011	.003	.001	.006	—	.027	.019	.004	*	*	*	*	*
4. Lumber & Wood Prod.	.002	*	—	.048	—	—	*	—	—	—	—	.005	.002	—	—	—	*	*
5. Furniture & Fixture	.004	.001	*	*	.290	.052	*	*	—	—	*	.001	.006	.002	.004	.002	.002	.008
6. Furniture & Fixtures	—	—	—	—	.002	.024	—	—	—	—	—	—	—	—	—	*	.018	.001
7. Paper & Allied Prod.	.002	.041	.009	.008	.038	.021	.277	.203	.189	.009	.013	.009	.021	.001	.013	.002	.010	.003
8. Printing & Publishing	*	.004	.001	.001	.022	.002	.003	.059	.008	.001	.003	.001	.002	.001	.001	.004	.002	.010
9. Chemical & Chemical Prod.	.016	.004	.027	.001	.033	.021	.029	.015	.181	.035	.108	.028	.028	.007	.028	.002	.008	.004
10. Petroleum Refining & Prod.	.037	.004	.004	.001	.002	.003	.007	.001	.017	.072	.002	.003	.016	.016	.005	.006	.002	.002
11. Rubber & Misc. Plastic Prod.	.002	*	*	.001	*	.010	.014	*	.002	.001	.007	.009	.004	*	.008	.004	.010	.009
12. Leather & Leather Prod.	—	—	.001	—	—	*	—	—	—	—	—	.137	—	—	—	*	—	—
13. Stone, Clay, & Glass Prod.	.002	.007	.003	—	.019	.004	—	—	.010	.004	*	—	.110	.016	.004	.003	.012	.004
14. Primary Metals	—	*	*	*	.002	.144	.001	.005	.002	.004	.006	.004	.020	.132	.299	.182	.069	.146
15. Fabricated Metal Prod.	.003	.018	*	.001	.106	.049	*	.001	.008	.032	.002	.009	.011	.001	.017	.048	.028	.036
16. Machinery (excl. Electric)	.003	*	*	*	*	.002	*	.009	.001	*	.002	*	.001	.014	.007	.059	.011	.080
17. Electric Machinery	—	—	—	—	.008	—	*	—	*	—	—	—	*	*	*	.056	.210	.033
18. Motor Vehicles	.001	—	—	—	—	—	—	—	*	—	.002	...	—	—	—	*	*	.087
19. Misc. Manufacturing	*	—	.007	.007	.005	*	*	.003	—	—	*	.039	—	—	—	*	*	*
20. Professional & Scientific Equip.	—	—	—	—	—	—	*	.003	—	—	—	—	—	—	.002	.001	.004	.003
21. Coal, Gas & Electric Power	.004	.007	.009	.005	.013	.011	.017	.005	.015	.019	.008	.005	.021	.017	.008	.009	.006	.006
22. Transportation	—	*	—	—	—	—	—	*	—	—	—	—	—	—	—	—	*	—
23. Wholesale Trade	—	—	.001	—	*	—	—	*	—	.002	—	*	—	*	.021	.003	*	—
24. Retail Trade (excl. Eating Places)	—	—	—	—	—	—	—	—	—	—	—	—	—	—	—	—	—	—
25. Communications	.003	.003	.004	.004	.003	.005	.003	.014	.004	.002	.003	.003	.004	.004	.004	.006	.004	.003
26. Finance & Insurance	.006	.006	.010	.010	.008	.006	.007	.008	.010	.009	.006	.007	.011	.009	.008	.007	.004	.004
27. Real Estate & Rentals	.001	*	.001	.001	.001	.001	*	.001	.001	*	.001	*	*	*	*	*	.001	*
28. Business Serv. (incl. Advertising)	.008	.026	.012	.011	.006	.013	.011	.046	.070	.023	.024	.018	.013	.009	.011	.011	.017	.013
29. Hotel, Personal, & Repair Serv.	.005	.001	.003	.003	.003	.002	.001	.001	.001	—	.001	.002	.002	.001	.001	.001	.001	*
30. Automobile Repair	.002	.005	.001	*	.010	.002	.001	.001	.001	.001	*	.001	.003	*	.001	.001	*	*
31. Private Household Serv.	—	—	—	—	—	—	—	—	—	—	—	—	—	—	—	—	—	—
32. Amusement & Recreational Serv.	—	—	*	*	*	*	*	*	*	—	*	*	*	*	*	*	*	*
33. Eating & Drinking Places	—	—	—	—	—	—	—	—	—	—	—	—	—	—	—	—	—	—
34. Misc. Industries	*	*	—	—	—	—	—	—	*	.005	—	—	.040	.001	*	—	—	—
35. Nonprofit Orgs.	.002	*	—	—	—	*	—	—	—	—	—	—	—	—	—	—	—	—
36. Construction	.012	.004	.001	.001	.001	—	.005	.004	.001	.002	.001	*	.006	.001	.001	.001	.001	.002
37. Research & Development	—	*	*	—	—	—	*	—	.001	.001	—	—	*	.001	*	.001	*	.001
38. Medical, Health, & Hospital Serv.	*	—	—	—	—	—	—	—	—	—	—	—	—	—	—	—	—	—
39. Elem., Sec., & Higher Educ.	*	—	—	—	—	—	—	—	—	—	—	—	—	—	—	—	—	—
40. Local Gov't.	.014	.016	.016	.016	.012	.016	.015	.013	.013	.015	.032	.010	.014	.012	.013	.013	.019	.014
41. Private Households	.180	.158	.238	.297	.211	.268	.220	.366	.160	.089	.263	.316	.274	.207	.310	.360	.301	.351
42. Unallocated	.004	.167	.161	.231	.135	.255	.157	.104	.230	.044	.105	.164	.229	.168	.158	.102	.135	.077
43. Imports (Noncompetitive)	.060	.020	.096	.016	.010	.017	.097	.024	.071	.442	.216	.152	.056	.152	.010	.015	.030	.008
44. Gov't Taxes Fed. & State	.019	.021	.021	.014	.016	.018	.039	.052	.056	.038	.040	.016	.031	.064	.025	.037	.033	.037
45. Profits & Dividends	.015	.203	.015	.010	.014	.013	.034	.029	.035	.036	.031	.008	.028	.056	.023	.029	.027	.036
46. Capital Allowance	.022	.076	.026	.009	.020	.023	.032	.022	.047	.109	.025	.016	.042	.029	.020	.026	.021	.013
47. Scrap & Misc. Charges	.005	—	.016	.005	.005	.007	.024	.010	.016	.007	.010	.005	.007	.052	.012	.010	.013	.009
Total	1.0	1.0	1.0	1.0	1.0	1.0	1.0	1.0	1.0	1.0	1.0	1.0	1.0	1.0	1.0	1.0	1.0	1.0

*Less than 0.0005. Figures have been rounded to nearest 0.001.

Table 7.1 (cont'd.)

19. Misc. Manufacturing	20. Prof. & Scientific Equip.	21. Coal, Gas, & Electric Power	22. Transportation	23. Wholesale Trade	24. Retail Trade (excl. Eating Places)	25. Communications	26. Finance & Insurance	27. Real Estate & Rentals	28. Business Serv. (incl. Advertising)	29. Hotel, Personal, & Repair Serv.	30. Automobile Repair	31. Private Household Serv.	32. Amusement & Recreational Serv.	33. Eating & Drinking Places	34. Misc. Industries	35. Nonprofit Orgs.	36. Construction	37. Research & Development	38. Medical, Health, & Hosp. Serv.	39. Elem-, Sec-, & Higher Educ.	40. Local Gov't.	41. Private Households	42. Unallocated
.030	–	.025	*	–	*	*	*	–	–	*	–	–	.002	–	–	.002	.001	.006	.003	.003	.001	.018	–
.025	–	*	.001	*	.001	*	*	–	–	.001	–	–	*	–	–	.015	–	.001	.020	.013	.005	.128	.006
.007	.005	*	*	.036	*	*	–	–	*	.012	.002	–	.001	–	–	–	*	–	.002	*	*	.009	.002
*	–	.001	*	*	*	*	*	–	.001	.019	.002	.001	.001	*	–	*	–	–	.001	*	.003	.024	*
.052	*	.003	.001	.001	*	–	–	–	–	*	–	–	–	–	*	*	.033	*	-	.002	.001	.004	*
–	.001	*	*	–	*	.002	*	–	–	.001	–	–	–	–	–	*	.005	.014	*	.005	.001	.005	*
.033	.011	–	*	.013	.012	*	*	–	.002	.014	.001	–	.001	.012	--	.002	.002	.003	–	.001	*	.002	.089
.005	.004	.003	.002	.011	.008	.021	.009	.012	.200	.006	.005	–	.012	.002	.001	.026	.002	.020	.003	.013	.003	.004	.210
.059	.018	.005	*	.002	*	*	–	–	.001	.023	.009	–	*	.004	.017	.007	.015	.016	.022	.002	.006	.014	.003
.006	.004	.050	.041	.004	.008	.003	*	.016	.004	.012	.003	–	.001	.017	.054	.017	.009	*	.015	.003	.014	.019	*
.009	.005	*	.007	*	.001	*	–	–	.002	.006	.035	–	*	–	*	–	*	.001	.001	*	*	.001	.002
.001	*	–	*	–	–	–	–	–	*	.001	*	–	.002	–	–	–	–	–	–	–	*	.006	*
.045	.006	*	*	*	*	*	–	–	*	.005	.017	–	–	.002	–	–	.069	.003	.002	.002	.005	.002	*
.054	.087	.027	.002	*	*	*	*	–	–	.001	.001	–	–	–	.001	–	.028	.001	–	*	.003	*	.001
.015	.021	.009	.001	.029	*	*	*	–	*	.002	.015	–	–	*	.004	*	.040	.005	*	.002	.004	.001	.003
.024	.020	.007	.008	–	.001	.010	.005	.006	.022	.003	.014	–	–	*	.008	*	.017	.030	*	.004	.008	.001	.003
.005	.081	.066	*	–	–	.002	*	–	*	.026	.020	–	–	*		.029	.049	.001	.002	.010	.005	–	
–	–	.005	.006	–	*	*	*	–	.001	.001	.145	–	*	–	–	–	–	*	.001	.006	.025	*	
.013	.006	*	*	*	*	.001	–	–	.010	.022	*	–	.016	.001	–	.008	.001	.001	.001	.002	.002	.013	.050
.001	.030	.005	*	–	*	*	–	–	.006	.013	.002	–	.004	–	*	.001	.039	.035	.004	.002	.001	.003	
.008	.006	.013	.006	.010	.022	.009	.002	.015	.009	.019	.019	–	.008	.040	.026	.018	.001	*	.004	.024	.016	.023	.029
–	–	.023	.115	*	.002	.001	*	–	–	–	*	.040	–	–	–	*	–	.001	.001	.001	.001	.012	.348
–	–	–	*	–	–	–	–	–	–	–	–	–	–	–	–	–	–	*	–	*	–	.044	.073
–	–	–	–	–	–	–	–	–	–	–	–	–	–	–	–	–	–	–	–	–	–	.162	*
.005	.005	.003	.007	.021	.011	.009	.006	.013	.149	.005	.007	–	.006	.007	.004	.006	.002	.003	.006	.005	.003	.014	.014
.008	.006	.063	.036	.036	.036	.018	.049	.032	.010	.015	.024	–	.021	.036	.025	.010	.019	.001	.013	.051	.040	.039	.039
.001	.001	*	.001	.003	.003	.001	.009	.003	.002	.003	.003	–	.004	.003	.001	*	*	.001	.001	.003	*	.035	–
.018	.013	.009	.005	.044	.056	.018	.017	.031	.017	.020	.016	–	.030	.016	.036	.008	.028	.003	.015	.003	.011	*	.048
.002	.001	.001	*	.003	.002	.001	*	.004	.005	.029	–	–	–	.014	.001	.001	–	.001	.002	*	.001	.052	*
.001	*	.002	.034	.010	.008	.002	.003	.002	.004	.009	.017	–	–	.001	*	.002	.005	–	.003	*	.001	.007	.003
*	*	–	.001	.001	.001	.015	*	.002	.001	–	–	–	.236	.001	*	.003	–	.001	.002	.003	*	.013	–
–	–	*	.001	–	–	*	–	–	–	*	*	*	–	*	–	–	*	–	–	.001	*	.030	.002
.004	–	–	*	–	–	–	–	–	–	–	–	–	–	*	.007	–	–	–	.001	*	.001		
–	–	.001	*	*	–	.001	.004	.010	*	*	*	–	*	–	–	.133	–	.001	.005	*	.005	.016	.002
.002	*	.021	.029	.009	.006	.030	.005	.084	.001	.003	.014	–	.022	.015	.001	.053	.261	.038	.025	.006	.010	*	.032
*	*	–	*	*	–	*	.001	–	*	.001	.001	–	.001	–	–	.021	–	–	.002	*	.002	–	
–	–	–	–	–	–	*	.001	–	*	*	*	–	*	–	–	.278	–	–	.001	.023	.379	.014	.038
.014	.014	.047	.031	.006	.017	.059	.022	.035	.012	.021	.018	–	.029	.027	.014	.007	.014	.004	.009	*	.012	.021	–
.284	.431	.258	.471	.446	.394	.342	.398	.582	.324	.319	.223	.958	.255	.405	.289	.303	.283	.485	.343	.683	.402	–	–
.157	.095	.046	.064	.142	.296	.060	.213	.010	.048	.260	.298	*	.200	.280	.357	.057	.052	.131	.012	.042	.006	.012	–
.027	.021	.142	.016	.056	.049	.016	.117	.036	.039	.050	.041	–	.049	.046	.014	.005	.002	.012	.020	.044	.005	.005	
.024	.045	.083	.033	.023	.009	.149	.045	.060	.030	.009	.007	–	.012	.012	.016	.003	.018	.010	.014	.004	.006	.173	
.023	.033	.030	.012	.061	.017	.090	.072	.017	.035	.020	.002	–	.019	.012	.011	–	.026	.054	.311	–	–	–	–
.026	.018	.046	.056	.025	.035	.114	.008	.016	.054	.045	.039	–	.067	.043	.109	–	.022	.054	.027	–	–	–	–
.010	.012	.005	.013	.008	.003	.022	.012	.014	.009	.005	.002	.001	.003	.002	.010	.013	.006	.011	.023	.036	.015	–	–
1.0	1.0	1.0	1.0	1.0	1.0	1.0	1.0	1.0	1.0	1.0	1.0	1.0	1.0	1.0	1.0	1.0	1.0	1.0	1.0	1.0	1.0	1.0	1.0

were to go across any row of the table, we would see how the total physical output of the sector corresponding to the row was distributed among all sectors.

Further, if we were to develop the constant technical production coefficient table corresponding to the flows table, then going down any column, say the column of the fabricated metal products sector, would tell us the pounds of steel, the man-hours, the pounds of chemicals, etc. required per unit of output. It is to be noted that when prices are assumed constant, using either set of tables gives the same results—we get the same results for a capitalistic society, such as the United States, whether or not we view flows in dollar terms or physical terms. Also, when prices are assumed constant, we get the same results for the Leningrad region whether or not we express the flows in rubles or physical quantities, or coefficients in rubles of steel per unit of output or pounds of steel per unit of output.

THE USES OF INPUT-OUTPUT TABLES

Having the set of constant production coefficients (in dollar terms) or the set of constant technical production coefficients (in physical quantity terms) and the associated flows table, we may ask how they may be used effectively. To demonstrate their use, we shall first consider development in a simple backward rural economy, and later the planning of new towns.

Use for Regional Planning and Development

Let us consider a simple backward rural economy with a population of 1,000, in which there is a small village. The economy is comprised of the following sectors: agriculture, services, and households. The agriculture sector produces simple crops. Per dollar output, it requires 10 cents of agricultural materials (for example, seed), 10 cents of services, and 40 cents of labor as inputs. The other 40 cents per dollar output flows out of the community as rent and interest payments to absentee landlords. Per dollar output of the second sector, services, inputs of 5 cents of agricultural products, 5 cents of services, and 50 cents of household labor are required. The rest of its dollar, 40 cents, is paid out to absentee landlords and capitalists as interest and rent on plant, equipment and land. Per dollar income of the third sector, households, meeting consumption needs requires 80 cents of agricultural products and 20 cents of services. Table 7.2 summarizes the data on these constant production (and consumption) coefficients.

We now present in Table 7.3 a snapshot of this economy's flows on an annual basis. Going across the first row of this table, we see that the total

Table 7.2   Inputs (in dollars) Per Dollar Output, By Sector

Sector	Agriculture	Services	Households
Agriculture	0.1	0.05	0.8
Services	0.1	0.05	0.2
Households	0.4	0.5	0.0
Rent, Interest, and Other Payments	0.4	0.4	0.0
Total	1.0	1.0	1.0

output of the agriculture sector is $50,000. This output is allocated as follows:

$ 5,000 to the agriculture sector
$ 1,000 to the services sector
$24,000 to the household sector
$20,000 to be exported to absentee landlords

The $20,000 total output of the services sector is allocated as follows:

$5,000 to agriculture
$1,000 to services
$6,000 to households
$8,000 as exports to absentee landlords

The $30,000 labor services, which represents the output of the household sector and which also constitutes income received as payment for the services, is allocated as follows:

$20,000 to agriculture, which also constitutes income received from agriculture
$10,000 to services, which also constitutes income received from the services sector

Finally, we see that absentee landlords and capitalists receive $20,000 from agriculture in payment for the plant, equipment, and land made available to this sector; and $8,000 from the services sector in payment for plant, equipment, and land made available to this sector.

Table 7.3   Input-Output Flows for a Simple Economy

Sector	Agriculture	Services	Households	Exports	Total Output
Agriculture	$ 5,000	$ 1,000	$24,000	$20,000	$50,000
Services	5,000	1,000	6,000	8,000	20,000
Households	20,000	10,000	—	—	30,000
Rent, Interest, and Other Payments	20,000	8,000	—	—	28,000
Total Inputs	$50,000	$20,000	$30,000	$28,000	

We see from Table 7.3 that the total output of the agriculture, services, and household sectors are $50,000, $20,000, and $30,000, respectively. Correspondingly, their total expenditures for inputs are $50,000, $20,000, and $30,000, respectively. We also see that absentee landlords receive $28,000 of products in payment for the plant, equipment, and land made available.

Undoubtedly, Tables 7.2 and 7.3 oversimplify the situation in any rural economy. However, they do capture some of the essential aspects of the situation. There is the large fraction of output of each production sector which flows to absentee landlords and capitalists (or local chiefs and elites) who may use these funds for purchasing luxury and conspicuous consumption goods from other regions or who may sell the product in export markets and hoard the monies received. There is a low per capita income. In our case the population is 1,000, total income received by the household sector is $30,000; thus per capita income

126

is $30. Note also that approximately two-thirds of the income is earned in the agricultural sector and one-third in the services sector.

Now, suppose a central political authority is concerned with the welfare of the people in this backward rural economy, which is one of many units over which the authority has jurisdiction. Suppose the authority has determined that because of ethnic, cultural, and historical factors the population of this region should not be forced to locate elsewhere. The authority decides to introduce an industry into the economy even though the industry must be subsidized in order to offset its relatively high cost of operation. Such a subsidy, for example, might involve the construction by the government of a large food-processing factory fully equipped with modern machinery. It might be made available at zero rent to an enterprise, provided the enterprise operates it efficiently and continues to operate it over the next fifty years. Because of this gift, the enterprise will have no annual fixed interest charges, a major advantage in its operations relative to an enterprise in the same sector producing in another region that does not have this subsidy. This advantage of zero interest charge may thus completely offset other disadvantages, such as higher transportation costs on the finished product to the market.

Now, the operation of this new food processing factory, which we view as a *basic* economic activity, will have important effects on the other sectors of the economy. Let us say that the technology of this plant is such that it requires 10 cents of locally produced agricultural products, 10 cents of locally provided services, and 30 cents of locally provided labor per dollar output. The other 50 cents per dollar output is used in buying raw materials which must be imported, in obtaining skilled and managerial labor who in effect will come from outside the native community, and in meeting interest and rent on plant and equipment. Further, suppose the total output of the plant is $20,000 annually. We therefore can list the input coefficients for this plant and its total inputs requirements in a separate table, Table 7.4. Column 1 of this table lists input requirements per $1 output. Column 2 lists the dollar amounts of inputs that must flow into the plant on an annual basis.

As before, we ask: From where do the inputs of $2000 of agricultural products, $2000 of services, and $6000 of household services come? Given the low level of per capita income in our economy and the underutilization of its resources, the obvious answer is: From the expansion of the sectors of the local economy. We see that to produce the $2000 additional agricultural products,

Table 7.4   Input Requirements of New Food-Processing Plant

Sector	Inputs Per $1 Output	Total Annual Inputs
Agriculture	.10	$ 2,000
Services	.10	2,000
Households	.30	6,000
Imports and Other Payments	.50	10,000
Total	1.00	$20,000

Table 7.5   Calculation of Second-Round Expansions

| Sector | First Round Input Requirements (Expansions) | | | Total Annual Inputs |
	$2,000 Agriculture Output (1)	$2,000 Services Output (2)	$6,000 Households Output (Income) (3)	
Agriculture	$ 200	$ 100	$4,800	$5,100
Services	200	100	1,200	1,500
Households	800	1,000	0	1,800
Subtotal	1,200	1,200	6,000	8,400
Rent, Interest and Other Payments	800	800	0	1,600
Total	$2,000	$2,000	$6,000	$10,000

which we designate a first-round input requirement and at the same time a first-round expansion of the agriculture sector, we need still more inputs, as listed in column 1 in Table 7.5. In line with the constant production coefficients of column 1 in Table 7.2, we need $200 of agricultural products, $200 of services, and $800 of household labor. Moreover, from column 2 in Table 7.5 we see that to produce the $2000 additional services that are first-round inputs into the factory, we need (in line with the coefficients of column 2 in Table 7.2) $100 of agricultural products, $100 of services, and $1000 of household labor. Finally, from column 3 in Table 7.5 we see that when $6000 more labor is hired by the new factory, this $6000 becomes income to households, and will lead to demands (in line with the coefficients of column 3 in Table 7.2) for $4800 of agricultural products and $1200 of services. So if we add across the rows of Table 7.5, we find that to produce the first-round input requirements of the factory as listed in the second column in Table 7.4, we are going to require as the second round of input requirements $5100 of agricultural products, $1500 of services and $1800 of household labor.

This second round of input requirements will be provided by expansion of the local economy and so constitutes the second round of expansion. But the second round of expansion requires inputs. The inputs required by the $5100 of second-round expansion of agriculture are given in the first column in Table 7.6, based on the production coefficients in Table 7.2. The inputs required by the $1500 second-round expansion of the service sector, and $1800 second-round expansion of the households sector are given in columns 2 and 3, respectively, in Table 7.6. These second-round expansions give rise to the third round of input requirements: $2025 of agriculture, $945 of services, and $2790 of households, which are listed in the totals columns in Table 7.6. In turn, we consider the third round of input requirements to constitute a third round of expansions, requiring a fourth round of input requirements. We calculate the fourth round of input requirements as we have calculated the second and third rounds. This fourth round involves

128

Table 7.6   Calculation of Third-Round Expansions

Sector	Second-Round Input Requirements (Expansions)			Total Annual Inputs
	$5,100 Agriculture Output (1)	$1,500 Services Output (2)	$1,800 Households Output (Income) (3)	
Agriculture	$ 510	$ 75	$1,440	$2,025
Services	510	75	360	945
Households	2,040	750	0	2,790
Subtotal	3,060	900	1,800	5,760
Rent, Interest and Other Payments	2,040	600	0	2,640
Total	$5,100	$1,500	$1,800	$8,400

   $2,481.75 of agricultural products
      807.75 of services
   1,282.50 of household labor

We consider this fourth round of input requirements to constitute a fourth round of expansions, which gives rise to a fifth round of input requirements. And so forth.

We have gone through all the necessary calculations. We present the results summarily in Table 7.7. There we see that the new industrial development initially requires from the local economy $2,000 of agricultural products, $2,000 of services, and $6,000 of household labor, or a total of $10,000 of local inputs. But it leads directly and indirectly to $16,000 expansion of output of the agriculture sector, $7,000 expansion of output of the services sector, and $16,000 expansion of the household sector (corresponding to new income received), or all told a total of $39,000—as indicated in the last column of Table 7.7. In sum, the direct and indirect effects, namely $39,000, are roughly four times as great as the direct effects, namely $10,000—a substantial multiplier effect. Or the indirect effects are roughly three times as great as the direct effects. Though the outcome varies greatly from situation to situation, in general indirect effects are truly significant and cannot be ignored. They must be made explicit. Hence, the great utility of the input-output technique.

Before commenting further on the technique, let us note one more point. Total household income has been increased by $16,000. For the rural economy it is now $46,000. If the population were to remain unchanged, per capita income would now be $46 rather than $30, a significant increase. However, as most of us know, in many economies that are barely subsisting and where there is high infant mortality due to insufficient food supply, it is likely that a good part, if not all, of the potential per capita income increase will be swallowed up by more mouths to feed. We will say more about this point in Chapter 15.

Limitations in Projecting Change and Growth

In the use of input-output analysis, we should be aware of its several shortcomings. First, we should note that the rounds of expansion which we have been discussing do not take place instantaneously in an economy, as we have been hypothesizing. They take time. So it may take some years before all the indirect expan-

Table 7.7   Successive Rounds of Input Requirements (Expansions)

Sector	Rounds of Inputs Requirements						Total Annual Inputs
	1st	*2nd*	*3rd*	*4th*	*5th*	...	
Agriculture	$ 2,000	$ 5,100	$2,025	$2,481.75	$1,314.56	...	$16,000
Services	2.000	1,500	945	807.75	545.06	...	7,000
Households	6,000	1,800	2,790	1,282.50	1,396.58	...	16,000
Subtotal	10,000	8,400	5,760	4,572.00	3,256.20	...	39,000
Rent, Interest and Other Payments		1,600	2,640	1,188.00	1,315.80	...	10,000
Total	$10,000	$10,000	$8,400	$5,760.00	$4,572.00	...	$49,000

sions and induced growth take place. Further, we have assumed that forces fore-stalling change would not be present. There may well be such forces. The local chieftains may regard development as dangerous in the sense that it may lead to increases in per capita income, standards of living, education, etc. The local population may then demand a larger voice in government, and increasingly resist exploitation. Hence, the elite and existing power structure may place obstacles in the path of economic development, which might significantly reduce the multiplier effect. Note, however, that the rent and other payments to landlords increase by $10,000 because of expansion of the local economy, a factor that can modify resistance to change by entrenched power groups.

Keep in mind that the data of Table 7.7 may well underestimate the indirect effects. We know that a new factory in a community can disrupt the social-cultural setting, stir imaginations, set in motion creative minds and free them from the tentacles of tradition, upset business ways, and facilitate the emergence of local entrepreneurship. Consequently, it may produce the spark for industrial development, such as the oil refinery–petrochemical industrial complex has done for Puerto Rico, which we will discuss in Chapter 17. In sum, by providing new stimuli, major industrial development can result in tremendous multiplier effects.

Moreover, sooner or later the factory might be induced to produce food products which require further processing. This can lead to other food products factories locating in the same community of this economy. Their very presence may make possible localization and urbanization economies, making the community a more desirable location for certain industries. Or in time a new plant may be constructed to produce products that initially the factory had to import from elsewhere. This new plant would not only have a transport cost advantage from its market (or part of its market) being right at hand but also could gain from localization and urbanization economies now possible in this community that did not exist before the development of the initial food products factory. If such takes place, the community in effect becomes a "growth pole," a point at which forces of growth focus and later spread to surrounding areas and other parts of the regional economy.

And so there are many other economic factors that must be considered to qualify the findings of Table 7.7. Additionally, there are environmental, social, and political factors (costs and gains) which need to be examined. In Table 7.7 we do not mention the impact on the ecological system. As indicated in Chapters

2 and 14, we should, and to some extent can, evaluate the costs of BOD and other water pollutants, and SO_2, particulates and other air pollutants to the rural economy. Political and social costs and gains are much more qualitative. Although we may be able to roughly measure effective participation in an election by the percent of population that votes, man-years of education, or percent of illiteracy, we do not know how to translate these measures into social and political gains and costs. Much more work needs to be done in this area.

Now that we have made clear the need to consider many other economic, political, social, and environmental factors than those examined in our most simplified input-output framework, let us proceed to some further evaluation of its virtues and limitations.

One serious limitation arises from the fact that we have assumed constant production coefficients. We have assumed that whenever we change (increase or decrease) output by some factor, say 50 percent, our input requirements will likewise change. This is a very poor assumption. In Chapter 5, we discussed scale economies—how floor space and rent for such space, or management services, etc. decline per unit of output as scale increases. With increases in output up to a certain level, they decrease and give rise to "increasing returns to scale." We noted that such scale economies are present in most important industrial operations. We also noted in Chapter 5 that, after a certain scale of operations is reached, variable costs per unit output can be expected to increase because of more complicated management problems, the need to obtain inputs from supply points that are more and more distant, or for a host of other reasons. Also, because of decreasing returns to scale in cultivating any given plot of land, we can anticipate rising variable costs per unit in agriculture, too. These factors mean that there is a certain amount of error resulting from the use of constant production coefficients.

Moreover, as development proceeds, we can expect old-fashioned technology in the agriculture and services sectors to be replaced by modern technology, so that input coefficients for at least some columns of Table 7.2 no longer pertain.

Further, we have postulated that there are no limits on the availability of resources needed for the expansion of the agriculture, services, and household sectors. We have already pointed to the phenomenon of diminishing returns in the cultivation of any piece of land. This "restricting" effect on growth is not encountered as long as there exists plenty of good soil lying idle which can be brought under cultivation. But when the supply gives out, we cannot expect the agriculture sector to expand with the same ease. It will be able to expand only under conditions of diminishing returns, which will decrease the potential rate of expansion of the economy.

We also assumed that the facilities of the services sector could be automatically expanded. But if such facilities involve investment of new capital, say in a lathe or sewing machine, that capital must be available. Or, if a new building is required, it must be possible to effectively use the unemployed or underemployed labor force to construct the building. In practice we often may not be able to assume these conditions. There may be a shortage of foreign exchange, little unemployment, or severe difficulties in mobilizing a local labor force for erecting a new building.

Likewise, we cannot assume the existence of an adequate labor force at all times. There may be a limited amount of labor in the local population possessing the skill or know-how that is required for production; and educational facilities may be inadequate to train enough labor to meet the increasing demand. Further, households may respond to the new demand for labor in ways rational to them, but not to us–namely, to reduce the supply of their labor as we raise wages in our effort to obtain a greater supply of that labor.

With all these serious qualifications to the assumptions we have made, coupled with our inability to take into account numerous social, political, and environmental factors, we may conclude that perhaps it is misleading to use input-output calculations; and, when we are in a critical mood, we may be inclined to discard this technique as a tool of analysis. If we do so however, we have nothing better to put in its place, and in all probability can only find something that is worse. The literature on national, regional, and urban growth is replete with bold attempts to dig effectively into development phenomena. So far, nothing has emerged that is superior as a tool to the linear systems approach that characterizes input-output, although there are some techniques and analytical approaches, some of which will be discussed later, which can be claimed to be as useful as input-output.

Use for New Town Planning and Development

Let us now turn to a second type of application of the input-output framework, with full recognition of all its limitations. Suppose a central governmental authority has decided to plan and construct a new town. In accord with welfare considerations to be discussed in later chapters, suppose the objective is not only to alleviate congestion, exposure to pollution, and the diverse social problems of growing urban masses but also to provide additional job opportunities for ghetto residents and a more satisfactory environment for their work and play.

A new town, to be economically sound, must be anchored to a solid economic base. Suppose the decision has been reached that its basic industry shall be some government-operated facility, say a major research laboratory probing the causes of cancer and other diseases. The initial level of operation of this facility may be set by the government, as well as its growth pattern over the next ten years. It would be desirable to know how many new jobs there will be in the town at the end of the ten years, broken down by categories such as skilled, semiskilled, or unskilled–or, even better, by different types of unskilled work–in order to evaluate the effectiveness of the new town in meeting the goal of providing new jobs for those in the urban ghettos currently unemployed.

Suppose we are given by the government a column listing of the inputs required for the new research facility, such as the listing for the research and development sector corresponding to column 37 in Table 2.1. We may characterize this column listing as the vector of inputs for the new research facility. Suppose also that we study what has historically taken place around other government research facilities of this type from the operation of market forces. We then can estimate roughly the column listing or vector of inputs for a set of pharmaceutical and other companies that might locate around this new facility. Then we can proceed as we did in connection with the new food-processing factory for our developing rural economy. We add the two vectors together to obtain a total set of inputs for all these basic economic activities. This set can be considered the vector of *first-round input requirements*.

We next go over each input carefully to determine how much of that input might be produced economically within our new town. If one of the inputs is electric power, we might reasonably assume that 100 percent of it will be provided by a power plant to be located in or close to our town. If another input is research labor, again we might reasonably expect that close to 100 percent of it will be provided by the households sector in our town. In contrast, if a basic input is fuel oil for heating purposes, and if not only do we want to keep oil refineries out of our new town but also want our new town to only be a high-cost location for the operation of an oil refinery, we might conclude that zero percent of fuel oil will come from the oil refinery sector of our town. In effect, like any other sector that operates at zero level, we do not need to list the refinery sector in our input-output table, either as a column or as a row.

Suppose another input is chemicals, such as chlorine and sulfuric acid. Again we might conclude that zero percent of these inputs will be provided by production facilities within our new town. Further, we might assume that the level of operation of the entire inorganic chemical industry in our town will be zero, partly because we may want to zone such industry out of our town. Hence, we will not need to have either a row or a column for this sector in our input-output table.

Between these two extremes are many inputs of which only a fraction will be provided by production facilities in our town. Take the input of cardboard boxes and similar items produced by paper and allied products sector. Though we might expect a factory to operate in our town which will manufacture cardboard boxes and similar items (particularly because such a factory would provide a fair number of jobs for unskilled labor, which ghetto residents of metropolitan regions might competitively supply), there are other specialized products, such as filters and stationary, which would need to be imported from factories in other regions. Scale economies dictate that these paper products be produced by only one factory for the entire national economy. Another input might be business, legal, and professional services. Here we might expect most, say 90 percent, of these to be provided by the residents of the town; the other 10 percent might pertain to highly specialized services available from consultants and other professionals residing in New York City, Washington, Chicago, and elsewhere.

So for each input in the vector of first-round input requirements for the research laboratory and pharmaceutical companies, we determine the percentage that would come from the appropriate sector of our new town. We then multiply each of these inputs by its respective percentage figure to obtain the vector of inputs which we expect the sectors of our town to supply. This new vector of "reduced" inputs represents the vector of *first-round expansions*.

Now, we consider in turn each item of this new vector. The first item is likely to represent expansion in the output of the food products sector. (We probably will have decided that none of the agricultural products that might be required by our research laboratory and pharmaceutical companies, and later by households, will be produced by our new town. Hence, we will already have deleted the agriculture sector, which typically appears as the first column and row in any input-output table.) We expect that some of the companies might buy certain food products from this industry. This expansion in output of the food products sector represents not only inputs of certain fats and oils required by the research laboratory and pharmaceutical companies but also products from bakeries, meat processors, and dairies needed by the cafeterias which they operate. This tells us, then, that we do want a food products sector as a column and row in the input-output table for our new town. It should be noted that, at this point of our analysis, we do not want a table of flows, but rather a table of coefficients. Hence, the first column of our table should list the coefficients of the food products sector of our town. These coefficients should characterize the food-processing operations in our new town. That is, they should be constructed to reflect not the mix of food processing that one finds in the national economy or within a huge metropolitan mass such as New York City, but rather that mix that characterizes operations in a relatively new urban area somewhat similar in structure to the one we have in mind.

The next item in the vector of first-round expansions may correspond to the output required of a textile sector reflecting our decision that a textile activity can be efficiently operated in our new town. We then want to list in the second column of the input-output table the set of coefficients which we judge to characterize the operations of the new textile plants to be constructed in our town.

In this manner, we proceed to consider each item in the vector of first-round expansions, and to set up a column of appropriate coefficients for its corresponding sector. On the basis of the discussion above, there would be a paper products sector, an electric power sector, and a business and professional services sector. There will also be an automobile repair sector because the research laboratory and pharmaceutical companies, as well as households, require repair services for motor vehicles. There will be a wholesale sales sector, a retail sales sector, etc. Finally, we know that the research laboratory and the pharmaceutical companies require labor from households; so there will be a household sector.

However, there are still other sectors which we need to include in the coefficient table for the new town. We know that the vector of first-round input requirements refer to the demands of the research laboratory and pharmaceutical companies only. But the households in the town will be demanding products, too. Very likely they will be demanding some products which the laboratory and pharmaceutical companies do not require in their operations. Hence, we must also include columns for other sectors that can operate competitively in our new town.

Moreover, the food products sector, the textile sector, the electric power sector, etc. may demand selected products that neither the research complex nor the households demand. Again we will need to add columns to the coefficients table for the sectors producing these products, provided we consider these sectors to be desirable for and able to operate efficiently in our new town.

In this manner, we develop an input-output coefficients table for our new town embodying all sectors that will be operating in it, either because they export to other regions (like the pharmaceutical companies) or because they serve local demands and are considered both desirable and able to compete. This table is similar to Table 7.2, except that it has many more rows and columns.

With a table bigger but of the same form as Table 7.2 and the vector of first-round expansions, we are ready to obtain the second round of input requirements. We do so in a way similar to the way in which we derived Table 7.5 from Table 7.2 and the totals column of Table 7.4, where the totals column in 7.4 corresponds to the vector of first-round expansions. We focus on the first number in the vector of first-round expansions, which refers to the inputs that we expect the food products sector to furnish to the research laboratory and pharmaceutical companies. We take this number and multiply it down the first column of the coefficients table to derive the first column of the table required for the calculation of the second-round expansions. Similarly, we take the second number listed in the vector of first-round expansions, which refers to the textile inputs to be provided by textile factories in our town to the research lab and pharmaceutical companies, and multiply it down the second column of the constant coefficients table to obtain the second column of the table for the calculation of second-round expansions. We do this for every other item in the vector of first-round expansions. Accordingly, we obtain a full table, similar to Table 7.5 except that it has many more rows and columns, for the calculation of the vector of second-round expansions. We already know that when we sum across the rows of the table—just as we did in Table 7.5 for the calculation for second-round expansions for our developing rural economy—we obtain a totals column that represents the second round of input requirements for the new town.

Our next step is to recognize that not all of the second round of input requirements will be provided by production facilities in our new town. Some will be, such as electric power, so we can multiply these by 100 percent to obtain the second-round expansions of the sectors that produce them. For other second-round input requirements—for example, items like food products and textiles— we must multiply each by a percentage figure that indicates the percentage of that input which we expect our town's production facilities to provide. When we do so, we obtain the second-round expansions of output for their corresponding sectors, and in this way complete the vector of second-round expansions.

In short, we must multiply each of the items in the vector of second-round input requirements, as given by the totals column of the table for the calculation of second-round expansions, by an appropriate figure indicating the percentage of the second-round input requirements which we expect to be produced by that sector in our town. When we do so, we obtain the column vector of second-round expansions.

Now we already know the process whereby we go from second-round expansions to third-round input requirements to third-round expansions to fourth-round input requirements to fourth-round expansions, etc. Ultimately we obtain a table like Table 7.7, except that we have many more rows and columns. When we sum across the rows of this table, we obtain in the totals column a figure indicating for each sector our first crude estimate of its total level of operations.

We have already indicated that the input-output technique must be used with considerable caution. That is why we can consider the items in the totals column just derived as only crude estimates. They serve as reference points or benchmarks which are subject to drastic revision, as any seasoned planner and regional scientist well knows.

CHECKING THE FEASIBILITY AND CONSISTENCY OF DEVELOPMENT PLANNING

The illustration just given pertains to a new town where we are able to specify beforehand the particular type of research laboratory that will serve as the economic base, as well as its level or scale of operations. Knowing these, we are able to project a reasonable new town for which the research laboratory serves as the central driving force. The first crude set of output levels allows us to make initial estimates of other important factors. Knowing output levels, we can estimate the total number of jobs, by type, and then total wage and salary payments. With the use of data on the typical participation of a population in the labor force (a figure often used is 40 percent), we can determine the expected total population of our new town. With information on the breakdown of jobs and other population census data, we can estimate the number of families and the age-sex distribution of the population. From here we can proceed to estimates of the number of different types of housing, schools, and other facilities required. Knowing the level of operation of different sectors, we can estimate the tax base of the town and whether, with reasonable tax rates, this base will yield sufficient revenues to meet the costs of operating municipal facilities and providing such services as police and fire protection. We also might test for feasibility in terms of estimating capital requirements. We want to be able to obtain sufficient capital from both private and public sources to construct housing, schools, roads, municipal buildings, and all the other facilities required.

Other feasibility checks can be made for land and other resources, the transportation system, the shopping center system, and the ecologic system. Land requirements can be crudely estimated by collecting data developed in other studies on land requirements per unit output of each sector, which reflects past market operations and individual location decisions. Multiplying this by the output of each sector yields total land required by that sector. Summing over all sectors, including households and transportation, yields a total figure that can be checked against the total land available for development and the amount of land allocated to each sector in a comprehensive land-use plan.

Transportation requirements can be determined in a number of steps. First, given the job data, we can estimate the number of journey-to-work trips. The length of these trips will be determined in large part by the land-use plan which designates areas for residential development and for the location of industries and research laboratories. Likewise, the transportation network that is designed for the new town would affect the number, average length, and distribution of journey-to-work trips. The shopping center locations in the land-use plan and the distribution of residential areas would provide the basis for estimating the number and length of shopping trips. Similarly, data on land use, provided by census and other studies, would lead to estimates of the number and length of other types of trips.

The data on person trips must be augmented by data on commodities that might be shipped by trucks and rail. Again, the areas designated by a land-use plan for the development of industries and research laboratories would, together with the information on the types of commodity inputs required by each sector and that sector's level of output, provide the basic information for estimating commodity movements. Taking the transportation facility requirements for both person trips and commodity movements and comparing it to the supply of transportation facilities provided by the transportation network of the land-use plan allows us to check for feasibility.

Further, given (a) total wages and salary payments (as derived by an input-output computation); (b) profit, rent, and interest payments that households might receive (estimated on the basis of census data and other studies); and (c) the distribution of residential areas, we then might estimate shopping center requirements. These might be checked for feasibility against the set of shopping center facilities provided by a land-use plan.

In making feasibility tests—whether they are related to the adequacy of the tax base to yield revenues for meeting municipal costs, the availability of land to meet land requirements, the capability of a transportation network to meet the town's transportation requirements, or the provision for a shopping center system to meet the shopping center requirements—we can of course alter our assumptions and our land-use plan in order to achieve consistency. If the tax base is inadequate, we might seek industry that can provide a large tax base to replace some industry that provides only a small tax base, although the latter may have advantages in other respects.

If the needs of our school system, estimated on the base of certain standards of education we would like to meet, are too costly for the tax base we can develop, then we can lower some of these standards. If the transportation required by our projected urban system exceeds the capacity of the network we are able to provide, then we can design industry and residential areas closer together, provide for greater density of residential and industrial land development, and otherwise revise our land-use plan to achieve consistency.

Further, we may find that a number of facilities that we would like to have in our new town cannot be used at a sufficiently large scale to achieve low enough cost to justify their existence. We may need to forego some of these facilities.

In these and numerous other ways we would check the feasibility of our projections, test their consistency, and in doing so revise and alter the assumptions behind our projections. In particular, we would need to introduce, at several strategic points, nonlinearities such as scale economies into the model; and to relax some of our standards and program goals so as to develop a set of projections that are more reasonable but still consistent. In Chapters 13, 15, and 16 we shall dwell further on the constant revision of our analysis, reformulation of our plans, resetting of our goals, and rerunning of our projections to achieve reasonableness, consistency, and where possible, *equity* and *social justice*.

At this point, we must point out that in many situations we are not told beforehand what the size of the central economic activity will be. In many cases it is up to us to determine the optimal size of a central driving activity. That is, we may be in a position to consider the construction of a new town without any directive as to the level of the basic economic activity. Under these circumstances we need to do much more cost analysis than in the case where the central driving activity and its level are specified beforehand.

Let us be more specific. Suppose we have in mind establishing a new town around an industrial district, to be composed of research and development, space-age and government facilities. The level of the industrial district, its size, and its composition are not specified beforehand; they are to be determined as part of the analysis.

We can immediately see that scale economy, localization economy, and urbanization economy analysis must be pursued. We must explicitly consider economic factors that are nonlinear, which we discussed in Chapter 6. But linear systems analysis is still very useful. We might proceed by selecting a range of industrial districts to be considered. We might consider one range in terms of size, and another range in terms of the percentage composition of different kinds of activities in the industrial district. Within this two-dimension range we might select a half dozen or a dozen districts representative of the different sizes and compositions that are possible.

We might then do an input-output computation for each of these representative industrial districts. We would then obtain a half dozen or dozen different conceptions of a new town. These are only first conceptions because they are based on a linear system projection. After we have made feasibility checks, we might modify each to take into account scale and other economies. Then we might choose the one that is best, given the need for economic efficiency as well as our desire to achieve noneconomic goals.

Thus far we have talked about two types of applications. There are, however, many possible ones. Suppose we are concerned with the recreational development of an unexploited coastal area. The basic economic activity will be recreational activity, to be measured by man-days (or man-weeks, or man-months) of use by people. As will be indicated in Chapter 14, corresponding to one man-day of use might be the use of so many square feet of beach (or feet of coast or shore), so much marine area for docking and for boating use, so many square feet of land for boat storage, so much capacity of the street system for automobile travel, so much retail store sales, electric power, medical services, police and fire protection services, and so forth. Given the vector of input requirements per man-day of recreation, we then might crudely estimate successively the first round of input requirements, the first-round expansions, the second round of input requirements, the second-round expansions, etc. In this way we develop rough, initial conceptions of a recreational development fully provided with diverse services. We then must check whether the land base is adequate, whether the ecologic system can maintain itself given this development, whether the necessary capital is obtainable, whether municipal costs and revenues will balance, whether the profit rate is sufficient to induce necessary private investments, and so forth.

Or we might have in mind a specialized city such as a political capital, a new university town, or a city for old people. Or we may have in mind reinvigorating a depressed mining area or textile town, or even rehabilitating a city. In all these cases we use the same approach. We obtain a vector of total inputs required. After many rounds of computations, we develop a vector of total expansions and check for feasibility. Again, in each case there are numerous shortcomings to the use of the input-output framework, but in each case we cannot currently replace the technique with one that is both more valid and more effective.

A SIMPLE EXPLANATION OF THE ALGEBRA OF INPUT-OUTPUT

Hitherto we have considered input-output computations in a nonalgebraic manner. Now that we have grasped the nature of the computation, we might as well use mathematics where it can serve us as a shorthand. After all, we do have powerful computers that can quickly provide us with different kinds of projections we would like to have for new town planning, provided we give the computer (1) the information in proper form, and (2) a set of consistent and meaningful numbers for the different kinds of assumptions we would like to try out. Computers can be a tremendous resource for input-output and any linear system analysis. Moreover, there exists an extremely useful shorthand which, with the use of a relatively few mathematical symbols, permits us to consider many different kinds of structures of new towns and to have their implications immediately made explicit through computer use. Hence, it is quite reasonable to learn this shorthand.

The Symbols and Notation

We begin with a simple notation. Consider the rows of an input-output table. There may be few or many. In our rural developing economy, we treated only four sectors. In our new town, we might require as many as 100. In our shorthand, we let the symbol i stand for any row (that is, for any one of the commodities produced under the category in a particular row). In the case of the four-sector rural economy, we let $i = 1, 2, 3, 4$—which means that the row i can be row 1, row 2, row 3, or row 4. In the case of our town we let $i = 1, 2, 3, 4,$ 5, 6, ..., 98, 99, 100—which means that i can refer to any one of the 100 rows. Now consider the letter j. We use that letter to refer to any column, representing economic sectors (activities). In the case of our rural economy with four sectors and thus four columns we let $j = 1, 2, 3, 4$. In the case of our new town with 100 sectors, we let $j = 1, 2, 3, 4, ..., 99, 100$. We use the symbol a_{ij} to refer to the dollar's worth of input of any commodity i used to produce a dollar of output of sector j. For example, a_{ij} might refer to the steel (ith row) which was used to produce a refrigerator (jth row).

To make this point clear, let us go back to Table 7.2. This table has three columns and three rows. In each cell of the table is a number, a coefficient, which we have already assumed to be constant and unchanging. Let us take the coefficient in the third row and first column. If we let a stand for a constant coefficient in general, without being specific as to the exact number, we can write $a_{3,1}$. This can represent the constant in the third row of the first column of Table 7.2, namely, 0.4. The symbol $a_{2,1}$ must then stand for the constant coefficient in the second row and first column, which is 0.1.

Likewise, the constant $a_{1,1}$ refers to the constant 0.1 in the first row and first column of Table 7.2, and the constant $a_{1,3}$ refers to the constant in the first row and third column, which is 0.8. Immediately we see that we can rewrite Table 7.2 in more general form, such as in Table 7.8 below.

Table 7.8   Symbols of An Input-Output Coefficients Table

Sector	A	S	H
A	$a_{1,1}$	$a_{1,2}$	$a_{1,3}$
S	$a_{2,1}$	$a_{2,2}$	$a_{2,3}$
H	$a_{3,1}$	$a_{3,2}$	$a_{3,3}$

However, we can do better, We can rewrite Table 7.2 or Table 7.8 as in Table 7.9. There we simply use the symbol a_{ij} with brackets around it, where we specify that i successively stands for rows 1, 2, and 3 and that j successively stands for columns 1, 2, and 3. We can be even a little more efficient by writing Table 7.9 as in Table 7.10.

Table 7.9

$$[a_{ij}], \; i = 1, \; 2, \; 3$$
$$j = 1, \; 2, \; 3$$

Table 7.10

$$[a_{ij}], \; i, j = 1, \; 2, \; 3$$

Now the reader may well state that what we have done in representing Table 7.2 by Table 7.10 does not represent any major saving of the time and effort that we claimed would be realized. This may be true with regard to Table 7.2. But now consider a coefficients table for a new town, such as Table 7.11, with 100 sectors and so with 100 columns and 100 rows. Try writing this down, as we have started to. Then write it down as in Table 7.12. Note the tremendous saving in time.

Table 7.11   Input-Output Coefficients Table for a New Town

Sector	#1	#2	#3	#4	. . . .	#100
#1	$a_{1,1}$	$a_{1,2}$	$a_{1,3}$	$a_{1,4}$	. . . .	$a_{1,100}$
#2	$a_{2,1}$	$a_{2,2}$	$a_{2,3}$	$a_{2,4}$	. . . .	$a_{2,100}$
#3	$a_{3,1}$	$a_{3,2}$	$a_{3,3}$	$a_{3,4}$	. . . .	$a_{3,100}$
#4	$a_{4,1}$	$a_{4,2}$	$a_{4,3}$	$a_{4,4}$	. . . .	$a_{4,100}$
.	.	.	.	.		.
.	.	.	.	.		.
.	.	.	.	.		.
.	.	.	.	.		.
.	.	.	.	.		.
.	.	.	.	.		.
#100	$a_{100,1}$	$a_{100,2}$	$a_{100,3}$	$a_{100,4}$	. . . .	$a_{100,100}$

Table 7.12

$$[a_{ij}], i, j = 1, \; 2, \; 3, ..., 100$$

Moreover, try writing down a table that has 496 rows and columns, such as the Philadelphia region input-output table. Try writing it with a's — $a_{1,1}, a_{1,2},$ $a_{1,3}, a_{1,4}$, etc. Further, try writing it with numbers that have six decimal digits Then write it down as in Table 7.12, except put the number 496 in place of 100 in Table 7.12. Are you convinced of the tremendous saving?

Of course, you may argue that the numbers representing the relevant coefficients need to be set down at some time. This is true. They are punched out on IBM cards once and for all, and then stored for use whenever we need them. In the meantime, for our thinking and analysis, all we need is Table 7.12, once we know the shorthand.

Now let us consider another element of the shorthand. Suppose we go back to Table 7.4 and concentrate on the totals column. That column represents input requirements that were required by the new food-processing plant constructed in our rural economy. Looked at another way, they are the demands that the new food-processing plant place on the rural economy, which must be met if the plant is to operate as planned. Let us represent "demand" by the symbol Y. The food-processing plant then has three demands, which can be represented by the column vector

$$\begin{bmatrix} Y_1 \\ Y_2 \\ Y_3 \end{bmatrix}$$

where Y_1 represents the demand for agricultural products, Y_2 the demand for services, and Y_3 the demand for labor from households. Now because the letter i can stand for any row, we can write that column vector as follows:

$$[Y_i], i = 1, 2, 3$$

Note that we do not use the letter j and we say nothing about the number of columns, because we are talking about a set of numbers in one column only. This is how we define a column vector. Such a vector has as many elements in it as there are rows, and the number of rows will be indicated by the last number to which the subscript i can refer.

If we were to consider the example of our new town for which there are 100 relevant sectors and thus 100 rows and 100 columns in a relevant coefficients table, then the first-round input requirements of our research laboratory and pharmaceutical companies listed as the totals column in a table like Table 7.5 could be represented by

$$[Y_i], i = 1, 2, ..., 100$$

The Basic Equations: The Case of an Underdeveloped Region

Now that we have illustrated how we can use mathematical symbols as shorthand, let us consider the practical advantage of this shorthand notation. Assume we are studying a growth pole in some underdeveloped region. It might be Appalachia, some coastal location in an African nation that has been undeveloped for centuries, or some site in an abandoned or idle agricultural area. Again imagine that we are treating a simple economy. This time, however, the economy must be fiscally in balance in the sense that its exports must pay for its imports. Also, the products that it produces and that are left over after exports are deducted, *plus* the products that are imported, must permit the people of this economy to survive.

Consider the sectors of this economy. Again, agriculture is present but, as in the past, the land is not too fertile and does not produce crops in sufficient quantity and of a high enough quality to allow this sector to compete on the world or export market. The sector produces goods strictly for local consumption—by the people in the economy and by the services and manufacturing sectors, as well as by itself. The second sector is manufacturing, in particular food processing. The sector is able to export to the world market. The third sector is the services sector, which provides inputs to agriculture, manufacturing, households, and itself. Like agriculture, it is not sufficiently productive to compete on the world market. Finally we have the households sector, which provides labor to all four sectors but is not in the position to export any services to the world market.

We list these four sectors in Table 7.13. In addition, we list imports as a row and representing the foreign trade sector. We assume that imports comprise goods that cannot be produced at all in the economy and that are either essential for production or constitute items for which households can afford to pay. We let I_1 represent imports per dollar (unit) output of agriculture, I_2 imports per dollar (unit) output of manufacturing, I_3 imports per dollar (unit) output of services, and I_4 imports per dollar (unit) output or income of households.

Table 7.13   A Table of Constant Production (and Consumption)
Coefficients for a Developing Economy

Sector	A	M	S	H	Exports
A	$a_{1,1}$	$a_{1,2}$	$a_{1,3}$	$a_{1,4}$	—
M	$a_{2,1}$	$a_{2,2}$	$a_{2,3}$	$a_{2,4}$	—
S	$a_{3,1}$	$a_{3,2}$	$a_{3,3}$	$a_{3,4}$	—
H	$a_{4,1}$	$a_{4,2}$	$a_{4,3}$	$a_{4,4}$	—
Imports	I_1	I_2	I_3	I_4	—

Table 7.13 is a coefficients table. Hence, it has four columns which refer to the four producing sectors, including households. Each column records the production coefficients for the sector at the head of the column. To ease the analysis, we assume that all items imported are included in the imports row. Hence, as before, the coefficient $a_{1,1}$ in the first row and first column refers to the input of local agricultural products per unit output of the agriculture sector. The coefficient $a_{2,1}$ in the second row and first column refers to the input of local manufacturers per unit output of the agriculture sector. And so forth. In addition to the four regular columns, we have in Table 7.13 a fifth column designated "exports." We shall say more about this column later.

We want to develop a flows table that corresponds to the coefficients table of Table 7.13. However, we do not know what the flows will be because we do not know the output of the different sectors. We may let the unknown X_1 represent the level of output of the agriculture sector, the unknown X_2 represent the output of the manufacturing sector, the unknown X_3 represent the output of the services sector, and finally the unknown X_4 represent the output of the households sector. Now, we see that we can make four specific statements. We can state:

1. *The output of the agriculture sector, less the amount of the output that the agriculture sector consumes, less the amount that the manufacturing sector consumes, less the amount the services sector consumes, less the amount households consume, must be the output that is left over for exports.*

We can put this statement into simple mathematical form. X_1 is the total output of the agriculture sector. Also, we know that $a_{1,1}$ is the amount of agricultural products (for example, that used for seed) that is required per unit output of agriculture. So if we produce X_1 units of agricultural output, we must consume $a_{1,1} X_1$ amount of agricultural output in this production.

Consider the amount of agricultural products consumed by the manufacturing sector. The coefficient $a_{1,2}$ indicates how much agricultural output is required per unit output of manufacturing. So if we produce X_2 units of manufacturing output, then we must consume $a_{1,2} X_2$ of agricultural output in the manufacturing sector.

Next consider the amount of agricultural output consumed by the services sector. The amount of agricultural products required to produce one unit of services output is $a_{1,3}$. So if X_3 represents the services output, then $a_{1,3} X_3$ must be the amount of agricultural output consumed by the services sector. Further, we know that $a_{1,4}$ is the amount of agricultural output required per unit output (or dollar income) of the households sector. If the output of the households sector is X_4, then $a_{1,4} X_4$ is the amount of agricultural output consumed by the households sector. Finally let us represent the export of agricultural output by the symbol E_1.

Now we can return to the above italicized statement. In mathematical symbols (and omitting the comma between any two successive subscripts) it is:

$$X_1 - a_{11} X_1 - a_{12} X_2 - a_{13} X_3 - a_{14} X_4 = E_1 \qquad (7.1)$$

Each of the flows in equation 7.1, you will note, is represented in the first row in Table 7.14.

Table 7.14   An Input-Output Flows Table in Mathematical Form

Sector	A	M	S	H	Exports
A	$a_{11}X_1$	$a_{12}X_2$	$a_{13}X_3$	$a_{14}X_4$	E_1
M	$a_{21}X_1$	$a_{22}X_2$	$a_{23}X_3$	$a_{24}X_4$	E_2
S	$a_{31}X_1$	$a_{32}X_2$	$a_{33}X_3$	$a_{34}X_4$	E_3
H	$a_{41}X_1$	$a_{42}X_2$	$a_{43}X_3$	$a_{44}X_4$	E_4
Imports	I_1	I_2	I_3	I_4	

In similar manner we can make a second statement:

2. *The level of output of the manufacturing sector, which is* X_2, *less the amount consumed by the agriculture sector, which is* $a_{21} X_1$, *less the amount consumed by the manufacturing sector itself, which is* $a_{22} X_2$, *less the amount which is consumed by the services sector, which is* $a_{23} X_3$, *less the amount which is consumed by households, which is* $a_{24} X_4$, *is what is left over for exports, which we designate by* E_2. This statement is contained in the following equation:

$$X_2 - a_{21} X_1 - a_{22} X_2 - a_{23} X_3 - a_{24} X_4 = E_2 \qquad (7.2)$$

Likewise, we can make a statement concerning the allocation of the output of the services sector, to obtain the equation

$$X_3 - a_{31} X_1 - a_{32} X_2 - a_{33} X_3 - a_{34} X_4 = E_3 \qquad (7.3)$$

Finally, for the households sector, we can state:

3. *The output of the households sector,* X_4 *(corresponding to total labor made available), less the amount that goes to the agriculture sector,* $a_{41}X_1$ *(labor provided to the agriculture sector), less the amount that goes to the manufacturing sector,* $a_{42}X_2$ *(labor provided to the manufacturing sector), less the amount that goes to the services sector,* $a_{43}X_3$ *(the amount of labor provided to the services sector), less the amount that goes to the households sector itself,* $a_{44}X_4$ *(labor provided itself) is what remains for exports. This is designated* E_4. Thus we have

$$X_4 - a_{41}X_1 - a_{42}X_2 - a_{43}X_3 - a_{44}X_4 = E_4 \qquad (7.4)$$

Note that each one of the equations or statements is simple. Each says that there is a pie to be divided among all possible groups of consumers—in this case, the four local groups represented by the four local sectors, and a fifth group represented by all other consumers in the world and whose share of the pie we have designated exports. The first pie is of agricultural products. The second pie is of manufacturers products. The third pie is of services output. The fourth pie is of household labor services.

A convenient way to set down the allocation or sharing of each pie among the five consuming groups is to depict each group's share along a row, as in Table 7.14 where the specific pie to be divided is indicated at the left-hand tab. Note that Table 7.14 is also an input-output flows table, showing the flows of the output of any sector to itself, to the three other local sectors, and to exports.

The Solution of the Equations: Determining the Relevant Sector Outputs for Different Export Plans of the Region

Now the only thing we do not know is the size of each pie. This is what we need to determine. As a starting point, it is helpful to rewrite the four equations so to line up vertically the unknowns. We obtain

$$
\begin{aligned}
(1-a_{11})X_1 - a_{12}X_2 - a_{13}X_3 - a_{14}X_4 &= E_1 \\
-a_{21}X_1 + (1-a_{22})X_2 - a_{23}X_3 - a_{24}X_4 &= E_2 \\
-a_{31}X_1 - a_{32}X_2 + (1-a_{33})X_3 - a_{34}X_4 &= E_3 \\
-a_{41}X_1 - a_{42}X_2 - a_{43}X_3 + (1-a_{44})X_4 &= E_4
\end{aligned} \qquad (7.5)
$$

In these four equations, the a's are constant coefficients that we know beforehand, because we know the technology being employed. Therefore, if we also know the values of E_1, E_2, E_3, and E_4 (which we might be able to determine by comparative cost analysis), we will have a system of four unknowns, X_1, X_2, X_3, and X_4 (the size of the four pies), and four equations. From high school algebra, we know that if the four equations are independent and consistent, we can solve for the size of the pies—for example, we can use the substitution process. Of course, if we use the longhand of high school algebra, it might take us a few days to solve these four equations and check the solution. In this process, we would obtain a very long algebraic expression. In fact, it is so long for the four equations of 7.5 that we cannot put all the symbols on one page. So, we use a shorthand notation.[3] But even with this shorthand notation we obtain clumsy equations, each of which contains a large number of symbols. One of these, we present in a footnote.[4] The important thing to keep in mind, however, is that our shorthand notation, for example D as defined in the footnote 3, stands for multiplication, addition and subtraction of constants only. A computer can do these operations for us. Also, if we concentrate on the long numerator that multiplies E_1 in footnote 4, we see that only multiplication, addition, and subtraction of constants are involved. Again the computer can do this for us, as well as divide that number by D as is required. Thereby it yields another number (a constant) which we designate A_{11}. This constant accounts not only for the direct input (per dollar output) of the agricultural sector into itself as given by the a_{11} coefficient, but also tells us the additional inputs of agriculture required by the round-by-round expansions in all sectors resulting from a dollar's increase in agricultural output, say for export purposes. Put otherwise, A_{11} represents the direct and indirect requirements of agricultural output necessary to produce one unit of agriculture for exports.

Similarly, the long-term multiplying E_2 in footnote 4 consists of constants only; so we use the computer as just indicated to obtain another constant A_{12}. Again, the constant A_{12} accounts not only for the direct input of the agriculture sector required by a dollar's increase in the output of manufacturing sector, as given by the a_{12} coefficient but also tells us the additional inputs of agriculture

[3]In solving Equations 7.5 we find it convenient to let D stand for the value of the denominator which we obtain from our algebraic operation. That is:

$$
\begin{aligned}
D = (1 - a_{11})[&(1 - a_{22})(1 - a_{33})(1 - a_{44}) - a_{32}a_{43}a_{24} - a_{42}a_{23}a_{34} \\
&- a_{24}(1 - a_{33})a_{42} - a_{34}a_{43}(1 - a_{22}) - (1 - a_{44})a_{23}a_{32}] \\
+ a_{21}[&- a_{12}(1 - a_{33})(1 - a_{44}) - a_{32}a_{43}a_{14} - a_{42}a_{13}a_{34} \\
&- a_{14}(1 - a_{33})a_{42} + a_{34}a_{43}a_{12} - (1 - a_{44})a_{13}a_{32}] \\
- a_{31}[&a_{12}a_{23}(1 - a_{44}) + (1 - a_{22})a_{43}a_{14} - a_{42}a_{13}a_{24} \\
&+ a_{14}a_{23}a_{42} + a_{24}a_{43}a_{12} + (1 - a_{44})a_{13}(1 - a_{22})] \\
+ a_{41}[&- a_{12}a_{23}a_{34} + (1 - a_{22})(1 - a_{33})a_{14} - a_{32}a_{13}a_{24} \\
&+ a_{14}a_{23}a_{32} - a_{24}(1 - a_{33})a_{12} - a_{34}a_{13}(1 - a_{22})]
\end{aligned} \tag{7.6}
$$

[4]With D defined in the previous footnote, the equation that gives the solution for X_1 is

$$
\begin{aligned}
X_1 = \frac{1}{D}[&(1 - a_{22})(1 - a_{33})(1 - a_{44}) - a_{32}a_{43}a_{24} - a_{42}a_{23}a_{34} \\
&- a_{24}(1 - a_{33})a_{42} - a_{34}a_{43}(1 - a_{22}) - (1 - a_{44})a_{23}a_{32}]E_1 \\
- \frac{1}{D}[&- a_{12}(1 - a_{33})(1 - a_{44}) - a_{32}a_{43}a_{14} - a_{42}a_{13}a_{34} \\
&- a_{14}(1 - a_{33})a_{42} + a_{34}a_{43}a_{12} - (1 - a_{44})a_{13}a_{32}]E_2 \\
+ \frac{1}{D}[&a_{12}a_{23}(1 - a_{44}) + (1 - a_{22})a_{43}a_{14} - a_{42}a_{13}a_{24} \\
&+ a_{14}a_{23}a_{42} + a_{24}a_{43}a_{12} + (1 - a_{44})a_{13}(1 - a_{22})]E_3 \\
- \frac{1}{D}[&- a_{12}a_{23}a_{34} + (1 - a_{22})(1 - a_{33})a_{14} - a_{32}a_{13}a_{24} \\
&+ a_{14}a_{23}a_{32} - a_{24}(1 - a_{33})a_{12} - a_{34}a_{13}(1 - a_{22})]E_4
\end{aligned} \tag{7.7}
$$

The person who has studied determinants will recognize that we are using Cramer's rule with longhand notation.

required by the round-by-round expansions in all sectors resulting from the dollar's increase in manufacturing output, say for export purposes. Put otherwise, A_{12} represents the direct and indirect requirements of agricultural output necessary to produce one unit of manufacturing output for export. Likewise, we find that the terms multiplying E_3 and E_4 are constants that may be designated A_{13} and A_{14}, respectively. Hence, we obtain from solving 7.5 for X_1:

$$X_1 = A_{11}E_1 + A_{12}E_2 + A_{13}E_3 + A_{14}E_4 \qquad (7.8)$$

Now what specifically does this equation mean? It simply states that the output of the agricultural sector, X_1, is equal to

1. The direct and indirect requirements of agricultural output to produce one unit of agriculture for exports, namely A_{11}, times the total amount of agriculture to be exported, namely E_1; plus
2. The direct and indirect requirements of agricultural output to produce one unit of manufacturing output for exports, namely A_{12}, times the total amount of manufacturing output to be exported, namely E_2; plus
3. The direct and indirect requirements of agricultural output to produce one unit of services for exports, namely A_{13}, times the total amount of services to be exported, namely E_3; plus
4. The direct and indirect requirements of agricultural output to produce one unit of household services (that is to meet household demands corresponding to that unit), namely A_{14}, times the amount of household services to be exported, namely E_4.

If we now proceed to solve for X_2, X_3, and X_4, we will obtain equations of similar form, namely:

$$X_2 = A_{21}E_1 + A_{22}E_2 + A_{23}E_3 + A_{24}E_4 \qquad (7.9)$$

$$X_3 = A_{31}E_1 + A_{32}E_2 + A_{33}E_3 + A_{34}E_4 \qquad (7.10)$$

$$X_4 = A_{41}E_1 + A_{42}E_2 + A_{43}E_3 + A_{44}E_4 \qquad (7.11)$$

Each of these can be interpreted as equation 7.8.

It is important to repeat that it is only a matter of seconds for a high-speed electronic computer to derive the $A_{11}, ..., A_{44}$ for us, once we give the programmer the a's of Table 7.13. To be specific, suppose the coefficients of Table 7.13 are

$$\begin{bmatrix} 0.10, & 0.10, & 0.05, & 0.6 \\ 0.20, & 0.15, & 0.20, & 0.2 \\ 0.10, & 0.15, & 0.05, & 0.2 \\ 0.40, & 0.35, & 0.40, & 0.0 \end{bmatrix} \qquad (7.12)$$

Then the computer calculates the A's in Equations 7.8 to 7.11. If, for convenience, we arrange the A's as

$$\begin{bmatrix} A_{11}, & A_{12}, & A_{13}, & A_{14} \\ A_{21}, & A_{22}, & A_{23}, & A_{24} \\ A_{31}, & A_{32}, & A_{33}, & A_{34} \\ A_{41}, & A_{42}, & A_{43}, & A_{44} \end{bmatrix} \qquad (7.13)$$

the computer gives, as values for these constants

$$\begin{bmatrix} 2.40, & 1.30, & 1.22, & 1.94 \\ 1.14, & 2.03, & 1.03, & 1.30 \\ 0.78, & 0.78, & 1.66, & 0.96 \\ 1.67, & 1.54, & 1.51, & 2.61 \end{bmatrix} \tag{7.14}$$

So we can write equations 7.8 to 7.11 specifically as

$$\begin{aligned} X_1 &= 2.40E_1 + 1.30E_2 + 1.22E_3 + 1.94E_4 \\ X_2 &= 1.14E_1 + 2.03E_2 + 1.03E_3 + 1.30E_4 \\ X_3 &= 0.78E_1 + 0.78E_2 + 1.66E_3 + 0.96E_4 \\ X_4 &= 1.67E_1 + 1.54E_2 + 1.51E_3 + 2.61E_4 \end{aligned} \tag{7.15}$$

Now let us go back to Table 7.14, which is a flows table. In connection with the discussion of that table and Table 7.13, we stated that only the manufacturing sector was able to compete on the world market. We might then consider a set of exports involving the export of 1,000 units of manufactured output and zero units of output of other sectors. That is, we suggest

$$E_1 = 0; E_2 = 1,000; E_3 = 0; E_4 = 0.$$

If we now put these values into the equations, we obtain the following outputs for our four sectors:

$$\begin{aligned} X_1 &= 1300 \\ X_2 &= 2030 \\ X_3 &= 780 \\ X_4 &= 1540 \end{aligned} \tag{7.16}$$

These are the sizes of the pie that we wished to determine.

We immediately see how we can obtain implications of different kinds of reasonable export plans that we may consider for the economy. If, instead of 1,000 units, we plan to export 1,500 units of manufactures, the output of the different sectors are

$$\begin{aligned} X_1 &= 1.30 \,(1,500) = 1,950 \\ X_2 &= 2.03 \,(1,500) = 3,045 \\ X_3 &= 0.78 \,(1,500) = 1,170 \\ X_4 &= 1.54 \,(1,500) = 2,310 \end{aligned} \tag{7.17}$$

If we judge that we can export 500 units of agricultural products as well as 1,500 units of manufactured products, then we obtain for the outputs of the different sectors

$$\begin{aligned} X_1 &= 2.40 \,(500) + 1.30 \,(1,500) = 3,150 \\ X_2 &= 1.14 \,(500) + 2.03 \,(1,500) = 3,615 \\ X_3 &= 0.78 \,(500) + 0.78 \,(1,500) = 1,560 \\ X_4 &= 1.67 \,(500) + 1.54 \,(1,500) = 3,145 \end{aligned} \tag{7.18}$$

Some More Algebra, and Planning for Different Sizes and Economic Structures of New Towns

Now let us return to our new town example. Instead of an economy geared to the demands of the export (world) market it can serve—that is, to the independent variables E_1, E_2, E_3, and E_4—we have an economy geared to the demands of the research laboratory and pharmaceutical companies that will provide the central driving force for the economic development of the town. These demands are the first round-input requirements. There are the demands of the lab and pharmaceutical companies for inputs of agricultural products, which we can represent as Y_1 and which we assume to be zero, because we do not anticipate that our town will have an agriculture sector within it. There are the demands for the output of the town's food products sector, designated by Y_2. There are the demands for the output of the town's textiles sector, designated Y_3. Finally, because there are 100 sectors in our new town, there are the demands of the lab and pharmaceutical companies for the output of the sector represented by the 100th row, designated by Y_{100}.

Thus we have a vector of input requirements from our town, which is at the same time a vector of demands for the outputs of our town's economy. This vector may be represented by the following column:

$$\begin{bmatrix} Y_1 \\ Y_2 \\ Y_3 \\ Y_4 \\ \cdot \\ \cdot \\ Y_{98} \\ Y_{99} \\ Y_{100} \end{bmatrix} \qquad (7.19)$$

which we have called a column vector.

This vector is cumbersome to treat. It takes a long time and much space to write down 100 Y symbols with appropriate subscripts. So we use our shorthand. Specifically, we represent the column of 100 Y's with subscripts by

$$[Y_i], i = 1, 2, ..., 100 \qquad (7.20)$$

where i can represent each of the 100 rows, and thus each of the 100 Y's.

Now, if we properly construct the coefficients table for our town's economy so that each coefficient, a_{ij}, represents the amount of input from the local sector in any row i per unit output of the local sector at the head of any column j, and where the rest of the input of that same commodity is covered in the imports coefficient, then we can give the computer the set of a_{ij}'s, say a matrix of 100 rows and 100 columns. We ask the computer to give us in return a matrix of A_{ij}'s like in 7.14, except that this matrix must have 100 rows and 100 columns. We then have the data with which to calculate the required output of each of our local sectors. For example, the output of the electric power sector, say the 15th sector, would be given by

$$X_{15} = A_{15,1}\, Y_1 + A_{15,2}\, Y_2 + \dots + A_{15,99}\, Y_{99} + A_{15,100}\, Y_{100} \quad (7.21)$$

The output of our households sector, say the 98th sector, would be

$$X_{98} = A_{98,1}\, Y_1 + A_{98,2}\, Y_2 + \dots + A_{98,99}\, Y_{99} + A_{98,100}\, Y_{100} \quad (7.22)$$

And so forth. But once again we find that it takes much time and space to write down the output equations for all 100 sectors. Again we want a shorthand. Further, although we do not mind doing four multiplications and summing the products to obtain the output of each one of our sectors in the underdeveloped economy characterized by Equation 7.15, we certainly will mind doing 100 multiplications and adding the 100 products to obtain the output of one of the sectors of our new town, especially when we must do this 100 times to obtain the outputs of all 100 sectors of our local economy. So, not only do we want a shorthand to avoid writing down all the mathematical symbols, but we also want a computer to do all multiplications and additions and to give us the results in a simple print-out. We want the print-out to list the required output of each of these 100 sectors in a single column of 100 items. That is, we want the computer to give a column of numbers which corresponds to

$$\begin{bmatrix} X_1 \\ X_2 \\ X_3 \\ \cdot \\ \cdot \\ \cdot \\ X_{98} \\ X_{99} \\ X_{100} \end{bmatrix} \quad \text{or} \quad [X_i],\, i = 1, \dots, 100 \quad (7.23)$$

To develop the desired shorthand, let us go back to Equations 7.8 to 7.11. They are

$$\begin{aligned} X_1 &= A_{11}E_1 + A_{12}E_2 + A_{13}E_3 + A_{14}E_4 \\ X_2 &= A_{21}E_1 + A_{22}E_2 + A_{23}E_3 + A_{24}E_4 \\ X_3 &= A_{31}E_1 + A_{32}E_2 + A_{33}E_3 + A_{34}E_4 \\ X_4 &= A_{41}E_1 + A_{42}E_2 + A_{43}E_3 + A_{44}E_4 \end{aligned} \quad (7.24)$$

We already know that $[X_i]$, $i = 1, 2, 3, 4$, stands for

$$\begin{bmatrix} X_1 \\ X_2 \\ X_3 \\ X_4 \end{bmatrix} \quad (7.25)$$

the four symbols at the left-hand side of the four equations. We also know that $[E_i]$, $i = 1, 2, 3, 4$, stands for

$$\begin{bmatrix} E_1 \\ E_2 \\ E_3 \\ E_4 \end{bmatrix} \quad (7.26)$$

a vector column of E's where the four E's are the ones that occur in the same order in each of the four equations above. We also know that $[A_{ij}]$, $i, j = 1, 2, 3, 4$, or $[\ A\ ]_{4 \times 4}$ stands for

$$
\begin{bmatrix}
A_{11}, & A_{12}, & A_{13}, & A_{14} \\
A_{21}, & A_{22}, & A_{23}, & A_{24} \\
A_{31}, & A_{32}, & A_{33}, & A_{34} \\
A_{41}, & A_{42}, & A_{43}, & A_{44}
\end{bmatrix}
\tag{7.27}
$$

Now let us adopt just one simple convention. Let us say that when we premultiply a column vector $[E_i]$, $i = 1,2,3,4$, by a matrix $[A_{ij}]$, $i, j = 1,2,3, 4$, we get another column vector of four items (rows). The first item in the resulting column vector is obtained by premultiplying each of the four items in the E column vector by its corresponding item among the four items in the first row of the matrix and summing the four products—that is, by premultiplying the first item E_1 in the column vector by the first item A_{11} in the first row of the matrix, then premultiplying the second item E_2 in the column vector by the second item A_{12} in the first row of the matrix, then premultiplying the third item E_3 in the column vector by the third item A_{13} in the first row of the matrix, then premultiplying the fourth item E_4 in the column vector by the fourth item A_{14} in the first row, and finally summing all products. So the first number in the resulting column vector is the sum

$$A_{11} E_1 + A_{12} E_2 + A_{13} E_3 + A_{14} E_4$$

To obtain the second number in the resulting column vector, we premultiply each of the four items in the column vector E by its corresponding item among the four items in the second row of the matrix and sum the four products to obtain

$$A_{21} E_1 + A_{22} E_2 + A_{23} E_3 + A_{24} E_4$$

To obtain the third and fourth items in the resulting column vector we premultiply the four items in the column vector E by the four items in the third and fourth rows, respectively, of the matrix and then sum the four products to obtain

$$A_{31} E_1 + A_{32} E_2 + A_{33} E_3 + A_{34} E_4$$

$$A_{41} E_1 + A_{42} E_2 + A_{43} E_3 + A_{44} E_4$$

So by this convention we have

$$
\begin{bmatrix}
A_{11} A_{12} A_{13} A_{14} \\
A_{21} A_{22} A_{23} A_{24} \\
A_{31} A_{32} A_{33} A_{34} \\
A_{41} A_{42} A_{43} A_{44}
\end{bmatrix}
\cdot
\begin{bmatrix}
E_1 \\
E_2 \\
E_3 \\
E_4
\end{bmatrix}
=
\begin{bmatrix}
A_{11}E_1 + A_{12}E_2 + A_{13}E_3 + A_{14}E_4 \\
A_{21}E_1 + A_{22}E_2 + A_{23}E_3 + A_{24}E_4 \\
A_{31}E_1 + A_{32}E_2 + A_{33}E_3 + A_{34}E_4 \\
A_{41}E_1 + A_{42}E_2 + A_{43}E_3 + A_{44}E_4
\end{bmatrix}
\tag{7.28}
$$

But by Equation 7.24 the sum of the four products in the first row of the right-hand brackets is X_1; and the sum of the four products in the second, third, and fourth row is X_2, X_3, and X_4, respectively. So we can write

$$\begin{bmatrix} X_1 \\ X_2 \\ X_3 \\ X_4 \end{bmatrix} = \begin{bmatrix} A_{11}, & A_{12}, & A_{13}, & A_{14} \\ A_{21}, & A_{22}, & A_{23}, & A_{24} \\ A_{31}, & A_{32}, & A_{33}, & A_{34} \\ A_{41}, & A_{42}, & A_{43}, & A_{44} \end{bmatrix} \cdot \begin{bmatrix} E_1 \\ E_2 \\ E_3 \\ E_4 \end{bmatrix} \qquad (7.29)$$

or using the shorthand we have adopted

$$\underset{4 \times 1}{[X]} = \underset{4 \times 4}{[A]} \cdot \underset{4 \times 1}{[E]} \qquad (7.30)$$

or simply

$$X = AE \qquad (7.31)$$

if it is understood that we have four sectors.

Let us go back to the problem that prompted us to employ this notation, namely the excessive time and space required to write things down for our new town economy. If we replace the symbol E by Y, the vector of input requirements of our new town's complex of the research laboratory and pharmaceutical companies, we have

$$\underset{100 \times 1}{[X]} = \underset{100 \times 100}{[A]} \cdot \underset{100 \times 1}{[Y]} \qquad (7.32)$$

or simply

$$X = AY \qquad (7.33)$$

where we know that X is a column vector standing for a properly ordered listing of required outputs of each of 100 sectors; where A is a 100×100 matrix of properly ordered constants A_{ij}, each A_{ij} being electronically computed from the a_{ij} of a 100×100 coefficients matrix for our new town; and where Y is a properly ordered vector of first-round requirements of inputs (expansion of output) from the town's sectors.

We are now at the end of our exploration into the use of shorthand. We see that with it we are able to incorporate in a simple equation, $X = AY$, a large amount of knowledge, thinking, and planning for our new town. We can consider different sizes and compositions of a complex of the research laboratory and pharmaceutical companies. Any particular complex can be set down as a vector Y of demands (first-round input requirements). We then make various assumptions about the desirability of having different sectors in our town and judge their competitive position through comparative cost and other analyses. With these assumptions and analyses, plus information provided by engineers on technical requirements for production, plus data from censuses and other government and industrial publications, we set up a matrix of constant coefficients, a_{ij}, say one which is of order 100×100. We then tell the computer to derive another matrix of constants, the A_{ij}, which is of order 100×100, and which is customarily designated the "inverse" matrix. We next instruct the computer to premultiply the Y vector by the inverse matrix to give us a column vector X of the required outputs of the sectors.[5]

[5] This gives the same results as a round-by-round computation, which has been discussed in the section entitled "The Uses of Input-Output Tables" in this chapter. See the appendix to this chapter.

For the high-speed computer, all this work is done in a matter of minutes. The important thing is the basic analysis that goes behind (a) the fashioning of a complex of the research laboratory and pharmaceutical companies and (b) the determination of the relevant a_{ij}'s for the coefficients table of our town. In Chapter 17, we shall discuss at some length the thinking that must go on in designing a complex.

It is very important to note that this approach can be generalized for any type of new town planning. Instead of a complex of the research laboratory and pharmaceutical companies, the economic base of a new town might be a complex of electronic and space-age industries; or a complex of universities and research and development activities; or a complex of food-processing, fertilizer, and leather-processing activities for an agriculturally oriented region; or a complex of oil refineries, petrochemicals, fertilizers, and synthetic fibers for an underdeveloped region whose only advantage may be the capability of its ecologic system to absorb pollutants at low social and economic cost. For each of these complexes we may consider different levels and compositions of activities. Then for each of the new towns, we need to develop relevant a_{ij}coefficients or consider several sets of a_{ij} coefficients, each set relevant for a particular set of assumptions. Once we have organized all our thinking and analysis about alternatives, we can then let the computer spell out the implications of our thinking and analysis in terms of column vectors of outputs of the required industry. We then proceed to check for feasibility and consistency along lines already discussed.

In conclusion, there are tremendous advantages to using the input-output (linear system) format for examining the difficult problems of underdeveloped and developed regions as well as new towns and existing cities. The resulting estimates are still only as good as the basic information, assumptions, and relationships that we feed into the computer. But the computer then gives us a tremendous capability for examining the implications of our thinking about the complex interdependent social, economic, and political framework of growth and development of any region or urban area, and for checking for consistency and feasibility in our planning.

OTHER APPLICATIONS

The input-output format is also useful for thinking about and probing into the problem of unemployment in a city or region, and in particular the problem of providing new jobs for its unskilled population. If we were to think just in terms of the data directly available on each industry—for example, its material inputs and its labor requirements—we might conclude that those industries which employ little unskilled labor per dollar output, say the petrochemicals industries, are not the ones to encourage. We might be inclined to say that other industries, like the food-processing industries, should be encouraged instead. But there are fallacies in this kind of thinking. First, even though an industry employs a large amount of unskilled labor, it might be undesirable for development in a metropolitan region because it would have to operate at high costs and could not compete against firms operating at much lower costs in other regions. This, for example, is true of textiles in the Philadelphia region. On the other hand, industries that employ few unskilled laborers may be just the type to encourage, particularly if these industries are growing at a rapid rate nationally. They may be able to operate at very low costs in the city with which we are concerned.

More importantly, their demand for inputs from other industries or firms in the city may lead indirectly to significant expansion of those industries or firms which are in a position to provide a significant number of jobs for the unskilled. It is by making explicit the linkage of industries, and thus the jobs they create, that input-output analysis is a powerful tool for helping to evaluate the job-creating programs.

But in one sense we can probe even more deeply than might be initially suggested. One of the major advantages of an input-output approach is that it allows us to set up a classification of sectors and commodities and services that is most useful for attacking the problem on hand. If our problem is to attack unemployment in a ghetto area, then it is grossly inadequate to have one sector only for households. We need several. At first glance, we might consider breaking households down into high-income, middle-income, and low-income classifications. But even this disaggregation of households is not satisfactory. What we want is a disaggregation that can provide us with a specific estimate of new job opportunities for those occupations which the ghetto population can fill. Hence, we want to break down the households sector into subsectors corresponding to different kinds of occupations or labor services. At the one extreme might be occupations requiring unskilled, low-education labor and occupations requiring very simple skills that can be acquired within a month's training period. At the other extreme might be occupations requiring Ph.D.-type engineering labor associated with the upper-middle income or high-income households. When we do this and run the input-output computation, we can come up with the detailed estimate of new jobs, by different types of occupation, for the different complexes and government programs under consideration. Once again it will be the indirect as well as the direct demands of the different complexes or programs that will be important.

HISTORY AS A TESTING GROUND

In this and the previous chapter we have been talking about both central driving forces in the development of cities and regions and the structure of economic activities surrounding the basic activities that function as driving forces and lead to the full-scale, comprehensive development of industrial regions and urban masses. At this point, we want to provide another check on our ideas—are they consistent with the historical record? Specifically, if we had done our analysis at some time in the past, say 1800 or 1875 or 1920, could we have predicted what took place subsequently?

Now, perfect prediction is impossible. First of all, at any point in time we possess limited knowledge. For example, although anyone can predict that there will be technological progress, no one can predict the specific shape it will take. No one in 1900 or 1930 could have predicted the space-age industry and activity that we currently have; nor in 1800 could one have predicted the railroad and highway systems which currently gird our society. In short, the specific kind or direction of technological progress is unpredictable. Hence, we cannot consider it a shortcoming of any analysis if it fails to forsee specific technical advances.

Another area in which we do not seem to be able to predict with any assurance concerns consumer tastes. Who in 1910 or 1920 would have predicted one or more cars in every home? In 1930, when birth rates in the industrialized nations were declining rapidly, who would have predicted the baby boom of World War II and our population growth problems of today? Again, we cannot consider it a shortcoming of a technique if it fails to make accurate demographic forecasts and forecasts of other items associated with changing consumer tastes and social values.

The techniques that we have are only applicable when we assume that technological structure, demographic rates, and household behavior do not change drastically.

Now let us see what history does tell us. Let us concentrate on the history of the United States. We observe that major cities like Boston, New York, Philadelphia, and Baltimore have arisen on the East Coast. Why? One reason comes to mind immediately—we could have anticipated that initial settlement of immigrants from Europe would take place on the East Coast of North America simply because the time and cost of transportation to reach these points were lower than to interior points or points on the West Coast. But this kind of statement is inadequate. Why was it that Philadelphia developed initially and not Barnegat, Atlantic City, or other points along the eastern shore of New Jersey? Here the answer lies in the port facilities that were available. The Philadelphia site, from the standpoint of harboring ships, involved much less risk and insecurity from weather than Atlantic City or Barnegat. Similarly, Baltimore, New York, and Boston offered excellent port facilities. But the next question that arises is: Why did both Philadelphia and New York grow to much larger size than Boston? Here a good part of the answer must be linked to the functions of ports in regions undergoing agricultural development. When agricultural development takes place, there is a need for transportation services to get the agricultural products to the market as well as essential goods to the farm and farm households.

In the case of the United States, there was a need to collect and ship the locally produced grains to the markets of Europe and to distribute a variety of manufactures and other goods to local farmers and their households. Hence, port services, as well as the actual transportation services in moving the goods along waterways and roads, had to be provided (produced).

If we consider the provision of port services as a production operation, comparative cost analysis tells us that the location that can produce such service at the lowest cost, everything else being the same, wins out in the competition. In this regard, it is clear that the Boston site was among the lowest cost sites in New England, New York City in the Hudson Valley, Philadelphia in the Delaware-Schuylkill Valley, and Baltimore in the Chesapeake-Potomac system.

There were, however, other selective factors at work. There was a scale factor. The hinterland serviced by Philadelphia via the Delaware and Schuylkill Rivers had a more productive soil and was more extensive than that of Boston, New York, or Baltimore. A larger farming population, with a greater demand for services, could be supported. Hence, Philadelphia could get ahead in terms of realizing scale economies. These scale economies could be partly passed on in the form of lower port and shipping charges to the farming population. This in turn encouraged a more intensive cultivation and a still greater demand for services, leading to greater scale economies. Moreover, access to the hinterland was easier along the Delaware and Schuylkill Rivers than along the waterways leading into Baltimore and Boston.

In addition to the scale economies in providing port services at the harbor in Philadelphia, the city could take advantage of the lower cost of shipping along its waterways. Consequently, Philadelphia experienced a snowballing effect with respect to its advantages.

There was still another cumulative effect in Philadelphia's favor in the precanal era. We have already pointed out the tendency for import substitution to take place as an agricultural area develops. There is a tendency to undertake the production of goods locally which are closely linked, either in a forward or a backward fashion, to agriculture. The combination of a large hinterland, easy access to it, and lower unit costs in producing port services made Philadelphia more attractive than other major cities as a location for new manufacturers trying to grab a part of the import-substitution market. So it is not surprising that Philadelphia got the lead in developing a diversity of import-substituting manufacturing operations. In contrast, Boston fell behind in the race, primarily because of relatively poor soil in its hinterland and relatively poor access to it via New England waterways. In fact, Boston had to seek other activities to assure growth and remain dynamic. For example, it participated in the triangle trade with the West Indies. Slaves were brought from Africa to the West Indies in exchange for sugar, which was then shipped to New England for the manufacture of rum, which was then shipped to Africa to pay the traders for the slaves obtained there.

While Philadelphia, Boston, New York, and Baltimore were vying with each other on the eastern side of the Alleghenies in the precanal era, a system of cities was developing west of the Alleghenies in connection with agricultural cultivation in the Ohio valley. The locally produced wheat was collected at superior inland ports, such as Pittsburgh and Cincinnati, and shipped down the Ohio and Mississippi Rivers to regional markets and to New Orleans at the mouth of the Mississippi, a natural break in the water transport system.

But a major change in the process of economic development took place with the construction and emergence of the canal as the dominant mode of transport. Baltimore, Philadelphia, and New York vigorously promoted the construction of canals into their interiors. Because of severe difficulties in the terrain, Baltimore was never able to complete the Chesapeake and Ohio Canal—the shortest route to the interior. It completely lost out in the competition for the trade west of the Alleghenies. Philadelphia promoted and constructed the Pennsylvania Canal from Philadelphia to Pittsburgh, which successfully opened the interior. But New York City, with the more circuitous Erie Canal, was able to avoid mountainous terrain (by going through the Mohawk Valley, the only break in the Allegheny chain) and thus to tap the interior at much lower transport cost than Philadelphia. It was said that the Philadelphia to Pittsburgh route, with all its costs, was equivalent to 600 canal miles, while the New York City to Buffalo route was equivalent to around 420. Moreover, beyond Buffalo there were 1,000 miles of navigable Great Lakes waterway. Consequently, New York City came to monopolize the grain and other trade from the interior (central and northern Ohio, northern Indiana, northern Illinois, southern Michigan, and southeastern Wisconsin). Philadelphia was able to move forward, but only on the basis of serving markets east of the Alleghenies plus some trade in light manufacturing with the interior. This in large part explains why New York City forged ahead of Philadelphia and, once ahead, was able to take advantage of its greater potential for scale economies in developing leadership in financial markets and related central administrative and communications services, as well as in garment and other manufactures. The national money market, always a sensitive indicator of urban leadership, shifted from Philadelphia to New York.

Equally interesting is the shift in the dominance pattern of cities west of the Alleghenics. In the precanal era, New Orleans was the foremost city. But once the canals were able to penetrate the interior, it was more economical for the grain trade headed for Europe to take the low-cost Erie Canal route via New York City rather than the longer route via New Orleans. So New Orleans declined in relative importance.

Shortly after the development of the canal, another major transportation innovation, the railroad, came on the scene. By the mid-nineteenth century, it was clear that a city had to emerge in the Midwest to serve as a major collection and distribution point for diverse agricultural and manufacturing products—to be a hub for many connecting railroad lines radiating in all directions. At the same time, long-distance water shipment was less costly than rail shipment, so such a city also had to have excellent port facilities. Because the Erie Canal route had such a great advantage in connecting the interior to the Eastern Seaboard, only ports having easy access to that canal were really eligible for the competition. Among others, these included Buffalo, Cleveland, Detroit, Toledo, Chicago, and Milwaukee—ports on the Great Lakes water system. Of these, Chicago was the southwestern-most point and thus most centrally located for serving as a railroad hub to the Midwest. It also had an abundance of vigorous entrepreneurs and risk capital. St. Louis was out of the competition because it did not have easy access to the Erie Canal. And so Chicago emerged as the dominant node. Yet observe that Detroit too emerged as a major city. In part it was a matter of chance. Henry Ford, who successfully innovated automobile production, was born and raised there. A pool of skilled automotive labor developed in his back yard. It was there that new enterprising automobile manufacturers had to gravitate to steal one another's secrets. Once started in Detroit, each had to continue operations and expansions there in order to reap the major scale economies in automobile production. These scale economies had to be realized if a manufacturer were to survive the competition.

We can go on to tell the story of San Francisco, London, Paris, Buenos Aires, and innumerable major cities. But in simple terms, their growth was dependent upon (1) a favorable comparative cost position in producing a product—most often because of port and related transportation services, (2) taking advantage of scale economies in such production through serving a larger rather than a smaller market or hinterland (farming or nonfarming), (3) taking advantage of a favorable transportation situation for marketing the product at low cost, (4) taking advantage of opportunities for import substitution in the production of new goods, and (5) exploiting all opportunities for reaping localization and urbanization economies—through forward and backward linkage, as well as mere increases in their size and the size of the tributary regions for which they served as primary nodes.

APPENDIX TO CHAPTER 7. *Equivalence of the Use of a Round-by-Round Expansion and the Inverse Matrix*

If we use matrix notation, and if we define

$$a = \begin{bmatrix} a_{11}, & a_{12}, & a_{13}, & a_{14} \\ a_{21}, & a_{22}, & a_{23}, & a_{24} \\ a_{31}, & a_{32}, & a_{33}, & a_{34} \\ a_{41}, & a_{42}, & a_{43}, & a_{44} \end{bmatrix}$$

then we can rewrite Equations 7.1 to 7.4 as

$$\begin{matrix} X & - & a & X & = & E \\ (4 \times 1) & & (4 \times 4) & (4 \times 1) & & (4 \times 1) \end{matrix}$$

Or if we replace E by Y and allow for 100 activities, we can rewrite Equations 7.1 to 7.4 as

$$\begin{matrix} X & - & a & X & = & Y \\ (100 \times 1) & & (100 \times 100) & (100 \times 1) & & (100 \times 1) \end{matrix}$$

We can further rewrite this equation to obtain

$$(1 - a) X = Y$$

Dividing through by $(1 - a)$ we obtain

$$X = \frac{Y}{1 - a} \equiv (1 - a)^{-1} Y$$

Now when the $a_{ij} < 1$ and other appropriate conditions are met, as they are with input-output coefficients, this equation is equivalent to

$$X = (1 + a + a^2 + ... + a^\infty) Y = Y + aY + a^2 Y + ... + a^\infty Y$$

Of the terms at the right of the equation, the first term, Y, is the vector of first-round input requirements. For an economy in which there are no exports and imports, that is, one that is closed, first-round input requirements also represent first-round expansions. The second term aY, represents the second-round input requirements (expansions). The third term, $a^2 Y$, represents the third-round input requirements (expansions). In short, X is the sum of round-by-round expansions.

Now we also know that the inverse matrix A which the computer derives for us is simply

$$A = \frac{1}{1 - a} \equiv (1 - a)^{-1} \equiv 1 + a + a^2 + a^3 + ... + a^\infty$$

Thus the use of an inverse or a round-by-round calculation yields approximately the same result—approximately, because in practice we do not carry the latter to an infinite number of rounds.

When first-round expansions are not the same as first-round input requirements, these statements need to be refined; the basic idea is still valid.

Chapter

8

Trade, Migration, Spatial Flows, and Exploitation in our Multi-Region Society

INTRODUCTION

In the previous chapter we focused on a particular underdeveloped region or new town. We recognized that this region or new town was not isolated—it had connections with the outside world. These connections were summarized in a column headed *exports* and a row designated *imports*. Clearly, however, we cannot think of the rest of the world as being simply a column of exports or a row of imports. The rest of the world is just as important as our region or new town, if not more important. The people, institutions, and government of the rest of the world are equally as significant as the people, institutions, and government of our region or new town. Accordingly, our framework of analysis must make this point explicit. It must not look upon the rest of the world as embodied simply in export and import figures.

AN INTERREGIONAL INPUT-OUTPUT SNAPSHOT

In trying to understand the phenomena of trade, migration, and spatial flows, it is easiest to think initially of a world of two regions. Suppose, in the century before the advent of aircraft, there were two regions, each confined to a valley surrounded by impassable mountains. Imagine that in each of these isolated regions a simple economy of agriculture (A), crafts manufacture (M), services (S), and households (H) had developed over time. We may also imagine that the agriculture and crafts had developed rather differently. Each economy, in this century of isolation, is representable by an input-output table.

A new century arrives and so does aircraft. The isolation of each region can be destroyed. Social resistance to change might impose sufficient obstacles to the use of aircraft so that it has little, if any, effect on a society. But for at least some societies, curiosity, as well as the new experiences made possible by the consumption of different goods available through trade, breaks down resistance to change. Certain segments of each of these societies begin engaging in trade.

Table 8.1   Input-Output Flows, Valley A

	A	M	S	H	Total
A	≠ 8,000	≠3,000	≠ 5,000	≠24,000	≠40,000
M	10,000	3,000	2,500	4,500	20,000
S	8,000	8,000	7,500	1,500	25,000
H	14,000	6,000	10,000	—	30,000
Total	40,000	20,000	25,000	30,000	

Table 8.2   Input-Output Flows, Valley B

	A	M	S	H	Total
A	$20,000	$ 9,000	$ 6,000	$45,000	$80,000
M	12,000	3,000	6,000	9,000	30,000
S	16,000	6,000	12,000	6,000	40,000
H	32,000	12,000	16,000	—	60,000
Total	80,000	30,000	40,000	60,000	

Before trade, let the flows Table 8.1 represent a four-sector economy for a valley A, whose currency is indicated by the symbol ≠, and the flows Table 8.2 represent another four-sector economy for a valley B, whose currency is indicated by the symbol \$. Corresponding to the flows tables of 8.1 and 8.2 are the coefficients tables of 8.3 and 8.4, respectively.

Table 8.3   Input-Output Coefficients, Valley A

	A	M	S	H
A	0.2	0.15	0.2	0.8
M	0.25	0.15	0.1	0.15
S	0.2	0.4	0.3	0.05
H	0.35	0.3	0.4	—
Total	1.0	1.0	1.0	1.0

Table 8.4   Input-Output Coefficients, Valley B

	A	M	S	H
A	0.25	0.3	0.15	0.75
M	0.15	0.1	0.15	0.15
S	0.2	0.2	0.3	0.1
H	0.4	0.4	0.4	—
Total	1.0	1.0	1.0	1.0

Imagine that some fruit is grown in valley A which cannot be cultivated in valley B, and that nuts are grown in valley B which cannot be produced in valley A. Further, let the households of both valleys come to prefer some combination of fruits and nuts to either fruits alone or nuts alone. A first condition for trade is then met. To keep things simple, suppose we assume that the craft articles produced in one region are not of interest to the other. Trade in these articles, or in services, does not materialize. Moreover, assume that neither region is interested in hiring the labor services of the other.

We may anticipate that, after trade, the household consumption patterns of each region are different. In each region, the households sector consumes some of the agricultural products of the other. In order to represent this phenomenon in input-output fashion, we need to construct a new type of table, which we shall call an *interregional input-output flows table* because interregional trade is involved (see Table 8.5). In this interregional input-output flows table, we depict the internal economy of each region in a major block along the principal diagonal running from the upper left to the lower right. Valley A's economy is represented by the major block of cells at the upper left, and valley B's economy is represented by the major block of cells at the lower right. Except for two cells, all the cells in the upper right major block and the lower left major block are empty. One cell that is not empty is the cell in the households column of region A and the agricultural sector row of region B. The figure in this cell

Table 8.5   Two-Region Interregional Flows Table

Sector		Valley A				Valley B			
		A	M	S	H	A	M	S	H
V A L L E Y A	A	≠ 8,000	≠3,000	≠ 5,000	≠21,000		||||		$ 6,000
	M	10,000	3,000	2,500	4,500	||||	||||		||||
	S	8,000	8,000	7,500	1,500				
	H	14,000	6,000	10,000	—				
V A L L E Y B	A		||||		≠3,000	$20,000	$9,000	$6,000	$39,000
	M	||||	||||		||||	12,000	3,000	6,000	9,000
	S					16,000	6,000	12,000	6,000
	H					32,000	12,000	16,000	—
Total		≠40,000	≠20,000	≠25,000	≠30,000	$80,000	$30,000	$40,000	$60,000

represents (in the currency units ≠) the export of nuts of valley B to the households of valley A. It also represents the imports of households of valley A from the agricultural sector of valley B. The second cell that is not empty is the cell corresponding to the households column of valley B and the agricultural row of valley A. The number in this cell represents (in the currency units $) the export of fruit of valley A to the households of valley B, which also constitutes imports of the households of valley B from the agricultural sector of valley A.

We can go from the interregional flows Table 8.5 to an interregional coefficients Table 8.6. In doing so we follow the standard procedure already discussed in Chapter 7. We divide the items in the cells of each column by the total of that column to obtain the relevant input coefficients. It is evident that as one economy expands or both expand, so will interregional trade.

Table 8.6   Two-Region Interregional Coefficients Table

Sector		Valley A				Valley B			
		A	M	S	H	A	M	S	H
V A L L E Y A	A	0.2	0.15	0.2	0.7	—	—	—	0.1
	M	0.25	0.15	0.1	0.15	—	—	—	—
	S	0.2	0.4	0.3	0.05	—	—	—	—
	H	0.35	0.3	0.4	—	—	—	—	—
V A L L E Y B	A	—	—	—	0.1	0.25	0.3	0.15	0.65
	M	—	—	—	—	0.15	0.1	0.15	0.15
	S	—	—	—	—	0.2	0.2	0.3	0.1
	H	—	—	—	—	0.4	0.4	0.4	—
	Total	1.0	1.0	1.0	1.0	1.0	1.0	1.0	1.0

It is easy to generalize our framework. We can imagine that trade takes place in products other than agricultural products. We can imagine that the households of each region would like to buy some manufactured goods from the other. Accordingly, the cell in the household column of any region that relates to the manufacturing sector row of the other will have a number in it. We have lightly striped in these cells in Table 8.5. Likewise, the agricultural sector of each region might use some of the manufactured products of the other. Once again we lightly stripe in the cell in the agriculture column of each region that relates to the manufacturing sector row of the other. Also, the manufacturing sector of each region might use inputs from both the agricultural sector and manufacturing sector of the other. So we stripe in four more cells. In this way we can take into account the different kinds of trading relations between the two regions.

Note that those cells not in the major blocks on the principal diagonal are the cells providing information on trade—that is, imports and exports. Note also that, in a sense, we have taken the imports row of our four-sector economy for valley A (corresponding to the imports row of Table 7.13) and broken it down into the imports from each of the four sectors of valley B. Likewise, rather than leaving imports of valley B in undifferentiated form, we have disaggregated the imports of valley B into four parts representing imports from the agricultural, manufacturing, services, and households sectors, respectively, of valley A. Looked at another way, we have disaggregated the exports sector of valley A into exports to each of the four consuming sectors of valley B; and the exports sector of valley B into exports to each of the four consuming sectors of valley A.

At this point, the reader might question the need to have information on the sectors of another region to which goods are exported. After all, doesn't a dollar's worth of exports have the same significance to a person in a region whether it is consumed by the manufacturing sector, households sector, or some other sector of a second region?

In reply to this question, consider a small economy like Finland, which exports to major economies like the Soviet Union and the United States. In planning the development of the Finnish economy in a way that hopefully insulates it from the international politics of the two big powers, it is critical to know whether exports will be going to the military or the households sectors of the Soviet Union and the United States. If they are going largely to the military sector, they may be resting on a shaky foundation. World politics and disarmament agreements can drastically affect the level and composition, and thus demands, of the military sectors of these two powers. In contrast, if the exports are going to the household sectors, they are not likely to be subject to as sudden and unpredictable changes. Household behavior generally changes slowly over time, and slowly enough that an economy like Finland's has time for adjustment without confronting catastrophe.

Table 8.7   Interregional Flows Table

Now that we understand the importance of keeping both imports and exports disaggregated, let us proceed to generalize our two-region situation to a many-region situation. Imagine that the airplane brings many isolated regions into contact. Or we may imagine that we are studying the nations of the European Common Market, COMECON, the sterling bloc, the regions of Yugoslavia, or the regions of Mainland China. The interrelations of these nations or regions might be depicted by the Interregional Flows Table (8.7). (The corresponding coefficients can be presented in another table with a similar structure.) Note once again that in Table 8.7, the internal economic structure of any nation or region is depicted by a major block of cells on the principal diagonal, and that its trading relations with other nations or regions are depicted in cells in major blocks which are off the principal diagonal. There are of course problems in getting data for these tables, but these are not insurmountable and are discussed elsewhere in the technical literature. It should be noted that the data for several interregional situations have already been collected and effectively utilized. Japan is a case in point.

COST AND PRICE ANALYSIS FOR INTERREGIONAL TRADE

An interregional flows table provides an excellent snapshot of a current situation. Its data furnishes a detailed description of the intricate interrelations that exist among the regions (nations) of a system. If the analyst desires to make projections and if he is willing to assume that a linear system has some validity in representing the functioning of an interregional system, he can easily proceed to employ an interregional coefficients table and its inverse. We will say more about such a potential application in a later section.

At this point, we wish to do careful cost analysis and examine the way prices of goods in different regions (nations) are related to each other. Let us reexamine the case of our two regions.

Trade Under Conditions of Pure Competition

Consider the two regions after they have been in contact with each other for some time and have established a fruitful trading relationship. A new kind of merchant has evolved, namely the trader, who is motivated to make profits by shipping goods from his own region to the other region, or by importing goods from the other region and selling them to consumers in his own region. We imagine also that a rate of exchange of one region's currency for the other has emerged. Suppose the basic unit of currency in one society is a standard basket (or other container) of fruit; in the other the basic unit is a standard bag (or other container) of nuts.

Prices in one valley are therefore in terms of baskets of fruit. A cow might be valued at 100 baskets of fruit (instead of $500 in the U. S. society) and a particular craft object might be valued at 3 baskets of fruit (rather than $15 in the U. S. society). Prices in the second valley are in terms of bags of nuts. A cow might be valued at 300 bags of nuts, a particular local craft object at 8 bags. Now, once trading relations have been established, the two societies may find themselves exchanging 2 bags of nuts for 1 basket of fruit, and there may be general agreement that this is a fair rate of exchange. After a rate of exchange is established, the different prices in the two regions become automatically inter-related. Let us see how.

In one society the cow was worth 100 fruit baskets, and in the other society 300 bags of nuts. Shortly after trading relations were established, a sharp merchant in valley *A* would have figured out that it made sense to transport a cow in a C-47 aircraft from his region to the other, provided it did not kill the cow and provided the cost of transporting the cow was not excessive. Say the transport cost was 30 baskets of fruit. He would have figured out that he could obtain 300 bags of nuts for the cow in valley *B*, and exchange the 300 bags for 150 baskets of fruit (at the exchange rate of two bags of nuts for one basket of fruit). He could then pay the original owner of the cow in valley *A* the 100 baskets of fruit he demanded, pay the transport cost of 30 baskets of fruit, and have 20 baskets of fruit left over for himself.

If other sharp traders had figured out this trade gain or had observed that this merchant was making a substantial profit by buying cows in one economy and selling them in the other, they too would have started trading cows. However, it can be easily seen that the profits from trading cows would soon start to decrease and even disappear. We can imagine that after a while, the first trader found he could no longer sell cows in valley *B* for 300 bags of nuts. After the most eager buyers in valley *B* had bought cows, the trader would have found that he could sell cows only to less eager buyers—buyers who were willing to pay only 290 bags of nuts. Also, the exporter might have found that he could no longer buy cows in region *A* for 100 baskets of fruit, the price he had to pay to the most eager sellers. He might have found that he could buy cows from only less eager sellers—sellers who demanded more than 100 baskets of fruit for a cow, say 110 baskets. Under these conditions he would have been selling cows for 290 bags of nuts, exchanging these bags for 145 baskets of fruit, paying 110 baskets for a cow, and 30 for transport of the cow, thus having only 5 baskets left over for himself as profits. Pretty soon his surplus profits would have disappeared, especially if other traders in both regions had entered into this export trade. New traders would bid up the price for cows in region *A* because of their new demand and force down the price for cows in region *B*, through the supply of more cows on the market at *B*. Sooner or later, the situation would have been reached at which no excess profit could be made from trade in cows. The price in region *B* would have fallen while simultaneously the price would have risen in region *A*, so that the difference between the two prices (when stated in terms of baskets of fruit) was just equal to the cost of transporting the cow from valley *A* to valley *B*. Put otherwise, the price in region *A* *plus* the transport cost from *A* to *B* would just equal the price in region *B*.

This simple illustration underscores the basic principle governing interregional trade in a highly competitive situation. This principle holds for any pair of regions, whether we are considering a system containing only two regions or more than two regions, As long as monopoly elements do not dominate—that is, as long as new traders are free to enter or leave the export business—the equilibrium prices of any standard commodity in this pair of regions must be related in one of two ways:

1. If there is trade between the pair of regions, the price of the good in the region of higher price must exceed the price in the other by the amount it costs

to ship a unit of the good from the region of lower price to the region of higher price. (We have seen that if the price spread is greater than the cost of transport, there will be excess profit from trade. This will stimulate more traders to enter the business and simultaneously induce existing traders to increase their export shipments. The consequence will be a rise in the price in terms of the standard commodity in the region of export and a fall in the price in the region of import, reducing excess profits. This process will continue until excess profits are eliminated.)

2. If there is no trade between the pair of regions, the price in the region of higher price (when the two regions have unequal prices) does not exceed the price in the other by an amount equal to the cost of shipping a unit of the good from one to the other. Accordingly, a sharp trader will not export this good. If he were to do so, he would incur a loss, because the price he would receive would not cover the cost of the good plus the cost of transport. If the two regions have the same price, no trader will export for the same reason.

Note that it is theoretically possible for the difference in prices between the two regions to just equal the cost of transporting a unit from the region of lower price to the region of higher price and yet no trade to occur, because of zero profits. Such a situation, however, represents a limiting case which rarely exists in reality because of reasons too technical to discuss at this point.

The above discussion can now be summarized by the use of mathematical symbols. If we let p^A represent the price in region A, p^B the price in region B, $\pi^{A \to B}$ the cost of shipping a unit of a good from A to B, and $s^{A \to B}$ the amount of shipments from A to B, we can state the following.

If $s^{A \to B} > 0$ at equilibrium, then

$$p^A + \pi^{A \to B} = p^B \qquad (8.1)$$

If $s^{A \to B} = 0$, then

$$p^A + \pi^{A \to B} > p^B \qquad (8.2)$$

Or, in a rare, trivial case

$$p^A + \pi^{A \to B} = p^B$$

We may also rewrite Equations 8.1 and 8.2 in another way:

if $p^A + \pi^{A \to B} = p^B$

then $s^{A \to B} > 0$

$$\text{(or } s^{A \to B} = 0 \text{ for the rare, trivial case);}$$

if $p^A + \pi^{A \to B} > p^B$

then $s^{A \to B} = 0$.

In more general terms: if we have a system of regions comprising region A, region B, region C, ..., region U, and if we let the letters J and K refer to any of these U regions, then the conditions can be generalized for any pair of regions J and K by substituting the symbols J and K for A and B, respectively, in Equations 8.1 and 8.2.

Trade Under Monopoly Conditions

Let us now introduce monopoly elements into the situation. Suppose valley A produces a unique product like tea. Let the condition of supply of tea for export be depicted by curve $S^A S^A$ of Figure 8.1. Tea cultivators as a whole are willing to supply more tea for export as the price increases. Let there be no production of tea in region B because of improper soil. However, let there be a demand for tea in region B as given by demand curve $D^B D^B$ of Figure 8.1. The population of region B is willing to purchase more tea as the price decreases. Now, if there were no restrictions on trading between A and B, we could consider these two curves as relevant, and could start to determine the equilibrium price and amount of trade. Recall from Chapter 4 that the equilibrium price and the amount of goods exchanged are determined by the intersection of the demand and supply curve. If transport costs were zero, we could say the same thing with respect to Figure 8.1; the intersection of the two curves determines the equilibrium price and amount of trade. But transport costs on shipping a good from one region to another are not zero, except in rare cases. These transport costs must be paid, either by the supplier or demander or both. Consequently, the equilibrium conditions cannot be described by the intersection point.

One way to determine the equilibrium outcome is as follows. Let the suppliers be responsible, either directly or through a broker, for delivering their

Figure 8.1 Demand for Tea in Region B and Supply in Region A

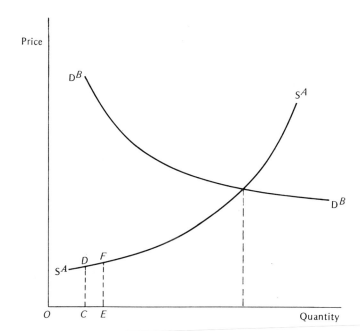

goods to the market in region B. Then each supplier of tea in region A, in effect, pays the transport cost. If he is willing to supply 100 pounds at $1 per pound to the market in his region, then he is willing to supply 100 pounds to the market at B at a price of $1 plus the transport cost, say $.10—that is, at a price of $1.10. Thus, for him to supply any given amount on the market at B, it is necessary to offer him $.10 more than is necessary to have him supply that same amount on the market at A. Likewise with all other tea suppliers. Accordingly, at the market in region B, the supply curve is not $S^A S^A$ as in Figure 8.1, but $S^B S^B$ as in Figure 8.2, where the $S^B S^B$ curve is derived by shifting all points of the $S^A S^A$ curve vertically upward by a stretch equal to $.10 in price. Now, the intersection of this "adjusted" supply curve $S^B S^B$ and the demand curve $D^B D^B$ determines the equilibrium amount of trade, namely OM, and the equilibrium price on the market at B, namely MN. Note that the vertical stretch RN represents the transport cost. If we subtract it from the equilibrium price MN on the market at B, we have MR, which is the equilibrium price on the market at A—that is, the net price (after transport cost is deducted) which the suppliers in region A must receive in order to induce them to supply the equilibrium quantity OM.

Figure 8.2   Demand and Supply of Tea on the Market of Region B

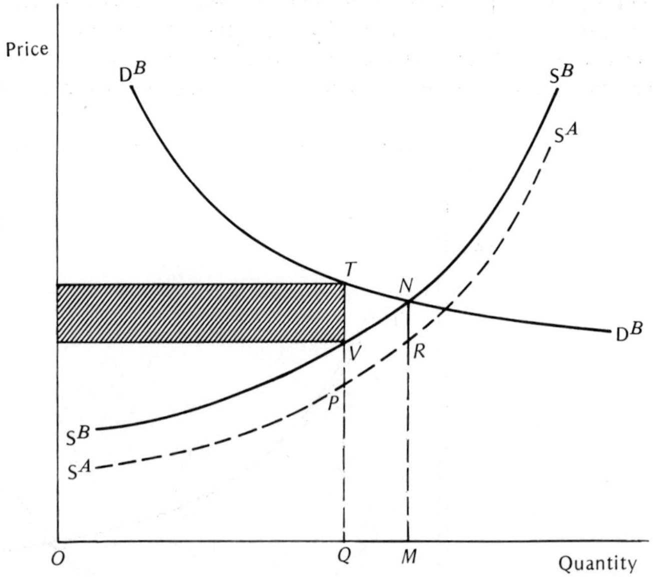

With this analysis we are ready to examine the effect of monopoly elements. Suppose the tea-producing region A is a colony of region B, and suppose also that a tea trading company is given, by law or some edict, a complete monopoly of the tea trade. We assume, of course, that it cannot dictate to consumers in B how much they should purchase and at what price, nor dictate to the tea cultivators in region A how much they should produce and at what price. However, the tea trading company can determine how much will be exported from A and imported to B.

Note from Figure 8.2 that if *OM* is exported from *A* and imported to *B* there are no excess profits from trade. The company would have to pay tea suppliers the price *MR* to obtain the quantity *OM*; and the transport cost per pound of tea would be *RN*. The price the company could get from purchasers in region *B* if it were to market *OM* quantity of tea is *MN*, which equals *MR* + *RN*—or, as indicated above, zero excess profits. However, the tea company is a monopoly. It can restrict the quantity of tea exported to any amount—say to *OQ*. In this case, it has to pay tea suppliers a price of only *QP*. It can also charge purchasers the higher price of *QT*. Thus, if it subtracts the transport cost *PV* from the difference *PT*, it has a surplus profit of *VT* on each unit sold. Over the *OQ* units sold, its total profits are given by the striped rectangle of Figure 8.2.

But why should the tea company restrict its trade to the quantity *OQ*? Perhaps if it restricted its trade by one more unit, its total profits would be greater; and if it restricted the quantity by still another unit, its total profits would be still greater. In short, having control of the amount to be traded, the company can seek that quantity of exports and thus imports which will maximize its total profits. In doing so, the company can employ the same marginal cost and marginal revenue analysis which we found to be relevant for the industrial firm and public body in the section in Chapter 5 on marginal analysis.

First, the tea trading company might construct a marginal revenue curve, given the demand curve $D^B D^B$ of Figure 8.2. This is depicted in Figure 8.3 by the curve labeled *MR*. Note it is not a straight line, as it is in Figure 5.5. of Chapter 5. Recall that in Figure 5.5 the firm was not large enough to be able to influence the ruling market price. It was so small that it took the prevailing price as given and marketed as much output as it desired at that price. In this situation, the tea trading company is the only one marketing tea in region *B*. Therefore, it can and does influence price. It cannot market all the tea it desires at any given price. If it wishes to market more and more tea it needs to induce less and less eager demanders of tea to purchase that tea. It can do so only if it offers that tea at lower and lower prices. The demand curve of Figure 8.1 reflects this situation. However, in order to market more tea the company must accept a lower price not only on the additional pounds of tea it wishes to market but also on all the pounds of tea it could have sold at the higher price. (It could have received this higher price if it had decided not to market more tea.)

The net effect of marketing more tea is embodied in the marginal revenue curve which indicates the additional revenue from selling an additional pound of tea, taking into account the loss of revenue on all previously sold pounds of tea (the nonmarginal tea), because they must be sold at a somewhat lower price. To make the point more clearly, we construct Table 8.8. Column 2 presents the demand schedule for tea corresponding to the demand curve $D^B D^B$ of Figure 8.1. Column 3 presents the total revenue schedule, obtained by multiplying the price in column 1 by the corresponding quantity demanded in column 2. Column 4 presents the marginal revenue schedule, obtained by dividing the difference between the total revenue figures in any two consecutive rows (as listed in column 3) by the corresponding difference in quantity demanded for those two consecutive rows (as listed in column 2). When graphed, the marginal revenue schedule yields the marginal revenue curve of Figure 8.3.

Consider the derivation of the marginal cost curve of Figure 8.3. To the tea trading company, the supply curve of $S^B S^B$ of Figure 8.2 is an average cost

Price (1)	Demand (2)	Total Revenue (3)	Marginal Revenue (4)
$1.00	100	$100.00	
.90	130	117.00	.57
.80	170	136.00	.48
			.42
.70	230	161.00	
.60	330	198.00	.37
.50	530	265.00	.34
			.32
.45	740	333.00	

Table 8.8   Demand Schedule for Tea

curve, telling the tea company the unit cost it must incur. This covers both the price it must pay to obtain different quantities of tea from tea suppliers and the transport cost of getting the tea to the market in B. The $S^B S^B$ curve is derived as any industry supply curve (see the discussion in the appendix to Chapter 5). Now, because we already know how to construct a marginal cost curve from an average cost curve, we can derive from the $S^B S^B$ curve of Figure 8.2 the company's marginal cost curve graphed in Figure 8.3.

Figure 8.3 Equilibrium Price, Output, and Profits Under Monopoly Conditions

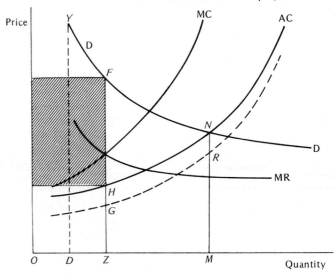

From the discussion in the marginal analysis section of Chapter 5, we know that the intersection of the marginal cost and marginal revenue curves defines the quantity that the company should supply to the market in order to maximize profits. From Figure 8.3 we see that this quantity is OZ. If the tea trading company were to market one more pound of tea, the additional costs would exceed the additional revenue. Hence, it would not pay the company to do so. Or, if it were to market one less pound of tea, the revenue foregone would be greater than cost savings. Again it would not pay to do so. Corresponding to the equilibrium quantity OZ is the average cost ZH (inclusive of transport cost) and the price ZF. Profits per pound of tea are HF; and total profits are shown by the striped rectangle of Figure 8.3.

We have now determined the equilibrium quantity that would be traded, namely OZ; the equilibrium price that the tea company receives, namely ZF; its equilibrium average cost (inclusive of transport cost), namely ZH; and the equilibrium price paid to tea suppliers in region A, namely ZG. We now evaluate this outcome. First, note that the quantity OZ is traded, rather than the quantity OM, which would be traded if conditions of free competition existed. Second, the suppliers of tea who are able to supply goods at the equilibrium price of ZG receive only that price ZG rather than the price MR, which they would receive if the trading were freely competitive. In this sense there is clear exploitation of tea suppliers (and/or local landowners who might have received as rent part or all of the surplus profits of tea producers). There is further exploitation, of a less dramatic character, in the sense that the tea suppliers who would have supplied the units corresponding to the quantity ZM no longer do so because there is no market for that tea. There is no opportunity for gainful employment in producing that quantity of tea.

From the standpoint of consumers there is also exploitation. The price paid by each consumer in region B is ZF. In the competitive situation the price would be only MN. Here the consumers who buy at price ZF are clearly exploited. Moreover, there is exploitation in the sense that consumers who would normally have been able to buy ZM quantity of tea, at prices they would be willing to pay, are no longer able to do so because of the higher monopoly price.

EXPLOITATION: COLONIALISM AND DISCRIMINATION

Figures 8.2 and 8.3 clearly demonstrate how monopoly elements not only restrict trade but lead to exploitation, benefiting the monopolist at the expense of consumers and suppliers. This type of monopoly analysis is particularly relevant for understanding one force militating, both in the past and present, against the development of backward regions. Grants of trade monopolies have frequently characterized relations between an industrialized mother nation and a colony, to the clear detriment of the colony.

Let us now illustrate other aspects of exploitation which have occurred in the past and which are still possible today. Consider the supplier, whether he be a tea or banana supplier or a supplier of some other commodity. We see from the $S^A S^A$ curve of Figure 8.1 that there are those who, in total, are willing to offer as much as OC of the commodity at the low price of CD. The price must be raised to obtain a greater quantity. A price increase induces existing suppliers to offer more of the good, and new suppliers to begin furnishing some of the commodity. To obtain a still greater quantity, still higher prices must be offered. At these higher prices, of course, the suppliers who would supply the quantity OC goods at the price CD now receive a surplus for these first OC units—that is, a price greater than necessary to induce them to supply. An exploitative monopolist may recognize this and at the same time be able to get around the normal operation of the market. He may offer to the first "low-cost" or efficient producers a price no greater than *CD* for their supply. If these producers have come to rely solely on the commercial sale of their crop for their means of livelihood, if the price *CD* allows them to subsist, and further, if they cannot sell their crop to any firm other than the monopolist, they are stuck. They must accept the price. Now, having obtained a supply *OC* at price *CD* (or less), the monopolist may then proceed to purchase the additional quantities that he desires, say *CE*, but only at the price *EF* necessary to induce suppliers to make additional quantities available. This may mean of course that some suppliers can get only the price *CD* on the first batch of goods they supply while they obtain the price *EF* on their second batch.

In short, the monopolist may not pay the supplier of the good a competitive price—such as *ZG* in Figure 8.3, the equilibrium supply price under nondiscriminating monopoly conditions. Rather, he pays that price which is necessary to induce the additional supply of one or more units. Except for the last units, this is always lower than *ZG*. In this way the monopolist discriminates among the units of supply and thus the suppliers. He assures for himself much, if not all, of any surplus that might be forthcoming to a supplier because of his greater ability to cultivate the soil and manage operations, or to the landowner because of the more productive soil he works or rents out.

This kind of discrimination can also take place in the labor market. The monopolist need not pay the same price to every laborer if his operation is the only one at which a laborer can obtain employment, or if all the employers collude rather than compete with each other. If he is able to determine the lowest wage that will induce a laborer to offer his services, he can pay just that wage and not the competitive wage. Of course, the monopolist may have evolved a situation that gives him still further control over supply conditions. For example, he may make it impossible for a laborer to shift from one employer to another. He may also offer credit at his store for the purchase of general supplies (food, clothing, etc.) while paying an inadequate wage. The laborer gets so far in debt to the monopolist that he (the laborer) loses all independence of action.

Note that in this last situation the monopolist may have been able to convert the normal upward-rising supply curve of labor to a flat line like the SS curve in Figure 8.4, where this curve indicates an unlimited supply of labor at a constant (subsistence) wage level. In this figure, we also construct a special type of a marginal revenue curve which reflects the additional revenues obtainable from the sale of the output of an additional worker, after payment of all costs other than labor. The intersection of this marginal revenue curve with the supply curve (which becomes the new marginal cost curve for the monopolist, because the cost of each additional laborer or man-hour is constant at the subsistence wage) yields the new equilibrium employment level, OM'. At this employment level, average revenue accruing to the monopolist per unit of labor hired, after payment of all costs other than labor, is $M'N'$ (N' lies on the AR—average revenue —curve). Profits per unit labor hired is thus $M'N' - M'K' = N'K'$. Total profits are then given by the rectangular striped area in Figure 8.4, such profits being significantly greater than the ones associated with a normal rising supply curve of labor.

Clearly this type of exploitation, and diverse variations of it, has marked not only colonialism but also the use of immigrant labor in the major metropolitan regions of the United States. In various forms it frequently occurs in the hiring

Figure 8.4   A Monopoly—Subsistence Wage Situation

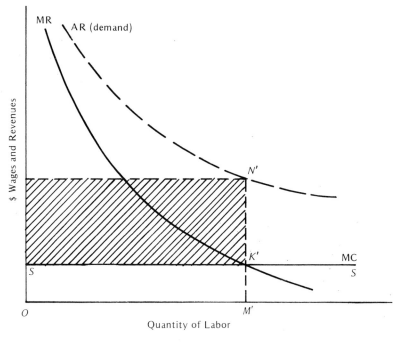

Quantity of Labor

of migrant farm and rural slum labor in the United States and many other parts of the world.

The monopolist may also discriminate with respect to consumers. Consider Figure 8.3, and assume that each consumer is interested in buying one and only one unit of product, say a refrigerator, from a monopolist. We note that the monopoly price is *ZF*. However, the demand curve shows that the most eager buyers would be willing to pay the price *DY*. If the monopolist recognizes this, he might charge a price of *DY* to his most eager buyers. But he is able to do this only if that part of his market represented by the most eager buyers is isolated from the part comprising less eager buyers. That is, it must not be possible for a less eager buyer to sell the unit he purchased at a low price, say *ZF*, to one of the most eager buyers for a higher price, say a price somewhat below *DY*. If that were possible, the most eager buyers would tend to purchase directly from less eager buyers, some of whom would be acting as middlemen or arbitrageurs. Thus, the discriminating monopolist must be able to register each unit of commodity sold, sell each unit under a contract that forbids resale, or use some other device to preclude resale; in practice this is often difficult to do, except where there are subgroups of consumers who are geographically isolated or at great distance from each other. Under such conditions, resale operations are not feasible because of high transportation cost. The monopolist can then discriminate, charging a higher price in one region where the consumers are generally more eager to buy than in another. Often, too, the monopolist sets aside one region in which he "dumps" the goods he cannot sell in his major profit-making markets (regions), acquiring some added revenue from sales at whatever price the goods can fetch.

Many variations of exploitation and discrimination have existed and continue to exist. They often explain the backwardness of a given region. Such exploitation and discrimination are present, as already indicated, in mother country-colony relations. They are also present in backward regions, in equally vicious form, where there is a high concentration of wealth and power in the hands of a few local landowners and political leaders who practice exploitation of the local population.

HUMAN MIGRATION: LONG RUN

Another very important spatial flow within the world's social system is the movement of people from one location to another. These movements can be long-run, middle-run or short-run—extending from lifetime movements as when a Ukranian Jew migrates to Israel, or daily movements as when a wealthy suburbanite commutes to his work on Wall Street. The great variety of movements suggests a variety of balances and imbalances in the world's settlement patterns that we wish to understand, particularly as they relate to social problems we wish to attack.

Let us begin with the long-run, lifetime migrations, which often are over considerable distances. In some cases, there is a pushing force; in others, a pulling force; and in still others, both. In the past, religious persecutions have been pushing forces, as with the migration of Pilgrims, Quakers, and many other religious groups to the United States. The lure of gold, silver, or uranium—that is, the search for a quick, easy fortune—has been a pulling force, as in the development of California and Alaska. The chance to farm at a level above subsistence, coupled with subsistence farming and religious persecution in the home region, represents a joint operation of pulling and pushing forces, as with the Irish and Russian migrations to the United States.

The diverse, noneconomic reasons for long-run migration have not been systematically and analytically examined by scholars. For example, political theory and analysis have not been cultivated sufficiently so that we could have anticipated the political crises in South Asia subsequent to British withdrawal from the Indian continent, and to have projected the major, long-run migrations resulting from a combination of religious and political factors. Accordingly, in this social-political-religious area, we cannot probe any more deeply than the intuitive historian possessing considerable acumen.

Predictions of Classical Trade Theory

When we examine economic forces leading to migration, we can say much more, analytically speaking. Suppose we consider two regions—a highly industrialized region in the United States, say New York City, and an underdeveloped region, say Southern United States or Southern Italy. Consider the labor market in each. We set down the demand and supply curve for labor in the developed region A in Figure 8.5. We measure quantity of labor along the horizontal and to the right, and wages along the vertical. We also set down these curves for the underdeveloped region, region B. However, in order to facilitate analysis we change our convention here. Instead of measuring quantity of labor from the origin O to the right, we now measure it (for the underdeveloped region B alone) from

Figure 8.5   Migration and Wage Determination in Two Regions

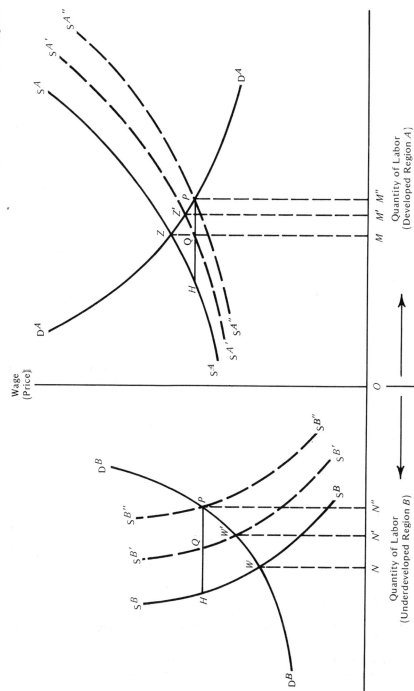

the origin O to the left. Thus the supply curve $S^B S^B$ slopes upward from the lower right to the upper left; and the demand curve $D^B D^B$ slopes downward from the upper right to the lower left. We thus obtain a back-to-back set of demand and supply curves. Note that the equilibrium wage in region A is MZ and in region B at the considerably lower level of NW. Now, classical trade theory usually assumes that complete (or almost complete) information about demand, supply, and prices in each market is generally available. It concludes that the labor in the underdeveloped region will eventually find out about the higher wage paid in the developed region and will tend to migrate to that region. Therefore, a situation will ultimately develop in which the wage differences would be eliminated, except for a proper allowance for migration costs.

Let us examine in some detail how the classical trade theory operates. Note that if the two regions were isolated, the equilibrium wage would be MZ in region A, the developed region, and NW in the underdeveloped region B. Because the wage rate in region A is considerably higher than the wage rate in region B, some of those in B who are paid the lower wage NW migrate to region A. In a sense, they increase the supply schedule of labor in A and lower the price there, while they decrease the supply schedule of labor in B and increase the price there. This migration theoretically continues as long as there is a discrepancy between the wage of region B and that of region A which exceeds a proper migration cost allowance.

For example, we may imagine that as much as HQ of labor has migrated from region B to region A. If this labor was available at all possible supply prices, the supply curve in region B would have shifted to the right to position $S^{B'} S^{B'}$, and the supply curve in region A would have shifted to the right to position $S^{A'} S^{A'}$. At these new positions, the equilibrium price in region B would have risen to $N'W'$ and the equilibrium price in region A would have fallen to $M'Z'$. Still the equilibrium price in A would be higher than that in B. This discrepancy would, theoretically speaking, induce still more migration from region B until HP amount of labor had migrated. At that level of long-run migration, the supply curve in B would have shifted to $S^{B''} S^{B''}$ and the supply curve in A would have shifted $S^{A''} S^{A''}$. The new equilibrium price would be $N''P$ in region B, and $M''P$ in region A. These prices are almost equal, their difference being the proper migration cost allowance. The net force for long-run migration would have been reduced to zero.

The above discussion illustrates the type of analysis derived from classical trade doctrine. It holds not only for the migration of labor but also for trade in any commodity. That is, if transportation costs are zero, the commodity will be exported from the lower-price region to the higher-price region, tending to raise the price in the lower-price region and lower the price in the higher-price region until the two are equal—or, if the transportation cost is positive, until the difference between the two decreases and finally equals the transportation cost. In this sense Figure 8.5 illustrates the basic trade principle that we developed in the previous section.

In considering the migration of labor, transportation costs include the costs of relocating a family, the losses incurred in selling property and other items in the home region at prices less than those at which these same items must be purchased in the new region, the wages that would have been earned during the period of migration, and similar factors. Hence, we do not expect the price of labor to be exactly equalized. However, the price of labor should be almost the same in the two regions because relocation and similar migration costs should be spread over the period of work remaining in the life of the migrant.

The Reality of Regional Poverty and Inequality: Why Classical Trade Theory Does Not Work

Classical theory tells us there is a strong tendency toward equalization of wages for a given type of labor in all regions. But when we observe reality, we find quite a different picture. We find major discrepancies in the wages paid the same kind of labor in different parts of the United States, the Soviet Union, and the world. We do not find that unskilled labor in India and Brazil migrates in volume to the United States, raising the level in India and depressing that in the United States until equality is approached. Nor do we find this to be the case for semi-skilled, professional, or Ph.D.-type labor.

If classical theory held, many of the problems of the world would not exist. There would be less inequality in per capita incomes. For example, in that part of the United States east of the Mississippi River, there would not be major discrepancies in income—the poor whites of Appalachia, the poverty-striken blacks of Louisiana, and others would have migrated in sufficient volume to the higher-paying areas in the Northeast and Great Lakes states. Equality would have been approached. In practice we know that this has not occurred. The absolute differences in per capita incomes in different regions and subregions continue to persist at approximately the same level despite minimum wage legislation in the United States.

Why has classical theory not worked? One major reason is the imperfection of markets. Imperfection takes on many aspects. One concerns the question of information. The poor white in Appalachia may not even know about New York City. If he does, he may not know that jobs for which he is qualified exist in New York City. If he does know that, he may not know that there is a difference in wage payments between New York and Appalachia. Even if he has all this information, he may not know where a job is or how to go about looking for a job. Even if he knows how to look for a job in New York City, he may not want to. He may not like New York City. He may not have friends there. He may find its way of life repelling. He may see all kinds of disadvantages and sacrifices involved in living in New York City. Still more, he may have no incentive to move. He may be satisfied with his lot and be quite happy, even though he suffers from malnutrition and is in poor health. In effect, in his own mind he may judge himself much better off in Appalachia than he would be, or than any person is, in New York City.

Moreover, we must consider various institutional barriers to migration that exist in the social system—for example, disdain for manner of dress, speech, and religious practice, as well as racial discrimination in employment, housing, and other aspects of life in the higher-price region.

It is not necessary to point out the many restrictions and exclusions that blacks, Puerto Ricans, Mexican-Americans, and women have encountered in the past in their search for gainful employment. We then realize that classical economics, at least in part, is in a wonderland of its own making. Social, cultural, and political forces, as well as economic forces, play an important role in determining migration. We cannot expect the economic forces to lead to equalization or anything approaching equalization. At best, only a fraction of the population in a low-wage region is sensitive to and has an opportunity to gain from the operation of economic forces. Therefore, we can expect major discrepancies in per capita earnings to persist among regions. Adam Smith's view that the operation of the market in a laissez-faire economy automatically leads to harmonious conditions for all participants does not hold in the world of reality, partly because freedom of exit and entry in all markets does not prevail, and partly because economic forces are only a subset of the total forces at play.

In this connection it is interesting to examine the findings of the many recent studies of migration undertaken in the United States.

We find, for example, that information plays a large role. Outmigration from one region to any other region J increases with increase in the number of friends and relatives in J, everything else being the same. For most people, friends and relatives are the major source of information concerning job opportunities and other advantages elsewhere. We also find some evidence that the degree of education influences the likelihood of migration. Those with very low income and little education have low propensity to migrate, partly because of lack of knowledge and partly because of lack of jobs for them in other regions. Clearly, of course, differences in wage rates for the same kind of job play a role in stimulating outmigration from the lower-wage to the higher-wage region when an opportunity for a job does exist in the latter. Also, differences in existing, potential, or expected rates of unemployment seem to encourage outmigration to a region with a lower existing, potential, or expected rate. As we might expect, the greater a region's stock of migrants (population subject to migration, which is partly determined by previous local birth and death rates), the greater the amount of outmigration, everything else being the same.

Also, the smaller the distance between a region of outmigration and any other region J, the greater the outmigration to that region, partly because transportation costs are lower, and partly because there are likely to be more friends and relatives in nearby than in far regions. They are there because of lower transportation costs in the past which affected their decision to migrate.

But again we must keep in mind, as noted in Chapter 3, that there are a number of different kinds of distances influencing one's decision to migrate or not to migrate—and if to migrate, where. Economic (transport cost) distance is only one. Others are political distances (for example, ideological differences), cultural distances (such as religious factors), and social distances (for example, differences in family and sex roles). Associated with these distances are social-political-cultural costs of movement. Often, too, the extent of outmigration from a region to any other region J depends on the number and kinds of opportunities in regions through which the migrants must pass; that is, the number of intervening opportunities that might induce them not to take advantage of an opportunity in the more distant region J.

Finally, we must mention differences in degree of urbanization as a major factor. The more urbanized the region of destination compared to a region of origin (and to other regions), the more attractive it is for potential outmigrants, at least up to a point. Frequently associated with greater urbanization are perceptions of more job opportunities, higher wage rates, better educational opportunities, fewer restraints on behavior, more cultural and social amenities, and more excitement and stimuli.

These and other findings attempt to "explain" migration. Note that they clearly indicate that although differences in wage rates and costs of migration influence migration, as classical theory states, there are many other factors at play. More important, the findings do not explain why there has not been more migration. That is, they do not explain why so many people decide not to migrate, either consciously or unconsciously (by not thinking about the matter). True, many of these people do not behave in a "rational" manner as we social scientists define rationality, which of course is based on our values. Or perhaps they simply behave in a rational manner according to their values (of which we social scientists know little).

This point, together with the findings that the extent and volume of migration are not in accord with classical trade theory, is fundamental for questions concerning economic development. We must constantly ask: Do the inhabitants of a backward region really want to migrate to better jobs, or do they want to be able to take on new jobs in their own region that might arise as a result of a development program? In answering this question social scientists in the upper-middle or high-income classes of a developed region are, to repeat, highly biased. We tend to project our value system onto others. We are incapable of sensing the values of those living under conditions of malnutrition and poor health. It is difficult, if at all possible, for us to imagine that the lot of some of these people can possibly be better than our own.

But the poor white in Appalachia may in fact be a happier person than the middle-income, or high-income white in New York City. That hypothesis has not been proven or disproven, nor will it ever be. The lot of the subsistence farmer in an underdeveloped region who has just enough food to live on and some housing, however poor, for shelter—but no air, water, sonic, visual, or other environmental pollution, and with no congestion and tension—may well be better than that of the New York resident with low infant mortality rate, high educational level and literacy, etc. Thus it is dangerous to assert that the population in the underdeveloped or backward region should be encouraged to migrate, or be offered development assistance, or anything of that sort. For similar reasons, it becomes dangerous to assert that, within the United States, the lot of the urban ghetto population is worse than that of white suburbanites.

Before concluding this section it may be wise to survey broadly certain aspects of world society in a somewhat different manner. The analysis of this section indicates that at least to some extent long-run human migration may be expected because of economic reasons, and that this migration is a force leading to a reduction in the discrepancies in per capita incomes among the different regions of the world. But this force toward reduction is more than offset by the forces leading toward greater discrepancies.

First, we must keep in mind that the different parts of the world are not equally endowed with either arable soil and grazing land capable of cultivation and yielding output or with coal, oil, ore, and other mineral resources that are sources of energy and raw materials to be processed into desired goods. Also, the different parts of the world are not equally endowed with river systems and waterways that can facilitate trade. Some have more than their fair share of mountains and deserts which impede development. It naturally follows that the people in these different regions do not find it equally easy to settle and to eke out an existence or to live in affluence.

But our thinking must go beyond this point. We see that in some regions having an abundance of resources (like many parts of the United States), much fruit is gathered from the land; much output is produced with the coal, ore, and oil resources; a large population can be supported; and further, if the population so desires, it can maintain a high material level of living. In contrast, there are other regions of the world, also with an abundance of resources, where the population has developed a society whose religious and cultural values place few if any restrictions on population growth. Here, high birth rates exist, leading to large numbers living at a subsistence level. High infant mortality, high death rates from malnutrition, and the like set limits to the growth of the population.

We may find still other parts of the world whose resource endowment is sparse. A cultural system that would tend to lead to higher material standards of living, were resources sufficiently abundant, may be present; but the sparse character of these resources compels the population to live at, or close to, subsistence.

Many liberal thinkers, particularly those schooled in the tradition of the laissez-faire, Adam Smith type of economics, believe that harmony basically underlies the process of development in all regions of the world when proper conditions, such as free competition, are present. Others place great stock in the role of democratic-type governments to ensure equality of opportunity for all and to eliminate the unequal distribution of wealth and discrepancies in per capita incomes. Such liberals may think it possible to approach equalization of material standards of living throughout the world by making financial assistance, equipment, and know-how available to the backward and sparsely endowed regions of the world, and by encouraging change in political institutions toward democratic-consensual forms. But such thinking flies in the face of historical reality. The historical record does not show any reduction in discrepancy in the material living standards among the peoples of the world. Rather, it points to increasing discrepancy.

This point is easily appreciated when one does some further analysis. For large parts of Asia, Latin America, and Africa we must conclude that the local population has a cultural system that leads to increases in population to the point where people live at the subsistence level and suffer from malnutrition. Starvation and high death rates are the effective checks on population growth. Moreover, the fraction of the world's population living in such a cultural system has not decreased over the last decades. It has increased.

In contrast, consider the population in cultures that have already embodied the tenets and characteristics of advanced urbanization-industrialization and within which there is developing an intense concern for environmental quality. These cultures tend to restrict population growth and lead their populations to invest large quantities of current output in the construction of new plants and equipment, in education and the like. Per head, both their capacity to produce output and their actual output increases. Accordingly, so does their material level of living, given current ethics on distribution of goods and the role of the market in allocating goods. As a consequence, the discrepancy between the material level of living of these cultures (and regions) and that of the cultures (and regions) of the subsistence populations becomes greater and greater. This outcome is almost certain, if not inevitable, provided drastic change or revolution in political, economic and social systems does not occur. Any large volume of human migration that might be provoked by major discrepancies between wages paid in different regions (such as we have analyzed in this section) will act at most to mitigate the increase in the discrepancy. It will be more than offset by the different savings, investment, consumption habits, and population growth patterns of various regions of the world.

This Malthusian type of conclusion is not necessarily a pessimistic one. It is so only if the analyst also assumes that those with the highest material levels of living or those with moderate levels of living are better off than those whose level is at or slightly above the subsistence level. We have already concluded that employing material level of living, longevity, or nutritional standards as a yardstick of happiness and true social welfare is dangerous. We will say more about "true social welfare" in later chapters of this text.

A DIGRESSION ON ENVIRONMENTAL QUALITY, EXPORT TRADE, AND REGIONAL DEVELOPMENT

As we well know, undesirable commodities such as air, water, and sonic pollutants are generated as a result of (1) activities going on at a particular location (for instance, production within a factory or heating within a house); and (2) movement of people and goods over space by various transportation modes. Management of environmental quality requires that we manage the way things are both produced and consumed and the way people and goods are moved over space. Such management, however, is not achieved easily. Transportation functions are complexly woven into the fabric of society. We have already seen that underdeveloped economies depend on the increase of industrial exports in order to reduce unemployment and raise per capita income; they are automatically dependent on the shipment of those export goods by some transportation mode. The regulation of that transportation mode—say by standards putting a ceiling on the kinds and amounts of air pollutants it may emit or on the decibels of sound it may generate—affects the cost of shipment from the region of export to the region of imports. Hence, the quantity that it can export is affected. We can see this if we look at Figure 8.6. There we reproduce from Figure 8.1 a typical demand curve of the region of import and a typical supply curve of the region of export. In Figure 8.2 we saw that the equilibrium output was *OM*. The equilibrium price was *MN* in the receiving region and *MR* in the exporting region, the difference being the transportation cost. If the transportation cost via a particular mode rises because of regulation, say from *NR* to *N'R'*, then clearly the spread between the two equilibrium prices must be greater. In Figure 8.6 we see that this is possible only if there is both an increase (to *MN'*) in equilibrium price to consumers in the market of the import region and a decrease in equilibrium price (to *M'R'*) to producers in the export region. Additionally, we note that the equilibrium quantity of goods traded is reduced to *OM'*.

If the export region depended on the increase of exports to combat unemployment, we see that the regulation of transportation interferes with the achievement of this goal, because such regulation leads to decreases in the equilibrium level of exports. Likewise, consider a poor exporting region within an industrialized nation like the United States, which relies on assistance from various federal welfare programs when high local unemployment exists. In this case, the regulation of transportation which decreases export trade tends to lead to an increase in federal welfare expenditures, and thus in the size of the federal budget and the amount of taxes all people in all regions must pay.

Figure 8.6   Effect on Equilibrium Position of Pollution Regulations on Transportation

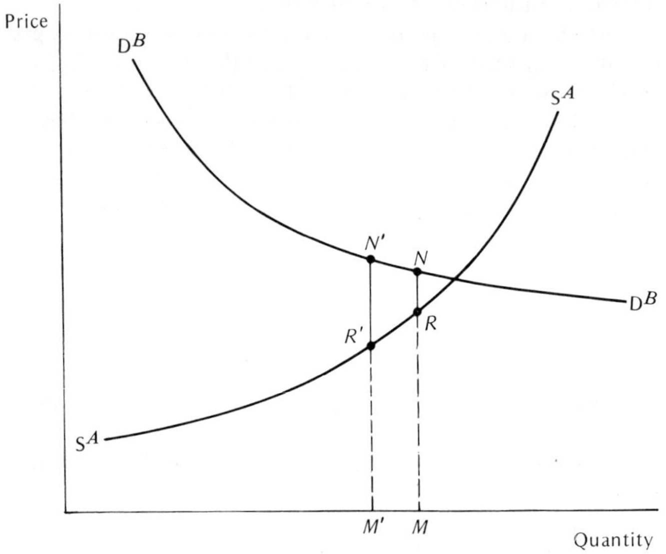

Regulating the transportation mode carrying export goods also results in higher prices in the import region. Consumers there must pay higher prices for import goods. Those who choose to consume the same quantity of the import good at the higher price have less income to spend on other goods. This means that the output of other goods declines, and with it the number of jobs associated with the production of this output. Thus the economic welfare of the importing region may be adversely affected, as well as the economic welfare of the whole society, because in general there are fewer goods available for consumption. On the other hand, there is less pollution as a consequence of regulation.

POPULATION MOVEMENT (MIGRATION): SHORT-RUN

With some perspective on the forces controlling long-run migration of population and, therefore, some insight into some of the world's problems and our ability to cope with them, we now turn to *short-run* migration—that is, short-run population movement. But before doing so, let us say a few words about *middle-run* migration.

Middle-run migration may be defined as that movement of population which takes place for a period of more than a season but less than a lifetime. Included here is the movement of those who ultimately migrate, say to a capital city like New York City or Paris, but who do so in two or more steps. For example, people might migrate from a rural area, staying several years in a small town. Then they migrate from the small town to a middle-sized town. Finally they migrate from the middle-sized town to a large metropolis. This step-by-step migration does not involve basic forces different from those we have already discussed with respect to long-run migration. The forces are frequently the push and pull of economic factors, such as the attraction of higher-paying jobs. Hence, we will not say anything additional about step-by-step migration—we will just recognize its existence.

Another type of middle-run migration is that associated with the movement of population because of shift in occupation, or position in the hierarchical structure of a particular enterprise or in the structure of society as a whole. Here we include migration associated with people moving up the administrative ladders of their companies and therefore shifting from one location to another because the jobs to which they are successively assigned are at different locations. This is the case in large companies such as General Electric, United States Steel Corporation, General Motors, and the like. Such migration also takes place outside private enterprise. A person who chooses a career as an administrator or in an educational system must be ready to shift, for example, from a position of high school principal in a small town to one in a large town to one in a metropolitan area. He may then move to the position of assistant superintendent of a regional public school system covering several counties in a lightly urbanized region, and finally to a position of administrator of a metropolitan system. Again, this migration is basically tied to economic opportunity, and is explainable in terms of location theory, trade theory, and other economic analyses which we have begun to develop. We do not have much more to say about this and a host of other forms of middle-run migration.

We now wish to consider short-run migrations. These cover journeys to work (commuting), journeys to shopping centers, journeys to schools and the sites of other cultural activities, and other daily and weekly trips of a population. We also include in short-run migration the seasonal migration largely associated with the recreational activities of an urbanized-industrialized society like the United States. During vacation periods and weekends, there are large movements of population between permanent residences and temporary ones at desirable recreational sites. We could discuss this type of movement at some length by itself. However, we shall not do so because the problems that arise here are mostly the same as those we confront in discussing other kinds of short-run migration.

In Chapter 3 we began to describe and analyze short-run population movement. We discussed how the volume of any type of traffic generally tends to fall off as the distance between the originating point and terminating point increases. We have already pointed up the importance of being able to forecast volume of traffic, especially by type of traffic, for effective transportation planning—for example, doing a good job in constructing a highway system for a normal metropolitan region that is expanding at a significant rate into its hinterland. We also have indicated how the study of short-run population movements can help expose the nature of basic social problems—for example, racial discrimination. Such study is essential also for an effective attack on air-pollution problems, and in general raising the quality of our urban and rural life.

In Chapter 3 we also suggested that one of the most effective tools for studying short-run population movement is the gravity model. We discussed its usefulness in describing the expected pattern of total daily trips of a population, or journey-to-work trips, or other particular types of trips. Often it can provide a reference framework, deviations from which provide us with new insight into social problems. We now wish to probe more deeply into these potentials.

The Gravity Model Once Again

To begin, let us make a specific application of the gravity model. Suppose we are planning a particular industrial district with 10,000 employees. We have in mind the housing requirements of these employees. To meet our requirements we consider utilizing existing vacant housing that is scattered in subareas, constructing new housing in subareas where underdeveloped land exists, or tearing down dilapidated houses. Suppose further that we wish to estimate the amount of new traffic that will be generated and its contribution to the existing stock of pollution. We know at the one extreme that the 10,000 new employees will not distribute themselves evenly over the commuting area distance, which is roughly 50 miles. At the other extreme, we know that they will not live in housing next to the industrial district, were 10,000 new homes to be constructed there. We know that there will be a falling-off effect; that is, as we go along any transportation route, we expect decreasing density of employees' residences with increased distance from the industrial district. We expect this falling-off effect to be generally comparable to that found in empirical studies of other metropolitan regions or urban industrial districts, particularly if all land is undeveloped.

We cannot argue this way, however. The land available for new development or housing is spread erratically and not evenly throughout metropolitan regions. If we go along one radial road where all land is usefully developed and where the existing structures are in great demand, we do not expect to find many new employees along this radial, although the distribution will be consistent with a falling-off effect. In contrast, if we go along another radial where there has been very little development and where land is relatively idle, though it has equally desirable attributes, we predict a much higher density of settlement of new employees along it. Again, there is a falling-off effect. This effect, however, would be different from the falling-off effect along the first radial.

Now, we want to set down our expectations of density and traffic with a set of numbers. To do so we must define the situation in terms of a relevant concept of mass—namely, the capacity of any subarea to provide housing for the 10,000 employees. For the moment, we do not consider housing for administrative officials or other specialized personnel. We concentrate on housing for production workers whose income is about \$8,000 to \$10,000 per year. We divide the metropolitan region into relevant subareas, assigning to each subarea a mass representing ability or capacity to produce or make available housing for the production employees. We consider the distance from each subarea to the industrial district, and then allocate housing units (residences) among the subareas in accord with a set of ratios developed below.

Mathematically speaking, let M_j be the mass of any subarea j. Let its effective distance, measured as a combination of transportation time and cost, be d_j. Then the relevant ratio for that subarea (for a simple gravity model) is M_j divided by d_j. When we consider fifty subareas, we have fifty such ratios—the pie is to be divided among these areas according to their ratios. We add all these ratios together to get:

$$\frac{M_1}{d_1} + \frac{M_2}{d_2} + ... + \frac{M_j}{d_j} + ... + \frac{M_{50}}{d_{50}} = \sum_{i=1}^{50} \frac{M_i}{d_i}.$$

We take the ratio of each subarea ratio (M_j divided by d_j) over the sum of all the ratios, i.e., $\dfrac{M_j}{d_j} \Big/ \Sigma \dfrac{M_i}{d_i}$. This gives us a simple method for estimating the fraction of the 10,000 employees who will eventually reside in subarea j. We now wish to consider possible improvements of this simple method.

We have already discussed the difficulty of measuring mass. The relevant mass of an area is reflected not only in its physical ability to provide housing (existing, rehabilitated, and new) for the employees but also in its other attributes —quality of shopping facilities, schools, police and fire service, environment, and taxes. Moreover, as we shall state below, this mass may be very large for a white population, but very low for a black population because of realty practices.

Another problem is the measurement of distance. We are not certain how to measure it. What index of transportation cost and time should be used? This, of course, is related to such factors as the presence of other kinds of traffic on the radials, and current and future capacity of these radials. (We have a dilemma, because in the long run the capacity of any radial largely depends on the demand for use of that radial by the population moving along it. But in this case, we are implying that the population that will move along any radial in the long run is a function of its capacity. This is a chicken and egg problem.)

Also, should not distance be raised to some power? There is much disagreement among regional scientists in this regard, and each has his own pet exponent.

Moreover, although the gravity model formulation involving an inverse relationship with distance is very useful for sharpening our thinking, many say it should be discarded in favor of some other model, one that uses a different mathematical formula and that may also appear to be more reasonable.

We do not purport here to choose among the various models that might get at the transportation flow. We are simply saying that certain available models, when combined with good thinking, allow us to attack the transportation problem. They allow us to make different kinds of projections about different kinds of trips over a network of certain highways, leading to certain results. After these projections are made, we can then make planning suggestions depending on the parameters we think are relevant. The important thing is to recognize that we are better off carrying out our thinking and analysis within some framework or with a given model. This is true whether they are simple or highly sophisticated. (The highly sophisticated ones introduce price of housing, price of land, residential quality, level of municipal services, accessibility to shopping centers and other sites (in addition to the job site), and various other factors to explain or project the location of behaving units in an urban region.)

Now let us consider another aspect of the study of short-run human migrations. This aspect is important to recognize in trying to get at some of the basic factors affecting our diverse social problems. It is concerned with opportunities for minority groups.

The relevant mass of the industrial district itself may not be the same for the several social problems we may wish to study. In the example above we assumed there would be 10,000 production employees in an industrial district. We assumed that these jobs would be available to the whole population. But this might not be the case. The 10,000 jobs might be a relevant figure for the majority population, but not for Mexican-Americans, Puerto Ricans, or blacks. For them, the relevant mass would be much smaller, depending upon the extent of formal and informal racial discrimination.

Consider the distance variable. A team of engineers and economists might be able to make some crude but good estimates of time- and dollar-cost distance that might be relevant for the subpopulation to which they belong. But once again these estimates may not be relevant for minority groups. Going through strange neighborhoods and unfamiliar territory might be psychologically difficult. For example, a black might avoid a road if it goes through a wealthy suburb. This section of the road may represent an insurmountable barrier socially and emotionally to the minority worker. (And, of course, the same may hold for middle-income whites when a road traverses a ghetto area.) Put in other words, the research analyst to a planning commission might well estimate a distance—but that distance might not in fact reflect the relevant variable; namely, the distance as perceived by a worker of the minority group.

We also recognize that the use of a gravity model pertains to a single point of time. Over time the relevant masses and distances change. Again, for a minority-group worker the mass might increase as discrimination decreases or the distance of separation might decrease as discrimination decreases. On the other hand, the distance might increase because of increasing pressure within a minority group to achieve cohesiveness and greater solidarity as its value structure changes.

In addition, we must bear in mind that different income, ethnic, and racial groups perceive physical environment quite differently. For example, a member of one group may feel that once you have heard one birdcall, you have heard them all. One tends to get quite distinct distributions and clusterings of these groups. There are different sensitivities to the density variable, the noise variable, and the light variable. There are different values placed on an hour of one's time. And so forth. As a result, the perception of the available housing in each subarea is different, and we get quite different views of the masses in these subareas, each group assigning a different mass to any particular subarea.

Consequently, it is impossible to use the gravity model or any similar model of population flow and population location without qualification. Ideally, we should modify the model for each possible set of conditions that might emerge, for each kind of subpopulation that exists, and for each type of trip. At the same time, we should keep in mind the total picture and the need to achieve consistency in terms of the total picture.

Also, we want to stress again the usefulness of the gravity model in focusing on the relevance of certain variables, or in testing a hypothesis about the relevance of certain variables. As an example, consider some facility that is equally available to all populations. We might observe, however, that a majority population utilizes it twice as frequently as a minority population. If, generally speaking, the majority population and the minority population are similarly distributed, then one might hypothesize that the minority population perceives the distance as greater. Hence, sociological and psychological distance is involved; and a bold investigator might try to develop quantitative estimates of it.

Or suppose there is some transport route that is normally used by majority and minority groups for journey-to-work trips. Suppose this transport route also extends to a cultural facility or an educational complex. Then if per capita use, after adjustment for other variables, is higher for the majority than minority population, we must assume that the minority group's perception of the mass of the facility is much smaller.

Commuting and Environmental Management

The preceding discussion illustrates one strand of interrelationship. Consider another. We all know that daily commuting by automobile is a major source of air pollution. There are various ways to reduce substantially the pollution generated by this source. In each of these ways the gravity model turns out to be a useful tool.

One simple and direct way is to make the cost per trip mile much higher. We may levy an excessive tax (federal, state, or local) on a gallon of gasoline and make automobile travel so expensive that few people can afford it. Most people would be forced to use urban mass transit. Because this mode of transportation is much less expensive than automotive transit, the overall cost of transportation to society would be significantly reduced. However, this approach puts the burden of change on the middle- and low-income groups and can well be viewed as inequitable. Its political feasibility is also questionable, because it involves such a drastic change in consumption patterns. However, if this approach were adopted, the transport cost distance for travel via the automotive mode between any two subareas j and k would be substantially increased. By putting into the denominator of the gravity model this greater transport cost distance (see p. 45 of Chapter 3), we could project significant decreases in automotive traffic over all distances.

Another approach is to require automobile manufacturers to modify the engine in such a way that pollution emissions per car mile are substantially reduced. This approach has been adopted by the Environmental Protection Agency. Because producers are required to develop a technically more elaborate engine, there will be an increase in the cost of the automobile. The burden again tends to fall more on the low- and middle-income population than on the high-income population. The cost of automobile travel becomes higher, and the number of cars produced and consumed is substantially reduced. Again the transportation cost or the economic distance increases and we can use the gravity model for making projections of new traffic volume.

Another alternative is to affect the spatial distribution of industry and people via a differential regulation. This is a policy that has not been followed and should be followed. In differential regulation it is not necessary to regulate a factory operating in an isolated region and producing just small amounts of air pollutants. There is no need to force it to adopt the most advanced and costly techniques. On the other hand, it is important to impose the highest standards possible on the same kind of factory in the major metropolitan regions, where the probability of crisis conditions is high. Such differential emission regulation is one way of attacking the problem. Note that its impact is to encourage more industries to expand and relocate in areas where there is considerable excess and unused capacity to absorb pollutants.

Such regulations mean that not only does the industry relocate, taking with it its output of pollutants, but also the chief breadwinners (and their families) who work in the industry. Thus, automotive and house-heating pollution are also reduced in the region of exodus.

Another possibility, of course, is to regulate both industries and households at their locations. Then the cost of operation of an industry is higher—and part or all of the increase in the cost of its product may be passed on to consumers. In a similar manner, the cost of operation of a residence is higher. In both these cases, households tend to have less income to spend for other things. They are, however, forced to consume (be exposed to) less pollutants.

Another possibility is to bring industry closer to the location of residences, thereby reducing journey-to-work travel and the pollution associated with it. Still another possibility is to bring workers closer to industry. Still other possibilities are to plan new towns or rehabilitate parts of existing cities so that the journey-to-work-distance is reduced. Walking to and from work, bicycling, and the use of other modes of travel that do not generate pollutants can be encouraged.

Thus, we see that there are a variety of ways of managing the environment by both direct and indirect regulation of daily trip patterns of population and daily commodity movements. This is why it is important to study the gravity and other models that can increase our understanding of short-run population movements and their potential for change.

However, they must be used with assumptions made explicit and variables carefully defined. And they must be modified to reflect changing conditions, specifically by changing weights, masses, and other relevant parameters.

MONEY AND CAPITAL FLOW: THE MIGRATION OF CAPITAL FUNDS

In addition to population flow and commodity flow, it is vital in our present world system to consider the flow of capital funds. Specifically, we refer to the gold and currency of one region which can be exchanged for currency of other regions in order to purchase capital goods and other productive resources in these regions. We are aware of the flow of money from, say, the Polish community in Chicago to relatives and friends in Poland, as a process of sharing income and wealth within the family. To some extent remittances of this sort are important, but not important enough for thorough discussion here. Nor are other remittances or transfers of a unilateral character significant at this point.

What is more important for us is that flow of purchasing power which takes place when for speculative and security purposes, individuals or enterprises decide to shift their wealth from one region to another—for example, when U.S. dollars are sold for German marks (by either U.S. or non-U.S. behaving units) and deposited in the banks of still other nations and regions, such as Switzerland. To study this problem, however, would lead us into a highly technical analysis of the balance-of-payments problem, which is not appropriate for an introductory text.

Most important is that flow of capital funds which takes place when the owners of capital funds in one region judge that the most profitable investments for their funds are in other regions. As noted in Chapter 3, New England capitalists have historically invested large sums of money in other parts of the United States and Canada. So have British capitalists. Also, large corporations in the United States frequently take undistributed profits and invest them in plants and equipment in Peru, Kuwait, France, and numerous other countries of the world, as do corporations in Japan, West Germany, and other nations.

From a social standpoint, such flows of capital funds can be desirable, everything else being the same. They can be desirable if consumer demand (which, after all, represents the votes of consumers on the economic market) is more profitably served by production establishments in a country other than one's own. Such a situation might exist if a firm can operate at lower costs in a foreign country and can deliver goods to your market at a lower price than a plant in your own country can. As a consumer you then face a lower price and can purchase more of this and other goods with your income. From this standpoint, which is one of efficiency, such a flow of capital is very desirable. It is consistent with the decision to undertake the construction and operation of a plant at the least-cost location, where the required capital comes from outside the region of location.

To a large extent the simple location theory in Chapter 6 explains the multi-regional or spatial pattern of investment. When the spatial pattern of investment is compared with the spatial pattern of funds available for investment, we can explain in large part the spatial flow of such funds.

However, a number of problems crop up because everything else is not the same. Consider the situation from the standpoint of the region of investment. First, if the investments in a region are made by foreign capitalists, then the profits from production may flow out of the region. They go to capitalists residing in other regions, who then make decisions as to their subsequent use. But if the region of investment and production is a low-income region, it might be more desirable for profits to be retained in this region. In this way the local demand in the region of production might be built up. In time, it might be able to support a variety of local service activities and other infrastructure which can help spark development.

Beyond draining profits from an area, absentee ownership, as already indicated, can lead to less awareness of and sensitivity to the needs and working conditions of the local population. This can result in undesirable exploitation.

Further, all kinds of balance-of-payment problems can arise. We already know that when a United States capitalist wants to invest in another country, he must sell his dollars on the money market for the currency of this country. The increased supply of dollars on the market tends, according to the law of supply and demand, to depress the price of dollars and concomitantly raise the price of the currency of the country in which the U.S. capitalist wishes to invest. When too many American capitalists want to invest in foreign countries, their demand for the currency of these countries leads to a decrease in the price of the United States dollar relative to the currencies of these other countries. That is, the dollar depreciates, leading to numerous problems. The fact that the United States dollar can no longer be regarded as a Rock of Gibraltar, as it was in the Fifties and Sixties, introduces undesirable uncertainties into economic relationships between trading countries. Many have regarded the dollar as a secure factor in an insecure world, have carried on many transactions with each other in terms of it, and have held dollars as a stock of wealth whose value would never diminish and always could be immediately realized. Other stable noneconomic relationships may be upset by a depreciating dollar, which in turn may have still other undesirable economic and noneconomic repercussions.

On the other hand, we must recognize that capital does not exist in many parts of the world. There is no means by which a local population can go out and buy necessary equipment from advanced industrial countries, or construct a facility to supply power necessary for the operation of such equipment. Hence there is a certain crucial dependence on foreign capital that cannot be ignored. This, of course, suggests a positive role for economic assistance or foreign aid. Ideally, economic assistance would be tied to a world government structure such as the United Nations. But there are at least two problems associated with the administration of foreign aid by such a world authority. One concerns the political problem within that authority. It is difficult to achieve an allocation of funds for economic assistance which reflects the direct needs of underdeveloped countries rather than the self-interest of the voting nations, or coalitions of voting nations. The second problem stems from the fact that the United Nations itself must obtain funds from supporting nations. The supporting nations may not be very generous when making available capital indirectly to countries through the United Nations, because each supporting nation knows that the U.N.'s allocation will in all probability not correspond to the allocation in the best interest of the supporting nation.

In these respects, then, foreign aid via a world government has severe limitations. But so does direct foreign aid from a big power. It allows the big power to have an influence on both the economic and political development of the dependent world region. Often the outcome is benign colonialism. Also, the region receiving the financial assistance may become accustomed to receiving aid, and may not vigorously attempt to develop local savings and investment habits that can lead in time to independence from the standpoint of capital supply.

Thus, there is no simple answer to the question of what is a desirable spatial pattern of capital flow. A whole series of factors are relevant: the degree to which unit costs are reduced and the welfare of consumers increased, the extent to which profits remain in or leave the region of production, the particular situation on the foreign exchange market, the particular structure of world government and its capability of administering economic assistance, the particular culture of the receiving nation and its ability to forge ahead on its own, the sense of impersonality and lack of local visibility that might result from foreign private investment, etc. All these and many others must be taken into account in determining the best spatial capital flow pattern.

THE FLOW OF IDEAS: COMMUNICATIONS OVER SPACE

In addition to people, goods, and money, ideas flow. They flow when interaction and exchange take place involving individuals acting either as independent units or on the behalf of groups and institutions. Unfortunately, this very important area of study has been sorely neglected. We know too little about it and cannot be as rigorous in examining the flow of ideas as we can be in examining the flow of goods, capital, and people.

First, consider the flow of know-how or knowledge, including technology. Here some good empirical studies have been undertaken—especially in terms of a diffusion process over space. These studies confirm the fact that distance acts as a friction or resistance which must be overcome if an idea is to flow. There is a cost of transportation or transmission. Specifically, the studies of the spatial diffusion of innovation indicate that, at any point of time, the probability of an individual adopting an innovation falls off with the increase in his distance from the point where he can acquire the know-how or where the know-how is generated in the form of a communication.

We also know that messages via telephone, telegrams, cables, and letters have a tendency to fall off with distance—again suggesting that some variation of the gravity model is relevant. On the other hand, a bias may be involved. The people to whom one sends telegrams, writes letters, or contacts by telephone are friends, relatives, and others who are culturally close. But we have already observed that the migration of these friends, relatives, and other close people tends to decrease with distance from the point of origin. Thus, the number of one's friends, relatives, and close people at a given location tends to fall off with increased distance between that location and one's residence. However, after correction for this bias, the falling-off effect with distance still shows up clearly in personal communications.

In studying the flow of ideas and communications, subtle forms of distance are frequently relevant. Consider the elite of the world, many of whom are among the key decision makers. By and large they have been educated at the few distinguished universities of the world, such as Oxford, Cambridge, Harvard, and the Sorbonne. By being closely associated with each other during their period of education, the elite have often become close socially and culturally. When they finish their education and return to their different parts of the world, physical or economic distance is no longer a good measure of their separation. Nor are the cultural and psychological distances that exist between their native societies. They continue to interact, at a more intense level than physical distance or cultural distance might suggest, and effectively hasten or facilitate the diffusion of ideas concerning economics, politics, music, art, religion, and other matters. Thus, when the usual forms of distance are discussed, it becomes very important to know as well the frequency and intensity of elite interactions and exchanges—interactions and exchanges that are so critical for world development and organization. This is a key to understanding basic problems of communication between the Soviet leaders and Western leaders, Asian and African leaders, African and Western leaders, and Asian and Western leaders.

In this connection a tool called a sociometric matrix is useful. We present one on interactions (communications) in Table 8.9. Along the rows is listed each

Table 8.9   An Interactions (Communications) Matrix

	1	*2*	*3*	. . .	*m−2*	*m−1*	*m*
1	–	10	6	. . .	1	1	0
2	9	–	6	. . .	1	0	1
3	8	7	–	. . .	1	0	0
.	.	.	.		.	.	.
.	.	.	.		.	.	.
.	.	.	.		.	.	.
m−2	2	0	0	. . .	–	4	5
m−1	1	1	0	. . .	4	–	6
m	0	2	1	. . .	3	7	–

person in a population (or group). Each person is also listed, in the same order, along the columns. In each cell we list the number of interactions between the person of that row and the person at the head of the column. We thus obtain some notion of the frequency of interaction between different pairs and some notion of the effective distance of each individual from every other one. In this sociometric matrix, we can substitute for each interaction a value that weights the importance of the interaction. We then obtain the weighted intensity of interactions between any pair of individuals, and thus a more appropriate measure of effective distance separating them.

The sociometric matrix, like the gravity model, can provide useful insights into the interaction of individuals in elites or other groups. For example in Table 8.9 persons 1, 2, and 3 interact much more with each other than with persons m, m-1, and m-2. They are closer to one another than to the others. They may be the political elite, or foreign ministers of common market countries, or the very wealthy, or next-door neighbors, or members of the subpopulation of those individuals holding Ph.D.'s. Also, persons m, m—1, and m—2 have more interactions with each other than with persons 1, 2, and 3, although they do not interact with each other as intensely as do 1, 2, and 3. They may be average citizens who live in the same community, or low-income residents of a ghetto, or members of an ethnic group, or assembly workers in a Ford production plant. Thus, the data of a table such as Table 8.9 provide are another set to complement economic, travel, and other data we have already considered for use. They also allow us to test hypotheses, such as who influences whom, and suggest the direct and indirect paths of influence.

We must further consider: (1) the relative decline in the cost of communications that can be forecast from technological innovations already on hand; (2) the exchange of ideas stemming from airplane, railroad, and automobile trips; (c) the dissemination of information through newspapers (in particular worldwide newspapers like *The New York Times* and the *International Herald-Tribune*), radio and satellite communication, research papers, reports and books, word of mouth, rumor and gossip, schools and other educational institutions, churches, political groups, social clubs, professional associations, international student organizations, and a host of other social, political, and economic institutions. All are important for studying the flow of ideas.

However, there are more subtle relationships to the study of the flow of ideas than just discussed. To perceive this, we might make certain comparisons with flows of commodities. As we pointed out in Chapters 6 and 7, there are heavy, bulky commodities and some perishable commodities which cannot be shipped long distances. Manufactured ice is an ideal illustration; others include gravel and sand, limestone, and cement. These are cheap commodities with relatively high transportation costs. If they are shipped over long distances they become so expensive that no one wants to buy them. For example, one does not think of a bottle of Coca-Cola being manufactured in San Francisco and shipped to New York City.

On the other hand, there are many other manufactured commodities for which transportation costs are a very small part of the total costs. Diamonds are an excellent example, toothpaste is another, and high-quality cameras are still another. Transportation costs from any point of production throughout the nation are so small that the sale of a unit of commodity in any region of the nation yields pretty much the same profit.

Then we can think of various commodities in between, which can effectively absorb the transportation cost of 200 to 500 miles, but nothing greater. In fact, if one examines the extent of the market area of different commodities, one finds a continuum from highly localized items like those sold at retail in a corner grocery store or barber shop, to those specialized goods such as transistor devices or diamonds which can be shipped all over the world.

In parallel fashion, we can think of ideas and their diffusion and transmission. If there were only one school at which reading, writing, and arithmetic were taught and to which all children of the nation had to come, the transmission of information would involve excessively high transportation costs. The process would be like distributing manufactured ice to all parts of the United States from a central point like Chicago, in an age (say 1890) when we did not have refrigerated railroad cars or aircraft. That is, the flows of certain ideas must remain in highly restricted markets or areas if they are to be effected. Thus, we find primary schools all over the United States in a small range of sizes, corresponding to the ice dealers of the 1890s.

When it comes to ideas at another level of specialization, say that of a secondary school, we have a larger service area over which ideas and knowledge are transmitted. With a community college we have still a larger area, and so forth, until we come to the highly specialized department of a university whose market and service area is worldwide. We should think of a communication transmission structure as one involving a continuum of different markets, corresponding to different specializations in the diffusion of information. We will discuss this structure somewhat further in Chapter 12.

THE FLOW OF INTANGIBLE, NONECONOMIC COMMODITIES

Before closing this chapter we should say a few words about flows of certain noneconomic commodities which, like ideas, are intangible. An idea is something represented by a relationship of symbols in an individual's mind—it has no material substance. Likewise, certain commodities which we have designated c-power, c-respect, c-solidarity, c-rectitude, c-well-being, c-skill, c-enlightenment, and c-affection (see p. 15) are commodities that have no material substance.[1] They cannot be defined as Grade A meat can be; yet a considerable amount of social welfare in our advanced society is dependent on the exchange and flow of these commodities and the ideas associated with them.

Consider the commodity political power, or just c-power. For the moment assume we have an ideal democracy wherein each representative duly elected by his constituency truly represents the interests of that constituency. When he goes to Washington, each such representative has a stock of political power, represented by the authority vested in him by his constituency. In Washington, he meets with other representatives and exchanges his political power with them. For example, let there be two issues or programs. The first program is of critical importance to the constituency of the first representative. The second program is of critical importance to the constituency of the second representative. It is quite common and natural to expect the first representative to exchange his vote

---

[1] Again, for definitions of these commodities, see W. Isard et al., *General Theory: Social, Political, Economic and Regional* (Cambridge: M.I.T. Press, 1969), Chapter 12.

(power) on the second program for the vote (power) of the second representative with regard to the first program. Thus, the representative from the agricultural state supports a low-income housing program deemed important by a representative from a major metropolitan region in exchange for that representative's vote for a program that fixes agricultural prices. What we have, in effect, are two flows of power (through the vote)—from the representative of the agricultural state to the representative of the metropolitan region, and vice versa.

Consider the flow of another intangible commodity. Imagine an international competition, whether it be the Olympics, or tennis or chess championships. World society is organized in such a way that it is considered desirable to maintain certain kinds of competition. They are characterized by a lack of violence and the undesirable aspects associated with it; inputs by each participant of time, labor, and other items; and an outcome, primarily of c-prestige and c-respect. When a country wins the Olympics, considerable c-respect flows to it from groups and individuals within all other countries. These flows of an intangible commodity play a great role in certain social activities and in achieving stability, friendliness, and compatibility in world society.

Again, when a scientist from some country receives a Nobel prize or the Stalin Peace Prize, there are flows of intangible commodities like c-respect and c-prestige to that person. The possibility of receiving such c-respect and c-prestige is, of course, a consideration in the effort and other resources each research scholar devotes to his work.

Compensation for work—partly with salary and partly with reward of intangible commodities—is much more common than is recognized. The structure and functioning of religious organizations is highly dependent upon the flow of c-rectitude. For example, within the hierarchial structure of the Roman Catholic Church, there are tremendously large flows of c-respect and c-rectitude in and out of the Vatican City, from and to all second-order nodes, third-order nodes, fourth-order nodes (see Chapter 12).

The organization of many nonprofit units, such as the Women's International League for Peace and Freedom, the United Nations Associates, and the International Red Cross, are based on major spatial flows of intangibles. They reflect the specific combination of intangibles significant to the specific objectives and structure of each unit.

Unfortunately, it is very difficult to measure the flows of intangible noneconomic commodities and develop models of the operation of noneconomic sectors and institutions. The Roman Catholic hierarchy, for example, has been with us for many, many centuries. There has been great opportunity to accumulate data concerning its operation and function. There is no question of its major significance in understanding the structure of world society. Yet the analysis of this hierarchy and the development of a model to simulate its operation have not been achieved.

There are still other aspects to the spatial flows of noneconomic commodities. As already suggested, political power is often considered equivalent to decision-making authority. One very interesting area of exchange of political authority or decision-making power is involved in the operations within a political party, such as the Democratic party. In particular, consider the functioning of a convention in choosing a presidential nominee. Within certain constraints, representatives of different constituencies come to a single location where they engage in trading, each seeking an outcome that is most preferred by his respective constituency. There are certain rules to this exchange of power—for example, on the first ballot some representatives are obligated to vote for a person already designated a favorite son. There are other rules governing the way in which a representative may join and leave coalitions, and the way in which a representative may participate in any decision of a coalition of which he is a part. There are also rules determining when a candidate becomes the party's nominee.

Now the whole process involves each representative making proposals in one or more rounds of action and interaction. At each round, particularly after the first one, an intricate pattern of exchanges of the intangible commodity, c-power, takes place. Ultimately, this process leads to a particular decision, the selection of the nominee. In an analogous situation, we shall discuss this process at greater length in Chapter 16, when we take up the problem of development programs.

CONCLUDING REMARKS

This chapter, unlike others, has ranged over a wide variety of phenomena. The common element is that each relates to flows.

The first sections deal with the flow of economic goods. Here the analysis has been pursued furthest. We are able to develop interregional input-output tables to provide snapshots of existing patterns of flows of economic goods and to help forecast how flows of economic goods might change over time. We are also able to develop relevant cost and price analysis with respect to regions to and from which goods flow. We can do so for situations under which conditions of either pure competition or monopoly obtain. We can accordingly examine different aspects of exploitation, colonialism, and discrimination.

However, in the study of flows of goods, money, and capital, we make the implicit assumption that the other region is much like our own. We know the market in our own region. We know how consumers, producers, and other behaving units in our region react to changing demand, supply, price, and profit conditions. When the other region is like ours—urbanized and industrialized—then our analysis is most valid. But when the other region is not like ours, then our implicit assumption that the other region is like ours—that its consumers, producers, and other behaving units act as ours do—often leads to results that have little correspondence to reality. This is particularly true when the other region is an undeveloped region with a substantially different culture. The type and volume of trade, capital flows, and development activities predicted by our theory and analysis do not occur.

These same kinds of considerations explain why our theories pertaining to long-run human migration frequently do not work. In particular, the classical theory, suggesting that labor should migrate from the low-wage region to the high-wage region until wages are equalized, is just an abstraction. Although the labor in a highly urban-industrialized region of our type (which is apt to have received a college education and been instilled with the motive to achieve) might respond in this way, the labor in backward regions (and even in our urban ghettos) does not. Because we are not members of the labor force of a backward region, our premises cannot adequately reflect their motivations, values, and thoughts on migration. So once again our theory and analysis are most inadequate, applicable at best to only a highly restricted subpopulation of the world.

With regard to short-run population movements, and with reference to the subworlds we know, the gravity model seems a useful tool. It is still a young tool, having been in use for less than twenty years. It still needs to be tested against the historical record and in other parts of the world. But when properly formulated and qualified, it seems quite useful for identifying the attenuating effect of distance on the volume of short-run population movements and communications and for providing helpful insights into the nature of certain difficult social problems.

Finally, with respect to the flow of ideas, communications, and intangible, noneconomic commodities, our theories and analyses have the least to say. Because ideas and noneconomic commodities are intangibles, our scientific approach based on measurement runs into major difficulties. Thus far we are unable to conduct satisfactory analysis even for our own region, where we have some notion of the motivation of individuals in the exchange of ideas and in the production and trade of noneconomic commodities. Here is where cultural values strongly enter the picture—values that we know are at least as important in most societies as the economic values (which embrace efficiency and the desirability of profit) to which our theories and analyses are oriented. Hence it is not surprising that economic theory and analysis, even at their best, fall far short of the mark in trying to explain and predict behavior, because noneconomic values are omnipresent in such behavior. Here then lies a most rich area for research.

Chapter

9

Private and Public Decision-Making in Urban and Regional Development

INTRODUCTION

Up to this point, we have been assuming that most behaving units—business-men, household consumers, political leaders, public bodies, and others who make decisions—were completely informed. That is, except for the very poor and those belonging to groups against which discrimination has been practiced, we have assumed that each behaving unit had all the necessary information at hand. Thus each was able to act in a simple rational way. We have been assuming that the businessman, knowing the outcome of each of his possible actions, chooses that plant location and output which maximize his profits (or his satisfaction from operating a business and consuming his income). We have been assuming that the normal wage-earner has complete information on possible jobs. He then chooses that type of work, puts in that amount of work, and consumes that income earned so as to maximize his (or his household's) utility or satisfaction from life. In doing so, he takes into full account the disutility of labor. We have been assuming that the political leader knows the outcome of each of his possible actions. He chooses that action which maximizes the welfare of his constituency, if in that way he maximizes his political support or power. If not, he chooses on the basis of some weighted combination of the welfare of his constituency and his political influence and interests. We have been assuming that the interregional trader knows completely world, national, and regional markets and chooses to export goods to and import goods from other regions to maximize his gains from trade. We have been assuming that an administrative agency, with an allocated budget for a given program, spends the budget so as to maximize the production and distribution of services connected with the program, having complete knowledge of the results of each of the ways it can spend its budget.

In reality, these simple assumptions are usually not valid—considerable uncertainty exists in most situations of life. For example, no one can predict the behavior of the natural environment. Who can predict the weather? Yet this influences the outcome of business operations in recreational industries. Who can predict an earthquake or a hurricane? Yet such phenomena can greatly affect the satisfaction you derive from your choice of a place to live. The same is true of non-natural phenomena such as wars, economic depressions, foreign exchange rate movements, inflation, strikes, breakdowns in power systems, and automobile, truck, and airplane accidents. Thus, we must ask how behaving units act when they have incomplete information and when they confront uncertainty or risk.

Consider the businessman who chooses to produce a new product, or the real estate operator who chooses to develop a new industrial district. In each case there are great uncertainties. Will consumers take to the new product? Will competitors produce a still better and more appealing product? Will a sufficient number of new plants want to locate in the new industrial district? In each case, the businessman is less than 100 percent certain that the most desirable state of affairs will transpire. He must attach some probability to other, less desirable states of affairs that may materialize. Part of the problem is that neither he nor anyone else has complete information about what consumers will want, what competitors will do, how industrialists will react to a new industrial district, or the state of the economy and whether or not it will encourage industrialists to set up new plants.

Or, for example, take the household unit that decides to locate in Los Angeles and build a house on the side of a fairly steep hill. This unit may well know of the probability of earthquakes in the area, or of landslides from rainfall and other natural forces. It has to attach a certain probability to the occurrence of a disaster, and perhaps a greater probability to a near-disaster. So it needs to make a decision with these risks in mind. But then how does it, or should it, make such a decision?

Finally, consider the political leader. He could support the Republican nominee, the Democratic nominee, be completely neutral, or take some other position. In any case, whatever he does, there is great uncertainty about who will win. Not having a good method of calculating precise probabilities, it is very difficult to know what action to take. Anyone who has studied the behavior of political leaders knows their vacillations when making decisions in highly uncertain situations. Let us note however that decisions are made. "Doing nothing" is also a decision, in the sense that it is a decision not to take any action.

Because so many key actions are taken when it is known that only incomplete knowledge is available, we want to see whether we can acquire any insight into the process of decision-making in risky or uncertain situations.

THE CASE OF A LOCATION DECISION BY
A GREEK INDUSTRIALIST

We will begin with the simpler kinds of situations and move on to the more complex ones in the next chapter. That is, we will begin with situations in which there is one individual, group, or organization choosing an action, and in which the outcome is completely independent of any action taken by other behaving units. Suppose we take the case of a Greek industrialist—a case that was realistic in 1960, and one that may still be realistic at this point of time.

His case is of direct interest to us because (1) Greece consists of several regions, some of which are considerably underdeveloped, and (2) this industrialist has at his disposal a large sum of capital for investment purposes, which could be used for the development of a textiles complex in the underdeveloped region of northern Greece.

Like most men, he has a limited amount of both time and mental capacity to consider the implications of different actions. Therefore, he is willing to, and does, consider only a few, say four. These four possible actions make up his *action set* or *action space*. Let them be:

A. Develop a textiles complex in the underdeveloped region of northern Greece, taking advantage of the presence of an abundant supply of cheap labor;
B. Purchase foreign currencies and securities of foreign companies, and deposit them outside the country, in particular in the banks of Zurich;
C. Construct an integrated steel works in Athens; and
D. Construct a metals-fabricating complex in Athens based on the import of steel and metal ingots and shapes.

Note that the action of the Greek industrialist is of concern to quite a number of groups. It is of concern to the national or central planning agency (the Ministry of Coordination), the banks of Greece, and other groups interested in national growth. It is of concern to the regional planning agencies and others, like us, interested in attracting new industry and employment to an underdeveloped region, thereby decreasing unemployment and raising per capita income and social welfare. It is of concern to urban and metropolitan planning units and related groups, interested in projecting and guiding the future land-use pattern and transportation structure of Athens. In 1960, environmental pollution was an incidental factor. Today, it is not. Today, the action chosen by the Greek industrialist would be of great concern to those interested in the environmental management of the Athens region, the eastern Mediterranean, and nearby areas.

Like us, the Greek industrialist has limited perceptions of the possible *states of affairs* of the world. He finds that he can perceive and consider only four possible states of international and national affairs without getting confused. For him, in 1960, these four were as follows:

I. Greece joins the common market, her present political regime stays in office, and political stability obtains;
II. Greece does not join the common market, her present political regime stays in office, and political stability obtains;

198

III. Greece does not join the common market, political revolution occurs, and the new regime socializes all industries without compensation; and
IV. Greece does not join the common market, her present political regime loses the election, and the new government nationalizes all heavy industry with partial compensation.

Note that in 1960, neither the Greek industrialist nor many of us concerned with the urban and regional problems of Greece would have considered as very likely the political situation that exists today (spring 1974)—a military regime in power. For our analytical thinking we may, however, substitute the current state of affairs in Greece for II above.

Needing to make a decision, the Greek industrialist calls in his right-hand man and tells him to develop the best set of estimates of possible profits for the different actions he might take for each state of affairs that might materialize. Specifically, he states: "Estimate my profits for each one of my possible actions if state of affairs I materializes—that is, if Greece joins the common market, her present political regime stays in power, and there is political stability. List these profits in a table. Do the same assuming the second state of affairs materializes; also for the third and the fourth state of affairs". He is then given a table like Table 9.1.

Table 9.1 A Hypothetical Outcome, or Payoff, or Profits Matrix
(in thousands of dollars)

| | | States of Affairs: International and National | | | |
		I	II	III	IV
	A	225	196	0	100
Industrialist's	B	100	100	81	144
Actions	C	0	361	0	25
	D	100	324	0	25

Before we speculate on the Greek industrialist's reaction to the numbers in the table, we might ask how these numbers were derived. His right-hand man might have reasoned as follows: "If Greece joins the common market and all remains stable, then a textiles operation based on cheap labor in northern Greece can do very well. It would have a definite labor cost advantage compared to most other locations in the common market nations. This would more than off-set its transport cost disadvantage in selling in the markets of these nations. Furthermore, in time tariffs would be lowered and even eliminated entirely, so the output of the Greek plant would have full access to these markets. Thus, per $2 million of investment I calculate profits of $225,000 for action A." He would have entered 225 in the first cell of the first column of Table 9.1.

Further, he might go on to reason: "If action B is taken, I calculate a rate of return [dividends, interest, and rents] averaging 5 percent, or $100,000 per $2 million investment." He would have entered 100 in the second cell of the first column of Table 9.1. Proceeding with his thinking, he might state: "If action C is taken and Greece joins the common market, the outcome would be disastrous. An integrated iron and steel works in Athens would be a relatively high-cost operation. There would be high transport costs on ore and coal, and high transport costs on any finished products that might be marketed in Northwest Europe. Moreover, efficient producers in Germany, France, Belgium, and Italy would be able to deliver steel to steel fabricators in Athens at a lower price than we could. Our profits would be zero." He would then have entered 0 in the third cell of the first column of Table 9.1. He would continue: "We might even incur losses. The only situation in which an integrated iron and steel works could make large profits—and these profits would be very large—is one in which Greece does not join the common market [in other words, state of affairs II] and sets very high tariff duties on imports of steel. In that way, we could have a monopoly of the Greek market for steel. We could charge high enough prices to meet costs and, in fact, to yield an annual profit of $361,000 per $2 million investment.

"If action D is taken, we could make a normal 5 percent return on a $2 million investment. Steel fabrication in Athens should on net be able to meet competition from elsewhere, at least in certain lines." He would have entered 100 in the last cell of column 1.

Now the Greek industrialist's right-hand man moves on to consider the outcome of each action if state of affairs II materializes; that is, Greece does not join the common market, the present political regime remains in office, and political stability occurs. Under these circumstances "profits in a textiles complex in northern Greece would not be as great. We could not easily penetrate the markets of Northwest Europe and Italy. But on the other hand, we have a big developing market at home. It would be protected by high tariffs from the competition of foreign producers. We should be able to make almost a 10 percent return, let us say 9.8 percent. That would realize profits of $196,000 per $2 million investment.

"As I already said, investment abroad would yield roughly 5 percent, or $100,000 per $2 million investment; and investment in an integrated iron and steel works would yield $361,000 annual profits.

"As for steel fabrication, this too should be highly profitable if Greece does not join the common market. We would be protected by high duties and have pretty much of a monopoly of the market. However, the plant would not be quite as profitable as the construction and operation of an integrated iron and steel works. I estimate that profits would be approximately 16.2 percent, or $324,000 per $2 million investment."

The right-hand man would then derive the relevant figures that he would enter in column 2 of Table 9.1. Following similar rough-and-ready reasoning, he would derive the figures that he would put into columns 3 and 4.

ATTITUDES OF THE GREEK INDUSTRIALIST AND THE PROJECTION OF HIS BEHAVIOR

We can now return to the Greek industrialist and consider his reaction to the numbers presented to him by his right-hand man. Say he agrees with the analysis and considers the estimates reasonable, except that he is less optimistic about the profitability of a textiles complex in northern Greece under state of affairs IV. He thus reduces the profit estimate from $196,000 to $100,000 and confronts the data of Table 9.1.

Now what action is the Greek industrialist likely to take? We may want to know this just out of curiosity or because we are scientists and want to understand behavior. Or we may want to know because if he is likely to take an action that we (as planners, or political leaders, or citizens concerned with our community) consider undesirable, we may want to exert pressure on him to choose another action.

Without further information, however, we cannot project the likely behavior of the Greek industrialist. Let us see why. If he is a born *optimist*—self-centered and certain that the world is on his side—he will choose to construct and operate an integrated iron and steel works in Athens (action C) because God will certainly see to it that Greece does not join the common market, the present regime stays in office, and political stability obtains (state of affairs II). He will then receive profits of $361,000, and nothing better is possible.

However, suppose the Greek industrialist is a born *pessimist*—again self-centered and certain that whatever he does, the world is out to get him. So when he considers action A, he is convinced that state of affairs III will materialize and his profits will be zero. And when he considers action B, he is sure state of affairs III will be realized; his profits will be $81,000. And if he chooses C or D, again a state of affairs will surely occur to make his profits zero. Hence, when the world is out to get him he chooses action B, because that action will yield the highest profits.

Thus, we can see that we need information about the attitude of the Greek industrialist before we can project his likely behavior. And we can see that the attitude variable is critical whenever we want to understand and project behavior in situations in which more than one state of affairs may materialize—and where the decision maker is aware of this. The psychological factor cannot be ignored, as it too often is, by economists and other social scientists when attacking urban and regional problems and problems of economic development. As soon as we admit that the state of affairs that can materialize is not a given, but a variable in the sense that more than one can be realized, we must simultaneously introduce the attitude variable in order to understand the behavior of a decision maker.

We can see this point in another way. Suppose the decision maker can perceive only one possible state of affairs, say II. Then Table 9.1 reduces to a single column. Whether he is an optimist, pessimist, or neither, he looks up and down the single column to find that profit figure which is highest. Because only one state of affairs is possible, he is sure of realizing that amount of profits if he chooses the corresponding action. This certainty of realizing the maximum possible profits exists whether he considers four possible actions as in Table 9.1, or 10, or 100, or 1,000. Single-column situations are the types frequently assumed by economists and other social scientists. However, as soon as we admit the reality of several possible states of affairs, which exist for most urban and regional problems, we have a multicolumn table and the psychological factor of attitude must be explicitly introduced into the analysis.

Let us now consider several attitudes one may encounter among decision makers. Our first type is that of the *Complete Conservative*. He is willing to consider only "sure things." He goes along each row, finds the lowest profit figure in the row, and assigns that figure as the value of the action corresponding to that row. Thus in Table 9.1, he assigns a value of 0 to action A, 81 to action B,

0 to action C, and 0 to action D. Then he chooses the action that yields the maximum of these sure things, namely action B. Note that in effect he identifies the minimum along each row, assigns it as the value of the action corresponding to the row, and then chooses the action associated with the maximum of these minimums. Put another way, he pursues a *max-min* strategy. Typical people with this attitude are bankers, especially those whose families have been in banking for generations; parents who are old and cannot easily adapt to big changes; and religious and political leaders unwilling to confront risk and thus change in policy, no matter how little risk of major loss such change entails.

In contrast to the Complete Conservative, expectations enter into the thinking of some decision makers. We have already encountered this type of decision maker. Take the *100 Percent Optimist*. He looks along row A and assigns a probability to each number along that row. However, he assigns a 100 percent probability to the highest of these numbers, namely 225, and zero to all others. So, with regard to Table 9.1, his expected payoff for action A is $1.0 \times 225 + 0.0 \times 196 + 0.0 \times 0 + 0.0 \times 100 = 225$, namely the maximum value along that row. Similarly, his expected payoff for action B is 144; for action C, 361; and for action D, 324. He then chooses the action whose value is the maximum of these maximum numbers—in effect, he adopts a *max-max* strategy. In real life, there are few 100 Percent Optimists around. They tend to be young and not yet exposed to the bitter experiences of life that most of us have confronted. Are they the Alexander the Greats and Napoleons of real life?

A third type, the *100 Percent Pessimist*, also uses probabilities. In contrast to the 100 Percent Optimist, he assigns a probability of 100 percent to the lowest profit figure along a row. Thus the value of action A in Table 9.1 is $0.0 \times 225 + 0.0 \times 196 + 1.0 \times 0 + 0.0 \times 100 = 0$. The values of actions B, C, and D are respectively 81, 0, and 0. He then identifies the maximum of these values and chooses the corresponding action, namely action B. In effect, like the Complete Conservative, he adopts a *max-min* strategy. Individuals with this type of attitude are not rare—they tend to be the Jeremiahs of our world.

Observe that the 100 Percent Optimists and 100 Percent Pessimists use probabilities to calculate expected profits (payoffs) for each action. They then choose that action which maximizes expected payoff. They are special types of *Expected Payoff-Maximizers* in the sense that when they derive the expected payoff for any action, they assign a probability of 1.0 to one state of affairs and 0.0 to all others. There are, of course, other kinds of expected payoff maximizers. Consider that individual who recognizes that four states of affairs are possible, and that each one has some probability of occurrence. But he cannot assign a probability to any of them. He may take the easy way out and say that each is equally likely to occur. That is, he assigns a probability of 0.25 to each. Accordingly, he calculates:

Value of action A = $0.25 \times 225 + 0.25 \times 196 + 0.25 \times 0 + 0.25 \times 100$
$= 130.25$
Value of action B = $0.25 \times 100 + 0.25 \times 100 + 0.25 \times 81 + 0.25 \times 144$
$= 106.25$
Value of action C = $0.25 \times 0 + 0.25 \times 361 + 0.25 \times 0 + 0.25 \times 25 = 96.5$
Value of action D = $0.25 \times 100 + 0.25 \times 324 + 0.25 \times 0 + 0.25 \times 25$
$= 112.25$

He then chooses action A, yielding expected payoff of 130.25, the maximum associated with any of the actions. Another individual combines elements of both optimism and pessimism—he is a *Mixed Optimist-Pessimist*. He may consider the best and the worst possible payoff for each action, and say that each has a 50 percent chance of occurring. In effect, he takes the average of the highest and lowest payoffs associated with each action. He chooses the action that gives the highest average, namely action C.

Several other special cases are worth noting. We are familiar with the person who always regrets that he chose some action when he could have done better by choosing another. His regret is usually measured by the difference between the maximum payoff he could have realized for the state of affairs that materialized and the payoff he does realize from the action that he chose. For example, suppose the regretter chose action D and state of affairs I of Table 9.1 materialized. Then the regret associated with D is 125. That is, it is the difference between 225 (the maximum in column 1 of Table 9.1), which he could have realized if he had chosen action A, and 100, the payoff he realized because he chose action D. Similarly, we may calculate the regret associated with action C when state of affairs I materializes as 225, with action B 125, and with action A zero. These regrets are recorded in column 1 of the Regret Matrix of Table 9.2. Likewise, we can calculate the set of regrets for each other state of affairs were it realized, and each of the several actions chosen. We record these in the other columns of Table 9.2.

Table 9.2   A Hypothetical Regret Matrix
(based on the Outcome Matrix of Table 9.1)

		State of Affairs: International and National			
		I	*II*	*III*	*IV*
	A	0	165	81	44
Industrialist's	B	125	261	0	0
Actions	C	225	0	81	119
	D	125	37	81	119

Once again we may consider different kinds of regretters. For example, consider the *100 Percent Pessimist-Regretter*. He knows that whatever he does, the world is out to make him as miserable as possible. If he chooses A, he knows that state of affairs II will materialize. He will be subject to the maximum regret, namely 165, when he chooses that action. If he chooses action B, he expects to realize the maximum possible regret associated with that action, namely 261. For action C, he expects the regret 225; for action D, the regret 125. Because he wants to avoid regret as much as possible because it is unpleasant, he chooses that action in which the maximum regret is the least. That is, he chooses action D, with a maximum regret of 125. In effect he chooses a min-max strategy.[1]

In Table 9.3 we list selected attitudes of the Greek industrialist and corresponding strategies, actions, and payoffs (outcomes). What we wish to establish is that in many important situations of reality—important to us and to others— we cannot understand or project the action of a decision maker without knowing

[1] In the appendix to this chapter we discuss other types of regretters.

more about his attitude. However, even if we know his attitude *and* his decision-making process, it does not necessarily follow that we can project his behavior.

Table 9.3   Selected Attitudes of the Greek Industrialist and Corresponding Strategies, Actions, and Payoffs (Outcomes)

Attitude	Strategy	Action	Profit or Regret (Anticipated or Expected)	
			Profit	*Regret*
Complete Conservative	Max-min	B	81	
100% Optimist	Max-max	C	361	
100% Pessimist	Max-min	B	81	
Expected Payoff-Maximizer who assigns equal probabilities to all states	Choose action with highest average	A	130.25	
Mixed Optimist-Pessimist (50–50)	Choose action with highest average of the best and the worst	C	180.5	
100% Pessimistic-Regretter	Min-max	D		125

For example, suppose the Greek industrialist is a careful, calculating individual who maximizes expected profit. He may not consider each state of affairs equally likely. Suppose he assigns unequal probabilities to these states of affairs, and we do not know these probabilities. Then we cannot project his behavior. We can see that if he were to assign a high enough probability to state of affairs I, he would choose action A; on the other hand, if he assigns a high enough probability to state of affairs IV, he would choose action B. Not knowing the probabilities he does assign, we can only speculate as to what his behavior will be.

ON INFLUENCING DECISION MAKING

Though we have only begun to examine the many different kinds of situations in which we are interested in understanding and projecting behavior, it is desirable to pause and consider the vital question of influencing behavior. As citizens we may exercise our right to vote and thus take the opportunity to participate in the choice of our representatives. Through this process, we can influence the set of programs that might be proposed and political actions that might be taken. As participating members of other organizations, we may also have this opportunity. However, on particular decisions we may want to exercise a more direct and greater influence. In the case of the Greek industrialist, we may want, for esthetic and other reasons relating to social or personal welfare, to keep an integrated iron and steel works out of Athens. We can see from Table 9.1 that this is not an easy thing to do if the Greek industrialist is a born optimist. However, we do have various courses of action at our disposal.

One standard course of action is to provide subsidies as an inducement for the Greek industrialist to choose some other action. For example, suppose we want to keep the Greek industrialist out of Athens. He is planning to construct and operate either an integrated iron and steel works or a metals-fabricating complex there, being sure that state of affairs II will materialize. If key officials and other individuals in northern Greece very much desire to have a textiles complex developed and operated in their region, they may be able to muster enough financial resources to provide the Greek industrialist with a subsidy of $166,000 annually. Together with the expected profits of $196,000, this would yield $362,000 annually, a sum greater than the $361,000 he perceives he can achieve with an integrated iron and steel works in Athens.[2]

This is an expensive procedure. An alternative might involve a combination of subsidies and penalties. A steel works in Athens means additional pollution, exceeding the natural absorption capacity of that region's ecologic system. There undoubtedly will be some social cost to the citizens of Athens and perhaps additional municipal costs in treating pollutants. So an additional or "special" tax may be levied on steel operations in Athens. This tax may be fixed at a high enough level to meet also the increase in social costs from the additional traffic congestion and other undesirable effects directly and indirectly associated with steel operations in Athens. (Of course, one can contend that there are many benefits.) Suppose this special tax amounts to $60,000 annually. Then the subsidy needed to induce the Greek industrialist to choose to operate a textiles complex in northern Greece will be $106,000 annually.

A third course of action might be to persuade him that the numbers of Table 9.1 do not depict the whole truth. There are other outcome elements besides profits. If he sparks industrial development in northern Greece through his operation of a textiles complex, he will receive much c-respect and c-reverence from the people. He may even become a regional hero, if not a national hero. On the other hand, if he contributes to the deterioration of the environment in the beautiful capital city of Greece, he will reap a negative amount of c-respect and c-honor. By making the outcomes of such noneconomic commodities explicit, one may be able to dissuade the Greek industrialist from moving ahead in Athens.

Moreover, the Greek industrialist's right-hand man may have used procedures and techniques for estimating the profit figures of Table 9.1 that understated the advantages of a textiles complex and overstated the advantages of a steel works. Let us see how.

First, we must recognize that there is no procedure or technique for estimating profit of different activities at different locations that is foolproof or that has a high degree of accuracy. There are many questionable aspects of most procedures. For example, in calculating labor cost differentials between a textiles site in northern Greece and a site elsewhere (say in Athens, or in some location outside Greece), the potential efficiency of labor in northern Greece may have been

---

[2] Note that one may argue that a subsidy of only $137,000 annually is required, because the value of action A as perceived by the Greek industrialist (if he is a 100 Percent Optimist) is $225,000. Together, they yield a sum of $362,000.

underestimated. We know that this is frequently the case when an established enterprise considers location in an underdeveloped region. By underestimating the efficiency, the right-hand man may have overstated labor costs and under-stated profits for the textile complex. He may have failed to foresee, on the one hand, falling power and transport costs as a result of the economic development that textiles might spark. On the other hand, he may have failed to allow for the increasing power and transport costs in Athens from the overdevelopment that might be provoked by an integrated steel works. So the figures of Table 9.1 should be corrected. The difference between the profit estimate of a textiles complex under state of affairs I and that of an integrated steel works under state of affairs II might be considerably reduced.

Further, the right-hand man is probably using a technique that is not the most modern. He may be using a comparative cost technique by itself, trend projections in market estimation, and so forth. He may not be combining these approaches with input-output (discussed in Chapter 9), linear programming (to be discussed in Chapter 15) and other more recently developed techniques that have been found valid. If he were to do so, he might come out with different results, perhaps more favorable or less favorable to the textiles complex.

Beyond examining these aspects of the problem in order to see if there is a sound basis for influencing the Greek industrialist's decisions along more de-sirable directions, we may try two other attacks. We may ask, after all, what is sacred about considering four and only four possible actions. There may be a fifth action, action E, which did not occur either to the Greek industrialist or his right-hand man. The action might involve the joint construction and operation of a textiles complex and a fertilizer complex. Through their joint use of power, male and female labor, and one or more raw materials, great cost savings may be effected relative to a textiles complex alone. If we were to estimate profits for each of the four possible states of affairs, they might be as follows:

Action	I	II	III	IV
Joint Textiles-Fertilizer Complex	375	296	0	150

In this case, the Greek industrialist, being a 100 Percent Optimist, would choose this fifth action. This point suggests that additional basic research is often desirable.

Finally, let us try one other attack. If there is nothing sacred about consider-ing four and only four actions, the same is true about considering four and only four states of affairs. Conceivably, there is a fifth and even sixth state of affairs that ought to be brought to the attention of the Greek industrialist. Suppose we considered a possible state of affairs in which not only Greece but Great Britain, Sweden, Denmark, and other European countries joined the common market, as in fact has occurred since 1960. This would mean that the textiles operation in northern Greece would be able to sell at a profit to additional markets, and in time under lower tariffs. Hence action A might yield an estimated profit of $400,000 annually under this state of affairs. It thus would be the choice of the Greek industrialist, if he were a 100 Percent Optimist and were persuaded of the reality of this possible state of affairs.

By now it should be clear that there is nothing inviolable or final in the figures that a major decision maker perceives. That is, there is no "Absolute Truth," in the sense that there is no one "rational" or best action for him to pursue. The best action is a relative one—relative to the knowledge that is made explicit in terms of possible actions, states of affairs, techniques of analysis, ways of making estimates, and so forth. As a consequence, we see that there is both an *art* and a *science* to influencing decision-making. This point, which is very important for each of us to recognize, will become more apparent as we proceed.

DECISION-MAKING IN POLITICS:
THE CASE OF A MAYOR

Because decision-making is such a basic aspect of life, and because the decisions taken by political leaders are so crucial for urban and regional development and for attacking urban and regional problems, it is worthwhile to examine a situation in which the choice of social welfare programs is involved. This one is easily recognized by the student in U.S. society.

Let us consider the case of a mayor of the central city of a typical U.S. metropolitan region. The central city contains a large minority population living under poverty (ghetto or slum) conditions. Municipal operations and functions (for example, education and police) have become relatively inefficient; property and other taxes are high, and the urban services provided are of relatively low quality. The private sectors of the economy are growing slowly, if at all; and unemployment in the central city is high, reflecting the presence of old factories and industries. Let the city's basic economy lean heavily on defense expenditures, either directly through military contracts let to industries in the city or indirectly through the industries' export goods used in military production elsewhere (either within the nation or outside). Many central cities in the United States, such as the city of Philadelphia, fit this description.

Let there be a political leader in this city, say the incumbent mayor, who is known to be concerned with getting ahead politically. He faces a problem: What position should he take with respect to social welfare programs, about which citizen discussion and agitation have been widespread? Such programs are tied to local initiative and administration. Standards, however, are set by the federal government, which funnels national subsidies for this purpose to the locality. Suppose the mayor is limited in his perspective, as many political leaders and mayors are, and sees only three courses of action as possible:

    A. Take no stand (a do-nothing approach);
    B. Support social welfare programs at a small scale; and
    C. Support social welfare programs at a major scale.

He contemplates the various possible states of affairs and his position vis-à-vis the opposition. (In order to keep things simple, we shall assume that the opposition is either a single party or a coalition that acts as a single party.) With respect to states of affairs, he sees four possibilities:

    I. International tensions are aggravated, leading to stepped-up military expenditures by the federal government;

II. The international situation and the level of national defense spending do not change;

III. Major national disarmament takes place; released resources are funneled primarily into a foreign aid program directed at underdeveloped areas abroad; or

IV. Major national disarmament takes place, with released resources devoted primarily to domestic purposes such as educational, medical, and other social welfare programs.

The first four columns of Table 9.4 refer to situations in which the opposition presents no effective program. However, the opposition may develop such a program—for example, one of a balanced budget with no increase in taxes. The four perceived states of affairs must be considered under this eventuality also. Thus, we have the eight columns of Table 9.4.

Consider the numbers in each cell of Table 9.4. Each number is an indicator or index of the political position of the mayor. His current (reference) position may be 100, associated with a *do-nothing* action on his part and a *no-change* state of affairs. The number 200 represents a better position, the number 75 a poorer position.

For some cases, these figures may be best estimates of *numbers*. They may indicate the number of unaligned (independent) voters whose support is forthcoming. Thus, the figure 200 could stand for 200,000 votes from the unaligned constituency, to be added to the votes of those who belong to the party of the mayor and who will vote for him out of party loyalty. For another group of cases, each number may indicate a *qualitative* score on position. For example:

0 represents political suicide
20 represents close to political suicide
50 represents major deterioration in political standing
60 represents slightly more than noticeable deterioration
75 represents noticeable deterioration
90 represents slight deterioration
100 represents no change
125 represents noticeable improvement
200 represents major improvement
350 represents potential for becoming a senatorial nominee
700 represents potential for becoming a presidential nominee

Alternatively, where the mayor is an appointed official, the figures might represent the number of people who speak or write favorably of him. Or they might reflect a relative score which his political party places on his worth.

Now, consider the mayor himself. What action will he choose? If he is a "sure-thing" conservative or a 100 Percent Pessimist, he will pursue a max-min strategy. He will choose action B (support a social welfare program at a small scale) because in that way he will obtain an (expected) payoff at worst equal to 60. This is the best of the minimums associated with his three possible courses of action. At the other extreme, the mayor may be a 100 Percent Optimist and judge that for him the best of all possible worlds will obtain. He sees the 700 and 350 figures in row C despite the possibility of political suicide resulting from the pursuit of action C. He will then be choosing in accord with a max-max strategy.

Table 9.4   A Mayor's Payoff (Outcome) Matrix

Mayor's Alternatives	Opposition has No Program				Opposition Adopts a Program			
	Stepped-Up Military Program (1)	No Change (2)	Major Disarmament		Stepped-Up Military Program (5)	No Change (6)	Major Disarmament	
			Foreign Aid (3)	Social Welfare (4)			Foreign Aid (7)	Social Welfare (8)
A. Do Nothing	200	100	20	50	200	100	50	75
B. Minor Social Welfare	75	100	75	125	60	90	125	200
C. Major Social Welfare	20	100	200	350	0	75	350	700

Or, the mayor may be a much more calculating person. He carefully considers the full range of states of affairs and opposition actions. He assigns to each column—1 to 8—a probability between 0.0 and 1.0. Suppose he estimates that the probability of occurrence of situations 1, 2, 5, and 6 are 0.2 each, and the probability of situations 3, 4, 7, and 8 occurring are 0.05 each. Then the expected number of votes (or improvement in political position) would be maximized if he were to follow course A. See Table 9.5.

Table 9.5   Computation of Expected Payoff

Course of Action		Expected Payoff
A	$0.2(200) + 0.2(100) + .05(20) + .05(50) + 0.2(200) + 0.2(100) + .05(50) + .05(75)$	$=130$
B	$0.2(75) + 0.2(100) + .05(75) + .05(125) + 0.2(60) + 0.2(90) + .05(125) + .05(200)$	$= 91$
C	$0.2(20) + 0.2(100) + .05(200) + .05(350) + 0.2(0) + 0.2(75) + .05(350) + .05(700)$	$=119$

EXTERNAL AND INTERNAL PAYOFFS AND UTILITY

Before proceeding to consider whether or not we want to influence the behavior of the mayor and if so, how, we should recognize one important difference between the situation of the Greek industrialist and that of the mayor. In the case of the Greek industrialist, the decision involves the investment of a small fraction of the wealth he controls. If the investment turns out to yield zero profits (or if it is expropriated by a new revolutionary government), he has plenty of other investments elsewhere and great wealth stored away in the banks at Zurich. His position in Greek and world society is not much affected. The same is true if he chooses course C and state of affairs II materializes, in which case he receives the highest of all possible perceived returns on his investment at the time of his choice. This is not so for the mayor. If he chooses to propose social welfare programs on a major scale, he in effect commits political suicide if it turns out that international tensions mount. The national government would respond by drastically increasing military expenditures and drastically cutting financial support for urban social welfare programs. In this eventuality, the mayor would be "lost." No one in his constituency could anticipate much, if any, financial support from the federal government for the social welfare programs the mayor would be strongly advocating. He would be proposing major deficits in the municipal budget, and this situation would be particularly politically suicidal for him if the opposition had taken a strong position on a balanced budget.

On the other hand, there is the possibility that international tensions decrease considerably, and the federal government passes all kinds of legislation offering municipalities major subsidies for well-developed social welfare programs. The mayor may be 58 years old, and the presidential convention may take place within a year. This is, in effect, the last chance he may have to try for a presidential nomination, for by the time the next presidential convention comes around he will be too old. Internally (within himself), he may place a very high value on the outcome 700, which represents the potential for becoming a presidential nominee. In fact, it may be so high that even after multiplying it by a low probability such as 0.05, it gives an expected "value" that leads the mayor to choose course C.

Along another line of thought, note from Table 9.4 that the zero value may be an outcome if course C is chosen. The mayor may not be aspiring to be a presidential candidate, but may consider himself a true representative of his constituency and be very sensitive to his performance in this role. If he were to score zero, he would be so embarrassed and ashamed to face his constituency that he could do nothing but resign immediately. So, if he sets a high "value" on his continued representation of his constituency, the outcome "0" would imply a high internal loss to him. Even if the probability of this outcome were small, it would represent such a great loss that it would lead to a negative expected "value" for course C from his standpoint. He would avoid course C.

In short, we must realize that another set of magnitudes or values may be involved in decision-making. The values set forth in Tables 9.1 and 9.4 are "external" values. They are profits in terms of dollars that are countable, where the value of a dollar is very well-defined in terms of weight of gold. They are votes, which are well-defined in terms of the number of times one of the levers of a voting machine is pushed down. These items are external to the decision maker. But the decision maker is a personality, and has his own set of internal values, developed during his entire life through the processes of socialization and acclimation to his environment. He may agree with other individuals that a lever has been pushed down 200 times. But he may disagree completely with them on what that means. That is, he attaches to that number 200 an internal value that is unique to himself.

In sum, we must talk of internal as well as external values. Internal values are often associated with the words *satisfaction* and *dissatisfaction*. Sometimes economists, psychologists, regional scientists, and other social analysts use the words *utility* and *disutility*. If a starving beggar and a fat prosperous merchant see a slice of bread in the window of a bakery at the same point of time, they as well as most individuals will agree that there is a slice of bread in the window. But they will sharply disagree on the value of that loaf. The beggar may plead for it, be willing to scrub the floor of the bakery for it, and even more. It has a high positive utility to him in the sense that it can satisfy his tremendous hunger and relieve his internal discomfort. The merchant, who perhaps has just finished a large noonday meal and is now starting to feel discomfort in his stomach, may consider the slice of bread as having zero utility to him because it cannot provide him with any satisfaction or relieve him of any displeasure. In fact, it may have negative utility in the sense that it would only cause him additional discomfort if he were to eat it. Also, if he had it in his hands at that moment there would be a certain inconvenience in getting rid of it. Thus, to understand the behavior of both the beggar and the merchant at the given space-time point, we would need to possess knowledge of their internal valuation processes—that is, of the utilities they assign to the slice of bread.

In many real-life situations, we need to convert numbers of items (dollars, beads, cows, votes, letters, favorable statements, citations, hours of work, etc.) to utilities or other internal values in order to understand behavior. However, this is extremely difficult to do. For centuries economists, and for decades psychologists (who have not been around as long as economists) have been trying to measure utility. They have typically defined utility as equivalent to the internal satisfaction derived from the consumption or possession of goods and services.

But they have been dismally unsuccessful in measuring utility. Today, most economists and at least some psychologists try to avoid the problem whenever possible. The closest approach comes from experiments in which subjects are asked questions like: If you have $100 and are happy as a result of this, what will make you twice as happy? Frequently the answers are $400 or sums close to $400. As a consequence, there is a tendency for these and other kinds of experimenters to state that

$$\text{utility} = \sqrt{\text{payoff}} \qquad \text{or} \qquad u = \sqrt{p} \qquad (9.1)$$

within a limited range of payoff.

The lesson we learn from the numerous unsuccessful attempts at utility measurement is that it is very dangerous to try to estimate utility values. The same is true of comparing one person's utility with another—most social scientists agree that that is impossible to do. On the other hand, we must not ignore the utility valuation for many situations of reality. For example, consider two situations for which the payoff matrix of Table 9.6 pertains:

Table 9.6   Matrix of Outcomes (in Terms of Pennies)

	I	*II*
A	16	16
B	0	36

The states of affairs pertain to general weather conditions on a given day—I representing weather of one kind, and II representing weather of a second kind. Let the two kinds of weather cover all possible weather conditions. Suppose these states of affairs are so defined that over a long period of time each occurs with the same frequency, and thus the probability that each will occur tomorrow is 0.5. The payoffs are pennies; the decision maker is free to accumulate them and spend them as he wishes. He has two alternatives, A or B. If he prefers more pennies to less he will always choose B, unless, of course, other factors enter in, such as boredom or a desire to test whether the rules of the game have been changed while he is playing it. On the other hand, if the payoffs are pennies which must be spent that day on cups of coffee (one cup costs 16 pennies, and 2 1/4 cups 36 pennies), and if his utility function resembles that of Equation 9.1, then he will choose A. For the payoff matrix in terms of cups of coffee becomes:

Table 9.7   Matrix of Outcomes
(in terms of Cups of Coffee)

	I	*II*
A	1	1
B	0	2¼

which when converted to utility in accord with Equation 9.1 becomes:

Table 9.8   Matrix of Utilities

	I	*II*
A	1	1
B	0	1.5

By choosing A, his expected utility is: $0.5(1) + 0.5(1) = 1.0$. By choosing B, his expected utility is: $0.5(0) + 0.5(1.5) = 0.75$.

Clearly this little example oversimplifies many of the real choice problems of life. It is used to illustrate a basic point, namely that when payoffs are well-defined external items and are viewed as such by the behaving individual, we may be able to project that he will adopt one specific course of action. If, however, he internalizes these items by converting them into utilities, we may find that we must project another specific action on his part.

This point becomes particularly clear in the case of the mayor who is aspiring for the presidency. His utility transformation may be:

Table 9.9   Conversion of Votes to Utilities

No. of Votes	*Utility (in units of utils)*
0	0
10	10
20	20
50	50
60	60
75	75
90	90
100	100
125	125
200	200
350	$(350)^2 = 122{,}500$
700	$(700)^3 = 343{,}000{,}000$

Note that up to and including the level of 200 votes, he has a regular type of utility function. Beyond this level, his utility function changes drastically. Thus, if he were not making internal valuations under the probabilities set forth in Table 9.5, we might project that he will adopt course A because it maximizes the expected number of votes. If he does make internal valuations and aspires for the presidency, then he will certainly adopt course C, because it clearly maximizes his expected utility.

There are many other interesting and important aspects of utility and related concepts which we cannot discuss here. We shall examine some of them further in Chapter 10.

Gambling as a Payoff Element

We should look at still another important aspect of decision-making, at least in the context of the urban and regional problems which we must attack. This new aspect arises when we pause and ask where gambling enters into the picture. How often do we hear political and civic leaders state: "Well, we'll have to take a gamble." Frequently, such a statement is an explicit recognition that several states of affairs are possible, each leading to different outcomes, and that some probability is associated with each. But also, there may be a real gamble going on, and a real satisfaction and utility being realized (derived) from gambling itself.

Let us be more specific on this point. There are promoters and the like who often have great influence on the manner and way in which cities and regions develop. These individuals may be great optimists, but they also derive much satisfaction from taking a chance and winning, especially when the odds are against them. In many ways, these individuals perceive two elements in the outcome of any action that they may choose and any state of affairs that may materialize. A relevant payoff matrix for this type of decision maker is:

Table 9.10   Matrix of Outcomes,
Each of Two Elements

	I	II
A	100, 0	100, 0
B	0, −1	750, +1
	.9	.1

In each cell there are two numbers. The first measures the usual payoff item; the second has reference to the activity "gambling." If the second figure is zero, it indicates that no gamble has been taken. If the second figure is −1, it indicates that a gamble has been taken and that the outcome of the gamble is a "loss." If the second is a +1, it indicates that a gamble has been taken and that the outcome of the gamble is a "win." We have also indicated at the bottom of each column of the payoff matrix the probability that the state of affairs listed at the top of the column will materialize.

If the decision maker is motivated simply to maximize expected payoff as recorded by the first figure in each cell, he should choose course A with an expected payoff of 100, rather than course B with an expected payoff of 75. But in choosing course A, there is no gamble whatsoever, no fun from trying to outwit nature, no excitement from seeing if you can beat the odds. On the other hand, there is such fun and excitement when one chooses course B. If the fun and excitement are worth more than the difference of 25 (the different in expected payoffs of actions A and B), then we must project that the decision maker will choose action B. More rigorously, if to the decision maker the utility of gambling in this situation and winning rather than losing exceeds the difference in the utilities assigned to the expected payoffs 100 and 75 of courses A and B, respectively, he should choose action B.

Among the key urban-regional decision makers are real estate, business, civic, and other operators who obtain much utility from gambling in the urban scene and in avoiding the routine but "sure" approaches and decisions. The number of these, of course, varies greatly from culture to culture. They are willing to pay for such gambling in terms of expected profits, utilities, and other values. To a lesser, but still significant extent, we find some political, civic, and other leaders who like to live in at least somewhat "risky" situations and who often unconsciously avoid those courses of action and approaches which give rise to little opportunity for agitation, controversy, and heated debate. Certainly there are great leaders in the past—Franklin D. Roosevelt, Fiorello La Guardia (Mayor, New York City), Joseph S. Clark (Mayor, Philadelphia), John F. Kennedy, Theodore Roosevelt—who have behaved in this manner.

In any case, it is quite clear that when gambling is involved, the outcome must be described by at least two elements. (For the mayor, the outcome associated with any combination of a course of action, state of affairs, and opposition choice may often need to be described by three or more elements—for example, votes, win or loss in a gamble, amount of c-respect received from the public, political power, etc.) When two or more elements are involved in an outcome, then it becomes necessary to weight them, or to take into account these elements in a more complicated utility or other value function. Thus, if we are to project the course of action of a mayor or other decision maker, it becomes necessary for us to know not only his attitude but how he goes about assigning values to the outcome elements recorded in any cell. Put otherwise, we cannot project behavior for the outcome matrix of Table 9.10. We need to convert the pair of numbers in each cell to a single index (say an index of utility), as in Table 9.11, before we can employ our knowledge in the projection of behavior.

Table 9.11   Matrix of Utilities (Values)
(based on Matrix of Table 9.9)

	I	II
A	10	10
B	−1	150
	.9	.1

ON INFLUENCING THE DECISION OF THE MAYOR

We now want to reconsider the potentiality of influencing a decision maker—in this particular case, the mayor whose actions can be critical for successful attacks on urban problems. We return to the situation depicted by the outcome matrix of Table 9.4, bearing in mind that the mayor may evaluate the elements of this matrix in terms of his own system of values or utility function. He also has or does not have inclinations to gamble.

Suppose we consider Table 9.4 as recording votes of the nonaligned constituency. Suppose we also know that the mayor is likely to pursue a max-min
strategy; he is a Complete Conservative, a 100 Percent Pessimist, or has another
attitude which leads him to employ this strategy. Accordingly, he will be motivated to choose course B. But let us say that we represent a part of the constituency (covering some of the nonaligned voters) which strongly supports major
social welfare programs. We wish to influence him to choose course C. Clearly
one way to achieve this is to guarantee him political support, to the extent of
61, should a stepped-up military program materialize. Then the minimum outcome of actions A, B, and C would be 20, 60, and 61, respectively, and the value
assigned to action C would correspond to the maximum of the minimums.

However, the mayor may be of a somewhat different type. He may be a mid-
dle-of-the-roader. He does not want to follow the one extreme (as he perceives
it) of doing nothing; on the other hand, he does not want to go to the other
extreme of supporting major social welfare programs. He is inclined to choose
a middle course—do something, but nothing major that will cause disruption.
He is inclined to choose course B. In this situation, it may be more difficult to
induce him to choose course C. We may need to guarantee him political support
of at least 90. After doing so, we can point out to him that whatever state of
affairs materializes and whatever the opposition does, he will always be at least as
well off, and most often better off, with action C than with action B. That is,
action C would dominate action B. Each cell on the bottom row would contain
the number 90 or greater, and would equal or exceed the number in the cell directly above it (corresponding to the choice of action B). That is, the bottom
two rows of Table 9.4 would appear as:

B	75	100	75	125	60	90	125	200
C	90	100	200	350	90	90	350	750

Only a most unusual mayor would not prefer action C to action B.

Finally, suppose the mayor maximizes expected payoff and assigns the probabilities already discussed in connection with the computations of Table 9.5.
Accordingly, he would be inclined to choose action A, where the expected payoffs calculated for actions A, B, and C are 130, 91, and 119, respectively. Again,
if we were to guarantee him political support of at least 60 from the nonaligned
voters, should a stepped-up military program materialize, his calculation of expected payoff from action C would rise to 131. This would then represent the
maximum of the expected payoffs and become the most preferred course of action in the eyes of the mayor (under the assumptions we have made regarding
his behavior).

We have considered that we need to guarantee the mayor in terms of political
support under different assumptions regarding his attitude and ways of behaving.
But we must also now ask: What is the *cost* of guaranteeing a minimum political
support, say of 61 or 90? Unfortunately (or fortunately), the estimate of this
cost will vary from one individual to another, whether he be a scientist, planner,
or civic leader.

Say a minimum political support of 90 is required from nonaligned voters to
commit the mayor to action C. If the individual who calculates the cost is

"conservative" and concentrates on the highest possible cost, i.e., obtaining 90 nonaligned voters, the estimate would cover

1. The cost of 40 votes from nonaligned members of a group such as the League of Women Voters (which might be obtained simply through door-to-door canvassing of nonaligned members of the group); plus
2. The cost of 30 votes from independent labor unions (which would have to be obtained through promise of 100 percent support for certain social welfare programs which they favor); plus
3. The cost of 20 votes from businessmen (which could be obtained only through a very costly commitment of support for certain "tax relief" legislation for which they are lobbying).

However, the individual may take into account probabilities: only 0.2 that a stepped-up military program materializes and the opposition has no program (in which case he will need to provide a subsidy of 70 to supplement the payoff of 20 [see Table 9.4] in order to guarantee a minimum political support of 90); only 0.2 that there is a stepped-up military program and the opposition adopts a program (in which case he will need to provide a subsidy of 90); and only 0.2 that there is no change in the international situation and the opposition adopts a program (in which case he will need to provide a subsidy of 15 to supplement the payoff of 75 in order to guarantee a minimum political support of 90). Then the individual estimates the cost as

0.2 X the cost of obtaining 70 votes
+0.2 X the cost of obtaining 90 votes
+0.2 X the cost of obtaining 15 votes

His estimated cost is clearly much lower than that of the conservative individual.

Last, if the individual calculating the cost is a 100 Percent Optimist, he does not admit the possibility of a stepped-up military program or no change in the international situation. He sees only the possibility of a major disarmament program. This individual considers the cost to be 0, because he is certain that major disarmament will occur.

Hence, we often observe the situation, in our study of urban and regional development, in which many groups can agree on the general desirability of major social welfare programs, but are not able to act together because they disagree sharply on the political and other costs involved in effecting such programs. Some judge the costs (political and other) to be so high as to preclude their active involvement in support. Others see the costs to be so low that they not only actively support the programs, but cannot understand why other groups who are inclined to favor major social welfare programs do not in fact actively support them.

THE SIMPLE-MINDED, SATISFICING POLITICAL LEADER (DECISION MAKER)

Before closing this chapter, let us examine one more case. It can rightly be claimed that in most of the analysis of this chapter, we have been hypothesizing a decision maker or political leader who is much more sophisticated than we typically find in real life. It may be claimed that we should consider an example of the very unsophisticated political leader, say a mayor, who thinks in terms of "win" or "lose." He does not appreciate, nor is he sensitive to, the *extent* by which he wins or loses. After all, by the time the next election rolls around, what will primarily count is not the extent of his victory, but what he has done. Thus, he determines the amount of votes that will just win an election. That number of votes, plus any greater amount (which also wins the election), is assigned (transformed into) the number +1, a "win." Any number of votes less than that amount is a loss, and is assigned (transformed into) a number 0, a "loss." Put otherwise, the +1 payoff or win may be viewed as "satisfactory" and the 0 pay-off or loss as "unsatisfactory." Such an individual is often called a "Satisficer,"[3] because he is motivated to obtain a "satisfactory" outcome, and is not motivated to "maximize."

Assume that in order to win, the mayor needs 90 votes from the unaligned constituency in addition to the votes he completely controls through his party machine or other organization. Again let the elements in Table 9.4 represent additional votes from nonaligned voters which can be anticipated for different combinations of actions on his part, states of affairs, and opposition action. The Satisficer then transforms the matrix of Table 9.4 into the binary matrix of Table 9.12. Examining each row of Table 9.12 offers no clue as to which course will be chosen—at least in terms of the categories of attitudes we have discussed so far. The conservative political leader will value each course of action as 0, because the worst element in each row is 0. The 100 Percent Optimist will set a value of +1 on each row, because the maximum element in each row is +1. The calculating political leader who thinks in terms of probabilities is likely to find one of these courses of actions (corresponding to one of the rows) as best, but until we know the probabilities he assigns to the occurrence of the several states and opposition actions, we cannot project his behavior.

However, suppose we do the amount of research necessary to establish the attitude of the leader. Suppose we determine he is "conservative," and suppose too that we are intensely concerned with achieving major social welfare programs. We wish to establish conditions such that the political leader will choose course C. In terms of Table 9.12, the elements 0 in columns 1, 5, and 6 of row C must therefore become +1 in the eyes of the mayor. Examination of Table 9.4 suggests that this would take place if he were guaranteed additional support so that his total support from nonaligned voters would be at least 90, *should* either the state of stepped-up military expenditures or the state of no change occur. Under these circumstances, row C would contain all +1 elements for the mayor, while each of the other rows would contain at least one 0 element. We could then project that the conservative satisficing mayor would opt for major social welfare programs.

---

[3] This term was originated by Herbert A. Simon. See his *Models of Man*, New York: John Wiley, 1957.

Table 9.12 A Satisficer's Hypothetical Payoff Matrix

Mayor's Alternatives	Opposition has No Program				Opposition Adopts a Program			
	Stepped-Up Military Program (1)	No Change (2)	Major Disarmament		Stepped-Up Military Program (5)	No Change (6)	Major Disarmament	
			Foreign Aid (3)	Social Welfare (4)			Foreign Aid (7)	Social Welfare (8)
A. Do Nothing	+1	+1	0	0	+1	+1	0	0
B. Minor Social Welfare	0	+1	0	+1	0	+1	+1	+1
C. Major Social Welfare	0	+1	+1	+1	0	0	+1	+1

CONCLUDING REMARKS

In bringing this chapter to a close, one very important point needs to be reiterated. For much of the decision-making that takes place in the world—and for most of the basic decisions regarding social welfare programs of urban and regional societies—there is uncertainty in the sense that several states of affairs may materialize. We and the decision maker may or may not be able to assign probabilities to these states. But in any case, we do not confront the single state of affairs that much of economics and social science analyzes. Similarly, we do not confront a situation in which the several possible outcomes associated with an action can be easily discounted for risk and other elements, thus providing a single column of numbers—one for each possible course of action—among which we can identify the maximum in our capacity as "rational" actors. In some cases, we may be able to assign a single value to the possible outcomes of an action once the attitude of the decision maker is established. Often we can not even do this. Thus the "rational," optimizing approach of economics does not apply. In effect, in the community of decision makers of urban-regional life, we confront a rich variety of ways and procedures for assigning values (explicitly and implicitly) to actions and for choosing among them. It is in this context of reality that we must attack problems and try to exercise influence (based on our own values)—taking into account the probabilities that decision makers objectively or subjectively assign to states of affairs, the particular behavior of other behaving units, the utilities they attach to payoff items, the gambling and other items they perceive in outcomes, and so forth. Finally, we must introduce the major consideration that not only are they behaving in a situation, but other units may also be behaving in the situation. What these other units do may be greatly influenced by what the decision maker does, or what they anticipate he will do. To this major consideration we turn in the next chapter.

APPENDIX TO CHAPTER 9.   Additional Payoff and Regret
Calculations

Payoff Calculations

In this appendix we wish to define more precisely certain of the concepts employed in the text, and to deepen the analysis in certain directions.

Consider the payoff matrix of Table 9.1. We designate it π. It consists of payoffs, π_{ij}, where i represents a row (i = A, B, C, D) and j represents a column (j = I, II, III, IV).

Now consider the concept of *expected payoff*. There are several ways it can be calculated. One way is to assign a probability α_j (j = I, II, III, IV) that state of affairs j will materialize, where $0 \leqslant \alpha_j \leqslant 1$ and $\sum\limits_{j=1}^{IV} \alpha_j = 1$. Accordingly the value of any action i (i = A, B, C, D) is the sum

$$\sum_j \alpha_j \pi_{ij} \qquad (j = \text{I, II, III, IV}) \qquad (9A.1)$$

Another way to define expected payoff is to order the payoffs in any row by size such that

$$\pi_{i(1)} \geqslant \pi_{i(2)} \geqslant \pi_{i(3)} \geqslant \pi_{i(4)}$$

where the subscript in parentheses refers to rank only, and not to any specific state of affairs. Let $\beta_{(1)}$ be the probability that the decision maker associates with the realization of the largest payoff along any row, $\beta_{(2)}$ with the second largest, $\beta_{(3)}$ with the third largest, and $\beta_{(4)}$ with the smallest. Then when $0 \leqslant \beta_{(k)} \leqslant 1$, and $\sum\limits_{k=1}^{4} \beta_{(k)} = 1$, the value of any action i is the sum

$$\sum_k \beta_{(k)} \pi_{i(k)} \qquad (k = 1, 2, 3, 4) \qquad (9A.2)$$

Now, consider those who are motivated to maximize expected payoff. The 100 Percent Optimist defines the expected payoff of any action by Equation 9A.2. Further, he sets $\beta_{(1)} = 1$ $\beta_{(2)}, \beta_{(3)}, \beta_{(4)} = 0$. Thus in selecting that action which maximizes expected payoff, he chooses that action which is a maximum of the maximums; that is, he pursues a max-max strategy.

The 100 Percent Pessimist also defines the expected payoff of any action by Equation 9A.2. However, he sets $\beta_{(1)}, \beta_{(2)}, \beta_{(3)} = 0$ and $\beta_{(4)} = 1$. Thus in selecting that action which maximizes expected payoff, he chooses that action which is a maximum of the minimums; that is, he pursues a max-min strategy. (Note that the Complete Conservative also pursues a max-min strategy. However, he does not think in terms of expected payoff. Rather, he deals with "sure" things, the sure thing associated with any action being the lowest possible payoff that can result from that action. As a maximizer, he therefore chooses the action that yields the highest of these sure things, there being only one sure thing for each action.)

Now consider the Expected Payoff-Maximizer, who recognizes that there is a probability that each state of affairs will materialize but who, for want of information, considers that each is equally likely to occur. He defines the expected payoff of any action by Equation 9A.1. He sets $\alpha_I, \alpha_{II}, \alpha_{III}, \alpha_{IV} = 0.25$ and thus obtains the value

$$0.25 \sum_j \pi_{ij}$$

for each action i. He selects that action having the highest value, and we can project this choice.

In the general case, however, when we do not know the α_j assigned by the decision maker, we are unable to project his behavior.

Consider the case of the Mixed Optimist-Pessimist, who defines the expected payoff of any action by Equation 9A.2, and who assigns a 50 percent chance each to the best payoff and the worst payoff in each row. For him, we have $\beta_{(1)}$, $\beta_{(4)} = 0.5$; $\beta_{(2)}$, $\beta_{(3)} = 0.0$. Accordingly, the value of each i (i = A, B, C, D) is the sum

$$0.5(\pi_{i(1)} + \pi_{i(4)})$$

and we can project his behavior. In the general case, when we do not know the $\beta_{(k)}$ we cannot project the behavior of this expected payoff maximizer.

Regret Calculations

We have already defined the 100 Percent Pessimist-Regretter in the text. For any column he identifies the highest payoff element. $\pi_{j\,max}$. The regret ρ_{ij} (i = A, B, C, D, j = I, II, III, IV) associated with any payoff π_{ij} in a cell is $\pi_{j\,max} - \pi_{ij}$ where by definition $\pi_{j\,max} - \pi_{ij} \geq 0$. Because we can calculate a ρ_{ij} for every π_{ij} in the payoff matrix π, we construct a corresponding regret matrix R.

Now consider the concept of *expected regret*. There are several ways in which it can be calculated. One way is to assign a probability α_j, j = I, II, III, IV, that state of affairs j will materialize, where $0 \leq \alpha_j \leq 1$ and $\sum_j \alpha_j = 1$. Accordingly, the regret value of any action i (i = A, B, C, D) is the sum

$$\sum_j \alpha_j \rho_{ij} \tag{9A.3}$$

Another way to define expected regret is to order the regrets in any row by size such that

$$\rho_{i(1)} \leq \rho_{i(2)} \leq \rho_{i(3)} \leq \rho_{i(4)}$$

where the subscript in parentheses refers to rank only, and not to any specific state of affairs. Let $\beta_{(1)}$ be the probability that the decision maker associates with the realization of the smallest regret along any row, $\beta_{(2)}$ with the second smallest, $\beta_{(3)}$ with the third smallest, and $\beta_{(4)}$ with the largest. Then when $0 \leq \beta_{(k)} \leq 1$, and $\sum_{k=1}^{4} \beta_{(k)} = 1$, the regret value of any action i is the sum

$$\sum_k \beta_{(k)} \rho_{i(k)} \tag{9A.4}$$

Consider those who are motivated to minimize expected regret. The 100 Percent Pessimistic-Regretter defines the expected regret of any action by Equation 9A.4. He sets $\beta_{(1)}$, $\beta_{(2)}$, $\beta_{(3)} = 0$ and $\beta_{(4)} = 1$. Thus in selecting that action which minimizes expected regret, he chooses the action whose value is a minimum of the maximums; that is, he pursues a min-max strategy. (Note that the Complete Conservative Regretter also pursues a min-max strategy. However, he does not think in terms of expected regret. Rather he deals with "sure" things, the sure thing associated with any action being the highest possible regret that can result from that action. As a minimizer, he chooses the action that yields the lowest of these sure things, there being only one sure thing for each action.)

The 100 Percent Optimistic-Regretter defines the expected regret of any action by Equation 9A.4. However, he sets $\beta_{(1)} = 1; \beta_{(2)}, \beta_{(3)}, \beta_{(4)} = 0$. Thus, in selecting the action which minimizes expected regret, he chooses that action which is a minimum of the minimums; that is, he pursues a min-min strategy.

Now, consider the Expected Regret-Minimizer who recognizes that there is a probability that each state of affairs will materialize but who, for want of information, considers that each is equally likely to occur. He defines the expected regret of any action by Equation 9A.3. He sets α_I, α_{II}, α_{III}, $\alpha_{IV} = 0.25$ and thus obtains the value

$$0.25 \sum_j \rho_{ij}$$

for each action i. He selects that action having the lowest value, and we can project this choice.

Usually, however, when we do not know the α_j assigned by the decision maker when he defines expected regret by Equation 9A.3, or the $\beta_{(k)}$ when he defines expected regret by Equation 9A.4, we are unable to project his behavior.

Generalization

We can generalize and consider decisions involving any number of actions, $i = 1$, $2,..., m$, and any number of states of affairs, $j = 1, 2,..., n$. Then there are m rows and n columns, and altogether mn elements in both the payoff and the regret matrices. Expected payoffs are still defined as in Equations 9A.1 and 9A.2, and expected regret as in Equations 9A.3 and 9A.4, except that i runs from 1 to m, and j runs from 1 to n.

Games, Conflicts
and Dilemmas

INTRODUCTION

One thing is clear in life. Conflict is omnipresent. Whether we consider at
one extreme the two Big Powers, USA and USSR, vying for global political
control or, at the other extreme, a five-year-old boy torn between spending his
10 cents for an ice cream cone or taking a ride on a merry-go-round, conflict
occurs and its management is constantly with us. There is no field of the social
sciences in which conflict does not enter as a basic phenomenon. This is so, despite the fact that in some fields the tradition among scholars has been to close
their eyes to it and concentrate on elements of natural harmony in the situations
with which they are concerned. Witness, for example, the field of economics.
The work of Adam Smith and the laissez-faire tradition naively disregard the
struggle between classes, whether capitalists and proletarian workers, landowners
and peasants, plantation owners and slaves, or large commercial farm operators
and migrant farm workers.

Those analyzing or engaged in urban and regional affairs are all too familiar
with conflict. There are the conflicts that arise between the individual pursuing
his self-interest and the community concerned with the general welfare (e.g.,
John Doe who litters and burns trash in his backyard versus the neighborhood

association concerned with maintenance of residential quality); between the businessmen who want lower taxes and the labor unions and civic groups who want a higher quality of education services (e.g., the local or national Chamber of Commerce versus The National Education Association); between those who want to protect the environment and derive great satisfaction from its esthetic qualities and those who view the environment as a set of materials to be exploited for amassing wealth and political power (e.g., the Sierra Club versus Consolidated Edison Power Co. of New York); between those who adhere to one set of religious symbols and rites and those who adhere to another (e.g., the Catholics versus the Protestants in Ireland, or the Hindus versus the Moslems in India); between those who have one color of skin and those who have another (e.g., the blacks versus the whites in America); between those who inherit and control wealth and those who do not (the Rockefellers versus slum-dwellers); between those who seek to maintain existing institutions and those who seek radical change (the John Birch Society versus the leftist Democrats in the USA, or the white business community versus the Black Panthers); between those who live in regions of great resources and those who do not (the Turinese versus the Sicilians, American socialites versus the Bengalis, or the Croatians versus the Bosnians); between suburbanites and central city inhabitants (the Philadelphia Main-Liners versus the Columbia Avenue gang members); between those who have political power and those who do not (the Moscovites versus the Georgians); between the cosmopolitan region and the rural hinterlands (Paris versus Brittany); and between males and females.

In short, conflict pervades all areas of life. Its very presence and the overriding problems it generates lead an ordinary layman to question why this subject is not the center of a formal discipline. Why, in books like this one and the standard texts of economics, sociology, political science, and geography, does conflict as a subject appear so late, and sometimes not at all, in the discussion? One answer is that conflict analysis and resolution are *implied* in many of the analyses of standard texts. But this kind of reply is simply a convenient way of avoiding responsibility for a major gap in traditional social science studies, which is in part being bridged in recent scholarly investigations in the peace research and peace science fields.

Regardless of whose responsibility it is to study and analyze conflicts, and who has or has not carried through on this responsibility, the omnipresence of conflict in urban and regional affairs requires that we understand some of its basic factors, especially as it treats interdependent decision-making situations. Also, we frequently want to help avoid dissension, inefficiency, and other undesirable aspects which result from conflict. At times we try to influence the way in which conflicts are managed and/or resolved and the way in which the welfare of each of the various participants is affected.

INTERDEPENDENT DECISION-MAKING AND GAMES

We can begin our analysis by recognizing that, in the case of the mayor of the last chapter, the action the opposition takes is partly dependent on the mayor's action, just as the mayor's action is partly dependent on the opposition's action.

In the case of the Greek industrialist, we may find him in a decision situation at a later time—for example, deciding whether or not to construct an oil-refining–petrochemicals–synthetic-fiber complex in Greece—where a second Greek industrialist is involved as a potential competitor. What one does depends in part on what the other does. But then, looking at the present, if what Onassis does depends in part on what Niarchos does, and if what Niarchos does depends in part on what Onassis does, we have a chicken and egg problem. Who goes first?

The Case of the In-Group (Majority) versus the Out-Group (Minority)

In attacking this question, let us develop a situation, typical of many existing conflicts, in which a deadlock, stalemate, or some other equilibrium has been reached, but in which improvement is possible for each of the participants involved. In order to use graphic analysis, we must assume that only two participants are engaged in an interdependent decision situation and that only two programs or issues are at stake. Later we shall generalize. We take the two participants to be an "out-of-power" group, usually a minority group, and an "in-power" group, usually a majority group. The members of a given group are assumed to behave by and large in the same way and, in particular, in the way their leader thinks best. We have in mind such situations as those which pitted the Black Panthers against the white business community in many major urban regions of the USA during the late 1960s and the 1970s, the Catholics against the Protestants in Northern Ireland since 1970, or a group of underprivileged central city residents against a privileged group of suburbanites (so often encountered in the post–World War II period). The in-group typically has political control, determining tax rates and the level of social welfare programs. Usually through self-interest or failure to perceive the pressing needs of the minority group, the in-group fails to levy adequate taxes and take other steps to provide social welfare programs (education, housing, medical services, and the like) at an adequate level and of satisfactory quality. Typically, unrest develops in the out-group, the minority. The outlet for this unrest may and frequently does take the form of vandalism, crime, and violence.

One can hypothesize that the set of alternative actions for the in-group centers around the level of diverse social welfare programs which it legislates and makes available. This level is its key instrument of *control*—short of restrictive police-military action. Because one effective way of measuring the level of social welfare programs is in terms of dollar expenditures, we can define the action set of the in-group by all points on the vertical axis in Figure 10.1, which measures dollar expenditures. We do not wish to imply that dollar expenditures is the one and only element of any action of the in-group. However, more than any other single measure, it reflects the basic set of actions typically available to an in-group. Note that in this action set, all levels (up to one penny) of dollar expenditures are possible. Hence, we take it to be continuous.

Now consider the minority group. It has little, if any, direct control over the level of expenditures on social welfare programs. However, it has significant control over the level and type of vandalism, crime, and violence that take place.

Figure 10.1   The Joint Action Space

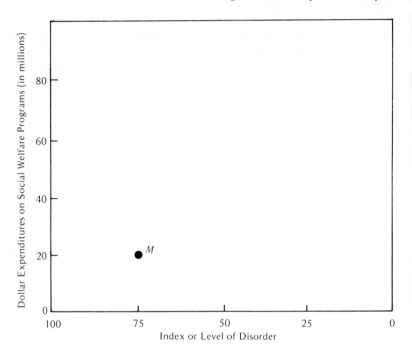

Suppose we measure this level in terms of some weighted index of dollars' worth of property destroyed or stolen; number of persons molested; number of casualties from shooting, knifing, and the like; and number of deaths from violence. For the moment assume that expert criminologists and sociologists are able to construct such an index. We then measure values of this index along the horizontal axis of Figure 10.1. Again we take it to vary continuously. Different levels of this index constitute the action alternatives of the minority. Thus the horizontal axis depicts the action set of the minority group.

We now define a *joint action* as a set of actions where one and only one is taken by each of the participants in a decision situation. An action can range from a simple, elementary act, as in saying "No," to a very complex series of acts taken over time and space—as in the construction and operation of an integrated steel works in Athens, or of legislating and putting into effect a set of social welfare programs. Recall that to "do nothing" is considered an action.

Having defined a joint action, we may define the *joint action set* as the set of all possible joint actions, each participant selecting an action from his own set. The box of Figure 10.1 can be taken as the joint action set for our particular problem. If the in-group chooses the action "to spend $20 million on social welfare programs" and the minority group chooses the action "to vandalize and molest to an extent corresponding to the value of 75 on the index of disorder," then we have a joint action which is represented by point *M* in Figure 10.1.

Because this box contains an infinite number of points, we see that an infinite number of joint actions are theoretically possible.[1]

The result of any joint action is, of course, a set of outcomes. In the case of the two Greek industrialists, these outcomes might be a certain amount of annual profits for the first Greek industrialist and another amount of annual profits for the second industrialist. In the case of the mayor, the outcomes might be a certain number of votes for the mayor in a specific election, another number of votes for the opposition, and a certain number of abstentions from voting. In the case of the in-group and the out-group, the outcomes may be described as a certain amount of taxes, crime, destruction, etc. for the majority members on the average; and receipt of the output and services of diverse social programs, sentences, penalties, and other negative sanctions connected with the generation of disorder for minority group members on the average.[2]

In all these cases, it is clear that the outcome to any participant, whether he be the first Greek industrialist, the mayor, or a member of the in-group, depends very much on what action the other participant chooses. In this sense, these situations, and all others in which the outcome to any participant depends on the action of one or more other participants, may be called interdependent decision situations, or simply *games*.

SATISFACTION, PREFERENCES, UTILITY, AND INDIFFERENCE CURVES

Before proceeding further in trying to project the action that each participant will choose, we must consider the satisfaction or dissatisfaction that might be associated with any outcome element or set of outcome elements of a joint action. Satisfaction and dissatisfaction, pleasure and displeasure, or happiness and unhappiness are concepts that are rather nebulous. Although some analysts might claim that these concepts can be measured, most would consider this to be impossible. Further, among those who claim that satisfaction, pleasure, and happiness can be measured, there will generally be considerable disagreement as to the amount of satisfaction to be assigned any given participant even when the outcome is clearly defined (say a loss, or a win).

To get around the problem of measuring the internal satisfaction or pleasure that any participant derives from an outcome, and to get around the additional stumbling block of trying to compare the satisfaction of one participant with the satisfaction of another participant, social scientists have used the notion of "preference." For most people in the lower- and middle-income brackets, who

---

[1] In practice, of course, budgets are approved which are rounded off, say to the last dollar or last $100, so that only a large finite number of budgets may be considered. Likewise, destruction from vandalism and number of killings are usually considered in terms of whole numbers (integers) so that only a finite number of values for the index of disorder are considered. Consequently, only a large finite number of joint actions are of relevance.

[2] All kinds of outcomes are possible. When two parties toss a coin, the outcomes are almost instantaneously realized; they are "win" for one and "lose" for the other (or sometimes a draw). In tic-tac-toe, the outcome is realized only after a sequence of at least three moves by one party and two moves by the other.

comprise at least 99 percent of the population of the world, we can usually state that having ten dollars (or rubles, pennies, marks, yen, lira, etc.) is preferred to having nine dollars (or rubles ...), and having nine dollars (or rubles ...) is preferred to having eight dollars (or rubles ...). And so forth. That is, if we speak of the internal satisfaction, pleasure, happiness or, to use a more neutral standard term, *utility* of having 10, 9, 8, 7, ... units of a standard currency unit, and if we use the shorthand $u(10)$, $u(9)$, $u(8)$, ... to designate the utility an individual derives from having respectively, 10, 9, 8, ... units of the standard currency, then we can state that

$$u(10) > u(9) > u(8) \qquad (10.1)$$

In short, each individual (except for a few in unusual circumstances) prefers to have more of the standard money rather than less.

Now, we can certainly pursue the analysis further. We can consider not only money but also another item that may be of general value, say land. We can say that, in general, 99 percent of the population would prefer to own more land than less; if the numbers in parentheses refer to square feet of land, we can state that for each individual

$$u(100) > u(90) > u(80) \ldots \qquad (10.2)$$

We can go further. We can state that if there exist two bundles of goods, where each bundle consists of an amount of money *and* an amount of land, then in general each individual will prefer a bundle that has more of each to a bundle that has less of each. That is, if we use the first number in the parentheses to represent the amount of money in a bundle and the second number to represent square feet of land, we can state for each individual

$$u(10, 100) > u(9, 90) > u(8, 80) \ldots \qquad (10.3)$$

Thus far, the analysis is simple. The problem becomes difficult when we compare two bundle of goods where, in one bundle, there is more of the first good but less of the second good. That is, how can we compare $u(10, 90)$ with $u(9,100)$?

In some situations, we may be able to get out of this dilemma. We may say that we cannot directly compare the satisfaction of having $10 and 90 square feet of land with having $9 and 100 square feet of land. But we can sell land and thereby convert our holdings of land to holdings of money. Once this is done, we can make comparisons. For example, suppose a square foot of land sells for $.01, then we are comparing $u(\$10.00 + \$.90)$ with $u(\$9 + \$1)$. Clearly,

$$u(\$10.90) > u(\$10) \qquad (10.4)$$

Thus, we indirectly derive

$$u(10, 90) > u(9, 100) \text{ when 1 square foot} = \$.01 \qquad (10.5)$$

Observe that we are able to give a precise answer because we are able to convert one element of an outcome to another element. This will generally be the case when all the elements of an outcome can be expressed in terms of a common currency or other item—when we can achieve an overall measure of the elements of an outcome in terms of a measure of a simple, generally accepted *unit*. But what if we can't, as is the case in many conflict situations of reality? Then what do we do?

For example, say we are talking about two kinds of goods in a situation in which the individual does not want to exchange them for money. Rather, he has a certain amount of money which he wants to spend on two goods. Say these goods are apples and oranges. Let the price of each be $.10. If he has $1 to spend, he can buy 10 apples, or 10 oranges, or 5 apples and 5 oranges, or 6 apples and 4 oranges, or 7 apples and 3 oranges, etc. Suppose we ask him to state the combination of apples and oranges which he most prefers, next most prefers, and so on, and finally the combination which he least prefers. Suppose he orders these combinations as follows:

Table 10.1   An Individual's Preference Ordering

Order of Preference	Combination of Oranges and Apples
1. Most preferred	5, 5
2. Next most preferred	6, 4
3.	4, 6
4. •	7, 3
5.	3, 7
6. •	8, 2
7.	9, 1
8. •	2, 8
9.	1, 9
10.	10, 0
11. Least preferred	0, 10

Then we can write his preference ordering as

$$u(5, 5) > u(6, 4) > u(4, 6) > u(7, 3) > u(3, 7) > u(8, 2) > u(9, 1) \quad (10.6)$$
$$> u(2, 8) > u(1, 9) > u(10, 0) > u(0, 10)$$

Now, if we assume that the individual wishes to maximize utility, then we can project his behavior. He will spend the $1 on 5 apples and 5 oranges. We see that in this problem we do not need to measure utility in order to project the individual's behavior. All we need to know is the preference ordering of Table 10.1.

Before returning to our in-group–out-group decision situation, let us see if we can say more. Suppose you are a traveller and have an hour or two to while away at an airport. I come along. Not having anything to do, you welcome my asking you a whole bunch of easy questions. I start this way: Suppose you have one glass of beer (8-oz) and a pizza pie (medium-size) and are happily contemplating a small but tasty supper. Along comes someone who has a bottle of beer but no pizza. He is not starving, and even looks overfed, so your conscience does not bother you if he continues to have no pizza. He asks you: "How much beer do I need to give you for a small piece (1/10th) of your pie?'' I now ask you what your reply would be. You contemplate the situation and say, "Well, for another 1/5 glass of beer I would give him 1/10th of my pie. I'd be just as content with 1 1/5 glasses of beer and 9/10 of a pie as with one of each." Letting the first number in the parentheses refer to the number of 8-oz glasses of beer, and the second to the number of pizza pies, I can thus write for you:

$$u(1.2, 0.9) = u(1, 1) \qquad (10.7)$$

After you reply to this question, I go on to ask how much beer he would have to give you for 1/5 of your pie. You think a while, calculating your desire for beer against your desire for pizza, and you answer 1/2 glass of beer. Thus, we may conclude:

$$u(1.5, 0.8) = u(1.2, 0.9) = u(1, 1) \qquad (10.8)$$

I respond by remarking that the well-fed man doesn't think the amount of beer you ask for in exchange for 1/5 of a pizza pie diminishes his stock of beer noticeably. So he may ask, "Well, how much beer for 3/10 of your pie?" You contemplate the situation again. You are starting to get too much beer relative to pizza pie, but then you consider that if the well-fed man is foolish enough to give up one glass of beer for 3/10 of a pizza pie, that would be okay with you. This reaction allows me to state:

$$u(2.0, 0.7) = u(1.5, 0.8) = u(1.2, 0.9) = u(1,1) \qquad (10.9)$$

We can plot these four combinations of beer and pizza pie in Figure 10.2. All seem to make your prospect of being happy and satisfied look equally good.

I abruptly change the situation. Imagine the loudspeaker announces the imminent departure of the well-fed man's plane, and before any exchange can be effected, he dashes off.

This sudden change in the environment, I point out, should not bother you. You would not have come out any better with any of the exchanges you contemplated. Now suppose I put you in another situation. As you get ready to partake of your 8-oz glass of beer and medium-size pizza pie, you notice a somewhat dejected man at the next table. You ask him what's wrong. He replies in a somewhat tipsy manner that he ordered a medium-size pizza pie and unwisely spent all his money on it, so he has nothing left over for a beer. You do not have much sympathy for him, because he has had enough liquid stimulation. I nonetheless ask you to consider possible exchanges that would leave you just as happy as if you had one beer and one pizza pie. You might say: "Well, for 1/10 of a glass of beer I should receive 1/10 of a pizza pie; for 2/10 of a glass of beer, 1/3 of a pie; for 3/10 of a glass at least 3/5 of a pie; for 4/10 of a glass, a whole pie; and for 1/2 a glass, 1 2/3 pies." So we can state that

$$u(1, 1) = u(0.9, 1.1) = u(0.8, 1.33) = u(0.7, 1.6) = u(0.6, 2) = u(0.5, 2.67) \qquad (10.10)$$

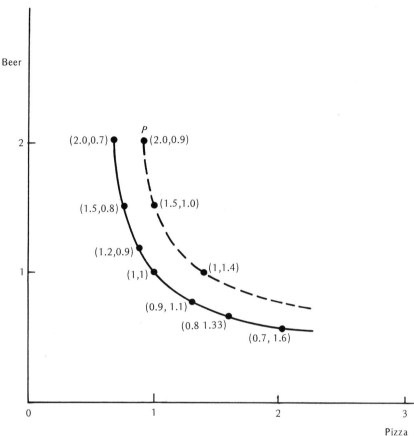

Figure 10.2   Two Possible Indifference Curves

We can plot in Figure 10.2 these additional combinations, which you prefer no more and no less than the combination of one glass of beer and one pizza pie. Because your preference for any of these combinations is neither more nor less than your preference for any other listed here and in Equation 10.9, we can say that you are *indifferent* between having any one of these combinations and having any other. If we connect all these points with a smooth curve, we can designate this curve an *indifference curve*. Roughly speaking, it connects all the points representing combinations of beer and pizza pie which give you the same satisfaction as the combination of one glass of beer and one pizza pie.

Again I change the situation. Suppose that just as you are about to start eating, the waiter comes along and apologizes for having made a mistake. He tells you that he mixed up your order with somebody else's, and replaces your 8-oz glass of beer with a 12-oz glass of beer. You have no objection to this replacement, and in fact you tell me that the situation has definitely improved and that you contemplate an even more satisfying meal. We plot this combination of

12 oz of beer, which is one and one-half 8-oz glasses, and one medium-size pizza pie as point N in Figure 10.2. From your statement you clearly prefer the combination represented by point N to the combination of one 8-oz glass of beer and one pizza pie, as represented by point M.

Now let us imagine that the waiter had corrected the mistake earlier, before the well-fed man had come along. Then you would have started your calculations from the reference point N, representing one and one-half 8-oz glasses of beer and one pizza pie. Clearly, for any amount of pizza that you are now willing to consider consuming, you will want to have more beer than you would have wanted earlier, when you began your calculations from the reference point M, representing one 8-oz glass of beer and one pizza. So any combination of beer and pizza pie which leaves you neither worse off nor better off than the combination represented by point N is going to lie on another indifference curve, which passes through N. It lies above and to the right of the solid curve in Figure 10.2, which passes through point M. For example, to induce you to be content with consuming only 9/10 of a pizza, you will want to consume 16 oz of beer (as represented by point P in Figure 10.2). If you were to be content with only 8 oz of beer you would need 1 2/5 pizza pies (as represented by point R).

Further, because the combination represented by point N is preferred to the combination represented by point M and any other point on the solid indifference curve, and because any point such as P or R is as preferred as point N, it follows that any combination represented by a point on the dashed indifference curve is preferred to any combination represented by a point on the solid indifference curve. In this sense we may characterize the dashed indifference curve as a *higher* indifference curve.

We can derive still other indifference curves which reflect your preferences. Suppose you had started off with 7 oz of beer and 1 pizza pie, or 6 oz of beer and 1 pizza pie, or 5 oz of beer and 1 pizza pie; or 8 oz of beer and 1 1/4 pizza pies, or 8 oz of beer and 1 1/2 pizza pies. Using each of these combinations as a reference point, we can derive for you an indifference curve, just as we have done for the two combinations represented by points M and N. You would, of course, need to be patient and take care that your replies to my questions are consistent with one another.[3] Then we can construct a figure such as Figure 10.3 with a selected set of your indifference curves. We use them to represent your preferences. Note that you do not need to assign any numbers to these curves, though you may want to do so. That is your privilege. Any set of numbers that preserves the ordering of the indifference curves is acceptable in many decision-making situations with which we will be concerned. Note also that the indifference curves have a particular shape. They are convex to the zero point; that is, "convex to the origin." We discuss in the appendix some of the rationale for this, as well as some of the relationships that such shape implies.

[3] For example, you should not tell me at any point in time that you prefer the combination of an 8-oz glass of beer and 1 1/4 pizzas to 1.1 glasses of beer and 1 1/6 pizzas when you had stated the opposite earlier.

Figure 10.3   A Set of Possible Indifference Curves
(A Preference Mapping)

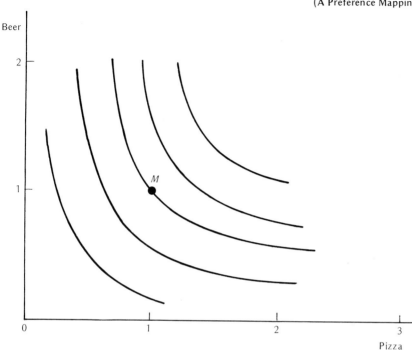

OBJECTIVES AND BEST-RESPONSE CURVES

Now, having derived a set of indifference curves for you—which you may wish to designate as a mapping of your preferences—we can imagine that a preference ordering or mapping by a set of indifference curves can be similarly derived for the leader (or average member) of a group in the interdependent decision situation discussed in connection with Figure 10.1. Recall that point *M* in this figure represents the joint action: $20 million of expenditures on social welfare programs and a combination of crimes, vandalism, etc. equivalent to the number 75 on an index of disorder. We may imagine a low level of utility (even a negative utility, or "disutility") associated with that outcome. There are many other outcomes which the in-group prefers to the one associated with the joint action *M*. Of all possible outcomes, the one that is most preferred is depicted by point *T* in Figure 10.4. This point corresponds to the joint action: $20 million expenditures on social welfare programs, and zero level of disorder. The in-group prefers $20 million of expenditures to zero expenditures because it prefers to control the rat population rather than let it grow without limit, to have a work force that is able to read elementary directions and instructions rather than one that is totally illiterate, to have some rather than no medical facilities to control epidemics, and to salve its Christian conscience rather than not. If *T* is the in-group's most preferred joint action, then *S*, involving added expenditures and the same zero level of disorder, is not. Also, if we consider joint actions involving zero level of disorder and less expenditures—that is, joint actions depicted by points directly below T—we will find, as we go vertically down from T, points that represent joint actions less and less preferred. After a while, we will come to a point, let us say U, which represents a joint action that is neither more nor less preferred than S. Hence, both S and U must lie on the same indifference curve.

Figure 10.4   A Set of Indifference Maps for the Average In-group Member

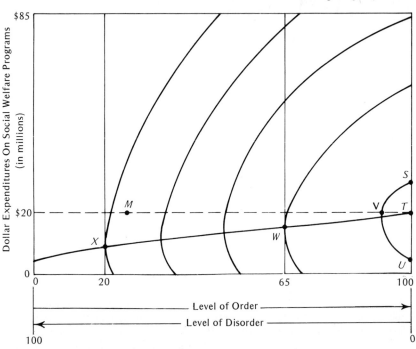

Further, we might consider joint actions representing the same $20 million level of expenditures on social welfare programs but more than zero level of disorder—that is, points on the horizontal line directly to the left of point T. Clearly we will come to a point, say V, which represents a joint action neither more nor less preferred than S and U. That point, too, will lie on the same indifference curve as S and U. Likewise, by going in all directions from T (but staying within the box), we will find other points neither more nor less preferred than S, U, and V. Connecting all these points, we obtain an indifference curve.

Similarly, we can construct any number of indifference curves, starting out with some random joint action (point) not already on a plotted indifference curve. In this manner we can obtain a set of indifference curves for the average in-group member. These are shown in Figure 10.4.

We now wish to examine these indifference curves more thoroughly. As we study them, we can see that it is possible to derive another locus of points, which we may call "best-reply" or "best-response" points. For example, suppose the out-group chooses an action corresponding to the level of disorder of 35 (or a level of order of 65). The in-group may respond (reply) with a choice of expenditures anywhere from $0 to $85 million, as given by the set of points lying along the vertical line constructed from and above the point corresponding to the index value of 65. Any point on this line represents a joint action. By going along it, we can find that joint action which the in-group most prefers. It will obviously be that point which, of all points on the line, lies on the highest indifference curve. This point is point W. We see that it is a point of tangency with an indifference curve.[4] Hence, the in-group will respond with an action that corresponds to the point W—namely a level of expenditures of $16.5 million.

Consider another action that might be taken by the out-group, say one that corresponds to the level of order of 20. Again construct a vertical from and above that point. The joint action that the in-group most prefers is given by point X, which, of all points on the vertical, lies on the highest indifference curve. Hence, the in-group will choose an action in response that corresponds to that point X—namely a level of expenditures of $9 million.

In this manner, we can determine the best response by the in-group for any action taken by the out-group. If we connect all those joint actions in which the action of the in-group is always a best response to the out-group's action, then we have the in-group's *best-response* or *best-reply* curve. Note from Figure 10.4 that the in-group's best-response curve falls off to the left from point T. This, of course, reflects the preference structure of the in-group, which is represented by the set of indifference curves in Figure 10.4. Looking at this preference structure, we can say that the in-group responds to an increase in the level of disorder (decrease in the level of order) by decreasing expenditures on social welfare programs. The in-group might be retaliating, in the sense that it feels that the more disorder the out-group creates, the fewer social welfare programs its members deserve—a view the in-group members do not find inconsistent with their Christian consciences. Or they may react to an increase in disorder with the feeling that the members of the out-group have too much education and, in particular, have acquired too much know-how about organization. Or they have had it "too soft"; or they need to be suppressed. Or the reaction propensities of the in-group as embodied in its best-response curve may simply be viewed as a "mean" type of reaction.

To illustrate other possible reaction propensities, we construct two additional types of reaction curves in Figure 10.5. Each starts from point T. The TZ best-response curve falls off sharply to the left from T. It reflects a very strong reaction, so strong that at a level of disorder of 50 or more, the in-group members on the average would retaliate with zero expenditures on social welfare programs. They would react very strongly with the view that education and social welfare are not good for the out-group members and only lead to trouble. Or they may react in an "eye-for-an-eye" Biblical manner.

---

[4] A point that represents a *most preferred joint action* must be a point of tangency. If not, it means that it lies on an indifference curve that cuts the vertical, implying that there is a higher indifference curve just tangent to the vertical. This contradicts the statement that of all points on the vertical, the point in question represents the most preferred joint action.

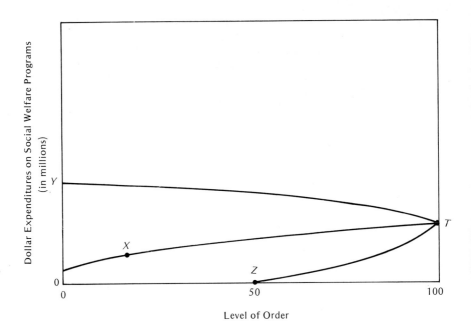

Figure 10.5   Possible Best-Response Curves for the Average In-group Member

Another possible "best-response" curve may slope upward to the left from point T, as does the curve TY. Here, with every increase in disorder there is a tendency for the in-group to respond with greater expenditures. This reflects the view that perhaps the out-group members have not been educated enough to realize the folly or fallacy of the "violent" approach, or that they are being given too few medical services and thus are not yet "happy" with the world. Or the in-group members may have been too "un-Christian" with their brothers, and God's way of making this point is through an increase in violence. In short, a "best-response" curve like TY indicates the propensity to increase expenditures in response to any increase in the level of disorder.

In practice, we know that the in-group includes a diversity of individuals with different views. Some are inclined to respond in accordance with TZ, others with TX, and still others with TY. Thus, the best-response curve of an in-group must be considered as some kind of weighted average of those of its members. Usually, it reflects the consensus of a dominant clique.

Just as we derived a set of indifference curves and a best-response curve for members (on the average) of the in-group, we can do so for members of the out-group. In Figure 10.6, point A represents the joint action that is most preferred by the out-group. It corresponds to the highest possible amount of expenditures on social welfare programs and a high level of disorder. The preference for such a high level of disorder, despite the level of social welfare expendi-

Figure 10.6   A Set of Indifference Curves for the
Average Out-group Member

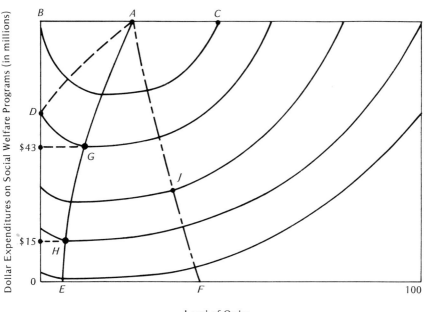

Level of Order

tures, may be associated with the enjoyment the out-group obtains from vandalism, molesting the in-group members, and inflicting violence on them. It may reflect a set of cultural values stemming from centuries of oppression and frustration. Note, however, that they prefer the joint action *B*, corresponding to the maximum level of disorder, less than *A*. This preference ordering may reflect the much higher cost to the out-group of maintaining a level of disorder corresponding to *B*—a higher cost reflecting the expectation of many more prison sentences, deaths from gunshot wounds, and other undesirable legal and physical consequences. Or it may reflect some hidden "Christianity" within the group. Or it may be a combination of these and other elements.

Now, as before, if *B* is less preferred than *A*, there is a point directly to the right of *A* which is also less preferred than *A*, but no more or less preferred than *B*. Say this is point *C*. There are still other points within the box, all involving less expenditures than *A* and more or less disorder than *A*, but which are neither more nor less preferred than *B* and *C*. We connect these with an indifference curve. Similarly, we construct other indifference curves on which points like *D* (less preferred than both *B* and *C*) lie; and so forth. As with the in-group, we are able to construct an indifference map for the out-group which reflects its preference ordering over all possible joint actions (see Figure 10.6).

Likewise, we can construct a best-response curve for the out-group. That is, for each possible action of the in-group, there is a best response by the out-group.

For example, if the in-group legislates and puts into effect a $43 million social welfare program, the out-group will respond with an action corresponding to point *G*, which, of all points on the $43 million horizontal line, lies on the highest indifference curve and so is most preferred. Or, for the action of the in-group corresponding to $15 million, the out-group responds with a level of disorder indicated by point *H*.

Note that the best-response line of the out-group indicates an increasing level of disorder with a decrease in the level of expenditures. This response function might reflect a decreasing willingness to curb violent instincts as social expenditures decline, an increasing willingness to bear the costs of increased disorder, a greater suppression of hidden "Christianity" because of feelings of "exploitation," a "mean" or punishing type of response, or some combination of these elements.

Of course, other possible best-response curves might be relevant, reflecting other indifference maps. The mean type of response may be very strong within the out-group, such that the response curve represented by the dashed curve *AD* of Figure 10.6 is relevant. Or the best-reply curve might be of a quite different character, as the long-and-short dash curve *AF* of Figure 10.6. Here, with a decrease from that level of social welfare expenditures associated with point *A*, the out-group becomes more cautious. It tends to reduce the level of disorder. Or, looking at the level of expenditures and disorder associated with joint *J*, the out-group considers it less dangerous to increase the level of disorder as the level of social welfare expenditures increases.

However we interpret the best-response curves, and whatever the slope and position, we are in a better position to pursue analysis with these curves in mind. But first, we must specify one more element of the situation. We must think of, or estimate, the objective of each group (sometimes we use the more technical term *objective function*). We realize this when we think of different kinds of individuals we have met in the past. Let me list some:

1. There is a type of individual who is self-centered, aggressive, and money-mad, who acts to maximize his profits or income.
2. There is the more casual philosophical individual who looks beyond money and perhaps questions its ability to provide undiluted satisfaction. He may be content with achieving a certain level of profits or income, and is not motivated to seek any further profits or income once he reaches it. This level is his goal and may be characterized as a *satisficing* level—even though he still continues to prefer more income to less. The point is that once he receives a certain level, he is not motivated to seek more and he withdraws from the mad race for income.
3. There is the individual who not only looks at his own income but at the income of his neighbor. Although he prefers more income to less, what really motivates him may be to maximize the difference between his income and his neighbor's income—or in war, the difference between the size of his army and his opponent's army.
4. There is the individual who may be out to minimize his opponent's satisfaction no matter what it costs him. Again he prefers to have more money than

less—but only after he cannot decrease his opponent's satisfaction any further. This is the mean type of individual.

5. There is the individual who considers his neighbor's welfare to be just as important as his own, and so is motivated to maximize the sum of his and his neighbor's welfare.

6. There is the still more godly individual who considers only his neighbor's satisfaction and is motivated to maximize it—of course, subject to the side condition that he (the individual) survives in order to be able to achieve this objective.

These are just some of the different kinds of objectives and aims that exist in reality and that come up in different kinds of interdependent decision situations or games. Each must be kept in mind. And more importantly, it becomes necessary for us to be able to specify or estimate what the objective function of each party is before we can project, forecast, or predict behavior.

SERIES OF ACTIONS AND REACTIONS
EQUILIBRIUM AND INEFFICIENCY

With this in mind, let us return to our case of an in-group and an out-group. We make the specific assumption that each is motivated to maximize its utility (that is, the objective of each participant is to maximize utility). Given this assumption, we can now project their behavior in different situations.

In Figure 10.7 we set down a pair of best-response curves, *TW* for the in-group and *AE* for the out-group. We have also put in this figure selected indifference curves for each group. Suppose that at some point in time, the joint action is represented by point *N* in Figure 10.7, corresponding to a level of expenditures of $76 million by the in-group and a level of disorder of 29 by the out-group. Note that *N* is not an equilibrium point. That is, it is not a position at which we can expect the situation to remain. It is on neither group's best-response curve. If the out-group were to increase its level of disorder from 29 to 78, so that the new joint action was given by point *P*, it would move to a higher indifference curve—that is, to a more preferred position. Hence, we expect the out-group to be motivated to increase the level of disorder.

From the standpoint of the in-group also, *N* does not represent the best it can do, given a level of disorder of 29. We see that by reducing expenditures from $76 million to $18 million, as given by point *Q*, the in-group would move to a higher indifference curve. It, too, will tend to shift away from point *N*.

The shift away from point *N* can proceed in several ways. One way would be in a leader-follower fashion, which might take place if the out-group is much quicker in its reaction than the in-group. The out-group, perceiving the situation and the possibilities for improvement earlier than the in-group, shifts from *N* to point *P* on its best-response curve. The more sluggish-moving in-group considers this change and eventually reacts by shifting from point *P* to point *R*, the point on its best-response curve consistent with a level of disorder of 78. The in-group can effect this shift by simply reducing the level of social expenditures from $76 million to $10 million. However, point *R* is not on the best-response line of the

Figure 10.7   Actions and Reactions in a Leader-Follower Situation

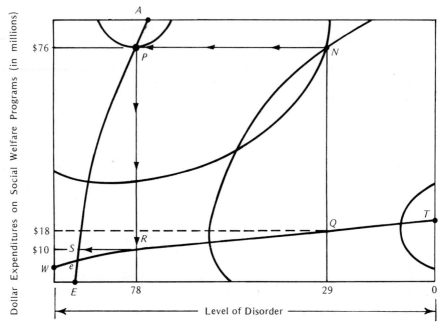

out-group. The out-group will therefore shift from *R* to *S*, a point on its best-response curve. In turn, the in-group will respond by some small adjustment so as to reach a point on its best-response curve. We can see that the series of actions and reactions come to a halt at point *e*, which may be viewed as an equilibrium point. It is an equilibrium point in the sense that it lies on the best-response curve of each group. Therefore, neither group is motivated to shift its position through change in the level of the variable it controls. Put otherwise, *e* is a mutual best-response point.

There is, however, another way in which point *e* might be reached. We might imagine that each of the parties starts to react by changing the variable it controls by small amounts. This is indicated in Figure 10.8 by the horizontal and vertical arrows from point *N*, which together shift the position from point *N* to point *G*. At *G* each party again shifts by a small amount, taking them to point *H*. At point *H* each party again shifts, bringing them to point *J*. The process continues in this manner until point *e* is reached. The process depicted in Figure 10.8 may correspond to one of gradual escalation. In contrast, the process depicted in Figure 10.7 may be looked upon as escalation by big jumps or by large increments. In both cases the same equilibrium point *e* is reached.

Similarly, we may study the set of responses when considering another pair of response curves. Figure 10.9 gives the result for the response curves *AF* of Figure 10.6 and *TY* of Figure 10.5. The resulting equilibrium point *e'* corresponds to a higher level of expenditures and lower level of disorder than the equilibrium point *e* in Figure 10.7. In contrast, however, the pair of best-response curves

Figure 10.8   A Series of Small Actions and Reactions

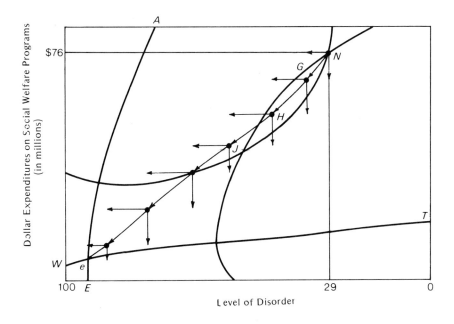

Figure 10.9   Some Inefficient and Efficient Joint Actions for a
Set of Best-Response Curves

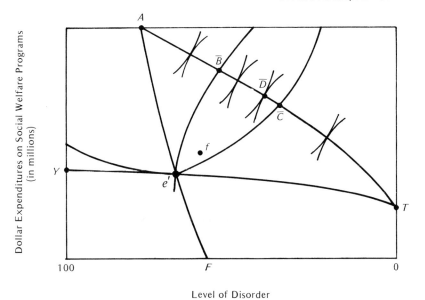

AD of Figure 10.6 and *TZ* of Figure 10.5 yields an equilibrium point e'' as depicted in Figure 10.10—a point which involves the minimum level of expenditures and the maximum level of disorder.

Again, we must keep in mind that no group is homogeneous. Each is typically comprised of a set of individuals and subgroups which are heterogeneous in character and thus have different preference orderings over the set of joint actions. Frequently, an equilibrium point such as e or e' or e'' is not reached. Various factors may act as obstacles or frictions which preclude the series of smooth, fine, and well-calculated moves implied by these figures. Thus we can imagine that the series of actions and reactions come to a rest at some equilibrium point like point f in Figure 10.9. It is not an equilibrium point, but some frictional elements bring the series of moves to a halt there.

Figure 10.10   Equilibrium Point for a Set of Best-Response Curves
for "Mean" Participants

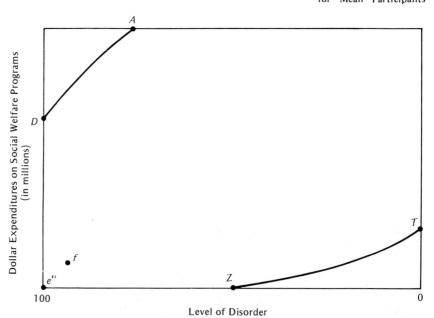

Observe, however, that in Figure 10.9 neither e' nor f is an efficient point. Point $\bar{D}$ lies on an indifference curve which is higher for the in-group than e'. Similarly, each of the points on the arc between $\bar{B}$ and $\bar{C}$ lies on a higher indifference curve for the in-group than point e'. And point $\bar{D}$ and every other point on the arc between $\bar{B}$ and $\bar{C}$ lies on a higher indifference curve for the out-group than point e'. Thus e' is dominated by all points on the arc. It is an inefficient point. Both parties would be better off if they could find a way to shift from e' to some point on the arc between $\bar{B}$ and $\bar{C}$. We thus see the need for negotiation, intervention, or arbitration by third parties. Put otherwise, we have seen how the two groups choose a sequence of actions and reactions converging to the joint action e'. At e' neither party is motivated independently to change its action. Yet at point $\overline{D}$ both could be better off than they are at e'. Hence it is desirable for them to use or develop a cooperative procedure that will enable them to select a joint action such as $\overline{D}$. Or they should have an arbitrator intervene to help them effect this result. We shall discuss this subject in the following chapter.

THE PRISONER'S DILEMMA AND RELATED GAMES

We now want to spend some time considering other types of game situations which are frequently encountered in reality and which are variations or further developments of the situation we have depicted. The simplest one is the prisoner's dilemma game. This game is given its particular name because it was originally made explicit for the situation in which two suspects are questioned separately by the district attorney. They are guilty of the crime of which they are suspected, but the district attorney does not have sufficient evidence to convict either. The state has, however, sufficient evidence to convict both of a lesser offense. The alternatives open to the suspects, A and B, are to confess or not to confess to the serious crime. They are separated and cannot communicate. The outcomes are as follows. If both confess, both get severe sentences, which are, however, somewhat reduced because of the confession. If one confesses (turns state's evidence), the other gets the book thrown at him, and the informer goes scot-free. If neither confesses, they cannot be convicted of the serious crime, but will surely be tried and convicted for the lesser offense.[5]

The Two-Person Dilemma

The two-person prisoner's dilemma situation is one involving interdependent decision-making, and hence is a game. It can be characterized by the simple payoff matrix of Table 10.2. Here, we shall name any two participants: Players 1 and 2. Each player may choose one of two actions: *to cooperate*, action c; or *not to cooperate*, action d. Player 1's actions correspond to rows c and d. Player 2's actions correspond to the columns c and d. The numbers in the cells of the matrix (Table 10.2) represent the payoffs to the players, when Player 1 chooses the action corresponding to the row of that cell and Player 2 chooses the action

Table 10.2   A Payoff Matrix

		Player 2	
		c	d
Player	c	−1, −1	−10, 0
1	d	0, −10	−6, −6

[5] Anatol Rapoport, *Fights, Games and Debates* (Ann Arbor: The University of Michigan Press, 1960), p. 173.

corresponding to the column of that cell. The first number in each cell is the payoff to Player 1; the second number is the payoff to Player 2.

We assume that each player is strictly self-interested and is motivated to maximize his payoff (or achieve his most preferred outcome). Thus, given the action of the other player, it is always best for a given player to choose d. For example, suppose Player 1 has chosen action c. Then Player 2 finds it better to choose d than c, for if he chooses d he gets a payoff of 0; if the choice had been c, he would get a payoff of −1. Or suppose Player 1 has chosen action d. Then Player 2 still finds it better to choose d than c, for if he chooses c his payoff is −10, whereas if he chooses d his payoff is −6.

Because this payoff matrix is symmetrical, it always pays Player 1 to choose d also for any given action that Player 2 may take. Hence, in this game, each chooses d, and the equilibrium payoff[6] to each is −6. It does not pay for either to change his action unilaterally.

It may be argued that if by chance each of the two players had erroneously chosen action c at the start, so that their payoffs were (−1, −1), this outcome would not be an equilibrium outcome. For where actions are independent, unrestricted, and retractable, and where this game is played only once, each player would then, out of pure self-interest, find it profitable to switch to action d.

Note how undesirable the outcome is when each player chooses action d. If somehow or other, the two players could cooperate and each choose action c in a way that binds them to c (no change allowed), then each would be much better off with the payoff of −1. Hence we are motivated to examine cooperative procedures as a means of breaking away from the deadlock equilibrium when each player chooses action d. We will do this in the next chapter.

The Three-Person Dilemma

We can generalize the prisoner's dilemma game to three persons or parties, Parties X, Y, and Z, or John, Tom, and Sam. We do so by constructing a tree in Figure 10.11. This tree is based upon a sequence of moves where John chooses first, then Tom chooses, and finally Sam chooses. Each party has two choices; to cooperate, action c; or not to cooperate, action d. Because John goes first we can go down two branches. One branch is where John chooses to cooperate (c). The other branch is where John chooses not to cooperate (d). We then come to two nodes; at each of them Tom chooses either action c (to cooperate) or d (not to cooperate). Then we come to four nodes where Sam can choose c (to cooperate) or d (not to cooperate). Finally, we come to eight nodes, where we indicate the resulting payoff to each of the parties by the triplet of numbers associated with each node. The first number of the triplet refers to John's payoff, the second number to Tom's payoff, and the third number to Sam's payoff. For example, if we consider the top node, it indicates that the payoff to each of the three parties is 3.

Suppose John is the first one to choose an action. If he chooses action c (to cooperate), he reasons as follows: "Tom can choose either c or d. If Tom

---

[6] An equilibrium joint action is defined to be one from which neither player is motivated to change his action unilaterally. Equilibrium payoffs and outcomes are payoffs and outcomes associated with such action.

Figure 10.11   A Decision Tree: A Sequence of Choices and Payoffs

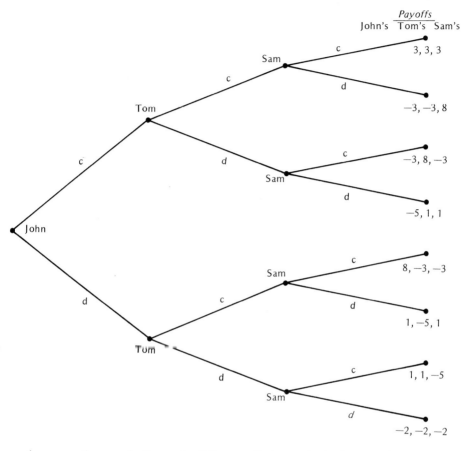

Payoffs
John's Tom's Sam's

c → 3, 3, 3
d → −3, −3, 8
c → −3, 8, −3
d → −5, 1, 1
c → 8, −3, −3
d → 1, −5, 1
c → 1, 1, −5
d → −2, −2, −2

chooses c, then surely Sam, who follows, will choose d. By doing so, he will get
a payoff of 8 rather than 3. So if I choose c and Tom chooses c, Sam will choose
d and my payoff will be −3."

However, John realizes that if he chooses c, Tom will probably choose d:
"If Tom chooses c and Sam chooses d, Tom's payoff is −3. On the other hand,
Tom knows that if I choose c and he chooses d, he will be better off whether
Sam chooses c or d. His payoff will be 8 if Sam chooses c and 1 if Sam chooses
d. So Tom will not choose c. He will choose d, and surely Sam, who comes after
Tom, will choose d. By doing so, Sam gets a payoff of 1, whereas he would get a
payoff of −3 if he chose c. Now, if Tom chooses d and Sam chooses d, then I,
John, will get a payoff of −5 if I choose c."

Thus John finds that if he chooses c, he cannot hope for more than −3, and
probably no more than −5, as a payoff. Because both these figures are negative,
John considers what would happen if he follows the other branch of the tree and
chooses d. If he does so, Tom might consider choosing c. In that case, if Sam
follows with c, John's payoff is 8; if Sam follows with d, John's payoff is 1. So
John reasons that he is better off with d than with c—at least so far. Now John

must also consider the possibility that Tom will choose d if he, John, chooses d. In that case, if Sam chooses c, John's payoff will be 1; if Sam chooses d, John's payoff will be −2. Again John comes out better than if he were to choose c. So John chooses d.

If John chooses d, Tom reasons that if he chooses c, his payoff will be −3 should Sam choose c and −5 if Sam chooses d. On the other hand, if Tom chooses d, his payoff will surely be better. For if Sam chooses c, Tom's payoff will be 1, and if Sam chooses d, Tom's payoff will be −2. So Tom chooses d.

If John chooses d and Tom follows with d, then Sam knows that his payoff will be −5 if he chooses c, and −2 if he chooses d. So Sam chooses d. As a consequence then, we arrive at the bottom node of the tree in Figure 10.11 where each participant receives the payoff of −2. Note that once again we arrive at the inefficient equilibrium situation. If all were to choose c, then we would reach the top node of the figure, where each receives a payoff of 3. But unfortunately, each participant acts independently and is motivated by narrow self-interest, leading to the outcome of −2 for each. Once again, the desirability and need for a cooperative procedure are illustrated.

It should be noted that the outcome of −2 for each participant follows even if John were to make a mistake and choose c initially. Because he is able to change his action, he will find that because his payoff will be −3 or more probably −5 if he chooses c, he will surely be better off if he switches from c to d. With d his worst outcome is −2.

We have now illustrated two cases of the prisoner's dilemma problem—one involving two persons and the other involving three persons. This type of situation is very important. Frequently, social problems arise because of the existence of this type of interdependent decision situation. One example is the problem of neighborhood deterioration, where landlords allow their houses to deteriorate in a slum or ghetto area. It frequently characterizes the situation of landscape deterioration, where landowners allow the environment associated with their particular land to deteriorate. It frequently characterizes the situation of sonic pollution escalation, which increasingly affects urban areas.

The Case of Residential Neighborhood Deterioration. Let us be more specific. Let us illustrate the case with regard to neighborhood deterioration. Let there be three landlords who own the houses in a neighborhood. We allow the numbers to represent profits. Suppose action c (to cooperate) represents the decision, and execution of the decision, to maintain housing through rehabilitation and net investment on a continuous basis. Suppose we allow the action d (not to cooperate) to represent an action involving no maintenance of the housing, thereby allowing it to deteriorate. We see from the tree of Figure 10.11 that the outcome is that each landlord chooses the action d. Thus no one maintains housing and the neighborhood deteriorates.

However, you may question whether the numbers of Figure 10.11 are realistic, and whether or not we obtain neighborhood deterioration just because of the particular set of numbers we have chosen. So we must justify or provide a rationale for the particular numbers of Figure 10.11. Suppose we assume that John and Tom have both chosen d (not to maintain housing). Then Sam can choose to maintain housing or not. If he chooses to maintain housing, he in effect makes significant outlays on painting, plumbing, etc.—but rents fall because John and Sam are not maintaining their housing. So his payoff is going to be less than if he does not maintain housing. By not maintaining his housing, perhaps rents fall still more, because the neighborhood deterioration will be still greater. But the resulting decline in his total rent receipts will be less than the costly outlays for maintaining his housing in this situation; so he chooses d. Put otherwise, in order for him to choose c he must obtain a sufficient return, namely a payoff of 3, to justify the costly outlays on maintenance. But this is only possible when rents stay high enough, which can only be the case if both John and Tom maintain their housing.

Suppose we go further to the left along the tree. Suppose John has chosen d and Tom considers c or d. He knows that, because of narrow self-interest, Sam is out to maximize his profits. Therefore, he knows that if he chooses c and makes the outlays to maintain his housing, Sam will choose d. For if Sam chooses c, Sam's payoff will be −3; by choosing not to maintain his housing, his payoff could be +1. In the case in which he (Tom) chooses c and Sam chooses d, then his (Tom's) payoff will be −5; hence Tom is not interested in choosing c and receiving the negative payoff of −5. He prefers to take the still lower rents that will materialize if he chooses d, in order to avoid the costly outlays on maintenance and large losses if he were to choose c. In this way he cuts losses from those corresponding to a payoff of −5 to those corresponding to a payoff of −3.

In similar fashion, we can argue that John will not choose c. If John chooses c, then he knows that even if Tom were to choose c, Sam will choose d. Sam will do so because it is more profitable for him to do so—he avoids the high costs of maintenance while suffering smaller losses in total rent receipts because of his failure to maintain his housing. So, he will choose d because his payoff will be higher—in particular, 8 instead of 3. But note that because Sam fails to maintain his property, rents decline and they yield lower payoffs for John and Tom. As a matter of fact, they yield negative payoffs. Hence John is not inclined to choose c. This is even clearer when John considers what happens if Tom chooses d rather than c. In this case, Sam will also choose d, and the payoff will be −5 for John. So John reasons that there is no way to achieve a better outcome and to justify costly maintenance, and so he chooses d.

Now suppose you question the validity of the specific numbers used, which you have every reason to do. Nonetheless, the outcome, namely that each participant chooses the action d (not to maintain housing, or not to cooperate), will always be realized for any situation where, as in the tree in Figure 10.12, the relations among the several possible payoffs to the parties are

$$P > R > S > T > U > V$$

Note that the numbers in Figure 10.11 satisfy these relations.

Also, we could change the number 8 in Figure 10.11, which corresponds to the letter P in Figure 10.12, to any other number greater than 3 (which corresponds to the letter R in Figure 10.12), and the outcome would be unchanged. Or we could change the number 3 of Figure 10.11 to any other number between +1, which corresponds to the letter S of Figure 10.12, and +8, which corresponds to the letter P, and the outcome would remain unchanged. Or, we could change both the numbers 3 and 8 in any way so long as the number corresponding to R always remains greater than the number corresponding to S, but less than the number corresponding to P.

Figure 10.12   A Decision Tree with Payoff Symbols

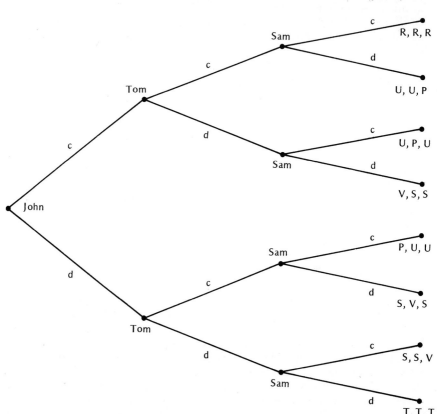

In brief, many combinations of numbers which might characterize payoffs in the landlord situation, and which preserve the P > R > S > T > U > V relations will yield the same outcome; namely, that each landlord chooses not to maintain housing. This is often the situation in real life.

'However, you might argue that this isn't the real world. In fact, you might argue that decisions in the real world cannot be retracted; they are not retroactive. People do make decisions when not certain what the decisions of others will be. Moreover, you may argue that they are not aware that other actors are going to take actions that will affect their outcomes or their profits. But surely this cannot be the case for a long time. In the landlord situation, suppose at some point of time one landlord, John, made a decision to maintain his housing—a decision made out of 100 percent narrow self-interest, which he judges will maximize his profits. Suppose some time elapses and a second landlord, say Tom, needs to make a decision whether or not to make the outlays to maintain his housing. Suppose he is not fully informed; and after making the best calculations he can, he also concludes that it is in his best interest to maintain the housing. Now a third landlord, Sam, comes along, and he has to make some decisions. Again he is motivated simply to maximize his own profits—his only interest is in money gains. He may see John and Tom making their investment which maintains or even increases rents. He then says to himself: "If I make the investment, there is a large outlay. This may enable me to charge even higher rents, and thus lead to some increase in revenue. On the other hand, if I do not make the outlays, I save a lot of money. Perhaps my rents will be lower, but the decline in the total rent payments that I will receive will surely not match the savings in dollar outlays which I can achieve. So it pays me not to maintain the housing."

So we have a situation where John and Tom maintain housing during the course of a year, while Sam does not. The payoffs to John and Tom are not high. In fact, they are negative because Sam's failure to maintain his housing has caused rents to fall, whereas both John and Tom have incurred the costly outlays of maintenance. So the following year, when another decision has to be made on whether to continue to maintain housing, Tom may reason that he will surely do better if he does not maintain housing. While rents will fall still more as a consequence, he will not incur the costly outlays. His payoff will be 1 if John continues to maintain housing and −2 if John does not continue. In either case, he will be better off than he is now with a payoff of −3, so he decides not to maintain housing.

In similar fashion, John, as a narrow, self-interested profit maker, will sooner or later see the wisdom of not maintaining his housing in this independent competitive action situation.

Note that even if Sam were initially to choose to maintain housing—say he happens to be slow-witted on the morning of the decision or temporarily imbued with a spirit of godliness (having been swept away at an evangelical meeting the evening before)—eventually one of the landlords, whom we assume are sharp-witted at least some of the time and are motivated by their own narrow self-interest, will see how his payoff can be increased by a decision not to maintain housing while the others do. He will then choose that action. And in similar fashion, each of the other landlords will choose not to maintain. So we have again the outcome of neighborhood deterioration. This is also a problem to be effectively attacked through cooperative procedures.

N-Person Dilemma

Now we might as well be frank. Probably you react negatively to landlords John, Tom, and Sam as they go about maximizing their profits without considering the negative social effects and costs that arise out of neighborhood deterioration. Perhaps you may even think of them as immoral. But if I divide the students I've had over the last twenty years in Regional Science, City Planning, Economics, Geography, Landscape Architecture, Political Science, Peace Science, Architecture, and Urban Design into two groups—one group which represents 1 percent of these students, and the second group which represents 99 percent of these students—and if you resemble the students in the 99-percent category, you are no better than landlord John, Tom, or Sam. For there are certain problems of social life which develop out of the inability of each one of us to perceive the implications of his actions in terms of social costs. Let us now develop this point.

The Case of Litter and Environmental Pollution. Take the very simple case of litter. I can definitely state that 99 percent of my students litter—whether they are economists who are not aware of visual qualities, or landscape architects and urban designers who talk loudly about visual pollution and the urgent need to improve the visual quality of the environment and hypocritically litter anyway. This point comes out very clearly when we use a simple diagram for our analysis. In Figure 10.13, we measure payoff along the vertical axis. We measure the number of persons who do not litter along the horizontal axis. Suppose we have in mind a park that is used by roughly 1,000 people. If everyone litters—that is, no one bothers to take his refuse and garbage to the litter baskets and garbage cans—then we have the worst possible situation. The number who do not litter is zero and the payoff to any non litterer is −80, as indicated by point W in Figure 10.13. On the other hand, if all 1,000 persons take their refuse and garbage to the litter and garbage cans, then we have the best possible outcome. We have 1,000 persons who do not litter and a payoff of 70, as indicated by point Z in Figure 10.13. If 600 people do not litter, then the payoff to those who do not litter is given by point V and is zero. If 300 people do not litter, the payoff to those who do not litter is −50, as given by point U. Or if 800 people do not litter, the payoff is +35, as given by point T in Figure 10.13. In short, the curve WZ is a curve of payoff to those who do not litter.

Now, because there are 1,000 persons who use the park, it is clear that each person has a very small effect upon the environment. If he litters, the deterioration of the environment that is associated with his action is very slight and perhaps just noticeable. On the other hand, the disutility avoided is significant to that individual. Being an independent actor concerned with the maximization of his own utility, he is inclined to take the easy course and litter. This situation is depicted in Figure 10.13 by the upper curve, which we have constructed in such a way as to lie above the lower curve by a fixed amount. This fixed amount represents the utility gain (the disutility avoided) by not taking one's refuse and garbage to the litter and garbage cans. Put in another way, suppose there are 600 people who do not litter, as given by point V. If you are the 600th person who does not litter you may reconsider whether or not you should litter. It is clear that if you do not litter your payoff is zero, whereas if you do litter you avoid a disutility (a nuisance) and so your payoff increases by +40 (the height of the vertical stretch RV). So, being a maximizer, you do not take your refuse or garbage to the litter or garbage can, and do litter.

If you are the marginal person, whether 1,000 persons do not litter, 300 persons do not litter, or 800 persons do not litter, you always gain +40 in payoff by littering. But this reasoning also holds for every other person. That is, no matter how many people do not litter, the marginal person always reasons "If I do litter I have a very small, hardly noticeable, effect on the total environment, while I avoid much nuisance. So why not litter?" Each marginal individual litters, and if each marginal person litters, the number who do not

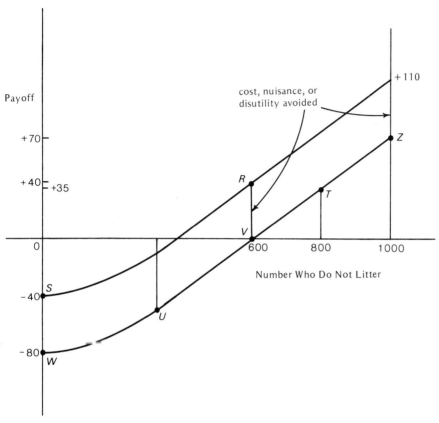

Figure 10.13   Payoff Curves to the Marginal Individual and
Group Members for a Litter Situation

litter becomes increasingly smaller. Ultimately we reach the zero point where all litter, and each individual receives the negative payoff of –40. Note, however, that if the 1,000 persons did not litter each would receive a payoff of +70. Hence we have another instance of a social situation in which independent action by each individual leads to a prisoner's dilemma kind of outcome–negative payoff to all individuals. However, if they could cooperate, they could achieve a significant amount of positive payoff. Thus, there is the need for cooperative procedures, third-party intervention, or new forms of laws and regulations.

We can immediately generalize this situation to the neighborhood deterioration problem. In our previous illustration we talked about a case involving three landlords. Now suppose there are 1,000 landlords in a large subarea. The rents in this area very much depend on the quality of the houses and their level of maintenance.   Each landlord owning one of 1,000 houses says, "If I do not maintain my house or just make the minimum outlay required by law to meet housing standards, then my action has a small, hardly noticeable, even negligible effect on the quality of the environment and therefore on the rents that can be obtained. But I avoid the significant dollar outlay on maintenance. So, why maintain any more than is absolutely necessary?" Hence, he doesn't. But if each landlord reasons in this manner, then no landlord maintains his house. If we look upon the horizontal axis of Figure 10.13 as measuring the number of landlords who maintain housing and consider the payoff to be net rents or profit, we see that the equilibrium outcome is —40. No one is motivated to maintain, yet if all would maintain in a cooperative manner, the payoff would be +70.

We can identify this social process in any number of other situations. Suppose we consider international fishing and assume there are 1,000 trawlers fishing for cod. The problem, of course, is the conservation and maintenance of the cod population. Each trawler has an insignificant effect on the fishing population. On the other hand, if it cheats by violating some international agreement concerning the size of catch and age of fish, it gains much. So why not? But if all behave in this manner—that is, if they all cheat—the fish population is decimated and as a result all lose. By cooperative action, however, they could all gain. Or take such problems as billboard advertising along the highway, making noise, burning leaves in one's back yard, or even polluting the air by using an automobile. All these kinds of situations involving independent action by a large number of individuals in a population lead to the same undesirable outcome. This outcome may be characterized as a social stalemate or a social deadlock, because the outcome is an equilibrium situation in which no individual actor on his own is motivated to change his behavior.

The Formation of Effective Coalitions. Now there are several interesting variations of this n-person prisoner's dilemma situation. First, we can see that if a coalition were to form, where a coalition is defined as a group of individuals who act as a body, things can be made better off. Consider the situation in Figure 10.13. Suppose a "nature-lovers" club is formed among the 1,000 persons who use the park. Suppose some one person acting as a leader is able to convince 600 of the 1,000 persons that they should join this club and abide by its decisions. Suppose one of its decisions is that no member shall litter. Then we see that the payoff to the 600 persons who do not litter is zero, as given by point V on Figure 10.13. This outcome is preferred to the outcome of —40, as given by point S, if all these individuals were to litter. Therefore, they are all better off. Of course, those who do litter are still better off than those who do not litter, for their payoff (+40) is given by point R. Nonetheless, everybody is much better off than they would be if there were no such coalition. Now, as long as the coalition exists, that is, as long as the Nature-Lovers Club is active and has full control over its members, this situation persists. But observe that it is very tempting for each member of the Nature-Lovers Club to defect. By doing so, he again says, "My littering will have little, if any, effect on the quality of the environment and I avoid the nuisance value of taking my refuse and garbage to the litter and garbage cans. Therefore my payoff is +40 rather than zero." Hence it becomes necessary for some other factor to exist, perhaps just social conscience or concern for social welfare, in order to make the coalition a meaningful group for the individual.

Another interesting variation concerns the payoff curve. Consider the problem of water pollution or air pollution. Up to certain levels, there are natural processes, such as oxygen replenishment, which naturally go on in a water system, enabling the water system to handle a certain amount of pollution (BOD) without leading to deterioration in the quality of the water. So a certain amount of pollution can be handled. In other words, the pollution of a certain number of polluters can be adequately handled by the natural system. Similarly, a certain amount of burning of trash in the backyard can be adequately taken care of by wind and other processes that go on in an airshed. Thus if there are 1,000 polluters in a community, perhaps as many as 200 can pollute the air without causing any deterioration of the environment. Thus, the payoff curve becomes flat at the scale of 800, as indicated in Figure 10.14. However, it is necessary for at least 800 not to pollute in order for the quality of the environment to be at a maximum. This, of course, means that there are 200 who can pollute and not only gain the utility of a maximum quality environment but also avoid the nuisance of not being able to burn the trash in the backyard. Thus there are two relevant payoffs. One is for the person who does pollute. The other, of lower value, is for the person who does not pollute. But note again that each individual acting independently is motivated to pollute and that the equilibrium outcome of independent actions is still given by point *S*, with a payoff of −40. However, in this situation we do not need a coalition of 1,000 persons to maintain a maximum quality of the environment, as was necessary in the case of the park, but one of only 800 persons.

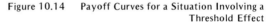

Figure 10.14   Payoff Curves for a Situation Involving a Threshold Effect

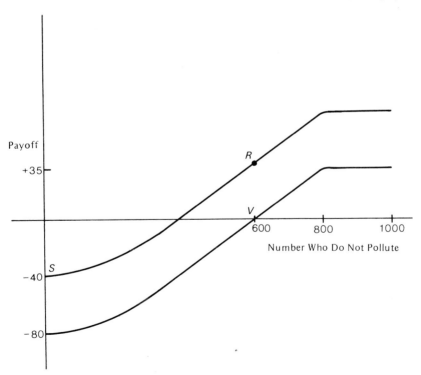

CONCLUDING REMARKS

In this chapter, we have considered the problem of conflict arising out of the fact that in many situations of life, the outcomes and utilities we derive depend not only on the action we take but on the actions that one or more other individuals or groups take. That is, in many situations of life we are involved in interdependent decision-making. When the joint action we most prefer is the same as the one most preferred by all other individuals and groups—that is, by all other behaving units—then we can have a situation of harmony wherein everyone obtains his most preferred outcome. But typically this is not the case. What you prefer, your opponent does not necessarily prefer. What Onassis most prefers, Niarchos does not. What the Black Panthers most prefer, the white business community does not. What the Irish Catholics most prefer, the Protestants do not. What the ghetto population most prefers, the suburban whites do not. What an in-group most prefers, an out-group does not. Thus, there are conflicts in all these two-participant interdependent decision situations we have just posed. This conflict frequently leads to situations that are inefficient and much less desired by each participant than other joint actions that could be achieved. We saw this to be the case for an in-group and an out-group in terms of indifference curves and best-response curves. (Recall that the indifference curve concept is extremely useful, for it allows us to depict preferences of an individual or group without requiring us to specify the exact amount of utility that might be realized from any joint action. That is, without measuring we can yet obtain much insight and potency for analysis.)

We then examined other cases of the prisoner's dilemma type. They involved two, three, and finally n participants. We saw how in many of these cases, if not all, the end result is an undesirable social outcome which is also undesirable for each participant. Thus we are motivated to analyze the possibility of developing ways and means of improving the outcome, not only from the standpoint of each participant but also for society as a whole. This pertains whether we are considering urban regions and conflicts among the individuals and groups in the urban areas; or whether we are considering a system of regions in a nation such as India, and are concerned with the social welfare of each region's population and that of India as a whole; or whether we are considering the nations of a world region, such as Denmark, Sweden, Finland, Poland, the USSR, East Germany, and West Germany, which comprise the Baltic Sea Region; or whether we are considering the nations that form our global society, where we consider each nation as a political region. We shall examine ways of improving outcomes and the properties of some appealing cooperative procedures in the next chapter.

APPENDIX TO CHAPTER 10. Indifference Curve Analysis
and Consumer Theory

In Chapter 4, in the section entitled "The Demand Schedule and the Demand Curve," we discussed the concept of a demand schedule. We considered the demand for Girl Fridays by businessmen who were concerned with maximizing profits, or maximizing some combination of (a) profits and (b) avoidance of disutility from work. Having developed in the text of this chapter the concept of an indifference map to represent an individual's preferences, we can now probe more deeply into what lies behind a demand schedule, and how the amount of goods you buy changes with your income.

Suppose on Sunday, August 15, 1971 you were at the London airport and, as before, contemplating eating a savory meal consisting of an 8-oz glass of beer and a medium-size pizza pie. You have a preference ordering for beer and pizza pie, as described by the indifference curves of Figure 10.3, two of which are reproduced in Figure 10A.1. Also, you are in a position to consume one 8-oz glass of beer and one medium-size pizza pie because you had, after budgeting $8 a day to live on, assigned $1 to the lunch meal. Now, the price of an 8-oz glass of beer is $.40 and that of a medium-size pizza pie is $.60. So the point *M* in Figure 10A.1 represents not only a combination of one 8-oz glass of beer and a medium-size pizza pie but also $1 of expenditure.

Now of course you can spend your $1 in a different way. You can have 2 1/2 glasses of beer and no pizza pie, as indicated by point *S* in Figure 10.4. Or you can buy no beer and 1 2/3 pizza pies, as given by point *T* in Figure 10A.1. (We may imagine that the restaurant sells pizza slices, each a sixth of a whole pie, at one-sixth the price of a whole pie.) Or you can buy 1 1/2 glasses of beer and 2/3 of a pizza pie, as given by point *U* in Figure 10.4. Or you can spend your $1 in any one of several different ways, as is indicated by the straight line that connects points *S* and *T* and courses through points *M* and *U*. This line is described by the equation

$$\$.60x + \$.40y = \$1 \tag{10A.1}$$

Figure 10A.1   Change in Quantity Purchased from Depreciation and Appreciation of the Dollar

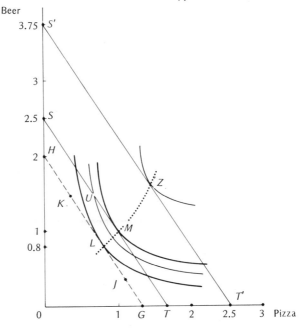

where x = number of medium-size pizza pies, and y = number of 8-oz glasses of beer. This line is, in effect, the locus of all combinations of glasses of beer and pizza pies which can be purchased with $1 at the stated prices.

Now perhaps you have no particular interest in this notion of a $1 expenditure line, but it does permit us to perceive better the rationality of your choice. Note that relative to point M, every other point on that line is less desirable to you. That is, every other point on the line ST lies on a lower indifference curve than point M, as you can easily observe. Hence, in choosing that combination M rather than any other which costs you $1, you have chosen that one which lies on your highest indifference curve. It maximizes your utility or, in general, your satisfaction. So this piece of analysis is somewhat useful, and suggests that we can perhaps act to maximize our utility without specifying how much utility we may be deriving from our choice.[1]

Changes in Demand with Change in Income: Your Consumption Expansion Path

The analysis becomes still more useful when we examine your reaction to a new piece of news. While you are eating your savory lunch, you hear a radio commentator analyzing the effect of the unexpected and most disturbing announcement by the president of the USA that the dollar will be allowed to float on the international money markets.

You learn, unhappily, that the traveller's checks (in dollars) that you have are likely to be worth 20 percent less—that from here on $1 can buy 20 percent less than previously. For example, $1 can buy only 2 glasses of beer (as represented by point H on Figure 10A.1) instead of 2 1/2 glasses (as represented by point S). So in effect the price of a glass of beer has risen from $.40 to $.50. Also, your dollar can buy 20 percent less of pizza pies, or 1 1/3 pies (as represented by point G) instead of 1 2/3 pies (as represented by point T). The price

---

[1] Note that this analysis allows us to see why indifference curves are generally shaped convex to the origin as in Figure 10A.1, and not concave to the origin as in Figure 10A.2, *when you consider consuming some of each of two goods like beer and pizza.* For suppose your indifference curves are concave to the origin like the ones in Figure 10A.2. Then with $1 to spend on beer and pizza, you can choose to consume any combination represented by a point on the $1 expenditure line. You can choose the combination represented by point M, which is a point of tangency of the $1 expenditure line with an indifference curve. But note that this combination does not lie on your highest possible indifference curve. It lies on the II indifference curve. You can move on to the higher indifference curve $I'I'$ by choosing to spend your dollar on a combination represented by point N. In fact, you will move to the highest possible indifference curve that has a point in common with your $1 expenditure line when you choose to purchase 2 1/2 glasses of beer and no pizza, as represented by spoint S. But this outcome possibility contradicts your initial statement of preferences (recorded in the text), where you imply that you want to consume at least some pizza pie with your beer and that you much prefer 1 glass of beer plus 1 pizza pie to 2 1/2 glasses of beer. So we see that regularly shaped indifference curves which are concave to the origin cannot represent your preferences *when you prefer to consume some of both goods rather than one alone.*

Now suppose you do have different preferences for a pair of goods, say ice cream and pickles, and choose to consume at a meal only one of them rather than both. Then indifference curves concave to the origin can represent your preference structure for these two goods. Also, the point M will represent your least desired combination of these goods were you required by law to spend your dollar and consume the goods purchased. For all other points on the $1 expenditure line lie on a higher indifference curve, as you can readily see by studying the curves in Figure 10A.2.

Figure 10A.2   Maximizing Utility with Indifference
Curves Concave to Origin

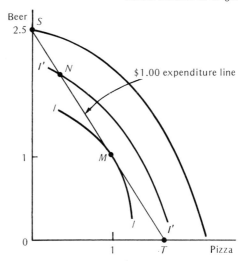

of pizza pie has thus increased from $.60 to $.75. You can no longer buy the combination represented by point *M*, but only a combination like *L, K,* or *J.* More specifically, what has happened is this. The price of beer and pizza pie at the London airport is stated in terms of shillings. In this changed situation, your dollar can buy 20 percent fewer shillings. So the price of beer and pizza pie have each gone up by 25 percent. If we now connect points *G* and *H* with a dashed straight line, which will necessarily course through points *K, L,* and *J,* we can see all combinations of beer and pizza pie that can be bought with your depreciated dollar. We see that with your depreciated dollar you will once again seek that combination of beer and pizza pie which gives you the most satisfaction. You will choose that point on the dashed straight line—whose points represent all possible combinations purchasable with your depreciated dollar—that lies on the highest indifference curve. We see that *L* is that point, representing .8 glasses of beer and .8 pizza pies. We see that you will have to be content with less of each—that the increase in price of each (as a result of the dollar depreciation) has forced you to decrease your effective demand for each.

Put another way, the increase in the prices of beer and pizza pie, and the subsequent decrease in the quantity you choose to buy of each of these commodities, represents a *real income* effect. With increase in prices in general, whether because of depreciation of the dollar or because of inflation, the real income (in terms of goods that you can buy) of any given amount of dollar income you have decreases. When your money income is fixed, as often is the case for those who are retired, then you face a declining real income in countries like the United States, where prospects of maintaining a constant price level are very slim.

Figure 10A.1 is useful for our thinking in a still more general way. Suppose you are having lunch at the London airport and you suddenly receive the very good news that the pound has *depreciated* relative to the dollar. Put otherwise, your dollar has *appreciated* relative to the pound. With your $1 you can now obtain 50 percent more pounds. Your $1 expenditure line now becomes the *S'T'* line of Figure 10A.1. If you choose to spend all your dollar on beer you can now obtain 3 3/4 glasses as given by point *S'*, rather than the 2 1/2 glasses before appreciation as given by point *S.* Or if you choose to spend all your dollar on pizza pies, you can now obtain 2 1/2 pies as given by point T', rather than the 1 2/3 pies before appreciation as given by point T. However, of all combinations which your appreciated dollar can now purchase, you most prefer that represented by point Z (which we see is the point on the $S'T'$ line lying on the highest indifference curve).

In similar fashion, we can derive your most preferred combination of beer and pizza for all percentage amounts of appreciation or depreciation of your dollar. If we plot the points representing these combinations on Figure 10A.1 and draw a dotted line through them, as we do through points L, M, and Z, then the dotted line indicates how your most desired combination of beer and pizza changes with change in your *real income*. This dotted line can then be designated your *consumption expansion line* as your real income increases.

The meaning of this line is perhaps clearer if we consider the guy sitting at the next table. He happens to be a typical Britisher. To him, all this business of exchange rates and depreciation is of no concern. He is in Britain. He works in Britain and gets paid in pounds. He buys goods whose prices are in terms of pounds. Suppose he is exactly like you in all other respects and thus has the same preferences, etc. If he has 2/5 of a pound to spend, which initially we assumed could be exchanged for $1, he will buy 1 beer and 1 pizza pie, as given by point M, just as you would. If he has 20 percent less, namely (1.6)/5 of a pound to spend, which exchanges for a dollar that is 20 percent depreciated, he will buy .8 glasses of beer and .8 pizza pies, as given by point L, just as you would with your depreciated dollar. If, however, he has 3/5 of a pound to spend, which exchanges for the appreciated dollar we have just talked about, he will buy the combination of beer and pizza represented by point Z, just as you would with an appreciated dollar. So the dotted line which connects points L, M, and Z also represents his *consumption expansion line*; it depicts the pattern of his consumption of the two goods as the amount (in pounds) he can afford to spend on these goods increases.

Suppose we were to do this analysis for each individual of a population and obtain for each a consumption expansion line. Then for various assumptions on how their incomes might change and how the amounts of income they allocate to beer and pizza might change in response, we can derive the changes in total demand for beer and pizza with income changes for the population of a region simply by appropriately adding up the demands of individuals.

Figure 10A.1 is also useful in another respect. The three straight lines represent three different amounts of incomes allocated to the consumption of beer and pizza. The first (lowest) line might be viewed as corresponding to the amount allocated by a low-income Britisher. The second line might represent the amount allocated by a typical middle-income Britisher. The third (highest) line might represent the amount allocated by a typical high-income Britisher. Thus we see how the consumption of these two goods might differ for typical members of different income groups.

Of course, the differences among income groups in their patterns of consumption will vary greatly depending on the goods being considered. What might be true for beer and pizza will not be true for mink coats and caviar. With regard to these last two commodities, the income allocated, and thus the corresponding expenditure line, will be zero for the low-income person. At the other extreme, consider turnips and cabbage. Because these goods are cheap and have high food value, the very low-income person buys much of them, even though he allots only a small total expenditure to the two of them. In no other way can he exist on his low income. In contrast, the high-income person who likes neither turnips nor cabbage allocates zero expenditures to their purchase and thus consumes none of them.

Change in Demand with Change in Price: Derivation of the Demand Schedule

We can now illustrate more clearly how your demand for beer is a function of its price. Suppose we construct in Figure 10A.3 three indifference curves from Figure 10.4 and the line *ST* which courses through point *M*. We have already shown that if you have $1 of income to spend at lunch time, and if the price of beer and pizza pie are $.40 and $.60, respectively, you will choose to consume one beer and one pizza pie. Now suppose your dollar neither appreciates nor depreciates, that your income stays the same, that the price of pizza pie does not change but the price of beer rises to $.50. What happens? First of all, if you choose to buy only beer with your $1, at that price you can buy only two beers. This outcome is depicted by point *H* on Figure 10A.3. Or, you can still choose to buy 1 2/3 pizza pies and no beer with your $1 income, as given by point *T*. Now we know that if we connect *H* and *T* by a straight line, that straight line will be the locus of points representing all combinations of beer and pizza pie that can be purchased with $1 income, given their prices of $.50 and $.60, respectively. We also know that the point on that new line which lies on the highest indifference curve will represent the combination of beer and pizza pie you will buy. That point is point *V*. At that point you choose to buy somewhat more than .8 of a beer and somewhat less than 1 pizza pie.

Figure 10A.3   Decrease in Demand with Increase in Price

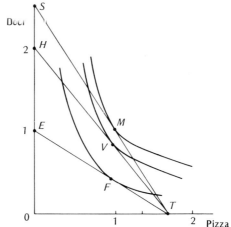

Consider a still higher price for beer, say $1, with the price of pizza pie unchanged. At that price you can have only one beer if you choose to spend all your money on beer, as indicated by point *E* in Figure 10A.3. Once again you can have 1 2/3 pizza pies if you choose to spend all your money on pizza, as indicated by point *T*. If we connect *E* and *T* by a straight line, this line will be the locus of points representing all combinations of beer and pizza that can be purchased with $1 income, given their prices of $1 and $.60, respectively. The point on this line that lies on the highest indifference curve is *F*, which indicates

260

that you will buy somewhat more than .4 beer and an amount of pizza somewhat less than one pie.

In similar manner, we can determine for each possible price of beer that amount that you will want to buy, given your preference structure, the $1 income you want to spend, and the price of pizza. We may list these prices and quantities in Table 10A.1 in demand schedule form, and construct a smooth demand curve as in Figure 10A.4.

Table 10A.1   Demand Schedule for Beer
($1.00 to be spent on beer and pizza at lunch, the price of pizza being $.60)

Price	Quantity
$1.00	0.4
.	.
.	.
.	.
$0.60	0.7
$0.50	0.8
$0.40	1.0
$0.30	1.4
.	.
$0.20	2.0

Figure 10A.4   The Individual's Demand Curve for Beer

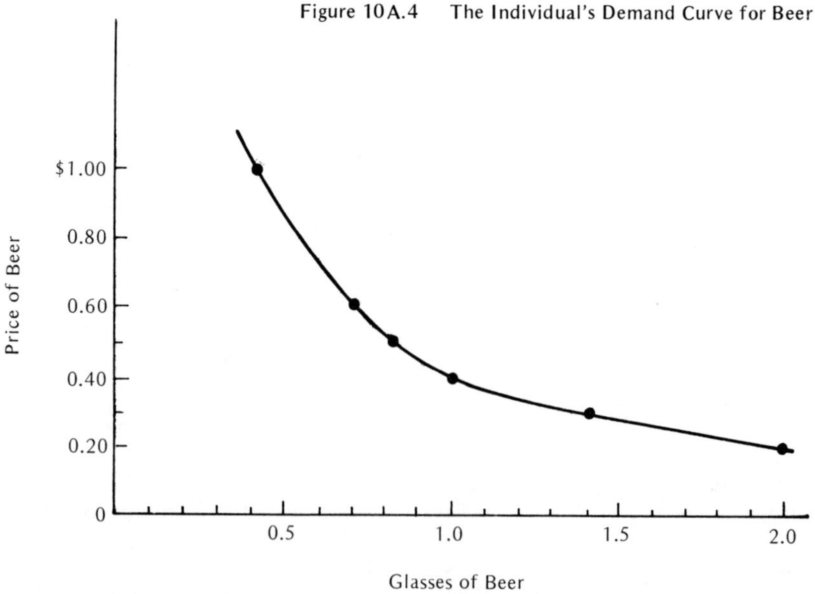

Price of Beer

Glasses of Beer

There are several additional points to make about this derivation. First, in practice beer does not come in variable-size glasses—a 4-oz glass, a 5-oz glass, a

6-oz glass, a 7-oz glass, and 8-oz glass, or in fractions of an 8-oz glass of beer. But this does not raise any basic problem in the analysis of how the equilibrium price of beer is determined. If we were to consider a cultural system in which the amount of beer was weighed on a scale, just as fruit and meat, there would be no problem. But more important, we are generally interested in your demand schedule for a much longer period of time than one or several hours, or one day; we are interested in a period of a month (or a year). Then instead of buying a 6.4-oz glass of beer or 4/5 of an 8-oz glass 30 times, when the price is $.50, which is 192 ounces of beer over the month, you buy an 8-oz glass 24 times during that month. That is, you tend to buy an 8-oz glass almost every day, refraining once or twice a week when the weather's not too hot, or when you have no great need for beer.

Moreover, suppose your demand curve is kinky, as in Figure 10A.5, where you decide to buy no beer if the price exceeds $.65, one beer per day if it is above $.35, but not $.65, and two beers per day if it is above $.10 but not above $.35. The fact that there are many people who demand beer, each having his own set of preferences, means that the kinks will occur at many different prices. For some, the kinks will occur at the same price as with you. For others the kinks may occur at prices slightly above $.60, $.30, and $.05; for still others slightly below $.60, $.30, and $.05. And so forth. When we add up all the individuals, a rather regular market demand schedule is obtained such as that in Table 10A.2. This allows us to represent the market demand schedule for beer by the smooth curve of Figure 10A.6, approximating this schedule. This then is the demand curve relevant for the determination of the equilibrium price of beer.

Figure 10A.5   A Kinky Demand Curve for Beer

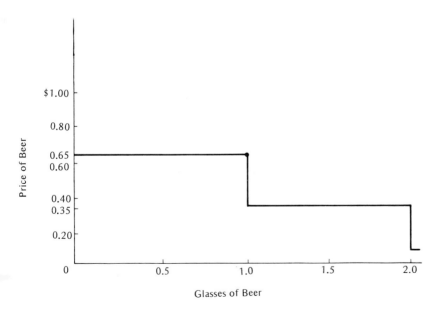

Glasses of Beer

Table 10A.2   Individual Demand and Total Demand Schedules for Beer (8-oz glasses)

| | Quantity of Beer Demanded (At Lunch) by: | | | | | | | |
| Price | You | Individual | | | | | | Total Demand |
		#1	#2	#3	#4	#5	. . .	
$0.75	0	0	0	0	0	0	. . .	10,000
0.70	0	0	0	0	1	0		13,500
0.65	1	0	0	0	1	1		17,300
0.60	1	1	0	0	1	1		21,200
0.55	1	1	0	1	1	1	. . .	25,300
0.50	1	1	1	1	2	1		29,600
0.45	1	1	1	1	2	1		34,000
0.40	1	1	1	1	2	2		38,600
0.35	2	1	1	1	2	2	. . .	43,600
0.30	2	2	2	1	2	2		49,600
0.25	2	2	2	2	2	2		56,000
0.20	2	2	2	2	2	2		64,500
0.15	2	2	2	2	3	2	. . .	75,000
0.10	3	2	2	2	3	3		90,000

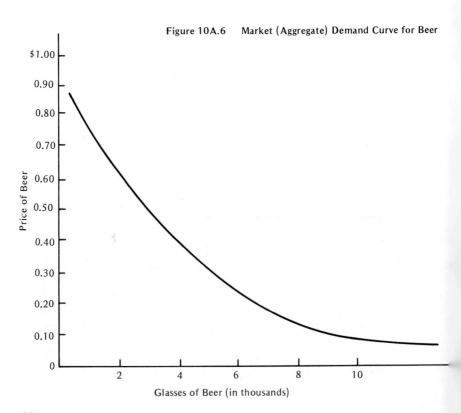

Figure 10A.6   Market (Aggregate) Demand Curve for Beer

Price of Beer

$1.00
0.90
0.80
0.70
0.60
0.50
0.40
0.30
0.20
0.10
0

2   4   6   8   10

Glasses of Beer (in thousands)

On Getting the Same Satisfaction from the Last Penny
Spent on Each Good

There is another useful way of thinking about that combination of goods which you most prefer for a given amount to be spent on them—say combination M in Figure 10A.1—when you can spend only $1 on beer and pizza. To see this, let us construct in Figure 10A.7 the $1 expenditure line of Figure 10A.1 and the indifference curve to which it is tangent. Now suppose you consider spending your $1 on combination X rather than M. We can immediately see that this would be irrational. For if you contemplate the purchase of combination X, you can say to yourself: "I can reduce my purchase of beer by a nickel, in which case I forego XY amount of beer. I can then take that nickel and spend it on pizza and get YZ additional pizza. Then I will end up with a combination of beer and pizza represented by Z. I observe that I prefer the Z combination to the X combination; and the former does lie on a higher indifference curve when I use indifference curves to map my preferences. That is, the utility I lose from giving up a nickel's worth of beer is more than compensated by the gain in utility from another nickel's worth of pizza. So it surely makes sense for me to buy the combination Z rather than X."

Figure 10A.7   Substituting Between Commodities to Maximize Utility

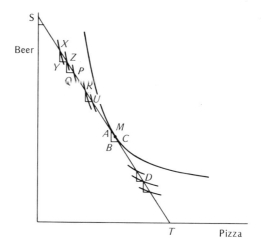

You might then reason that, if you are better off by spending one less nickel on beer and one more on pizza, maybe you could become still better off by reducing your consumption of beer by still another nickel's worth and increasing your consumption of pizza by still one more nickel's worth. You will be giving up ZQ amount of beer and obtaining QP more of pizza. You find this desirable, because you prefer combination P to combination Z; the former lies on a higher indifference curve. So you will spend less on beer and more on pizza. And you will continue, at least for a while, this process of substituting a nickel's worth of pizza for a nickel's worth of beer. But you also note that, as you continue to substitute a nickel's worth of pizza for a nickel's worth of beer, your net gain in utility becomes less and less. This is reflected in the fact that your indifference curves become less and less steep as you move down the $1 expenditure line from X to Z to P to R to U. Finally, when you reach the vicinity of point M, you see that the utility lost by spending one less nickel on beer just about equals the utility gained by spending one more nickel on pizza. That is, reducing your consumption of beer by an amount AB puts you on a lower indifference curve, but when you increase your consumption of pizza by an amount BC you return to ithe same indifference curve (as far as you can see), namely the one that is tangent to the $1 expenditure line at M. So once you get close to M, you gain nothing by further substitution of pizza for beer. The utility of the last nickel's worth of beer is about the same as the utility of the next nickel's worth of pizza, which also is about the same as the last nickel's worth of pizza. To make this point more strongly, suppose you initially contemplate consuming the combination represented by point D rather than point X. Then you see that by giving up a nickel's worth of beer you will be giving up much more utility than the utility from a nickel's worth of pizza. You will be moving on to a lower indifference curve. In fact, you find that you will be better off if you substitute in the other direction—that is, if you buy a nickel's worth less of pizza and a nickel's worth more of beer. For by doing so you will be moving on to a higher indifference curve. Further, you find that it makes sense to continue to substitute beer for pizza until you come close to point M. There once again you will find that the utility foregone from spending one less nickel on pizza just about equals the utility gained from spending one more nickel on beer.

So now you reach the conclusion that for your dollar, point M, which we have already identified as representing the combination you most prefer—that is, which maximizes your utility—also represents the combination where the utility you get from the last nickel's worth of each good is approximately the same. Of course, if we were to blow up the diagram to five times its size, we might find that our approximation was pretty crude. However, if we were to do this, we could then talk about substituting a penny's worth of beer for a penny's worth of pizza. We would find that the last penny spent on each good at or close to point M yields approximately the same utility. So we can state the principle that when you have a fixed sum to spend on two goods, and you want to by some of each, the last penny spent on each good must yield you the same utility when you are buying your most preferred combination. This, in more technical language, is a necessary (but only a necessary) condition for utility maximization.[2] And this principle makes sense—for if the last penny spent on pizza gives you perceptibly more utility than the last penny spent on beer, then you would be better off by spending at least one more penny on pizza and one less on beer. But this contradicts the assertion that you are already buying your most preferred combination.

[2]This necessary condition is often called the first-order condition for maximization of utility. When it is combined with another condition, namely that your indifference curves be convex to the origin (which is often called the second-order condition, and which we discussed in footnote 1), we have the necessary and sufficient conditions for utility maximizing behavior. Of course, we are implicitly assuming that any good that is consumed has positive marginal utility no matter how much of it is consumed (an assumption of insatiable consumer appetite), and that the marginal utility of a good diminishes as we consume more and more of that good.

Also, note that point M in Figure 10A.2 does satisfy the first-order condition for utility maximization, but does not satisfy the second-order condition. It therefore does not represent a utility maximizing combination. Rather, as we found out, it corresponds to a utility minimizing combination.

Conflict Resolution and Cooperative Procedures

INTRODUCTION

In this chapter we want to proceed in examining what can be done with regard to resolving conflicts. We hope to identify some basic principles for cooperative action. We want to see if we can develop cooperative procedures that can get parties out of the deadlocked and stalemated situations in which they so frequently get trapped. We realize, of course, that this is no easy job. From the earliest times, stalemates and deadlocks, as well as wars, have been recorded, and we do not seem to be much farther ahead now than centuries ago. Yet it is imperative that we continue to attack the problem.

To make headway on this problem, we find it useful to deal with specific situations. Let us return to the in-group–out-group conflict of the previous chapter. Suppose you are an influential citizen who happens to be respected by members of both the in-group and the out-group. You are concerned that the current situation is deadlocked or stalemated at a point that is highly undesirable (inefficient) socially. It may, for example, be characterized by point e in Figure 10.7, corresponding to a joint action involving a low level of social welfare expenditures and a high level of disorder. Not only are you concerned, but you are also aware that there are positions—sets of joint actions—each of which both the in-group and the out-group greatly prefer to the current situation. This situation is depicted in Figure 11.1. Here we have reproduced the relevant curves of Figure

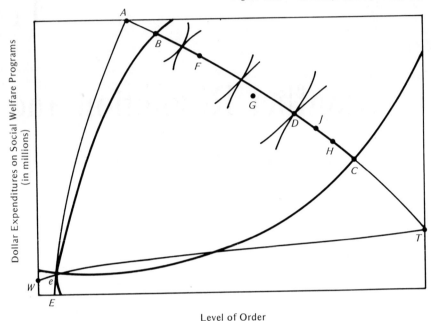

Figure 11.1   A Compromise Joint Action

10.7 We have charted the best-response curves AE and TW of the in-group and out-group, respectively. The equilibrium point e is indicated by the intersection of these two curves. We have also constructed selected indifference curves for these groups. In particular, we have indicated by bold lines the indifference curves of the in-group and out-group which pass through the equilibrium point e. We have also constructed a curve from A, the most preferred joint action of the out-group, to point T, the most preferred action of the in-group. We have constructed this curve so that it passes through points of tangency of pairs of indifference curves, one for the in-group and one for the out-group.

THE CONFLICT OVER THE DESIRED EFFICIENCY OUTCOME

You are a concerned citizen. You note the current deadlocked situation, characterized by point e. You easily recognize that both parties would be much better off if somehow they could move to a point such as point D in Figure 11.1. Point D lies on an indifference curve for the in-group which is much higher than that indifference curve of the in-group which passes through point e and which reflects the level of satisfaction currently being realized by the in-group. Also, point D lies on an indifference curve for the out-group which is much higher than the out-group's indifference curve which passes through point e and which reflects the level of satisfaction (dissatisfaction) currently being received by the out-group. So wouldn't it be desirable for the two groups to get together and jointly decide that the level of social welfare programs the in-group supports should be consistent with *D* and that the level of disorder the out-group controls should also be consistent with point *D*?

As a third person who is "neutral," you might get the leaders of the two groups together and show them (perhaps with a simpler figure than Figure 11.1) that at this point *e* each group receives a relatively low level of satisfaction. You might show them that by simple agreement on a compromise joint action, they could be at point *D* where each group would experience much greater satisfaction. That is, you suggest that they employ a simple *principle of a compromise joint action.*

But this obvious type of solution is not so simple if the leader of one or both of the groups is perceptive. The leader of the in-group, for example, might say: "Yes, we are both better off at *D*. But it is not really a fair point. A fair compromise joint action might be that represented by point *H*." (Note that point *H* corresponds to a higher level of satisfaction for the in-group than point *D*. It also corresponds to a lower level of satisfaction for the out-group.)

The perceptive leader of the out-group might say: "Yes, *D* does represent a much better position than *e*, but it would not be a fair compromise point to the out-group. A fair point would be *F*." (Note that point *F* corresponds to a level of satisfaction for the out-group which is higher than *D*, and a level of satisfaction for the in-group which is lower than *D*.) Thus a conflict exists: Which point along the arc *AT* should be the joint action to be cooperatively arrived at by both groups? Of course, this assumes that you have been able to convince the two groups that they should narrow down their considerations to points along the arc *AT, the efficiency frontier.* [1] You may have shown them that any point not on this arc is inferior to some point on the arc, in the sense that both could be better off by moving from a joint action off the arc to a joint action represented by a point on the arc. In doing so, both participants move to a higher indifference curve. But now we have a new conflict.

Strictly speaking, we can see that the in-group prefers to move to a position on this arc that is as close to *T* as possible. But it recognizes that it cannot get any closer than point *C*, because any point on the arc closer to point *T* provides the out-group with less satisfaction than it derives from the current joint action *e*. So of all the joint actions on the efficiency frontier that would not make the out-group worse off, *C* is the point that represents the joint action most preferred by the in-group.

In parallel fashion, the out-group would prefer a joint action on the efficiency frontier as close to *A* as possible. However, it recognizes that if the joint action were closer to *A* than *B*, the in-group would be worse off than with the joint action represented by *e*. So the out-group recognizes that it cannot get any closer to *A* than *B*. From these considerations, we can see that the joint actions represented by points along the arc *BC*, part of the efficiency frontier, form what we shall call the *realistic negotiation set.*

---

[1] The efficiency frontier *AT* is defined by the locus of points of tangency of the indifference curves. Once the participants are on the efficiency frontier, one of them cannot move to a higher indifference curve without the other moving to a lower indifference curve.

SIMPLE COMPROMISE SOLUTIONS:

Split the Difference (in the Joint Action Space)

If both leaders are informed, how would you go about resolving the conflict? You might think of one of the simple types of procedures that have been success-fully used in the past. You might suggest a simple 50-50 compromise over the joint action each proposes, or a split-the-difference compromise.

For this type of solution, you take point B as representing the realistic joint action most preferred by the out-group and point C as representing the one most preferred by the in-group. You then take the levels of expenditures associated with points B and C and propose something midway between the two. Likewise, you take the levels of disorder represented by points B and C and propose some-thing midway between the two. You suggest that the parties agree on this type of simple compromise and try to point out its fairness. In view of the respect that you command and the forcefulness of your arguments, you may convince both parties. Then the conflict would be resolved. Note, however, that you would be suggesting a joint action corresponding to point G. Point G does not lie on the arc BC and thus does not represent an efficient joint action. There is some point on the arc representing a joint action that both parties would prefer to that represented by point G. But then you may say to yourself: "Well, point G is rather close to the efficiency frontier. Let's not try to get too sophisticated by indicating that there is a still better point that they can achieve. In doing so, we would open up the discussion again and perhaps to a Pandora's box of problems." Being a wise arbitrator and knowing that group leaders usually are not rational (as defined by the rigorous economist or regional scientist), you follow the old adage "let well enough alone."

Weighted Average and the Conflict over Appropriate Weights

Of course, if you are a respected and skillful arbitrator, you do not need figures like 11.1. You bring the parties together. You percieve their differences and skillfully propose a compromise that leads each party to feel that it has gained much. However, it does not always work this way, particularly in important situations. For example, if you propose to split the difference between the most preferred joint actions (B and C) in the realistic negotiation set, the leader of the out-group might reply: "Well, a 50-50 compromise on actions has a certain amount of fairness to it, but it really hides the basic issues. It's not actions that count. It's the satisfaction that is derived from some action." And he might state that the in-group would get the better deal in a 50-50 compromise, for it wouldn't be giving up very much by paying the higher taxes required for the higher level of social welfare expenditures, whereas the out-group would be giving up an awful lot by not having more social welfare programs. That is, he might argue: "What would another \$10 million of expenditures mean to the in-group members? They would be paying higher taxes, but the money for these taxes wouldn't be providing that much additional utility, because they are in the high-income bracket. We wouldn't be depriving them of much satisfaction if they had to pay another \$10 million in taxes. On the other hand, consider the value of that additional \$10 million if the social welfare programs were effectively implemented and led to improved quality of education for the children of the out-group. Hence, a 50-50 compromise action is not really *just* or *equitable*. A much more reasonable compromise would be a weighted average where the importance of our proposal is given three times the weight of the proposal of the in-group."

Of course, you can imagine that the in-group has a counterargument. A member of the in-group might argue that excessive taxes will destroy incentive, the basic force behind the tremendous growth and strength of the free enterprise system. This is, after all, what made America what it is today. On the basis of this argument, he might insist that the proposals be weighted so that those of the in-group are set as only 50 percent more important than those of the out-group.

If you are a skillful arbitrator, you recognize that the conflict is now reduced to the problem of how to weight the two proposals. Both parties may be adamant in insisting that you employ their weighting in a compromise. If you continue to argue about the merits of the different sets of weights of the different parties, you will usually get nowhere.

It should be noted that this problem of choosing proper weights develops partly because we are not able to measure utility. If we were able to measure the utility of a typical member of the in-group and a typical member of the out-group, we might be able to resolve at least to some extent the differences between the two groups. We might be able to narrow down the range of compromise joint actions over which the debate is conducted. If we were able to measure utilities, we might be able to convince the out-group that some of its demands were excessive, in the sense that they would yield the in-group little additional utility compared to the utility currently received from the joint action given by point *e*. Also, you might be able to convince the in-group to relax some of its demands so that the out-group could realize additional utility.

Concession Procedures

Let us return to the typical situation in which utilities or levels of satisfaction cannot be measured. At best, we can derive indifference maps which represent the preference orderings of the two groups. As an arbitrator you say to yourself: "I cannot get the two groups to concentrate on a simple compromise, such as split-the-difference, over their most preferred joint actions. I cannot get them to agree on weights to be applied to their proposals—they just get into another type of stalemate over what weighting is proper. Hence, I'd better look around for something else on which the two groups might focus their attention and perhaps come to agreement." You might try, for example, forgetting about weights and absolute magnitudes, and shift to percentages. You might say to the two parties "Let's consider the question of concessions. Suppose we think of it this way. Each of you agrees to concede by the same small percent, say 5 percent, on your most desired proposal. If the result is two different proposals (joint actions) then let's agree that each of you will concede by another 5 percent. If the result is still two different proposals, let's keep this up until we reach proposals that come sufficiently close to each other so that it makes sense to split the difference."

In more precise terms, say we start off with joint actions represented by points *A* and *T* in Figure 11.2 (or *B* and *C* in Figure 11.1). In the first round of concessions, the out-group reduces its demand for social welfare expenditures by 5 percent and at the same time suggests an increase of 5 percent in the level of order from that corresponding to point A. Its new proposed joint action is A'. Likewise, the in-group—starting with the joint action corresponding to point T—reduces its demand for order by 5 percent and increases by 5 percent its offer of social welfare expenditures. Its new proposed joint action is thus T'. Because a considerable distance separates points A' and T', both the out-group and the in-group undertake a second round of concessions and concede by another 5 percent, arriving at proposed joint actions A'' and T'', respectively. In a third round of concessions, they arrive at proposed joint actions A''' and T''', respectively. After a sufficient number of rounds, their proposed joint actions, say A^{ix} and T^{ix}, are sufficiently close to each other that it is judged reasonable by both to split the difference. They thus arrive at the compromise joint action H.

Figure 11.2   A Series of Small Equal-Percentage Concessions

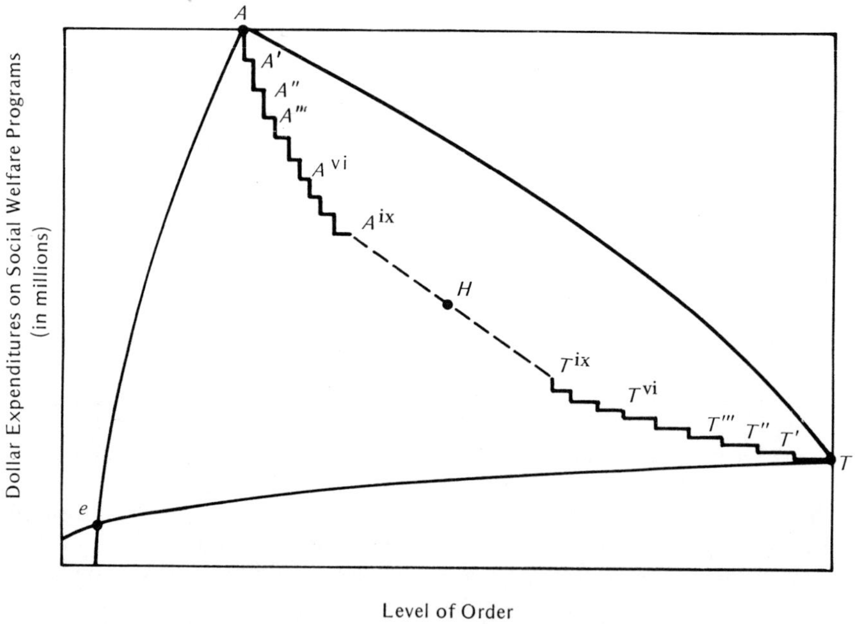

Level of Order

Again, skillful negotiators using this and similar kinds of procedures in the past frequently have been successful. An example is labor-management arbitration. On the other hand, we are aware of many stalemate situations where this procedure has been tried and has not worked. The out-group may, for example, argue: "You're just trying to hide the issues again. You're neglecting the fact that in conceding 5 percent of what we find important we give up much more than the in-group gives up through the same procedure." A smart leader of the out-group says: "We want $85 million worth of social welfare expenditures. You ask us in the first move to give up 5 percent of it, which is $4.25 million. The in-group is suggesting social welfare expenditures of $20 million. You are asking them to increase it by 5 percent, namely $1 million. What are you trying to put over on us?"

As a skillful arbitrator, you might have initially perceived this kind of argument and changed the situation so that the absolute amount $4.25 million, corresponding to the 5 percent reduction in the out-group's demand for social welfare expenditures, is also taken to be the amount by which the in-group is to increase its offer regarding social welfare expenditures. Likewise, the absolute amount corresponding to the 5 percent reduction in the in-group's demand for order is taken to be the amount by which the out-group is to increase its offer regarding the level of order. But even this ploy on your part does not handle the argument of inequity when the leader of the out-group states: "But $4.25 million of social welfare expenditures means much more to us than does the loss of $4.25 million in income to the in-group. This kind of concession procedure does not make sense. It's just a trick to conceal, with the notion of percentages, the basic inequities and injustices that are involved." The in-group retorts by pointing out that giving up 5 percent of its demands on the level of order means much more to it than does the corresponding concession by the out-group regarding order. But this may not carry much weight when the out-group is emotionally concerned with social welfare programs.

So once again you have to search around for new criteria. Anticipating this kind of argument, you might avoid comparisons by asking the out-group to concentrate only on concessions in its demand for social welfare expenditures (the issue of basic concern to it), and the in-group to concentrate only on concessions in its demands for level of order (the issue of most concern to it). Then after a series of concessions, you might reach a point where you propose a joint action corresponding to the demands for social welfare expenditures and for level of order reached by the out-group and in-group, respectively, in the last round of concessions. You leave implicit the fact that the joint action means willingness on the part of the in-group to levy more taxes and approve the higher level of social welfare expenditures, and willingness on the part of the out-group to control its activities so the level of order proposed can be achieved.

Or you might have to search around for other criteria on which to focus, or use other ploys to find some issue on which they can reach an acceptable compromise. This can then be used to define an acceptable compromise joint action.

Of course, if it were possible to specify the utilities that each group receives in connection with the diverse joint actions—for example, to associate a utility magnitude for each party with respect to points A and T (or B and C in Figure 11.1)—then the arbitrator might be able to suggest a joint action that would split the difference between their utilities. Or he might suggest a series of equal-percentage concessions in terms of utilities. But such a situation is very unlikely to develop. This is so not only because in most situations we as social scientists have been unsuccessful in measuring utilities but also because the groups might not agree on the utilities to associate with points A and T (or B and C in Figure 11.1)

SOME MORE SOPHISTICATED COMPROMISE PROCEDURES AND GUIDING PRINCIPLES

You have tried the simpler guiding principles to resolve the conflict—such as a split-the-difference porcedure in the joint action space, or a weighted average of the proposed joint actions, or equal-percentage concessions in the joint action space, or weighted percentage concessions in the joint action space, or a split-the-difference procedure over utility when utility can be measured, or equal-absolute or percentage concessions in a series of rounds. You have not been successful, and you now look around for a more sophisticated technique which, because it is more sophisticated and therefore further removed from the point of contention, may allow you to bring the two groups together more easily.

Desirable Properties of Cooperative Procedures

You think of different properties of a procedure that might be psychologically appealing to both participants. You want to induce them to consider the procedure as worth studying for possible use. One property that often has considerable appeal for vested interests and conservative groups is an approach that involves only a small change at any step or move. This has appeal because it allows the conservative party, usually an in-group, to be sure that it cannot suffer a disastrous loss or defeat from any move. If the conservative group does make an error, the fact that there is only a small change in actions assures the group that its loss will not be excessive. On the other hand, out-group members may not favor such a procedure because they are eager to get results soon, usually perceive that there is little they can lose, consider the series of small steps as involving too much time, and in general may be more impatient. Nonetheless, because the conservative in-group is likely to feel more intensely about the need for such a property in a cooperative procedure than the bold, risk-taking out-group does, such a property may be desirable. This property might be characterized as a *limited-commitment* property, or a *small action-change* property.

A second property, which usually goes hand in hand with the first, is the need for a series of steps, moves, or rounds in order to reach an effective resolution of the conflict. We might designate this property as *sequential resolution*. A series of small moves may have appeal because the parties are able to perceive a resolution which, though it gives only a small improvement on any *one* move, promises significant improvement after *many* moves.

A third property, which again may have more appeal to the conservative, vested interests, and those who would like to maintain the status quo (even though that is impossible), is one that guarantees improvement to both parties in each round. The rationale for this is obvious. However, if there are a long series or rounds of discussions, and the improvements on each round are of small magnitude, the out-group may become more impatient and even somewhat negative toward this process. Nonetheless, a *guaranteed-improvement* property may be not only acceptable but even desirable.

A fourth property is one that insures that a joint action is ultimately achieved that is efficient in the sense that both parties can not shift from that joint action to another which would make both better off (or at least make one better off while not making the other worse off). That is, the procedure should ultimately take the parties to a point on the efficiency frontier, specifically on the arc *BC*, in Figure 11.1. This property might be called *efficiency* or more generally, *objective achievement*.

A fifth desirable property is one that makes it impossible to forecast the end point of the process. We may designate this property preindeterminacy. Although we may know that a procedure with this property insures that the participants will ultimately adopt a joint action on the efficiency frontier, there should be no way of telling which efficient joint action it will be. Thus the parties cannot disagree at the start about the relative desirability of a procedure having this property as opposed to another procedure because the former may lead to a joint action which one participant prefers while the latter leads to a different joint action which the second participant prefers. For they cannot predict which joint action will be realized by the former procedure.

A sixth property that is desirable and may have considerable psychological appeal is the *veto* property. This property would give each group the power to exercise a veto at any time, and through exercise of this veto bring the participants back to the joint action, say *e*, from which they started. In this way, it is guaranteed that no one can be worse off than he was initially. But in a sense this property is redundant, because we already have guaranteed improvement on each move. Yet in the real world, where a concerned arbitrator is dealing in a conflict situation, there is often a high level of emotional involvement by one or more parties. Stating a property in two or more ways is often more effective for obtaining effective participation. We must also realize that words are, after all, cultural symbols. The terms *guaranteed improvement* and *veto* may have quite different connotations to the different parties in the conflict. The former may be clearly understood and the nature of the property clearly perceived by an in-group. But it may be easily misperceived or not fully understood by an out-group. On the other hand, the veto power may have a very clear and precise meaning to an out-group but have less significance to the in-group when compared to the property of guaranteed improvement. Thus, in some cases redundancy in properties is desirable.

There are still other properties that might be developed as relevant and significant for conflict situations. One such property might recognize the strategic potential of each party, though this concept is very difficult to define. Another property might represent equity or social justice, again a property that is difficult to define.

The Veto Incremax Cooperative Procedure

Let us now consider developing a procedure that incorporates several desirable properties. We call it the *veto incremax* procedure because it gives each participant the *veto* power and allows participants to approach a resolution of their conflict *incrementally*—that is, in a series of steps at every one of which each participant chooses a *maximizing* action. Suppose you start with the veto power. (Stating this property first might win over the out-group, or make it interested in examining the procedure—that is, might break down its resistance.) To it you add sequential resolution, limited commitment, and guaranteed improvement, which may appeal to the in-group and make it willing to consider the procedure. In addition, because of your concern for social welfare you want to see that the objective achievement property is incorporated into the procedure. That is, you want to insure that an efficient joint action from the standpoint of social welfare is achieved. (This property, however, may have little appeal to either group.) Finally, as an arbitrator you might want to have the preindeterminacy property in reserve. If either of the groups accuses you of playing favorites, you are in a position to state that it is not possible for anyone to forecast the outcome. In fact, you can ask the group that is complaining to call in a mathematician to prove this—although if it is the out-group that accuses you of favoritism, it is not likely that they will put much stock in the findings or statements of a mathematician. Nonetheless, it is good to retain the preindeterminacy property.

Rules in its Operations. Having in mind the six properties

veto power
sequential resolution
limited commitment
guaranteed improvement
objective achievement (efficiency)
preindeterminacy

we define a process which involves a series of moves for each party. On each move, the parties make a proposal for a joint action. The making of these proposals is, however, subject to several rules. To state the first rule, we must focus on the deadlock point *e* and the two indifference curves which pass through it. We stripe in the area lying between the two indifference curves, as shown in Figure 11.3. Any joint action in the interior of this striped area represents a joint action which makes each party better off than the joint action *e*, because for each party it lies on a higher indifference curve than the one going through point *e*. So every point in this striped area is consistent with the property of guaranteed improvement, if the joint action represented by that point were adopted rather than the joint action represented by point *e*. All these points make up a set which we call the *improvement set*. Now we state Rule 1: *In making a proposal for a joint action, each player shall not consider a joint action that would yield any participant an outcome less preferred than the joint action reached in the preceding move.* On move 1, this rule means that each participant's proposal for a joint action must lie within or on the boundary of the striped area in Figure 11.3. Or we may require that the proposal lie strictly within the striped area and not on the boundary line. On each successive move, we shall define a new set of indifference curves that defines the new improvement set.

Now, recall the property of limited commitment. We ask each party to specify along both the vertical and horizontal axes the maximum change that it is willing to consider on any move. For example, on the first move we ask each party to specify—from the base point *e*—the maximum change with regard to both social welfare expenditures and level of disorder that it is willing to consider or allow on that move. Suppose the in-group says it would not mind seeing as much as a $6 million change in the level of social welfare expenditures (measured along the vertical) and a change of 20 points in the index of level of disorder (measured along the horizontal). The out-group might specify that it would be quite willing to consider as much as an $80 million change in social welfare expenditures, but only a change of 3.5 points in the index of level of disorder. So we take the least of these maxima along the vertical and the horizontal axes, respectively, and construct a box around point *e* as indicated in Figure 11.3. Thus, the height of the box must represent an increase of $6 million in social welfare expenditures and the width of the box a decrease of 3.5 in the level of disorder, all with reference to the base point *e*. Now any point within or on the box represents a change in the joint action that does not exceed the maxima that

Figure 11.3   The First Move in a Veto Incremax Procedure

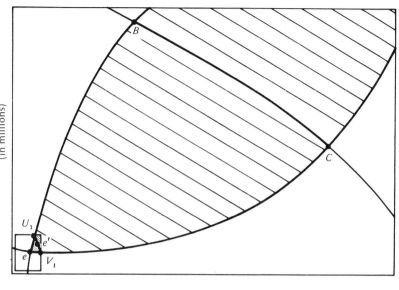

Level of Order

oither party can tolerate. Each point in that box is consistent with the limited-commitment property. So the set of points in the box and on its boundary can be viewed as the *commitment set* for the first move. In each subsequent move we will construct a new commitment set because, as we shall see, the base point will be different for each subsequent move. Now we are ready for a statement of Rule 2: *On each move, no player can propose a joint action that lies outside the commitment set.*

We can see that on the first move each participant must propose a joint action that lies, by Rule 1, within the improvement set but that also lies within the commitment set. Thus, each participant is restricted to the shaded area around point *e*, which is the overlay or intersection of the two sets, the improvement set and the commitment set. Now, if a participant is going to make a proposal from this shaded area, he will likely propose that joint action which maximizes his utility or is most preferred—in other words, that point in the shaded area on his highest indifference curve. As we can see from Figure 11.3, that point is point U_1 for the in-group and point V_1 for the out-group. Note that these points do not coincide, signifying that the two proposals of a joint action are inconsistent: We therefore need a third rule to obtain a consistent joint action.

In constructing Rule 3, we have in mind the need to effect a compromise on each of the small steps involved in the series of moves. Because each move is to be only a small move, because the difference between the two proposed joint actions is therefore small, and because a whole series of moves is contemplated, it is less likely that the two parties will disagree on a simple compromise procedure, which was the case when we proposed a compromise joint action once and for all for the total conflict. At this point, two simple compromise procedures

276

suggest themselves. One is split the difference, which means drawing a straight line connecting points V_1 and U_1 in Figure 11.3 and taking the midpoint of that line as a compromise joint action. This can then serve as a base from which improvement is sought on the second round. Alternatively, we might toss a coin to see who has his way on the first move, with the understanding, of course, that on the second move, the person who loses the toss will have his way. The parties will then alternate in having their way on the sequence of moves. This is an alternating leader-follower process or principle.

Suppose we opt for the first. Then we can state Rule 3 as: *If, on any move, the proposed joint actions of the participants are not identical, the participants shall adopt as a compromise proposal that joint action defined by the midpoint of the straight line connecting the proposed joint actions of the two participants.*

We see from the operation of Rule 3 that the midpoint e' of line $V_1 U_1$ is the new compromise joint action at the end of the first move. We then take it as the new base or reference point for the second move. In Figure 11.4 we plot e' and

Figure 11.4   A Sequence of Compromise Joint Actions in a Veto Incremax Procedure

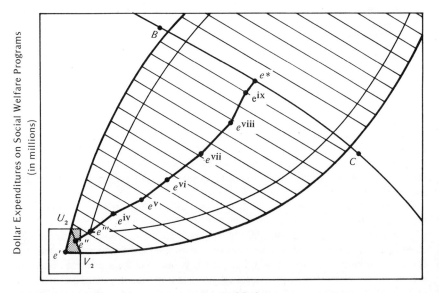

Level of Order

also the indifference curves of the in-group and out-group which pass through e'. We stripe in the area lying between these two indifference curves, thus defining the improvement set for the second move. We then ask each participant to specify the maximum change he is willing to allow along both the vertical and the horizontal axes on the second move. The in-group, for example, might be willing to allow as much as a \$7 million change in social welfare expenditures (because it did not do too badly in the first-round activity) and 20 points in the index of the level of disorder. The out-group might be willing to consider a change of 4 points in the index of level of disorder, and \$80 million in social welfare expenditures. From the statement of these maximum changes, we take the least vertical and the least horizontal change proposed to form a box around the point e', as illustrated in Figure 11.4. We once again shade the overlay or intersection of the box (commitment set) and the improvement set. We let each party propose a joint action in this shaded area it most prefers, say U_2 for the in-group and V_2 for the out-group. We connect these two proposed joint actions by a straight line and find the midpoint e'', representing the compromise joint action relevant for the next move. We apply the same procedure on successive moves, until finally we reach the efficiency frontier or are so close to the efficiency frontier that it makes sense to stop the process. This is indicated by the series of points we have plotted in Figure 11.4.

Qualifications to its Use. We should recognize that the veto incremax procedure detailed above is an overly refined sequence of the steps that can be expected. First of all, we know that preference orderings are not precise. They are often fuzzy in the minds of the leaders representing the groups, and so not rigorously depicted by a set of indifference curves. Often a leader is not sure whether one joint action is preferable to another; his opinion might fluctuate depending on the time of day you ask for it.

More important, we know that preference orderings do not stay the same when one enters a negotiation process. They change. First of all, each leader learns something from each step of the negotiation process in which he has been involved. This learning experience may lead to changes, perhaps drastic ones, in his preference orderings and so in his indifference maps. Often, too, the leader may be specifically motivated to maximize utility or satisfaction, but he unavoidably makes comparisons with the utility or satisfaction being derived by the other party. Thus relative utility enters in to some extent. This means that the problem cannot be precisely defined as one in which each of the two parties is bent on utility maximization. Their objective functions are more complex.

Not only do participants learn and find themselves with more complex objective functions, but their tastes, attitudes, and values may change during the negotiation process. They may learn that the next fellow is not so bad to deal with after all. They may become more Christian in the process. All this changes their indifference maps. It also changes their objective functions.

Moreover, there is no reason why the indifference curves should be well-behaved, as indicated in the figures. If they are not well-behaved and have concave sections, it may be impossible in some round to guarantee improvement.

Thus, many of the implicit assumptions and aspects of the process depicted by our diagrams may not be realistic. However, the procedure does suggest a series of steps that can in a rough way simulate what one might expect. In this sense it can be very valuable.

OTHER COOPERATIVE PROCEDURES AND GUIDING PRINCIPLES

We have outlined only one of the many possible cooperative procedures and sets of guiding principles that might be used in resolving a conflict. There are, of course, numerous others. We can see this if we go back and look at the list of desirable properties. For example, the property of efficiency may not be neces-

278

sary. We may well imagine that both parties are out to achieve a certain level of satisfaction and once they achieve this level are not strongly motivated to fight and bargain for any more. So if, in Figure 11.1, point G achieves the level of satisfaction which is greater than or at least equal to what each party is motivated to obtain, then G corresponds to a joint action that might be regarded as a satisfactory resolution of the conflict—though it is not socially efficient.

Or, as we have indicated, the veto power is in one sense redundant when the property of guaranteed improvement on each move is involved in the cooperative procedure. So the veto power need not be included. Or the veto power can be included and guaranteed improvement omitted. Or limited commitment may be omitted. After all, if one party can exercise a veto power and if he is conservative, he need not worry about the possibility of major loss from too big a change. He can always go back to the initial starting point, Or, as we have already noted, the property of preindeterminacy need not be an essential one; it can be omitted. Or, for that matter, given the veto power, the properties of sequential resolution and limited commitment can be omitted.

In addition to cooperative procedures that are combinations of some of the six properties of the veto incremax procedure, we can have procedures that introduce other properties. We have mentioned the property of maintaining strategic potential. We can think of a conflict situation in which it is inconceivable, from a psychological standpoint, for one of the parties—which has traditionally initiated proposals—to give up the right of having the first opportunity to make a suggestion. That is, we might have a cooperative procedure in which we preserve the right of one of the parties to be the first to suggest a joint action. We may be able to introduce another property, however, which in effect assures equity for the second party. For example, in taking weighted averages of the proposals we might give the second party twice as much weight as the first. More specifically, in each of the moves of the incremax procedure we might let the in-group, the traditional leaders of the society, propose a joint action. We then have a rule that states that the out-group can also make a proposal for a joint action, but the proposal must not be more than 5 percent different on any dimension than that proposed by the in-group. If the two joint proposals are incompatible, we take a weighted average, where the in-group's weight is one and the out-group's weight is two. This property can be said to preserve the leadership role of the in-group, which may be of extreme importance psychologically to that group. It may, however, allow the out-group to do even better on each move than it could do with the split-the-difference veto incremax procedure outlined in the previous section, or with the alternating leader-follower veto incremax procedure, which was hinted at in the previous section.[2]

Another variation involving new properties might be as follows. Suppose the out-group is impatient. Its leadership is very aggressive and demanding. There is a need for quick action and immediate evidence of sizable gains. This is frequently the case in real life. The out-group, because of decades of exploitation, frustration, etc., may not be able to contain itself in a situation where many moves are involved in the negotiation process and long, slow, and careful deliberation is required in each. On this count, the veto incremax procedure, though it has

[2] For a full technical discussion of the incremax procedure see Isard, Smith et al, *General Theory: Social, Political, Economic and Regional* (Cambridge: M.I.T. Press, 1969), pp. 309–28.

strong appeal, might be inconsistent with the need for evidence of immediate gain. Thus, the skillful negotiator must introduce a property into the procedure which establishes the assurance of significant gains from the very beginning, at least as far as the out-group is concerned. From the standpoint of the in-group, however, this property may not be a critical element. The in-group may, on the other hand, find limited commitment, sequential resolution, and other desirable aspects appealing. One might imagine then that the leader of the in-group—who perhaps is the mayor of a town, chairman of a Chamber of Commerce, or president of a Federal Reserve Bank, and who was previously a professor at a university—has some knowledge of game theory or has at his hand a number of friends he can consult for immediate advice. He might be willing to go along with a property guaranteeing that the social welfare expenditures, which are currently at the level of perhaps $10 million, shall be at least $50 million, provided the veto incremax procedure is followed and the resulting joint action is accepted by the out-group. Thus we have a seventh property to be added to the six already listed for the veto incremax procedure: *guarantee of at least a* k *level for some magnitude* z.

With this property, the skillful negotiator would meet the need for immediate evidence of significant gain for the out-group. He is able to propose this property because he can have a rational discussion with the leader of the in-group and his mathematical friends. He can point out to them that although we cannot determine beforehand what the outcome of a veto incremax procedure will be, it is clear that the probability is almost zero that this outcome will not involve an expenditure of at least $50 million for social welfare. In connection with Figure 11.1, he is stating that the probability is almost zero that the joint action on the efficiency frontier *BC* will lie below and to the right of point *J*.

So in effect a new property is introduced, which one might say is consistent with the strategic potential of the out-group in this particular situation. However one looks at it, it does the trick.

In short, there are innumerable variations of procedures that can be developed. There are certain *scientific* aspects to the development of these procedures, as suggested by the graphic analysis of the previous section. One wants to make sure that a procedure can achieve the objectives you have in mind; it will hopefully do so if the parties agree to the procedure. On the other hand, there is an element of *art* in designing a procedure to meet the needs of the parties in the conflict, as was illustrated by the last variation we discussed.

CONCLUDING REMARKS

We have now spent three chapters on decision-making. We have introduced (a) the attitude variable, when a decision maker faces uncertain outcomes because of different possible states of the environment; (b) the conflict variable, as it is involved in many interdependent decision-making situations; and (c) principles and cooperative procedures for resolving stalemates and other conflicts. We now want to imbed our thinking in the actual framework of the total society. There is, after all, an *economic system* interrelating all these behaving units of society in their economic roles, which are aimed at adapting society to the environment and the resources it provides. There is a *social system* comprising numerous and diverse social groups within which are various individuals behaving in accord with roles relating to family, education, and religious institutions. Here the forces of cohesiveness, solidarity, dissension, and consensus are at play. There is a *political system* that determines the specific goals and targets consistent with broad social and cultural values. This sets social welfare programs, and is characterized by a hierarchical structure of levels of government. There is a *cultural system* that determines the nature of the socialization processes and how patterns, know-how, and other aspects of the culture are maintained.

It is within this broad context that regional systems operate, any regional system being one of many systems. It is also within this broad framework that groups and individuals make decisions, and within which conflicts are resolved. It is quite clear that the kind of conflicts that arise, the kinds of decisions that are made, and the kinds of cooperative procedures that are adopted are all greatly influenced by the broad social, political, and cultural setting. Hence it becomes necessary for us to consider the processes of regional development, location decisions, investment actions, decisions to migrate, and decisions to leave one job for another within this broader framework.

Chapter

12

Organizations: Their "Why, How, Who When and Where"

INTRODUCTION

Watertown is a quiet city in upstate New York. Historically it has been the center of a region possessing timber resources and producing paper, pulp, and related goods. The paper industry of northern New York has been declining, and so has the economy of Watertown–though this decline is being offset in part by growing recreational activities. Unemployment is relatively high, at times as high as 10 percent. Watertown's economic base is shaky because many of its factories are old and operate at high cost. A number of those still operating are just able to survive. Although the town's water system is highly polluted, the quality of its air is excellent, if not outstanding, because of very favorable wind conditions.

In mid-December 1972, Knowlton Brothers, one of the older pulp and paper mills in the United States, became the first mill in northern New York to be placed under order by New York authorities to halt air pollution. This order required the abatement of smoke discharges. It meant a higher cost of operation for this plant and perhaps could have led to its closing down, particularly because a number of other pulp-paper plants elsewhere were not being as heavily regulated. Yet most residents of Watertown were not aware of any air pollution. The so-called "objective" or "scientific" engineer could have detected a slight sweet smell in and around the plant, and his equipment would have recorded some presence of air pollutants, but nothing of a significant magnitude for the town. Hence, given the existing unemployment problem, this order—which at best could marginally improve a high-quality air system and could well have led to the discontinuance of the Knowlton Brothers' operation and to further unemployment—seems to be a most irrational one. It seems to contradict our location cost analysis in Chapters 5 and 6. It seems to suggest that the basic decision-making of reality is not in keeping with the kinds of approaches we have suggested for finding industries that will provide jobs in high unemployment areas.

Yes, the issuance of the New York state order may seem irrational. Yet it was in part predictable and therefore, as some scholars would claim, it was in part logical and rational. Because similar kinds of decisions may be expected for other towns and regions with unemployment and low-income problems, we need to know why the issuance of this order was in part predictable, logical, and rational if we are to plan effectively. To understand why, we need to examine carefully the basic features of organizational structure and function within the United States and other societies. We now turn to this matter, and then we will point out why the Watertown decision was in part predictable, logical, and rational.

THE GENERAL SETTING: DIFFERENT KINDS OF ORGANIZATIONS

In previous chapters we have encountered certain elements of organizational structure and function. We have, for example, talked about the economic market. We spoke about the demand, supply, and wage rate for Girl Fridays. The way in which the demand and supply were equated and the wage rate determined involved a fairly informal market organization. By custom, a need for or the availability of a Girl Friday is made known by an advertisement in a local newspaper. Then through telephone calls, correspondence, and personal interviews, each need (demand) is usually matched with an availability (supply), and each availability is usually matched with a need. Although this procedure occasionally breaks down, by and large it works well. Society seems well satisfied with it.

Other markets are much more formally organized. The purchase and sale of a number of securities of major corporations in nations like the United States take place at formally organized points of exchange, like the New York Stock Exchange. There, all orders to buy and sell a particular stock come together at a single desk (post) and are taken care of according to certain rules and procedures. Many of these rules and procedures have been informally developed over the years. Others have been set down by the New York Stock Exchange itself in order to protect the interests of its members and to preserve the Exchange as a major institution within the financial world—and possibly to further enhance its influence in social, economic, and political circles. Still others are set down by the state of New York and the federal government in order to protect the interests of the people, their constitutents.

Other markets are organized in different fashion. The wheat market and the markets for a number of food products require that the product be classified in terms of several grades in order to minimize deception of consumers and exploitation of farmers. The market for Ph.D.s in economics requires that letters of reference be written testifying to the qualities and competence of each person coming on the market.

We have also discussed economic firms. Each firm is an organization. Perhaps the one-man corner grocery store is not much of an organization. But certainly General Motors and ITT are organizations. When talking about economic firms, we have made the very simple assumption that each firm is interested in maximizing its profits—or the satisfactions derived from work and living, in the case of a one-man operator—and nothing else. Though this simple assumption may hold for a number of firms, it certainly is inadequate for understanding the behavior of such conglomerates as ITT, Unilever, and Mitsubishi. As organizations, they have a number of other objectives, and we will have to look at the whole range of combinations of possible objectives in order to understand their behavior. Further, we will find that the organization's objectives are often closely related to the objectives of its members (its big chiefs as well as its little people); to the way in which it is structured; to its size, age, location, inputs and outputs; and in a sense to its total environment. On the other hand, we will observe that the objectives of an organization such as General Motors (or even a much smaller one, like the local supermarket) influences what kinds of people with what kinds of objectives become members of it.

Economic organizations are not the only organizations. Others of equal importance exist. There is the whole range of political organizations, from formal governments such as the government of the United States, New York state, the city of Philadelphia, and Delaware county to less formal ones, such as political parties (the Republicans and Democrats), SANE, and the League of Women Voters, and to still less formal ones, such as the Delaware County ACTION Group to Prevent World War III, or the Main Street Nixonites, or simply the gang that hangs out at Harvey's Pool Parlor. All these organizations are important to study.

Furthermore, political organizations may be cross-national and multinational, as well as national. We have organizations like the United Nations (presumably covering the entire earth and all its population); the International Geographic Union (relating to one set of specialists spread over the earth, SEATO, the Southeast Asian Treaty Organization (covering a set of nations which form a world region); the Central European section of the Peace Science Society (covering a set of scholars within a limited world region but with emphatic international orientation); and the former British Commonwealth (a loose, noncontiguous federation-type grouping of nations having certain common interests and subject to some common authority).

In a real sense, each of these political organizations, as any organization, is distinct just as is each region or each personality. Yet there are common features of organizations or subclasses of organizations which exist. It is useful to know about these features if we are to study and analyze both the set of decisions and the process of development which occur over time in cities, regions, and the world. We also know that political organizations, at least in the short and middle run, determine in large part how society's resources are allocated to different needs. For example, they determine how much tax monies are to be collected from individuals and other economic production units within the U.S. society and how these monies are to be allocated to various programs relating to social and individual welfare. This is greatly influenced by the way in which these organizations and their leaders perceive the needs of the people. Thus, they come to influence greatly urban and regional development by the priorities they set on education, health, transportation, crime control, defense, environmental management, and many other community service programs.

Another set of major organizations is oriented to social forces and much more social in character—the family, the teenage club in high school, the Rotary Club, the Kiwanis, the XYZ Sorority, the Main Liners, etc. There are many of these, kaleidoscopic in form and structure. Usually, however, they are small, local, and decentralized in terms of decision-making and authority. They provide opportunities for social activities and the development of affection and friendships among their members, encourage morale building, and control disruptive-deviant behavior through sanctions (rewards and penalties). These groups often provide the grass-roots integrative tissue of a social system.

A fourth set of organizations is much more concerned with long-run goals. These are cultural organizations like churches and schools. They serve to maintain a system, sustain its knowledge and know-how, and preserve its values and interaction patterns. They aim to provide a relatively secure and stable framework within which individuals and other institutions and entities concerned with short- and middle-run goals may function.

The operations of all these organizations are complex and intricately interrelated. They influence behavior and welfare in diverse ways. A political organization, like the government, can enact minimum wage legislation and thus greatly change the workings of the economic market and the per capita income of a region. Also, as we have seen, this organization can impose environmental regulations and significantly affect the employment potential of a region like the Watertown one.

To illustrate further, consider our consumption behavior. It is influenced in a variety of ways by organizations. Our attitudes toward the consumption of a number of goods are strongly conditioned by authoritative statements made and sanctions imposed by religious organizations. Further, the information we acquire about many goods that are and can be produced comes through the educational system and communications channels (TV, radio, newspapers, and just plain gossip). But most important, our tastes develop from interaction with members of our family and other social organizations. How often do we find certain particular demands of teenagers stemming from the goals and fashions adopted by their largely informal social groups?

Although all these organizations influence our behavior and welfare in diverse ways and with different intensities, we will tend to concentrate on studying those organizations which either directly or indirectly influence the decisions affecting cities and regions in the short and middle run. These are the organizations which have a direct bearing on the kinds of problems we wish to attack. Accordingly, we will give much less attention to cultural-type organizations (which determine cultural values over the long run and which are more properly studied by anthropologists), and to those social groups which do not have a major influence on decisions relating to the short and middle run. This bias should be kept constantly in mind as we develop the analysis.

Finally, note that we have avoided any specific definition of the term "organization." We have done so purposely, because we find no agreement on a definition among social scientists who study organizations and who are experts on one or more aspects of the why, how, who, when, and where of organizations. Some view organizations such as General Motors and the Chase Manhattan Bank as collections of people committed to achieving the goals of the members through an explicit and stable structure of task allocations, roles, and responsibilities. Another group of social scientists looks upon organizations as people interacting, and so focuses upon the various problems and conflicts that arise from such interaction, both within small and large groupings of people within the organization. Still another set of scholars looks upon organizations in terms of the roles people play rather than the nature of the personalities in the roles; they deal with the way these roles are intertwined in a social structure and with the various rewards, incentives, and expectations society places on people performing their roles. A fourth set of scholars looks upon organizations as systems, particularly as mechanisms for processing information for decision-making.

From our standpoint, the organization is *any collectivity (grouping) of people* that forms a *basic behaving unit* to be confronted in the study of society, in the analysis of its problems, and in whatever plans and actions we may propose to attack these problems. Our concern with organizations is therefore with trying to understand the way they behave in social-problem contexts and how we can influence such behavior, whether we are individual scholars and citizens, members of organizations themselves, or both.

THE SPATIAL-REGIONAL HIERARCHICAL STRUCTURE

Perhaps it would be appropriate at this point to ask: Why do organizations exist? How do they operate and function? Who are involved and what roles do they perform (leader, foreman, worker)? Which factors govern change (growth and decline) within organizations, and the ways in which they influence and are influenced by their surrounding environment? All these questions and others are relevant. They can be approached from several angles. The economist attacks these questions differently than the sociologist, the anthropologist differently than the political scientist, the psychologist differently than the historian. Because we are regional scientists, we shall approach these questions in a way that has most promise for facilitating an attack on urban and regional problems.

From our standpoint, the earth is a physical space, with whose control, use (exploitation and conservation), and management we are concerned. We immediately recognize that there is physical resistance (friction) to movement over this space, whether of an individual when he wishes to go from one place to another, or of a good being shipped to satisfy (directly or indirectly) some need of an individual. Movement involves the expenditure of effort—directly by the individual or indirectly because of the work required to produce the fuel burned up in transportation. Thus, whether human beings are guided by the principle of least effort, by their inclination to be lazy, or by their desire to consume as much as they can given the amount of effort they do allocate to work, they will tend to act so as to avoid unnecessary transportation. Whether they wish to interact socially (in a family and community) or culturally (at religious rites) or economically (because they wish to barter corn for beads, or sell and buy specialized labor services), they should be close to each other, everything else being the same. The varied set of family activities such as cooking, weaving, and rearing children in the household, and the set of agricultural activities for producing goods on the farm require spatial juxtaposition to avoid unnecessary time and effort spent in transportation. The coming together at a specific market location of farmers who want to sell their surplus vegetables and of consumers who wish to purchase some of this surplus leads these farmers and consumers to live relatively close to each other to minimize time and effort spent at transportation, everything else being the same. The assembly of people to discuss political concerns, such as defense against a common enemy or the operation of an elementary school system, implies relatively little separation among them in physical space.

In brief, there are numerous forces, some of which we shall discuss more extensively later, which lead to the clustering of population—to the tendency to agglomerate in one big city.

On the other hand, there are other sets of forces at work. Resources are not evenly distributed over the earth's space. Rich agricultural soil is not ubiquitous. Abundant stands of timber are not within reach of everyone. Streams, rivers, and seas abounding in fish are not accessible to all. Easily worked iron ore deposits appear infrequently. Excellent coking coal is limited to relatively few locations. The fact that resources, including climate and all other aspects of the environment, are unevenly distributed leads to at least some geographic specialization among different parts of the world. It makes sense for a region with excellent agricultural soil for growing wheat to trade with another area having excellent fish resources, or easily worked deposits of copper, iron ore, coal, and other mineral resources. Accordingly, trade in commodities takes place, and clusters of population oriented to different resources and allied economic activities emerge.

With time and the development of technology of greater complexity, the simple basis for geographic specialization and trade disappears. Some commodities come to be produced which are highly valued but which incur little transport cost because they are not bulky or heavy and do not involve much effort at transportation. If there is some one location that has a great advantage in the production of a commodity of this type, and if this advantage is further increased by the possibility of scale economies in production, this location may be able to ship the commodity all over the world at a competitive advantage.

At the other extreme, if there is a location that has a resource which yields a low-valued heavy commodity such as sand, and if this resource is generally present at many other locations, the commodity produced from it will be shipped only over relatively small distances.

In between, there are other commodities, such as steel, which are both heavy and highly valued. In this case a particular location with an excellent situation for production can ship over a substantial distance. Such a commodity can be competitively produced at an advantageously situated location for more and more distant markets as long as this location's production economies are not fully offset by increasing transport costs involved in marketing at these distances. When these economies are fully offset, then other locations may develop as steel producers, and restrict the first location's market to only a part of the world.

From these considerations and many others, we expect clusters of gainfully employed persons and their families to emerge at different locations in the world. These population clusters will have different importance for the world economy. Those which develop as locations for the production of critical commodities that are widely consumed (such as steel), or for the provision of critical services (such as finance) become large in size and acquire much economic wealth and political power. Those clusters at locations advantageous for the production of commodities of moderate importance, such as textiles and craft objects, become centers of generally lesser importance. Finally, at the other extreme, those clusters at locations or within regions with few resources and inferior production in most if not all respects remain small in size when they do appear, and are centers of negligible importance. A good illustration is the village in a poor agricultural region that exists to provide a few elementary services for the surrounding farming population.

Although mass-production economies, the avoidance of unnecessary transportation, cosmopolitan attractions, and other forces lead to the development of large cities of increasing importance relative to other population clusters, and may continue to operate in unrestricted fashion for some time, sooner or later key counterbalancing forces come into play. These latter may be associated with the increasing congestion as cities grow in size, as well as mounting environmental degradation, increase in crime incidence and insecurity, and increase in the cost of living from rising rents, taxes, and food prices (because of the need to bring in agricultural products from more and more distant locations). Hence the forces toward one or a few big cities are tempered, and a hierarchy of nodes (clusters) emerges: megalopolises, metropolitan regions, urban centers, cities, towns, villages, and crossroads hamlets.

In looking at historical development and in considering the interplay of political, social, and other noneconomic forces as they determine the key decisions that affect each of our lives, the geographer-regional scientist Philbrick has put forth a seven-order classification system of nodes, or centers, and population clusters. Four of these orders (levels) of organization are depicted in Figure 12.1. There is the grass-roots (first-order) level, indicated by the short vertical stretches at the bottom of the figure, which we may designate the individual or the family units in the society. Each node in the next higher level (the second-order) connects seven of the grass-roots units. We designate each one of these nodes as a village or hamlet. At the third level (order), each node connects seven second-order nodes; we designate each third-order node as a town. Finally, at the fourth order, there is depicted only one node which we designate the metropole, connecting seven of the third-order nodes.

It is easily seen that we can construct a more extensive diagram in which we connect seven of the fourth-order nodes (metropoles) to a single node, which might be viewed as the national capital, primary metropolitan area, or megalopolis of the nation (a fifth-order node). Moreover, we can proceed still further and connect seven of the national capitals (or primary metropolitan regions) to a still higher node, which might be designated a world region capital (a sixth-order node). Last, we might connect seven of the world region capitals (sixth-order nodes) to a single node representing an agglomeration of worldwide influence.

Figure 12.1   A System of Nodes of Four Orders

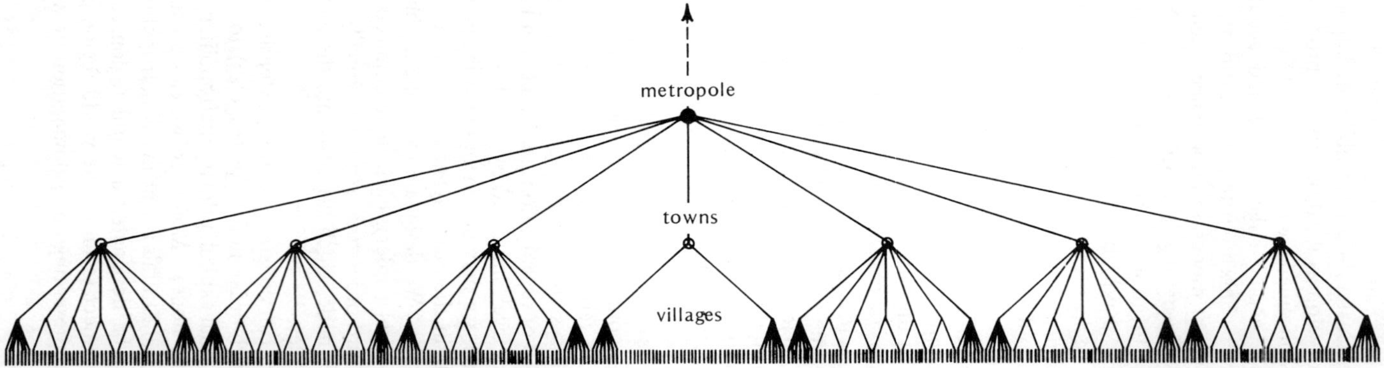

Another way of depicting hierarchical structure is through a figure such as Figure 12.2. It shows how a population regularly and systematically clustered over some segment of a nation might appear to an observer looking down on the earth from a position well above it (except that the lines would not be present and there would be much more irregularity in the pattern). At the center of the figure is a single fifth-order node, perhaps a national capital or a major metropolitan region. Around it are six bold black dots, each representing a fourth-order node corresponding, let us say, to a metropole. Each fourth-order node is surrounded by six centers, indicated by a "+" mark, each of which corresponds to a town. In turn, each of the third-order nodes, corresponding to a town, is surrounded by six second-order nodes (small black dots), each of which may be considered a village. Finally, in the six hexagons surrounding the national capital, we have depicted six first-order nodes about each second-order node, where each first-order node represents an individual or family unit. Strictly speaking, we should put individual or family units about all the second-order nodes (the black dots) in the figure. However, if we did so, we would make the figure confusing; so we have chosen not to. But the reader should imagine individuals and family units scattered around each second-order node in the figure.[1]

We have graphically depicted a hierarchy of four orders of nodes in Figure 12.1 and five orders in Figure 12.2. Now let us examine some of the rationale and evidence for the hypothesis that the world is roughly organized into world regions, nations, urban-metropolitan regions within a nation, town regions, village areas, and family farms and other family holdings.

Social Evolution And A Seven
To Eight-Order Hierarchy

We all know that there is a top to any pyramid representing a hierarchical structure. From our study of history, we know that at some time periods this peak is pointed and sharp, as in the heyday of the Roman Empire. Few if any scholars would dispute the statement that at this time the node represented by the city of Rome and its immediate surrounding territory held an unchallenged position at the top. In the quarter century preceding World War I, one could view London and its surrounding region as the node at the top of the pyramid. London was the financial center of the world, the pinnacle of the mighty British empire, and a center of technological know-how. And, among nations, England occupied the same position. Likewise, during the reign of Louis XIV in the early eighteenth century, Paris and France were at the top of the pyramid.

But history tells us that no one population agglomeration has been able to hold on to this position of dominance for too long. The march of time, whether it is associated with general advance or decline of world civilization, brings with it

---

[1] Note that each village in Figure 12.2 serves the six family units surrounding it plus the family unit that is located at (or immediately adjacent to) the village site—that is, seven family units in all, as indicated in Figure 12.1. Each town (indicated by a "+" mark) serves the six villages surrounding it and also serves as a village for the population immediately surrounding it—that is, seven villages and their populations, as indicated in Figure 12.1. And so forth. Thus each metropole site in Figure 12.2 serves also as a village and town site; the national capital serves also as a village, town, and metropole site.

Figure 12.2   A Spatial System Involving Five Orders of Nodes

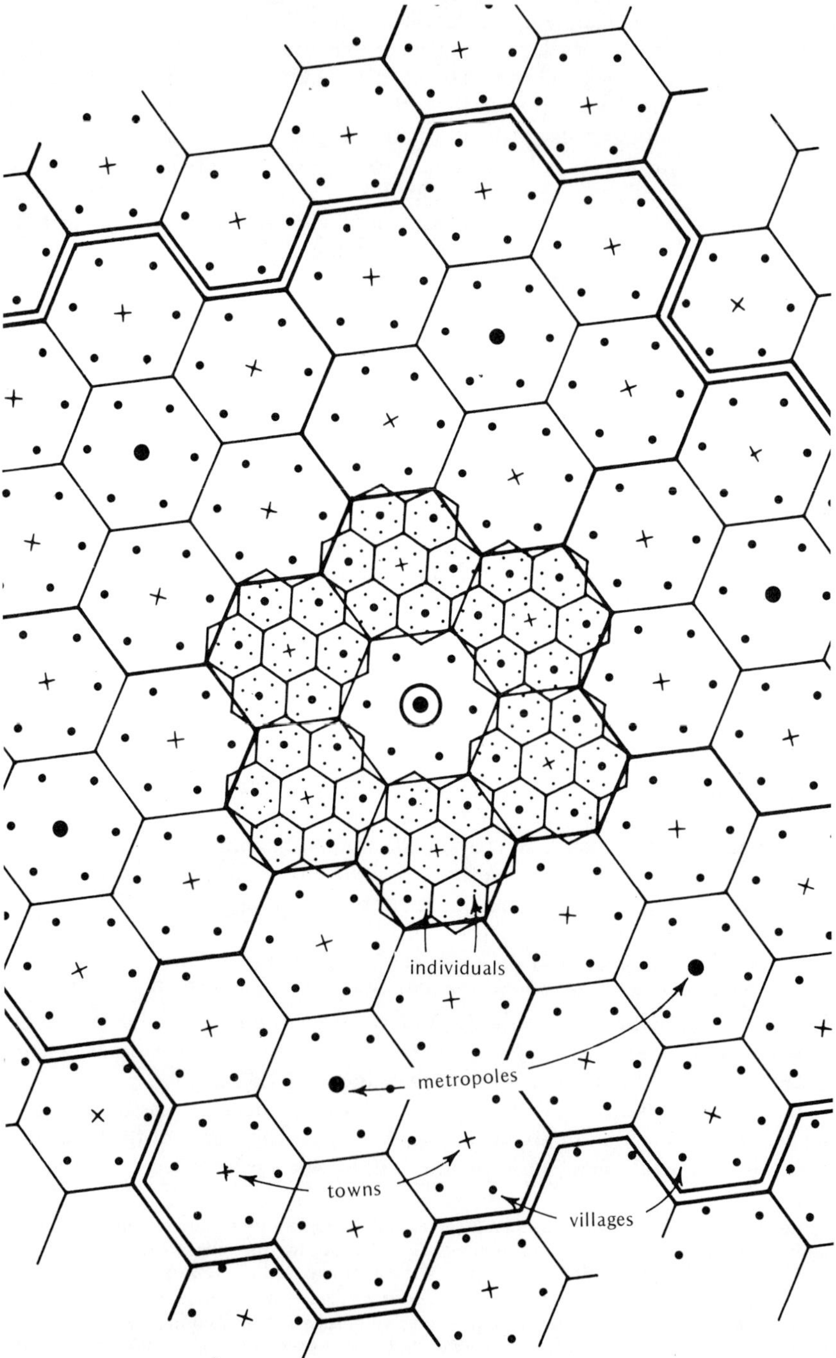

individuals

metropoles

towns

villages

new forces which undermine existing, seemingly invincible world elite groups. Decay sets in. And, as one elite group or population agglomeration slides downhill, another simultaneously swells in strength. For some time period at least, the top of the pyramid is not pointed and sharp, but rather flat. More than one elite group or population agglomeration vies for the highest position. Such was certainly true during part of the period between World War I and World War II, when the influence of the London metropole was waning and that of the Boston-Washington axis was on the increase. And though for a short time subsequent to World War II the megalopolis extending from Boston to Washington and centering around New York had almost unchallenged occupancy of the top of the pyramid, by the 1960s the peak had become less sharp with the rapid advance of the Moscow politico-socio-economic elite. More recently, the top has become still flatter with the mounting power of the population agglomerations and elites of Peking and Tokyo.

It is, of course, easier to interpret events at a distance in time. First, the analyst's mind is not cluttered by the numerous small events that occur and constantly impinge on his daily life; he cannot avoid exaggerating their influence. Second, he is not emotionally involved in historical happenings and thus can think much more clearly about them. For example, when we try to determine who is on top today, Washington or Moscow, our values unavoidably become trapped in our assessment. When we ask who was on top in the early eighteenth century or in the first century B.C., we are much less emotionally involved, if at all. Yet it is doubly interesting to speculate on the question of who is on top today—and who will be on top tomorrow. Not only does this question tease our intellectual curiosity, but it is also of real concern in terms of our goals in life and how we behave given the fact that we are human and have values.

But before anyone speculates on what is today and what may be tomorrow, he had better gird himself with more information about the structure of the pyramid of economic, social, and political power.

If there is a top to a pyramid, there must be a bottom. At the bottom, the grass-roots level, are the individuals of society and the family units or households which they form. They constitute the first-order nodes in the organization pyramid. The family unit makes basic decisions on the division of tasks among its active participants. Some are assigned to and specialize in food-growing activities, others in cooking, and perhaps still others in textile activities. Clearly, some organization is required whether just for survival (including the begetting, nurturing, and socialization of children) or for other purposes. Of course, certain activities of the individual, such as voting, do not require the family unit as an organization. For purposes of general analysis, however, it is best to consider the family as the primary elementary unit.

The next level of organization pertains to that type of unit which pulls together a set of families as participants, or which provides services for the set. The village store, to which goods are brought and made available for purchase and consumption by families, is an illustration. So is the primary school, at which the socialization process of the children of the family is extended and enriched. The local church, at which certain noneconomic functions, social and religious, are performed for the family, or for a pair of families in the case of marriage, is another illustration. Still another institution at the second-order level which facilitates the functioning of families and furnishes certain services for enhancing individual welfare is the town hall meeting, or similar local political discussion arenas. Here proposals are set forth and sometimes decisions made as to how much of the resources (income, labor, etc.) of each family and its members are taxed for the production of various governmental (public) goods and services for distribution and use to the families and their members.

When one or more stores, schools, churches, discussion clubs, and other second-order organizations are clustered together in geographic space, as typically occurs in order to minimize the time and effort spent at transportation and building roads and other facilities, this small-scale juxtaposition in space of activities and institutions is designated a hamlet, village, crossroads town, or a central place of lowest order, using the terminology of central place theory. (We will consider the theory of central places more extensively in the appendix.)

The third-order level in the hierarchy is associated with the linking of hamlets, villages, and other small centers into a pattern or set to be served by a sizeable town. Such a town may be required in order to provide adequate general hospital and medical services for the families in all the centers encompassed in the town's sphere of influence. Some higher-level educational services such as secondary schools may be provided by such a town. In addition, a town may provide the facilities for local religious festivities, rodeos, farmers' markets, visiting theatrical troupes, and the like. The town may also be considered a central place of the next-to-lowest order.

At the fourth-order level, where towns and their surrounding villages and populations are linked together in a metropole (a central place of the next higher order), we find the need for specialized hospital and medical units, wholesale and distribution facilities, colleges, technical and other specialized schools, and fairly specialized professional services. Many cultural facilities such as museums and symphonies may be best operated at the scale of an urban-metropolitan region. The same is true of some social units, like the Explorer Clubs and the Rotary units, and economic units such as department stores, newspapers, and producers of such things as manufactured ice and Coca-Cola. These are production establishments which require at least a fairly large demand to achieve scale economies—as indicated in Chapter 6.

The next higher level (the fifth order) in the hierarchy might be viewed as that order at which each node, a central place frequently corresponding to the national capital, combines urban-metropolitan regions into an effective system. Most frequently this system corresponds to the nation-state, for example Canada, United States, Mainland China, and Japan. In other cases, a system does not come to exist because national boundaries and differences in institutions (for example, in languages and religion) intervene to preclude this. It may be argued that to some extent this is the case for the Scandinavian countries, some of the smaller common market countries, and some of the smaller Middle East countries. Because of the intervention of national boundaries, and the presence of different institutions, many partial and incomplete systems, at times encompassing only one urban-metropolitan region, continue to exist. The incompleteness of systems at this level points up a place of major inefficiency in the world system, sometimes posed as the problem of "too many small nations." It suggests also the excessive importance of the role of traditional political boundaries (nations) and social-cultural institutions in the world structure, roles whose significance should perhaps be reduced.

Associated with nodes at this fifth level are many activities. There are those national economic activities for which scale economies and transportation costs are such that only the national market is the natural market area for the goods they produce. This might be the case for history books on the nation, magazines printed in the language of the nation, certain specialized food products which by and large are consumed only by the individuals of the nation, and in general goods for which the barriers to trade are sufficiently high as to be kept off world markets. Other activities involve such entities as a national university, a national museum, professional associations such as the American Sociological Association, cultural organizations like the American Legion, and state religions (Anglican in England, Lutheran in Norway). Also encompassed are national government units like the federal government and central planning authorities, national firms such as Hertz and Bell Telephone, and numerous financial institutions linked to the currency of the nation such as national banks, the Federal Reserve Board, and the New York Stock Exchange.

Above the fifth order there exists a set of nodes (the sixth order), each of which encompasses several nations. Frequently, spatial contiguity may lead directly or indirectly to the formation of world regions—such as the Latin American countries, the Scandinavian countries, and the nations of the Danubian confederation. Others are linked because they have a common language, a common political tie (the British Commonwealth), or a common need (to preserve the Baltic Sea). Others may form world regions because of economic factors (as in the case of the common market countries in Northwest Europe), or because of security considerations (as the Warsaw Pact nations). Within these multination groupings, organizations may have very limited power today. But the problem of world survival may lead to an increase in their authority with time, especially as the number and complexity of interactions among the nations and peoples of the world increases and as the friction of distance decreases with further technological development. Considerations of defense and military security, efficient resource utilization (for example in the management of river systems), wise environmental management, and wise monetary controls imply greater importance for multination groupings.

At a still higher level (the seventh order) exist the nodes (central places of the highest order) and their corresponding national (or world empire) units which correspond to total world influence and control. Such nodes are few in number—we have already implied that the Boston-New York-Washington megalopolis and the Moscow complex now occupy positions in this order. Perhaps the Peking and Tokyo agglomerations will soon join these two, if they have not already, and possibly replace one or both of them. In a somewhat different manner, with emphasis on particular functions, the United Nations and the International Court of Justice, as world organizations, operate at this level, although in a weak manner. So does the International Political Science Association and the Peace Science Society (International) for highly specialized subsets of the world's population (namely, political scientists and peace scientists, respectively), as well as the Vatican City and the Harvard-M.I.T. complex.

It may even be tempting to speculate that there is forthcoming an eighth-order node with corresponding eighth-order types of influence and activity. As man extends the domain of his control into space, the world in which man behaves encompasses more than the earth. Hence, nodes which control space activities and the exploitation of the physical world beyond the planet earth can be viewed as occupying an eighth-order level. In time it may be more appropriate to designate them galactic nodes, exercising galactic power and engaging in galactic activities. Currently the Boston-New York-Washington megalopolis and the Moscow complex are vying for such characterization.

We have now explored a tentative classification of organizations and nodes and their corresponding regions within a concept of world hierarchy. We have examined their spheres (spatial extent) of influence, interchange, political control, and so forth. The world hierarchy, of course, is the basic structure within which key behavior takes place, whether in the realm of economics, politics, culture, or social life. One cannot hope to conduct basic research on the welfare of different regions and cities and other areas of this world without taking into account their positions and roles within this hierarchy.

Of course, our classification is oversimplified, and many other factors should be discussed in order to depict this hierarchy more accurately and to suggest the way it has come about and how it is likely to change in the future. However, we do not have the time to consider these questions in this introductory text. Roughly speaking, the sketch presented is adequate for our present purpose.

Hierarchy and Structure in Subsystems

Before proceeding, we should recognize that the hierarchical structure of world society is frequently repeated within subsystems or sectors of society. For example, take the educational sector. At the top of this system at any point of time are a few universities that might be recognized as world universities. As indicated, Oxford and Cambridge Universities in England occupied these positions in the first quarter of the twentieth century. Today the Harvard-M.I.T. complex is in a position at the top, though not with regard to each and every field of knowledge. Below the world university are national universities such as the University of Tokyo, Moscow University, the University of Chicago, and University of Munich. Below national universities are state or metropolitan universities such as the University of Nebraska, Wayne State University, and Boston University. Next in order are community colleges, then senior high schools, then junior high schools, then primary schools, and lastly kindergartens and other preschool units. We are all acquainted with this hierarchical structure, so we need not elaborate upon it.

Hierarchical structure exists not only in terms of areal extent of influence, relevant for the educational subsector of world society and for our look at the distribution of generalized power within world society; it also characterizes the different positions in a decision-making structure or in an administrative-authority complex. Thus we have an ordering of positions within a major university starting with students at the grass-roots level, moving up to graduate teaching assistants, faculty, department chairmen, deans, provosts, and the president. Definite roles are assigned to each position, all in accord with the fairly regular structure of levels of nodes suggested by our Figures 12.1 and 12.2.

Such hierarchical structure can also exist when we emphasize a particular kind of function, say planning. Thus we can have (and in time undoubtedly will have) central world planners, world region planners, national planners, regional planners, metropolitan planners, and local area planners. In terms of transportation systems, we have feeder roads and walkways, secondary streets and thoroughfares, primary roads, metropolitan radial speedways and circumferentials, interstate turnpikes, and transcontinental highways. In communications, we have neighborhood news-sheets, local newspapers, metropolitan dailies (like the *Philadelphia Inquirer*), national newspapers (like *The New York Times*) and international newspapers (like the *International Herald Tribune*). Another type of hierarchy concerns communications within a large organization. There may be the statistical clerks and research assistants who collect relevant data and tabulate them. Data and tables from several research assistants and clerks are then communicated (transmitted) to an analyst. The analyst may develop the costs and benefits of diverse alternatives (actions) that might be considered. He, together with other analysts, passes on his evaluations in terms of a report to a director of research. The director examines the several reports he receives, each perhaps on a particular area of concern. He digests them and develops a set of policy recommendations which he transmits to his vice-president. The vice-president studies each set of policy recommendations made by the director of research and submits a classified or confidential document to the president, containing a succinct summary statement backed up by appendices with relevant data and analysis.

Having now outlined a notion of hierarchy with regard to several aspects of everyday life and in several contexts, we are interested in the ways we can look at organizational structure and function to understand behavior of institutions within the world hierarchy. We would particularly like to predict, as much as possible, this organizational behavior, especially when it influences what we would like to do for our region. Hence, we now want to consider the "why, how, who, when, and where" of organizations.

WHY ORGANIZATIONS EXIST

Consider the why of organizations. Why does ITT exist? Why does the United States or the Soviet Union exist? Why the local PTA? Why the family?

When we look at the family or the local PTA, the answer seems fairly simple. These organizations exist in order to be able to do things which individuals cannot do by themselves, or to do things in a much more efficient way than can individuals acting in their own independent way. For example, the PTA allows parents and teachers to exchange ideas on what is to be taught, how, and for what purpose. In that way, a more effective and satisfactory educational service can be provided. Other kinds of organizations exist in order to maximize the probability of survival of a group of individuals and to better meet the physical hardships of the environment. Several families might band together in order to protect themselves more effectively against attacks by outsiders, to hunt more effectively, or to construct a road so that they can have more time for other activities. Or they may band together, formally or informally, to provide other kinds of security; for example, they immediately construct a new barn to replace one struck and burned down by lightning. Or they band together simply because they find it enjoyable to sing, dance, and frolic as a group, and to be exposed to a wider range of stimuli than is available in family life.

Thus, numerous organizations emerge with an almost infinite variety of characteristics. However, it often happens that once an organization is formed to meet external demands, to provide new stimuli, or for some other purpose, it takes on a life of its own. It starts setting up its own goals and objectives, which are based on or related to the demands of the individuals internal to the organization. For example, a political club may form to provide its members with information concerning political issues and candidates for office, but in time it begins to provide a certain amount of sociality for its members. It takes on social as well as political functions. In addition, a certain specialization evolves within the organization in the sense that some tasks are to be performed by one individual, and other tasks by other individuals. At first, volunteers may perform these tasks, but later one or more individuals may be hired. A head of the organization may emerge. The head and other employees of the organization may become interested in making their jobs secure, and thus in maximizing the probability of a continuing healthy life for the organization. The organization then has a premium placed on its survival, in part to protect the interest of its active employees. In turn, each leader and each worker may be judged by his performance. In a culture in which positive values are ascribed to growth and development, the employees are motivated to strive for such. Of course, one way growth and development can be facilitated is through influencing decisions made outside the organization—influencing them in such a way as to create a more favorable rather than a less favorable climate for adding on staff and embarking on new ventures. So the organization takes on still another goal, namely to accumulate potential for influencing decisions—that is, to accumulate power over, or ability to exert pressure on, other behaving units.

In this manner, an organization which initially formed to meet simple demands develops into a much more complex grouping of individuals. It is concerned not only with meeting these first demands but also with its probability of survival, its position in the power structure, its capability for accumulating goods and other material and nonmaterial items of value to its leaders and nonleaders, and its attractiveness to the best kinds of employees. Thus a small local operation—involving two or more persons trying to construct a better piece of equipment for a farming job, or a better pump for extracting oil from a local deposit, or a better motor for an aircraft, or a better pharmaceutical product, or a better calculator—can lead in time to the emergence of a huge organization with a tremendous accumulation of wealth and a large working force. At the top of its hierarchical structure are leaders who can and frequently do exert tremendous influence on social, political, and economic decisions affecting the social welfare of the people not only in the home nation of that organization but also in other regions of the world.

When we are engaged in formulating and implementing plans concerning our region's development, we confront diverse organizations, big, medium, and small, as behaving units. Although initially set up to meet the immediate needs of their members, they may have taken on basic goals which involve the accumulation of power and wealth and which frequently run counter to meeting the welfare goals of our urban or regional community. We then need to have greater understanding and insight into why they function as they do, the way they impose constraints on our political leaders, and the kinds of actions we can expect our leaders to take. Further, we need to have some notion of how organizations should and must be regulated and constrained in their race, frequently mad, for economic and political power.

We must bear in mind that leaders of organizations are not unaware of the possible public reaction to their behavior. Take the leader at the top of an organization whose reward system provides him with strong incentives to amass economic and political power for use by the organization. Recognizing the likelihood of negative public reaction to the level of concentration of power he seeks, he changes the behavior of his organization somewhat in order to counter such negative reaction. He has his organization take on new kinds of roles, such as providing scholarships and fellowships for college and graduate students, subsidizing community organizations (like baseball clubs and local symphonies), or supporting cultural services (like sponsorship of Metropolitan Opera concerts). Though he spends a certain amount of his organization's resources on such endeavors, enough goodwill among the citizenry is generated to allow the organization to keep on accumulating power and to achieve effectively its other goals. If these public relations endeavors are wisely conceived and managed, a positive net gain accrues to the organization. In this way the organization ups its power position or more securely insures its status. Unfortunately, it also becomes still more entangled and intimately interconnected with society, more entrenched, more difficult to regulate properly, and more complex internally At times, an organization becomes so interconnected, entrenched, and complex that even its leaders are unable to comprehend what goes on within the organization and exert adequate control over basic actions taken by it.

A Scenario: The Committee of Concerned Citizens to Save Society

To illustrate these points, let us paint a scenario. We may think of a small group of concerned citizens in a community such as yours who get together to forestall a change in the local zoning laws that would make the location of a gasoline station possible. The group applies sufficient pressure so that the gasoline station is still excluded and the so-called residential values of your community preserved. But the group learns something. It must be constantly on the alert to see that no legal tricks or underhanded tactics are employed, enabling the gasoline station or other undesirable activities to get a foot in your community, particularly if location there could lead to big profits. So the group, which you may have joined, asks each concerned person to make a contribution to a small fund. It is to be used to compensate and meet the expenses of one of the members who knows the law and agrees to serve as a watchdog. This particular member, whom we shall call J.D., likes the sense of power (however small) that comes with the kind of work involved, as well as the generous compensation for the small amount of effort required on his part.

A neighboring community has the same problem. It too finds it desirable to band together, to meet in the house of one of its members whenever necessary, and to ask for contributions. Hearing about J.D. and his legal skills, it asks him to advise it in combatting a proposed zoning change and subsequently to serve as a watchdog. In time still other communities, hearing of the success of the initiative taken by your community and the neighboring one, find it meaningful to band together. J.D. becomes their watchdog as well. After a while, J.D. may find it more convenient and efficient to set up a somewhat more formal structure to serve all these communities, and further proposes to act as a watchdog for all the concerned communities in the county. The countywide nonprofit organization is a success. It is extended to cover the two neighboring suburban counties and a still more formal organization is set up. J.D. is assigned the leader role by being appointed president; a board of advisers of highly respected citizens is established to add weight to the venture; and a few workers are hired. J.D., as official leader, is now concerned with growth and development. Sooner or later he extends the organization to all the suburban counties of the metropolitan region. The organization grows in size and its internal hierarchical structure both widens and deepens, but J.D., the leader, is still completely on top of all its operations. And being a skillfull, capable person, he performs efficiently.

We can imagine that the stellar performance of this organization in the metropolitan region leads in time to the formation of branches in suburban communities of other metropolitan regions in a nation like the United States. Pretty soon the organization encompasses all the Middle Atlantic and New England states, then California, then Illinois, then Missouri and Washington, until most of the states and their suburban communities are involved. But the objective of the organization is now not only to perform a watchdog operation on land use, but also to grow—for amassing power as well as for growth's sake. Because it has been such a good land-use watchdog (at least in the minds of its constituents), it may gradually (and quietly) take on the additional function of being a watchdog of undesirable political or other behavior within these communities. Suburban communities in the United States are by and large higher-income communities with residents who have been successful and are inclined to approve of the existing social system. They want few basic changes, because the social system as presently constituted has dealt generously with them. They are generally negatively disposed toward any activity that might provoke revolutionary change—for example, overthrow of the existing form of government, drastic change in the family institution, or major overhaul of local churches that have failed to perform their brotherly Christian function with regard to nonsuburban populations.

In the process of assuming these new watchdog operations, the organization finds it appropriate to name itself *The Committee of Concerned Citizens to Save Society* (CCCSS). Its leaders, of course, get paid higher salaries because of its growth and success in achieving its objectives. Certain wealthy individuals react very favorably to the new organization and make large contributions. And pretty soon the organization starts advertising in *The New York Times* and other media to tell the world about its mission and to invite further contributions.

The organization grows within the United States. It spreads to Canada. It makes a leap and takes root in West Germany. It then leaps to Japan, where a new elite group of wealthy industrialists has emerged, taking on many of the cultural traits of the West. In time it may even spread to Moscow and Peking. In short, it becomes worldwide.

Obviously, an organization of this character eventually wields considerable influence. It includes among its membership many with tremendous wealth from most if not all the key industrial nations of the world. Because of their wealth, these individuals have economic and political power and influence within their respective countries. They are also accessible to the president who originally was the young, bright, capable suburbanite in your community. The organization also has power because of its huge treasury—it can advertise à la Madison Avenue. Or it can use part of its treasury as side payments to compensate individuals who perform certain questionable, under-the-table operations which influence decisions in somewhat unprincipled ways—but which are considered necessary "to save society." And it has become an organization that searches for power, opposes change of almost all types, and seeks to preserve the status quo.

Thus, what started as a negligible unit in the world society with meritorious goals turns out to be a powerful Goliath with its initial goal now of secondary, if not tertiary, importance. It has new goals, some of them very questionable to perhaps all the original members of the organization except J.D., who continues to reign as president. Yet there it is, an organization that now must be confronted by the members of the suburban community because of its strong influence on election of local as well as national political leaders and, perhaps at some future time, international leaders. Furthermore, it may be an organization that blocks local tax reform, educational innovation, provision of recreational services, and other activities desired by the majority in the local community, including many of the original resident members of the organization.

Other scenarios can be constructed in other ways. But this one suffices to suggest why organizations are set up and why, after some time period, they may develop objectives very different from, and perhaps even contradictory to, the initial ones.

The objectives and aims of organizations change, and so do their membership. Most of the organizers and early supporters of CCCSS may have left the organization, and the wealthy (including some of the *nouveau riche* of West Germany, Moscow, and Peking) may have taken their place. Moreover, the internal workings have taken on a drastically new pattern—the organization no longer works as a voluntary organization. As we have already suggested, this new internal structure affects the goals of the organization. This structure is in turn affected by the goals. The organization may now be too big for the president, say in his sixties, to sit on top of it and comprehend what is going on. He may be able to control only operations at or near to the top, and in effect cannot stay in touch with the many decisions and activities close to the grass-roots level—decisions that may augur major change at the top. For this reason the leader is likely to try to forestall any changes in the structure demanded at the grass-roots level or elsewhere. Knowing little of what is going on at these levels, he cannot evaluate the implications of such changes. Often, however, these changes take place anyway informally, if not formally, without the leader being aware of them. In this respect, the leader is often a pawn or mouthpiece of the organization; he is being led by the organization rather than vice versa. Perhaps he provides at most some nice window-dressing.

In fact, it has often been said that the president of the United States, sitting at the top of a huge hierarchy, is a tool of the organization, comprising in large part the organization of his political party and elite members of other groups (e.g., the military-industrial complex). He is at least partly impotent because of his inability to comprehend and effectively command the exceedingly complex society which he heads. He cannot, for example, be a leader with respect to economic affairs, unless by chance he was trained as a economist. For economic advice and determination of desirable policy, he is wholly at the mercy of his economic advisers, who are probably selected on the basis of recommendations by those in key positions of the party. In effect, in economic and many other important affairs the president is the distinguished official through whom the elite and other leaders of different interest groups, particularly those who have access to him, effect their objectives. Looked at from this standpoint, we see that in addition to knowing about the *why* of organizations we must have knowledge about the *how* and *who* of organizations—in particular, how the different nodes operate together to reach decisions of different sorts, how they communicate with each other, and how they compete for power and other rewards which the organization assigns.

THE HOW AND WHO OF ORGANIZATIONS

To begin to understand the *how* of organizations, we first recognize that early in its life, if not at the start, an organization requires specialization with respect to the roles and functions of its members. Typically, there is a need for a leader and one or more followers, or a manager and one or more employees. The leader should, from a rational standpoint, be the individual best able to reach decisions and solve problems. The manager should be the one best able to coordinate and handle the diverse business operations.

Organizations often grow with time. More individuals become associated as members or participants. It then becomes desirable to develop still further specialization. In decision-making and administration, leadership may be broken down into two types: *creative* (for example, perceiving the need for reorganization of the production operations to produce a new product and a way to achieve it), and *routine* (for example, keeping accounts and filing reports in accordance with diverse tax laws).

This additional specialization tends to occur side by side with the development of a hierarchy. At the top may be the person who possesses the scarcest skill, which is usually creative decision-making ability, especially under conditions of risk and uncertainty. Equally important, in many cases, is the ability to bring various individuals together as an effective and productive team, often through resolving interpersonal conflicts in what is perceived to be a "fair" manner.

Below the very top is a set of positions (or nodes) at which individuals are located who have other scarce abilities. Some may have the ability to organize the complex operations of a production process. Others may be able to keep the various accounts of the organizations in orderly fashion, or to carefully examine the legality and illegality of various operations with respect to different governmental regulations. Still others may be able to develop an incentive system and wisely change it according to the needs of the organization (so that the morale remains high and workers productive). Some may have the ability to make contact with different kinds of external behaving units, in order to exploit and develop existing and new markets.

In turn, each of the individuals at the next-to-highest level of nodes may oversee a number of persons at the next lower level of positions. These latter individuals may be the diverse foremen in the production process; or the diverse accountants, each of whom is concerned with a single operation of the organization; or the diverse lawyers, each of whom specializes in a particular type of law and government regulation. At the bottom of the hierarchy are the ordinary members of the organization, its workers of different types and with different skills. In the case of religious organizations, those at the bottom are the members of the church; in the case of an educational organization, the students; and in the case of political organization, the members of a party.

It is thus clear that hierarchy tends to develop and specialization takes place for reasons of efficiency or effectiveness in meeting the goals of the organization. Not all organizations must develop a hierarchy and specialization, but history records few organizations that have survived over a relatively long period of time without any hierarchy. We may, for example, look at the Religious Society of Friends (Quakers). Even in such a society, where each member is both a minister and a listener, and thereby potentially equal to every other member, there still exist "elders" or "weighty" Friends who are relatively few in number and, by implication, "nonelders" and "nonweighty" Friends who are the many. Although this simple organization is effective in meeting its goals, it is no more effective than is the Catholic church, whose organization, in contrast, involves extensive, multitudinous layers of authority and roles.

Along with the need for hierarchical structure and specialization, there exists the need for communication. As we have seen, the data on market prices, exchange rates, population trends, and other factors that the research assistant collects must be sifted and tabulated. The materials must be transmitted to an analyst at a higher-order node. The analyst must process the data, sifting through them in a different manner, and prepare a report on possible actions or interpretations for his chief. In turn, the chiefs of various divisions must develop a series of policy recommendations to be transmitted to those higher up the ladder. Ultimately different types of decisions are reached, involving the responsibilities of different nodes of an organization. Usually when a decision is reached, there is a leader who individually makes the decision or consults with members of the group (which may consist of middle or senior management people directly below him), and perhaps with outside technical consultants. Often in this communication process, much information that has been considered relevant at one level is put aside as irrelevant at another level. Often, too, the decision is predetermined, but nonetheless the process of decision-making is pursued for morale purposes, to preserve tradition, to permit consultation of the leader with those who oppose him for purposes of appeasement, or out of deference and respect for others in the organization.

Once decisions are reached, the information on them must be channelled through the organization in an appropriate manner. Hence, paralleling the upward communication channels, communication channels that lead down from decision-making points to various nodes must exist, identifying those elements of decisions that are relevant to these nodes and that require certain actions or the making of subdecisions by them. In turn, they must transmit to other nodes the relevant information on their actions and subdecisions. Ultimately, all these decisions, subdecisions, and actions influence the behavior of the grass-roots members of the organization, who now must work or vote or behave according to them.

We can see that a structure of communications must be developed within an organization for its efficient operation, that congestion of communication channels must be avoided, and that the network must be integrated with the decision-making structure. Further, the problem of communications raises certain basic issues. One is the extent to which decision-making and authority to make decisions should be centralized or decentralized. If there is too much centralization, it may be very costly to collect, process, and transmit all the information from diverse nodes up to the top and transmit information on the sequence of decisions and subdecisions downward. Accordingly, many routine decisions are often judged to be best made close to the grass-roots level rather than at or near the top. Overloading of communication channels, as well as costly transmission, can be avoided. Further, morale may be improved because more members of the organization participate in some decision-making. The quality of their performance and that of the organization may rise. Other advantages may also accrue, as is extensively discussed in the literature on centralization and decentralization, and on communications structure within organizations. However, there are also a number of disadvantages associated with decentralized decision-making. On average, a lower-level decision maker has less information on, and is less able to see, the overall behavior of the organization. His decisions are less likely to fit in smoothly with decisions elsewhere. They are less likely to be coordinated with decisions made at other nodes. He is more likely to make a bad decision once all the decisions of the organization are made and recorded. Also, when there are more rather than fewer decision makers in an organization, their average ability for making wise decisions is likely to be lower.

The optimal degree of centralization or decentralization within an organization is also related to the kinds of personalities that govern the organization. As already indicated, there should be different kinds of capabilities at the different nodes of the organization. At some nodes it is necessary to have an individual who is able to resolve a complex decision situation involving many kinds of conflicts. This is necessary when, for example, the vice-president in charge of rolling mills, who is interested in maintaining the output of his division, may insist on policies that conflict with those recommended by the vice-president in charge of marketing, who judges that changing consumer tastes necessitate a change in the types of products the organization produces. The policies the former insists on may also conflict with those proposed by the vice-president in charge of legal affairs, who points out the desirability of altering an efficiently rolling operation in order to comply better with environmental regulations, or with those supported by the vice-president in charge of accounts, who suggests that production levels should fluctuate from month to month in order to take advantage of certain tax loopholes. For the individual at the top to take an action in a complex decision situation involving conflicts among vice-presidents requires a certain toughness of personality, but often a toughness accompanied by outgoing friendliness and warmth.

At other nodes, requiring other capabilities, one is likely to find still other kinds of personalities—perhaps a personality that is highly sociable in order to maintain morale when the job is dirty and unpleasant, or a crisp and articulate type of personality when precise standards are required in manufacturing the product, or a conservative type of personality when the problem is to build a sense of stability and security into a unit of the organization.

In short, different nodes with their different task requirements need leaders with different kinds of personalities. This gives the organization a personality flavor that reflects the component personalities involved. An organization may develop as an aggressive type (such as ITT), a conservative type (such as the old Pennsylvania Railroad), a creative type (such as Bell Laboratories), or a non-creative type (such as the Amish church). Of course, within each organization there can be a considerable variety of personalities and so a common need for an individual with the ability to resolve conflicts, both because of the conflicting objectives of the organization and the conflicting personalities involved. An organization may be inclined partly to resolve these conflicts, or to avoid them in the future by recruiting new members with personalities that reinforce the personalities of those presently in the organization.

Alternatively, we might see the organization in another light—as a system which efficiently (or inefficiently) assigns tasks and the necessary resources for carrying them out to individuals at the different nodes. Usually, it is desirable to make this assignment and allocation of resources explicit so that everyone (employees, managers, customers, etc.) knows what to expect and who to go to for a particular problem. In this way, an overseeing official in the organization can judge whether the behavior of an individual is proper or improper, conforming or deviant. Other individuals, who mete out sanctions, know exactly how many sanctions to impose. Still other persons are then able to make clear decisions and issue precise orders—for example, choose a production function given the available technological know-how, and then issue orders as to how many raw materials of different kinds should be purchased and how much labor of different sorts should be put to work on what production tasks. On the other hand, it is desirable to permit a considerable amount of flexibility within the organization, a certain amount of indeterminateness and looseness in the definition of tasks and allocation of resources. The external environment changes and the organization must adapt. It must adapt the products it produces to new consumer tastes, so its rules must not be too rigid with regard to who should be employed and what tasks are done at what nodes. A new product, for example, may require a different kind of hierarchy, so that some nodes should disappear and new ones emerge. The labor market may change so that rules governing deviant behavior within the organization must change. Competition from new firms using the most modern technology may become so keen that the organization must automate in order to survive. This in turn may require the wiping out of a whole series of nodes and communication channels.

THE WHEN AND WHERE OF ORGANIZATIONS:
INTERNAL CHANGE AND EXTERNAL
ADJUSTMENT

It is now becoming clear in our discussion that organizations of different sorts have different relevance for different locations and points in space and for different times. The family has survived from early man to the present day. It has served, and still does serve, as a basic subsistence unit in many parts of the world. It is the unit most relevant for sexual gratification and for the begetting and nurturing of children. It is the unit through which a large part of world society regulates the socialization of children and the psychological development and maturation of the individual. It may be argued that it is absolutely essential for the survival of man in an era of low-level technology and know-how. But today, with the world developed in such a variety of ways and to different degrees in different parts, is it any longer an essential organization? Although it may be argued that the family is still necessary for simple peasant societies in many parts of the world, is it still essential for the Boston-New York-Washington megalopolis, or the San Francisco–Los Angeles axis? If it declines and disappears in these regions, what social units (if any) should come on the scene to assume its functions, either in whole or part? What organizations will provide at least some of the highly personal elements required for the psychological development and maturation of the individual? Can a family institution based on "open marriage" develop extensively and survive?

In contrast, we have the huge conglomerates like ITT, the State University of New York, and General Electric, whose functioning is based upon concentrations of populations. Because of the complexity in allocation of resources and tasks within these organizations and rapid changeover of personnel within them, the personal element is considerably reduced. Yet huge conglomerates, despite their impersonality, have become an increasingly important part of national and world societies. They seem to be very effective organizations for producing the great variety of goods and services for which individuals, as consumers, have acquired tastes, rightly or wrongly. Today, they invariably invade the domain of a local society as soon as its constituency acquires modern tastes, if not earlier, in order to obtain control of key resources.

Organizations emerge at different space-time points because basic (survival) needs arise at different times at different locations. The need for cooperative work to build dikes to prevent flooding, or irrigation ditches to provide a regular water supply, may exist in one agricultural area and not in another where rainfall is more regular and adequate. Accordingly, a community organization may appear earlier in the former than the latter. In still another area well isolated by mountainous terrain, the agricultural population may be much less subject to invasion by outsiders than the population inhabiting a plain. Some type of organization for defense purposes will tend to develop sooner in the second community. In fact, such organization may not appear in the former community until technology advances to the stage where mountains are no longer obstacles to invasion.

From another standpoint, an area with rich agricultural soil is more likely to have conditions of surplus food supply than other less fertile areas. This surplus is available for exchange for "luxury" items. Accordingly, the need for an effective economic organization, based on a standard currency and involving traders and perhaps port and banking facilities, induces the growth of a town economy with all its supportive organizations to serve this rich agricultural area. For the less fertile areas, this development of town organization may not occur until a much later period, if at all; and because there is less food that can be made available to support the inhabitants of a town, any town that does develop is likely to be smaller and less varied in organizational structure.

Still another way in which the location of population greatly influences the kinds of organizations that emerge is seen when we consider the organizational needs of rural versus suburban versus central city populations. In rural areas, where there is an abundance of opportunities to be in direct contact with nature and with the many pleasant facets of the physical environment, there is no need to organize hiking clubs like the Sierra Club, or bicycle groups like Wheelmen of America, or to have facilities such as YMCA gymnasiums for physical exercise. On the other hand, city residents require them at convenient central city sites. There is also less need to develop social clubs in order to provide a desirable level of sociality in rural areas, because the common problems which those who till the soil have in confronting the physical environment are apt to be a rallying point for social interaction—a rallying point we do not find among urban residents who are so highly specialized and are engaged in so many different occupations. However, rural inhabitants may need to organize a cooperative in order to combat exploitation. This exploitation may be in terms of excessively low prices paid on farm products, perhaps because of discriminatory monopolistic-type practices used by brokers who buy farm products; or in terms of excessively high prices charged for consumer goods, because of discriminating selling practices or because each village by itself is too small a market for delivering goods except at very high prices.

At central city locations, there are needs for organizations of a different character. A local organization may be needed to combat crime and drug abuse, or to expose corruption (which is much more tempting in the urban setting because of the tremendously higher payoffs possible.) Another type of organization may be needed to plug for reform government, or to fight an irresponsible or inefficient bureaucracy. Moreover, within a central city, ethnic groups may need to organize in order to preserve rich cultural traditions that are in danger of disappearing because of job specialization. Citizens may need to organize to control demands and pressures from other interest groups that exist, such as the Union of Transport Laborers or the teachers' union, to counteract their tendency to exploit the central city population as a whole.

Enough has been said to indicate how the different kinds of responsibilities, education requirements, intellectual stimuli, tensions, tempo of life, and speed of diffusion of ideas are associated with different locations and areas. They are factors that greatly influence *where* different kinds of organizations emerge, the points in time at which they appear, their size, their tasks, and their characteristics.

The *when* and *where* of organizations are, of course, closely associated with the process by which organizations grow and change in character over time. We have already indicated various elements that give rise to change within and around the organization. First of all, there may be technological innovations.

New ways of producing old products are developed. New products themselves appear. If an organization is to succeed in its objectives of making profits for the owners of its common stock, maintaining good-paying jobs for its employees, and continuing to provide quality products and services to its customers on a low-cost basis, it may need to completely reorganize its production processes. As we have noted, this may require drastic change in its hierarchy with respect to decision-making authority and communication, such as when production needs to be automated. Likewise, if the old products like horse buggies are no longer in demand, the organization must perhaps produce automobile bodies if it is to stay alive. Moreover, it may even need to shift its location in physical space, as when textiles plants moved from New England to the South, leaving in their wake large pockets of unemployment and ghost towns.

Major reorganization does not take place within economic organizations alone. Innovation may impinge drastically on noneconomic organizations. The development of communication and computing facilities, starting from the telephone, through radio and TV, and down to the latest giant IBM computer, has caused political parties to revamp their modes of operation. University organization and operation have been greatly affected, leading on the one hand to a presumably more efficient operation in the sense of cost-effectiveness budgeting, but on the other hand to the decline of the incidence of new creative ideas because they cannot be budgeted. Also, though modern communication and computing facilities have made feasible the administration of still larger universities, encompassing still greater specializations and democratization of college education, they have led to the breakdown of personal relationships among the faculty, between the faculty and the administrators, and between the faculty and the pupil, with this last relationship being increasingly reduced to the level of an IBM card. The revolution in communications and computers is even invading the domain of the most established and sacred organizations, namely the religious ones, and is leading to major changes there as well.

So technological innovation, by changing the nature of production, the ways in which organizations can operate internally, and the tastes and demands of the clients or the grass-roots members of organizations and society in general, leads to all kinds of changes within the organization's structure and function.

As already pointed out, these changes are frequently associated with change in objectives and size. Innovation in medical research which led to effective control of polio made the objective of the National Foundation for Infantile Paralysis obsolete. In order to preserve the organization and to maintain good-paying and satisfying jobs to its employees, the specific goal of the organization was changed from that of conquering infantile paralysis to conquering childhood diseases. We have already seen how the goals of our fictitious organization, the CCCSS, had to change in order to accommodate the need for growth and success, which were goals in themselves. We have also indicated how change in size and adaptation to new technology, new external demands, and scale economies have in turn led to the need for a new kind of leadership and new kinds of nodal structures internal to the organization. Without question the kind of aggressive, promotional, far-seeing leadership that was required during the nineteenth century to gird the territory of the United States with iron rails was totally different than the need for leadership within the railroad industry since the 1950s in

order to preserve an unwieldy, toppling, inefficient structure. This need for preservation stems not only from the desire of bondholders to receive their interest
payments (let alone the desire of stockholders for some profits) but also the
nation's desire to have an effective and efficient transportation mode for commodity traffic and a standby ground facility should the new airline system break
down at any time, especially at times critical for national security.

Change in size is also associated with the need to confront risks and uncertainty in an efficient manner. When an organization produces many different
kinds of products—as does General Foods—the organization is less likely to be
adversely affected by a sudden change in a particular consumer demand (say for
canned tuna because of some pollution incident) or by the failure of a particular
crop. Of course, this means a larger organization, greater specialization within
the organization—with specialists in each line of production concerned with the
efficiency of their particular line—and a greater need for an overall manager able
to resolve conflicts. But it also means a greater probability of a positive amount
of "success" (though perhaps a smaller probability of brilliant success).

When and where the forces for growth are at the maximum—where the organization seeks diversification to better meet unexpected contingencies of the environment, to amass influence and power in order to maintain its position, to
grow for the sake of growth, and so forth—then we find the modern conglomerate
such as ITT appearing on the scene. Where such forces will lead us in the future
we cannot yet foresee. One scenario might have the multinational corporation
not only achieving a stranglehold on political leaders within a number of important nations of the world—conceivably including the United States, the Soviet
Union, Mainland China, and Japan but also exercising a controlling interest in
a new United Nations or world organization. In such a scenario, the organization
might name itself *Concerned Multinationals to Promote the Healthy Resource
Development of the Milky Way.*

Of course, although most organizations tend to survive and grow, and though
their number keeps on increasing, some do die. But deaths do seem to be significantly less than births. Typically, a death occurs via absorption into another
organization or conglomerate. ITT takes over a dying industry because it is
profitable to do so, not only in terms of taxes saved but also in terms of still
further accumulation of power—more employees under its control, more dollar
assets, more constituent stockholders, and more customers whom it can influence. When they are dying, religious organizations and educational systems are
often absorbed into others.

But then some organizations do decline and die. The Shakers of Massachusetts
and the Freie Gemeinde of Sauk City, Wisconsin (a group of Free Thinkers) are
examples of such units. One can also see, in many of the old central cities of
metropolitan regions, church structures that have been abandoned, reflecting the
shift of an original constituency out of an area and succession by another ethnic
group which has no interest in the particular type of religion associated with
that structure. The deaths of *Life, Look,* and the *Saturday Evening Post* are
other illustrations. But it should be noted that it is harder for organizations to
die than to be born. An organization that has once prospered has in its vaults
some resources, such as titles of buildings, and land and stocks in old companies.
Older members may find these resources adequate for maintaining the organiza-

tion for many years. For example, the Freie Gemeinde will probably not totally go out of existence until all its older members die.

Finally, we must say a few more words about the organization as a forceful participant in society. We have discussed at some length how different cultures, different kinds of regions, different kinds of needs, and different kinds of resources determine somewhat systematically the kinds of organizations which emerge, the individual personalities involved in them, and their "when and where." We have said much less about how the organizations themselves influence cultures, the goals of society and the goals of individuals and their behavior. We must recognize that this type of influence is systematically exercised by organizations. Whether they advertise, as the airlines do; directly condition the thinking of individuals who are their employees, church or party members, or students; or indirectly exert influence through an intricate network of connections, there is a clearcut flow from organizations and their goals and behavior to individuals and social goals and behavior.

So we have a system of mutual interrelations among society, individuals, and organizations. Individuals and society restrict the action spaces of organizations by governmental regulation and the impact of "tradition." On the other hand, organizations restrict the action spaces of individuals in terms of the kinds of employment made available, income earned, and the ability to make profits that can be taxed for general social purposes. Organizations also determine the efficiency with which many resources are used, partly through decisions regarding expenditures on research and development. In this way they influence the number and kinds of jobs (and thus action spaces) available to individuals—and also the surplus profits which again are available for taxation for governmental purposes. Organizations, as we have already indicated, condition peoples' tastes and change their goals and behavior through advertising. Through contributions to different community services, charities, educational programs, and religious-cultural activities, they also have a systematic influence on the health and welfare of the individual and again on his goals and behavior.

Sometimes their exercise of influence is explicitly aimed at directly assisting individuals and promoting public welfare. More often the actions they take and the influence they wield is designed to increase or maintain their legitimacy and to counteract any nuance of illegitimacy in their operation.

Often, moreover, the path an organization pursues in moving through the power structure to exercise influence is not clearly identifiable. We have already suggested the hierarchical system of organizations. Given such a hierarchy, an organization may choose to exercise influence on individuals by influencing the goals and behavior of one or more other organizations (or institutions) which in turn influence (or restrict action spaces) of another subset of organizations (or institutions) and so forth, until we reach the individual at the grass-roots level. Of course, here, as in the hierarchy of regions we depicted earlier in this chapter, there is much overlapping among organizations. We observe that leaders in one organization may serve as directors in another, and vice versa. We also observe that by means of interlocking directorships and appointments, the basic decisions in society come to be controlled by a small elite and that power is concentrated in their hands. The existence of such interlocking frequently makes it difficult to identify the real source of an illegitimate action or exercise of an undesirable influence. But notwithstanding all these complications—that is, the interlocking of top officials, goal structures, and behavior of organizations, and the numerous kinds of constraints which they place on each other—there is no question that they do have systematic influence on social and individual goals and behavior. Thus, they play a significant role in controlling the environment that surrounds them.

CONCLUDING REMARKS

We have broadly painted the why, how, who, when, and where of organizations. We now wish to get a clearer notion of how these organizations influence the whole process of urban and regional development, and how in turn they can be influenced. We may wish to influence them in order to reduce obstacles they may impose on such development, or to encourage them to provide subsidies and other forms of assistance.

The Rationality of Irrationality

Recall the Watertown example used to introduce the subject matter of this chapter. We said that the apparently inefficient and irrational decision of the state government of New York in placing Knowlton Brothers under order to halt air pollution was in part predictable, and therefore logical and rational. It was predictable in the sense that the residents of the United States have become increasingly aware of the deterioration of the environment within which they live. They have demanded that environmental degradation be halted. To bring such degradation to an immediate halt, however, is beyond the capability of the society as it is currently constituted and operated. But the issue is perceived to be so important that the population makes a sharp distinction between political leaders who do nothing to control the environment and political leaders who do something. Because there are individuals in this society who aspire to the presidential office and who perhaps are not aware of the tremendous personal costs involved, each individual who is fortunate enough to have become a candidate to this office must have already committed himself and his party to action to halt environmental degradation. Whoever becomes elected is then obligated to do something, and although a leader and his party may welch considerably on this obligation, nonetheless they must take some action—do something—in order not to appear as irresponsible and deceptive.

The problem of wise environmental management is a complex one. So many variables are involved and intricately interconnected that we still know relatively little about what constitutes wise environmental management. For example, it differs widely from region to region. One region may have extensive wind movements, another hardly any. One region may have an extensive and abundant water system, another may not. One region's past growth and prosperity may have been dependent upon excellent deposits of coal that is good but that contains a high content of sulphur, such as Pittsburgh and West Virginia, while another region's past growth and prosperity may have been based on hydroelectric power, such as the Pacific Northwest. One region may have rich agricultural soil, with little need for fertilizer and pesticides; another may not. One region may have large, highly mechanized commercialized farms; another may not.

We have little knowledge about how to take account of these major regional differences in developing a wise environmental policy. Further. we have very little knowledge as to the links among the different kinds of ecologic systems. We know very little about how solid-waste disposal can contribute to the water-pollution problem, or how air and water pollution are interrelated. We know very little about how the simultaneous presence of different kinds of air pollutants affect an area. And to complicate matters still more, we have no clear notion of the different health effects of each of the different kinds of air and water pollutants. For example, to what extent are the "imagined" ill effects of strontium really and truly ill effects?

So the state-of-the art of environmental policy formulation is at a very low level. On the other hand, our presidential leader and his party—whether it be President Ford and the Republican Party as it is today or McGovern and the Democratic Party as it might have been—are committed to some rather immediate action. A political leader and his party cannot tell a constituency: "Before we take action we must have all the facts on hand, even if it takes ten years to accumulate them." To take some action now means he must set up some agency or unit in the government at the next-lower order of nodes, with the objective of proposing "good" legislation. It means that this government agency cannot do even short-run research but must call upon some experts to help in quickly drawing up good legislation, largely based upon hunches and views and a scarcity of facts and tested hypotheses.

An agency in a democratically run society, or in a society that purports to be democratically run, may know that a nonuniform kind of policy is desirable to attack a specific problem. But unless it can firmly justify nonequal taxation, nonequal charges, or nonuniform regulation, it will run into sharp criticism from the so-called equal-opportunity and equal-tax enthusiasts and others who are emotionally swept away with the egalitarianism of democracy and not its true welfare implications. Thus, given the extreme complexity of the environmental problem and our scant knowledge of it, there is nothing more consistent with the ethos of the U.S. society than uniform regulation—legislation which sets the same standards for pollutant concentrations and emissions for all people, for all organizations, and for all locations. So we have a law such as the Clean Air Act.

In line with democratic principles, we find that this act assigns to each of the nodes of the next-lower order—that is, the states—the task of developing its own program for implementing the standards set by this act. But if the federal government has not done research on wise environmental management, how can one expect any state, with its considerably smaller resources and smaller demand for research, to pursue basic research? The state does not, and therefore it too follows the basic principle of equal taxation, equal burdens, and uniform standards. Moreover, if standards are specifically defined by people who are experts on the problem from a technical engineering standpoint, *and whose involvement is absolutely essential*, then we cannot expect them to be aware of the important indirect social and economic implications.

Thus we must expect the appropriate officials in New York state to issue orders to all companies to abate in exactly the same manner, with the usual minor exceptions for special circumstances which always creep into any legislation. So the order imposed on Knowlton Brothers is in part predictable, logical, and rational for a society that is not too long on research and that is geared to the principle of equality and democracy. In fact, one might make the even stronger statement that this decision was predictable with high probability and therefore was "highly" logical and rational. And we can also predict that many similar decisions will be made. They will be justified at the higher-order nodes on the basis of equality of opportunity or equal sharing of burdens. But in fact, because of the lack of the leaders' knowledge at the higher-order nodes and their limited perceptions, there will be inefficiency and considerable social injustice at the grass-roots level. We can predict this more so when a conservative political administration is in power, committed to the principle of "no immediate payoff, no research."

As regional scientists, we must understand this situation as a decision situation within a system that embodies numerous kinds of organizations and many individuals, all of whom are subject to emotionalism and manias in mass behavior situations. These organizations are intricately interrelated, and there is a tremendous conflict among the goals, not only within any given organization but among all these organizations and individuals as well. This leads to predictable behavior by many political units in terms of decisions governing not only environmental management but also housing, education, transportation, medical care, business regulation, and other policy areas. All this influences the possibilities for development within our own city and region. We cannot afford to ignore this intricate pattern of organization and decision-making that exists. We must conduct our analysis in such a way that we can identify decisions of high probability, or identify the subset of decisions most likely to embrace the decision that is taken. Within this framework we must struggle for solutions to urban and regional problems with which we are concerned, and fight for change in the hierarchy so that social injustice is less likely to occur.

APPENDIX TO CHAPTER 12.   The Theory of Central Places

In close connection with the notions of hierarchy in the decision-making structure of world society, we can develop the theory on the system of central places. This theory stems from the work of Walter Christaller,[1] a geographer, and August Lösch,[2] an economist. It does provide additional insight into the process by which a hierarchical structure emerges—for example, of cities within a system, or of decision-making nodes within an organization.

As a beginning, we assume an "abstract" area, in particular a flat, even plain, which is homogeneous in terms of soil fertility and all other resource characteristics. Over this area, movement is possible in any and every direction. Further, the population is uniformly distributed and is identical in tastes, income, and most other ways.

Next we consider a set of economic activities that produces goods and services for the population. These activities require as inputs only ubiquitous goods and services—that is, those which are available everywhere in unlimited quantities as defined in Chapter 6. Such inputs might be land, labor services (because

---

[1] Walter Christaller, *Central Places in Southern Germany* (Englewood Cliffs, N.J.: Prentice-Hall, 1966).

[2] August Lösch, *The Economics of Location* (New Haven: Yale University Press, 1954).

population is uniformly distributed), air, and so forth. Highly localized inputs such as iron ore or coking coal do not enter into any production activities.

Already we see that this set of assumptions is not generally applicable to the real world. However, for some areas of the world (such as southern Germany in Christaller's time, and parts of Iowa and other agricultural areas in the past and present), these assumptions can be considered reasonable. This is so particularly when we are considering service-type activities such as retail trade, repair services, and crafts, which do not require many localized inputs, if any.

With a population having identical tastes, income, and needs, and being evenly distributed over space, we may imagine that many different-sized market areas for goods and services would emerge, because of the joint operation of scale economies and transport costs. As already suggested, we have at the one extreme scale economies that are small relative to transport costs, but significant enough to make it profitable for one individual to produce a good for one (or two) other individuals. Then we have the smallest-sized market area. We also tend to have the maximum number of producers for a given population. At the other extreme, where transport costs approach zero and scale economies are major, or where decreasing unit costs of operation always obtain, we have the largest-sized market area and the tendency to have a minimum number of producers, namely one. Thus, we may imagine that when we plot the number of producers with the size of market area, we obtain a figure such as that depicted by Figure 12A.1.

Lösch has pushed the theory further. Assume that the population (in terms of household units) is uniformly distributed, as are the dots in Figure 12A.2, and require that each household be served by a producer of a good. (All household

Figure 12A.1   Different Sizes of Market Areas, Due to Scale
Economies and Transport Cost Differences

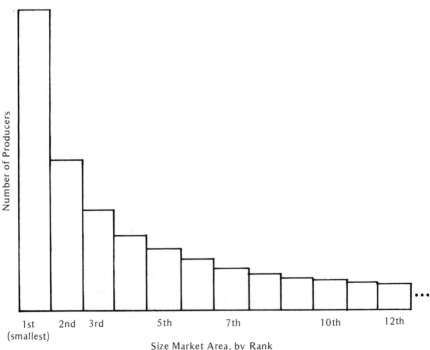

Figure 12A.2   A Uniformly Distributed Population

units are taken to be of the same size.) Then the normal circular-type market areas on the left-hand side of Figure 12A.3 are not possible, because the household units in the shaded areas are not served by a producer. Lösch goes on to show that the boundary line between the market areas of any two producers of a good must be a straight line, and that pure competition will ensure that the market areas of the producers of a given good will be regular hexagons. This is indicated on the right-hand side of Figure 12A.3.

Lösch develops sizes of market areas that are theoretically possible, though each theoretical market area need not occur in reality. The ten smallest possible market areas are listed in Table 12A.1. Sets of the three smallest-sized market areas are depicted in Figure 12A.4. If we take a location, say Z in Figure 12A.5, as the location of a major urban-metropolitan center which produces goods serving all theoretically possible market areas, then the ten smallest-sized market areas around the center Z can be depicted as in Figure 12A.5.

Often in our thinking about social problems in a particular cultural setting we know that not all theoretically possible market areas are consistent with the ways of a culture. From the set of possible market areas, we then are inclined to choose a subset that does have meaning. For example, in connection with the discussion of Figures 12.1 and 12.2 in the text, we choose the smallest market area, the village, to be one that serves 7 persons. Then, using a factor of 7, we develop a system of towns (each serving 7 villages), a system of metropoles (each

Figure 12A.3   The Movement from Circular-Type Market Areas
to Hexagonal Market Areas

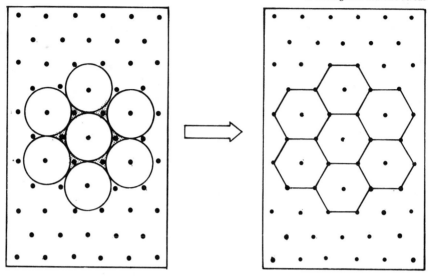

Table 12A.1   Size of the Theoretically Possible Market Areas

Order of Market Areas, by Size	1	2	3	4	5	6	7	8	9	10
Number of Household Units Served including the Household at the Location of the Unit of Production	3	4	7	9	12	13	16	19	21	25

serving 7 towns), and so forth. Such a system is useful to our thinking and similar, but not strictly identical, to one that Lösch might derive. In terms of
facilitating communications, Christaller and Lösch have suggested the utility of
a framework based upon *primary market areas* each serving 4 persons, which
thus corresponds to the second smallest of the theoretically possible market
areas—towns, each of which contains 4 primary market areas—cities, each of
which serves 4 towns; and so forth. Such an arrangement is presented in
Figure 12A.6.

Although it is possible to present many other interesting spatial patterns that
can be deduced from the basic Christaller-Lösch framework, we must at the same
time recognize its serious limitations because of the unrealistic assumptions it
makes. Perhaps its most serious inadequacy is that it initially assumes a uniform
distribution of population, as in Figure 12A.2, and then deduces a concentration
of economic activities at an urban-metropolitan center such as Z in Figure 12A.5.
Such a concentration of activities implies a concentration of jobs and thus households, contradicting the initial assumption of uniform distribution.

We cannot discuss the various limitations of this framework in this introductory textbook, nor other materials that might suggest some deeper insights
which this framework can provide for attacking the social problems that interest
us. These belong to more advanced courses.

Figure 12A.4   The Three Smallest Sets of Market Areas

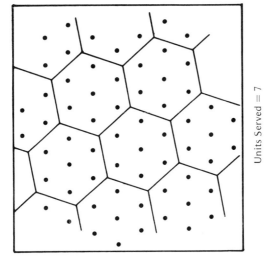

Units Served = 7

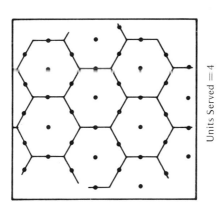

Units Served = 4

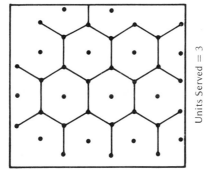

Units Served = 3

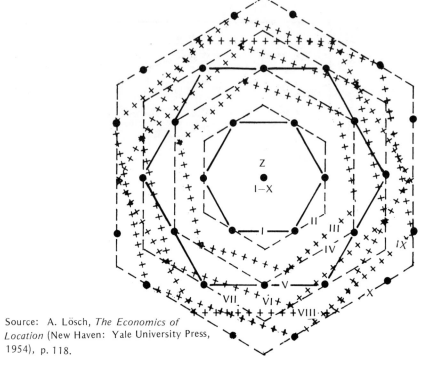

Source: A. Lösch, *The Economics of Location* (New Haven: Yale University Press, 1954), p. 118.

Figure 12A.6   A Löschian System, With a Market Area
Serving Four Units

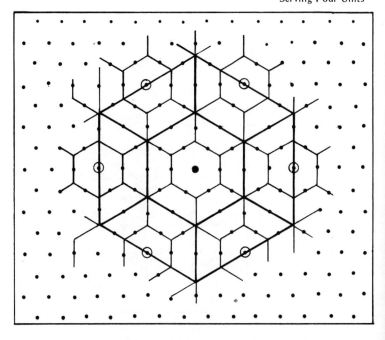

Chapter

13

Public Sector:
Activities and Welfare

INTRODUCTION

Social injustice is all about us. This is so whether we look at the slums while riding on an el (elevated transit facility), or whether we pass by the human slop yard of a capital city on a Caribbean jaunt, or whether we mistakenly wander in the alleyways of Moscow. The sight and knowledge of slums prick the conscience of some; they are thus motivated to improve the welfare of the much less fortunate. To others, the existence of slums merely spells high crime rates, a significant probability of riots and mass violence, and other insecurity and threat to their well-being. For more selfish reasons, they too are motivated to support measures to eliminate slums, urban poverty, and other kinds of social injustice which result in their own discomfort and disutility. As a consequence, in societies of affluence we witness a strong demand for the evolution and public administration of new kinds of programs. In recent times the rapid increase in this demand accounts for much of the tremendous growth of the public sector in the United States and many other parts of the world.

What one person (man or woman) does often affects the well-being of another. When one litters, numerous others are adversely affected—as already seen in Chapter 10. Likewise when one pollutes. When one pokes along a superhighway, he may raise the tension level of many drivers. Further, when one brings into the world a new life, the increased pressure on the world's limited resources is felt by all. As we have indicated, it is true that often the impact of a single person's action has negligible influence on all others. But we have also seen that when many persons behave in a similar manner, the accumulation of negative impacts on each one's welfare can be major. This problem of controlling the behavior of many, when each person on his own has little influence, has become increasingly important in terms of maintaining neighborhoods, conserving the environment, managing a transportation system, and the like. It is part of the larger problem of requiring behaving units to be more responsible for the negative externalities they impose on others. The public's demand that such responsibility be required is another major reason for the recent tremendous growth of the public sector in the United States and many other countries.

Additionally, we recognize the continued presence and growing importance of the more traditional demands for public sector activity. There are the needs for police and fire protection, education, adjudication, legislation, administration, monetary management, defense and security, and other services of a kind that cannot be easily marketed and that cannot be produced by a single citizen at low cost. These services are provided by local police and fire departments, the U.S. Treasury, the Defense and State Departments, and numerous other agencies. Another set of traditional functions encompasses the regulation of the activities of one or a few selected behaving units in order to protect the welfare or the interests of the larger group. Examples include regulation that eliminates the exploitation of labor, as was discussed in Chapter 8, or regulation to preclude consumer exploitation by big firms in industries where decreasing costs lead to natural monopolies. Here services are provided by the Antitrust Division of the Justice Department, the Federal Power Commission, and the Interstate Commerce Commission, among others. Finally, there is the traditional function of the public sector to provide job, market, scientific, and other information of a strategic character not generally available to individuals, in order to increase their mobility and to facilitate the wise use of their resources and labor. Such functions are provided, for example, by the U.S. Departments of Labor, Agriculture, and Commerce.

As a result of both new functions and the growing importance of old ones, the public sector has become an increasing presence in our everyday life. When we did input-output studies in the old days, we looked upon government and the public sector as a single major sector—like the iron and steel sector, transportation sector, or agriculture sector. But now, with the tremendous amount of public expenditures on a highly diverse set of programs, we can no longer consider government as comprising one sector in an input-output table. It must be considered as comprising many sectors, perhaps as many as there are economic sectors.

For this chapter, public sectors are simply defined as the sectors that produce public goods and services; they traditionally comprise governmental units in all their diversity. A public good itself is not as easily defined. There are differences of opinion among experts as to what a public good is. Clearly, we can include those goods, such as national defense or the services of a lighthouse, that can be consumed by any one person without decreasing the consumption of the same good by another person, where it is not feasible to try to exclude someone from consuming the good if he so desires. We should also classify as public goods those which are collective goods in the sense that some segment of the public collectively wants them, is prepared to pay for them, and cannot buy them at the normal economic market. An additional requirement here is that such collective goods be publicly provided. This is the case for low-income housing, recreational facilities, and toll roads, which can be subject to user charges, thereby excluding some people from consuming them. There are still other kinds of public goods of which we will become aware as we proceed with our discussion.

Just as we study the activities of the numerous economic sectors in order to see their impact on the urban and regional economy and how we can alter such impact, we must do the same for each of the many public sectors. In what follows, we shall first examine and analyze the more traditional public sector activities. Then we shall move on to the more interesting, new types of activities.

ANALYSIS OF TRADITIONAL PUBLIC SECTOR ACTIVITIES

Production of Nonmarketable Goods

Consider such traditional activities of governments as the provision of fire and police protection, national defense and security, and other *nonmarketable goods.* The reasons these activities fall under the jurisdiction of a governmental unit are very simple. First, the goods may be of such a character that once they are produced no one can be excluded from their benefits. Once the borders of a country are policed to exclude undesirable characters, no one within the country can be excluded from benefiting from (that is, consuming) those services. Once a sign is posted warning people of thin ice, no one passing by can be excluded from having such information and gaining utility from it. Second, the provision of these services may be achieved by collective or government action at a much lower unit cost per person than when each person has to provide the service for himself—as is the case for checking the thickness of the ice, or looking out for hurricanes and slide areas.

These points are clearly demonstrated with the use of Figure 13.1. Suppose we have a small village community consisting of three families. There exists a lake, which is public property. When the lake freezes in winter, the children of all the families skate upon it. Suppose each family is concerned with the danger of drowning should the ice crack and give way. Therefore each is motivated to spend some money to check the thickness of the ice. Each family may then be said to have a demand for ice-testing services, measured say in man-hours spent at testing the ice. Let the demand curves D_A, D_B, and D_C, represent the demand curves of families *A, B,* and *C,* respectively. There is a professional ice-tester in the neighboring community whose services are available. The schedule of the rates that he quotes for supplying different amounts of services is given by the SS curve.[1] If family *A* were living there alone, it would purchase Oq_A of these services; if family *B* were living there alone, it would purchase Oq_B amount; and if family *C* were living there alone it would purchase Oq_C amount. But these families do live together in the same community. If we were to con-

[1] His rates fall at first with increase in amount to be supplied, reflecting the fact that he incurs certain transport and start-up costs in taking on a new job. His rates rise sharply when large amounts are to be supplied because he may judge that it is unwise to be too dependent on a single customer or set of customers.

320

sider the *sum* of the amounts of services they would be purchasing, were each living alone in the community—that is, $Oq_A + Oq_B + Oq_C$—we would obtain the amount Oq_E. But this amount of ice-testing services is not the most desirable when they are all living in the village. We can see this when we construct a vertical line at Oq_E. Observe that for Oq_E amount of services, family A would be willing to pay a price of p_A in accord with its demand curve D_A, family B would be willing to pay p_B in accord with its demand curve D_B, and family C would be willing to pay p_C in accord with its demand curve D_C. All told then the three families would value the last unit of ice-testing services at the sum of the three prices $p_A + p_B + p_C$. Note that this sum is given by the vertical stretch OT. Because it well exceeds the actual price at the level Oq_E, as a collective they would all gain from the provision of an additional unit of ice-testing services. In fact, they would continue to gain from the provision of an additional unit until we reach the level of services represented by Oq_F, at which level the sum of the three prices the families would be willing to pay for an additional unit equals price.

Figure 13.1   Demand and Supply Curves for Ice-Tester's Services

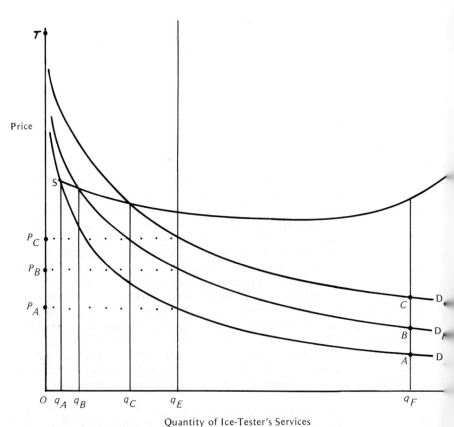

Quantity of Ice-Tester's Services

At the start, let the three families be very cooperative and recognize the potential for their mutual gain. They work out, and follow year after year, an arrangement with the ice-tester whereby he provides Oq_F amount of services with family A paying a price corresponding to the vertical stretch q_FA, family B paying a price corresponding to q_FB and family C paying a price corresponding to q_FC. Fortunately or unfortunately, time does not stand still. One spring a real estate developer appears in the village and puts up 100 new homes, which are soon occupied by new families. Winter comes along. None of the new families can be excluded from the use of the public lake. Each considers Oq_F amount of ice-testing services more than adequate to insure the safety of its children. So at least some of the families will say: "Why chip in to pay for the ice-testing services? The lake belongs to all of us. No one can exclude us. Why not be a 'free-rider'?" Of course, the original three families might feel that they are "suckers." They may terminate the arrangements with the ice-tester. Then no family would obtain the benefits of having a lake for their children to skate on without worry. Perhaps some other families may get together, be willing to be the suckers, and not mind the fact that they will be paying for services which others get free of charge. But such might not happen. Clearly, then, we would have a case where a public sector is needed. It is needed to arrange for the provision of a service that is *nonmarketable*—that is, a service for which a market cannot be established with people paying for the units they consume.

Of course, the case for collective or public sector activity becomes stronger when we relax the assumption that all families are fully cooperative. We can see how family A might reason that because family C has a more intense demand for ice-testing services than it (family A) has, family C is likely to purchase some, say an amount roughly corresponding to Oq_c. Family A may then ask why it should purchase any on its own, because it is likely to be able to benefit from Oq_c amount of services free of charge. Family B may also reason in this way. But then family C, realizing what is happening when it finds itself buying Oq_c of services and families A and B buying none, may refuse to be a sucker. It may reduce its purchase to zero. In this case no one pays for or gains from having the ice tested; all are worse off than they could be from some kind of collective action.

Another kind of situation requiring public sector intervention is one in which none of the families' demand curves crosses the average and marginal cost curves, as indicated in Figure 13.2. No one family by itself can afford the ice-tester's services and therefore none of the children skate on the ice without worry. But if we were to construct a "collective" demand curve D*, indicating the aggregate price the three families would be willing to pay for different amounts of services, collectively they would be able to purchase Oq_G amount of services. They could do so because family A would be willing to pay a price corresponding to the vertical stretch Aq_G, family B would be willing to pay a price Bq_G, and family C a price Cq_G. In total the three families would be willing to pay a price $Hq_G = Aq_G + Bq_G + Cq_G$, a price that meets the average cost (and supply price) of the ice-tester for Oq_G amount of services. Everybody would be better off.

In similar manner, we can consider the supply and demand for fire protection, police protection, and many other goods and services which are non marketable.

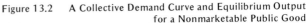

Figure 13.2   A Collective Demand Curve and Equilibrium Output
for a Nonmarketable Public Good

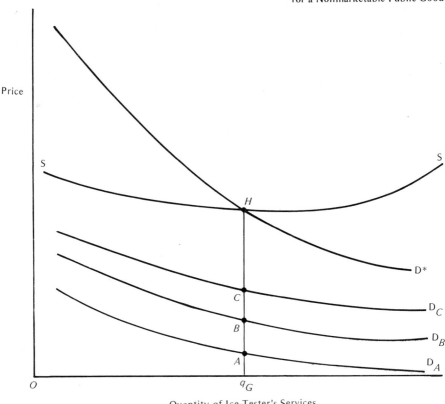

Quantity of Ice-Tester's Services

The justification for public service involvement is crystal clear, particularly when no one family can afford to support say a fire station and a fire-fighting force by itself, but thousands of families as a collective can.

Regulatory Activities

A second kind of demand for public sector activities stems from the traditional need to regulate. In Figure 8.4, which we reproduce as part of Figure 13.3, we noted the exploitation of labor when a monopolist can get away with a subsistence wage payment of OS^A. The monopolist's exploitation profits are given by the rectangle $S^A ZN'P$. Clearly there is a need for regulation on the part of society that would both require a wage higher than the subsistence wage and try to maintain employment opportunities at the same time. If we look at Figure 13.3, we can see that the wage rate as defined by the vertical stretch OS^A can be raised by shifting the horizontal line upward to correspond to the new vertical stretch OS^*. The new intersection point of the marginal revenue and the marginal cost curves is at T, suggesting that the monopolist, operating on his own out of self-interest, would cut back employment from OM' to OR. However, the regulation could be such that both the employment OM' and the minimum wage OS^* are required. We can see from Figure 13.3 that this is possible, because the profits to the monopolist would still be positive. His profit per unit would be $P*N'$ and his total profits would be $P*N'ZS*$.

Figure 13.3   A Regulated Monopoly and Wage Situation

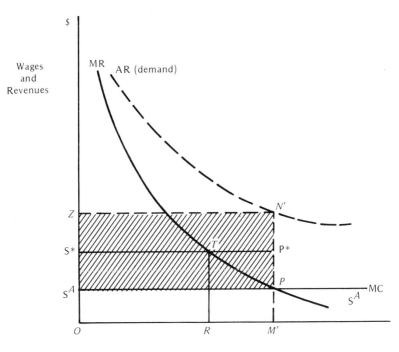

Quantity of Labor

Still another need for regulation arises when, because of decreasing costs, a condition of natural monopoly exists within an industry and the monopolist does not hesitate to exploit consumers as much as possible. This situation can be illustrated by Figure 13.4. Here we employ another set of regular demand (AR) and marginal revenue (MR) curves. However, we now depict a situation in which average costs continue to fall until we reach a significant level of output. See the average cost (AC) curve in the figure on which we also construct the corresponding marginal cost (MC) curve. Clearly, the monopolist maximizes profits when he chooses the output corresponding to the intersection point E of the marginal cost and marginal revenue curves. We indicate his profits by the shaded area. But note the high price that consumers must pay, namely OY. Note also that, for the quantity OZ of output which they purchase, the price they pay is much higher than the marginal costs to the producer. According to some social welfare analysts, this outcome is undesirable. These analysts often state that marginal costs are the proper costs to be met in production. As long as the consumer is willing to pay a price greater than marginal costs, a good should continue to be produced. Its production should be increased, even with price falling (from increased supply) and marginal costs rising, up to the point where marginal costs equal price. Accordingly, in a social welfare society the output of the good should be increased to the level OW in Figure 13.4, corresponding to the intersection point U of the marginal cost and demand curves.

324

Figure 13.4   Monopoly versus Social Welfare Price and Output

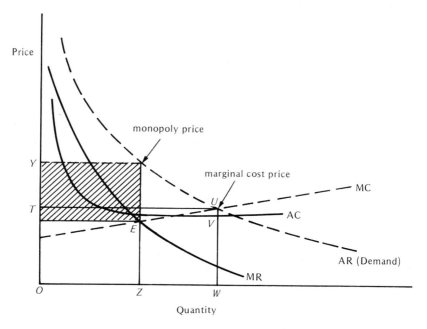

Note that this would involve a significant decrease in price from OY to OT and a significant increase in output from OZ to OW. The monopolist still makes a profit of UV per unit, the difference between the average cost curve and the price at the output level OW. Thus some analysts intensely concerned with social welfare demand that a public regulatory authority intervene in monopoly-type situations, insuring that consumers obtain the lower price and larger output which is possible through marginal cost pricing while still leaving the monopolist with some surplus profit. Stronger social welfare advocates would argue that profits be fully taxed away for use in other programs.

However, situations can arise in which this kind of marginal cost pricing raises problems. Suppose the average cost (AC) and marginal cost (MC) curves are as in Figure 13.5, reflecting decreasing unit costs for all levels of output. If we pursue marginal cost pricing, the result is that the output should be OW, as given by the intersection point U of the demand and marginal cost curves. But at this output, price is lower than average cost. Therefore, a subsidy of UV per unit of output would have to be provided the monopolist in order to keep him producing. Some welfare theorists would insist that this is what should be done. Others, however, would be horrified at the thought of subsidizing a monopolist. They would propose in this situation that price be set to meet average cost, with the output level being determined accordingly. Thus, in Figure 13.5 an output of OR should be produced, a level corresponding to the intersection of the demand (AR) and the average cost (AC) curves. Note, however, that with average cost pricing the level of output available for consumers is smaller, being OR

Figure 13.5   **Welfare Pricing under Conditions of Decreasing Cost**

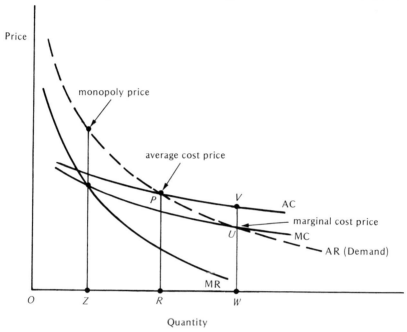

rather than *OW*; and the price is higher, being *RP* rather than *WU*. Some social welfare analysts would prefer marginal cost pricing to average cost pricing, for although the former involves subsidizing a monopolist, it also makes available to consumers larger output at lower prices by taking advantage of the scale economies which give rise to decreasing costs. They would contend that the benefits to consumers outweigh the cost of subsidies.

Whatever situation is judged by decision makers, political leaders, and citizens to be the more desirable, it is clear that a public sector must be actively involved in telling the monopolist what price he can and cannot charge.

Supply of Information

The third traditional area of public sector involvement concerns the provision of useful information to citizens. For example, in connection with Figure 8.5 we discussed the possibility of labor migration from areas where wages are low because of small demand and abundant supply to areas where wages are higher because of greater demand and less supply. However, as we pointed out, in order for migration to occur, those in the less developed regions must know of the employment opportunities in the more developed regions. Hence we need a job information source such as the Bureau of Labor Statistics to provide such information.

In the area of production, there has always been a wealth of new patents filed and new technologies tried. It is impossible for any one businessman to go through more than a small fraction of the technical journals bearing upon product developments which might be of interest to his enterprise. Therefore it is important, especially for the small businessman, to have a technical information service that can efficiently summarize developments and indicate where more information can be obtained. This is a traditional function of the Department of Commerce.

In farming, it is again impossible for each small, independent farmer to keep abreast of new kinds of crops, new ways of cultivation, new types of equipment, and all kinds of information concerning prices and markets. Again, it is important to provide such information for efficient farm operations. This service has always been performed by the Department of Agriculture.

In these and many other ways, public sector activities in the provision of information and similar services are required for the welfare of people. Further elaboration of this point is not necessary.

THE PUBLIC SECTOR AND EXTERNALITIES CONTROL AND MANAGEMENT

We have discussed three traditional areas of involvement of the public sector. Let us now move on to consider its involvement in the area of externalities control and management—an involvement which, strictly speaking, is not new, but which has attained a new level of significance because of a whole set of critical externalities that have emerged. By externalities, we mean spillovers and

Figure 13.6   Supply and Demand Curves for Gasoline

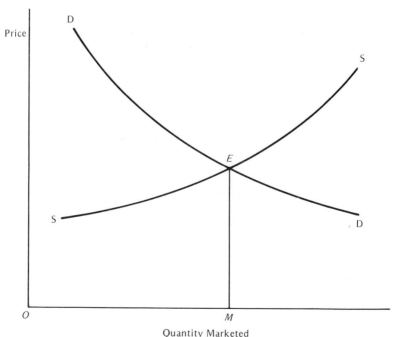

Quantity Marketed

other effects—positive or negative, desirable or undesirable—which result from a person's actions but which fall upon or accrue to other parties that are not directly involved in that action. A classic case is the discomfort from noise pollution to the individuals in a neighborhood when one person mows his lawn early on Sunday morning. With reference to an economic transaction involving two parties, a buyer and a seller, these externalities are sometimes called "third-party effects." A classic case here is the unpleasantness caused many passersby when a highly visible piece of land is rented and put to use as a junkyard.

The analytics of the externalities problem can be simply presented. In Figure 13.6 we present the demand (DD) and supply (SS) curves of a commodity, say gasoline. The price of gasoline established by the market is given by the intersection point *E* of these two curves, namely *EM*. However, the oil refineries which produce gasoline throw off a whole bunch of pollutants into the environment. These pollutants have adverse health effects as well as other negative impacts. We should take these into account by considering them as costs imposed on society. The oil refineries should be held responsible for these costs and should contribute an amount of funds equal to them to society. The oil refineries should then add them on to their regular production costs and determine their supply curve accordingly. For example, suppose the costs per unit output are as indicated by the dashed curve PP of Figure 13.7. (The costs rise with increase in quantity supplied, reflecting the fact that more and more output means more and more pollutants thrown out upon the environment, everything else being the same. This results in greater and greater negative impacts from each additional

Figure 13.7   Pollution Costs Per Unit Output and the Adjusted Supply Curve for Gasoline

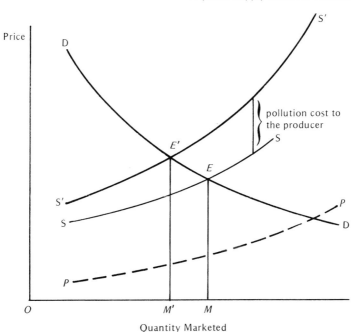

Quantity Marketed

unit of output.) The costs for any output, as given by the dashed curve, are to be added to the regular supply price of that output, as given by the SS curve, to yield the adjusted supply price of the output, as given by the $S'S'$ curve. The latter price and the $S'S'$ curve would be the relevant price and curve if oil refineries were required to meet the costs described by the dashed curve. As a consequence, the market price would be higher, corresponding to the intersection point E' of the $S'S'$ curve and the regular demand curve. The equilibrium output OM' would be smaller.

We can also use the curves of Figure 13.7 to represent another relevant situation. We may imagine that because of the negative impacts of pollution, the oil refineries are regulated and required to limit the amount and kinds of pollutants they generate. They may be told that they can emit only XX tons of SO_2 per day, or YY amount of BOD per hour. This restriction might vary with different levels of output, becoming more stringent per unit of output as the level of output increases. The oil refineries would need to invest in pollution control equipment and to incur labor and other costs in operating the necessary equipment to stay within the law. Thus the dashed curve of Figure 13.7 can be viewed as portraying the pollution control costs per unit output in supplying different quantities of gasoline to the market. If this were so, then the effective supply curve would once again be $S'S'$, the equilibrium price $E'M'$, and the equilibrium output OM'.

As late as the decade of the Sixties, the oil refineries were permitted to sell gasoline to consumers without incurring any of these costs. But this laissez-faire convention is no longer possible in the United States society. In the early Seventies, the public became alarmed by rapidly mounting environmental degradation. It compelled its political leaders to act and to outlaw uncontrolled generation of pollutants. The Environmental Protection Agency (EPA) was set up to serve as a watchdog. Unfortunately, it is very difficult to identify health deterioration and other negative impacts, and to associate with these a cost. Hence the public sector activity of the EPA is largely concerned with setting limits on the amounts of pollutants that an oil refinery or any other economic, social, and political entity may emit.

Not only do the producers of gasoline pollute, but so do consumers. Each consumer pollutes when he drives his automobile, or heats his home, or burns trash in his back yard. Thus he too should be required to bear the costs to society of the pollution for which he is responsible. Therefore, another amount ought to be added to the market price of gasoline which he pays, representing the social cost of the pollution associated with the consumption of that gallon of gasoline.

In terms of his demand schedule, such as the one depicted in Table 8.8 in Chapter 8, the price the consumer pays must cover both what the producer is to receive and what is to be levied on the consumer by society to compensate for the cost of his pollution. In terms of net price after social cost, which is what is relevant at the market, his demand curve would shift downward and to the left; and so likewise with every other consumer. In short, if we take the dashed CC curve of Figure 13.8 to represent the social cost of pollution per unit of consumption for different levels of consumption, the demand curve would drop to the position D'D' as indicated in Figure 13.8. Its intersection with the new supply curve leads to both lower net price (E"M") received by the producer at the market and smaller sales (*OM"*). This result might be considered a move in the right direction. On the other hand, in terms of the full price the consumer pays, the old demand curve DD is still relevant. The outcome is a higher price $M''F$ paid by the consumer. The difference between $M''F$ and $M''E''$ (what the producer receives) represents the cost per unit consumption levied by society on the consumer.

Alternatively, because it may be difficult for society to levy a charge per unit of consumption on each consumer, it may choose, as it does today, to regulate the pollution emissions from automobile use through the Environmental Protection Agency. With such regulation, society requires that each automobile contain additional machinery and equipment to reduce pollution emissions to a satisfactorily low level. This in turn means that each automobile is more costly to both purchase and operate. Thus we might consider that each individual consumer incurs additional costs per mile of automobile use, for different volumes of use, as given by a curve such as the CC curve of Figure 13.8. As before, each consumer's demand curve in terms of net price is effectively lowered. The D'D' curve of Figure 13.8 may now be taken to represent the demand for gasoline in terms of the net price at the market, the net price being the gross price consumers are willing to pay less the costs to them from the higher price of the automobile and its increased cost of operation.

Figure 13.8   Pollution Cost Per Unit of Consumption and the Adjusted Demand Curve for Gasoline

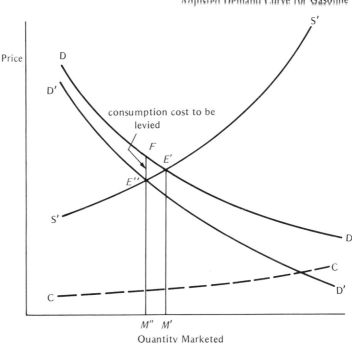

330

The accompanying discussion and set of graphs illustrate just one kind of pollution situation that can arise, involving costs to society because of both production and consumption. There are many cases like this one. There are also many where pollution costs enter in on the production side only (as in the case of mass transit), or on the consumption side only (as in the consumption of canned beer and food products).

There are also many cases where externalities give rise not to *costs* but to *benefits*. A classic case here might be the education of an urban slum population. We may, for example, imagine that there is a demand curve for educational services by a slum population. At all prices demand may be very small, relatively speaking, reflecting the low income of the population, its low aspirations, and its low perception of the benefits from education. There is a hypothesis often advanced that the education of the disadvantaged yields benefits to society in the sense that a low rate of crime incidence and of welfare costs (from unemployment), and a high rate of labor productivity are associated with a more educated population. In Figure 13.9 we let the BB curve represent the benefits to society per unit of educational services to an urban slum population for different levels of educational services that might be provided. Thus, though the demand curve for educational services by the slum population might be as indicated by the DD curve, the demand curve by society inclusive of this population's demand might be given by the D'D' curve, which lies above and to the right of the DD curve. For any level of output of educational services, the difference between these two

Figure 13.9   Equilibrium Price and Output with Externality Benefits

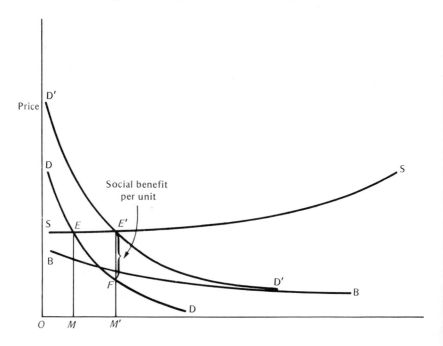

Quantity of Education Service

curves should depict the benefits to society at large per unit of services from having that volume of educational services provided to its subpopulation. Observe the change in the equilibrium position. When social benefits are not taken into account, the amount OM at a price EM should be provided. When social benefits are taken into account, the amount provided should increase to OM', at the slightly higher price of $E'M'$. But note that the subpopulation pays a price of only FM', society being responsible for the difference between FM' and $E'M'$, namely $E'F$. In effect, society pays a subsidy for the education of this subpopulation, which is just equal to the "externality benefits." In many other cases, we find similar justification for subsidization of subpopulations or other groups because of externality benefits. Many of the social welfare programs are justified in terms of the analysis just presented.

All this illustrates the need to develop thoroughly the analysis pertaining to externalities. One of the interesting and challenging things of life is that these externalities become increasingly important as population densities increase and as the social system becomes more and more urbanized (and less and less rural). A more urbanized system, as we are all aware, is a more impersonal system. In a more impersonal system, each individual is less concerned with every other individual. Thus we see more litter. We see more vandalism. We see less concern for public property, or with helping a stranger when he is in trouble. And so forth. Hence, externality analysis becomes increasingly important for those of us who study urban and regional problems.

Also, from another standpoint (which will become clearer in a later chapter), the increasing neglect or misuse of the environment beyond its capabilities by a population that is growing at a rapid pace and with many of its members having an insatiable demand for the goods of affluence generates negative externalities increasing almost exponentially in significance. The need for public sector intervention mounts likewise. So does the need for study by regional scientists, because environmental problems are by and large spatial and regional problems.

THE PUBLIC SECTOR AND SOCIAL JUSTICE

Major discrepancies in per capita income among people in different locations in the world, in a nation, in a region, or in other kinds of areas has always been a key issue for the regional scientist. Until the 1960s other social scientists had relatively little concern with this problem. However, with the developing political power of the poverty populations these other social scientists have found that they can no longer afford to neglect the study of the problem of sharp inequality in the distribution of income, wealth, and power. Also, to reiterate what we have said in Chapters 3 and 8, the problem has become intensified with time. Much of the world's population still lives at or below subsistence levels. Both in absolute and relative numbers such population is on the increase.

Further, while poor people continue to exist at subsistence level, the rich people have become even richer. This is so whether we think of the rich people in the United States, Sweden, Japan, Arabia, or India. And perhaps this fact has intensified the unrest of the poor, their insistence upon having greater involvement in political processes, and their demand that the public sector evolve and administer more and new kinds of welfare programs to eliminate deprivation.

In fact, if we think of development as leading to more orders of nodes with more nodes at each order, we can well see that with the key decisions still concentrated at the top of the hierarchy, the poor and deprived, all of whom are at the grass-roots level, have come to have less and less influence upon critical decisions because they are more and more removed from them. That is, because of the increasing height and size of the pyramid, they are at greater and greater distances from the points of key decision-making.

Social welfare is a very complex matter and no one has been able or will ever be able to define it adequately, let alone depict it by some mathematical formula. In the tradition of the grand political theorists of the nineteenth century and earlier, we might view social welfare as related to the trinity of values: *liberty, equality,* and *fraternity.* In the twentieth century, we might add *security* (political and social stability) as another sweeping variable. But clearly such a broad definition of social welfare is not very helpful when we focus on per capita income discrepancies, for we cannot directly relate these discrepancies to the presence or absence of any of these broad, vague values.

We might go to the other extreme and find a very precise magnitude, say gross national product (GNP), with which we might associate social welfare. But such an association leads to a very narrow view of social welfare, one which would be clearly unacceptable to most people except businessmen, economists, and those political leaders who are conscious of economic power. We then might broaden our definition to cover not only gross national product but also the distribution pattern of that GNP among a population. We might then add a third aspect, namely the division of that product among different kinds of goods (those that are necessities such as basic food, clothing, and shelter required for subsistence and/or for healthy living; and those that are non-necessities, such as mink coats). Further, we might wish to consider as relevant to social welfare the breakdown of the non-necessities into those for conspicuous consumption and those for the spiritual, cultural, and educational development of individuals and society.

Alternatively, we might consider social welfare to be measured by the productivity of the total labor force, or by such productivity and the allocation of that labor force to the production of essential goods and nonessential goods. Or social welfare might be measured in terms of literacy rates, crime rates, and family solidarity, as well as GNP and the distribution pattern of goods produced. And so forth.

It is evident that there is no single, clear defintion of social welfare. Everyone has a different notion of what variables are important, and the weights to assign to them. Despite the wide disagreement as to what social welfare is, we nonetheless can do some useful thinking and analysis. For example, when two people barter with each other and each finds the outcome a more desirable state than that previous to the barter, and when no other individual in society is affected by this barter, we can say that social welfare has increased; for the welfare of each of the two individuals has increased, while that of all others in society has remained the same. Or if we consider a cooperative that has worked out arrangements for production and the sharing of the environment which leaves each member of the cooperative better off, and if there are no externalities in the sense that the actions of this cooperative have no spillovers or other effects upon the welfare of all other cooperatives and behaving units in the society, then we can say that social welfare has increased.

We can go beyond general statements such as these to make other basic analytical points, which by and large are reasonable and generally accepted

despite our inability to define social welfare. To begin, take a very simple concept—as usual, an oversimplified and overexploited one. Suppose we consider the
classical utility function of the individual. This function indicates the different
amounts of satisfaction or utility that a typical or representative individual might
receive from wisely spending different amounts of money. We illustrate such a
utility function by the UU curve in Figure 13.10. If we could measure utility,

Figure 13.10   Possible Utility Functions for an Individual

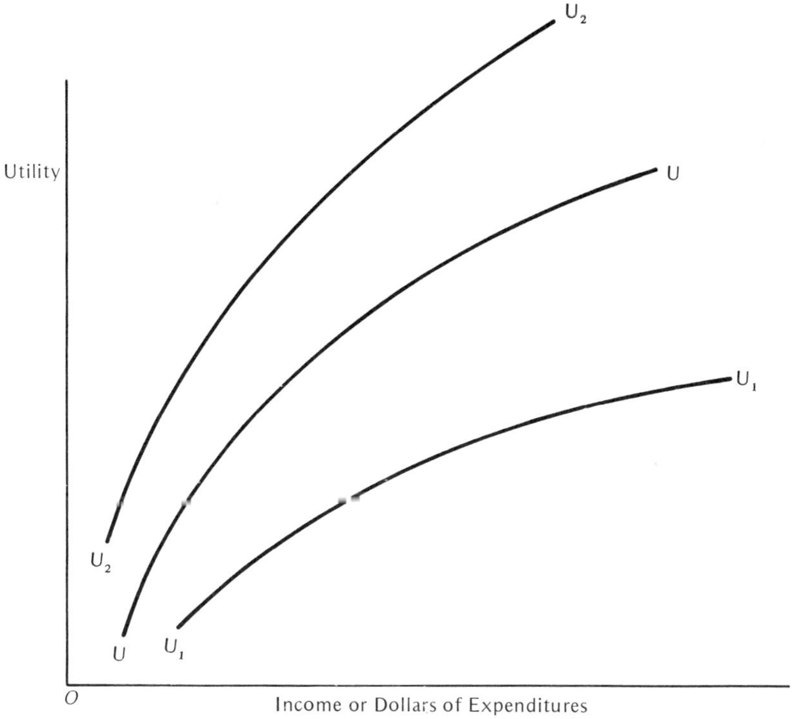

we would indicate quantity of utility along the vertical axis and amount of income
available for use, or dollars of expenditure, along the horizontal axis. As we have
discussed in Chapter 10, it is not possible to measure utility. Thus we could just
as well construct other curves, such as the $U_1 U_1$ and the $U_2 U_2$ curves, to suggest
the relevant utility function. One keen social welfare analyst might consider the
$U_1 U_1$ curve most representative, another the $U_2 U_2$ curve, and still another the
UU curve. However, if we tried to depict the utility function as a straight line
from the origin as in Figure 13.11, most scholars would seriously object. For it
is generally believed—and this belief may simply be an inherited notion with
little if any scientific basis—that as the typical individual has more and more
money to spend he derives less and less utility from each additional dollar. That
is, the margianl utility of income (money) decreases with increase in the size of
one's income; this is the principle of diminishing marginal utility of money. This
belief or hypothesis is inconsistent with the constant marginal utility implication
of a straight-line utility function such as the one on Figure 13.11. Likewise, most
social science analysts would object to a utility functions such as $U_3 U_3$ in Figure
13.11, which depicts increasing marginal utility with increase in income.

334

Now if we accept the notion of diminishing marginal utility of money, we are accepting some crude idea of how social welfare can be increased. This is evident when we consider one of the relevant utility functions, say UU, of Figure 13.10. Particularly in a society with an ethos that each person is born equal and has equal rights to life, liberty, and the pursuit of happiness, it is natural to suggest that the very wealthy individual having a low marginal utility of income, say the one with a $100,000 income, ought to transfer the last dollar of his income to the very poor person whose marginal utility is extremely high because he is at the starvation level. Such a suggestion becomes even more natural if we accept the hypothesis that starvation interferes with the realization of liberty and the pursuit of happiness. But why not suggest a transfer of $2 of income, of $3 of income, and so on? Assuming that individuals are not that much different in their makeup and their requirements for basic living, realization of liberty, and pursuit of happiness, the whole notion of a major redistribution of income makes sense to the social welfare analysts in most cultures, even in cultures as divergent as the USA and India.

Figure 13.11   Unlikely Types of Utility Functions

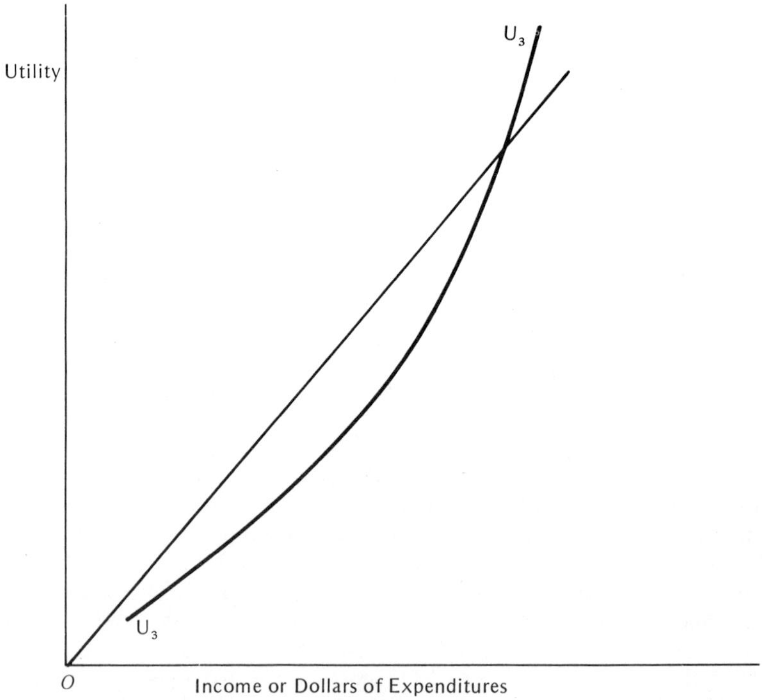

It is easy to go from the oversimplified diagram in Figure 13.10 to a principle for income redistribution. The principle might state that individuals ought to be allocated income in such a way that the marginal utility from the last dollar spent is the same for all. In this way, one might argue, we would be maximizing the total utility of society. Unfortunately, life and society are much too complex for such a simple principle to be put into effect. First, we know that the very pro- duction of income—that is, the production of goods and services generating income—is strongly motivated by the desire of individuals to accumulate wealth and goods and to amass the power that stems from income. If an individual knows beforehand that incomes will be so allocated that most of the surplus income or differential in income which he can earn by hard work will be channelled to others, this knowledge destroys his incentive to work hard or be imaginative and creative. In turn this means a much smaller GNP available for distribution. This suggests that the above principle for income redistribution must be qualified to preserve at least part of our incentive system so that we can reap most of this system's benefits.

In addition to the need to preserve incentives, there is the need to create pools of slack resources, surplus funds, or other stockpiles in society that can be drawn upon by creative entrepreneurs (economic and administrative) to try out new ideas, products, ways of production, and methods of organization. Thus, stocks of capital must be available at different points in the social system, easily tapped by appropriate individuals, to facilitate the achievement of greater productivity. These individuals must possess or have quick access to the wherewithal for investment in physical plant and equipment.

Beyond these, there is the need for capital for investment in the training of human beings as such. Again the process must be such that individuals who are born with different capabilities and talents can move in different directions, and that they are motivated to do so by an incentive system. Access to different amounts of resources is essential, as well as prospects for appropriately increased compensation for the greater amounts of effort, hard work, risk, and hardship necessitated by different careers.

It is possible to go on and on, listing the differentials in terms of opportunities, access to resources, income and possessions, etc. which are needed to achieve at least moderate rates of increase in productivity, and which to a large extent are justifiable in the sense that all individuals are better off as a result of them. So we conclude that the simple principle for income redistribution must be severely qualified in its applications. But we have no real scientific notion of what the qualifications should be. Over the centuries, these qualifications have been and still are great in the USA and other capitalist countries. In comparison, the much more even distribution of incomes in Mainland China suggests that the qualifications to the operation of such a principle are or would be much less there; likewise in the Soviet Union.

We can say that no large society has yet found the magic formula for defining and shaping a qualified principle for income redistribution. On the other hand, few of us would want to suggest that some qualified principle for income redistribution should not be in effect to a significant extent. We suggest that the public sector be involved in some program of pure direct income redistribution, or positive and negative income taxation, or something similar that effects income redistribution and fosters social justice.

EQUATION OF MARGINAL SOCIAL WELFARE AND MARGINAL SOCIAL COST: THE SIZE OF THE PUBLIC SECTOR

We have suggested that the public sector be involved in the production of certain kinds of goods, the regulation of exploitative organizations and behaving units, the provision of basic information, the management of activities generating both negative and positive externalities, and the alleviation of social injustice. But how *big* should the public sector be? Are there not diminishing returns in its operations, just as in agriculture, most businesses, and other activities?

Once again we are posing a complex question without a simple answer. Further, because we cannot measure many of the specific benefits of different public sector activities and government services, we can only attempt a very broad reply. We start with the use of Figure 13.12. In this figure we indicate along the vertical axis some nonquantifiable magnitude which we call social benefits (utility). As with the vertical axes in Figures 13.10 and 13.11 measuring utility, the vertical axis in this figure is used to *order* states of higher or lower social welfare without specifying magnitude. Along the horizontal axis we might measure some property of the public sector which suggests its size, such as dollar expenditures. Another could be the number of its employees.

Figure 13.12   Social Benefits from Government Expenditures

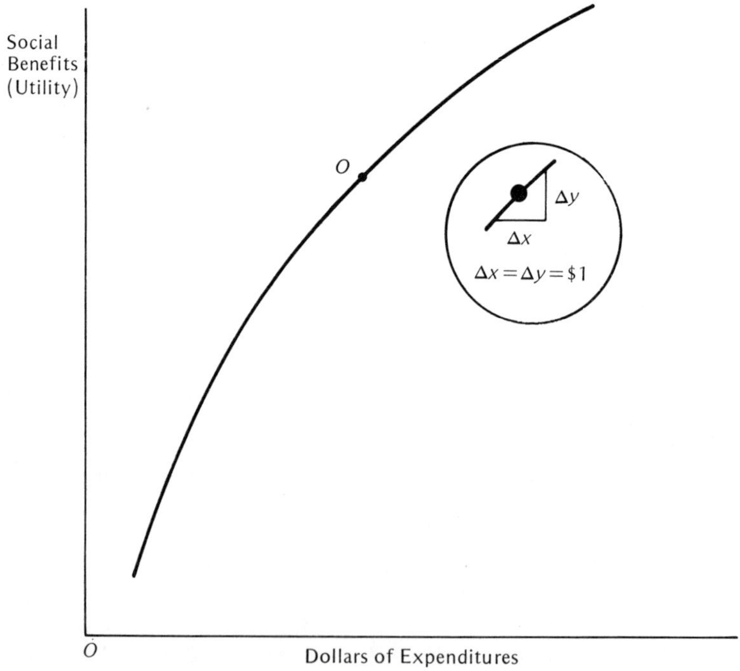

If we measure dollar expenditures, and if it were possible (which of course it is not) to assign dollar values to social benefits, then both axes could be measured in terms of dollar units. Now, if the curve of Figure 13.12 were viewed as relating amounts of social benefit (in dollar terms) produced by different levels of government expenditures, we should clearly increase government expenditures (the size of the public sector) as long as each additional dollar of expenditure (marginal social cost) yielded more than one dollar's worth of social benefit (marginal social benefit)—that is, up to the point where an additional dollar of expenditures just yields an additional dollar's worth of social benefit. That point, point O on Figure 13.12 which equates marginal social cost with marginal social benefit, determines the "optimum" size of the public sector. (Point O and its immediate surrounding area is enlarged in the inset of Figure 13.12.) Beyond that point, given our assumption of diminishing returns from public sector activity, each additional dollar of government expenditure yields less than a dollar's worth of social benefit.

There are serious and valid objections to any analysis that assigns a dollar value to social benefits. However, it should be realized that if social benefits were measurable, we would be able to employ the standard marginal cost-marginal revenue analysis to help determine an optimal size of the public sector. Moreover, there is some indirect value in this exercise, as can be seen when we proceed to attack the next question. This question arises when we examine a large public sector or government for internal balance. When we break that public sector down into its parts, are some parts too large and others too small? Is the justice (courts) sector too small? Is the treasury too big? Is HUD (Department of Housing and Urban Development) too small? Is DOD (Department of Defense) too large? Or if we disaggregate the public sector into programs and activities rather than administrative units, is the low-income housing program too small? Is the highway construction program too large? Is the foreign aid program too small?

Priorities among Public Sector Units and Individual Programs

Having been initiated into marginal thinking for the public sector, we see that such marginal thinking is applicable for analysis by administrative units or by programs. Clearly, the level of expenditure on each program of the public sector should be increased up to the point at which the last dollar spent on any administrative unit or program yields one dollar's worth of social benefit, however each one of us defines the latter. We can draw a graph just like Figure 13.12 for each administrative unit and each program. Along the vertical axis we measure the social benefits that results from that administrative unit's operation or program, and along the horizontal axis dollars of expenditure. As before, there will be much disagreement among different social scientists about the benefit function, some contending that it should be flat like the $U_1 U_1$ curve in Figure 13.10, others that it should rise sharply like curve $U_2 U_2$. Again, we have no objective way of really determining how much should be spent on each program.

However, we may be able to do some additional analysis. Suppose social scientists *disagree* on the social benefit function, some attributing much social benefit to government expenditures and others little. They may *agree*, however, that money should be allocated among the different programs in such a way that the last dollar spent on each program yields the same amount of social benefit. Further, they may agree on the relative importance of the several programs. They may agree that roughly one-tenth of the government's budget ought to be assigned to housing programs, one-twentieth to transportation, one-fifth to defense, and one-twenty-fifth to agriculture. That is, they may be able to agree on the division of the federal budget, although they sharply disagree on its size.

This point is illustrated in Figure 13.13. In this figure we measure dollars of expenditure on one program, say low-income housing, along the vertical axis, and

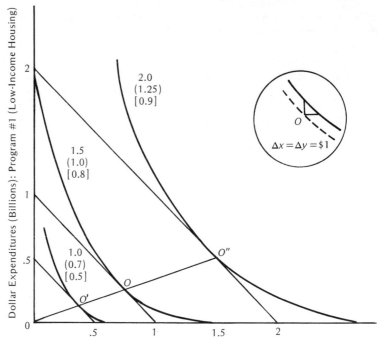

Figure 13.13   Indifference Curves for Two Social Welfare Programs and their Best Combinations

dollars of expenditure on a second program, say education, along the horizontal axis. We have also drawn three indifference curves. Each indifference curve represents the different combinations of expenditures on these two programs which an ordinary knowledgeable citizen might consider equally desirable. Observe that this set of indifference curves signifies that too much expenditure (in percentage terms) on one program and very little on the other is considered less desirable than a more balanced combination. This is reflected in the fact that the combination represented by point *O* (on the middle indifference curve), involving an expenditure of $.75 billion on education and $.25 billion on low-income housing, a total of $1 billion, is considered to be equally desirable from a welfare standpoint as the expenditure of $2 billion on low-income housing and $0 on education, or as the combination $0 on low-income housing and $1.5 billion on education. Or, if $2 billion is available for expenditure, the highest possible indifference curve is attained by spending approximately three-quarters of it on education and the rest on housing, and the lowest indifference curve by spending it all on housing.

We have not assigned a number to any of these indifference curves. Individual *i* might say that the social benefits corresponding to the three curves are $1, $1.5, and $2 billion, respectively. He would urge that the federal budget be $2 billion, spent as indicated by *O''*. Individual *j* might say that the social benefits corresponding to the three curves are those given by the numbers in the parentheses—namely $0.7, $1, and $1.25 billion, respectively. He would urge that the federal budget be $1 billion and spent as indicated by point O. Finally, individual k might say that the social benefits are those given by the numbers in the brackets—namely $0.5, $0.8, and $.9 billion, respectively, and urge a federal budget of $.5 be spent as indicated by point O'. Thus, although i, j, and k disagree greatly on the social benefits to be associated with the indifference curves, they all agree that approximately one-quarter of it should be spent on program 1 (low-income housing) and three-quarters on program 2 (education). If Congress were to legislate $1.5 billion to be spent on some combination of these two programs, the three individuals could pretty much agree on the combination that is best.

In the inset on Figure 13.13 we have blown up the area around the point O. Reduction of a dollar of expenditures for education shifts society from the higher solid indifference curve to point O on the lower dashed indifference curve. However, an increase of a dollar of expenditure for low-income housing corresponds to a shift from point O on the lower curve back to a point on the higher curve. That is, at an equilibrium point such as point O the last dollar spent on each program yields the same marginal utility.

In short then, although a constituency comprised of Republicans, Democrats, American Independents, and Peace and Freedomites may differ as to the benefits of public expenditures, they may differ much less, and even agree, on the percentage allocations of funds to be spent on the several programs.

CONCLUDING REMARKS

In bringing this chapter to a close, we may both briefly summarize and indicate areas in which additional analysis and deep thinking are required. We have already specified the rationale for public sector activities. There are the traditional needs (1) to produce goods that are in the general welfare—most often nonmarketable goods but sometimes, as in the case of post office services and railroads, goods that could be marketed but where the working of the market does not properly reflect social welfare needs; (2) to regulate organizations and other behaving units that are prone to exploit consumers, laborers, or other groups; (3) to provide basic information to agriculture, business, commerce, the family, and many other groups; (4) to manage production, consumption, and other activities in order to make them more sensitive and subject to social costs and benefits from diverse externalities; and (5) to alleviate social injustice by various tax schemes, programs, and the like.

We have also indicated that public sector activities are on the increase—mostly because the advances in technology, industrialization, and communication have greatly increased the number of interactions among individuals and their potentiality for having negative spillovers and impacts on third parties. We have also suggested that public sector activity reaches a peak level in the huge metropolitan regions and megalopolises currently emerging. When population is densely clustered, the potential of negative impacts of any individual's actions upon others is greatly increased. Therefore, in our urban metropolitan and regional planning we cannot ignore either the presence of or the potentiality for public sector activities.

Because this is not a book on the public sector, we have only touched lightly upon many important aspects of it in this chapter. We have crudely defined public goods, externalities, and social welfare. Closely associated with the concept of social welfare is that of public interest. What is the public interest? Is it the interest of the majority, or is it the interest of the majority somewhat qualified to take into account the interest of the minority? If so, how should we weight these two interests, should they both be well-articulated and well-defined? Further, what if there are subgroups within the majority that have different opinions and react to alternatives with different intensities? How should we weight these? Should the public interest entirely ignore the individual? If not, how should he be introduced into the weighting scheme? Should the public interest be estimated before or after income redistribution?

So we have all these problems of determining what the public interest is. And though we may view the political process as helping to identify the public interest, it is clear that the way the political process operates today, it only partially determines it.

It is desirable not only to identify public interest and social welfare, if we can, but also to identify a good structure of government—for by and large, public sector activities are government activities. Thus all our discussion relates to the questions of what the structure of the government should be: What is the proper set of checks and balances to be imposed? What is the proper areal division of power (among central, state, metropolitan, and local governments)? What is the proper degree of decentralization? These are issues which we have already touched upon in previous chapters. They of course relate to such questions as: What is the purpose of government? To what extent should or does government operate as a quasi-market?

Moreover, when we think of public sector activities, we must be aware of the many ways in which the government or the public sector can provide goods and services. It can produce them directly. It can encourage the formation of cooperatives and other voluntary groups to produce the right kinds of goods. It can offer subsidies, penalties, rewards, and bribes. It can regulate and even prohibit. All these matters should be taken up and discussed in great detail.

Finally, we have not gone into the subject of taxation itself. We are aware of the many different ways in which taxes can be levied to raise revenue to meet the cost of public sector activities. Each way has a different impact on social welfare of the various groups and individuals in a region, because each way takes money away from people in different patterns. Each way, in a sense, leads to a different pattern of income after taxes. Thus each way involves a different form of income redistribution. Again, taxation is a subject matter that is extremely important but is beyond the scope of this introductory text.

Thus, although we must leave open many critical questions of public sector involvement in urban and regional life, we do so with the thought of returning to their study at a more advanced level.

Economic-Ecologic Conflict and Environmental Quality

INTRODUCTION

On Armistice Day, 1919, a lad could join in the celebration by jumping off a Philadelphia pier and splashing around gleefully in the Delaware River. He could look forward to a world of eternal peace, so he was told, and partake in full of the blessings of the environment. Fifty years later, things had changed. He could only look forward to a world of continual strife and conflict, and an environment already heavily despoiled and possibly deteriorating to a point of no return. The drastic change from one of bright, rosy dimensions to one of gloom may perhaps be exaggerated. A very wise man would not have been swept away by the mass enthusiasm of Armistice Day, 1919. Nor would he be swept away today by the prophecies of doom. The world system as we know it is an exceedingly complex one and cannot be simplistically labeled as either brilliantly hued or sinfully degraded. Today, we perceive its vast intricacies and know that the economic system cannot possibly be separated from the ecologic system—as we sincerely thought it could be in 1919, whenever we did do some thinking about the ecologic system. We implicitly assumed that we could not do it harm or disturb it. We realize now that only painstaking study of the basic processes going on in the interconnected economic, ecologic, political, social, cultural, and other systems will allow us to cope with our mounting problems. We know that it is impossible to consider the growth of cities, development of regions, and improvement of social welfare without taking into full account the environmental impacts of different actions and decisions. In short, we must engage in much hard work in studying and designing effective social-environmental policy.

Of course, one may reflect upon the past and easily perceive how the slogan of World War I, "the war to end wars," could have swept people away and how the emotional release at the signing of the Armistice could have so exaggerated the rosiness of future prospects. Also, in 1919 one could hardly have foreseen the environmental problems with which we are cursed today. No one could have predicted the tremendous growth of the economic system which has taken place since 1919. No one could have foreseen the tremendous variety of material goods that has come to exist and the voraciousness of consumer appetites. Hardly anyone could and would have anticipated the increase in population numbers.

All this has led to increasing pressure upon the use of the limited resources and capabilities of the environment, to the point where environmental processes no longer remain negligibly undisturbed. In their normal operations, they can no longer overcome the destruction wreaked by man's activities.

Further, there is no indication that the world's population is by and large willing to alter its aspirations for large increases in the number and variety of consumption goods, such as air conditioners, more elaborate kitchen appliances, and automobiles. In addition, high rates of productivity, as they become the province of more billions of people, will intensify the problem. So we face the possibility of exponential increase in population—and of exponential increase in affluence, effective demand, and realized consumption of the average member of that population. This possibility is considered a certainty by the prophets of doom.

There are those of us who may be numbered among these prophets of doom. Then again, there are many who are more optimistic and judge that we can successfully attack our problems. In either case, certain steps based on sound analysis can be taken. We can at least soften or delay that doom predicted by the pessimist, or realize in part the effective attack which the optimist hopes is possible. Hence we must conduct such analysis, whatever our outlook.

AN INPUT-OUTPUT DESCRIPTION OF THE COMBINED ECONOMIC-ECOLOGIC SYSTEM

One promising approach to analysis stems from the descriptive framework of an input-output format. As pointed out in Chapter 2, an input-output table of an economy at any point in time is an exceedingly useful description of what is. We are given numbers on the jobs in each industry. We are given numbers on the sales of each industry to households and every other industry. We are given numbers on the purchases of industries and households. It would seem that this extremely useful descriptive function might also be performed by an input-output framework for the ecologic system. If so, we would have another very valuable set of consistent data for our studies.

Consider the data on the economic system. Advanced industrial societies, like that of the United States, have been collecting large amounts of such data over time. Censuses of human population have been taken for centuries. Official censuses of manufactures have been taken in Great Britain since 1907, and in the United States since 1905. And every time a census is taken, we learn about our mistakes and how to make the next census better or what additional processing of data to undertake.

All these censuses were considered necessary—for establishing numbers of representatives in Congress, estimating tax revenues that could be collected, estimating markets, promoting economic development and regulating industries, planning for schools and transportation, and so forth. So today we have a rather extensive set of data pertaining to population, the economic system, and the economic behavior of businesses, consumers, and other units in the system.

Unfortunately, as pointed out in Chapter 2, there has not been much pressure or felt need for collecting similar data on the ecologic system. It has never been considered necessary to count the gallons of water flowing through the mouth of a river system as we have counted the number of automobiles coming off the production line. Gallons of water flow is not an item which enters into an estimate of gross national product; numbers of automobiles appropriately valued are. It has never been necessary for us to estimate the value of a mountain lake or other environmental features, as we must with regard to buildings and other structures designed for economic production in order to estimate economic wealth which can be taxed. Consequently, though there have been innumerable studies by natural scientists, engineers, and others related to different processes going on in the environment and its different populations (species, fauna, etc.), it has not been considered necessary for such data to be collected in a systematic and comprehensive fashion. Hence, the set of data pertaining to the environmental system which we inherit today is tremendous in variety and amount, but almost completely unorganized for social welfare planning. We therefore confront difficulty in trying to develop a systematic input-output description of the ecologic system. The data of a marine biologist are not comparable to those of an agricultural soil scientist—nor are the data collected by one marine biologist on one species of fish even likely to be comparable to those collected by another marine biologist on a second species.

Notwithstanding the fact that it may take decades before systematic collection and processing of ecologic data can be achieved, it is useful to try to visualize or depict now what such a systematic organization of data might look like. With this in mind, we see that the input-output framework can be very useful. Further, the attempt to impose an input-output framework on the ecologic system can be a valuable first step in encouraging natural scientists to employ comparable units in their work and, where desirable, to follow fairly standard procedures in collecting and processing data so they can be integrated for systematic analysis. It should be recalled, though, that when one states the input-output system in the form of coefficients, one is making the very unrealistic assumption that the relationship among the basic variables is linear.

Let us begin by concentrating on a particularly heavy polluter, say the oil-refining industry. As indicated in previous chapters, we wish to make explicit *all* its inputs and outputs—the inputs of water and air taken from the environment as well as the inputs of economic commodities, and the outputs of pollutants dumped on the environment as well as the outputs of economic commodities. To do this, we must specify in well-defined units the set of inputs and outputs of *ecologic commodities* from and to the environment. We define an "ecologic commodity" very loosely. We exclude those commodities which can be priced at the market. We exclude a live chicken, fish, or cow ready for purchase at the market, though each of these animals can be viewed as a product solely of natural

Table 14.1   Water Pollution Commodity (WPC) Code

WPC Code	Water-Related Item	Units
1000	Water Intake, Total*	1,000 gals
1001	Sanitary Use	"
1002	Production Use	"
1003	Cooling	"
1004	Boiler Feed	"
1008	Irrigation	"
1009	Other, n.e.c.	"
1010	Water Discharge, Total	"
1011	Sanitary Use	"
1012	Production	"
1013	Cooling	"
1019	Other, n.e.c.	"
1020	Water Consumed	"
1031	Biochemical Oxygen Demand, BOD 5-Day	1,000 lbs
1032	Ultimate Oxygen Demand, UOD	"
1033	Chemical Oxygen Demand, COD	"
1040	Solids, Total$^+$	"
1041	Suspended Solids	"
1042	Settleable Solids	"
1047	Turbidity	"
1048	Color	"+
		+
1051	Alkalinity	"
1052	Acidity	"
1061	Oils and Greases	"
1062	Surfactants	"
1070	Pathogenic (Disease-Causing) Organisms	—§
1080	Temperature	—§
1090	Other Pollutants	"
1095	Toxic Material#	"
1096	Radioactive Waste	—§
1099	Not Classified	"

* *Cost of water intake is given by SIC code 4941—water supply.*

\+ *1040 = 1041 + 1042.*

‡ *In addition, color should be specified by kind by its wavelength.*

§ *No one satisfactory measure was decided upon at this time, although thermal pollution may be specified most satisfactorily in terms of millions of BTU.*

\# *Phenols, which fall in this category, may be identified by a five-digit code such as WPC 10951.*

Source: Walter Isard, "Some Notes on the Linkage of the Ecologic and Economic Systems," Regional Science Association: Papers, XXII, European Congress (1968), p 89.

production processes. We *include* all those commodities, such as air, water, algae, marsh grass, nitrogen, phosphorus, and birds, which are not priced properly at the market. Yet all these commodities are almost infinite in number; we must restrict our set of ecologic commodities to those that are important from the standpoint of environmental management, judging importance on the basis of our limited knowledge of environmental processes. We might exclude such commodities as orchids, spruce trees, ants, skunks, and helium. Even so, we are likely to find that we still have more commodities than we can possibly handle in any environmental study. Hence, for study purposes we must specify the number of ecologic commodities which we can possibly consider, say fifty, and then select the fifty most important ones for inclusion in the study, taking into account the linkages among these commodities.

For studies dealing with water pollution, we list in Table 14-1 some of the critical commodities, such as water itself, BOD, solids, and radioactive wastes. This table also records a proposed water pollution commodity (WPC) code. For studies

Table 14.2   Air Pollution Commodity (APC) Code

Units: Tons (or lbs)

APC Code	Commodity	APC Code	Commodity
1000	Gases	1500	Acids
1100	Sulfur compounds	1510	Hydrochloric acid
1110	Hydrogen sulfide	1520	Sulfuric acid
1120	Sulfur oxides	1530	Phosphoric acid
1121	Sulfur dioxide	.	.
1122	Sulfur trioxide	.	.
1130	Methyl mercaptan	.	.
1140	Dimethyl sulfide	1700	Inorganics
1200	Carbon compounds	1710	Metals
1210	Carbon monoxide	1711	Mercury
1211	Carbon dioxide	1800	Other (Specified)
1220	Aromatics		
1230	Hydrocarbons	2000	Liquids, entrained droplets
1231	Methane		and saturated vapors
1232	Acetylene	2100	Acid mists
.	.	2120	Sulfuric acid mist
.	.	.	.
.	.	.	.
1300	Nitrogen compounds	2200	Water vapor
1310	Nitrogen oxides	2300	Smoke and oil vapors
1320	Ammonia	2400	Aerosols
.	.		
1400	Halogens	2500	Oil mists
1410	Chlorine		
1411	Chlorides	3000	Particulates, conglomerate
1420	Fluorine		
1421	Fluorides	4000	Particles, larger than 1
1430	Iodine		micron
		.	.
		.	.
		.	.
		5000	Particles, smaller than 1
			micron

346

dealing with air pollution, we list in Table 14-2 some of the critical commodities, such as hydrogen sulfide, sulfur dioxide, carbon monoxide, and hydrocarbons.

After the full range of ecologic commodities is examined and a relevant set of ecologic commodities defined, we must make explicit their involvement (as inputs or outputs) in every economic activity upon which we focus. For instance, when we consider the petroleum-refining activity, whose code in the Philadelphia input-output study is RIS 2911, we set down our relevant ecologic commodities together with economic commodities. For a narrow water-pollution study, we might list the set of coefficients indicated in Table 14.3. The lower part of this table refers to relevant ecologic commodities.

With such coefficients for each economic sector of a region, we could then construct an input-output table of the form of Table 14.4. At the head of the columns would be listed the various sectors of a region (for example, the 496 endogenous and the 86 final demand sectors for the Philadelphia region). In the upper section of rows would be listed coefficients pertaining to inputs and outputs of economic commodities. In the lower section would be listed coefficients pertaining to inputs and outputs of ecologic commodities.

However, a narrow study that is just concerned with how much water pollutants of various kinds are dumped on the ecologic system is not very satisfactory from the standpoint of wise environmental policy covering both short-run and long-run impacts on health and other issues. We need to consider the air, solid wastes, and other pollutants of the oil refinery and every other industrial operation as well. So we would like to extend the set of rows, corresponding to ecologic commodities, to cover these pollutants. This we do in Table 14.4, where we specify several air pollutants and solid wastes.

Bear in mind that when we extend a table we must revise our notation suitably. Recall that in Chapter 7, we considered 100 different economic activities for a town and we used the symbol j ($j = 1,..., 100$) to represent any of these activities. However, for many urban studies, 100 sectors may be inappropriate. For regions like Philadelphia, 496 sectors may be appropriate. Hence we find it convenient to avoid specifying the number of sectors. Instead, we list the sectors in order as 1, 2, 3,..., $n - 1$, n. The number n is to be determined in terms of the specific needs of a particular study. Accordingly, we let $j = 1,..., n$.

Also recall that in our discussion of new town planning, we spoke about 100 different commodities, one and only one being produced by each economic activity. We used the symbol i ($i = 1,..., 100$) to represent any one of these commodities. We were then able to speak of the coefficient a_{ij} as representing the dollar's worth of input of commodity i used to produce a dollar of output of sector j. We now state our set of economic commodities in more general form as 1, 2,..., $n - 1$, n. If we add to them 50 pollutants as ecologic commodities, we may number the latter as $n + 1$, $n + 2$,..., $n + 49$, $n + 50$. Further, if we designate such commodities by the letter e ($e = n + 1, n + 2,..., n + 49, n + 50$), then we can use the notation a_{ej} to indicate the output of pollutant e per dollar output of sector j. If so, we can represent the lower part of Table 14.4 by the matrix

Sector		Coefficient
RIS 1311	Crude Petroleum and Natural Gas	−.612006
1509	Construction, Maintenance, and Repair	−.001410
2652	Set-Up Paperboard Boxes	−.008054
2655	Fiber Cans, Tubes, Drums, and Similar Products	−.001557
2812	Alkalies and Chlorine	−.000935
2818	Industrial Organic Chemicals, n.e.c.	−.027180
2819	Industrial Inorganic Chemicals, n.e.c.	−.009190
2911	Petroleum Refining	+.954950
2992	Lubricating Oils and Greases	−.014954
3411	Metal Cans	−.005294
4811	Telephone Communications	−.001210
4890	Telegraph and Other Communications	−.000100
4911	Electric Utilities	−.007629
4920	Gas Companies and Systems	−.012336
4941	Water Supply	−.001082
4990	Sanitary and Other Systems	−.000142
6020	Interest	−.005088
6301	Insurance, Nonlife	−.001242
6510	Real Estate Services	−.007680
7301	Business Services excluding Advertising	−.017228
7310	Advertising	−.002312
7400	Research and Development	−.000390
7500	Automotive Repair	−.001040
9000	Local and State Taxes	−.008049
9100	Federal Income Tax	−.014755
9826	Office Supplies	− .000280
9842	Transportation Costs	−.040831
9888	Wages and Salaries	−.089378
9899	Residual	−.063589
WPC1001	Water Intake, Sanitary Use, 1,000 Gal./$ Output	−.000455
1002	" Production "	−.022827
1003	" Cooling "	−.114861
1011	Water Discharged, Sanitary Use "	+.000323
1012	" Production "	+.070219
1013	" Cooling "	+.050100
1031	Biochemical Oxygen 1,000 Lb./$ Output Demand BOD, 5-Day, "	+.000065
1032	Ultimate Oxygen Demand, UOD "	+.000076
1033	Chemical Oxygen Demand, COD "	+.000169
1041	Suspended Solids "	+.000084
1042	Settleable Solids "	+.000124
1047	Turbidity "	+.000365
1051	Alkalinity "	+.000051*
1052	Acidity "	+ n.a.
1061	Oils and Greases "	+.000012
10951	Phenols "	+.000003

*The pH factor for this industry is in the range of 4.5–10.7, with 7.0–8.0 most likely.
Source: Walter Isard, "Some Notes on the Linkage of the Ecologic and Economic Systems,"
Regional Science Association: Papers, XXII, European Congress (1968), p 88.

Table 14.4 An Input-Output Coefficients Table Extended to Cover Selected Ecologic Commodities

CODE	COMMODITY	UNIT	2033 (Canned fruits & vegetables)	2071 (Candy & other confectionary products)	3111 (Leather tanning & finishing)
0122	Fruit & nut tree farms	Dollars	–.090423	–.025180	
0123	Vegetable farms	"	–.035098		
2011	Meat-packing plants	"			
2021	Creamery, butter	"		–.000512	
2026	Fluid, milk	"		–.017067	–.135061
2033	Canned fruits & vegetables	"	+1.000000		
2037	Frozen fruits & vegetables	"	–.032090		
2046	Wet corn milling	"		–.033293	
2062	Cane sugar refining	"		–.123477	
2071	Candy & other confectionary products	"		–1.000000	
2072	Chocolate & cocoa products	"		–.076803	
2087	Flavoring extracts & sugars	"		–.068082	
2641	Paper coating & glazing	"		–.005689	
2651	Folding paperboard boxes	"	–.058751	–.039886	
2654	Sanitary food containers	"	–.000364		
2751	Commercial printing (except lithography)	"		–.034197	
2812	Alkalies & chlorine	"			–.000275
2815	Dyes & organic pigments	"			–.001946
2816	Inorganic pigments	"	–.000241		–.001946
2818	Industrial organic chemistry	"			–.012588
2819	Industrial inorganic chemistry	"			–.000722
2842	Specialty cleaning preparations	"			–.005189
2843	Surface active agents	"			–.042151
2861	Gum & wood chemistry	"	–.003584		–.105116
2899	Chemicals & chemical preparations	"	–.007256	–.009120	–.013460
2911-0	Petroleum refining	"			
2911-1	Petroleum refining (fuel)	Gallons			

Code	Item	Units	Col 1	Col 2	Col 3
3111	Leather tanning & finishing	Dollars	+.877532		-.051705
3221	Glass containers	"			-.026872
3411	Metal cans	"			-.000728
39999	Unallocated produced inputs	"	-.002595	-.016646	-.006168
4911	Electricity	"	-.014698	-.010582	
4920	Gas	"	-.000155	-.004449	
9888	Wages & Salaries	"	-.326719	-.285878	-.026972
WPC 1000	Water intake—total	1000 Gallons	-.019965	-.003180	-.019277
WPC 1010	Water discharge—total	"	+.017816	+.002542	+.003279
WPC 1011	Sanitary use	"	+.000376	+.001268	+.000446
WPC 1012	Production	"		+.000566	
WPC 1013	Cooling	"		+.000708	
WPC 1019	Other	"	+.017440		
WPC 1031	BOD, 5 day	1000 Pounds	+.000094		+.002833
WPC 10311	Settleable 5-day BOD	"	+.000038		+.000118
WPC 1033	COD	"	+.000228		+.000206
WPC 1040	Solids, total	"	+.000361		+.000172
WPC 1041	Solids, suspended	"	+.000107		+.000017
WPC 1042	Solids, settleable	"	+.000254		+.000155
WPC 1051	Alkalinity	"	+.000046		+.000025
WPC 1052	Acidity	"	+.000009		
WPC 1091	Chromium	"	+.000004		
WPC 1092	Chloride	"	+.000112		
APC 1121	SO₂	Pounds	+.071271		+.000154
APC 1663	Methyl ethyl ketone	"			
APC 1699	Misc. halogenated hydrocarbons	"	+.000384		+.000154
APC 1712	Toluene	"		+1.155897	
APC 1919	Misc. inorganic gases	"			
APC 3000	Particulates	1000 Pounds	+.099185	+.012159	+.000768
SWC 1000	Food	1000 Pounds	+.101938	+.017108	+.119670
SWC 2000	Paper	"	+.048698	+.114622	+.171944
SWC 3000	Wood	"		+.009806	
SWC 4000	Glass	"			+.051200
SWC 5000	Ferrous metals	"	+.005384	+.010408	+.054384
SWC 6000	Plastic	"		+.003446	
SWC 8000	Soil/sand/ash	"	+.073048		
SWC 9000	Other	"	+.092246		

$$\begin{bmatrix} a_{n+1,1} & \cdots & a_{n+1,2} & \cdots & a_{n+1,n} \\ a_{n+2,1} & \cdots & a_{n+2,2} & \cdots & a_{n+2,n} \\ \cdot & & \cdot & & \cdot \\ \cdot & & \cdot & & \cdot \\ \cdot & & \cdot & & \cdot \\ a_{n+50,1} & \cdots & a_{n+50,2} & \cdots & a_{n+50,n} \end{bmatrix}$$

or simply by

$$\begin{bmatrix} a_{ej} \end{bmatrix} \qquad j = 1,...,n$$
$$(50 x n) \qquad e = n + 1,..., n + 50$$

But we want to study still more. We know that the BOD and thermal units dumped in the water system disturb the natural production processes which produce fish. We want to know to what extent. We know that the increased turbidity of the water caused by economic activity and the dumping of pollutants affects the photosynthesis process which produces phytoplankton, the ultimate food of fish and many other species. We also know that some of the air pollutants emitted, such as sulfur dioxide, are subject to chemical transformation under certain conditions. Some of the products of this transformation, for example sulphuric acid, have important implications for health beyond the immediate pollutants. We therefore want to have information about such chemical transformations.

In short, we are stating that we want to study not only what is emitted but also the diverse ecologic production processes that, together with the economic processes, generate the set of economic and ecologic commodities (including "goods" as well as "bads") which we can consume and to which we are exposed. Accordingly, it is insufficient just to list economic processes as we have done in Table 14.4. We must add a set of relevant ecologic processes. We define an "ecologic process" as one involving inputs and outputs of economic and ecologic commodities, but one in which a payoff-maximizing behaving unit (such as a human being, group of human beings, or public body) is not involved.

As with ecologic commodities, the number of ecologic processes is almost infinite. So we must constrain ourselves, limiting ourselves to a manageable number of ecologic processes. We must set priorities and determine for our environmental study the 20 to 50 or 100 ecologic processes of most relevance. again taking into account their linkages.

Let us be specific. Suppose we are concerned with a problem of water pollution and its effects upon those who use a river system for recreational purposes (fishing, swimming, and the like). Here we would need to treat explicitly the set of ecologic processes embodying the food chain in fish life. For a situation in which winter flounder is the key sport fish, we would need to have information on the specific production processes in the food chain which yield winter flounder as an ultimate output. Such information is incorporated in Table 14.5. There, we note in the last column that to produce one pound of winter flounder, we require as inputs .71 pounds of crustacea, 2.30 pounds of mollusca, 3.36 pounds of annelida, 2.73 pounds of algae, and approximately .04 acres of water area. To produce one pound of crustacea, we need 10 pounds of detritus (dead plant matter); so 7.1 pounds of detritus is required to produce the crustacea needed to

Table 14.5   Inputs and Outputs in the Winter Flounder Food Chain

CODE	COMMODITY	UNITS	Ecologic Production Processes						
			PMX 60 Marine Plants (including Algae)	PMX 611 Algae	PMX 6001 Detritus	PMX 712 Annelida	PMX 713 Mollusca	PMX 717 Crustacea	PMX 723 Winter Flounder
MX 31	Bay or estuary water area	acres							− .04
MX 32	Intertidal & subtidal shoal water area	acres		−8 $\times 10^{-6}$					
MX 51	Muddy & sandy bottom area	acres	−8 $\times 10^{-6}$			−7550 $\times 10^{-6}$	−2265 $\times 10^{-6}$	−7550 $\times 10^{-6}$	
MX 60	Marine plants (including algae)	lb	+1		−1				
MX 612	Algae	lb		−1				−10	−2.73
MX 6001	Detritus	lb			+1	−10	−10		
MX 712	Annelida	lb				+1			−3.36
MX 713	Mollusca	lb					+1		−2.30
MX 717	Crustacea	lb						+1	− .71
MX 723	Winter Flounder	lb							+1

352

produce one pound of winter flounder. Similarly, we need detritus to produce the mollusca and annelida. To produce one pound of detritus, we require one pound of live marine plants, including algae. In turn, the marine plants and algae are related to plankton and other production activities which we do not include in the table. They have been detailed elsewhere.[1] Accordingly, our water-pollution study requires that a full input-output table incorporate the activities described in the columns of Table 14.5.

For other fishing areas, we would want to look at other ecologic processes involved in other food chains. For example, if we are concerned with commercial cod fishing, we find that the production of one pound of cod requires on average 8.333 pounds of carnivorous invertebrates, 1.667 pounds of small fish, and 1.167 pounds of herring. In turn, one pound of herring requires 10 pounds of plankton. And so forth.

In still other environmental studies, we might be concerned with such processes as the nitrogen cycle, shellfish production, and phytoplankton production from photosynthesis. One study shows, for example, the amount of solar radiation, in terms of gram calories per square centimeter per minute, that is required to produce a gram of phytoplankton under different conditions relating to water transparency and the presence of phosphorus as phosphate in ocean water. Other studies consider the phosphorus flow through a mussel population, in which the output of one activity might be phosphorus ingested by mussel populations and inputs might be particulate matter, dissolved phosphate, and detritus.

In this introductory chapter, we cannot spell out in full what any particular environmental study might involve. However, we can suggest the dimensions of a complete input-output table for a given region. This we do with Table 14.6.

Here, we use bold lines to identify four major sectors. In the first set of columns, we list those activities which are economic activities. The set summarily depicts what we have outlined in Table 14.4, which in turn is a condensation of the corresponding part of a full input-output table for a regional economy. For illustrative purposes, we note, by plus and minus signs, selected inputs for only one economic activity, namely *leather tanning and finishing*. Listed along the upper set of rows of the table are relevant economic commodities. Thus, when we go down the column for the leather industry we meet the usual inputs of skins from meat-packing plants, alkalies and chlorine, and dyes and organic pigments that we recorded in Table 14.4.

Continuing down the first set of columns, we list ecologic commodities in the lower set of rows. We list these in greater detail than previously, but not in as great detail as we would like. One useful classification of commodities is the following, comparable to agricultural, manufacturing, and service activities in the economic system:

1. Abiotic
   a) meteorologic (climatic)
   b) geologic
   c) physiographic
   d) hydrologic
   e) soils

[1] See W. Isard et al., *Ecologic-Economic Analysis for Regional Development* (New York: Free Press, 1972).

Table 14.6 An Input-Output Coefficients Table for a Combined Economic-Ecologic System.

ECONOMIC

ECOLOGIC

ABIOTIC — BIOTIC

CLIMATIC / GEOLOGIC / PHYSIOGRAPHIC / HYDROLOGIC / SOILS / PLANTS / ANIMALS / HOUSEHOLDS (POP.)

LEATHER: TANNING . . . . COMMERICAL FISH / SULFURIC ACID

STRAWBERRIES / CRUSTACEA / WINTER FLOUNDER

ECONOMIC	FISH		+			+		−
	MEAT PACK.	−	**ECONOMIC SYSTEM:**			**ECOLOGIC PROCESSES:**		−
	:							
	ALKALIES . . .	−	Intersector			Input and Output Coefficients		−
	DYES	−	Coefficients			Re: Economic Commodities		−
	LEATHER	+						−
	:							
ABIOTIC	CLIMATIC							
	:							
	SO₂	+			−			±
	H₂SO₄				+			
	Particulates	+						±
	:		**ECONOMIC SECTORS:**			**ECOLOGIC SYSTEM:**		
	GEOLOGIC							
	:		Input and Output Coefficients Re: Ecologic Commodities			Interprocess Coefficients		
	PHYSIOGRAPHIC							
	:							
	LAND AREA	−						−
	WATER AREA	−						−
	:							
	HYDROLOGIC							
	:							
	WATER INTAKE	−						
	:							
	B.O.D.	+						±
	C.O.D.	+						±
	:							
ECOLOGIC	SOILS							
	:							
	PLANTS							
	:							
BIOTIC	DETRITUS							−
	:							
	ANIMALS							
	:							
	CRUSTACEA						+	−
	WINTER FLOUNDER			−				+

353

2. Biotic
   a) plant life
   b) animal life

We have tried to follow this classification in listing ecologic commodities in Table 14.6. As commodities oriented to hydrologic processes, we list water (as intake) and diverse water pollutants. As commodities oriented to meteorologic (climatic) processes, we list the air pollutants. And so on. Last, as commodities oriented to animal life, we list the fish which we have already encountered in Table 14.5, in particular winter flounder and crustacea. Thus we are able to visualize with the help of Table 14.6 a complete listing of all the inputs and outputs of economic and ecologic commodities for a given industry.

It is desirable to classify ecologic processes in the same manner as ecologic commodities. Accordingly, we have a set of ecologic processes in the second set of columns (after the column listing of economic sectors). Under the biotic processes are those production processes whose outputs are winter flounder and crustacea; we have also noted some of their inputs in the lower right-hand part of the table.

To understand the table better, we have designated in bold type the different types of entries that are involved. In the upper left-hand block, referring to the economic sectors, the set of coefficients indicated is designated *economic system: intersector coefficients*. The meaning of these coefficients has been fully discussed in Chapter 7.

In the major block at the lower left, the set of coefficients indicated is designated *economic sectors: input and output coefficients re: ecologic commodities*. We now understand the meaning of these coefficients. We include the various pollutants which are produced by economic activities and which are exported to or forced upon the ecologic system. Specifically noted by plus signs are some pollutants of the leather industry, which are simultaneously exports from the economic system to the ecologic system and imports of the ecologic system from the economic system.

In the lower right-hand block of the table, the set of coefficients indicated is designated *ecologic system: interprocess coefficients*. They simply cover the various inputs and outputs of ecologic commodities involved in ecologic processes. Using minus signs we note in the next-to-the-last column, which refers to winter flounder production, the inputs of crustacea and other items required per pound of winter flounder, discussed in connection with Table 14.5.

Finally, in the upper right-hand block of the table, the set of coefficients indicated is designated *ecologic processes: input and output coefficients re: economic commodities*. These coefficients pertain to the production and use of economic commodities by the ecologic processes themselves. It should be noted that not many economic commodities flow directly from the ecologic system as *final* goods for consumption by the households (or governments and other non-producing units) of the economic system. For example, the fish that the ecologic system produces are inputs for the commercial fishing sector, because they are raw materials in a production activity which processes the fish and delivers them to the market site at the right time. Therefore, under the commercial fishing column in the economic set of economic sectors, we list at the bottom of the column a minus sign to indicate the inputs of winter flounder into commercial fishing. These inputs come from the output of winter flounder which is indicated by a plus sign at the bottom of the winter flounder column, the next-to-last in the table. Similarly, fruit that is produced in orchards must be picked, put into containers, and delivered to the market before they become final goods for consumption. The same is true for corn and most other ecologic outputs. These outputs are indicated by plus signs in the lower left-hand block of the table and not in the upper right-hand block. Therefore, there are relatively few entries in the upper right-hand block.

But there are some ecologic outputs that may be viewed as final products for household consumption. Wild strawberries picked by a family on a picnic are final products which require no further processing, unless one wishes to consider the labor spent by a person at picking as an input. Fruits picked off trees in one's backyard, nuts gathered, or fish caught while camping can be similarly considered final goods. These are not, however, major items for the environmental studies we have in mind.

The presentation of a table of the form of Table 14.6 is very important in making explicit the total set of inputs and outputs of all commodities in the functioning of an economic system in a region. We of course need to have a similar table for each region of our nation, world region, or even world. Such a table is also extremely important in making explicit the complex transformations that take place in the environment, such as the set of processes involved in the phosphorus cycle or a food chain. If we consider constructing a landfill causeway over a marsh that is a particularly rich producer of plant-type nutrients, we are able to trace out, at least qualitatively, the indirect effects upon winter flounder and other fish populations supported by that marsh. In devising air-pollution policy, we are at least qualitatively able, with the aid of pluses and minuses, to trace out transformation of the SO_2 emitted by automobiles into sulfuric acid, a dangerous pollutant.

Note that at the extreme right of the table we list the households (human population) column, frequently designated a final demand column. The entries here have important implications for human welfare. We list all the goods that enter here as inputs (final deliveries for consumption purposes), and all the pollutants (ecologic commodities) to which the population of a region is exposed (which is, in one sense, forced consumption). For example, the sulfur dioxide that is breathed in represents an input just as bread does, and thus is indicated with a minus sign. But a large part of the sulfur dioxide that is breathed in is also breathed out. So we must indicate that amount with a plus sign, the difference between the minus and plus being the sulfur dioxide absorbed in the systems of the human population.

We must also list in the households column the various outputs of pollutants that the households generate in their consumption and other activities—including the air pollutants from house heating and the solid wastes from eating (garbage). In doing this we have a complete accounting for all commodities, economic and ecologic.

It is not the purpose of this textbook to discuss or analyze the physiological processes within the human body and the conditions which lead to different levels of physical health and welfare. However, the data that enter into the households column are clearly of direct relevance for those medical researchers expert in this area.

The data in a table like Table 14.6 are organized to depict *what is*. We might similarly organize our data to help project *what could be* or *what will be*. This point is particularly relevant for those activities in the table, mainly economic activities, which are subject to our control. For each economic sector, we are

Table 14.7   Air Control Systems Code: A Selected List

No.	Control
E0000	No control
0100	Closed system
E1000	Mechanical separation
1100	Cyclone
1110	High-efficiency cyclone
1120	Low-efficiency cyclone
.	.
.	
1200	Floating roof tank
1210	Fixed roof tank
1300	Vapor manifold
1310	Vapor recovery system
.	.
.	.
1700	Stack baffles
1710	Steam injected stack baffles
.	.
E2000	Electrostatic precipitation
2100	Electrostatic precipitator
2110	Cottrell electrostatic precipitator
2200	Irrigated electrostatic precipitator
E3000	Filters
3100	Fabric filter, baghouse
3110	Glass bag filter
.	.
.	.
E4000	Wet scrubbers
4001	Wet cap
4010	High-efficiency scrubber
4020	High-energy scrubber (60" water)
4100	Venturi scrubber
4110	Water scrubber
.	.
.	.
4700	Centrifugal gas scrubber
4710	Multiple centrifugal scrubber
4720	Dynamic centrifugal scrubber
4800	Orifice-type scrubber
E5000	Incineration
5100	After burner
5200	Flare
5210	Steam injected flares
.	.
.	
5500	Fume burner

able to obtain the data indicating not only what its current inputs and outputs are but also what its inputs and outputs would be if it used different kinds of equipment for pollution control. If industries were required to use specific kinds of control equipment, we could project the decrease in the amount of pollutants dumped on the environment. We would then be in a better position to judge whether the benefits from decreased pollution justify the increased costs of production from investment in and operation of control equipment. Some of the specific kinds of control systems relevant for reducing air pollution are recorded in Table 14.7

Finally, we should indicate that the format of Table 14.6 may not be the most appropriate one now, and in all probability will not be the most appropriate one for future analysis. As in any social science study, the classification that is best for analysis changes as the problems change. In the past, it was very useful to class populations by religion, but this is no longer as important. Today in the United States, we make distinctions by color of skin. However, in most other cultures color of skin is not a meaningful item for classification.

For effective attacks on environmental problems, it is very likely that within the next decade we will find our present regional classification system obsolete. Metropolitan regions, such as New York and Chicago, or census regions, such as New England and the Pacific Northwest, are not likely to be useful for environmental studies. This point is easily seen when we recognize that river systems do not correspond to any of these man-made regions. Nor do air systems which may be identified by meteorologic studies. Moreover, the area covered by water systems differs greatly from the area covered by air systems. Thus one might speculate that to attack water-pollution problems we need a different set of regions than to attack air-pollution problems.

The problem, however, does not stop here. Water, air, and land pollution are all interrelated. We know that when industries and populations are regulated so as to reduce their emissions of water pollutants, they tend to change their respective production processes and living habits, which may result in different kinds of pollutants being produced. Wastes that can no longer be carried away by water stream and dumped into a river may be burned in an incinerator, or treated and deposited as solid waste in some dump. This intensifies the air or solid-waste pollution problem. Hence, wise management requires a joint attack on air, land, and water quality rather than independent piecemeal attacks. In turn, we need to develop a set of regions relevant for such a comprehensive attack, a task much more difficult than merely identifying water system regions. To start the process of thinking in fresh directions, we suggest in Table 14.8 a regional breakdown which emphasizes the three major types of environmental regions, namely land, air, and marine. This table depicts how a familiar geographic region, like the Philadelphia one, can be embraced as a subregion of the major environmental regions.

RECREATIONAL DEVELOPMENT AND COASTAL WET-LANDS: A RELATIVELY SIMPLE CONFLICT PROBLEM

We have talked much about conceptual materials. It is now time to ask the $64 question: How do we go about putting the knowledge we have to use? This is

Table 14.8 A System of Environmental Regions

			LAND		AIR		MARINE	
			Economic	Ecologic	Economic	Ecologic	Economic	Ecologic
			Phila	Phila				
LAND	Economic	Phila						
	Ecologic	Phila						
AIR	Economic							
	Ecologic							
MARINE	Economic							
	Ecologic							

Source: W. Isard and T. Langford, Regional Input-Output Study, (Cambridge: M.I.T. Press, 1971).

a tough question to pose, at a time when serious environmental research by social scientists is less than a decade old. But let us sketch some beginnings in analysis.

Take the problem of zoning coastal wetlands. Consider a marina development on a bay. Involved in the marina development will be a set of facilities. There will be facilities for pleasure boating, with rowboats and with some boats having outboard motors and others inboards. There will be facilities for sport fishing, again with rowboats and with some boats having outboard and others inboard motors. There may be facilities for sport fishing off a pier or jetty, party boat fishing, and surf sport fishing. All of them may need to be designed for both transient population and seasonal population. Say the plans are to develop a marina with the capacity to handle as many as 400 boats. To handle them when the marina is being operated at full capacity, we need as much as 450,000 sq ft of water surface for docked boats and 100,000 sq ft for moored boats.

In addition to inputs of water surface, we need inputs of land surface. We require as much as 55,000 sq ft for indoor storage, 6,000 for repair facilities, 3,500 for sales area for boats and marina accessories, 2,000 for administration and diverse services, 2,000 for restrooms for related facilities, and 365,000 for parking. We also need at least 40,000 man-hours of diverse labor, and inputs of fuel, bait, and a host of other items.

Associated with the day-to-day operation of these facilities will be the generation of pollution—from burning fuel in motors, generating the power for the facilities, littering, and other behavior associated with the use of recreational areas.

Beyond inputs and outputs for current operations, the development of the marina itself requires the dredging of both harbor access and secondary service channels (costing as much as $300,000 in 1970 for a marina in Kingston Bay, Massachusetts), and the construction of bulkheads for shore protection, breakwaters, access roads, and sewage disposal systems. Also, land structures must be constructed. All this causes disturbance to the natural ecologic system. In the study of a marina for Kingston Bay, we judged that it would be necessary to dredge an access channel of 1,800 feet, involving the removal of 35,000 cubic yards of bottom material. This could destroy the crop of as much as 20 acres of spartina grass, which is a source of organic detritus. The detritus in turn is an input into soft-shell clam production. Hence, one (but only one) cost of the marina would be the loss of the shellfish which the spartina grass area could have supported. However, other ecologic costs would also be involved in this disturbance of the natural environment. They are too complex for us to evaluate here.

In short, a thorough study evaluating the benefits and costs of a marina development would have to take into account not only the actual economic dollar costs, both for the structures that are built as well as inputs for day-to-day operations, but also the ecologic costs. These latter would be associated with the disturbance of the shellfish food chain and other natural processes from the construction of channels and other facilities, as well as the generation of pollutants in the use of the marina.

There is no acceptable way of estimating ecologic cost. We could say that one element of it was the loss in the dollar value of the shellfish crop. But then how calculate the costs to be attributed to destroying the natural state of a coastal environment, on which some fraction of the U.S. society places a high value? How place a dollar value on the negative health effects of the additional sulfur dioxide, particulates, hydrocarbons, and carbon monoxide generated by the user population? Note that these costs may be trivial to the transient who spends a day or two at the marina. They may be much more significant to the fishermen and other residents who live close to the bay.

On the other hand, there are major recreational benefits. Some of these benefits can be measured by the dollar amounts that users of the marina are willing to pay for the various marina services provided. (For the Kingston Bay site, we estimated in 1970 that these would be $550,000 annually.) But there are other gains both to individuals and society. For many persons, the marina may provide *real* recreation—their use of it relieves tensions and leads to greater personal happiness. In turn, these individuals become more productive workers in the economic system, clearer-thinking citizens in the political system, and more effective contributors to the cohesiveness of society.

Hence, the problem of evaluating the costs and benefits of any *simple* development of an area, particularly one critical to the ecologic system, is exceedingly complex. All we can do is try to set up a comprehensive list of the significant benefits and costs that are likely to result, and allow the political process to determine whether or not such a development should occur.

Note that in any such determination, major conflicts arise among different interest groups. There are the economic and real estate promoters (entrepreneurs) who are swept away with the ethic of capitalism and judge that any development that provides more jobs, greater tax base, and more output that can and will be counted in the gross national product is *per se* good for society. (In the case of the Kingston Bay marina, the equivalent of twenty full-time jobs would be created, and GNP would be increased by at least $250,000.) They may look upon the ecologic system as something that is simply there to be manipulated and exploited. These promoters often take the attitude that marshes, for example, are of no value unless they can be drained and developed.

In contrast are the "overly concerned" conservationists who look upon any development whatever as involving ecologic costs which cannot possibly be met by any economic gains. They would put a halt to any development that involves the least amount of environmental degradation. They ignore the fact that most of the population of the United States enjoys and expects a rising standard of living, and that these expectations can only be met by paying a price in ecologically valuable marine resources.

Clearly, this and many other conflicts must be resolved or managed through the development of wise environmental policy, embodying appropriate compromises. Involved is comprehensive planning in the sense that conservation priorities must be assigned to various parts of the coastline and the earth's surface in general. Involved are the increasing demands placed upon ecologic resources by a growing population with ever-mounting and even insatiable demands. Involved is the danger of major disruption of the ecologic system, and the loss of most of the benefits that come from living in (and enjoying) an environment close to, if not in, its natural state. The development of wise environmental policy will surely require all the wisdom man has in analyzing system interrelations and in working out suitable compromises for managing conflict.

LAND-WATER-AIR QUALITY MANAGEMENT: A REGIONAL PERSPECTIVE

If the marina development problem looked simple but turned out to be complex, how much more complex is the problem of managing the land-water-air use of the earth as a whole? It is in fact so complex that all we can do is to point up some of the key factors that we currently perceive—knowing that the key factors we see now are only a small fraction of the total set that are relevant and that we will be able to see a decade from now. By trying to identify some of these key factors, we may be able to avoid some unwise decisions we might otherwise make. On the other hand, we run the risk that we may be dealing with situations where "a little knowledge is worse than no knowledge at all." For with a little knowledge, we may be misled into believing that we can develop wise policy when in fact nature can do better without our interference, even while we continue to exploit and disrupt it.

Suppose we consider the problem of pollution in a major megalopolis—say New York or Tokyo—or in a somewhat less complex region like Philadelphia. We must be concerned with air, land (from disposal of solid wastes), water, sonic, visual, and all other pollution. People live in Philadelphia. For each household in each income class we can estimate the amounts of different kinds of pollutants generated. For each industrial plant, commercial facility, and governmental unit, we can do the same. In short, for each behaving unit we can estimate pollutants generated per unit of its activity. So if the Philadelphia region were considered a point at which all its population, production, and consumption activities were concentrated, we could estimate the total set of pollutants generated.

We can be very specific here. We have already indicated that for a base year, say 1970, or the current year, we can roughly determine the level of each economic activity in the Philadelphia region. In Chapter 7, we used the symbol X_j to represent the output of the jth economic sector, where j can represent any one of the n sectors in our region. That is, $j = 1, 2, ..., n$.

We must multiply the output X_j by the coefficient $a_{a+1, j}$ which indicates the amount of pollutant $n + 1$ generated per dollar output of economic sector j. We obtain $a_{n+1, j}X_j$, the amount of pollutant $n + 1$ generated by the economic sector j. If we do this for all economic sectors in the region and add the amounts of pollutant $n + 1$ generated by each of the n economic sectors, we obtain

$$a_{n+1,1}X_1 + a_{n+1,2}X_2 + a_{n+1,3}X_3 + ... + a_{n+1,n}X_n = \bar{P}_{n+1}$$

where $\bar{P}_{n+1}$ is the total amount of pollutant $n + 1$ generated by all the economic sectors in the region. If we follow the same procedure for every other pollutant, to obtain the total amount of each other pollutant generated, we have

$$a_{n+2,1}X_1 + a_{n+2,2}X_2 + ... + a_{n+2,n}X_n = \bar{P}_{n+2}$$
$$a_{n+3,1}X_1 + a_{n+3,2}X_2 + ... + a_{n+3,n}X_n = \bar{P}_{n+3}$$
$$\vdots \qquad \vdots \qquad \vdots \qquad \vdots$$
$$a_{n+50,1}X_1 + a_{n+50,2}X_2 + ... a_{n+50,n}X_n = \bar{P}_{n+50}$$

Using our definition of a_{ej} on p. 346 and recalling from Chapter 7 that we can let $(50 \times n)$

$$X = \begin{bmatrix} X_1 \\ X_2 \\ \cdot \\ \cdot \\ \cdot \\ \cdot \\ \cdot \\ \cdot \\ X_{n-1} \\ X_n \end{bmatrix} \qquad \bar{P} = \begin{bmatrix} \bar{P}_{n+1} \\ \bar{P}_{n+2} \\ \cdot \\ \cdot \\ \cdot \\ \cdot \\ \cdot \\ \cdot \\ \bar{P}_{n+49} \\ \bar{P}_{n+50} \end{bmatrix}$$

X $(n \times 1)$ $\quad$ $\bar{P}$ (50×1)

we can calculate the vector $\bar{P}$ listing the total amount of each of the 50 pollutants generated in our region by all its economic activities as

$$\begin{bmatrix} P \end{bmatrix} = \begin{bmatrix} a_{ej} \end{bmatrix} \begin{bmatrix} X \end{bmatrix}$$

$$(50 \times 1) \qquad (50 \times n) \quad (n \times 1)$$

or simply

$$\bar{P} = AX.$$

Of course, economic sectors are not the only sectors that pollute in a region. The government sectors do, in burning fuel for heating and in their diverse activities. And so does every other activity we may cover in calculating the Y (final demand) vector for our region. In the case of the new town in Chapter 7, we must take into account the pollutants of the government research laboratories and the pharmaceutical companies. In the case of the Philadelphia region, we must take into account the pollutants of the U.S. Naval Shipyard, the U.S. General Services Administration, the Internal Revenue Service, and each of the other thirty-three federal sectors operating there, as well as the other activities we might classify as final demand activities to be covered by the Y vector for the Philadelphia region. Specifically, for each of the final demand activities we must and can calculate appropriate pollution coefficients, which we shall not specify here in order to avoid using complicated notation. And again by multiplying these coefficients by the levels of these final demand activities, which can easily be determined, we obtain a vector of pollutants,

$$\begin{bmatrix} \bar{\bar{P}} \end{bmatrix}$$

$$(50 \times 1)$$

which lists the total of each of the 50 pollutants generated by all final demand activities. This vector of pollutants is of course to be added to the $\bar{P}$ vector.

Fortunately, neither the Philadelphia region nor any other is a point in space. It is spread out and forms a geographic area. This means that the generation of pollution is also spread out. So if we divide up the geographic area of a region into subareas—for example, census blocks or neighborhoods—and obtain for each of these subareas the data on its population, industrial, commercial, and government activities, we can estimate the total amount of pollution generated at each of the subareas by such population and activities.

Specifically, if we recognize that the output X_j of any economic sector j is divided up among the subareas of a region, and if we designate the subareas of the region by $a, b, c, ..., u$, then we may write:

$$X_j = X_j^a + X_j^b + X_j^c + ... + X_j^u$$

where $X_j^a, X_j^b, X_j^c, ..., X^u$ are the outputs of economic sector j in subareas $a, b, c, ..., u$, respectively. Next we can take the vector of outputs of industries in any subarea c, that is:

$$X^c_{(n \times 1)} = \begin{bmatrix} X^c_1 \\ X^c_2 \\ \cdot \\ \cdot \\ \cdot \\ \cdot \\ \cdot \\ X^c_n \end{bmatrix}$$

and premultiply it by the pollution coefficient matrix $\underset{(50 \times n)}{a_{ej}}$ to obtain

$$\underset{(50 \times 1)}{[\bar{P}^c]} = \underset{(50 \times n)}{[a_{ej}]} \ \underset{(n \times 1)}{[X^c]}$$

where $\bar{P}^c$ is a vector listing the total amount of each of the 50 pollutants that are generated by all industries in subarea c of our region. To this amount of pollution we must of course add the vector $\bar{\bar{P}}^c$ of pollutants generated by the government units and other final demand activities in subarea c.

For example, we have divided the Watertown region of upper New York State into subareas. For its subarea 3 we set down in column 1 of Table 14.9 our estimates for 1971 of the daily emissions of seven air pollutants by the economic sectors of this subarea. In column 2, we record our estimates of the daily emissions of these pollutants by final demand activities, taken in this study to cover government units and households.

Table 14.9   Crude Estimates of Selected Pollutants by Source, Subarea 3 Watertown Region, lbs/day

APC Code No.	Pollutant	Industry (1)	Households and Government (2)	Automotive Transportation (3)	Total (4)
3000	Particulates	8,485	515	-----	9,000
1120	Sulfur Oxides	2,655	1,345	-----	4,000
1121	Sulfur Dioxide	400	-----	-----	400
1122	Sulfur Trioxide	5	-----	-----	51
1210	Carbon monoxide	300	-----	50,000	50,300
1230	Hydrocarbons	600	-----	10,100	10,700
1310	Nitrogen Oxides	600	-----	6,800	7,400

But if the population and industrial, commercial, and government facilities are spread out, the system is forced to transport people and goods. We know that transportation, whether by rail, truck, boat, pipeline, or tankers, generates pollution. And it generates pollution at each subarea that contains origination and termination points of traffic and through which transport routes cut. Specifically, we can estimate the traffic volumes by type on each transport route (road, railway, waterway). Further, we have accumulated data on the pollutants (for example, hydrocarbons, carbon monoxide, and nitrogen oxides) generated per car mile at specified speeds when the car is of a certain vintage (type), and when the traffic is subject to a specified number of accelerations (and decelerations). So by multiplying car-miles of each type of traffic in a subarea by the relevant pollutant coefficients, and by summing by type of pollutant, we can crudely estimate, at a given point in time, the pollutants generated for each subarea of a region. Thus, we list in column 3 of Table 14.9 our estimates of selected pollutants emitted daily from automotive transportation within subarea 3 of the Watertown region in 1971.

However, we cannot stop here. Pollutants that are emitted do not stay in place nor do they remain wholly unchanged chemically. The fallout of BOD at any point in a river system is diffused and carried downstream, and in part chemically transformed. The SO_2 that is emitted at any point source into the atmosphere is diffused and partly transformed chemically, and it and its products come to reside in a number of different subareas. Hence, we need to apply diffusion-transformation models.

Essentially, a diffusion model takes each pollutant emitted in a subarea (strictly speaking, at each point source) and allocates it to every other subarea of a region. Thus, if P_h^c is the amount of pollutant h emitted in subarea c and we use the symbol D_h^c to represent the appropriate diffusion operator, we have

$$P_h^c \times D_h^c = P_h^{c \to a} + P_h^{c \to b} \, P_h^{c \to c} + ... + P_h^{c \to u}$$

.

where $P_h^{c \to a}$, $P_h^{c \to b}$, ..., represent the amount of h that comes to reside in subareas a, b,..., respectively, as a result of emissions in c. In the same way we must apply a diffusion operator to the pollutant h emitted in every other subarea. Thus for all h that is emitted in all subareas we have

$$P_h^a \times D_h^a = P_h^{a \to a} + P_h^{a \to b} + ... + P_h^{a \to u}$$

$$P_h^b \times D_h^b = P_h^{b \to a} + P_h^{b \to b} + ... + P_h^{b \to u}$$

$$\vdots$$

$$P_h^u \times D_h^u = P_h^{u \to a} + P_h^{u \to b} + ... + P_h^{u \to u}$$

We then wish to derive R_h^k, namely the total amount of pollutant h that becomes resident in subarea k from the emission of h in all subareas. This we do by simple addition:

$$R_h^k = P_h^{a \to k} + P_h^{b \to k} + ... + P_h^{u \to k} = \sum_{j=a}^{u} P_h^{j \to k} \qquad j, k, = a,..., u$$

The diffusion model depicted in the previous paragraph of course takes a different specific form for each type of pollutant that is generated. Further, we have not indicated with this model the chemical reactions that occur, such as the reactions that convert SO_2 into SO_2, into sulfuric acid, and finally into suffates of metals, which occur while SO_2 is being distributed over space. Yet the above model is sufficient to indicate that if we apply an appropriate model to each type of pollutant, and project correctly the transformations that take place during the diffusion process, we can obtain the resident pollutant concentration vector

$$R^k = \begin{bmatrix} R^k_1 \\ \cdot \\ \cdot \\ \cdot \\ R^k_h \\ \cdot \\ \cdot \\ \cdot \\ R^k_p \end{bmatrix}$$

which lists the amount of each of the different pollutants that becomes resident in subarea k for the relevant unit of time. This vector allows us to establish crudely the ambient air and other qualities of subarea k's environment. In similar manner we establish this quality for every other subarea in our region. Although our current diffusion-transformation models are very poor and do not provide us with the quality of data we desire, they should be much improved in the near future.

Once we have estimates of pollutants by type that may come to reside in different subareas from the current operations in a region, analysis must be pushed in other directions. We need to estimate different health effects of different pollutants, about which, as we have indicated, we have little knowledge. Further, we know that in many situations the public sector will introduce regulations which in one way or another will require abatement of emissions. (Recall our discussion of the Watertown region at the beginning and end of Chapter 12.) Such abatement means that the estimates of emissions in Table 14.9 must be modified in light of new technologies put into use because of the regulations. So must our estimates of diffusion and health effects.

Another area in which additional analysis is required becomes clear if we go back to the problem of establishing a new iron and steel plant or a new textiles operation, which was discussed in Chapter 6. To determine whether or not there should be iron and steel expansion in a given region, we must pursue comparative cost analysis. Accordingly, we construct a table like Table 6.6 in Chapter 6 for the iron and steel operation, in which we list eligible locations by row and major locational cost differentials by column. We put in Table 14.10 all the information embodied in Table 6.6. However, now that we have made explicit the environmental impact variable, we must add another column or several columns to account for air, water, and other pollution costs per ton of steel produced at the different locations. We summarize them as ecological costs per ton steel.

Table 14.10   Some Economic and Ecologic Costs Per Ton Steel for
Selected Producing Locations Serving New York City*
(Figures in parentheses are hypothetical)

Location	Transportation Costs on				Ecological Costs	Total
	Ore	Coal	Finished Product	Subtotal		
New London	$3.68	$5.42	$ 8.80	$17.90	$ (8.00)	($25.90)
Pittsburgh	5.55	1.56	12.40	19.51	(10.00)	(29.51)
Cleveland	3.16	3.85	14.00	21.01	(10.00)	(31.01)
Sparrows Point	3.68	4.26	8.40	16.34	(12.00)	(28.34)
Buffalo	3.16	4.27	11.60	19.03	(12.00)	(31.03)
Bethlehem	5.56	5.06	5.80	16.42	(9.00)	(25.42)
Trenton	3.68	4.65	4.80	13.13	(15.00)	(28.13)
Middle Susquehanna Basin	(6.50)	(5.00)	(10.00)	(21.00)	(3.00)	(24.00)

*Source: Partly based on W. Isard and J.H. Cumberland, "New England as a Possible Location for an Integrated Iron and Steel Works," Economic. Geography 26 (October 1950), p. 257.

Suppose we set down the figures that are indicated in the parentheses in these columns and that are strictly wild guesses of the author. Suppose also we add another site to the list of eligible locations, a site in the Middle Susquehanna Basin. It is to be considered because of its favorable environmental situation with regard to air and water movements and low levels of pollutant-generating activities.

Table 14.10 immediately suggests that when we add the hypothetical ecologic costs, Trenton loses its attractiveness for new steel expansion. The environmentally superior site, the Middle Susquehanna Basin, comes out best, primarily because of its lower ecological costs. The ecological cost differential is thus critical, dominating the transport cost differential of Trenton.

The formulation of the problem, however, needs to be refined. We have already indicated that when inputs are excessively dear, such as at a high labor cost location, one tends to use less of the high-cost inputs and more of the relatively cheap inputs (see the discussion of factor substitution in the appendix to Chapter 6). Similarly with respect to a Trenton site. A new iron and steel plant at Trenton would cut back on its use of air as a media for dumping pollutants (which incurs high negative social sanctions) and use more of less expensive inputs. In particular, it would use more capital inputs in the form of equipment to remove or reduce emissions so that it would need to use less of the services of the air resources. (If the plant did not make this decision, society would soon force it to do so—that is, society would soon require that iron and steel plants in areas like Philadelphia employ the best pollution control [state of the art] technology currently available.) So we would have to revise the table to reflect the additional capital requirements for operating steel plants in Philadelphia as against the Susquehanna site, and also adjust the ecologic costs. Hence, Table 14.10 might now look like Table 14.11. Note that the ecologic cost differential remains dominant, and the Middle Susquehanna Basin remains the cheapest location for steel expansion in this hypothetical case.

Now this is one way to approach the problem. When the figures in parentheses are taken into account, they say that for locations like Philadelphia there should

Table 14.11   Adjusted Economic and Ecologic Costs Per Ton Steel
for Selected Producing Locations Serving New York City
(Figures in Parentheses are Hypothetical)

Location	Subtotal from Table 14.10	Fixed Charges on Control Equipment	Ecological Costs	Total
New London	$17.90	$(0.75)	$ (7.00)	($25.65)
Pittsburgh	19.51	(0.90)	(8.90)	(29.31)
Cleveland	21.01	(0.90)	(8.90)	(30.81)
Sparrows Point	16.34	(1.00)	(10.80)	(28.14)
Buffalo	19.03	(1.00)	(10.80)	(30.83)
Bethlehem	16.42	(0.85)	(8.00)	(25.27
Trenton	13.13	(1.00)	(13.50)	(27.63)
Middle Susquehanna Basin	(21.00)	(0.60)	(2.30)	(23.90)

be no additional steel plants because the social costs are high when compared to steel plants in the Susquehanna Valley (or at New London or Bethlehem). They state that the use of the air, water, and land in the Philadelphia region for dumping pollutants is a very costly input when compared to the Susquehanna Valley. But we must recognize that this conclusion is based on the use of the cost figures in the parentheses of Table 14.10. It becomes very relevant to ask: Whose costs are these and how are they derived? For the person in the Philadelphia region who is unemployed, who might find employment in a new iron and steel plant, and who may also neither be aware of air pollution in Philadelphia nor concerned with the water quality the ecologic costs noted are irrelevant. aside from the possibility that they might be exaggerated. For the conservationist in the Philadelphia region, who may also be a professional, these costs may be excessively low. He may be very much concerned with the possibility that the SO_2 emitted may combine with oxygen to form SO_x and other sulfur compounds and lead to a higher incidence of cancer, let alone decrease the pleasantness of living in the Philadelphia region.

For the real estate promoter who lives and promotes in a suburban area not in the path of the wind movements diffusing the air pollutants of the steel plant, these costs might be excessively high. For the administrator who drives to his place of employment and must breathe in some of these pollutants during his journey to work, these costs may be excessively low. In short, there are likely to be significant differences of opinion among the diverse groups as to what ecologic costs are: the poor unemployed versus the conservationist; the real estate promoter versus the high-income professional; the conservative laissez-faire capitalist versus the social-welfare oriented quasi-socialist.

Moreover, the problem is still more difficult. We know from our discussion in Chapter 7 that when we put a particular industry like iron and steel in a region, other things change. The new industry requires inputs, at least some of which will come from the local area and lead to the expansion of the other industries in the local area. The new industry will require labor services, which will largely come from the local area (from labor already there or immigrants). This will lead to new income from wages and salaries, a large part of which will become effective demands for many products. Some of the products can only be provided economically by industries in the local area—such as retail services, professional services, and Coca-Cola, for example. Thus there will be additional expansion. We do not need to repeat this round-by-round expansion effect described in Chapter 7 and this chapter. What happens, then, is that the vector of outputs which before the introduction of new industry was

$$\begin{bmatrix} X \end{bmatrix}$$
$$(n \times 1)$$

now becomes

$$[X + \Delta X]$$
$$(n \times 1)$$

Using our set of pollution coefficients, we estimate the set of emissions before the introduction of new industry as

$$[a_{ej}] \qquad [X]$$
$$(50 \times n) \quad (n \times 1)$$

which now, with the introduction of the new industry and the prospective growth, becomes

$$[a_{ej}] \qquad [X + \Delta X]$$
$$(50 \times n) \quad (n \times 1)$$

But we know that the problem does not stop here. There will be additional pollution not only because of the new industry and the resulting industrial growth but also because there are more people around who consume more and who pollute in their consumption and living habits. So this must be added to the set of pollutants. Further, people do not live right next door to their workplaces. Many live at a distance, and commute in transportation vehicles that pollute. We must add on this dimension to obtain total pollutants generated because of the steel plant. Moreover, the pollutants are dispersed to the various subareas of a region and subject to transformation while being dispersed. Thus the estimated levels of additional pollutants generated by industry and population must be disaggregated by subarea. To them must be added the pollutants generated by the additional traffic. Then the dispersion of these must be estimated via a diffusion model.

So we might reach the conclusion that the figures presented as ecologic cost differentials in Table 14.11 are not the relevant ones. They cover only some of the ecological costs and fail to come to grips with the major ecological costs associated with the multiplier effects of iron and steel expansion. If these latter costs (together with possible benefits) are taken into account, then the conservationist might rightly claim that the ecologic costs listed doubly underestimate the true costs, while the promoter with his eyes focused on the new employment generated (and the benefits associated with such) might claim that they are doubly overestimating net costs, if not being doubly irrelevant.

Moreover, the problem of identifying these ecologic costs in any scientific manner that may be agreed upon is extremely difficult, for reasons already mentioned. To each of the pollutants that becomes resident in each of the subareas (directly and indirectly as a result of a new steel plant) we need to assign a price, taking into full account the health effects. But how can we do this, especially when the populations in some subareas are very poor and others very rich, and when the populations and their perceptions of welfare differ greatly? Further, the relative effects of the several pollutants on current, in contrast to future, population are different. Still more, some of the pollutants may have minor short-run impacts (today and tomorrow), but major long-run impacts (ten to twenty years from now). How can we weight an individual's current health against his future health? And how allow these weights to change in accord with what the population thinks is important?

Because we can only guess at what the social costs of different pollutants in the different subareas of a region are, how can we put down figures in the ecological costs column of Table 14.11? Because we cannot justify any of these cost figures, many may argue that we should not list them. But then if we do not list these figures, the data of the table would indicate that we should treble the iron and steel capacity in the Philadelphia region. But if we do so, everybody knows that the air and water resources of the region would not be able to handle the additional pollutants generated. The ecologic system would break down in terms of its ability to support a healthy population. It thus turns out that we must put some figures in the ecological costs column, however poor they might be, if we hope to have anything that approaches wise environmental management. But this still leaves us with the dilemma of estimating relevant figures for the iron and steel facility as well as for a number of other heavy polluting operations such as a power plant, a cement plant, a pulp and paper mill, a steel foundry, a chemical plant, or an oil refinery.

So we must conclude that however hard we try and however rapid our research and scientific analyses proceed, we face a problem bristling with difficulties. But the problem of wise environmental management must nonetheless be squarely confronted.

LAND-WATER-AIR QUALITY MANAGEMENT: A MULTIREGIONAL PERSPECTIVE

The preceding discussion pertains to some of the basic aspects of environmental management for a particular region. But as we well know, environmental processes do not recognize and confine themselves to man-made regions. The disturbance of the environment which occurs in one region has effects upon the environment of a second region. The agricultural practices followed in one region can lead to major hydrologic changes in the second region. The pollutants of one region, when dumped in a river system, can destroy the fish life of a second region. One region's emissions of black smoke under normal wind conditions can become particulate deposits in the lungs of the people of a region next door. The radioactive wastes discharged in one region can lead to significant strontium intake by people in all regions. Thus, it becomes necessary to extend the management of the environment beyond any particular region and its subareas and to cover a multiregion system, ideally the entire earth and its atmosphere. To do so, however, is not an easy task. There are tremendous difficulties.

These become obvious when we go back to Table 14.6 for a single region. For a multiregion system, we need to have one such table for each region. Moreover, we would need to extend a table such as Table 14.6 in order to take into account the flows into the region (imports) of diverse pollutants from each other region and to make explicit the flows out of the region (exports) of diverse pollutants to every other region. Of course, this is no easy job. It will take decades, if not a century, to develop an adequate interregional accounting of this order.

Beyond the difficulties in depicting what is or what might be with basic changes in the level of agriculture, industrial activities, and patterns of population settlement, there are tremendous difficulties in coping with the many conflicts that will arise. Consider the general conflict between the developed and the developing nations (regions). First, difficulties arise because of different perceptions of economic progress. As already noted, progress in New York City would be indicated by zero black smoke curling out ot the smokestack of a power plant, whereas in some underdeveloped region it would be measured by the blackness and density of the smoke.

Next we have the major differences in needs among different people. Clearly, in the industrialized nations, the need for additional power for a new electric kitchen gadget does not compare with the need in a developing region for additional power to operate a school or a small steel plant. How to equate these two? This problem is associated with the fact, to which we have frequently alluded, that the marginal utility of income is in general much higher for those in developing regions than for those in developed regions. Thus, in general the gains from having a smokestack belching forth black or any other color smoke are much greater for the former than for the latter.

Then there are the major differences among regions in per capita generation of pollutants. The industrialized nations, even with their advanced pollution-control technology, emit much more pollutants per head than the developing regions. What, if any, should be a "fair difference" in allowable pollution generation per head? Why not allow each nation to pollute by an amount equal to its population times some constant number? Looked at from the world standpoint, this approach has the same appeal as a "one person–one vote" procedure. But then this denies the existence of the political and economic power network of reality, and might imply major retrenchment in consumption in the major industrialized nations.

Then there are the differences in the cumulative amount of pollution generated per head. In industrialized regions, we can broadly estimate the amount of resources cumulatively used up by each region, and pollutants cumulatively imposed on the environment over the last century or two, per head. This figure will be high. We can do the same for underdeveloped regions. This figure will be low. Why should not the underdeveloped regions be given the same opportunity to exploit resources and damage the environment from here on into the future? Why should the latter not be permitted to operate without control, at least until they have caught up with the developed regions in the cumulative exploitation of resources, while the industrialized nations are forced to comply with the strictest regulations that are technically feasible and even forced to contract their output so as to reduce the absolute amount of pollutants they dump upon the environment?

Then there is the issue associated with an infant industry argument. This argument would hold that in order to spark industrialization, all regulation that adds to the costs of operation of a critical development industry for a developing region should be foregone until the "takeoff" is achieved in that region. Once it has passed the takeoff stage, the region's critical development industry can then be regulated as all others.

Additionally, we must consider the fundamental differences in the goals and values that exist among the different regions, as has been discussed in previous chapters. They must enter here, too. There are some nations, particularly the affluent ones, which are likely to give much more weight to long-run implications of *current* use of the environment than others. When we distinguish between pollution by land, water, and air, we expect land-locked nations out of which flow river systems to have relatively little concern with ocean pollution and to be much more vociferous about the management of the air environment. Their views are likely to be quite different from nations that are completely surrounded by water, such as Britain and Japan, and others that have extensive beaches. Regions within which there are considerable wind and water movements are less likely to be concerned with pollution control than regions with less favorable meteorologic and hydrologic conditions. Nations possessing nuclear bomb capabilities are likely to propose much less stringent regulations on the use of nuclear power than others.

We conclude this chapter by repeating the point that the dimensions of the environmental problem compel us to be more multinational in our thinking than ever before. In the past, when we set up a steel plant in one nation, we could think of this in the international arena as a decision that had little direct effect on any other nation. Now, if we set up a steel plant in a region such as Germany and the pollutants are blown over to Copenhagen, intensifying the air-pollution problem there, we do have a significant effect on another nation. In short, because of the tremendous load of pollutants currently being dumped on the environment, and because of the dispersion processes, we confront a multinational problem. It is one that is likely to be more intense than most social problems.

We inevitably reach the conclusion that the environmental problem is one that will require intensive discussion and extensive action on a multination basis—from a world region standpoint, if not a world standpoint. We have already seen development in this direction—witness the United Nations Conference on the Human Environment held in Stockholm, and the extensive discussion of the law of the seas. In the last chapter of this book we will focus more on possibilities for desirable developments in this direction.

Chapter
15

Development Theory and
Social Welfare Analysis

THE DEFINITION OF REGIONAL DEVELOPMENT

"Development" is a word that has many interpretations. To some, it means almost the same thing as "civilization." It implies something good, something positive. It is progress. To others, "development" means much less. But it is clearly a word that has grown out of the thinking of those scholars and leaders in advanced industrialized regions of the world who have been motivated to improve society and to increase the "happiness" of its members. Such factors are associated with progress and "development." The word has not, to any significant extent, been part of the indigenous thinking of those in nonindustrialized regions. The word has come to them through exposure and contact with scholars and leaders in the already industrialized regions.

It is unlikely that this word, with the sense or meaning that we give it, exists in the languages of isolated cultures; it is also unlikely that one would find in the isolated, "static" cultures the problems that are associated with efforts to achieve development. One can even speculate that members of these isolated cultures are happier and more developed in a noneconomic, social sense than are people in cultures in which "development" has been a key word, and in which individuals are locked into economic growth processes through their specialized activities and the complex social environment that surrounds them.

It is fruitless for us to debate who is happier—a member of an isolated culture or a person caught in the spiral of development and unable to extricate himself from it. We, at least, are trapped, for who among us is able to break from the mainstream and settle in an isolated Alaskan or Andean area? So we must perforce come to grips with development, to try to restrict its bad effects while nurturing its good ones. This we must do whether we view development as generating *on net* negative or positive effects.

Webster defines "development" as "the act, process, or result of developing." In turn, "develop" is variously defined as

To evolve the possibilities of
To promote the growth of
To make available or usable
To cause to unfold gradually
To expand by a process of growth

A key notion in these various definitions is *growth*, which is associated with the words "increase," "expand," "come into existence," "arise," and "produce."

Likewise in the literature on development, growth and consequently increase and expansion are central concepts. Increase and expansion may occur with respect to both material and nonmaterial things. Among the many material things that count in this world are

1. Income (or equivalently, purchasing power)
2. Wealth, or the amount of valuable economic or material goods one owns or whose use one controls
3. Guns, weapons, planes, bombs, and other items of potential destructive power which one can employ or threaten to employ in order to increase the probability of one's control over the use of material goods and other items one considers important
4. Number of offspring, sometimes only female, other times only male
5. Number of gadgets (refrigerators, automobiles, television sets, etc.) that can be conspicuously displayed
6. Number of supporters (votes upon which one can count)
7. Number of trophies (even scalps)

Because these material things are easily counted, people are able to talk about them clearly. They can be referred to in a precise and lucid fashion in discussions and writings. Naturally then, in the early years of a developing culture people refer to the increase in the numbers of things as a sign of progress. As culture and values are passed on through successive generations, a bias becomes cumulatively ingrained in the culture. Progress is increasingly measured in terms of these material things, especially in scientifically oriented societies in which much stock is placed on measurement.

Among the nonmaterial things that count in this world are

1. The ability to make wise and just decisions (something that is extremely difficult to measure, but has consistently been deemed important in both pre-Biblical and post-Biblical society)
2. The amount of respect accorded an individual by his peers, associates, and countrymen
3. The amount of love and affection extended to an individual by his kin, friends, and other members of society
4. The spiritual level of an individual's or a community's life
5. The level of solidarity, sense of security, and cohesiveness within a group, community, or society

It is extremely difficult to measure these nonmaterial things, to indicate whether there has been an increase, decrease, or no change in their levels over a period of time. Hence, it is difficult to discuss or write about development in the context of nonmaterial things. Slowly these nonmaterial things often count for less and less in the thinking and literature of a people, especially as scientific knowledge accumulates and scientifically validated statistical procedures are established and required in justifying policy proposals and making decisions.

Against this background, we may set down some of the definitions of development that we find in the literature. A definition which we like but which is not extensively employed is that of David Barkin, writing in the United Nations' *International Social Development Review*. He states, "Development, whether on a national or a regional level, is a dual process of enrichment and structural change. On the one hand, it raises incomes by using available resources more productively and accumulating additional resources to facilitate and increase production. On the other hand, it usually involves the transformation of an economy from one on a primarily agricultural and subsistence basis to a more diversified commercial structure in which a surplus is generated to permit further investments and diversification. This dual process has its counterpart on the human level—a level all too often ignored by people interested in economic development—which also involves enrichment and structural change. In this case, however, the structures that must be altered are those of social class and the distribution of income."[1] Another conception of the goals of development, one identified by member states of the United Nations, includes "the elimination of all forms of discrimination and exploitation, the assurance at all levels of society of the right to work, equal opportunity for social and economic advancement, and the assurance of a steady improvement in levels of living and of a just and equitable distribution of income. Among the means required to achieve these goals are: an increasing rate of popular participation; democratically based social and institutional reforms, including land reform; the establishment of forms of ownership of land and of the means of production that would preclude any kind of exploitation of man; and the introduction by Governments of necessary changes in the social structure for attainment of the goals."[2] According to still another expert, who writes more in terms of traditional approaches, especially those found in the already industrialized regions of the world, "In the literature of economic development, the term *development* is usually defined as an increase in real per capita income which occurs over some specified period of time. In the case of regional development, however, we are frequently inclined to regard development in terms of increases in aggregate income or increases in levels of population and employment. This is a perfectly acceptable view of development, particularly since changes in overall levels of economic activity within a region are frequently the focus of interest. Nevertheless it is important that this distinction be recognized."[3]

[1] *International Social Development Review*, No. 4, "Regional Socio-Economic Development" (1972), p. 84.

[2] Ibid., pp. 3–4.

[3] John Parr, "Regional Development," in *Focus on Geography*, Philip Bacon, ed. (Washington, D.C., National Council for the Social Studies, 1970), p. 122.

Many other definitions of development can be cited. In most of them, the relevance of the nonmaterial items is grossly understated or ignored.

Now, though we would like to set forth our own definition of development reflecting our ideas on what is important, we find that we are unable to do so. First, we do not have in the English language, the French language, or the other languages of the industrialized world, a sufficient variety and number of words to describe what we have in mind. The language we inherit has ingrained in it the cumulative biases of past generations of scholars, leaders, and writers on all kinds of subjects.

Second, if we tried to do so, we would need to use words that are distinctly new but that also suggest some notion of the meaning we wish to give them. For example, when speaking of the outputs or yields of a religious organization, we prefer to coin the word c-rectitude rather than *zyzzos* (a word that suggests nothing). Other new words we might consider using are c-spirituality, c-affection, c-respect, c-well-being, c-enlightenment, c-participation, and c-solidarity. We must define each in a much tighter way than Webster defines the corresponding words spirituality, affection, respect, and so on. We need as tight a definition as possible in order to begin effecting some measurement with respect to each, however crude. We need to be able to state whether there has been an increase, decrease, or no change at all in these nonmaterial things (or commodities) during a period of time. Unfortunately, at this moment we cannot set down definitions of such new words that are generally accepted and meaningful to use in an introductory textbook. Perhaps twenty years from now we will be able to do so.[4] Hence, we cannot put forth our own definition of development.

In the discussion that follows, we will employ the Parr type of definition, but with a very critical eye. We will constantly refer to its narrowness. With the analysis we shall try to move our thinking in those directions necessary for reaching a better definition which is equally precise.

THE SOCIAL WELFARE FUNCTION AND SOME WELFARE ANALYSIS.

We often use the term "social welfare" in our studies on development. This means that we think of social welfare as increasing, decreasing, or not changing as each of the variables to which we relate it changes or stays unchanged. Generally we have in mind a social welfare function which states that social welfare, W, is a function of the level of a first variable x, the level of a second variable y, the level of a third variable z, and so forth. We state this relation mathematically as

$$W = f(x,y,z,...) \tag{15.1}$$

It is often useful to think of the ratio of the change in social welfare, designated ΔW, resulting from a change in one of the variables, say x, where we designate the change Δx, when the levels of the other variables, y, z,... stay unchanged. This ratio as then indicated by the symbol $\dfrac{\Delta W}{\Delta x}$. Or, when we think

---

[4] However, see W. Isard et al., *General Theory, Social, Political, Economic and Regional* (Cambridge: M.I.T. Press, 1969), Chapter 12, for some exploratory definitions.

of Δx as being an infinitesimally small change, we can use the symbol of calculus, namely $\dfrac{\partial w}{\partial x}$. This last symbol is designated a partial derivative.

As already indicated, we cannot measure social welfare, and so cannot obtain the ratios just mentioned. However, we can still develop some useful concepts for social welfare analysis and for evaluating development. We can, for example, think in terms of curves each of which define various combinations of the variables that are equally beneficial for, or desired by, the members of society. We have already treated such curves in Chapter 10 and its appendix. They are indifference curves. The indifference curve HH depicted in Figure 15.1 is a locus of

Figure 15.1   Indifference Curves Regarding c-Spirituality and c-Cohesiveness

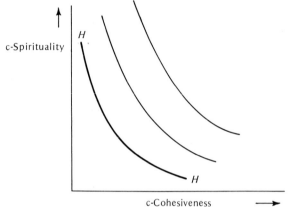

points representing the various combinations of c-spirituality and c-cohesiveness that lead to the same level of social welfare, all other things being the same. In Figure 15.2, the indifference curve GG connects points representing the various combinations of c-spirituality and income that lead to some given level of social

Figure 15.2   Indifference Curves Regarding c-Spirituality and Income

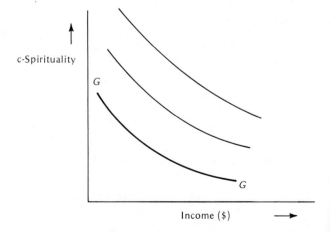

Figure 15.3   Indifference Curves Regarding Housing Expenditures
and Education Expenditures

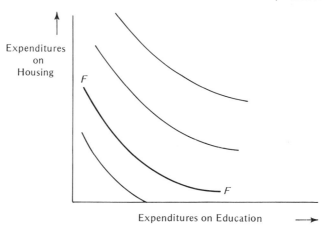

Expenditures on Education ⟶

welfare, all other things being the same. In Figure 15.3, the indifference curve *FF* is the locus of points representing various combinations of expenditures on housing (that is, purchasing power devoted to housing) and expenditures on education (that is, purchasing power devoted to education) that yield some given level of social welfare, all other things being the same.

We can now talk about sets of indifference curves in each diagram. As we move from one indifference curve to the next, going from the lower left to the upper right, we are moving to higher levels of social welfare. In each case, we do not specify by how much social welfare has increased as we pass from one curve to the next. We simply indicate an increase in an ordinal sense. Now the key problem is to determine how to use our various resources to achieve the highest level of social welfare. In doing so, we include in resources not only the coal, water, air, personal labor, accumulated machinery, factory buildings, and other goods that we possess, but also the so-called spiritual and other nonmaterial goods that we have at our command. That is, we include our total culture.

Let us see how we can use these indifference curves. Suppose one of the key commodities is c-enlightenment, or the educational level of a population. For the moment assume that the political, social, and economic leaders of a particular culture or society are able to specify the best set of educational programs for every level of education expenditures. For example, they may have decided that a mix of programs which involves equal per capita expenditures is best. Or they may have decided on equal per capita expenditures for situations where less than $10 million (equivalent say to $100 per year per child of school age) is available for educational programs. Where more than $10 million is available, they may have decided to devote half of the amount above $10 million to specialized education of the 10 percent most able student population (selected by some tests considered to be objective). Or they may have judged that the first $10 million allocated to education should be spent on the enlightenment of the select 10 percent of the students, and that all additional monies should be spent equally on the total student population. And so forth. At this point we do not wish to discuss the conflicts involved in establishing wise and/or fair educational policy. We assume that some policy has been arrived at through regular political, social, and economic processes, and that whatever funds are devoted to education will be spent effectively to implement the policy.

Suppose we are also concerned with c-well-being, the general mental and physical health and vitality of the population. Suppose here too that a body of political, social, and economic leaders has arrived at what it considers to be the best set of programs for every dollar amount that might be allocated to the production of c-well-being. The programs would include the provision of medical services, housing, and diverse social-cultural services. Suppose also that the educational programs are viewed as distinct and independent of the c-well-being programs, although strictly speaking they may not be. Then we might plot in Figure 15.4 expenditures on c-enlightenment (efficiently spent, given the best policy) along the vertical axis, and expenditures on c-well-being (again efficiently spent, given the best policy) along the horizontal. We can construct a rough set of indifference curves for these two types of expenditures, assuming that all other components of social welfare are held constant.

Suppose there were $20 million available for the two commodities, c-enlightenment and c-well-being. We can imagine that all of the sum was spent on c-enlightenment and zero was spent on c-well-being. This would be indicated by point T in Figure 15.4. Or suppose all of the $20 million was spent on c-well-being and zero on c-enlightenment. This would be depicted by point S. Or, $10 million might be spent on c-well-being and $10 million on c-enlightenment, as

Figure 15.4   Best Combination Line for c-Enlightenment Expenditures
and c-Well-Being Expenditures

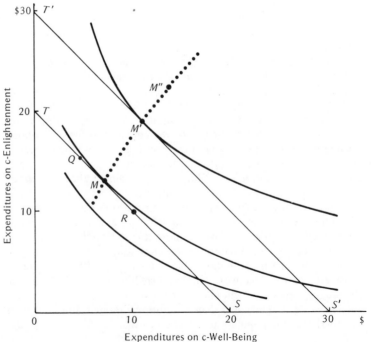

given by point R on the straight line TS. Or $15 million might be spent on c-enlightenment and $5 million on c-well-being, as given by point Q. As is obvious, the $20 million might be spent in numerous ways. Each would correspond to a point on the straight line TS, representing the locus of all combinations of non-negative expenditures on c-enlightenment and c-well-being which add up to $20 million.

It is clear from Figure 15.4 that neither of the end points, T or S, represents the best that is achievable in terms of social welfare. Each of these points lies on a lower indifference curve than other points on the line TS. In fact, if we search for the best combination,—that is, the one lying on the highest indifference curve—we find it given by point M, which is a point of tangency of an indifference curve with the $20 million expenditures line.

Suppose with time that the tax base of society (that is, its taxable property, income subject to taxation, and import duties) increases so that $30 million is available for these two sets of programs. Or suppose that technological innovation or increased managerial efficiency leads to increased average productivity of the labor force and thus to increased incomes and taxable base. Again, we may have $30 million of revenues available from taxation. Or suppose that at some point in time, political leaders have decided that a higher tax rate should go into effect (because of the noneconomic needs of society), so that the $30 million becomes available. Then we would plot another line on Figure 15.4, namely the $T'S'$ line, or $30 million expenditure line. It represents the locus of all combinations of non-negative expenditures on programs, leading to the production of c-enlightenment and c-well-being, which would add to $30 million. We see that point M' would correspond to the best combination of programs at this higher $30 million level. In similar manner, we can consider other totals available for the production of these two commodities (that is, to be spent on these two sets of programs), and determine for each total the best combination. By connecting these points we determine the *best combination line $MM'M''$* ... of Figure 15.4.[5]

People can count dollars, and most have a clear perception of what a dollar is, although their perception of what $20 million is may vary greatly. However, when we come to social welfare, there is little agreement among different individuals as to its specifics, although many would agree that social welfare should be related to such broad undefined ideas as the right of every individual to life, liberty, and the pursuit of happiness. Disagreement on specifics is, as we well know, pervasive and gives rise to both minor and major conflicts. In the section following and in the next chapter, we shall discuss the nature of these conflicts, and show that in some cases these conflicts may be resolved. Then we can roughly sketch the indifference curves underlying social welfare, such as the indifference curves of Figure 15.4. For the moment, however, we assume that society has been able to identify its relevant indifference curves. We want to move on to a deeper consideration of how we determine, given a particular situation, the level of total expenditures (government revenues) that might be available for the production of such noneconomic goods as c-enlightenment and c-well-being. For this, we must return to a discussion of the basic factors that determine

[5]The student who has read the appendix to Chapter 10 may note the parallel in determining the best combination line and the consumption expansion line of the individual consumer. There are other parallels of social welfare analysis to the consumer analysis in the appendix of Chapter 10 which he may wish to work out for himself.

the level of agricultural, industrial, and commercial development of a region. Such development sets the levels of aggregate income, population, and employment. From these, we can proceed to calculate the tax base and then the government revenues potentially available for different social welfare programs.

EXPORT INDUSTRY, IMPORT SUBSTITUTION, EXTERNALITIES, AND OTHER GROWTH-POLE ANALYSES

What forces influence the levels of aggregate income, population, and employment and their changes? In Chapter 6, we discussed the kinds of industries that might be located in a region. We discussed key location factors, one of which was transport costs on finished products, or access to markets. It was clear that when the market lay outside the region, we were discussing the possibility of an export industry. Therefore, a basic concept in the literature relates to the set of export industries, or the *export base*, of a region. The growth, development, and economic well-being of a region tend to increase, everything else being the same, when the number of outside (export) markets which the region's industries can profitably serve increases. To serve these markets profitably, however, often requires that, in addition to favorable transport costs on finished products, our region have advantages, relative to other regions, regarding transportation costs on raw materials, labor costs, power costs, taxes, or other location factors. On *net*, the locational cost differentials must be positive for our region when compared to any other region well-situated for competing for the export markets under consideration.

The levels of income, population, and employment are not determined by the level of export activities alone. We know from our discussions in Chapters 7 and 8 that once an export industry is established, it requires inputs (as in our input-output table). They constitute new markets within our region, which may induce other industries to locate here. That is, there may be *backward linkages* via input requirements leading to additional industrial growth. Similarly, the export industry produces output, which constitutes a source of supply of inputs for other kinds of industries. These latter industries may desire to save on the transportation cost of the good which they use as an input. They too might come to our region because of savings that are due to *forward linkages* in industrial interconnections.

Besides these, there are other possible growth effects. The new industries provide new jobs, resulting in more wages, salaries, and other income to residents of the region. The added income increases the demands for products at the markets in our region, which in turn may lead other activities to locate here and contribute further to the round-by-round expansion discussed in Chapter 7.

Moreover, as these different industries grow, there may be additional stimulus from possibilities for agglomeration economies—scale, localization, and urbanization economies—as discussed in Chapter 7, and to be discussed further in connection with the industrial complex analysis in Chapter 17. These economies tend to make every industry still more profitable and tend to attract still more industry, leading to a snowballing effect. Generally this results in increased productivity and health in the region. Of course, we must keep in mind that this cumulative process continues only up to a point. After a certain mass of industry and population is reached, further industrial growth leads to various deglomeration economies, or diseconomies, already discussed in Chapter 7.

Still another factor touched upon in Chapter 7 was *import substitution*. There, we pointed out that in the early stages of development, the market in the region for numerous products is too small to justify locating plants producing those products there. They must be imported. However, as the markets in the region expand with its growth in industry, income, and population, the markets can grow to sufficient size to attract industries producing products hitherto imported. An excellent example today is the iron and steel industry. As discussed in Chapter 6, it is a market-oriented industry. However, because it needs to take full advantage of scale economies, an integrated iron and steel works cannot afford to locate in a region until the region's demand for steel is large enough to fully absorb its output.

In short, possibilities for import substitution mount as a region grows, becoming another important source for generating new jobs and income. Moreover, as industries based on import substitution develop in the region, their presence attracts other industries. We know that the introduction of an integrated iron and steel works induces steel fabricators to locate at adjacent sites. This latter effect has been designated by Parr as *secondary import substitution*.

In a sense, all these import substitution effects increase the region's self-sufficiency, at least with respect to the new industries locating in the region. Moreover, the development forces that emerge because of initial resource advantages, agglomeration factors, and import substitution effects are interactive and become mutually reinforcing. In a sense, they tend to attract other diverse, "foot-loose" type industries which generally find location in many different regions equally attractive because no location has a particularly strong advantage over any other. On the other hand, as a region grows it may demand a greater variety of products, many of which may not be locally produced because of advantages other regions have in their production. Hence the imports of our region may increase and its self-sufficiency decrease.

There is a host of other factors that are becoming increasingly important in current regional development. Many relate to amenities, the quality of life, and the environment. They include climate, character of schools and municipal services, and cleanliness and physical design of the man-made environment (particularly his manipulations of the landscape). Their importance increases as the differences among regions in the costs of production (including transportation to the market) diminish for many of the new types of professional and service activities.

Recall also that, in certain respects, regional development occurs in stages. The first stage might involve the development of an export industry oriented to an agricultural or food-processing activity at the village level. In time, a second stage is achieved—the village grows into a town, taking on new functions as it services its population and that of several surrounding villages. Later, a third stage is reached when the town becomes a metropole. It develops still other service functions and production to meet the demands of its own population and that of several surrounding towns and villages in its hinterland. And so forth. This stage process of development is frequently associated with economic activities concentrated first in the agricultural and mining sectors (primary activities), then spreading to manufacturing (secondary activities), and finally moving into professional and service employment (tertiary activities). Often, the village, town, or small city at which the strong development impulse occurs is designated a *growth pole*, a term frequently used in development literature. This signifies a location where major concentrated development has occurred or can be sparked because of the location's resource base, import substitution possibilities, externalities, exploitation of amenities, and a host of other factors. Such concentration involves developing a great variety of skills in the labor force and of managerial risk-taking abilities among the entrepreneurs of a local elite group. This in turn serves as a propulsive force not only at the growth pole but also at several other favorably situated villages and towns in a region. This *spread* effect is closely associated with the fact that industrial growth in other villages and towns can be oriented to the newer and larger markets emerging at the growth pole—from increasing demands by industry for input requirements and increasing demands by households for diverse types of goods owing to their rising incomes. In short, as a growth pole develops, it can pull the whole or a large part of the region along with it. However, it can also have *dampening* effects on the growth of villages and towns in the surrounding areas and subregions. By providing better-paying jobs it may draw the best and most skilled labor from these villages and towns. Because of agglomeration economies accruing to industrial plants at a growth pole and their access to more modern transport and other facilities, these plants may be able to eliminate from competition the plants producing in the villages and towns of the surrounding areas and subregions. But the notion of growth pole is simply another way of looking at the whole process of development which we have discussed in Chapters 6, 7, and 8, and which we shall discuss again in Chapter 17.

We have now briefly reviewed some of the key factors relating to regional development which have been covered in the previous chapters. As we can easily imagine, such regional development builds up the stock of wealth of the economy, its level of income, and its population and human resources. This suggests that for any policy specifying a tax rate or type of taxes to be levied, we can calculate the levels of tax revenues that will be available as dollars of expenditures for the production of c-enlightenment, c-well-being and many other nonmaterial products. These, together with economic products available for consumption by a population, lead to hopefully greater and greater social welfare as regional development proceeds—especially if larger and larger amounts of income and resources become available for the production of nonmaterial commodities. Used in connection with such regional development and the usual taxing powers of a society's government, the social welfare analysis of the preceding section takes on significance.

However, we should bear in mind that our discussion has been biased. It overemphasizes the factor of demand—demands from outside the region for the products of its export sectors and demands internal to the region for its products to meet industry, government, and household demands and to substitute for imports. From this standpoint, we have maintained the bias of the input-output framework. There, exports represent final demands from outside the region. The sales of each sector to every other sector and to itself represent demands of the sectors—whether they be agriculture, manufacturing, and service sectors, or households and governments. In its less sophisticated versions, the input-output approach simply assumes that the demands will be met, in the sense that the goods demanded will be automatically produced. No direct consideration is given to the costs of production—that is, to conditions of supply. It fails to give proper weight to the fact that resources are scarce, and that any region or society in the process of development must allocate scarce resources among many competing programs and demands. To be specific, we are all familiar with the extreme shortage of capital that exists among underdeveloped regions. This precludes the development of industry, infrastructure, and social investments of the type that are urgently demanded and sorely required. Hence, we wish to turn to a new kind of analysis, programming analysis, which can cast some light on the process of allocating scarce resources. We want to know how that allocation can be efficiently designed, in order to make a greater amount of tax revenues available to support the production of needed food, clothing, and shelter, *and* such social welfare programs as those producing c-enlightenment and c-well-being.

PROGRAMMING ANALYSIS FOR THE EFFICIENT ALLOCATION OF RESOURCES

To begin to develop the programming approach, let us take a very simple example. Suppose there exists a region that wishes to maximize the net income it can obtain from foreign trade—that is, its foreign exchange earnings. This income will be used to purchase equipment and other goods from foreign countries urgently required for internal growth and welfare. Let us say its government has decided that the following amounts of its scarce resources shall be made available for the production of goods for export trade.

Table 15.1   Resource Supplies Available for Use by Export Activities

Resource	Supply (in number of relevant units)	Symbol
Water	6 MM	R_1
Land	1.8 MM	R_2
Labor (skilled)	3 MM	R_3
Capital	24 MM	R_4

Let us imagine that the region recognizes that only two of its activities can compete successfully in world markets. Call them activities 1 and 2. In time, though, it may develop the know-how and competitive capability for other export production. Moreover, think of this region as a small region. Whatever it produces constitutes only a small fraction of the world output. Therefore, it will not have any influence on the prices it obtains. So, if the level of output of the first activity is X_1 and of the second X_2, and if the price on the world market of the output of the first activity is p_1 and the second is p_2, then clearly the income (foreign exchange earnings) from the first will be p_1X_1 and from the second, p_2X_2. The sum of its earnings in foreign trade will be

$$Z = p_1X_1 + p_2X_2$$

Clearly, the objective of the government is to maximize Z.

To facilitate our analysis, let us redefine our unit level of activity to be that which yields one dollar's worth of product. Hence, if we let $V_1 = p_1 X_1$ = total dollar product of the first activity, then we can use V_1 to represent the level of the first activity. Also, if we let $V_2 = p_2 X_2$ = total dollar product of the second activity, then we can use V_2 to represent the level of the second activity. Consider the inputs required per unit level (per dollar output) of each of these activities. We record these inputs in Table 15.2.

Table 15.2   Resources Required Per Dollar Output

Required Units of	Activity	
	1	2
Water	0.5	0.6
Land	0.2	0.15
Labor	0.4	0.2
Capital	3.0	2.0

From our input-output analysis, we know that if the input requirements per unit of output are constant and if prices are also constant, then the inputs per dollar output can be taken to be constants. Thus the first column of Table 15.2 tells us the amounts of water, land, labor, and capital required per dollar output of the first activity. Specifically, .5 units of water, .2 units of land, .4 units of labor and 3 units of capital are required. Similarly, the second column tells us the amounts of water, land, labor, and capital required to produce one dollar's worth of output of the second activity.

Now consider the various combinations of our two activities that can be supported by each of our scarce resources. Take the water resources first. If only activity 1 were carried on, then our 6 MM units of water could be used to produce 12 million units of activity 1. This situation is depicted on Figure 15.5 by point N. Or, if we were to carry on only activity 2, then our 6 MM units of water could be used to operate activity 2 at a level of 10 million units. This is depicted by point U. Or we might consider devoting half the water resource to activity 1 and the other half to activity 2. In this situation, we could operate activity 1 at a level of 6 million units and activity 2 at a level of 5 million units. This is depicted by point G on line NU in Figure 15.5. Or we can consider any other allocation of the available water between these two activities. In each case, the combination of levels at which the two activities could be operated would lie along the straight line connecting points N and U. In short, line NU is the locus of all points representing non-negative combinations of levels of activities 1 and 2 that are possible, using in full the 6 million units of water available. This line is the water constraint line, for it effectively constrains the level of operation of any one of the activities when a feasible level of operation of the other is given. Combinations of the two activities represented by a point lying above and to the right of the line are infeasible, because they require more than the 6 million units of water available. For example, point C represents an infeasible combination. It requires 3 million units of water for activity 1 and 4.8 million units for activity 2, totaling 7.8 million units of water. That amount is not available.

Note also that the points lying below and to the left of line NU represent combinations of operating levels of these two activities that can be realized. In each case, however, the combination does not fully use up the available 6 million units of water. In this sense, each of these combinations is inefficient, for with

Figure 15.5   Graphic Solution to a Simple Linear Program

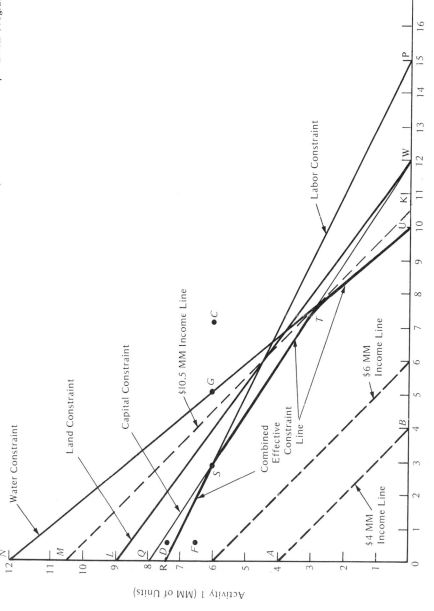

the leftover water we could produce more of the output of each activity. From this point of view, line NU is often considered to be an "efficiency frontier" with respect to water use.

In similar manner we can consider the use of the other resources. Take land. If the 1.8 million units of land were devoted solely to activity 1, the level of operation of activity 1 would be 9 million units, as depicted by point L on Figure 15.5. Or if all the land were devoted to the operation of activity 2 it would be possible to operate activity 2 at 12 million units, as depicted by point W. If we then connect points L and W by a straight line, the straight line is the locus of all combinations of non-negative levels of the two activities that fully use the available land. All points lying above and to the right of line LW represent infeasible combinations of the two activities. They require more land than is available. At the same time, all points lying below and to the left of line LW represent inefficient combinations because they do not use up all the land available. Thus, line LW reflects the land constraint. It effectively constrains the level of any one activity, given a feasible level of the other. Line LW is also an efficiency frontier with regard to land use.

In a similar way we construct the labor constraint line RP and the capital constraint line QW. Now we have three sets of combinations of the two activities with respect to *each* resource. One set contains those combinations represented by points lying above and to the right of the corresponding constraint line. This is the set of *infeasible* combinations. A second set contains those combinations represented by points below and to the left of the corresponding constraint line. This is the set of *feasible* and *inefficient* combinations. The third set contains those combinations represented by points lying on the corresponding constraint line. This set is the set of *feasible* and *efficient* combinations.

Our problem now is to identify the set of combinations of the two activities that are technically feasible and efficient not with respect to only one resource, but with respect to all four resources. That is, we need to identify efficient combinations that satisfy all four constraints. We want a set of combinations, each one represented by a point which does not lie above and to the right of any of the four constraint lines, and which does not lie below all four. For example, we cannot choose the combination represented by D. Although it lies below the water, land, and capital constraint lines, and thus does not require all the water, land, and capital available, it does lie above and to the right of the labor constraint line. Therefore this combination does require more labor than is available. It is infeasible on this score, and hence must be ruled out as a possibility for development. In contrast, point F represents a feasible combination because it lies below and to the left of all four constraint lines. But it is inefficient, for it does not use the supplies of any of the four resources in full; we can produce more of each activity than represented by point F.

Our problem is not as difficult as it appears at first. Suppose we start with point A on the y-axis. It lies to the left and below all four constraint lines, and so it is feasible. Suppose we proceed vertically from A, increasing the level of activity 1 and leaving the level of activity 2 unchanged at the zero level. As we proceed upward, every combination is feasible until we try to go beyond point R. Point R represents a feasible combination which requires all 3 million units of the labor available. If we go beyond point R, we are considering a combination of activities whose requirements of labor exceed the 3 million units available.

Each one of these combinations is technically infeasible. Hence, we cannot move vertically beyond point R.

At point R we reach the labor constraint line. If we now consider moving horizontally from point R, we find we cannot do so without violating our labor constraint. The only way we can move horizontally is to simultaneously shift downward so that we move along stretch RS. In this way, we are able to consider a series of combinations, all of which just meet the labor constraint and require less of water, land, and capital than is available. At point S this situation changes. Point S lies on the capital constraint line QW as well as the labor constraint line RP. The combination uses up all the available capital and all the available labor, but does not use up all the available water and land. If we try to move along line RP beyond point S, we find we cannot do so. All points lying on the SP stretch (except for S) of the labor constraint line lie above and to the right of the capital constraint line. They represent combinations of activities that require more capital than the 24 million units available. In fact, in order not to exceed the capital constraint we must lower our sights. That is, if we move horizontally from point S we can only do so if simultaneously we move down along stretch ST, which is part of the capital constraint line. In that way we will not violate the capital constraint. Note that in doing so, we move through a series of points that are below and to the left of all the other constraint lines, so that these points represent combinations which do not fully use the water, land, and labor resources. Thus, from R to S the labor constraint is binding; and from S to T the capital constraint is binding—that is, effectively limits the levels of our two activities.

When we reach point T, we observe that the combination represented by this point not only uses all the capital available but also all the water available, because point T lies on the water constraint line. Also, at point T we observe that we can no longer continue to move along the capital constraint line—that is, move along stretch TW. All points on the stretch TW (except for T) lie above and to the right of the water constraint line NU; the combinations they represent require more water than is available. Hence, in order not to violate the water constraint we must move along the stretch TU of the water constraint line NU. Note that in doing so, we move through a series of points that are below and to the left of the land, labor, and capital constraint lines so that these points represent combinations which do not use up all the land, labor, and capital available. From T to U the water constraint is binding.

We now have completed the task. By putting together the three stretches RS, ST, and TU, we form a "combined effective constraint line." Any point lying above this line is technically infeasible. It represents a combination of activities that requires more of at least one resource than is available. Any point lying below the line is technically feasible, for it represents a combination that would use in full none of the four resources available; but it is also *inefficient* because we would be in a position to produce more of each activity. Any point lying on the line is technically feasible and also efficient because it does use in full at least one of the resources.

We have narrowed down our problem considerably. We have identified the *combined effective constraint line* as the locus of points representing combinations of the two activities that are feasible and efficient with respect to all four resources. We now wish to find the combination that will maximize earnings of foreign exchange for the region. We can start off by asking the simple question: Is it possible for the region to earn $4 million of foreign exchange? We see that this is possible if the region chooses to operate activity 1 at a level of 4 million units and activity 2 at a level of zero units, as depicted by point A in Figure 15.5. Or the region could earn $4 million in foreign exchange if it were to operate activity 2 at a level of 4 million and activity 1 at zero level, as depicted by point B. Or the region can earn $4 million in foreign exchange by operating both activities at a level of 2 million units. In short, it can earn $4 million in foreign exchange by choosing any combination of these two activities represented by a point on the dashed straight line AB, which we designate the $4 million line.

Can we do better? Clearly the answer is yes. For example, the region can earn $6 million in foreign exchange by operating activity 1 at a level of 6 million units and activity 2 at zero level, or by operating activity 1 at zero level and activity 2 at a level of 6 million units. Or it can choose a combination of levels of these two activities corresponding to any point lying on the straight dashed line designated the $6 million line.

Can the region do still better? The answer again is yes. In fact, we see that we can keep drawing lines parallel to the two dashed lines representing higher and higher income lines until we reach a line that does not cut through (intersect) the combined effective constraint line, but has one point in common with it. In Figure 15.5 this is the $10.5 million line. Thus, this line contains only one point that is technically feasible—namely, the combination represented by point T. If we try to move to a $10.6 million line, we find that it contains no point that does not violate at least one constraint. If we were to be satisfied with just $10 million of foreign exchange, corresponding to a dashed line lying to the left and below the $10.5 million line, there would still be quite a few points in the neighborhood of T that would be technically feasible. We would not yet have found the best combination. In the situation depicted in Figure 15.5, it is only by going to higher and higher income lines that we finally reach that technically feasible combination depicted by point T. It is optimal, in the sense that it, and only it, lies on the highest possible foreign exchange earnings line, given our constraints. By this graphic analysis, we have identified that combination of the two activities that will maximize the foreign exchange earnings of this region. Because these earnings will be used for developing new income-generating and employment opportunities in the region, thereby increasing the region's tax base, we can see how going from a nonoptimal to an optimal combination of the two activities will permit a higher dollar expenditures line for Figure 15.4. Larger amounts of both c-well-being and c-enlightenment, associated with various sets of health and educational programs, can then be produced.

THE ALGEBRA OF PROGRAMMING ANALYSIS

We have presented a simple graphic analysis of linear programming, confining ourselves to two activities and four resources. But if we use the algebra that we have covered in Chapter 7, we can easily expand our thinking to cover many different types of activities and many different kinds of scarce resources. Suppose we are interested in several different activities that can compete on the world market, where $X_1, X_2, ..., X_n$ represent the level of activity 1, the level of activity

2, and finally the level of activity n. Again we take our region to be small and to have no influence on world market prices. Let the world market prices be $p_1, p_2,..., p_n$, where p_1 is the price of a unit of output of the first activity, p_2 is the price of a unit of output of the second activity, and finally p_n the price of a unit of the output of the nth activity. We can then designate foreign exchange earnings as the sum of earnings over all activities. That is,

$$Z = p_1X_1 + p_2X_2 + ... + p_nX_n = \sum_{i=1}^{n} p_iX_i \qquad (15.2)$$

The problem is to maximize Z, subject to the limited resources at our disposal. We can be specific here. Suppose there are m scarce resources. Let $R_1, R_2,...,$ R_m be the amount of resource 1, the amount of resource 2, and finally the amount of resource m, which we have available for use by all n activities we wish to consider. Let us list the input requirements of each of these resources for each activity. This we do in Table 15.3. In the first column we indicate the set of resource inputs required by one unit of activity 1; these inputs are, in order, a_{11} of resource 1, a_{21} of resource 2, a_{31} of resource 3, and finally a_{m1} of resource m.

Table 15.3   Resources Required Per Unit Level of Activity

Resources	1	2	3	4	...	n	Available Supply of Resource
1 (water)	a_{11}	a_{12}	a_{13}	a_{14}	...	a_{1n}	R_1
2 (land)	a_{21}	a_{22}	a_{23}	a_{24}	...	a_{2n}	R_2
3 (labor)	a_{31}	a_{32}	a_{33}	a_{34}	...	a_{3n}	R_3
4 (capital)	a_{41}	a_{42}	a_{43}	a_{44}	...	a_{4n}	R_4
.	.	.	.	.	.	.	.
m (uranium)	a_{m1}	a_{m2}	a_{m3}	a_{m4}	...	a_{mn}	R_m

As in Table 15.2 and Table 7.1, these a's are constant production coefficients. In the second column we list the resource inputs required per unit level of the second activity. Once again the number of the input is given by the first subscript, and the using activity by the second subscript. Similarly, we list inputs for every other activity.

Now consider the demand placed on the use of each resource. Take the first resource (water). Per unit level of activity 1, a_{11} units of water are required. If the level of activity 1 is X_1, then the total demand of activity 1 for water is $a_{11}X_1$. Per unit level of activity 2, a_{12} units of water are required. Hence, if the level of activity 2 is X_2, then its total demand is $a_{12}X_2$. Similarly, the total demands of activities 3, 4,..., n for water are $a_{13}X_3, a_{14}X_4,..., a_{1n}X_n$, respectively. Adding these demands, and recognizing that their overall sum must not exceed R_1, the supply of the first resource available, we obtain

$$a_{11}X_1 + a_{12}X_2 + a_{13}X_3 + ... + a_{1n}X_n \leqslant R_1 \qquad (15.3)$$

Equation 15.3 thus states the constraint on the use of the first resource. We derive a similar constraint for every other resource, which states that the sum of demands for it must not exceed supply. Altogether the constraints may be set down as

$$a_{11}X_1 + a_{12}X_2 + a_{13}X_3 + ... + a_{1n}X_n \leqslant R_1 \qquad (15.4)$$
$$a_{21}X_1 + a_{22}X_2 + a_{23}X_3 + ... + a_{2n}X_n \leqslant R_2$$
$$a_{31}X_1 + a_{32}X_2 + a_{33}X_3 + ... + a_{3n}X_n \leqslant R_3$$

$$\vdots$$

$$a_{m1}X_1 + a_{m2}X_2 + a_{m3}X_3 + ... + a_{mn}X_n \leqslant R_m$$

We must add on one more set of constraints, in order to avoid meaningless solutions. This constraint states that no activity is to be operated at a negative level. A negative level of activity is unrealistic for an economic system. That is,

$$X_1 \geqslant 0, \ X_2 \geqslant 0, \ X_3 \geqslant 0,..., \ X_n \geqslant 0 \qquad (15.5)$$

Having stated the constraints 15.4 and 15.5, it becomes a simple problem for the computer to find a set of levels $X_1^*, X_2^*, X_3^*, ..., X_n^*$, of the different activities that maximize foreign exchange earnings Z as defined in equation 15.2. This problem for the computer is as simple as the linear programming problem we solved graphically, if not simpler. Note that this programming problem is linear because all relations are either linear equalities or linear inequalities. Nonlinear relations are not involved.

Note also that if we use the algebra of Chapter 7 (the section entitled "A Simple Explanation of the Algebra of Input-Output"), we can state the linear program problem much more simply. Let

$$X = \begin{bmatrix} X_1 \\ X_2 \\ X_3 \\ \vdots \\ \vdots \\ X_n \end{bmatrix}_{(n \times 1)} \quad R = \begin{bmatrix} R_1 \\ R_2 \\ R_3 \\ \vdots \\ R_m \end{bmatrix}_{(m \times 1)} \quad \text{and } a_{ij} = \begin{bmatrix} a_{11}, a_{12}, ..., a_{1n} \\ a_{21}, a_{22}, ..., a_{2n} \\ \vdots \\ a_{m1}, a_{m2}, ..., a_{mn} \end{bmatrix}_{(m \times n)} \qquad (15.6)$$

and let $p = [p_1, p_2, ..., p_n]$.
$_{(1 \times n)}$

Then 15.2, which represents the objective function—that is, the function that defines the object or item that is to be maximized or, in other kinds of problems, minimized—is

$$\underset{(1 \times 1)}{Z} = \underset{(1 \times n)}{p} \underset{(n \times 1)}{X} \tag{15.7}$$

Our program is subject to the constraints 15.4 and 15.5, which may be rewritten as

$$\underset{(m \times n)}{a_{ij}} \underset{(n \times 1)}{X} \leqslant \underset{(m \times 1)}{R} \tag{15.8}$$

and

$$\underset{(n \times 1)}{X} \geqslant \underset{(n \times 1)}{0} \tag{15.9}$$

Still more simply, our problem is

$$\begin{aligned} \max \quad Z &= pX \\ \text{subject to:} \quad aX &\leqslant R \\ X &\geqslant 0 \end{aligned} \tag{15.10}$$

There are many other kinds of programming models. As indicated, we have presented only a linear programming model, because, to repeat, all the relationships it covers are linear equalities or inequalities. We know, of course, that many relationships in life are nonlinear, and sometimes jumpy or kinky. So other programming models have been developed, such as quadratic programming and integer programming. In one way or another, they may correspond more closely to reality. Of course, the techniques they must use to derive solutions are more complex, but in many cases solutions are possible, and therefore available for use by planning, development, and other interested agencies. The study of these kinds of programming models is more appropriate for advanced courses.

What we are concerned with here is the usefulness of the results of these programming models. As we have already indicated, these programming models are very useful in identifying the program that is best for meeting a goal. In the case examined, we were interested in maximizing foreign exchange earnings. We implicitly hypothesized that as more foreign exchange earnings are available, the region can industrialize more, more economic development can take place, and more funds can be available for the production of such goods as c-enlightenment and c-well-being. In this respect then, the programming models are valuable. In another context, they are useful for making explicit various conflicts and thereby, at least in the minds of some scholars and thinkers, making a faster and better resolution of the conflicts possible. We turn to this matter in the next section and in Chapter 16.

REGIONAL DEVELOPMENT: CONFLICTS OVER BASIC VALUES

Up to this point, our discussion has been either extremely broad, or very specific. We have discussed the social welfare function and welfare analysis, and have spoken very generally about noneconomic commodities such as c-enlightenment and c-well-being. We did not discuss the priorities that different societies might attach to the production of these goods, and to the specific programs that might be involved in this production. In our third section in this chapter, we left the world of nonmaterial noneconomic values and concentrated upon nurturing economic activities that generate income and employment. Then we developed a programming technique primarily to help in identifying an optimal combination of production activities for maximizing foreign exchange earnings or achieving some other objective expressed in terms of economic goods, items, and values.

In this section, we turn to a further discussion of priorities in the allocation of resources as they relate to the basic values and principles of a society. We wish to obtain further insight into the process of setting goals and levels of programs, and determining the amount of tax revenues that might be made available for programs to produce such noneconomic goods as c-enlightenment and c-well-being.

In this regard, it is useful to contrast the basic values that come out of a single nation entity and the values that emerge from a world grouping of nations.

Take the United States. Although there may be considerable disagreement about a precise statement of the values that have dominated United States society, by and large we may state that the values are oriented to the individual's uninhibited right to life, liberty, and the pursuit of happiness. This has meant that there should be individual freedom to enter any trade, to compete in any economic activity, to preach, to lead, and to conquer nature and use its resources. Such an approach has led to the development of political, social, and economic institutions on a pragmatic, flexible, and experimental basis. Together with the seemingly unlimited resources available to this society in the first centuries of its development, it has led to an unqualified faith in the desirability of science and technology to facilitate the individual in his various pursuits.

In time, the society came to recognize that permitting persons with large amounts of economic, social, and political power to have unrestricted freedom leads to serious encroachments on the freedom of other individuals. In such cases, constraints on the actions of individuals and other behaving units have been set, such as those imposed by antitrust legislation and civil rights legislation, to preclude excessive interference with the freedom of other individuals. Often, these constraints have been set reluctantly and belatedly.

Most recently, the sanctity of individual freedom has been questioned as problems have emerged because of negative externalities such as those discussed in Chapters 13 and 14, and because the U.S. society has come to abandon isolationism as a foreign policy and to exercise increasingly a role of leadership in the world community. By assuming this role, U.S. society has had to consider the impact of its actions on the welfare of other nations and on the political and social support forthcoming from them.

In contrast to the basic values of the U.S. society are the values that seem to be emerging in the United Nations and in other organizations representing the world community. There, increasing emphasis is being placed on cooperative developments (joint actions), subject to certain guarantees of individual freedom. The principle of both popular participation and democratically determined policies exists as in the U.S. society, but a major constraint is imposed on their exercise. There should be consistency in the overall set of joint actions relating to planning, development, and growth of the world community as a whole as well as to its various parts (world regions, nations, and regions within nations). As a consequence, the use and conservation of resources (and the associated problem of environmental management) are viewed as involving many more joint actions and considerably more restrictions on individual actions. Advances in science and technology are viewed as having great potential for enlarging the scope of joint actions for the good of mankind, and for increasing their effectiveness. But the potential of such advances for increasing the destructive capabilities of both individual and joint actions is also clearly recognized—both in terms of warring actions and major disruptions of the environment. Accordingly, the advances of science and technology are viewed as processes that must be carefully guided and overseen.

Because of the joint action orientation of the United Nations and world organizations, considerations of individual welfare frequently yield to considerations of social welfare. Consequently, indicators of social welfare rather than indicators of individual welfare play a greater role in policy formulations.

In analyzing regional development, we confront conflicts stemming from the differences in basic values. For example, consider the possible use of the programming technique discussed in the previous section. Comprehensive planning and programming of economic development within a nation is a notion acceptable to the United Nations as a whole, and to many of its member countries. They see the need for institutions, such as a central planning authority, to control the allocation of key resources such as capital, land, labor skills, coal, oil and other energy sources, iron ore and other strategic minerals, and foreign exchange. In contrast, the existence of such an institution in the United States would be considered a serious abridgement of the individual's right to engage in economic activities of his own, to bid freely at the market for resources and obtain those resources for which he can pay the asking price, to own and amass property to whatever extent he can through purchase at the market, and to deposit his money and liquid assets in whatever bank in whatever country he desires. Thus, because of this background of different values, we run into major conflicts regarding policies for developing regions of the world. The United Nations views development assistance as a cooperative effort. It involves constraints upon the actions of the various regions and nations of the world, constraints consistent with at least a limited amount of total planning authority at the central level. In contrast, a nation like the United States frowns upon such broad-scale planning. Acceptable forms of contribution to developing regions include unilateral gifts directly or indirectly through the United Nations, and making resources available to such regions at relatively low prices, especially when such resources are surplus in the U.S. (This has been the case with food and outdated equipment in the past.) The differences in basic values, leading to different approaches in studying and analyzing regional development, environmental management, and other problems of the world, can result in serious conflicts.

Of course, the United States does not stand alone in its individualistic tradition. Britain, France, West Germany, and Japan are among other nations which by and large are in the same boat. This tradition, as already indicated, has led to the exploitation of the mineral and human resources of underdeveloped regions by large and often monopolistic enterprises of Western Europe, Japan, and the United States. Because of this, many underdeveloped regions, especially former colonies, now view the world as a community. They feel that the resources of each part of it must be properly protected; something possible only by joint cooperative effort. The full social cost to the world of resource exploitation must be made explicit and borne by individual enterprises or other involved units. Also, all excesses of individual enterprises and behaving units must be properly controlled, and the constraints involved must have a worldwide orientation rather than a nationalistic framework. Such control implies that taxation powers, particularly of a progressive character, should be given to worldwide regulatory authorities.

This immediately generates conflicts among the "haves" and the "have-nots." Two major reasons exist for conflict over the role and desirable extent of worldwide legislation, adjudication, and administration. The first arises from the fact that the individuals or behaving units who practice excessive exploitation of resources and infringe on the rights of others are those in the "have" countries. They would thus be most restricted by such legislation, adjudication, and administration. Second, these same individuals, behaving units, or nations would be subject to the largest amounts of taxation for the support of such operations.

These conflicts arising from differences in basic values relate not only to legislative, adjudicative, and administrative procedures that might be adopted by the United Nations but also to the constitution of a possible new world government, or the establishment of institutions of a worldwide character and the powers, structures, and functions of such institutions. As we have indicated, they also involve conflicts over the extent to which central planning should be undertaken by world, regional, and national authorities—and thus the extent to which a technique such as programming should be used for resource allocation on worldwide, regional, and national bases.

CONCLUDING REMARKS

In the first section of the chapter, we discussed some of the different definitions of regional development, and the problem of arriving at a precise definition that might be adequate. We related the notion of development to social welfare in general. In the second section, we focused upon social welfare. We pointed up the problem of defining social welfare or identifying a social welfare function, and suggested the use of indifference curves in welfare analysis. We clearly linked the level of expenditures of governmental units on educational programs, medical care, housing, and cultural functions to the revenues obtainable from taxation to support these programs. In turn, the revenues obtainable by government were directly related to the level of economic development (in the narrow sense) of a region—that is, to its level of industrial production, employment, income, and investment.

In the third section we discussed a set of factors that determine the level of economic development achievable in a region—factors that emphasized the *demand* for its export products in world markets, *demand* of its own population for goods, the *demand* of its industry for inputs from other industries, and so forth. But this approach toward economic development must be broadened to consider the *supply* side as well. One way to effect this broadening is through programming analysis. A very important by-product of such analysis is that it permits more effective controls on the course of economic development. Specifically, through setting appropriate constraints, we can shape such development so as to be consistent with the notions of minimum standards regarding noneconomic commodities (education, quality of environment, quality of life) which we consider important from the standpoint of social welfare.

But this property of a programming analysis requires us to be able to specify the kinds of constraints we should place upon any economic development plan. In the last section of this chapter we began to see some of the major difficulties in specifying such constraints. There exist major differences in basic values among different regional and national cultures. In the next chapter we shall expose still other difficulties, which arise because of conflicts among regions and nations regarding goals and programs to achieve these goals. In the last sections of the next chapter we shall discuss some methods of resolving these differences (and conflicts) so that we can put appropriate constraints into a programming analysis. These constraints should be sensitive to what we believe to be the needs of people, both material (food, shelter, and clothing) and non-material (education, culture, and physical and spiritual well-being). After this is done, the student should have a better grasp of how development planning can be guided toward the achievement of greater social welfare, taking into account the direct and indirect demands on a region's resources which stimulate its economic growth, and the constraint factors (planning guidelines) which we can impose from the supply side through the allocation of resources.

Development Theory, Coalition Analysis and Conflict Resolution

INTRODUCTION

In this chapter, we continue with our discussion of how programming analysis can be used to shape the path of a region's development so as to be more consistent with a broad definition of social welfare. Specifically, we shall concentrate on our ability to specify the constraints of a development program, in order to steer that program in the direction of greater social welfare, as we perceive it. In doing this we must remember that there are conflicts, which we have already identified, among the basic values of different regional and national cultures, as well as conflicts among regions and nations in terms of both the goals they find most relevant and the specific programs to achieve these goals. We will discuss the latter conflicts in the sections to follow. Also, we will find it necessary to give some attention in the last sections to the possibilities of resolving such conflicts, so that we can specify precisely the kinds of constraints we would like to see a planning authority or a set of political leaders consider imposing on any development program.

REGIONAL DEVELOPMENT: CONFLICTS OVER BASIC GOALS

When we come to specific goals, the conflicts among societies, whether national or international, can be posed explicitly with a programming framework. For example, we can consider a nation with a number of underdeveloped regions. It may be a planned socialistic economy such as that of Poland, Hungary, and Yugoslavia; or countries such as India and several Latin American ones, which view central planning in a favorable light. There may be many goals prevalent in such a society. One may be to eliminate or reduce the discrepancies in the per capita incomes of its several regions. Another may be to achieve minimum standards of living in all regions. A third may be to realize a more even distribution of capital investment in the different parts of the nation. In each case we need to extend our programming model to cover more than one region. We now turn to this task.

The Algebra of a Simple Multiregion Programming Model

For simplicity's sake, imagine that there are only two regions in a nation, say North and South—as in Italy, or the United States in the Civil War era, or Korea, or currently in Vietnam. We can think of production activities taking place in each of these regions. We let $X^N_1, X^N_2, X^N_3,..., X^N_n$ represent the levels of activities 1, 2, 3,..., n, respectively, in the North. We let $X^S_1, X^S_2, X^S_3,..., X^S_n$ represent the levels of activities 1, 2,..., n, respectively, in the South. Correspondingly, we let $p^N_1, p^N_2, p^N_3,..., p^N_n$ be the prices of the output of activities 1, 2,..., n in the North and $p^S_1, p^S_2,..., p^S_n$ be the prices of the output of activities 1, 2,..., n in the South. We now define the gross regional product for the North and South, respectively, as

$$Z^N = p^N_1 X^N_1 + p^N_2 X^N_2 + ... + p^N_n X^N_n = \sum_i p^N_i X^N_i \quad i = 1,...,n \quad (16.1)$$

$$Z^S = p^S_1 X^S_1 + p^S_2 X^S_2 + ... + p^S_n X^S_n = \sum_i p^S_i X^S_i$$

We can also sum over the regions to determine, as one indicator of gross national product, that

$$Z = Z^N + Z^S = \sum_J \sum_i p^J_i X^J_i \quad J = N, S; i = 1,...,n \quad (16.2)$$

Let the objective be to maximize Z, gross national product.

For each activity in each region, we posit a set of constant production coefficients. If two regions produce steel in the same way, then the coefficients for steel production activity in the two regions will be the same. But if they produce steel in different ways, perhaps because they use different ore sources or different mixes of fuels and electric power, then these production coefficients will be different. We specify coefficients for each activity in each region, by associating the appropriate superscript N or S with each coefficient. Thus, in Table 16.1 the first column of a's records the amount of each resource needed per unit operation of the first activity in the North. Of course, the resources must be available in the North. Note that the lower half of the first column contains only zeros, indicating that the operation of an activity in the North consumes no resources that may be available in stockpiles or at the markets in the South. Once resources availabe in the South are transported to the North, and thus become resources in the North, they can be consumed in the production activities in the North.

Table 16.1 Resource Inputs Per Unit Level of Activity: Interregional Model

RESOURCES	ACTIVITIES								TOTAL SUPPLY AVAILABLE
	IN NORTH			IN SOUTH					
	#1	#2	$\cdots$	#n	#1	#2	$\cdots$	#n	
NORTH									
#1	$a_{11}^N,$	$a_{12}^N,$	$\cdots \cdot,$	a_{1n}^N					R_1^N
#2	$a_{21}^N,$	$a_{22}^N,$	$\cdots \cdot,$	a_{2n}^N					R_2^N
$\cdot$ $\cdot$ $\cdot$	$\cdot$	$\cdot$	$\cdot$						$\cdot$
#m	$a_{m1}^N,$	$a_{m2}^N,$	$\cdots \cdot,$	a_{mn}^N					R_m^N
SOUTH									
#1					$a_{11}^S,$	$a_{12}^S,$	$\cdots \cdot,$	a_{1n}^S	R_1^S
#2					$a_{21}^S,$	$a_{22}^S,$	$\cdots \cdot,$	a_{2n}^S	R_2^S
$\cdot$ $\cdot$ $\cdot$					$\cdot$	$\cdot$	$\cdot$		$\cdot$
#m					$a_{m1}^S,$	$a_{m2}^S,$	$\cdots \cdot,$	a_{mn}^S	R_m^S

Also, note the last column of a's in Table 16.1. It lists, per unit of the nth activity in the South, the amount of each resource required which must be available in the South. Again, the upper half of the column contains only zeros. indicating that no resources present in the North are consumed by activity n in the South. Resources in the North do not become available and are not consumed in the South until they have been transported to the South, becoming part of the resource stocks of the South.

Hence, in constructing a multiregion framework, we must make explicit the shipment of resources from one region to the next. Let $E^N_1, E^N_2,..., E^N_m$ represent the *net* export of resources 1, 2,..., m, respectively, from the North to the South; and $E^S_1, E^S_2,..., E^S_m$ represent the net exports of resources 1, 2,..., m, respectively, from the South to the North. Now we know from Chapter 8 that, in a two-region world, what one region exports the other must import. Each region cannot *on net* export wheat. If E^N_i is positive, representing positive exports and equivalently negative imports, then it must follow that E^S_i is negative, representing negative exports and equivalently positive imports. And if E^S_j is positive, then E^N_j is negative. So for any resource i we can state:

$$E^N_i + E^S_i = 0 \qquad i = 1,..., m \qquad (16.3)$$

With this relation in mind, we must adjust our statement of the resource constraints discussed in the last chapter in connection with Equations 15.3 and 15.4. For any given resource in any given region J, say the ith resource in the North, we must consider not only the demands for this resource because of the economic activities operating in the region, that is:

$$a^N_{i1} X^N_1 + a^N_{i2} X^N_2 + a^N_{i3} X^N_3 + ... + a^N_{in} X^N_n$$

but also the amount E^N_i. When the North exports i to the South—that is, when the amount E^N_i is positive—this amount represents an additional demand for resource i in the North by the exporters in the North. Thus our resource constraint becomes

$$a^N_{i1} X^N_1 + a^N_{i2} X^N_2 + ... + a^N_{in} X^N_n + E^N_i \leqslant R^N_i \qquad i = 1,..., m. \qquad (16.4)$$

When the North imports i from the South—that is, when the amount E^N_i is negative—this amount represents an additional supply of resource i in the North made available by exporters in the South. So to the quantity R^N_i, the existing supplies in the North, we must add $-E^N_i$, which is a positive quantity because E^N_i is negative. Thus, our resource constraint now becomes

$$a^N_{i1} X^N_1 + a^N_{i2} X^N_2 + ... + a^N_{in} X^N_n \leqslant R^N_i - E^N_i \qquad i = 1,..., m. \qquad (16.4a)$$

If in 16.4a we transfer E^N_i from the right side of the inequality to the left side, we see that we obtain Equation 16.4. Thus, 16.4 can serve as a statement of the constraint when E^N_i is either positive or negative.

Generally speaking, we set down the resource constraints for our two region case as

$$a_{11}^N X_1^N + a_{12}^N X_2^N + \dots \quad + a_{1n}^N X_n^N + E_1^N \leqslant R_1^N \tag{16.5}$$

$$a_{m1}^N X_1^N + a_{m2}^N X_2^N + \dots + a_{mn}^N X_n^N + E_m^N \leqslant R_m^N$$

$$a_{11}^S X_1^S + a_{12}^S X_2^S + \dots \quad + a_{1n}^S X_n^S + E_1^S \leqslant R_1^S$$

$$a_{m1}^S X_1^S + a_{m2}^S X_2^S + \dots + a_{mn}^S X_n^S + E_m^S \leqslant R_m^S$$

Suppose we are able, as we have done elsewhere,[1] to conceive and design a set of shipment activities between the two regions involving only linear relationships, as in our production activities. If we impose the further constraint that no activity be operated at a negative level either in the North or the South—that is,

$$X_1^N \geqslant 0,\dots, X_n^N \geqslant 0; \quad X_1^S \geqslant 0,\dots, X_n^S \geqslant 0 \tag{16.6}$$

then we can ask the computer to solve for a set of activity levels for both regions—that is, for $X_1^{N*},\dots, X_n^{N*}, X_1^{S*},\dots, X_n^{S*}$ to minimize Z of Equation 16.2, subject to the constraints expressed in Equations 16.5 and 16.6 and Equation 16.3.

To state the problem in compact form, let

$$X = \begin{bmatrix} X_1^N \\ \vdots \\ X_n^N \\ X_1^S \\ \vdots \\ X_n^S \end{bmatrix} \quad R = \begin{bmatrix} R_1^N \\ \vdots \\ R_m^N \\ R_1^S \\ \vdots \\ R_m^S \end{bmatrix} \quad E = \begin{bmatrix} E_1^N \\ \vdots \\ E_m^N \\ E_1^S \\ \vdots \\ E_m^S \end{bmatrix} \quad \begin{aligned} E^N &= \begin{bmatrix} E_1^N \\ \vdots \\ E_m^N \end{bmatrix} \\[2em] E^S &= \begin{bmatrix} E_1^S \\ \vdots \\ E_m^S \end{bmatrix} \end{aligned}$$
$$(2n\times 1) \qquad (2m\times 1) \qquad (2m\times 1)$$

and $a_{ij} =$ $(2m\times 2n)$

$$\begin{bmatrix} a_{11}^N ,\dots a_{1n}^N & \\ \vdots & \\ a_{m1}^N ,\dots, a_{mn}^N & \\ & a_{11}^S ,\dots, a_{1n}^S \\ & \vdots \\ & a_{m1}^S ,\dots, a_{mn}^S \end{bmatrix} \tag{16.7}$$

[1] See W. Isard, *Methods of Regional Analysis* (Cambridge: M.I.T. Press, 1960), Chap. 10.

and let

$$p \atop (1 \times 2n) = p_1^N, ..., p_n^N, p_1^S, ..., p_n^S \qquad (16.8)$$

Our aim is then to

$$\max Z = pX \qquad (16.9)$$

subject to

$$aX + E \leqslant R \qquad (16.10)$$
$$X \geqslant 0$$
$$E^N + E^S = 0$$

Per Capita Income Equalization as a Constraint

We now have a framework for multiregion linear programming analysis. Next consider the specific goals that motivated us to formulate this framework. One goal is per capita income equalization between regions. What does this mean? If we specify the population of the North and South as Q^N and Q^S, respectively, and the income earned in these regions as Y^N and Y^S, respectively, then per capita income equalization implies

$$\frac{Y^S}{Q^S} = \frac{Y^N}{Q^N} \qquad (16.11)$$

For our problem we can imagine that the populations Q^N and Q^S are given beforehand, so that Equation 16.11 becomes

$$Y^S = \frac{Q^S}{Q^N} Y^N = kY^N \qquad (16.12)$$

where k is the ratio of the South's population to the North's. For example, it may be 2. Income cannot be given beforehand. It is directly related to gross national product, and in maximizing gross national product we necessarily treat it as a variable. However, we can define income fairly well after we solve for the X's.

Take the first industry in the North. Its level of output is X_1^N. Per unit level of output, it uses a certain amount of labor, which we designate our l resource. The input of labor (in man-hours) per unit output of industry 1 in region N is a_{l1}^N and the total amount of labor (in man-hours) used by industry 1 in the North can be represented by $a_{l1}^N X_1^N$. Now let p_l^N represent the price of a unit of labor in the North; that is, the wage paid per man-hour. Then $p_l^N a_{l1}^N X_1^N$ represents the wages earned by labor in industry 1 in the North. Similarly, $p_l^N a_{l2}^N X_2^N$ represents the income earned by labor in industry 2 in the North, and $p_l^N a_{l3}^N X_3^N$, ..., $p_l^N a_{ln}^N X_n^N$ represents the income earned by labor in industry 3, and finally industry n in the North. Altogether, total wages earned by labor in the several industries in the North are

$$Y^N = p_l^N a_{l1}^N X_1^N + p_l^N a_{l2}^N X_2^N + ... + p_l^N a_{ln}^N X_n^N = \sum_i p_l^N a_{li}^N X_i^N$$

Likewise, we can obtain Y^S, total wages earned by labor in the South, as

$$Y^S = \sum_i p_l^S a_{li}^S X_i^S$$

We now impose on our linear program the per capita income equalization constraint of Equation 16.12. It is

$$\sum_i p_l^S a_{li}^S X_i^S \geqslant k \sum_i p_l^N a_{li}^N X_i^N \tag{16.13}$$

for a situation in which the North would have the higher per capita income were there no constraint. The meaning of this constraint is most easily perceived if we suppose the populations, Q^N and Q^S, of the two regions to be the same so that $k = 1$. The computer will then solve for a new set of optimal outputs

$$X_1^N {**},..., X_n^N {**}, X_1^S {**},..., X_n^S {**}$$

consistent with the old and this new constraint.

For some nations, such as Japan, where the per capita income differences among regions are not too sharp, per capita income equalization may be considered a reasonable and feasible constraint. In most nations, however, it would not be. A more reasonable constraint would focus on narrowing the existing discrepancies in per capita income among regions. For example, if for a given base year the lowest per capita income region had one-sixth of the income per head of the highest per capita income region, a reasonable program might specify that per capita income in any one region not be less than one-fifth that in any other. For a two-region society, our constraint might then read

$$\sum_i p_l^S a_{li}^S X_i^S \geqslant \frac{k}{5} \sum_i p_l^N a_{li}^N X_i^N \tag{16.14}$$

Again the meaning of this constraint is most easily perceived when $k = 1$.

Any time a constraint is imposed and becomes binding, in the sense that it is effective and disturbs what otherwise would be, it forces the system to be less efficient from the standpoint of achieving the objective stated in the objective function. For example, suppose the objective is to maximize gross national product and we run the program without constraints. Suppose it turns out that per capita income in the North would exceed the per capita income in the South by more than a factor of five. Then when we require the system to operate subject to Equation 16.14, we disturb the otherwise efficient operation of the system. In a sense, we force the system into a certain mold and introduce by fiat a certain amount of inefficiency into its operations. The maximum amount of GNP that is achievable is reduced. This reduction represents the cost of imposing the constraint.

Note that we now have at our disposal a very important tool for central planning societies. We can develop cost functions that tell us how the amount of GNP foregone (a cost) changes as we change the magnitudes of different kinds of constraints. For example, suppose there are two regions with equal population so that k as defined in Equation 16.12 is unity. Then we may restate constraint 16.14 as

$$\sum_i p_l^S a_{li}^S X_i^S \geq \frac{1}{\nu} \sum_i p_l^N a_{li}^N X_i^N \qquad (16.15)$$

where we let ν be the factor by which per capita income in the highest per capita income region (the North) cannot exceed per capita income in the lowest (the South). Suppose in Figure 16.1 we measure the ν factor along the horizontal. Suppose we let ν successively take the values 12, 11, 10, 9,..., 1. When we run the program without a per capita income constraint, it may turn out that the highest per capita income region has six times the per capita income of the lowest. This means that if we set the factor at 6 or higher, our constraint will not interfere with the operation of the system. Consequently, there will be no cost. However, if we reduce ν below 6, then we force costs upon the system. For example, if ν were set equal to 5, the cost in GNP might be $4 million. We indicate this cost by point E in Figure 16.1, where we measure GNP foregone or cost in terms of GNP along the vertical.

If we set $\nu = 4$, the cost in GNP might be $12 million, as indicated by point E' in Figure 16.1. If we set $\nu = 3$, the cost might be $23 million, as indicated by point E''. In brief, we can consider all possible values for ν (except 0) and put them in the computer, which then tells us the amount of GNP foregone. We can

Figure 16.1   GNP Foregone as Related to Constraint Magnitudes

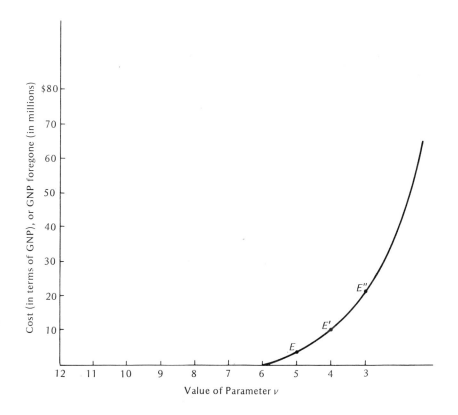

plot these results to yield the cost curve depicted in Figure 16.1. Note how valuable a tool this curve is. It presents in dollars-and-cents terms the cost to the nation in foregone GNP. It indicates that although some regions in a nation may gain by having their per capita incomes rise, on the average each person in the nation loses, as binding constraints result in reduced GNP. There comes a point where any further move toward income equalization may not be justified because of the excessive cost in terms of GNP foregone. In fact, a situation might develop, if the constraint of equal per capita income were imposed, in which GNP and per capita income in most of the regions would be greatly reduced. It then might be better to relax the constraint and simply transfer income from one region to the next by taxing incomes in the rich regions and distributing some of the tax receipts as food and rent subsidies to the needy in the poor regions.

We have now illustrated one powerful use of the linear programming approach. Clearly, even for such a simple goal as the narrowing of per capita income differences, major conflicts arise. Why should the region of highest per capita income (say Croatia in Yugoslavia) support the region of lowest per capita income (say Macedonia in Yugoslavia)? Why should the former's resources and gross regional product be taxed in order to foster development in the latter? Residents of the high-income region can easily argue that it would be inefficient to shift resources in this way. They can argue that opportunities for capital investment and industrial development are most profitable in their region and least profitable in the lowest per capita income region. This is why the observed differences in per capita income have arisen. They would argue that all development should be in their high-income region, and perhaps that population should be shifted out of the low-income region. In this way, they would contend, the nation as well as all its population would be better off. This is an old argument, which we have already encountered in Chapters 3 and 8. There we raised the question: Should people be moved to well-paying jobs (which generally exist in the high-income regions) or should jobs be moved (provided) to the people in the low-income regions by investing capital in new plants and equipment there? We do not wish to repeat the pros and cons of this argument.

However, we can now push our thinking a bit further. Suppose that on the basis of moral and humanitarian (Christian) principles, those in the high-income region are persuaded to make some contribution to the welfare of the low-income region. They might be persuaded to set aside say 2 percent of their gross regional product for investment in the low-income region. They consider this amount to be a very generous contribution. But though such an amount may slow down the rate of increase in the discrepancies, it may not forestall an increase in absolute amount. Thus, it is not consistent with per capita income equalization. Accordingly, political leaders of the low-income region may insist on more than a 2 percent contribution. They may want a contribution of 10 to 20 percent of the gross regional product of the high-income region. A major conflict therefore arises, namely the determination of a fair or reasonable contribution from high-income to low-income regions. In general, those in the high-income region will propose a low figure and those in the low-income region a high figure. The difference between the two will be major. This problem has in fact been confronted by countries such as Italy, where the two regions were North and South. The central government there passed legislation in the 1950s specifically making available at least a certain minimum amount of funds for investments in the

South. The problem has also been confronted in Poland, India, Yugoslavia, Japan, and other countries. It is a problem that has been discussed not only in political circles but also among economists, regional scientists, planners, lawyers, and many other social scientists and professionals. No appropriate basis for resolving the conflict has been developed in the past, except what results from the hap-hazard, random, and emotional interactions of political leaders and their con-stituents. But now we are able to pose the problem in more explicit form by approaching development from a programming standpoint. As we have shown in the discussion of Figure 16.1, we are now able to identify one of the major costs of achieving a particular goal, namely GNP foregone.

Balanced Industrialization as a Constraint

Per capita income equalization is only one specific goal that has been discussed widely in the literature and in the political arena. Another goal that has come under widespread debate and discussion is that of balanced industry or balanced industrial development. Now, what is meant by balanced industry? Again, there are many possible interpretations. One very broad interpretation would insist that no less than a certain percentage (say 20 percent) of the labor force be employed in the manufacturing sectors, and no less than another percentage (say 25 percent) in the service and tertiary sectors. This view of balanced industrial development is particularly prevalent in regions where income earnings in agricul-ture are low. The populations of these regions look to greater balance in the sense of having more jobs in manufacturing and services and relatively fewer jobs in agriculture. However, in regions having high agriculture productivity and incomes, especially where the soil is fertile and access to markets excellent, the need for jobs in manufacturing is less pressing; and if any drive for balanced industrial development exists, it is likely to be weak. This has been the case for Denmark.

Other views of balanced development focus on other kinds of classifications of economic activity. For example, one view may be stated with reference to the two-digit SIC classification of industry, as recorded in our input-output tables (see p. 122). The categories, food processing (SIC 20), textile mill products (SIC 22), apparel (SIC 23), leather and leather products (SIC 31), are older-type industries. They usually require less skill on the part of workers. They involve less investment per worker, turn out less dollar value of product per worker, and pay less wages. In contrast stand electrical machinery (SIC 36), mo-tor vehicles (SIC 37), and professional and scientific equipment (SIC 38). These are industries in which more skill and training are required per worker, more capital is invested per worker, more dollar value of product per worker is yielded, and thus higher wages paid. In this context, balanced industrial development for a region endowed with older-type, low-wage industries means more jobs in the newer-type, high-wage industries. Sometimes this approach is presented in terms of the categories of old, oldish, newish, and new industry, or of durable and nondurable manufacturing, or other broad classes.

Balanced development may also be viewed in terms of different kinds of proc-esses. There are early-stage production processes which primarily involve working ores and processing agricultural crops. They often turn out low-valued products and pay low wages. There are other processes at later stages in production, where more skill and investment are required. These include steel fabrication, fine glass manufacture, and dress design; they often turn out high-valued products and pay high wages. Hence, those regions with a heavy concentration of industry in agriculture, mining, and related processing activities view balanced development as bringing more of the processes involved in the later stages in production.

Balanced development might be approached from the standpoint of reducing the cyclical instability of one's economic structure or export activities. There are certain products whose prices on the world market fluctuate widely from month to month, or even week to week, and for which demands change rapidly. There are other products for which both demand and prices are very stable. Balanced production might mean a shift toward producing less of the former and more of the latter.

Balanced development is often viewed in terms of self-sufficiency (autarchy). In certain respects, there are advantages to being self-sufficient. The region can be less dependent on imports for certain basic products and on exports to obtain the foreign exchange to purchase essential imports. In this sense, balanced development means moving in the direction of reducing import dependence—it means reducing the amount of imports even at the expense of exports and foreign exchange earnings. This particular version of balanced development is particularly significant for cities and regions that are one-industry economies, or are completely dependent on the export of one raw material. Such an economy is very vulnerable to middle-run and even long-run changes in the export price and markets for its product. Therefore, economists and regional scientists generally concede that it is worthwhile to trade off some efficiency for some stability, obtained by engaging in new, but less profitable economic pursuits.

Each version of balanced industrialized development can be made explicit and at least partially effected in the operation of a programming model. For example, take the first view. The requirement that 20 percent of the labor force be in the manufacturing sectors means perhaps 3,000 jobs in those sectors. Suppose the manufacturing sectors run from numbers 3 to 10 in our sector classification. If the coefficient a_{li} represents the labor input (man-hour) per unit output of the ith industry, and a full-time employee works 2,000 hours per year, then this requirement can be stated in constraint form as

$$\sum_i \frac{a_{li} X_i}{2000} \geqslant 3000 \qquad i = 3,4,\ldots, 10$$

The additional requirement that there be at least 25 percent of employment in the service trades, corresponding say to sectors 11 to 17 in our classification scheme, can be stated as

$$\sum_j \frac{a_{lj} X_j}{2000} \geqslant 3750 \qquad j = 11,12,\ldots, 17$$

Similarly, we can develop meaningful constraints for other notions of balanced development. To cite one more example, if the labor force is 50,000, and we are concerned with self-sufficiency, we might set up a series of constraints

$$\frac{a_{l1}X_1}{2000} \geqslant 1500$$

$$\frac{a_{l2}X_2}{2000} \geqslant 2100$$

$$\frac{a_{l3}X_3}{2000} \geqslant 1200$$

$$\begin{matrix} \cdot & & \cdot \\ \cdot & & \cdot \\ \cdot & & \cdot \end{matrix}$$

$$\frac{a_{ln}X_n}{2000} \geqslant 1000$$

where

$$\sum_{i=1}^{n} \frac{a_{li}X_i}{2000} \geqslant 50{,}000$$

As with the per capita income equalization goal, conflicts among regions emerge with regard to a balanced-industry goal for each region. These regions where the low-income activities are concentrated and where labor productivity is low will strongly support balanced-industry goals and the imposition of appropriate constraints on development programming. Those regions with a very large share of industries and service activities with high-paying jobs and a small share of those with low-paying jobs will, of course, strongly resist the imposition of such constraints. Again, the conflict must be resolved either through the explicit use of cooperative procedures or through the political process. Of course, one real alternative is to do nothing at all.

**Constraints Relating to Land Reform, Agricultural
Subsidy, and other Goals**

Still other specific goals can be considered in a programming format for development. For example, the focus might be on total employment rather than income. Instead of constraints relating to per capita incomes there might be a constraint assuring a minimum number of jobs in each region (where, in view of the different populations of the different regions, each region may have a different number). Or the concern might be with insuring a healthy overall growth rate for each region. An appropriate constraint here might specify that the gross regional product of each region increase by at least 4 percent per annum. Or the concern might be with full employment, with a constraint perhaps requiring that employment in each region be not less than 90 percent of its total labor force.

As suggested by our discussion, other concerns and constraints might be relevant. One constraint might read: Imports from the rest of the world should not exceed some dollar magnitude. Another might read: Exports to the rest of the world should be at least as large as some other dollar magnitude. Others, relating to environmental quality, might require that the emissions of any particular pollutant, say particulates, not exceed a certain level for the region, or that the ambient air quality not fall below a certain level. (See the discussion in Chapter 14.)

Even more broadly, one may distinguish between agricultural activities pursued on the large landholdings of big business, wealthy capitalists, or others of great power, and agricultural activities pursued on small, or very small, landholdings by small independent farmers. Even though these agricultural activities may produce the same product, they can be kept quite separate in a programming format. Often, too, their input coefficients are quite different, so that from a technical standpoint they should be viewed as two unique sectors.

If, then, one is concerned with land reform (or other reform within the agricultural sector) one might require, in a development plan extending over several years, that the ratio of agricultural output by small landowners to that by large landowners increase by at least a certain percent, say 5 percent, per year. Of course, still more drastic constraints associated with agricultural and land reform can be imposed.

Still another goal in regional development planning might relate to the amount of investment in a region based on foreign capital, or the extent to which local industries are managed by foreign personnel. This concern is linked to the fairly common belief in some underdeveloped regions that the effect of foreign investment is very undesirable. It is true that such investment might enable each local laborer to be more productive, in the sense that he has more machinery of a higher quality with which to work. Moreover, if the plant in which the foreign investment is made is operated by managers, engineers, and other personnel brought into the region, the local worker may be more productive simply because he is managed by more experienced and better-trained personnel. The latter can provide superior assistance to help the local worker to understand better the operation of his machine. Yet the very presence of efficient foreign capital and management means that the most profitable local opportunities are gobbled up by outsiders, and are not available for exploitation by the less efficient local capital and management. The potential for accumulating local capital on the basis of savings from local profits is dried up. Also, the less efficient local managers are denied the opportunity to learn from experience. (Such experience may be desirable despite the many mistakes that may be made.) Consequently, there is little tendency for a managerial class or engineer class to develop within the local population. A state of long-run dependence and subservience to foreign capital and management results. Hence, with the objective of getting rid of such dependence and subservience, we can imagine a region or nation imposing constraints requiring that the number of native engineers or amount of local capital employed be an increasing percent of total engineers or total capital employed, respectively. This might be in terms of its industries in general or of certain key sectors like steel, petrochemicals, and research and development.

As indicated earlier, a programming framework has strongest appeal for those countries in which there is a tradition of central planning or in which recent changes in political and social life have made people favorably disposed toward the notion of central planning. In societies like the United States where the tradition of laissez-faire capitalism is still strong, the possibilities of comprehensive programming and planning are much more restricted. Nonetheless, from the standpoint of regional development, there are sectors in these societies in which the programming approach may be fruitfully used. For example, consider the agriculture sector in the U.S. economy. It is notorious for being a sector that is slow to change, where much rural poverty (often hidden) exists. It is subject to severe fluctuations in prices and in the income of its enterprises, whether they be small independent farmers or large commercial operations. Also, this sector has a considerable history of subsidization. A government bureaucracy has developed to handle this subsidization. In the minds of some, it is highly inefficient. Because the federal government is extensively subsidizing the agricultural sector, with little hope that it can extract itself from much of its heavy commitment, it is appropriate for the federal government to seek to minimize that subsidy where it can. It should at least move in a direction of making the subsidy more efficient in terms of support given to the agriculture sector.

Hence, it makes sense to pursue programming analysis for the agricultural sector of the United States, treating the country as a set of regions delineated in terms of soil and other characteristics relevant to agricultural production and markets. Constraints should reflect political, social, and economic needs and realities, as well as possible states of affairs with regard to such factors as markets for different products, technology, and levels of gross national product and population. Then programs can be run to determine the most efficient level (output) of each type of agricultural activity in each region. With a programming solution on hand for each of several reasonable sets of assumptions and constraints, the federal government should be in a position to make desirable changes in its pattern and types of subsidies. That is, policies with regard to subsidies and operations of the Department of Agriculture can be examined explicitly in terms of their effectiveness in achieving the goals established by legislation. Multiregion linear programming analysis of the agricultural sectors has been conducted in the United States and has thrown useful light on both appropriate national and regional development policies. Much more insight is possible with further research in a programming framework, both within the U.S. and other parts of the world.

In short, innumerable relevant constraints can be imposed in a programming format for development, and frequently can yield penetrating insights for evaluating the feasibility and outcomes of alternative policies. However, the resolution of the conflicts among interest groups that have different preferences for different goals is not resolved. Here it is interesting to refer to the central assistance program for projects of national importance developed in the late sixties for the states of India. As Lefeber and Datta-Chaudhuri note, "The problem of central assistance became urgent in connection with NDC's [National Development Council's] deliberations on the Fourth Five Year-Plan for the period 1969–70 to 1973–74. In the autumn of 1968 the Chief Ministers of the States agreed that objective criteria were needed for the distribution of central assistance and that each of the criteria must be suitably weighted to show its relative importance. Accordingly, NDC accepted the principle that the extent of a State's participation in central assistance should be determined by the size of its population and income, together with its performance measured by tax effort and its development expenditure in a well-defined classification. In order to make these four criteria operationally applicable, NDC also agreed on a set of weights to establish the relative importance of each of them, namely 0.6, 0.1, 0.1, and 0.2 for population, income, taxation and development expenditure, respective." [2]

By placing a high weight on population and low weights on performance (tax effect and development expenditure) and on income, the NDC was clearly placing primary emphasis on narrowing the per capita income differences among regions— that is, on the achievement of a more equitable income distribution. As a consequence, it may be asserted by some, especially those concerned with maximizing investments in basic industry, that the usefulness of central assistance to motivate development effort was seriously diminished.

REGIONAL DEVELOPMENT: CONFLICT OVER PROGRAMS

Suppose that in some way or other all the basic conflicts over both values and goals have been resolved. There still remain a number of conflicts to be faced. Again, these conflicts become more explicit when we use a linear programming format.

Suppose we confront a particular situation where goal-oriented constraints like per capita income equalization and balanced industrialization are not as relevant as other kinds of constraints. A central government, sensitive to public opinion, might judge that public response would be more favorable if certain specific and tangible programs—relating to the provision of low-income housing, supplementary food, education, and medical care—were effected, rather than the more nebulous objective of narrowing per capita income discrepancies among regions. Or, the government might doubt that its population, especially those who have known only poverty, would know how to spend its increased income wisely. It may fear that too much of this increase would go for the purchase of conspicuous consumption items, such as color television sets, second-hand automobiles, and fancy kitchen gadgets, and not enough for meeting basic nutrition, schooling, and medical needs. This concern might be particularly acute where widespread conditions of poor diet habits, inadequate medical care, and illiteracy have resulted in a labor force of low productivity and where scarce resources make it essential that the productivity of the labor force be increased. Put more pointedly, because constraints generate costs in terms of GNP and profitable investments foregone, the government may be very much concerned that such costs are balanced by real benefits in terms of a more productive labor force as a result of better nutrition, housing, medical care, and education, and not by the questionable benefits resulting from added income being frittered away in satisfying nonessential needs.

Further, the economic markets of one or more regions, especially if they are low-income, may be working very inefficiently and imperfectly. Monopolists may be exploiting consumers, charging high prices for low-quality goods. They may capture a good part of the added income of a poverty-stricken population which has little experience for judging whether or not it is being cheated. And the government may feel that it is not in a position to control this exploitation.

---

[2] Louis Lefeber and Mrinal Datta-Chandhuri, *Regional Development Experiences and Prospects in South and Southeast Asia* (Paris Mouton & Co., 1971), p. 55.

Moreover, there may be a number of negative externalities that the government would like to avoid. Some of these may arise from the independent behavior of many consumers, the behavior of each having only a negligible effect—as discussed in connection with the litter problem in Chapter 10. For example, if too many people buy automobiles, the road network might become seriously congested. This, in turn, would cause a major slowdown of truck movement of the commodities essential for the efficient operation of the industrial sectors. To combat such congestion, more investment in roads would be required. But this could take place only at the expense of other sorely needed undertakings, such as a new cement plant.

In short, the government may prefer not to think just in terms of broad goals such as per capita income equalization or balanced industrialization, but rather in terms of some of these goals (perhaps only to a small extent) *and* specific, tangible programs.

With regard to specific programs, the government might wish to set some or all of the following constraints: (1) the deliveries of certain basic foods to each region should be not less than a certain amount per capita, with the food to be offered at modest price; (2) the number of low-income housing units to be constructed in each region should be not less than a prespecified amount, which might vary considerably from region to region; (3) the number of hospital beds, doctors, and nurses in each region must not be less than certain prescribed levels, with free medical services and supplies up to a certain amount per capita; (4) the number of schools and teachers at the primary level should be not less than what is required by proposed legislation on compulsory education to combat illiteracy.

Or, suppose the government is distrustful of the existing pool of entrepreneurs in the several regions. They may already possess excessive amounts of economic and political power. They may be insufficiently innovative, excessively corrupt, or inattentive to the needs of the poor laboring population. Hence, speaking about general employment and balanced-industry goals does not strike a responsive chord among concerned government officials. These officials know the realities of a colonialistic-type, oligarchical power structure. The government may want to upgrade the small, restricted pool of entrepreneurs and managers by bringing in new faces. It might therefore want to encourage undertakings by small businessmen capable of initiative. It may opt to subsidize local firms that are independent of the large regional and national enterprises having all kinds of interlocking directorates. It may want to provide specific kinds of infrastructures in small impoverished communities to facilitate new local ventures, so that these communities can pull themselves up by their own bootstraps. In terms of constraints of a linear program, it may require the following: (1) the level of expenditures for the construction of local roads (to enable small independent ventures to ship their output to other regions) must be above some minimum level; (2) the amount of funds available for low-interest loans for small business in each region is to be not less than another minimum figure; (3) the amount of assistance, in the form of services of business consultants, engineers, lawyers, and others should be not less than still another minimum level; and perhaps (4) a small office of area development specialists is to be established in each region, of at least some minimum size.

In short, numerous kinds of specific programs can be visualized, each able to be stated as a constraint in a programming model. For example, on deliveries of

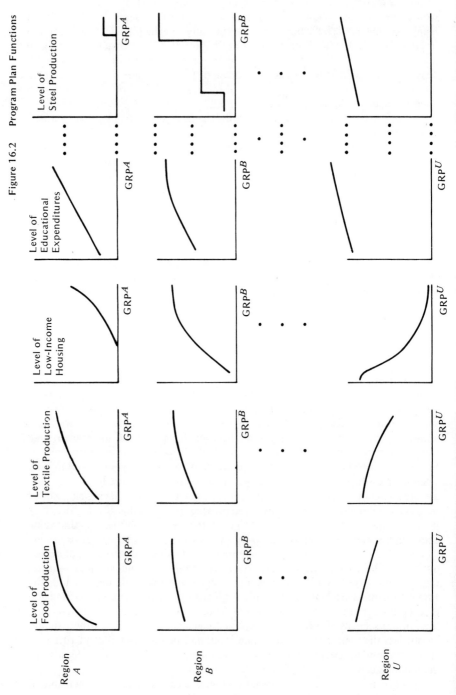

Figure 16.2   Program Plan Functions

a basic food (rice), which we shall now designate by the symbol g, to the households (sector h) in region S (the South), the constraint states that the output X_g^S of rice in region S *less* the amount $\sum_i a_{gi}^S X_i^S$ consumed by various industries in region S *less* the amount E_g^S exported (or *plus* the amount imported) shall be greater than the established per capita minimum consumption level a_{gh}^S times the South's population Q^S. That is, the constraint reads

$$X_g^S - a_{g1}^S X_1^S - a_{g2}^S X_2^S - ... - a_{gn}^S X_n^S - E_g^S \geq a_{gh}^S Q^S$$

At this point, we do not wish to get involved in the technicalities of setting up the many other possible constraints in proper form. The topic is appropriately treated in advanced courses. Rather, we wish to move on to the diverse kinds of conflict that arise when a government focuses on specific programs in its regional development planning, and more importantly, to a discussion of their resolution.

Clearly, when there are specific programs, there will be differences among individuals and interest groups as to their preferences for these programs. The construction industry and the industries furnishing inputs to the construction industry go all-out for a program for the construction of new roads. The agriculture sector fully supports specific food programs that will increase the market for their outputs, especially when the government is ready to provide whatever subsidies or other forms of incentives that are required to increase the food supply to achieve the minimum standards. The pharmaceutical manufacturers strongly favor more medical aid programs, though they may not be too happy with the increased level of business and income taxation that may accompany the programs. In general, those who are relatively well-off will disfavor such programs, because these programs do imply increased tax burdens, especially if the taxation is progressive. Those who are impoverished favor such programs, particularly when the taxation is strongly progressive. They may be less inclined to favor such programs if the taxation is regressive.

Such differences in preferences generate conflicts of all sorts. Even those of us having just a smattering of knowledge of the political process from reading about legislation proposed in Congress, platforms adopted at the national conventions of political parties in presidential election years, and local legislation and political fights know too well the great variety and different intensities of these conflicts.

We may imagine, however, that at times these conflicts may be resolved. In central planning types of economies there may emerge plans that specify targets and paths to these targets. With respect to each type of program, such a plan may be designated a *program plan function*.

We illustrate some program plan functions in Figure 16.2. The top row of graphs in this figure represents the functions pertaining to region A. The first one refers to the level of food production, and indicates the plan for increasing that level as the gross regional product of region A increases. Here, region A is viewed as being low-income and underdeveloped, so that large increases in food production with increase in GRP are judged highly desirable in order to improve the health and productivity of its population. The second graph in the top row refers to the level of textile production. We see that significant increases in this level are planned as GRP grows, both to provide more clothing for the population and to develop goods for export purposes. With such goods, credits can be earned outside the region to finance the purchase of equipment and materials for constructing new industrial plants. The third graph refers to the level of low-income housing. According to the plan, this level is to remain at zero until a certain level of GRP is achieved, at which time the region can afford to divert some of its scarce resources to low-income housing construction. The fourth graph refers to the level of educational expenditures. Here we observe that the plan involves steady increases as GRP grows. Finally, the last graph in the first row refers to the level of steel production. Although the region would like to undertake steel production immediately, the planning authorities are not able to set aside funds for investment in this industry until the GRP of region A has increased substantially.

The second row of charts pertains to region B, which we take to be farther along the path of development, having a substantially higher GRP and per capita income than that of region A. Because it already has a high level of per capita food production, the plan for region B involves a small increase in food production as its GRP increases. Likewise with textile production. In the case of low-income housing, however, region B will have the resources to engage immediately in a substantial program as its GRP increases, and to achieve a high level for that program with further GRP increases. With regard to educational expenditures, region B is already at a high level, and its plan calls for substantial increases in the level of educational expenditures as its GRP increases. Finally, with regard to steel production, the region is producing at a low level. It plans for substantial lumpy increases as its GRP grows.

Finally, we consider region U, a high per capita income region, highly industrialized, and in general very well-off. According to its plan, the level of food production will fall as its GRP increases. This reflects the long-run tendency for its labor force to shift out of agriculture to more remunerative trades, and the increasing desirability of importing agricultural products from other regions. Similarly, textile production falls off. With regard to low-income housing, the level of that program is high already and its plan calls for the completion of all required or desired number of units in the relatively near future. Both educational expenditures and steel production are already high, and its plan calls for steady increases in these levels as its GRP mounts.

Figure 16.2 summarizes, in a very simplistic manner, how a planned economy, having planning at both the national and regional levels, might put down a set of plans with respect to the future development of each of the regions. Each of these regional plans may be loosely or tightly articulated with respect to the national plan. If they are loosely connected, their tie to the national plan might involve just central assistance of the sort developed by the National Development Council in India, mentioned earlier. If these plans are tightly articulated, then in working them out, considerations of national efficiency and productivity as well as regional efficiency and productivity would be involved. Consequently, for a basic industry like steel, the planned increases in the several regions would need to be consistent with the overall development plan for steel in the nation. This would require that each location be a least-cost point for the markets it is designed to serve. We speak of least cost here in the same manner as we spoke about it in Chapter 6, where we discussed comparative cost analysis.

Also, if the regional plans are tightly articulated with the national plan, there must be a meaningful linkage between the projected exports of each region (e.g., the projected exports of textiles by region A) and the projected imports in each region (e.g., the projected imports of textiles by region U)—as well as the projected exports and imports for the nation as a whole.

Further, if these regional planning functions are finely articulated with respect to the national plan, they imply an allocation of the investment funds (as central assistance from the central planning authorities) to each of the programs in each of the regions in ways relevant for improvement of the social welfare of the nation. That is, the allocation must be related to an overall social welfare function for the nation, and one that is obviously sensitive to the income distribution variable. We have seen how the social welfare function can be illumined by the use of indifference curves, as discussed in the last chapter. The social welfare function must be consistent also with the program plan functions of Figure 16.2. Thus, the pattern of increases in national levels of expenditure for education and low-income housing associated with a maximum advance in social welfare (see Figure 15.3) must also be consistent with what is depicted in the charts for the several regions in Figure 16.2.

Observe that the expenditure levels for the different programs, with changes in the GRP of region A, can be represented by a point in Euclidean space. If there are ten programs, then the point would be in ten-dimensional space, where we would measure the level of each of the programs along a dimension. Our set of program plans for region A, as given by the charts along the first row of Figure 16.2, could then be represented by a series of these points (that is, a line path) in ten-dimensional space. In a finely articulated national plan there would be a series of points for each region, and all the series together might indicate an optimal development path—optimal in terms of maximizing social welfare for the nation over some planning horizon.

COALITION ANALYSIS AND CONFLICT RESOLUTION PERTAINING TO DEVELOPMENT POLICY

We have presented in graphic form what a central or regional planning authority might consider desirable with respect to specific programs for each of several regions. We do not need to repeat that the decisions they reach and the plans they formulate reflect the resolution of numerous kinds of conflicts through the political process. We also do not need to reiterate that we have relatively little knowledge of the basic rationale, logic, or behavioral properties (desirable or undesirable) that underlie the political process. Each political process that has been studied is unique in terms of historical setting, cultural background, specific institutions, personality of the actors, and numerous other factors. But we can make some beginnings at analysis to suggest a rationale for, or some desirable properties of, the political process—beginnings that are related to the kinds of joint actions and cooperative procedures we began to examine in Chapter 11.

Let there be a simple situation as follows. There are three regions: A, B, and C. Region A is heavily industrialized, with high per capita income and a strong, diverse economic base. It is most concerned with maintaining a high rate of growth of the national economy and a firm position in international trade. Region

B is a region having a modest per capita income, based primarily on the development of mining activities oriented to its mineral resources. It prefers a high rather
than a low rate of national growth. But its greatest concern is with developing
new kinds of industry in its area in order to become less vulnerable to the vicissi-
tudes of trade in the world markets, because its minerals are primarily exported
to such markets. It therefore sets highest priority on its own balanced industrial
development. Region *C* is a very low-income region with few resources and a
large population having low education and skill levels, poor housing, and grossly
inadequate nutrition and medical care.

Now, consider the operation of a central planning authority for this hypothetical three-region nation. We can do so either in terms of broad general goals or
specific programs. To simplify the analysis, suppose a budget for investment is
given to the central planning authority. Suppose that the broad goals guiding
investment decisions are (1) maximizing the growth rate of the economy or gross
national product; (2) the narrowing of per capita income differences among
regions; and (3) balanced industrial development for each region.

Region *A* most prefers to see the gross national product maximized. It advocates the choice of a pattern of investment consistent with the results of a linear
program designed to maximize gross national product, subject to none of the
constraints typically imposed to effect welfare programs. However, there would
be initial constraints explicitly stating the limited existing capacity of the nation's
industries for production and of its transport network to move goods. Region *A*
would prefer that all investment go into building up capacity in sectors where
bottlenecks might occur in the national growth process. Region *A* would prefer
that little of the investment funds be used to build schools, provide medical
facilities, or achieve balanced-industry structures. However, recognizing that a
revolution might possibly be fomented in region *C*, it does advocate some funds
for per capita income equalization programs (to nip in the bud any revolutionary
tendencies); and, in order to keep the second region moderately happy, it suggests
some funds for balanced industry programs. Let us suppose that it concludes that
it would be best if 60 percent of the investment funds were to be allocated for
investment in industry and transport where bottlenecks might occur, 30 percent
for per capita income equalization, and 10 percent for balanced industry programs.
Its most preferred action can be stated in terms of the allocation 60, 30, 10,
indicating the percentage amounts of the total investment funds to be devoted
to industry-transport investment, per capita income equalization, and balanced-
industry programs, respectively.

Region *B*, on the other hand, strongly prefers large investment in balanced-
industry programs, small investment for stimulating the growth of GNP, and
slightly larger investment for per capita income equalization. Its most desired
percentage allocation for national growth, per capita income equalization, and
balanced-industry programs is 10 percent, 20 percent, and 70 percent, respectively. That is, it most prefers the allocation 10, 20, 70.

In contrast, region *C*, having very low income, is only somewhat concerned
with national growth, still less concerned with balanced industrialization, and
intensely concerned with per capita income equalization. It most prefers the
allocation 20, 70, 10.

We have now stated the most preferred allocation of each of the three regions
with respect to three goals. It is easily seen that we could have done so with

respect to any three goals. Instead of maximizing national growth rate, region *A* might desire to minimize the tax rate, with the level of welfare programs approaching a level of zero. Region *B* might desire a modest tax rate, considerable financial assistance for metal fabricating and other manufacturing complexes to complement its existing economic activities, and low levels of social welfare programs. Region *C* might desire a very high tax rate and a progressive tax system, some assistance for the metals trades, and very large amounts for food, housing, and medical care programs. But whether we think of different goals or specific programs, we can have sharp conflicts.

At this point we may use some simple graphic analysis to clarify the nature of the conflict and possible ways of resolving it. In Figure 16.3 we measure, along the vertical axis, the percent of the budget that might go for investments in industry and transportation to avoid possible bottlenecks that might slow national growth. Along the horizontal axis, we measure the percent that might be spent on per capita income equalization. We connect the 100 percent points along these two axes by a straight line and shade in the area to the left and below that straight line. We obtain a triangular shaded area. This area, including the straight lines that bound it, contains all possible budget allocations for the three sets of programs.

Figure 16.3   The Budget Allocation Space

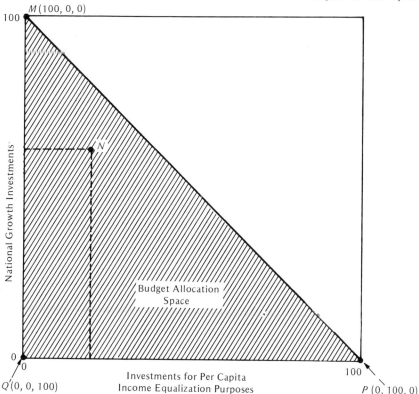

To show this, consider the three end points in Figure 16.3. Point *M* represents a situation where 100 percent of the budget goes for national growth investment, 0 percent for per capita income equalization, and 0 percent for balanced industrailization. We may designate this point with the three percentages 10, 0, 0. Point *P* corresponds to the budget allocation of 0 percent for industrial-transport investment, 100 percent for per capita income equalization, and 0 percent for balanced industrialization. We designate it by the three percentages 0, 100, 0. Point *Q* corresponds to 0 percent for industrial-transport investment, 0 percent for per capita income equalization, and 100 percent for balanced industrialization. We designate it by the three percentages 0, 0, 100. Any other point within the diagram, such as *N*, corresponds to an allocation to the three sets of programs, which adds up to 100 percent. For *N*, we have 60 percent for industrial-transport investment, 20 percent for per capita income equalization, and 20 percent for balanced industrialization. Note that in this diagram it is not necessary to measure the percentage to be allocated to balanced industrialization along a third axis. It must necessarily equal 100 percent less the percentage allocated to national growth and less the percentage allocated to per capita income equalization. To make this point clearer, consider the most preferred allocations of the three regions, with reference to Figure 16.4. As indicated, *A* most prefers the allocation

Figure 16.4   Most Preferred Allocation in the Budget Allocation Space

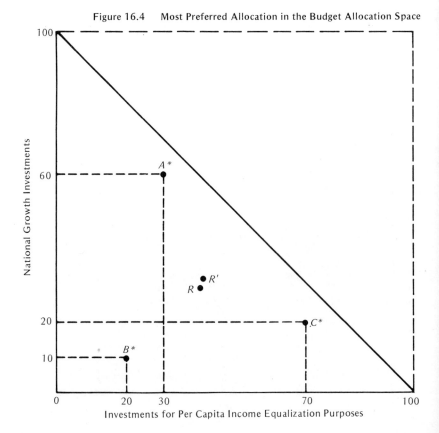

Investments for Per Capita Income Equalization Purposes

60, 30, 10. We determine the point A^* in the figure which corresponds to 60 percent along the vertical axis and 30 percent along the horizontal axis. Then the portion not allocated to these two goals, namely 10 percent, must be allocated to the third goal, balanced industrialization, which we do not need to measure along any axis. Likewise, B most prefers the allocation 10, 20, 70. Hence, to represent it we need only plot the two percentages 10 and 20 along the vertical and horizontal axis respectively, namely the point B^*, and the remaining 70 is automatically assigned to the third goal, balanced industrialization. So, too, with C's most preferred allocation of 20, 70, 10. Plotting the point (20, 70) on the figure, namely C^*, automatically implies the allocation 20, 70, 10.

We have plotted in Figure 16.4 the most preferred allocations of the three regions, A, B, and C. Because they do not correspond, there is conflict. In this situation, how can we establish the point (the percentage allocation) that corresponds to maximum social welfare? Should we apply weights to these most preferred positions? If so, should we take into account the intensity of needs of the three regions (as might be indicated by the marginal utilities of their last dollar of GRP)? Should we try to determine what is fair?

We have discussed all these questions in Chapter 13. We do not need to repeat that discussion. What we do want to do is see if we can develop a notion of political process that resolves the problem in some way that is reasonable, has elements of fairness, recognizes the strategic potential of each region in the situation, is consistent with constitutional mechanisms such as majority rule and other principles guiding the development of the culture, and appeals to all three regions because of these and other properties.

To begin, we must make another assumption: we specify the relative strengths, voting power, or economic might of the three regions. Suppose their strengths are 40 for region A, 25 for region B, and 35 for region C. Now consider region A. Suppose all the constituents of region A most prefer that allocation of funds by the planning agency corresponding to A^*. The leader of A is then 100 percent motivated to propose and fight for that allocation. In doing so, he receives 100 percent support from his constituency. However, the leader recognizes that he does not control sufficient votes to win in a situation in which a majority vote is required, which is the case here. He needs to form a coalition with at least one other party, B or C, in order to influence directly the percentage allocation that will ultimately be selected. He also recognizes that the percentage allocations most preferred by the other regions, B^* and C^*, respectively, are different than his. He therefore realizes that he has to compromise. That is, he must be willing to accept a less preferred outcome than A^* if he is going to be a member of a winning coalition. So he must ask: By how much will my support decline if I agree to a proposal for a different allocation than that corresponding to A^*? For example, he asks: How much support will I receive if I agree to the proposal represented by A' in Figure 16.5, which is at some distance from A^*? At this point we may imagine that he finds it convenient to construct a set of contour lines about A^*. For example, he estimates that with the allocation represented by A' in Figure 16.5, 75 percent of his constituents would support him. He would thus get 30 percent of the vote of the total nation. Likewise with all other percentage allocations represented by points on his 30 contour line. The allocation represented by point A'' would, according to his estimates, yield him

Figure 16.5   A Support Region in the Budget Allocation Space

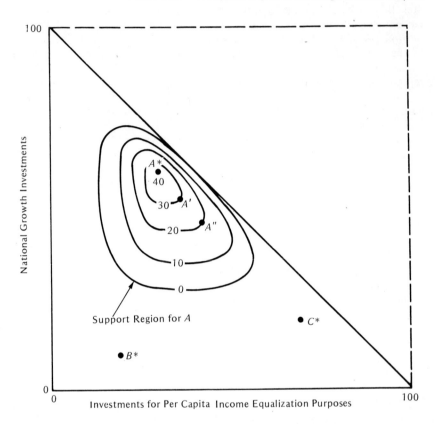

support from 50 percent of his constituents, and thus 20 percent of the vote of the total nation. So would all other percentage allocations represented by points on his 20 contour line. In similar manner he can construct his 10 and 0 contour lines. The contour lines in Figure 16.5 and others that *A* might construct can be taken to describe his support region. Any point within his zero support contour line yields him some positive support, and all others zero support.

In like manner, we can construct contour lines to describe the support regions of *B* and *C*, as they may estimate them. *B*'s contour lines circle around *B*** in Figure 16.6, where the percentage allocation corresponding to *B*** yields the leader 100 percent support, which corresponds to 25 percent of the national vote. The first dashed contour line around *B*** is the locus of points representing allocations that yield the leader 60 percent support from his constituency, or 15 percent of the national vote.

For the leader of *C*, the position *C*** yields 100 percent support from his constituency, corresponding to 35 percent of the national vote. All points on the 20 dotted contour line correspond to allocations which win him 57 percent support from his constituency, or 20 percent of the national vote. And so forth.

Figure 16.6   Support Regions in the Budget Allocation Space

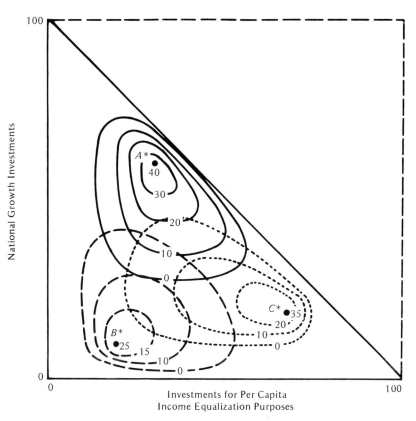

Now it is clear that if each leader refuses to compromise, none of the proposed allocations can achieve a majority vote. A deadlock situation arises, a frequent occurrence in the past. In time, as the deadlock continues and as costs rise in the sense that the benefits from investment are being postponed, we may imagine that one or more of the leaders begins to speculate that perhaps it is better to have some allocation of the funds than none at all. Also, he realizes that as time passes and nothing gets done, the support from his constituency may begin to dwindle and even reach the point at which it ceases to regard him as an effective leader, even though he has held out obstinately for its most preferred position. So he begins to think in terms of trade-offs and concessions. If he is the leader of *A* he asks: What would I have to give up in order to induce the leader of either *B* or *C* to join me in a winning coalition? Suppose he knows not only how his constituents feel about the different allocations but also how the constituents of *B* and *C* feel. Suppose, in effect, he is crudely aware of (or estimates) the support contours of Figure 16.6.

Now support contours do not represent preferences. But the leader might reason that the preferences of any constituency might be ordered in terms of the number of voters willing to support a given allocation. He might reason that if 75 percent of his constituency will support the allocation represented by point A' in Figure 16.5 and only 50 percent will support the allocation A'', then his constituency prefers A' to A''. In similar manner, the constituency prefers A'' to any allocation on the 10 contour line, and of course A' to any allocation on the zero line. In short, he can use the contour lines also to order the preferences of his constituents for the different allocations within his support space.

In similar manner, he can view B's contour lines as ordering the preferences of B's constituency for allocations within B's support region; and C's contour lines as ordering the preferences of C's constituents for allocations in C's support region. Thus, as a final example, B's constituents prefer any allocation on B's 15 contour line over any allocation on B's 10 contour line.

Having estimated all the support contour lines, A may then ask: With whom would it be better for me to form a coalition? For example, if he were to form a coalition with C, the coalition of A and C would control 75 percent of the votes, and would thus be a winning coalition.

The process by which a coalition is formed can be quite complex, and intricate subtleties can be involved. One can only guess what the process would be for any given situation. But clearly one consideration that would come to A's mind is this. If he forms a coalition with B, he, A, will be contributing 40 of the 65 votes that the coalition will control, somewhat more than two-thirds of the voting power. If he forms a coalition with C, he will be contributing 40 of the 75 votes, or somewhat less than 55 percent of the voting power. He may then reason that he could more easily dominate the $A-B$ coalition than the $A-C$ coalition. So we may imagine that he approaches B and suggests forming a coalition.

Clearly he must recognize that B is not interested in forming any coalition unless he has something to gain. He must be guaranteed that an allocation will be chosen that corresponds to a point lying within his (B's) support region—that is, within his zero contour line. For if it does not, B receives zero support and his constituents may be said to gain nothing by the formation of a coalition. In similar fashion, A recognizes that he is only interested in allocations that lie within his (A's) support region—that is, the region bounded by his zero contour line. Hence we can consider that A and B both realize that the allocations over which they can negotiate—that is, the *negotiation set*—must correspond to points within the shaded area of Figure 16.7. That area is the intersection of A's and B's support regions.

Within this shaded area, we expect A to prefer that allocation represented by the point which lies on A's highest contour line—that is, point $\bar{A}$. In turn, B prefers that point which lies on B's highest contour line, namely $\bar{B}$. Thus we have a conflict within the coalition $A - B$. However, the two parties may be able to compromise. They may adopt a split-the-difference procedure which yields them an efficient point E, or some other procedure yielding a point on their efficiency frontier $\bar{A}\bar{B}$. See Chapter 11 for a discussion of the efficiency frontier.

Now it is quite clear that C will not be happy about the formation of a coalition between A and B. First of all, he is excluded; he faces the prospect of being the losing minority. Second, the solution point E lies between his 0 and 10 contour lines and corresponds to an allocation for which his constituency's preference is low. So, out of self-interest, C is motivated to consider how he can disrupt the

Figure 16.7   The Negotiation Set: The Intersection of Two Support Regions

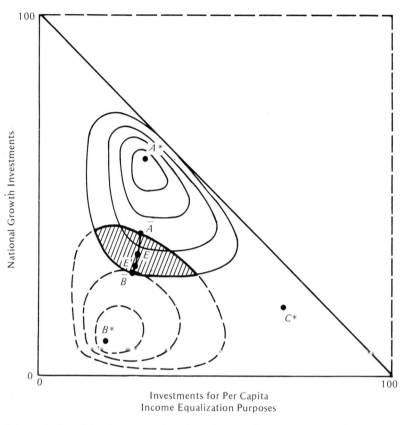

Investments for Per Capita
Income Equalization Purposes

coalition of A and B. He recognizes that A controls more votes and resources than B. *Everything else being the same* then, he prefers to form a coalition with B. In a $B-C$ coalition he might be the dominant party, because he would contribute 35 of the 60 votes. In an $A-C$ coalition he would probably be dominated, because he would contribute only 35 of the 75 votes. At the same time, he recognizes that if he is to induce B to defect from the coalition $A-B$, he will need to offer B a better outcome than B gets in the $A-B$ coalition.

We may imagine that, aided by the contour lines, C considers the situation. In Figure 16.8 we locate point E, the compromise allocation reached by the coalition $A-B$. C now wishes to do better for himself. So we construct C's contour line through E, to serve as a reference curve. Also, we construct B's contour line through E to serve as another reference curve. Now, if the formation of a coalition $B-C$ is to have meaning, it should result in an outcome that is better for both B and C than the outcome associated with point E. Hence, such an outcome must lie within the shaded area of Figure 16.8, an improvement set relative to E. This set contains all points lying within the two contour lines (B's and C's) which pass through E. It is the intersection of B's and C's support regions that yield support greater than or equal to what B and C receive at E.

Figure 16.8   The Improvement Set for a Disrupting Coalition

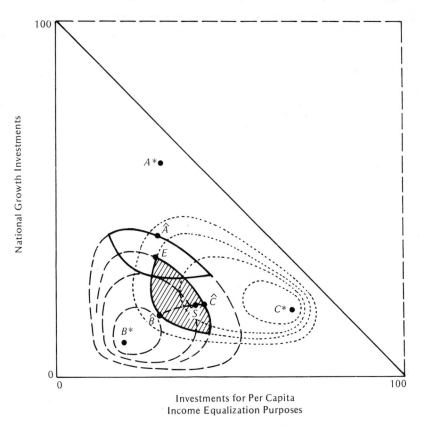

Because the improvement set is non-empty, we may imagine that C persuades B to defect from the $A-B$ coalition and join him in a new $B-C$ coalition. We may imagine that in the new coalition, an agreement is reached through some cooperative procedure to support the allocation S. This allocation is on the efficiency frontier of the coalition $B-C$, and is more preferred by both parties than the allocation E.

But in parallel fashion we can see that A becomes unhappy. He is no longer included in a winning coalition. For him, the allocation S is much worse than E. Point S lies outside A's support region, and so is an allocation highly disliked by his constituency. Thus, A is strongly motivated to break up the $B-C$ coalition and to form another coalition in which he is included. Because B controls fewer votes than C, A is motivated to form a new $A-B$ coalition and offer B an outcome that B prefers not only to E but also to S. Let us designate it by E' in Figure 16.7. But once again C is unhappy and reconsiders his offer to B in the $B-C$ coalition, making a still better offer to B. And so the process continues—B continually receives better and better offers from A and C. Such a situation often occurs in reality. It is a case where each of two .stronger parties seeks the weakest of the three parties as a member of a potentially winning coalition. The weakest party—

that is, the one controlling the least resources—is then able to bargain effectively to receive a payoff share of any coalition to which he belongs that is more than proportionate to his resource contribution to the coalition.

The blissful state of B, however, may not last too long. As the payoff he receives continues to increase, either A or C eventually recognizes that it is better not to do business with B. That is, the point may be reached at which B is receiving such a high payoff in a coalition, say $B-C$, that A considers it more profitable to persuade C to defect from the coalition $B-C$ than B; and he does persuade C to do so.

But now B, to his dislike, is excluded from the winning coalition. So we may imagine that B is willing to relax the price he insists upon for his participation in a coalition. He will approach A or C to form another $A-B$ or $B-C$ coalition. He probably would approach C, because C controls fewer votes than A. He, B, would control a larger percentage of votes in a $B-C$ coalition (25 out of 60) than in an $A-B$ coalition (25 out of 65). So we can imagine that B offers C sufficiently attractive conditions to cause C to defect from the $A-C$ coalition and join him, B, in a $B-C$ coalition.

Now once again A is excluded from a coalition. He finds this an unhappy state of affairs. He therefore starts luring away either B or C from the $B-C$ coalition. And the process continues on and on. It is a process which in many situations is inherently unstable. It is not unlike many actual situations in which it is impossible to form a stable coalition controlling a majority of the votes. It has been said that this kind of situation characterized the Republican convention of 1920. We observe it often in legislative bodies of nations having more than two political parties.

The question arises. Can we develop a procedure to cut through such cyclical instability—that is, cut through the unending process of coalition formation and disruption—and avoid the excessive costs of time and effort that are incurred? In the case of the Republican convention of 1920, a dark horse, Warren Harding, was finally nominated. This outcome has subsequently been judged by historians to have been an inefficient resolution of the conflict. In other cases, highly inefficient allocations may be chosen, with no party achieving any progress toward its objective. However, a sense of fairness *is* attained by the fact that they all incur losses, or forego significant gains, or are equally harmed.

In Chapter 11 we indicated the difficulty of finding good criteria for conflict resolution on the basis of welfare considerations. This difficulty stems from the different views and perspectives of the parties with regard to welfare. Nonetheless, let us reexamine the problem in the context of coalition possibilities.

First, consider again a split-the-difference procedure. The most preferred allocations of the three regions A, B, and C are, respectively:

$$A^*: \quad (60, 30, 10)$$
$$B^*: \quad (10, 20, 70)$$
$$C^*: \quad (20, 70, 10)$$

The split-the-difference procedure requires that we average the percentage support for each of these three allocations. We do so and obtain [(60 + 10 + 20)/3; (30 + 20 + 70)/3; (10 + 70 + 10)/3] or (30, 40, 30), an allocation represented by point R on Figure 16.4. But why should each of the three regions be satisfied with the unweighted average required by a split-the-difference procedure?

426

Why not weight by their voting strengths, which are 40, 25, and 35 for A, B, and C, respectively? That is, why not apply a weighted-average procedure? If we do so, we obtain the allocation (33.5, 41.5, 25.0), which is given by point R' in Figure 16.4. Immediately we see that B will be unhappy with this change of procedure. Having less weight than either of the other two, his wishes will be less reflected in the final outcome for this particular situation. In fact, we observe that the allocation R' assigns 25 percent of total investment funds to balanced industrialization. The allocation R, based on the unweighted-average, split-the-difference procedure, assigns 30 percent to balanced industrialization. B is therefore unwilling to accept a weighted-average procedure for resolving the conflict. Similarly, at least one of the regions is likely to object when weights are based on factors other than control of voting resources, as discussed in Chapter 11. Let us go on.

Reconsider another type of cooperative procedure, a gradual-improvement type of procedure, to break the cyclical instability in our coalition situation. Suppose an outsider comes along and points out to the three parties that they are getting nowhere by forming and disrupting coalitions in unending fashion, and that they ought to approach their problem more systematically. He suggests that they start at their respective zero contour lines. These are plotted in Figure 16.9. (Note that in this figure we are assuming a considerable larger support region for each leader than in the previous figures. We do so in order to make the analysis clearer in graphic terms.) The solid curve enclosing A^* is A's zero contour line. The dashed curve enclosing B^* is B's zero contour line. The dotted curve enclosing C^* is C's zero contour line. These zero contour lines define and bound the support regions of A, B, and C, respectively.

The next step is to see whether there are any allocations that would make each region better off than it would be if it faced an allocation represented by a point on its zero contour line. We can do this by seeing if the support regions of A, B, and C have an area in common. We see from Figure 16.9 that this is so. It is the area of intersection of all support regions, and is shaded (both heavily and lightly, and includes the striped area) in this figure. Any point in the shaded area corresponds to an allocation yielding more than zero support for all three participants. We may define this area as the first-round improvement set—it is also the negotiation set for the first round.

Now imagine that we can identify what would correspond to a small improvement, say 8 percent, for each of the three regions. Let this amount correspond, for A, to a shift from a point on the solid zero contour line to a point on the first solid contour arc $\tilde{B}\,\tilde{C}$ within this zero line. For B, this amount might correspond to a shift from a point on the dashed zero contour line to a point on the first dashed contour arc $\tilde{A}\,\tilde{C}$ within this zero line. For C, this amount might correspond to a shift from a point on the dotted zero contour line to a point on the first dotted contour arc $\tilde{A}\,\tilde{B}$ within this zero line. These three new contour arcs enclose a smaller set of points than the three zero contour lines. This smaller set of points is defined by the heavily shaded and striped area of Figure 16.9. Each point within this smaller area corresponds to an allocation that involves an improvement of at least 8 percent for each of the three participants. Hence, taking this first step insures an 8 percent improvement for each.

Observe, however, that conflict elements are still present. A would most prefer that allocation $\tilde{A}$ in the heavily shaded striped area. It lies on the highest

Figure 16.9   A Sequence of Negotiation (Improvement) Sets

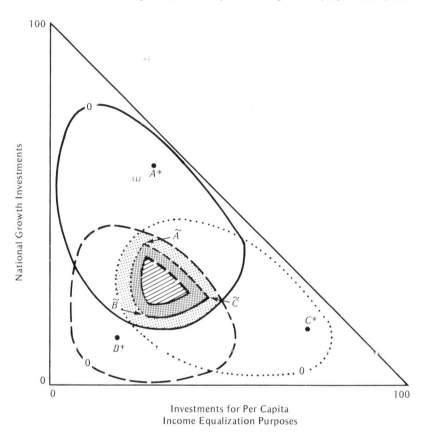

Investments for Per Capita
Income Equalization Purposes

of *A*'s contour lines going through that area. *B* prefers $\widetilde{B}$ and *C* prefers $\widetilde{C}$, for the same reason. Hence we need to eliminate this conflict element. To do so, we suggest that the three regions seek another small improvement, say a 6 percent improvement, for each. We then identify a new set of three arcs lying within the previous set of three arcs. These three arcs are the second solid contour arc within the solid zero contour line, the second dashed arc within the dashed zero contour line, and the second dotted arc within the dotted zero contour line. This second set of arcs encloses all points corresponding to allocations that insure each region, at the minimum, this further 6 percent improvement.

Again, we may expect there to remain some small area of conflict, which, however, can be resolved through one or more rounds of small, equal improvements for each region.

Now we have depicted a round-by-round gradual-improvement process. In doing so, we have glossed over some fundamental difficulties. For example, there may not be agreement among the three regions over what constitutes a comparable improvement—say a 10 percent improvement—for each party. Nor may there be agreement as to what is the zero support contour line for each.

As a consequence of these and other difficulties, we may want to look at still other procedures. Suppose we take the equal-concession procedure. In this procedure, each party states his most preferred allocation in his preferred winning coalition. For A, this would be point A indicated in Figure 16.7, which is also $\hat{A}$ in Figure 16.8. For B, this would be point $\hat{B}$ in Figure 16.8. For C this would be $\hat{C}$ in the same figure. Because $\hat{A}$, $\hat{B}$, and $\hat{C}$ do not coincide, each party is asked to make a small concession and accept an allocation corresponding to a small decrease in its welfare (or payoff)—say a 5 percent reduction. Doing so would bring them closer together. Perhaps after one or more rounds of concessions, they may be able to reach agreement on a desirable allocation. However, in a round-by-round concession procedure, we run into the same difficulties as in the round-by-round improvement procedure. In addition, for certain sets of contour lines it may not be possible to converge, after a series of rounds, to a desirable allocation.

We must emphasize again that even though we can demonstrate that the round-by-round gradual-improvement procedure (and others) are reasonable and yield allocations that leave each region better off than a situation in which there is an unending cycle of coalition formation and disruption, we still may not be able to get the regions to agree to use any one of these procedures. Being able to predict the outcome of each procedure, one region, say A, may strongly prefer one type of procedure, say procedure α, because for him procedure α would yield (directly or after a series of rounds) a better outcome than procedure β or procedure δ. On the other hand, regions B and C may strongly prefer procedures β and δ, respectively, for the same reason. Once again, a conflict over most preferred outcomes (allocations) becomes a conflict over procedures.

Recall from Chapter 11 that we introduced an incremax procedure which had several reasonable and appealing properties—above all, the property that it is impossible for any region to predict beforehand the outcome of an incremax process. Not knowing what the outcome will be, the regions may be induced to adopt the procedure. The incremax procedure can be adapted to this coalition situation. However, we prefer to illustrate still another procedure, which is less rigorous and sophisticated, but which may have more appeal to "average" pragmatic political leaders of regions.

Imagine that the three political leaders of regions A, B, and C have support regions as indicated in Figure 16.9. Now we have already indicated that a round-by-round gradual improvement procedure may not work because of disagreement over what constitutes comparable improvement and a host of other elements. Hence, it may be necessary to look around for other issues on which there can be agreement.

Let a mediator be introduced into the situation in order to break the cycle of formation of new and disruption of old coalitions—a situation that may be described as a *cyclic deadlock*. He recognizes the need to shift the focus from improvement, in terms of moving to higher support contour lines, to something else. He may consider placing the focus on specific material things. Knowing A's desire for a high rate of national growth, he may judge that the construction of a major world port facility with government funds will elicit a very favorable or positive response from A's leader and constituents. Therefore, he proposes that as one element of a package. Knowing *B*'s desire for balanced industrialization, he judges that a metals-fabricating complex, located efficiently in region *B* with respect to its mining activities, will elicit a strong positive response from *B*'s leader and constituents. Knowing *C*'s strong positive desire for per capita income equalization, he judges that a major program involving free food, zero rent, and free medical care for all families whose income is less than $6,000 will elicit a strong positive response from *C*'s leader and population. Of course, the mediator would have to be sensitive to the perceptions of the peoples in these three regions. For each region, the item it strongly desires must be so designed (whether it is the port, metals-fabricating complex, or the free goods, zero rent program) so that its appeal outweighs or dominates any objections and any sense of inequity or injustice that that region may have with regard to the relative magnitudes of investment required to effect the three components of the package. For example, the appeal of a world port facility should be strong enough to outweigh the objections *A* might have to the proposed metals-fabricating complex in *B*, or the free food, zero rent program to poverty families in *C*.

Having induced the three regions to accept a package of specific material things (which we assume can be financed fully from the investment funds available to the central planning authority), the mediator may be in a better position to obtain agreement from them on a percentage allocation of the remainder of the funds. This might be done according to certain notions or principles, of the sort we have already discussed.

The mediator might approach the problem of breaking a cyclic deadlock in another interesting way. He knows that the leader of each region desires to obtain an allocation that is as high as possible on the preference scale (ordering) of his constituents, for he thereby maximizes his support. On the other hand, the typical leader is sensitive to obtaining at least that amount of support which insures his staying in office, usually 50 percent in a two-party system. Now, the mediator may study carefully the contour lines characterizing the support regions for a particular situation. He examines the 50 percent support lines (or whatever other support lines are critical for a leader to stay in office), and plots them as in Figure 16.10. He observes that the 20 contour line for *A* (corresponding to 50 percent support from *A*'s constituents), the 17.5 contour line for *C* (corresponding to 50 percent support from *C*'s constituents), and the 12.5 contour line for *B* (corresponding to 50 percent support from *B*'s constituents) intersect. They bound an area, which is striped, common to all three support regions. Each point in this area corresponds to an allocation generating at least 50 percent support for the leaders of the three regions. Each point also represents, for the constituents of the region, a major improvement over what they would receive if an unending cyclic deadlock occurred. The mediator can propose that a procedure be adopted which insures each leader at least 50 percent support, but which allows the mediator otherwise to choose among allocations, perhaps randomly (through the toss of one or more coins), or in some split-the-difference or weighted-average manner, or in some other way. This insures each leader that he stays in office, and in addition has appeal because otherwise a continuing cyclic deadlock may lead to the gradual erosion of support from the leader's constituency.

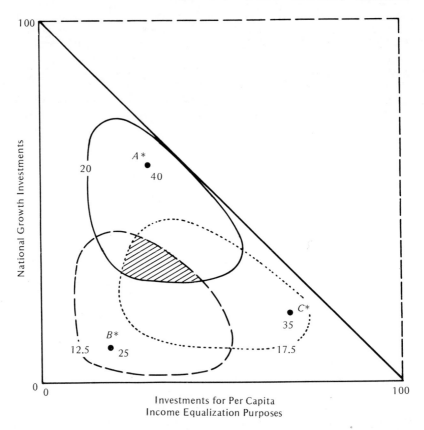

Figure 16.10   A Set of "Satisfactory" Allocations

In short, such a procedure establishes an area, such as the shaded area of Figure 16.10, which encloses a set of points representing allocations "satisfactory" to all leaders. It removes the potential for conflict by granting to the mediator full power to choose from among the set of points that are jointly satisfactory. This type of simple, pragmatic approach is, of course, exceedingly useful when each leader has confidence in the impartiality, integrity, and wisdom of the mediator.

This discussion points up one of the fundamental requirements of an effective mediator; namely, the ability to shift the conflict from one issue to another to still another, or to come at the conflict from one angle or from another or from still another, until he is able to find an issue or an angle from which a basis for a partial, or perhaps a full, resolution of the conflict is possible. In the case of the three political leaders, a partial resolution was possible by shifting the emphasis from the issue of maximizing on a preference scale (ordering) relating to constituency welfare to the issue of insuring that each leader be able to stay in office. However, if in the case examined, the three 50 percent support contour lines had not intersected and bounded an area common to all three support regions, then the mediator would not have been able to resolve the conflict in the manner indicated. He might have tried to resolve it using a different approach, or he might have found it fruitful to shift to still another issue, as for example, an issue of specific material things like a port facility or industrial complex, or an issue of specific nonmaterial things like establishing two or more official languages or state churches. In short, the skillful mediator must shift the issues and angles until he finds one that permits partial or complete resolution of the conflict, all the while being sensitive to each party's perceptions of how much they are gaining relative to other parties, and their notions of what constitutes fairness and progress.

Before concluding this section, we should mention at least some of the many assumptions we have implicitly been making. We have been assuming that no member of a leader's constituency will migrate to another region, perhaps because of dissatisfaction with the goals and proposals made by the leader of his region. It is equivalent to assuming that each voter belongs to one and only one party and cannot belong to any other. This assumption may be satisfactory when we speak of three distinct physical regions, in which the cost of relocation (migration) is substantial. But it may not be satisfactory for coalition analysis in situations in which it is possible for individuals to shift from the constituency of one leader to the constituency of another. In such situations, it would be necessary to consider also the intensity of support that each individual gives to each leader, the extent to which an individual's preferences correspond to those of the leader or what the leader perceives to be those of his typical constituent, and the costs incurred by any leader in inducing constituents of other leaders to defect.

Moreover, we have been generally assuming that each leader has full and complete information. In most situations, this is far from the case, and the amount of information possessed by the several leaders and regions may differ greatly. Furthermore, preference structures may change as coalitions are formed and disrupted, and learning may take place so that new information becomes available and new strategies may be perceived. In turn, incomplete information, changing perceptions, and learning make possible a rich variety of bluffing strategies and the use of misinformation to advance one's interest.

Still more, we must recognize that different institutions and cultural settings limit, in different ways, the range and possibilities of coalition formation and disruption. Certain laws may forbid the formation of certain kinds of coalitions. Others may be encouraged. Moreover, we should extend the analysis to cover situations with four, five, six, and in general n participants. Then the number and variety of possible winning or blocking coalitions greatly increases. Further, in real life there are always uncertainties about the future. Preferences must often be stated over *prospects*, rather than 100 percent certain outcomes. This has important effects on the participants' perceptions of the subsets of relevant coalitions, gains, losses, and so forth. We have seen this in connection with Chapter 9, where we discussed how the attitude variable affects locacation decisions.

Finally, we have left out entirely important psychological variables—such as personality traits and group characteristics—and how these influence the ways in which participants conduct discussions and form, identify, and define their relevant set of actions or their restricted action spaces.

In this and the preceding chapter we have discussed extensively issues and problems of regional development. We first encountered the difficulty of defining development and deciding what it is. There are narrow definitions which yield precise measurements such as GNP, but which are grossly inadequate from a social welfare point of view. There are much broader definitions, more adequate from a social welfare standpoint, but very inadequate from a measurement standpoint and therefore from the standpoint of evaluating different policy alternatives.

Equally nebulous are notions of social welfare. The measurement of social welfare remains a difficult problem, despite the possibilities for the indifference curve type of analysis.

Hence, if we do need measurement, and if we do need means of evaluating different policy alternatives in terms of magnitudes, symbols, or concepts on which everyone can agree, then we must rely, much too much, on the narrow, unsatisfactory definitions of development.

We discussed how demand factors, together with a favorable comparative cost situation, affect the level of export industry. We looked at possibilities for import substitution, and for taking advantage of externalities and related factors (such as forward and backward linkages) to spur economic development. We viewed this process in terms of the emergence of one or more growth poles with potentialities for significant spread effects.

The approach from a demand standpoint was then supplemented with an approach from a supply standpoint. This latter approach went beyond the comparative cost analyses of individual industrial operations conducted independently of each other. It started with the stark reality facing many developing regions; namely, the scarcity of resources such as capital, skilled labor, and foreign exchange with which to purchase critical items. It asked: How can we efficiently allocate scarce resources among different activities, given a stated development objective such as maximizing GNP? Programming analysis permits a development plan that is defined in terms of the level of operations of different activities, where outputs are then supplied to the several markets at the prespecified prices. From the standpoint of conducting sound analysis, it is important to complement the demand and comparative cost approaches with this programming (supply) approach, but it has certain additional merits. It allows us to specify the kinds of constraints we wish to impose on the operation of an economic system so that we can consider the implications of different values, goals, and programs which the several regions and interest groups of a nation may deem important. Then, implications can be examined in terms of certain identifiable costs, such as GNP foregone. By setting constraints, programming analysis allows us to shape the growth of a nation and its several regions.

But all our efforts in these directions are very much qualified by the fact that the sharp differences among regions and other constituencies with respect to preferences for diverse values, goals, and programs make it difficult to identify the best way to shape the path of development. We continually confront the problem of how to resolve conflicts from different preferences over values, goals, and programs. No matter how elegant the mathematics in our programming models, no matter how nice and reasonable the set of graphs we use to portray program plan functions, we still must come to grips with the age-old problem of bringing together different leaders and groups in conflict. How shall we weight their different demands? How can we be sensitive to the different intensities of their needs and aspirations? What kinds of cooperative procedures can we offer to improve the lot of each, to avoid deadlocks, and to bring to a quick halt forces that escalate conflicts or intensify distrust, anxieties, and hostilities?

This problem of conflict resolution forced us to begin looking into the area of coalition analysis. Frequently, through the formation of coalitions controlling blocs of votes, compromises can be effected in the political arena to set weights, and kinds and levels of constraints in the use of scarce resources. But as we well know, the coalition-based political process, even in the nations that profess high democratic ideals (such as the United States and India), is highly imperfect, if not subject to major corruption. Too often, in these nations the "haves" get the lion's share of scarce resources and the "have-nots" a piddling share.

This outcome, of course, is not unexpected. Partly it results from the fact that we still are not able to conduct coalition analyses and similar studies to suggest a way acceptable to all parties for reaching compromise solutions. There are many ways in which compromises can be effected, and each party has different preferences over the several ways. The conflicts over basic values, goals, and programs frequently become conflicts over what weights to use and what procedures to pursue to effect a compromise or some other resolution of a conflict. Hence, although we are able to set down several procedures that have appealing features, such as the veto incremax procedure detailed in Chapter 11 and the satisficing gradual-improvement procedure, we are still far from being able to suggest one or more procedures that would be generally acceptable to parties in a conflict. This sad state of affairs results from the fact that we cannot incorporate into procedures imperfect knowledge, bluffing, changing preferences, and learning, all of which are part of our everyday life. Nonetheless, it is important for us to cover this ground. As potential planners or mediators, we obtain insight into the difficulties of different procedures and therefore are better able to suggest the use of one, as we often must, to settle a conflict. We also know the kinds of additional analysis that are required in future research.

Perhaps most important is the fact that, in our diverse involvements as planners, mediators, and citizens, we are more aware of certain basic relationships and their complexity, which our various techniques—input-output, export base, and interregional linear programming analyses—help us uncover. Thus, we are better able to avoid bad decisions and to narrow down policy alternatives to a set of what we might call good alternatives. This point will come up in the next chapter when we study and evaluate a real-life situation. Decisions were made there, and decisions will always need to be made. They could have been made differently. The important thing is to be able to say that the decisions made were much better than other decisions that could have been made, and that might have been made in the absence of our analysis.

Regional Science
in Practice:
A Tale of Puerto Rico*

INTRODUCTION

We have now covered thirteen chapters of analytical material. They have been peppered with data and experiences of various sorts to support the different notions and relationships set forth. Nowhere have we supported the analysis with a case study of an actual city or region. We now wish to do so. We wish to relate an experience in regional development that was keyed to the use of our analytical techniques. The experience pertains to Puerto Rico, a region open to trade, subject to large in- and outmigration, culturally homogeneous, and responsive to decisions and events taking place both within and outside the region. For these reasons, its situation was appropriate for the use of regional science techniques. That is, it offers us a basis for evaluating the merits of the types of concepts, tools, and techniques we have been presenting in these pages. Further, this live experience in regional development is one in which the author and his associates were directly involved. Our use of it, therefore, allows us to record experience, first-hand. Yet there is the disadvantage that the author's values creep unconsciously into the text in the telling of the story. There obviously are several different perspectives for assessing this history.

*In the writing of this chapter the author drew very heavily upon materials developed by Thomas A. Reiner. However, the author alone is responsible for all statements and evaluations.

THE SETTING: RESOURCES AND
APPROACHES TO RESEARCH

In 1950, Puerto Rico was described as the *"Pearl of the Caribbean."* Its heritage of Spanish architecture blended serenely with the calm natural beauty of the island to overwhelm the unprepared observer. But just as serenely blended into the environment were its dilapidated shacks and children's pot-bellies, by the hundreds of thousands. Gastrointestinal deaths, though at one-third of the 1936 rate, were 127 per 100,000, still many times the U.S. figure. As one index of poverty, diarrhea-enteritis was the prime cause of death, though through the implementation of the first level of public health measures, the death rate was already very close to that of the U.S. (about 10 per 1,000), having dropped from double that figure in just one decade. Infant mortality and stillbirths, other indicators of poverty, were in 1950 at a rate of 68 and 49 per 1,000, very high by contemporary standards, though registering considerable decrease from the preceding decade. Puerto Rico was a region of extreme poverty. Its per capita income in 1950 was $279, way below anything comparable in the United States mainland. Malnutrition was omnipresent.

By 1950, the government and, in particular, the Economic Development Administration of Puerto Rico had attracted a number of factories to Puerto Rico, partly as an adaptation to the New Deal policies of Franklin D. Roosevelt. These factories were largely in the garment trades. Entrepreneurs found it profitable to employ Puerto Rico's cheap labor, which was especially skilled at needlework operations. Although this represented a significant step forward in terms of providing jobs, it brought with it certain disadvantages. The industrial growth was highly specialized to the garment and related trades. It tended to make Puerto Rico a "one-industry" region, subject to the typical "one-industry" instability and vulnerability. Moreover, the garment trades are particularly vulnerable because of their highly competitive character. Firms might come in and leave at the drop of a hat. So although the garment operations were welcome in that they did provide new jobs and income, the Economic Development Administration realized that these operations did not provide a solid, long-run base for an economy turning away from agriculture and toward manufacturing. Overcommitment to the garment industry would hardly represent an improvement over previous overcommitment to the sugar-based agricultural industry. Nor were such operations likely to spark basic industrial development. The search and drive was for a truly basic industry to spark a "take-off."

Regarding basic industry, Puerto Rico faced a dilemma. This would have been recognized by any regional scientist.[1] Any regional scientist would have started off in the usual fashion by asking: What are the resources of the region? He might first consider agricultural resources, but, as far as we and others were able to see, the land in Puerto Rico was not particularly rich. Considerable erosion was taking place because of poor agricultural practices. Crops such as coffee, pineapples, and bananas, which had been important to the economy in the past, were losing out more and more because of serious competition in the world markets. Other

---

[1] At that time, no term such as "regional scientist" was used. It came into use subsequently. In the early fifties, we talked of an economist with a regional bent. Even the term "regional economist" was not in general use.

agricultural areas were able to produce higher-quality crops at competitive prices. Cane sugar was about the only agricultural crop holding its own—barely holding its own, and due, in the next decade, to experience absolute as well as relative decline in importance. The control of its production, moreover, was highly concentrated in the hands of a few (many of whom were nonislanders) having few if any modern entrepreneurial ideas.

In short, there was not much hope in agriculture.

Were there any significant mineral resources? At that time, experts were not able to locate any, nor were the prospects good that some might be found.

Were there any other specific labor and other resources that were particularly attractive? Yes, there was cheap labor skilled in the needlework and apparel crafts. But, as already mentioned, this resource was being exploited, and the Economic Development Administration feared that increased exploitation of this resource alone would lead to a one-industry, highly unstable economy, comprising too many fly-by-night operations so characteristic of the garment industry. There were no special talents in the managerial class. In fact, the managerial class was small in number and lacking many skills. It was interested primarily in maintaining the great inequality in the distribution of wealth and income; that is, in maintaining the status quo and working the land in a short-sighted, exploitative manner much as it had done in the past. There were hardly any entrepreneurs with the vigor of the Carnegie, Rockefeller, and Ford brand, whatever their shortcomings. Further, there were few skilled in engineering and financial management. There were few, if any, facilities for training in the trades and the professions.

In short, there were no resources—land, mineral, venture capital, labor—except the cheap needlework labor. It was in this discouraging context that we began our work some twenty-five years ago. Though troubled, we did not give up. We tried another direction. Perhaps if we were to scan the Census of Manufactures systematically and examine carefully each of the many manufacturing operations listed, we might find one or two suitable for location in Puerto Rico. But every time we made a comparative cost analysis for one that looked promising, the answer was negative except when the operations would be based primarily on Puerto Rico's cheap needlework labor. We also noted that the prestigious consulting firm of Arthur D. Little, Inc. had already completed a research study on the industrial potentialities of Puerto Rico. It had recommended four types of operations for promotion. Accordingly, a glass bottling works, a boxboard factory, a brickworks, and a shoe factory were set up. Each one encountered severe difficulties and managed to use up a large part of the government surplus accumulated during the war years from excises on rum sales, without providing much employment.

The prospects were more discouraging than ever. In brief, resource studies and a systematic comparative cost approach suggested nothing new. There was, of course, the potential for tourism. This got off to a good start with the construction of the Caribe Hilton Hotel at about the same time the airline links were more strongly forged. But clearly, though tourism was welcome as a source of supplementary income, it was recognized as an activity that does not substitute for basic industrial development.

At that time, it was natural for several individuals to suggest that we put the input-output technique to work on the problem, especially because an input-output table was being constructed for Puerto Rico. But, as we indicated in Chapters 7 and 8, an input-output table cannot help us identify what new basic industry to bring to a region. Rather, it can furnish a useful statistical description of what is going on in a region, and provide us with good estimates of the direct and indirect impacts of a new basic industry.

In the early Fifties, linear programming, too, was starting to become accepted as a valid technique for analysis. But recall from our discussion in the last two chapters that it is a powerful tool for telling us how best to use a set of resources we have. But if we have *no* resources (except the needlework labor, which we already know how to use), of what use is linear programming?

THE NOTION OF AN INDUSTRIAL COMPLEX

It is often said that necessity is the mother of invention. This turned out to be the case in our Puerto Rico research. Here was a region that was poverty-stricken; in addition, there were no resources available. Yet the objective was to achieve development using an industrialization strategy. The comparative cost technique yielded negative results. The input-output and linear programming techniques were irrelevant at this stage. There were a number of other less sophisticated tools around, such as the basic-service ratios, location quotients, and coefficients of localization. But all these simply involved ratios and indices, which are fine for description but fail to identify propulsive forces for industrialization. They could tell us, for example, that Puerto Rico did not have a fair share of a number of manufacturing operations, considering the size of its population, but who didn't know that?

For months we tracked down false leads. Then one day, in unpredictable fashion, an idea came up. If no *one* manufacturing activity by itself could be profitably located in Puerto Rico, perhaps we could find some *combination* of activities that together might be profitably operated. Perhaps this possibility could be nurtured because the location of such activities next to one another would provide additional advantages to each. If one activity were to produce an output that was an input to a second, there would be a savings on transport costs on the output of the first activity. Conversely, if an operation could locate next to one that provided it with an input, then it would get that input at a lower delivered price. Further, an operation might produce a by-product that ordinarily is scrapped—dumped on the environment. (Recall that at that time the pollution-absorption capability of the environment was considered almost infinite, way beyond the foreseeable reach of man.) If we could arrange to place another operation close by that could use the by-product, then that by-product might fetch some revenue. Moreover, there were possibilities for "agglomeration economies" (of the urbanization type—see p. 116). If more than one operation required the same input (such as power or ethylene oxide), the input could be produced close by these operations at greater scale, and perhaps made available at a lower price because of scale economies. Or perhaps some items could be purchased in bulk, permitting transport cost savings. Or perhaps all operations could cooperate in using a common training facility to train workers in diverse skills, making training less expensive for each operation. Or when located next to each other (spatially juxtaposed), perhaps these operations would need to hire

1

only a single skilled machinist to keep their machinery in repair, thus saving on that wage item. And so forth.

In short, we began to think of ways of putting together sets of operations or industrial complexes meaningful for Puerto Rico. We defined an industrial complex as *a set of activities occurring at a given location and belonging to a group (subsystem) of activities which, because of technical, production, marketing, and other linkages, generates significant economies to each activity when spatially juxtaposed.*

However, it was difficult to conceive of industrial complexes for Puerto Rico. There were no resources to start off with, natural or human, except the cheap needlework labor. And one has to begin with something.

After several unsuccessful tries at getting started and getting nowhere, in desperation we said: "Well, if Puerto Rico has no resources, we'll have to look outside Puerto Rico. What meaningful resource lies closest to it?" With a compass we drew circles around Puerto Rico, gradually widening the radius until we struck oil in Venezuela, 600 miles away.

The ray of hope from oil was short-lived. Oil refining requires little labor and large amounts of capital. We knew that capital-intensive activities are not particularly favorable for development in backward regions, which are short of capital and generally must pay high interest rates for capital. In this case, the disadvantages of an oil refinery would be particularly severe, because the oil would need to be imported, and more importantly, the necessary type of petrochemical engineering labor and managers did not exist in Puerto Rico. If an oil refinery were to be operated there, chemical-petroleum engineers and managers would have to be brought in from the mainland, and at a much higher wage scale than on the mainland. Additionally, the most efficient refineries were huge and involved a tremendous investment of capital, which was just not practical for Puerto Rico at that time. Moreover, all the petrochemical operations most closely associated with oil refining would confront the same kinds of disadvantages.

So we quickly put aside the notion of an oil refinery for Puerto Rico.

Again, we sat back and scratched our heads. We examined all kinds of data relating to new possibilities for using agricultural crops as a basis for food products manufacturing, the possibilities of producing irradiated products simultaneously with the operation of a nuclear reactor (which as a "hot" thing in the early Fifties), new research and development ideas, and so forth. No hope. We looked at the export and import data once more. We knew that a careful examination of current export data, with particular attention to those exports which have grown rapidly, can throw light on emerging strong points of an economy that might be further nurtured. No good ideas emerged. Then we examined carefully the import data. Once again we saw how fertilizer stuck out like a sore thumb, because of its large magnitude of import. And then the obvious hit us like a thunderbolt.

We knew that after several production stages, fertilizer could be obtained from the gas streams of an oil refinery. We knew that numerous other products —such as synthetic fibers, plastics, paints, detergents, solvents, synthetic rubber, and explosives—could also be produced, after many operations, from these gas streams. Moreover, we knew that transportation costs on fertilizer from the Gulf Coast (the supplying region) to Puerto Rico were high. Thus, we hit on the notion of a complex using oil (Puerto Rico's most accessible resource), producing fertilizers (effecting a major transport cost savings in eliminating the haul from the Gulf Coast), producing a synthetic fiber or similar product (which would allow the complex to take advantage of the cheap needlework labor), and marketing products in the large Eastern Seaboard markets on the mainland (thus taking advantage of Puerto Rico's duty-free status relative to other cheap labor locations outside the mainland USA). Also, taken together, the activities of the complex might be able to spark the industrialization so intensely sought.

Excited by this prospect, we worked industriously and diligently at the problem. We soon recognized that it was no easy job. There were hundreds of different end products that could be made from crude oil, and many ways of producing each. This is indicated by Figure 17.1, which reproduces some of the possibilities in 1950. There we see that the basic raw material, crude oil, yields the familiar products: gasoline, kerosene, fuel oil, and lubricating oil. It also yields less familiar gases and liquid fractions such as hydrogen, methane, ethane, ethylene, propane, propylene, butane, bytylene, and benezene. Further, various products such as gasoline, kerosene, fuel oil, and lubricating oil can, under appropriate pressure and temperature, be cracked to yield more of these refinery gases and liquid fractions.

The various gas streams and liquid fractions coming out of the refinery can be used in many ways to produce numerous other end products, only some of which are listed at the extreme right of Figure 17.1. At the top, we see that methane can be made into hydrogen, and then successively into nitric acid, urea, and finally fertilizer. Methane also can be converted into methanol which, via formaldehyde, yields plastics. Or it can be used to produce HCN, then acrylonitrile, and finally the synthetic fibers Orlon, Dynel, and Acrilan. Or acrylonitrile can be obtained from acetylene, which in turn may be derived from ethane, ethylene, propane, or propylene. Acetylene may be channeled to produce acetic acid, which leads to rayon, or to vinyl chloride, which can yield polyvinyl chloride and plastics. Or the ethylene can be processed into any number of products and finally made into plastics, synthetic rubber, antiknock fluid, synthetic fibers, antifreeze, detergents, and explosives. From propane, we can go to propylene and then to many of these same end products. Or propane can go into LPG (liquid petroleum gas), a high-grade fuel. The naphthenes yield an interesting set of products. The most familiar are nylon, synthetic rubber, plastics, paints, insecticides, and synthetic fibers.

In brief, a tremendous number of ways existed for setting up a complex using crude oil, refinery gases, and liquid fractions. Our problem was to find a complex for Puerto Rico that could stand the competitive pressures from the mainland and other world regions, and that could operate profitably. We had limited resources for research. We knew that in all likelihood we would not be able to identify the very best complex, but we also knew that whatever we identified had to be close to the best for Puerto Rico. This was imperative because, except for the operations using needlework labor, each of the activities we would be considering would be unprofitable by itself.

To make a long story short, we arrived at several useful criteria to guide us through the maze of possibilities:

1. We recognized that in operating any one plant, such as an oil refinery, there most likely would be scale economies. We knew that in most cases we could not achieve the full-scale economies in Puerto Rico because of small markets

Figure 17.1   Flowsheet of Principal Petrochemical Raw Materials, Intermediates, and End Products

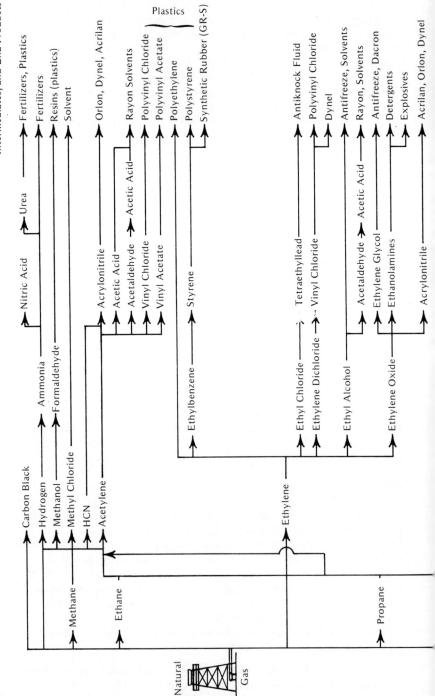

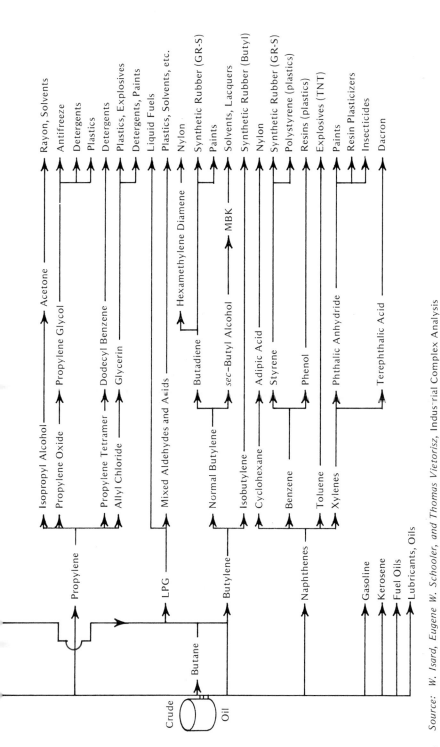

Source: W. Isard, Eugene W. Schooler, and Thomas Vietorisz, Industrial Complex Analysis and Regional Development (Cambridge: M.I.T. Press, 1959), pp. 30-31.

441

there and because of the large capital investments that would be involved. But we also knew that we would have to operate the plant at a level that would capture many of the scale economies. For example, the curve on Figure 17.2 shows how unit costs fall with increase in size of an oil refinery. We knew that in Puerto Rico we would have to operate an oil refinery at a scale within the range indicated by the elliptical shape on Figure 17.2 if we were to have any chance of finding an economically feasible complex. For each activity we set up a minimum plant size for being included in a complex. Of course, except for fertilizers, the output from a minimum-size plant in an activity would be above any conceivable demand level in Puerto Rico itself.

2. We required that there be an end product (from among those listed at the right-hand side of Figure 17.1) which would use a very large amount of the cheap needlework labor of Puerto Rico. Because of the decided advantage it had in the costs of this resource, the more such labor could be used, the more likely we could find a profitable complex for Puerto Rico. (We had in mind the exploitation of additional advantages that come from substituting cheap labor for other factors at a cheap labor location, as technically developed in the appendix to Chapter 6.) We found that synthetic fibers required the greatest amounts of such labor, generally speaking. So we almost always included the production of synthetic fiber in any complex examined.

3. We recognized that private mainland businesses (on which Puerto Rico would have to depend for substantial capital investment) would find an

Figure 17.2   Costs Per Barrel of Crude Oil Refined for Different Scales of Operation

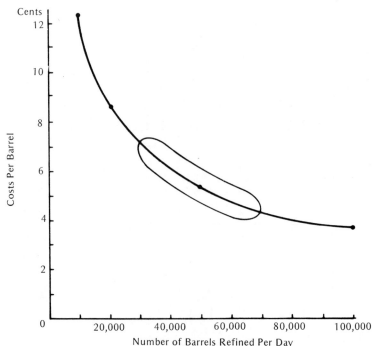

operation less risky if its outputs were products whose mainland markets were growing at a faster rather than a slower rate. Hence, we considered the production of only those synthetic fibers for which demand was growing rapidly in the United States in the Fifties and which was expected to continue in the Sixties. This led us to concentrate on Dacron, Acrilan, Dynel, Orlon, and Nylon.

4. We required that, where technically possible, no by-products should be wasted. Accordingly, we introduced the commodity LPG (liquified petroleum gas) as one to be produced (and sold on the local market) from the unused gas streams and liquid fractions of the refinery.

5. In order to spark industrialization, we almost always required that any complex considered be a "full" complex, in the sense that it contained the full range of activities in going from the refinery to fertilizers on the one hand, and from the refinery to the synthetic fiber end products on the other. In this way, we hoped to achieve maximum stimulus for development of entrepreneurship, management, and a pool of labor, with a diversity of key skills. Of course, we had to recognize that a few items might have to be imported from the mainland, because scale economy and other considerations would make production in Puerto Rico exceedingly costly.

THE ANALYSIS FOR SPECIFIC INDUSTRIAL COMPLEXES

With all these and other criteria in mind, we began testing and experimenting with diverse complexes. There is not the time and space to indicate the many times we fumbled in our analyses, and why. But through hit and miss procedures we did arrive at certain meaningful complexes. For example, in Figure 17.3 we present a *Dacron A* complex. At the extreme left of the figure is the oil refinery. It produces as main products: gasoline, kerosene, diesel oil, cycle oil and other fractions, coke, and LPG. It also produces gas streams. These gas streams are channeled into two different sets of production activities. The first is depicted above the heavy horizontal line in the figure. It indicates that ethylene is extracted from the gas stream and used to produce ethylene glycol. Ethylene glycol, combined with dimethyl terephthalate (produced from imported paraxylene) yields Dacron polymer. Dacron polymer is then worked upon by the needlework labor of Puerto Rico to produce the end product, Dacron staple.

The second set of production activities into which gas streams of the oil refinery enter are depicted below the heavy horizontal line in Figure 17.3. From hydrogen, methane, ethylene, and ethane, ammonia is produced to form an ammonia pool. From this pool, ammonia is used to produce nitric acid and urea. Nitric acid and ammonia are combined to form ammonium nitrate. The ammonium nitrate and urea together form fertilizer, the other main end product.

Now, we must be very precise in specifying the levels of outputs and amounts of inputs required in each of the activities. So we place numbers both inside and on top of the boxes in Figure 17.3. The number within the box simply records the number assigned to the production activity of that box and corresponds to the number of the column in Table 17A.1 in the appendix and in our master table of activities. (It parallels the number assigned to each sector in the input-output table. Giving each activity a number corresponding to a column facilitates the use of a computer.)

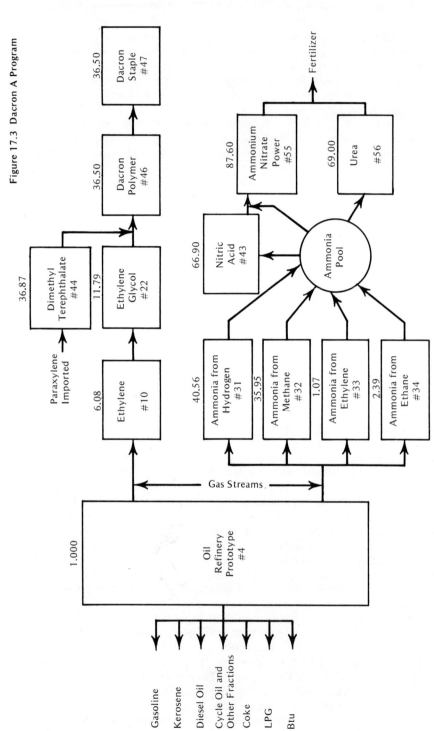

Figure 17.3 Dacron A Program

Source: W. Isard et al., Industrial Complex Analysis and Regional Development, 87.

444

The number on the top of each box specifies the level at which the activity of the box is operated. It is a level consistent with the efficient operation of the complex and is discussed at some detail in the appendix to this chapter. After these' levels are specified, we can compute (as described in the appendix) the total sets of inputs and outputs of the Dacron A complex which we list in column 1 of Table 17.1. Going down the column, we note that 9.428 million barrels of crude oil are required, 1.300 million barrels of straight-run gasoline are produced, 2.226 million barrels of cracked gasoline are produced,..., 0.707 million barrels of kerosene are produced,..., and 153.590 million lbs of LPG are produced. We see that 127.799 million kilowatt-hours of power are required, 2,756.42 billion BTU of fuel are required,..., 2.522 million lbs of methanol are required, and 25.072 million lbs of paraxylene are required (imported). Finally, 36.5 million lbs of Dacron staple are produced,..., 87.6 million lbs of ammonium nitrate (part of the fertilizer) are produced,..., and 5.284 million man-hours of textile labor and 2.229 million man-hours of chemical petroleum labor are required.

For every other kind of complex that we care to consider, we can construct a diagram similar to Figure 17.3. The diagram must be internally consistent, for example, in the sense that enough hydrogen is generated by the refinery so that the activity which converts hydrogen into ammonia can be operated at the level required. Likewise, there must be enough ethylene in the gas stream of the oil refinery so that we produce that amount of ethylene glycol needed to yield 36.5 million lbs of Dacron staple considered essential for the textile operation to be efficient, meaningful, or both in terms of major chemical-producing companies. And so forth. From each diagram of the type of Figure 17.3, we can derive for the corresponding complex the total requirements and yield of each of the several relevant commodities. Thus, in columns 2, 3, and 4 of Table 17.1 we list the requirements and yield of three more Dacron programs, Dacron B, Dacron C, and Dacron D. Each of these differ somewhat from the Dacron A program in terms of the set of intermediate processes they use to reach the final set of end products. In columns 5 and 6 we indicate total requirements and yield for two of the better Orlon programs examined. In columns 7 and 8 we list the the same for two of the better Dynel programs examined. For many other programs, including Nylon programs, we calculated total requirements and yield.

It is insufficient just to list the total requirements and yield of each commodity for each complex. Such a list does not make much sense to the businessman heading a major chemical-producing company or the president of a major investment house. He wants to know what the costs of the complex operations will be, what sales revenue he can expect, and how much savings he can realize if he develops a complex in Puerto Rico.

Now recall that our problem was to demonstrate, if we could, that there were one or more complexes that could operate in Puerto Rico at a greater profit than elsewhere. At the time of the study, there was no doubt in our minds and those of businessmen that there would be major increases in demand for refinery products, fertilizer, and synthetic fibers, as we know turned out to be the case. There was no doubt that new plants would be constructed to meet this demand. The question was whether some new plants could be operated at greater profits in Puerto Rico than on the mainland. That is, could a Puerto Rico complex be

Table 17.1 Total Requirements and Yields of Selected Industrial Complexes

	Dacron A (1)	Dacron B (2)	Dacron C (3)	Dacron D (4)	Orlon B (5)	Orlon J (6)	Dynel A (7)	Dynel F (8)
1. Crude oil MM bbl	-9.428	-9.428	-9.428	-9.428	-9.428	-9.428	-9.428	-9.428
2. Gasoline, straight-run MM bbl	+1.300	+1.300	+1.300	+1.300	+1.300	+1.300	+1.300	+1.300
3. Gasoline, cracked MM bbl	+2.226	+2.226	+2.226	+2.226	+2.226	+2.226	+2.226	+2.226
4. Gasoline, reformed MM bbl	+1.486	+1.486	+1.486	+1.486	+1.486	+1.486	+1.486	+1.486
5. Gasoline, polymerized MM bbl	+0.433	+0.428	+0.433	+0.428	+0.444	+0.415	+0.444	+0.415
6. Naptha, MM bbl	—	—	—	—	—	—	—	—
7. Kerosene, MM bbl	+0.707	+0.707	+0.707	+0.707	+0.707	+0.707	+0.707	+0.707
8. Diesel oil MM bbl	+0.896	+0.896	+0.896	+0.896	+0.896	+0.896	+0.896	+0.896
9. Gas oil MM bbl	—	—	—	—	—	—	—	—
10. Cycle oil MM bbl	+1.980	+1.980	+1.980	+1.980	+1.906	+1.887	+1.980	+1.980
11. Heavy residual MM bbl	—	—	—	—	—	—	—	—
12. Coke and carbon 10 × MM lb	+4.033	+4.033	+4.033	+4.033	+4.033	+4.033	+4.033	+4.033
13. LPG 10 × MM lb	+15.359	+15.270	+15.359	+15.270	+14.006	+15.050	+15.558	+15.050
14. Hydrogen MM lb	+0.788	+0.845	+0.470	+0.524	+3.553	+1.640	+2.793	+0.610
15. Methane MM lb	+15.088	+16.083	+9.549	+10.545	+9.658	-0.006	+3.536	+0.038
16. Ethylene (mixed) MM lb	+6.948	+9.794	+6.715	+9.561	+3.359	+0.950	+1.106	+5.451
17. Ethane (mixed) MM lb	+12.513	+17.812	+12.264	+17.564	+2.373	+1.528	+1.059	+9.805
18. Propylene MM lb	+2.971	+4.290	+2.971	+4.290	+3.542	-0.066	—	+2.331
19. Propane MM lb	+1.991	+2.875	+1.991	+2.875	—	+0.001	—	+1.562
20. Butylenes MM lb	—	—	—	—	—	—	—	—
21. Butanes MM lb	+0.003	+0.007	+0.003	+0.007	-0.012	—	+0.003	—
22. Pure ethylene MM lb	+18.356	+13.102	+18.356	+13.102	+0.004	—	+20.721	—
23. Pure ethane MM lb	-4.113	-4.192	-4.547	-4.342	-4.885	-5.021	-4.233	-4.401
24. Steam MMM lb	—	—	—	—	—	—	—	—
25. Power MM kw-hr	-127.799	-128.750	-132.386	-163.048	-140.933	-142.383	-219.177	-148.253
26. Fuel 10 × MMM Btu	-275.642	-277.528	-270.971	-272.855	-313.006	-277.014	-281.806	-272.244
27. Salt MM lb	—	-26.435	—	-26.435	—	—	-93.075	-26.469
28. Caustic Soda MM lb	—	+17.494	—	+17.494	—	—	+61.594	+17.516
29. Chlorine MM lb	—	-0.003	—	-0.003	—	—	—	—
30. Hydrochloric acid 100% MM lb	—	+0.311	—	+0.311	—	—	+14.329	—

31. Limestone MM lb	—	—	—	—	—	—	—	−29.927
32. Lime (hydrated) MM lb	—	−14.185	—	−14.185	—	—	—	—
33. Ethylene oxide MM lb	—	−0.005	—	−0.005	+0.013	—	—	+0.003
34. Nitrogen MM lb	+80.172	—	+80.172	—	+265.948	—	—	—
35. Ethylene glycol MM lb	+0.001	+0.001	+0.001	+0.001	—	—	—	—
36. Ethylene dichloride MM lb	—	—	—	—	—	—	—	−0.003
37. Acetylene MM lb	—	—	—	—	—	+0.002	+0.005	+0.002
38. Vinyl Chloride MM lb	—	—	—	—	—	—	+0.001	+0.005
39. Ammonia MM lb	−0.032	−0.024	−0.018	—	−0.003	−0.020	+0.001	+0.017
40. HCN MM lb	—	—	—	—	+0.002	+0.002	+0.002	+0.002
41. Acrylonitrile MM lb	—	—	—	—	+0.005	+0.005	—	—
42. Methanol MM lb	−2.522	−2.522	−2.522	−2.522	—	—	—	—
43. Sulphur MM lb	—	—	−1.777	−1.777	—	—	—	—
44. Sulphuric acid MM lb	—	—	−0.002	−0.002	—	—	—	—
45. Nitric acid MM lb	+0.061	+0.061	+0.065	+0.065	+0.060	+0.060	+0.061	+0.061
46. Paraxylene MM lb	−25.072	−25.072	−21.753	−21.754	—	—	—	—
47. Dimethyl terephthalate MM lb	+0.005	+0.005	+0.005	+0.005	—	—	—	—
48. Dacron polymer MM lb	—	—	—	—	—	—	—	—
49. Dacron staple MM lb	+36.500	—	—	—	—	—	—	—
50. Dacron filament MM lb	—	+36.500	+36.500	+36.500	—	—	—	—
51. Dynel polymer MM lb	—	—	—	—	—	—	—	—
52. Acetone MM lb	—	—	—	—	—	—	—	—
53. Dynel staple MM lb	—	—	—	—	—	—	−10.950	−10.950
54. Dynel filament MM lb	—	—	—	—	—	—	+36.500	+36.500
55. Orlon polymer MM lb	—	—	—	—	—	—	—	—
56. Dimethyl formamide MM lb	—	—	—	—	−8.395	−8.395	—	—
57. Orlon staple MM lb	—	—	—	—	—	+36.500	—	—
58. Orlon filament MM lb	—	—	—	—	+36.500	—	—	—
59. Ammonium nitrate MM lb	+87.600	+87.600	+87.600	+87.600	+87.680	+87.680	+87.600	+87.680
60. Urea MM lb	+69.000	+69.000	+69.000	+69.000	+68.960	+68.960	+69.000	+68.960
61. Carbon dioxide MM lb	−51.750	−51.750	−51.750	−51.750	−51.720	−51.720	−51.750	−51.720
Textile labor MM m-hr	−5.284	−5.359	−5.283	−5.358	−5.315	−5.280	−5.396	−5.334
Chemical petroleum labor MM m-hr	−2.229	−2.473	−2.226	−2.469	−2.329	−2.217	−2.590	−2.390

Source: W. Isard et al., Industrial Complex Analysis and Regional Development, pp. 90–91.

MM = million; bbl = barrel

designed to achieve cost savings relative to mainland operations in serving the Eastern Seaboard market with refinery products, the market in the South with synthetic fiber, and the market in Puerto Rico with fertilizer? To answer this question, we needed to determine which location would be best on the mainland for serving the markets just noted. Obviously, if we were to compare the Puerto Rico location with a highly inefficient location on the mainland, for example a location on Pike's Peak, there would be no question whatsoever that Puerto Rico would have major advantages. But the comparison would be meaningless and rather annoying to any busy executive hard at work in maximizing profits. It was clear that in this new and intensely competitive industry of petrochemicals and synthetic fibers, businessmen were making very careful cost calculations. We could make a convincing case for a Puerto Rico location only if we showed advantages in Puerto Rico relative to the best location on the mainland for serving the markets in mind.

On the basis of previous studies of the petrochemical and related industry, we knew that the Gulf Coast was an excellent location. However, we had to do still further study to find out whether it was the best mainland location for serving the indicated markets. After such study, we realized that it would be better to locate the synthetic fiber operation of any mainland complex in the cheap labor areas of the South (such as in Mississippi or Tennessee). For by locating this operation there, the additional transport costs in shipping a polymer or salt (such as Dacron polymer or Nylon salt) to a Southern factory would be fairly evenly balanced by the savings in transport costs in getting the finished product to the Southern market. At the same time, we could take advantage of the cheaper textile labor in the South. Accordingly, we determined that the most efficient mainland situation would involve a split complex, with the synthetic fiber operation in the South and all the rest at the Gulf Coast.

Having determined the best mainland location pattern, we were able to proceed with the next step. Because we were doing a comparative cost analysis, we were not interested in obtaining costs for inputs that would be the same everywhere. Rather, we were interested only in the differences in costs that might arise from the operation of a complex at different locations—in particular, Puerto Rico and the Gulf Coast. We proceeded, then, to look for these differences, commodity by commodity.

Let us illustrate. Consider the requirements of crude oil. At the start, we assumed that the Puerto Rico oil refinery would use the same kind and quality of crude as a Gulf Coast oil refinery. If the location were at the Gulf Coast, we calculated that the crude oil price at the Gulf Coast would be equal to the price of crude in New York less the transport cost in getting the Gulf Coast crude to New York. This point is consistent with the analysis we did in Chapter 8. There, we showed that when a major world market for a commodity exists in a region, and when the price in that market is determined by the forces of supply and demand, the supply coming from several regions, then the price in any supplying (exporting) region is equal to the price at the major market less the transport costs to that market. For the producer in the supplying region would be foolish to accept less; and if he insisted upon more, the importer in the major world market (if he paid the transport cost) would buy from another supplier who was willing to accept a price equal to the price at the world market less transport cost. So because New York and the surrounding Eastern Seaboard is a dominant world market for crude and receives crude from many supplying regions of the world, the Gulf Coast price was given by the New York price less the transport cost in getting the crude to New York from the Gulf Coast by tanker. We were able to calculate this transport cost.

Now, what would be the price of crude in Puerto Rico? Again we used the same kind of analysis. We started off with the price of crude in Venezuela. Because Venezuela is one of the major suppliers of crude to the New York market, by our reasoning the price in Venezuela must be the price in New York less the transport cost to New York, which again we were able to calculate. With the price of crude in Venezuela thus determined, we could derive the price of crude in Puerto Rico by recognizing that the transport cost in getting the Venezuelan crude to Puerto Rico must be added to the Venezuelan price. As a result of these calculations we derived the price of crude at the Gulf Coast and in Puerto Rico, and more importantly determined that Puerto Rico would have to pay 14.3 cents more for a barrel of crude than the Gulf Coast. When we multiplied 14.3 cents by the number of barrels of crude required annually (which was 9.428 million for a Dacron A complex), we obtained Puerto Rico's annual disadvantage with regard to crude.

The second commodity listed in Table 17.1 is straight-run gasoline. We made the reasonable assumption that there would be considerable new demand for this gasoline in the New York region and that this was a market for which both the Gulf Coast and Puerto Rico would compete. Here Puerto Rico would be better off, because it is closer to New York. We calculated what the cost would be for reaching the New York market by tanker from both locations and found that Puerto Rico would have an advantage of 7.3 cents per barrel. This was multiplied by the total annual output of straight-run gasoline (which was 1.3 million barrels for a Dacron A complex) to obtain Puerto Rico's annual advantage with regard to this commodity.

The third, fourth, and fifth commodities are cracked gasoline, reformed gasoline, and polymerized gasoline, respectively. For each of these we calculated a Puerto Rico advantage of 7.3 cents per barrel, and thus were able to obtain the annual advantage with regard to each.

In similar manner, we calculated for every other commodity, whether an input or output, the advantage or disadvantage of Puerto Rico vis-à-vis the Gulf Coast. We know, for example, that with regard to fertilizer, Puerto Rico would have a major advantage because location there would incur only negligible transport costs in serving the Puerto Rican market. However, the Gulf Coast location would incur major transport costs. With respect to Dacron staple, Puerto Rico would be at a disadvantage because it would have to ship the staple to the Southern textile plants, which would be much closer to the Dacron staple production on the mainland.

Once we obtained Puerto Rico's cost advantage or disadvantage for each commodity, per unit and then on an annual basis, we summed up the annual advantages and disadvantages over all commodities to obtain the overall net transport cost disadvantage of Puerto Rico. There was never an overall net transport cost advantage. For selected complexes, we list these disadvantages in the first column of Table 17.2. Note that the Dacron A program incurs an annual overall net transport cost disadvantage of $263,000, and that Nylon G incurs one of $772,000.

Table 17.2   Overall Net Advantage or Disadvantage of a Puerto Rico
Location, in $/yr, by Type Program* (On the basis of "Moderate"
Scale Disadvantage)

	(1)	(2)	(3)	(4)	(5)	(6)
Program	Transport Cost Disadvantage (approximate)	Advantage on Textile Labor	Disadvantage on Chemical and Petroleum Labor	Overall Net Advantage: Identical Complex Comparison	Scale and/or Process Disadvantage: Fiber and Fertilizer Production	Adjusted Net Overall Advantage or Disadvantage
Dacron A	− 263,000	+ 3,963,000	− 2,229,000	+ 1,471,000	− 1,160,000	+ 311,000
Dacron C	− 339,000	+ 3,962,000	− 2,226,000	+ 1,397,000	− 1,909,000	− 512,000
Orlon B	− 608,000	+ 3,986,000	− 2,329,000	+ 1,049,000	− 2,017,000	− 968,000
Orlon J	− 565,000	+ 3,960,000	− 2,217,000	+ 1,178,000	− 708,000	+ 470,000
Dynel A	− 760,000	+ 4,046,000	− 2,590,000	+ 696,000	− 2,916,000	− 2,220,000
Dynel F	− 437,000	+ 4,000,000	− 2,390,000	+ 1,173,000	− 1,445,000	− 272,000
Nylon A	− 457,000	+ 4,055,000	− 2,624,000	+ 974,000	− 2,543,000	− 1,569,000
Nylon G	− 772,000	+ 3,974,000	− 2,275,000	+ 927,000	− 335,000	+ 592,000

*All data rounded to the nearest $1,000.

Source: W. Isard, Methods of Regional Analysis (Cambridge: M.I.T. Press, 1960), p. 395.

Having obtained the overall net transport cost disadvantage for each complex, we needed to consider labor advantages and disadvantages. From conversations with a variety of knowledgeable persons, and from our own study of the data on wage rates and their changes over time, we estimated that a reasonable advantage for Puerto Rico in textile labor would be $.75 per man-hour. (Recall that this advantage is with respect to the textile South and not the Gulf Coast, because the most efficient mainland operation would involve synthetic fiber production in the South.) When we multiply this figure by the man-hour requirements of textile labor, we derive Puerto Rico's annual advantage on this count. From column 2 in Table 17.2 we see that it is $3,963,000 for the Dacron A complex.

Beyond textile labor, we require chemical and petroleum labor. For such labor we assumed that Puerto Rico would be at a disadvantage, as already noted. If we assume that the wage rate for such labor would be $1 greater in Puerto Rico than on the Gulf Coast, we can derive the annual Puerto Rico disadvantage on this count for each complex. In column 3 of Table 17.2 we see that it is $2,229,000 for the Dacron A complex.

At this point we can add together the annual overall net transport cost disadvantage (column 1), the annual textile labor advantage (column 2), and the annual disadvantage on chemical and petroleum labor (column 3) to get a first crude appraisal of possibilities. For the eight complexes of Table 17.2, we do this and obtain column 4. Column 4 shows that a Puerto Rico location would have an annual advantage of $1,471,000 for the Dacron A complex, and an advantage also for each of the other seven complexes noted.

At first glance, the figures in column 4 suggest that Puerto Rico ought to be a very desirable location for industrial complexes. But on further thought we see that our analysis must be extended to consider a number of other factors. However, the figures of column 4 suggest that Puerto Rico might be in the "ball-park."

First, we should recognize that we have been assuming that the structure of a complex on the mainland would be identical to one in Puerto Rico. In particular, we have been assuming in our cost computations that the same mix of inputs (factor proportions) would be used, the same mix of products would be produced, and the same production processes would be adopted. Such assumptions are bad. For example, we know that the Gulf Coast possesses both oil and natural gas. Its oil refineries, of course, yield fuel oil that can be used to provide the BTU requirements of the complex. We assumed that this happens, because the complex on the Gulf Coast is taken to be identical to the one designed for Puerto Rico. But in 1950, natural gas per BTU was much cheaper than fuel oil on the Gulf Coast. It was clear that the Gulf Coast producer would use natural gas rather than fuel oil for fuel. In this way, he would realize cost savings in the production process which a Puerto Rican location could not, because in Puerto Rico there were no natural gas deposits close at hand. So for each complex the Puerto Rico advantage had to be adjusted downward to recognize that a Gulf Coast complex could use a different, less costly fuel. Similar adjustments had to be made for other cost savings that the Gulf Coast could realize from using a different input mix.

Even after taking into account the different input mix factor, the production processes on the Gulf Coast would not be the same as in Puerto Rico. For example, it might be best in Puerto Rico to use ethylene oxide to make the required acrylonitrile in an Orlon program; at the Gulf Coast it would be more economical to use acetylene to make acrylonitrile. Accordingly, the cost savings at the Gulf Coast location from using the acetylene rather than the ethylene oxide would need to be subtracted from the relevant figures of column 4 in Table 17.2 to obtain a more accurate accounting of the Puerto Rico advantages.

Moreover, why should a Gulf Coast complex produce the same mix of products as Puerto Rico? The price received for fuel oil in Puerto Rico is higher than on the Gulf Coast. So we would expect the Gulf Coast location to produce less fuel oil and more of some other product from which greater revenues are obtainable.

We do not wish to set down all the complicated analysis involved in the use of different factor proportions, processes, and product mixes. Some of this is suggested in the appendix to Chapter 6; further analysis belongs to advanced courses. What we want to make clear is that major adjustments in the preliminary figures of column 4 in Table 17.2 must be made.

Still more, we must recognize that another set of cost differentials stems from the scale, localization, and urbanization economies, and in general agglomeration economies, discussed in Chapter 7. They enter here in a very important way. The level of operation of an oil refinery on the Gulf Coast would be at least four to five times that of Puerto Rico, as is suggested by Figure 17.2. This would mean that unit costs could be much lower on the Gulf Coast, and thus a major disadvantage for the Puerto Rico location.

For example, with reference to the Dacron A complex, we note that the ethylene glycol plant is operated at a level 11.79 in a complex for Puerto Rico. That is, it produces 11.79 million lbs of ethylene glycol annually. Such a plant would be much too small for the Gulf Coast. There, many different kinds of consumers of ethylene glycol exist. An ethylene glycol plant might run at a level of 50 million lbs annually, achieving moderate scale economies. We estimated these to equal $505,000 annually, relative to a 12 million lbs plant. Or the plant might operate at the very high level of 100 million lbs annually and realize economies of scale of $674,000 annually, relative to a 12 million lb plant. Similarly, the scale of operation of many other activities would be larger on the Gulf Coast than in Puerto Rico in order to take advantage of major scale economies.

As it turns out, it is frequently economic to use different factor proportions, processes, and product mixes for different scales of output, as already suggested in the appendix to Chapter 6. That is, factor proportions, processes used, product mixes, and scale are all interrelated. To avoid a complicated presentation, we lump together all the adjustments of the column 4 data which are required to take account of these factors. We present in column 5 of Table 17.2 the sum of the adjustments needed to recognize in full the additional advantages that could accrue to a Gulf Coast location. Subtracting the data in column 5 from that in column 4 yields the adjusted net overall advantage of Puerto Rico in column 6.

Note that in column 6 we find three programs that can operate profitably. Dacron A has a net overall advantage of $311,000 annually, Orlon J $470,000 annually, and Nylon G $592,000 annually. There were, of course, some others that showed advantages. Most confronted disadvantages.

At this point, one might think that our study was at an end—because we clearly identified some complexes that could operate at an advantage in Puerto Rico. However the study could not halt here. There are several other interesting considerations that must be evaluated and aspects that must be pointed out—considerations and aspects which crop up in every development plan.

First, we must recognize that the results very much reflect the nature of the assumptions we made. For example, we assumed that the disadvantage of Puerto Rican chemical and petroleum labor would be only $1 per man-hour. If it turned out to be $1.30 per man-hour, none of the programs would show a positive net advantage. Now, from where did this $1 figure come? It was the best crude estimate we could make. One could not have done otherwise. At the time of our study, there was no data on such labor, because no such labor was being employed in Puerto Rico. As can be expected, we were criticized for using this figure. Conservative chemical companies like du Pont claimed that the figure was too low. It should be at least $1.50 or $2. On the other hand, development enthusiasts at the Economic Development Administration of Puerto Rico said the figure was much too high. After all, the University of Puerto Rico would train chemical-petroleum laborers and engineers in Puerto Rico once the construction of the complex got started. It would be a matter of only a few years before well-trained Puerto Rican engineers would be available to work in the units of a new complex. The disadvantage might then disappear, or fall at least to $.25 per man-hour.

Also, we were sharply criticized from both sides for the use of the figure of $.75 as the advantage of Puerto Rico for textile labor. Conservative groups like du Pont said we greatly overestimated the productivity of the Puerto Rican labor force. According to them, Puerto Rican labor was much less efficient than mainland labor. Thus, even though one needed to pay less per hour of work for Puerto Rican labor, adjustments for the greater output of mainland labor could make the Puerto Rican labor much more costly.

In contrast, the Economic Development Administration of Puerto Rico stated that we underestimated the textile labor advantage. They claimed that in fact

Puerto Rican labor was more productive than mainland labor when it was given the same equipment with which to work. According to them, the Puerto Rican labor had more of a tradition in textile-type work, was less demanding of fringe benefits, and was not likely to be as highly unionized. Further, it had less rigid ideas, could be more easily trained in new ways of work, and could more easily adapt to new technology.

We were in a dilemma as to what figures to use. We could have refrained from using any figures. After all, we had constructed the methodology in such a way that each person was able to put in the assumptions he wished to make about the advantages and disadvantages of labor, or any other input or output. The figures that would come out of the computations, which we programmed so as to involve only a few minutes of time, could reflect his own assumptions. Thus, we were not compelled to use any labor cost differences, such as $1 and $.75, which admittedly reflected our value system. On the other hand, in making a decision a political leader or businessman must make the best assumptions he can at the time of the decision and put them into the computations. If we had been the decision makers in Puerto Rico in the early 1950s, we would have put in the figures of $1 and $.75, respectively, as we did.

Now, there are other points at which the investigator's assumptions must enter in if he is to arrive at a reasonable estimate of the net advantage or disadvantage. One important point pertains to the scale disadvantages of Puerto Rico. Naturally, if the Economic Development Administration of Puerto Rico estimated the scale economy advantages of a Gulf Coast location relative to Puerto Rico, it would probably be on the small side. The Administration might observe that there is a limit to the size of an oil refinery that can be tolerated on the Gulf Coast. Administrative complexities grow exponentially with size. So do disturbances to the ecological system, a point that would now be forcefully made. And so forth. The Economic Development Administration might thus find the maximum feasible size on the Gulf Coast to be three times that of Puerto Rico. Accordingly, its estimate of the scale economy advantages of the Gulf Coast would be much smaller. On the other hand, a Gulf Coast real estate promoter would judge that the relevant factor might be 7 or 8. Accordingly, his estimate of the scale economy advantages of the Gulf Coast would be much larger.

To point up the significance of the scale economy assumption, we made some calculations. Specifically, we made calculations for two different kinds of assumptions regarding scale economies. Under one assumption, which we call the *moderate scale economy* assumption, we assumed that plants on the Gulf Coast would operate at moderate scale while the plants in Puerto Rico would operate at minimum scale. Under the other assumption, which we call the *maximum scale economy* assumption, we assumed that the Gulf Coast units would operate at the maximum feasible scale. Accordingly, we obtain figures such as those in Table 17.3. Consider column 1 and the first four rows of this table. For our assumptions on textile labor advantage and chemical labor disadvantage, as given at the top of the column, we see that if the Gulf Coast scale economies are maximum, Nylon G, Dynel F, Orlon J, and Dacron A cannot operate at a profit. No possibility exists for a competitive operation of a complex in Puerto Rico. On the other hand, if we assume moderate scale economies on the Gulf Coast, we

Table 17.3   Overall Net Advantage of a Puerto Rico Location for Selected Full and Partial Complexes, in Thousands of Dollars Per Year

Complex in Puerto Rico	Assumed Wage Rate Differentials					
	Textile Labor: + 75¢/m-hr Chemical Labor: − 100¢/m-hr			Textile Labor: + 37 1/2¢/m-hr Chemical Labor: − 50¢/m-hr		
	Mainland Scale Economies			Mainland Scale Economies		
	Max. (1)	Mod. (2)	Min. (3)	Max. (4)	Mod. (5)	Min. (6)
1. Nylon G	−2841	592	927	−3691	− 258	77
2. Dynel F	−1122	−272	681	−1927	−1077	−124
3. Orlon J	− 569	470	1093	−1441	− 489	221
4. Dacron A: DMT *plus* Dacron polymer *plus* Fiber *plus* Refinery *plus* Petrochem-Fertilizer	− 790	311	1471	−1657	− 556	604
5. Dacron polymer *plus* Fiber *plus* Refinery *plus* Petrochem-Fertilizer	73	633	1426	− 794	− 234	559
6. Dacron fiber *plus* Refinery *plus* Petrochem-Fertilizer	983	1373	1662	− 99	291	580
7. Refinery *plus* Petrochem-Fertilizer	− 612	−222	67	− 498	− 108	181
8. Dacron fiber *plus* Petrochem-Fertilizer	1395	1785	2074	248	638	927
9. Petrochem-Fertilizer only	− 168	222	511	− 119	271	560
10. Refinery only	− 704	−704	−704	− 639	− 639	−639
11. Dacron fiber only	1563	1563	1563	367	367	367

Source: W. Isard et al., *Industrial Complex Analysis and Regional Development*, p. 207.

obtain the figures of column 2, which are the same as the figures in the last column of Table 17.2. We find that Nylon G, Orlon J, and Dacron A can operate profitably in Puerto Rico. Finally, if we assume that the Gulf Coast plants are at a minimum scale, just as assumed in Puerto Rico, then we obtain the figures in column 3. Here all four complexes can operate profitably in Puerto Rico, and most others are also favored over Gulf Coast locations.

However, as already indicated, there were serious questions about the nature of our assumptions on labor advantages and disadvantages. To show how profitability changes with a change in these assumptions, we calculated columns 4, 5, and 6, corresponding to assumptions of a textile labor advantage of $.375 per man-hour and a chemical labor disadvantage of $.50 per man-hour. Under these assumptions, no complex could operate profitably in Puerto Rico, unless the Gulf Coast plants were to operate at minimum scale. Of course, this was not to be expected.

Finally, we returned to a basic consideration—which we can now illustrate with cost computations. We made the point at the beginning of the chapter that we and the Economic Development Administration considered it very important that there be a full complex, in order to spark industrialization in Puerto Rico. There are, of course, disadvantages to such a requirement. This can be seen by studying some of the figures in Table 17.3. In rows 5 to 11 we present data for different complexes which are not "full." Row 5 refers to the operation of four activities rather than the complete complex. Row 6 refers to the operation of only three. Rows 7 and 8 each refer to the operation of only two, and rows 9 to 11 each refer to the operation of a single activity. If we study the first three columns of the table, we see that the production of Dacron staple alone is consistently positive. We should expect this, because of the Puerto Rican advantage on textile labor. Recall, however, that we did not want to set up just another textile plant. By the 1950s, Puerto Rico had enough of this type of industry and needed other kinds. A second good possibility, involving less than a full complex, is the combination of Dacron staple plus petrochemical fertilizers, as given by row 8. Because this combination involved two different operations, one of which was not textile, this was considered definitely superior to Dacron staple production alone. But again note that this combination did not involve oil refineries, or a host of interrelated activities that could spark industrialization. So, although it promised positive profits for all sets of assumption in Table 17.3, it did not fill the bill.

Row 5 refers to four types of activities, which almost comprise a full complex. When we compare row 5 with row 4, which relates to a full complex, we find in general that row 5 suggests better profit potentials. It is much better for the realistic assumption that the Gulf Coast plants might achieve either moderate or maximum scale economies. But again, the activities of row 5 do not comprise a full complex. If we then insist on a full Dacron A complex, under mainland maximum scale economies, the profit of $73,000 annually in row 5 becomes a loss of $790,000 annually in row 4, or a subsidy of $790,000 annually from the Puerto Rican government if an industrialist is to be induced to set up a complex. Under the assumption of moderate scale economies on the Gulf Coast, the figure of $633,000 (row 5) falls to $311,000 (row 4) when we go to a full Dacron A complex, a significant reduction.

Yet it was clear in the minds of the Economic Development Administration that it was worth an annual subsidy of $790,000, or a reduced advantage from $633,000 to $311,000 annually, in order to get going a full complex sorely needed, and to maximize the probability of takeoff. This point cannot be emphasized too much. In regional development planning, there are important trade-offs that occur, and here is one beautiful illustration of what in fact was faced. From all this analysis, we reached the conclusion that there was real potential for a complex being located in Puerto Rico. Being conservative, we. concluded that, "for at least a limited type of development, the advantages of a Puerto Rico location with regard to a relatively fully integrated industrial complex are clear-cut. Exactly how extensive this development should be—under favorable circumstances it could be quite extensive—and what its specific form should take obviously depend on a host of subsidiary factors which fall outside the scope of this study."[2]

[2] Walter Isard, Eugene W. Schooler, and Thomas Vietorisz, *Industrial Complex Analysis and Regional Development* (Cambridge: M.I.T. Press, 1959), p. 215.

SOME THOUGHTS IN RETROSPECT

Now that the study is done, it is of course important to evaluate the conclusions and impact. The conclusions of the study have held up. The procedures used in collecting, processing, and interpreting the data, as well as the kinds of methodology employed, have received much criticism. But, by and large, no major errors or shortcomings were found. The same approach has since been used elsewhere in the world, particularly for justifying the development of oil refinery–petrochemical fertilizers–synthetic products complexes. It is more difficult, however, to evaluate the impact. First of all, it must be recognized that a study has little or no impact if its findings do not reach the key decision makers, directly or indirectly. The same is true if they do reach them but are disregarded.

In the case of this study, the findings did reach key decision makers. Although the materials were too technical for presidents and vice-presidents to read (a reading of the summary was enough for them), the materials were not too technical to be read by the staff upon whom these key executives relied for the evaluation of the data, analyses, and alternatives. We do know that Theodore Moscoso, the dynamo of the Economic Development Administration of Puerto Rico, introduced his own assumptions into the study so that it could be used to paint what he perceived to be the golden opportunities for Puerto Rico. And he was sufficiently vigorous, energetic, and imaginative to see that the findings of the study were called to the attention of key industrialists and private investors on the mainland.

What was the outcome? It is sufficient here to record the current situation in Puerto Rico. As of 1973, some 7,000 jobs exist in the petrochemical sector. Moreover, other new jobs have been created, though some of the strong linkages anticipated have not materialized. But much more important is the drastically new industrial psychology that has come about. Businessmen are confident about Puerto Rico's capability for engaging in industry on a competitive basis, and thus are vigorous in their pursuit of further opportunities. Thus, one can definitely state that the impact was positive, and that successful economic development was generated. But here one must be very careful to make sure that the term "economic development" is used only in the narrow sense defined at the beginning of Chapter 15. For there were important outcomes, significant from the standpoint of measuring social welfare, which cannot be measured by dollar figures or number of jobs. Some of these have been discussed in previous chapters. We shall elaborate upon them in the next sections.

SELECTED PROBLEMS FROM ECONOMIC DEVELOPMENT

At this point, let us again go over the situation of Puerto Rico in the 1950s. Although not representative of the regions undergoing development in Asia, Africa, or the rest of Latin America, in 1950 Puerto Rico had the classic set of problems faced by regions of the Third World. There was grinding poverty. The political situation was ambiguous. There was much dependence and subservience to a dominant power, the mainland U.S. society. Puerto Rico looked to the outside through an "alien" society. Most of the decisions affecting its welfare were made by nonislanders. It had a typical dualistic economy, culture, and society. That is, it had a high concentration of wealth in the hands of a few. It operated at a low-level equilibrium, which meant widespread poverty.

In the decade after World War II, this vicious circle was somehow broken. Change suddenly was in the air, partly from the beginnings of growth and partly from far-reaching political changes. Commonwealth status was granted, giving the island a good measure of political independence. Probably most important was the appearance in the changed administrative setup of new leaders and decision makers (there did not have to be very many) with a program at hand, partly the result of recent studies analyzing the island's prospects.

The immediate goals were economic: more jobs, higher income, and a higher tax base to permit investment in more educational and health facilities, and in public improvement. The strategy was to support the establishment of many small and medium-sized factories to create new jobs; make the investments necessary to educate and train the labor force, and provide roads and other basic infrastructure for industry; and develop a few key basic industries to spark industrialization through forward and backward linkages.

Accordingly, the Economic Development Administration was set up to assess prospects, recruit, provide subsidies, build factories for zero or low rent, reduce taxes for the enterprises, and establish training programs. In addition, the Puerto Rico Planning Board, formed a decade earlier, was charged with the development of an overall economic, social, and physical plan.

During the decade of the Fifties, great progress was made. *Operation Bootstrap* had lured some 1,500 small factories to the island, mainly to take advantage of a favorable labor climate and supply. The construction of oil refineries and several petrochemical plants had been completed or was underway, and an industrial complex to spark industrialization was assured before the Sixties came along. Moreover, despite tax rebates to entice industry, public revenues had greatly increased, partly from funds from federal government programs. Thus it was possible to carry out a successful policy of training workers. Per capita income had risen from $279 in 1950 to $587 in 1960 (and was to pass $1,000 a decade later), and many of the artifacts of an affluent society had been widely distributed.

But it must be asked: Was this experience really regional development? Did it increase the welfare of the Puerto Rican society? Or was success in economic development achieved through the loss of basic social values—that is, through a trade-off for cultural well-being?

These points are raised because a number of new problems emerged, while some old ones persisted. First, unemployment remained high, despite the increased migration to the mainland during the Fifties, which was in part a result of development and social change. New jobs in manufacturing and the associated services could not keep up with reduced employment in agriculture and home needlework. Also, there was a rapid increase in numbers entering the labor force, because public health measures had reduced the death rate sharply.

Further, although a large number of factories were constructed on the island, many of these were located in the San Juan metropolitan area. In effect, the success of the Fifties meant improvements and new opportunities in a small part of the island, resulting in even larger discrepancies in per capita income and disparities in social welfare.

Problems from the success of the 1950s led the leaders and people to reconsider the goals and strategies that shaped public policy during the first Commonwealth decade. More people were now participating in the modern economy, and making new kinds of demands. They were asking new kinds of questions. By 1960 the time was ripe to assess what had happened: the good things and the unanticipated bad things. It was also time to ask: How good was the public administrative sector, how might it be changed to function even more effectively, and what new goals and strategies should be set to take advantage of new opportunities?

Excessive Urbanization and Increasing
Income and Other Disparities

Perhaps the main unexpected result was the rapid growth of the urbanized areas. At the start, it was thought that Puerto Rico would be able to keep roughly the same balance between rural and urban population, life styles, and activities. But this did not prove to be the case. To counter these trends, the administration gave preferential treatment to new industrial plants in the small towns and rural areas. Several programs were undertaken to support agricultural activities. Public facilities such as health centers, roads, and programs of assistance to local community organizations were provided extensively. Yet each year the growing population became more concentrated in the island's cities. Some migrants came to the large cities directly, others through a step-by-step process from rural areas to small towns to metropolises. Still others returned from New York City and other large metropolitan areas on the mainland to the San Juan metropolis. Because the population was particularly concentrated in the San Juan metropolitan area, some observers began to argue that for most purposes, the entire island was simply the hinterland of one city, the capital. Why did this happen, and why is the same phenomenon found in most developing nations?

Increased income played a major role. As the men and women turned to work in factories (that is, entered the modern sector), they acquired enough income to consider several possible life styles. For them, the wider range of goods and services offered in San Juan was especially attractive. At the same time, the number of employment opportunities was simply greater in the main metropolitan area, despite significant efforts by the government to diffuse factories throughout the island. These factors reflect the very important influence of economies of agglomeration in a small developing nation. The typical firm or service establishment in the private sector finds the best-trained labor in the main city. Communications and other facilities are much better there. Linkages to other firms can be more effectively made. A much wider range of services from other establishments can be easily and quickly obtained. In short, only in the main city can the full urbanization-type agglomeration advantages be found. So most new firms and service establishments decide to locate there. In turn, this leads to still more jobs there, still larger markets there, a still larger pool of skilled and managerial labor, and thus further concentration of activity. Just these phenomena took place in Puerto Rico with respect to San Juan.

Also, the way in which the public sector spent its monies helped to accentuate the differences, even though the public sector did not wish this to happen. When a nation's revenue grows, and when it aspires for still more growth, it needs to set up increasingly specialized services and facilities. These include an economic development administration, planning board, development bank, small-business advisory service, bureau of statistics to provide information required by both business and government, training institutes for engineers, public administrators, and managers, and in time a major university, major health center, and major international airport. Typically, jobs in these units will be found in the metropolitan area and will be well-paying.

Most of these specialized services and facilities had to be concentrated and spatially juxtaposed if they were to operate efficiently and achieve scale and urbanization economies. Also, they needed to be linked to the location of major demands, and located in a place where their employees would be satisfied to live. Skilled employees usually prefer a city location. Cities have the facilities they want as households and consumers, such as better schools for children, adequate telephone service, and good roads. Cities better meet their demands to be at the locus of communication exchange, to be close to other specialized personnel, and to have convenient access to transportation to the outside world. The result was that many major facilities representing the "new Puerto Rico" were built and operated in the San Juan area. This further reinforced its relative concentration and attractiveness.

Operations in nonindustrial sectors also were affected by forces for cumulative concentration in San Juan. The housing industry during the first decade of Commonwealth had to grow substantially. Further, for the first time a large share of new units was constructed on an industrialized, mass-production basis. Again, considering the need for an adequate market for housing units and the need to have at hand all the different building-trade skills, manufactured products, and business, financial, and legal services to achieve construction on a mass-production basis, it is no wonder that the bulk of the new units were found in the San Juan area, often in projects of many hundreds of houses or apartments. In turn, the availability of a relatively ample stock of housing, and at a good price because of mass-production economies, was a strong force in drawing households to the San Juan area—particularly those of the middle class and those with two wage-earners in the family.

Another sector was important. Given the fact that the island was a region with few resources, except for labor, it was to be expected that the natural beauty and other amenities of Puerto Rico should be exploited. With modern airplanes to replace boats for most interisland or island-to-continent travel, the effective distance of the island from large population concentrations was vastly reduced. After some rather hesitant starts, tourism became a major industry. Here, as in the previous cases, agglomeration economies, proximity to the airport, and the relatively central location of the metropolitan area all helped to concentrate the bulk of this new activity in and near San Juan.

Industry, housing services, and tourism all had other, less direct impacts through increasing wages and salary payments in the San Juan area. This meant more consumer demand and much more growth of market-oriented activites. In turn, a large multiplier effect required the provision of still greater amounts of appropriate public facilities. Some of these, of course, could be used by still other activities. Here we think of roads, schools, and the like. And the very mass of activities contributed to the attractiveness of the area for those functions which have been identified as "footloose," able to locate wherever the overall attractiveness is the greatest.

<h2 style="text-align:center">Undesirable Shifts in Demands and Life Style</h2>

A second type of impact deals with shifts in demands. With growing income, and with a wider range of opportunities identified (e.g., jobs, shops, recreation, public facilities), the typical household increasingly came to rely on the private automobile. This generated demands for the construction of highways, bridges, and public parking areas, and spawned a host of commercial and service activities linked to the needs of a driving public. New public and private institutions were required to finance large construction projects, as well as the purchase of automobiles. Repair garages, gasoline stations, and junkyards emerged. This in turn generated a series of counterpressures. Spokesmen on behalf of the poor nondriving public pointed out the unfair aspects of large-scale public expenses on behalf of those who could afford automobiles. Why should a large part of the island's income be spent on what appeared to some as a luxury? Also, the purchase of automobiles meant that island income was being spent on goods that could not be produced on the island rather than on goods that might possibly be made by island enterprises. There was opposition as well from the vocal, if not numerous, traditional forces who looked at the "automobilization" as one more malignant cancer fed by foreign ways and stimuli at the expense of those more in harmony with the local culture, society, and history. The "automobilization" of Puerto Rico was an example of unanticipated, yet deep and basic changes triggered by development.

Also, there were a number of undesirable impacts upon family structure. Most of the new jobs in the factories, particularly in those which were persuaded to locate in the smaller towns, were for women. In Puerto Rico the power in the family, and specifically the control of the cash income and how it was spent, had been traditionally vested in the husband. The earning of cash income by the women had devastating effects. Increasingly, when the husband lost his job because of mechanization in the agricultural sector (where he had typically been employed), he was inclined to migrate to the mainland. There he might become a seasonal farm worker or find a low-status urban job as a tentative migrant. Large numbers of family units broke down.

Another factor that brought about increased outmigration was the very fact of participation in the modern sector. Ideally, jobs in the modern sector would have provided the family with the wherewithal to function more effectively in the local setting, and to do so with greater comfort and satisfaction. In fact, the experience, new income, and changed motivation which the new work generally offered caused the Puerto Rican to want to live in New York, or at least San Juan, to partake of what he judged to be much greater opportunities. This revolution in thinking, ideas, and aspirations which the industrialization plan generated set in motion a still larger migration movement. This was especially so among those who found jobs in the new factories: the younger, the more educated, and those with greater experience.

Such "selective migration" is typical of the development process in Third World nations, and is one more reason to look at the Puerto Rican experience. Though it might have been possible to anticipate and even measure this kind of effect and include it in a rational calculation seeking to assess the worth of the development effort, a number of other unanticipated effects were observed. These, too, are rather typical of the impact of industrialization in developing nations. They reflect in part the uneven spread or diffusion of the development process among all strata and regions or subregions of the country. These effects, however, almost defy quantification in traditional cost and benefit measures, although they are equally important.

One such effect relates to retail trade. Until about 1955, virtually all retail trade in Puerto Rico was carried out by small shops, called *colmadas*, with small stocks, limited capital (perhaps one refrigerator), and real estate often consisting of the owner's home. Out of a mix of motives—one of them being the desire to offer a wider diet choice—a mainland supermarket chain was encouraged to open a unit in 1954. A decade later, almost half the food sales in Puerto Rico was in large units, with 60 percent of sales in the San Juan area accounted for by supermarkets. These were highly capitalized establishments. They were, for example, able to stock forzen foods. They were located on large lots to capture the automobile shopper's trade. They drew customers from a radius of several miles (rather than the colmada's three-or four-block "hinterland"). As a function of their larger scale, they stocked a much wider variety of goods—with rising income, families could purchase a range of foods going far beyond the traditional staples. In fact, local diets more and more came to resemble mainland diets.

The first result was to reduce sharply the number of "mom and pop" colmadas. This added a large number of the elderly, with limited alternative job possibilities, to the rolls of the unemployed. Second, though the retail chains did, without question, change and possibly improve the diets of the majority, they reduced the options and convenience of the minority who could not afford to patronize the new establishments, or chose not to for a variety of reasons (such as age). Third, a great deal of traffic congestion was generated during critical rush hours. For reasons of enterprise efficiency, most of the supermarket units were located on highways which also served to link home and work, link enterprises shipping goods to each other, and also to serve intercity traffic.

Fourth, the new supermarkets were not and could not function as informal neighborhood communication centers or neighborhood meeting grounds. The colmadas had frequently fulfilled this function. The owners of the colmadas knew their neighbors. They extended credit during times of family crises, and were breeding grounds, so to speak, of small-scale ventures (entrepreneurial activity). Thus the supermarkets destroyed a major force for cohesiveness and social integration within Puerto Rican society. Fifth, although without question functioning as more efficient units, the large retail food establishments had built-in vulnerabilities. Their stocks were more sensitive to power failures, shipping strikes, and other interruptions of service. The dependence on the outside world was further accentuated, in most cases, by off-island ownership.

Along another direction, development had the effect of causing (or possibly was accompanied by) shifts in the balance of power from country to city. Most of the development efforts were keyed to the industrial sector. Though efforts were made to channel some of the new enterprises to small towns, the major growth took place in the San Juan area and a few other points. At the same time, in order to survive world competition, agricultural activity was being mechanized, particularly in the production of sugar, which continued to be the main export crop. Thus, as there were gains in the industrial sector in terms of value of product, investments in plant and equipment, and number of workers, declining employment was being registered in the agricultural sector. This was particularly hard for the elderly, others with low mobility, and those who shied away from environments other than the familiar rural one. Also, there were rising expectations and demonstration effects. These were partly the result of widespread education and enhanced communications. The radio and TV became ubiquitous. Virtually everyone had the opportunity to visit San Juan, and perhaps New York also. As a consequence of all these factors, the family subsistence farm came to be seen as a nonviable economic and social unit. Thus a very important side effect of the development process was the overall decline in importance, acceptance, and functioning of the agricultural-rural sector and regions.

Loss of Identity

Students of development have established that there are different "styles" which define and describe the development process. The dimensions include: (1) the extent to which power is concentrated, (2) the relative reliance on free enterprise and the laissez-faire operation of the market as opposed to administrative devices in the economic sphere, and (3) the degree to which the fruits, as well as the costs, of development are equitably shared. One dimension of particular significance, given the context of Puerto Rican society, is the relative sense of identity—the ability to control the destiny of the society, and the maintenance of traditional patterns. The constitutional changes accompanying economic and social development promised to enhance this ability to function independently. But they also boxed in the society, perhaps more so than ever before. The development path chosen, partly made possible by these changes, reflected in good measure an alien model and alien methods of analysis used to describe and shape development. Development linked the Commonwealth more closely to the mainland and failed to increase the freedom of options of the local government. The Commonwealth business cycle began to mirror mainland cylces with a lag. As already noted, growing income had meant a larger proportion of income spent on off-island goods and services. In turn, a larger portion of locally produced goods was exported. To some, such trade and interaction were welcome signs of development. To others, they had all the earmarks of greater vulnerability, dependence, and inability to choose one's own options, because the trade and interaction were so predominantly oriented to the mainland. Nowhere was this more strikingly illustrated than in the way in which local programs such as housing, financed from U.S. federal funding sources, were limited in the way in which the programs were administered.

One final point pertaining to the outside world was the use made of the English language and the encroachment of English on the local Spanish. This was the consequence of the many English-speaking visitors, military personnel, and tourists, and of the flowback of English resulting from migration. To some observers, the high rate of bilingualism represented an opportunity. Puerto Ricans might function as a "bridge" between North and South Americans. Or the mixed language might be a symbol of "hybrid vigor." To others, it simply illustrated a decline of sharp identity, a loss of traditional ways without new ones to replace them.

OPERATION SERENITY: A THRUST FOR SOCIAL DEVELOPMENT

We have spent considerable time discussing a selected number of cultural and social problems generated by successful economic development. (As we concluded at the end of the second section, there was no question whatsoever that successful development in the economic sense had been achieved by the end of the 1950's. Puerto Rico had "taken off.") The cultural and social problems included persistent unemployment; increasing urbanization; increasing discrepancies in per capita income; increasing disparities in social welfare, and in what was perceived to be the attainment of the good life; increasing inequity between the urbanized and rural sectors and populations; increasing traffic congestion; psychic disutility from too rapid a rate of economic growth; increasing geographic concentration of power and wealth; too rapid an "automobilization"; breakdown of the nuclear family unit; destruction of important social bonds, linkages, and community cohesiveness; overall decline of family subsistence farming; loss of identity; increasing dependence on a single external power, the mainland U.S.; reduction in the choice of options in decision-making; greater economic vulnerability; language and cultural pollution; and breakdown of traditional ways.

Each of the problems generated by the development experience can be seen as an index of positive development and progress, or it can be considered an index of the society's inability to function effectively in the modern world. To the extent that it represents the latter, it poses a challenge. Can a society devise a development style that (a) preserves traditional ways and sharpens the sense of worth and identity, (b) raises the level of economic welfare for the society's population by increasing per capita income, and (c) decreases discrepancies among the poor and rich regions, populations, and sectors of the society? This question was confronted by at least certain key decision makers in Puerto Rico, and has been identified with the political position of the independence movement.

For in Puerto Rico, there has been a growing dissatisfaction with the single-minded development thrust, and a growing awareness of the type of undesirable social externalities of development which must be controlled. So even within the government—which in many ways has rejected an independence option, as has the population, at least insofar as it was able to express its preference in the electoral process—one looks for a redefinition of the development process through a new style.

One variant on the new ideology—itself an amalgam of several positions—was first announced by the then-governor Muños Marin some two decades ago. It

was seen as a further step in the development process. For a time it was expressed as "Operation Serenity" to contrast with, but also parallel, Operation
Bootstrap and Operation Commonwealth. It sought a Puerto Rican blend of
economic modernization and structural change as a stimulus to the island, but it
also sought to serve as a prototype of Third World development. The traditional
aspects of the society were not to be destroyed in the quest for the new. There
was to be a constant and intense search for ways to expand human freedom and
dignity. Rather than constantly striving to raise the level of economic well-being,
the sought-for mode was one that would permit statisfaction with a more modest
level of attainment and one that could permeate large segments of the society.
The energies available would be directed to predominantly cultural ends. In
more formal terms, it was as if some judicious weighted average of per capita
income, identity, and culture was to be optimized in the process of growth. In
the language of our earlier discussion of the issue, a blend of material goods,
c-enlightenment, and c-self-respect was to be sought, but only provided a threshold of each was attained. The style of development, then, was one in which several
objectives were to be pursued jointly. Although it was expected that Commonwealth status or some variant would continue (and with it close ties with the U.S.
and, necessarily, the functioning of the economy and society as part of an open
system), there was to be decidedly less emulation of the U.S. as a model of the
future. As we shall note in the next section, more recently this concept of
development was amplified by including an environmental objective: the
maintaining of the island as a homeland, and not one despoiled by industrialization or affluence.

As this position became more specifically formulated, it called for yet greater
investments and expenditures in education and health. The enlightened person
would be able to *use* the fruits of development. As a subsidiary element, considerable attention was given to public support for cultural activities like the
restoration of historical monuments and areas. A second major thrust was the
specification of the freedom objective in terms of a shift in the balance from
foreign to domestic capital. The third component was the intent to establish a
more desirable rural-urban balance, "so that rural areas will not only be cultivated
but also cultured; and the cities not only developed but also civilized."

The bundle of economic and noneconomic objectives developed by Puerto
Rico is illustrative of the revised ambitions expressed in many developing regions.
Because the commitment to such a direction is now a matter of record for about
a decade in Puerto Rico, it is perhaps worthwhile to consider what the results
have been.

Most observers feel that in the years following the articulation of this bundle of
objectives, those aimed at serenity have at best been only partly met. The development goals of a more traditional sort predominated and continue to predominate.
Notable gains were registered in GNP and GNP per capita, overall industrialization
and infrastructure installed. On the other hand, the degree of equity in terms of
income distribution has hardly changed. Traditional ways are no closer to being
maintained than formerly. Indeed, certain events of the last years have led to
even greater strains (e.g., the immigration of Cubans and Dominicans, and the
return of large numbers of "New Yorricans").

How does one explain this? In part it is the difficulty of making operational a
planning system based on the joint pursuit of multiple objectives. Indicators of

equity, cultural advance, and maintenance of traditional ways are hard to find. But the forces of institutionalization are even deeper. In the case of Puerto Rico, there'was built up a tremendous momentum in the bootstrap effort. The important role which the government agencies played became institutionalized. These agencies came to have vested interests, as well as public support because of their achievements. Hence, they made it difficult to set up an institutional structure more responsive to the new serenity thrust. This, combined with the continuous flow of federal funds in the more traditional directions, has caused the bulk of public expenditures to continue to be in the bootstrap direction.

Moreover, the values and aspirations of the individual members of a population do not change easily. It is difficult to start curbing material goods production in a society in which the population is having its first taste of the automobiles, household goods, and diverse luxury items for whose possession and consumption it has long aspired.

Further, it was very difficult to make the serenity goals specific enough for public decision makers, and to measure returns from programs designed to achieve serenity in such a way that they could be contrasted with costs so that the programs could be assessed. As a result, less priority was given to such efforts than the rhetoric would have suggested. Finally, the benefits from serenity-type programs were diffuse, and did not respond clearly to the needs of any wide or powerful constituency.

Looking back, and to repeat, it was as if, faced with a possible set of economic and noneconomic commodities, the ruling group set out to give appropriate weights to each; previously, full weight had been attached to material goods alone. The future, as envisaged by the ruling group, was to see relative increases in the production of such commodities as c-enlightenment, c-respect, and c-justice-rendered, as well as the exercise of power to make autonomous political decisions. But this concern with commodities other than the traditional economic ones was based on the belief that a threshold in the production and consumption of the traditional economic commodities had been crossed. The serenity operation was premised on an approach to societal objectives where, after some point in the development process, relative attainment of the *set* of these objectives was more critical than the dramatic attainment of only one objective. Such did not turn out to be the case. As new institutions took root and as new values of the island's population emerged in the initial development stages, rigidities developed that could not tolerate changes in the set of weights to be applied in the production of economic and noneconomic goods.

What is the moral of the Puerto Rico story? Takeoff in the economic sphere precluded takeoff, and in fact generated takedown, in at least some vital noneconomic spheres. *Perhaps the achievement of takeoff in* all *spheres requires* from the very start *the proper, long-run institutional framework and associated strategies.* As yet, these are only poorly understood and explored.

DEVELOPMENT AND ENVIRONMENTAL DEGRADATION

The Puerto Rican experience has several other lessons for developing regions of the Third World. These pertain to environmental management. Certainly, well through the Sixties and perhaps even up into the Seventies, there was little if any appreciation of another cancer from development, namely environmental degradation. In the case of Puerto Rico, the ecological impact of modernization took several forms. There was the direct pollution of surroundings brought about by the operations of the new enterprises. Despoilation of the air and water in and about the petrochemical complex in the southwest was one example; the steady contamination of the air in and around the major power plants in the San Juan area was another.

Changing patterns of living had an effect on the environment, too. Here the impact was incremental rather than one perceived suddenly. The widespread ownership and use of cars significantly altered the ambient air qualities. The very attractiveness of the beach area, which drew thousands of island and overseas residents to occupy or build cottages along the shore, significantly added to coastal pollution. Microclimate and local hydrological patterns were increasingly being affected by the lateral and vertical spread of settlement. The large residential subdivisions, which provided what clearly were improved housing opportunities, also led to flooding, erosion, and pollution of the water supply. Much more intensive use of recreational areas—in part a reflection of a higher income, in part one of changed attitudes toward use of leisure time—threatened repeatedly to break rather fragile natural and human ecological conditions which had initially made a rainforest, beach, or mountain village a cherished and attractive destination. In many cases, in fact, overuse destroyed.

Moreover, development brought with it another pernicious effect, a disconcern for surroundings. We have already mentioned the increasing breakdown of the family unit, the decreasing sense of community from the destruction of the colmada and many other cementing local institutions, the decreasing pride in and attachment to one's immediate physical spaces, and the increasing attachment and identity with some nebulous, bigger world. So the prisoner's dilemma effect inevitably took its count: the discarded coke bottle, the rusty beer can, the kaleidoscopic forms of litter.

So development runs into new problems of very significant proportions. The society is controlled politically and economically by a relatively few, each of whom can escape the undesirable effect of pollution because they have tremendous flexibility in choice of residential location or because they are nonresidents (externals) of Puerto Rico. Because these relatively few decision makers know how to manipulate the Puerto Rican society and how to trade in political power (c-power), and use their money to that effect, it is increasingly difficult for the Puerto Rican society to achieve the goals for its people. This is especially true when many of the people aspire so much for the "good" but highly materialistic life. Of course, this force pertains not only to Puerto Rico. It becomes a major force that must be controlled and shaped by all developing regions of the world.

We also have an intensified problem of management. So many more people are involved—through "automobilization," as well as demand for power in their use of electric gadgets and all the other things that spell success and for which they have been aspiring. Here, each person sees his own demands as having no effect whatsoever on the problem. Each is one of a million, or even a billion participants in the prisoner's dilemma game, in a setting that is becoming increasingly impersonal.

At the same time, there is another lesson from Puerto Rico's recent experience with environmental degradation from industrial development. It portends another major obstacle, yet opportunity for economic development. Because mainland residents find oil refineries and petrochemical plants obnoxious and many other industries environmentally undesirable, they raise almost insurmountable obstacles and new costs to their development in desirable mainland locations. Thus, in the minds of business executives, locations in Puerto Rico and in underdeveloped regions will have even more comparative cost advantages. Social costs from pollution elsewhere will offer Puerto Rico and these underdeveloped regions more opportunities for industrial development if they are willing to ignore the costs associated with their own environmental degradation, and thus to serve as "dumping grounds." Further, if decisions granting permission to locate are controlled by an elite, largely residing outside these regions, a new form of potential colonial exploitation is in the offing.

CONCLUDING REMARKS

Much of the thinking and analysis of this textbook comes to a head in this chapter. We have presented a case study in order to show how a regional scientist might use the techniques and methods of analysis in studying a region's real-world problems—in this instance, development.

In terms of Puerto Rico, a first goal in the development process was to bring in industry and other economic activity, not only to provide jobs and raise per capita income but also to spark change in the economic structure. In working toward this goal, basic information about the island was required. Though the available information was inadequate—it included an input-output table under construction, and limited data on movements of goods, people, capital, and communications—it was more adequate than that generally available for underdeveloped regions.

Against this background, we conducted analysis. It was clear that comparative cost elements had to enter into the situation; these elements included the basic cost analysis of Chapter 5 and the location factors listed in Chapter 6. Further, to obtain relevant cost differentials, we had to employ the market pricing mechanism given in Chapter 4 for making the best estimates of what the price of such items as crude oil, textile products, and fertilizer might be in Puerto Rico and elsewhere.

But comparative cost analysis was not sufficient. We had to identify forward and backward linkages. Therefore, we had to develop what we termed an industrial complex analysis, which was a synthesis of the comparative cost and of the input-output analyses presented in Chapter 7 and 8. In sum, all the analytic frameworks contained in Chapters 4 through 8 turned out to be essential for identifying the oil refinery–petrochemicals–fertilizer–synthetic products complex which we found economically sound for Puerto Rican development.

The results of applying the analytic techniques were a set of findings. They were based on a number of key assumptions. Three of them related to the wage rate differentials that would continue to exist between the mainland and Puerto Rico, the scale diseconomies under which a Puerto Rican complex would operate, and the future political situation (particularly with respect to the mainland United States). Because of the attitude variable in decision-making, as discussed in Chapter 9, our findings could be, and were, variously interpreted.

Conservative firms, like du Pont, interpreted them as negative. Promotion-bent enterprises, like the First Boston Corporation, considered them positive. Again, this points up the need for a proper psychological setting for development. And often this need must be coupled with changes in the institutional structure, so that vigorous individuals with innovative ideas can exercise leadership. In Puerto Rico, the establishment of the Economic Development Administration was an essential step, both in generating enthusiam on the island and in contacting the right kind of business leaders on the mainland. As this case study illustrates, proper development planning requires cognizance of how attitudes affect basic investments, and therefore how institutions must be structured and manned with the right kind of personalities.

What can we say about the results in Puerto Rico? It was a successful economic development experience, an unsuccessful social development experience, and a highly destructive experience regarding the environment. In short, economic success was diluted with social and environmental losses. On net, the experience was a "little" successful. We have to say a little successful on subjective grounds only. For if one visits the island, one no longer sees pot-bellies (unless he looks very hard). By and large, they have disappeared. Perhaps this is the factor that counts most in any index of social welfare.

On the other hand, development generated many problems. They are the result of changes in the sociocultural structure from economic forces. We can include the broken families, the scarred language, the evaporated or disintegrated neighborhoods, the despondent elderly, the lost adolescents, the hugh junkyards, the littered beaches, and the foul air. This experience clearly demonstrates why economic development cannot be equated with social development, as discussed at length in Chapter 15 and 16.

The attempt at an Operation Serenity in Puerto Rico signified that political leaders eventually recognized that economic development was taking place at the expense of community welfare, and was undermining strong community bonds and a rich cultural heritage. But the disappointing results of Operation Serenity suggest the dangers stemming from the rigidities of new institutions and socio-economic structure generated in the process of economic development. Here, all the knowledge we have about organizations, as discussed in Chapter 12, is essential for anticipating and hopefully avoiding the problem for future developing regions.

Specifically, a major force blocking a successful Operation Serenity was the presence in Puerto Rico of newly developed institutions with vested interests, such as the Economic Development Administration (EDA), the Puerto Rico Industrial Development Corporation (PRIDCO), and the many institutions in the private sector which gained from economic development. The EDA's history repeats several elements of the scenario we presented for the CCCSS in Chapter 12. By the time Operation Serenity was initiated, EDA was firmly rooted in the public sector and in the society of Puerto Rico. Operation Serenity involved a change in the weights to be applied to the production of various economic and noneconomic goods—and, in particular, the application of smaller weights to new production of economic goods. Because such production provided the basic justification for EDA's existence, it resisted, and in many ways its resistance was effective. It was concerned with the maintenance of its power base as an objective in itself, apart from the needs of the Puerto Rican people. Understandably, the Puerto Rico effort failed to anticipate this undesirable force. The next experience in development planning should not.

Other lessons come from the Puerto Rico experience. The Puerto Rico effort failed to establish from the start safeguards for preserving its abundant environmental heritage. Now it must face a gigantic problem in controlling the use of the environment. In large part, this problem is due to the very successful efforts of Operation Bootstrap. The basic industrial structure has expanded significantly. But more important, now that the first component units of basic petrochemical and refinery operations are in place, the potential for expansion is greater than ever because of major new agglomeration economies possible. This assumes that, as in the past, industry is not required to bear the social costs of pollution. So the thrust and momentum of Operation Bootstrap is likely to continue to encourage industrial growth. Even with the use of the best pollution-control technology, there will be a significant increase in the pollution load on the environment. At the same time, the conflicts of Operation Bootstrap with Operation Serenity and similar welfare programs will become more intense, particularly because we can expect more vocal and powerful antipollution interest groups to arise as the harmful effects of pollution become more and more evident.

We must conclude that both an Operation Serenity and an Operation Beauty must accompany any Operation Bootstrap. Successful economic development cannot be achieved with only one successful "operation." It must have at least two, and ideally three. This requires the foresight and the know-how to make a more effective assessment and consideration of the effects of economic development in order to temper the growth path and guide it in directions which are best, taking into account all social costs and benefits.

As we come to the end of the story we must ask: Was the outcome positive? Was it worth it? We certainly see the sharp increase in GNP, per capita income, and material level of living. We also see the sharp decrease in sense of identity, rich cultural traditions, and serenity. And we see the sharp and almost deadly degradation of the environment. In looking forward, we see all three becoming even more sharp.

As we have indicated previously, there is no way of evaluating the total effect. The only thing one can do is ask the people themselves whether it was worth it. We from the more advanced industrial regions can offer our opinions. But they mean very little. And we should go down to Puerto Rico and see the havoc wrought upon the environment. The Penuelas region of the petrochemical plants is a messy wasteland. The cities have not retained their traditional qualities, and all too often they exhibit congestion and squalor amid affluence. On the other hand, to repeat, the hundreds of thousands of pot-bellies have disappeared.

APPENDIX TO CHAPTER 17. Inputs and Outputs for Selected Oil Refinery, Petrochemical, and Synthetic Fiber Activities.

As clearly indicated in Chapters 15 and 16, any analysis aimed at identifying specific activities in connection with programming the economic development of a region requires information on the inputs and outputs of these activities.

Usually we find it easiest to state these inputs and outputs first in terms of constant production coefficients à la input-output procedure as discussed in Chapter 7. Then, whenever necessary and possible, we modify these constant production coefficients to reflect nonlinear relations.

In our industrial complex research for Puerto Rico, we found this procedure useful. Accordingly, we collected information from all kinds of sources—published literature, reports of consulting engineering firms, patents, and interviews with business officials and engineering experts.

For each activity we constructed a set of relevant inputs and outputs. In a systematic and comprehensive fashion we recorded them in a master table. Part of this master table is reproduced as Table 17A.1, which records inputs and outputs in terms of physical data. It is in such physical units that East European societies conduct their analyses. In contrast, in the USA and in Western European industrialized societies, inputs and outputs are stated in terms of dollars, marks, etc, as in Tables 7.1 and 7.2.

In Table 17A.1 each column represents one activity; the activity is given the number of its column. Also, each row represents a commodity, and the commodity is given the number of its row. When the commodity is used in an activity as an input, this is indicated by a minus sign. When it comes up as an output, this is indicated by a plus sign.[1] For example, column 1 records the annual inputs and outputs in operating at unit level a given hypothetical oil refinery (designated prototype 1).[2] Among its annual inputs are 9.428 million barrels (MM bbl) of crude oil (row 1); 0.801 billion pounds (MMM lb) of steam (row 24); 2.511 million kilowatt-hours (MM kw-hr) of electric power (row 25); and 1,390 MMM BTU of fuel (row 26). Among its annual outputs are 2.074 MM bbl of straight-run gasoline (row 2); and 1.484 MM bbl of cracked gasoline (row 3). The cells in column 1, where no figures appear, refer to inputs or outputs not involved in a significant way in the operation of oil refinery, prototype 1.

Many of the columns of Table 17A.1 deal with activities that produce just one output. For example, column 47 shows the annual inputs required to produce a unit amount (in this case 1 MM lb) of Dacron staple (row 49). These inputs include .05 MMM lb of steam (row 24), 1.2 MM kw-hr of electric power (row 25), and 1 MM lb of Dacron polymer (row 48).

It should be noted that the table does not list the full set of inputs and outputs associated with all the activities noted. A complete list including taxes, for example, would be necessary for constructing full cost and profit estimates. Here, such estimates are not required. The basic question is whether expected expansions should occur at sites on the mainland only, or on both the mainland and Puerto Rico. Thus, the only inputs and outputs that need to be considered are those leading to significant variations in cost or revenue between Puerto Rico and mainland locations.[3] Moreover, Table 17A.1 lists only those inputs and outputs whose amounts vary in direct proportion with the scale of production —for example, those that double when scale or level doubles. Inputs such as labor and capital services are excluded. These inputs must be considered individually at a later stage, because they generally vary nonlinearly with scale of production.

[1] Unlike input-output tables, this table reports the several outputs as well as inputs involved in a given activity. Hence, outputs and inputs must be differentiated by sign.

[2] This refinery includes a topping and vacuum flash unit, a fluid catalytic cracking unit, a catalytic polymerization unit, and a simple gas separation plant.

[3] This point has been developed in the discussion of comparative cost studies in the second section of Chapter 6.

Note also that alternative processes are included in the table. Several refinery prototypes could be considered, although only two are explicitly noted. Several ammonia production processes are recorded (columns 31–34). This procedure is consistent with the programming approach to development discussed in Chapters 15 and 16.

Once a table of linearly varying inputs and outputs of relevant activities is constructed, the next step is to determine the totals of these inputs and outputs for each of many complexes. We first put together several types of activities in a logical and consistent way, and at specific quantitative levels. In Figure 17.3, we outlined the Dacron A complex, in which the figure within each box indicates the number assigned to the activity of the box, and the figure on top of each box represents the level at which that activity is to be operated. To explain Figure 17.3, begin with the Dacron staple box at the upper right. A plant producing annually 36.5 MM lb of Dacron staple was considered, a priori, reasonable for Puerto Rico. It is large enough to achieve scale economies, and was consistent with estimated increases in the demand for Dacron. Because Dacron staple corresponds to activity 47 in Table 17A.1, and because a unit level of activity 47 yields 1.0 MM lb annually of Dacron staple, all the items in column 47 must be multiplied by 36.50 to obtain the inputs and outputs corresponding to an annual production of 36.5 MM lb of Dacron staple. Thus, we have placed the number 36.50 above the Dacron staple box. This indicates the level of operations at which activity 47 is to be pursued.

One of the chemical intermediates required for Dacron staple production is Dacron polymer. Specifically, we require 36.5 MM lb of Dacron polymer annually. Because Dacron polymer is activity 46, and because the unit level of activity 46 is 1.0 MM lb of Dacron polymer, all the coefficients of column 46 must be multiplied by 36.50. This number has been placed above the box designated Dacron polymer.

The production of 36.5 MM lb of Dacron polymer requires 36.87 MM lb of dimethyl terephthalate. Because a unit level of activity 45 yields 1.0 MM lb of dimethyl terephthalate annually, all the coefficients of column 45 must be multiplied by 36.87 to obtain the required dimethyl terephthalate. The number 36.87 is placed on top of the dimethyl terephthalate box. The paraxylene required to produce dimethyl terephthalate is programmed to be imported because it would be much more expensive to import the necessary raw materials that would be required to produce paraxylene in Puerto Rico.

The production of 36.5 MM lb of Dacron polymer also requires 11.79 MM lb of ethylene glycol. Therefore activity 22, whose unit level of operations yields 1 MM lb of ethylene glycol, must be carried on at a level of 11.79. Accordingly, all coefficients of column 22 of Table 17A.1 must be multiplied by 11.79; this number is placed on top of the ethylene glycol box in Figure 17.3.

Producing 11.79 MM lb of ethylene glycol via the oxidation process requires 9.79 MM lb of ethylene. Because a unit level of operations of activity 10, an ethylene separation process, yields 1.610 MM lb of ethylene, this activity must be operated at a level of 6.08; this number is placed on top of the ethylene box. Ethylene is part of the gas stream coming from an oil refinery. We assume an oil refinery with a cracking as well as a coking and a reforming unit. We operate it at a scale which corresponds to an annual input of 9.428 million barrels of crude oil. For convenience we designate the operation which involves this level of crude input as a unit level. Hence all the coefficients of column 4 are to be multiplied by 1,000; and this number is placed on top of the oil refinery box in Figure 17.3.

We follow a similar procedure in setting the level at which the fertilizer operation, and every activity directly and indirectly required to yield the necessary

Table 17A.1   Annual Inputs and Outputs for Selected Oil Refinery, Petrochemical, and Synthetic Fiber Activities

	Oil Refinery, Prototype 1 (1)	...	Oil Refinery, Prototype 4 (4)	...	Ethylene Separation Prototype 4 (10)	...	Ethylene Glycol (oxidation) (22)	...	Ammonia from Hydrogen (31)	Ammonia from Methane (32)
1. Crude Oil MM bbl	− 9.428		− 9.428							
2. Gasoline, straight-run MM bbl	+ 2.074		+ 1.300							
3. Gasoline, cracked MM bbl	+ 1.484		+ 2.226							
4. Gasoline, reformed MM bbl			+ 1.486							
5. Gasoline, polymerized MM bbl	+ 0.219		+ 0.415		+ .0029					
6. Naphtha, MM bbl	+ 0.660									
7. Kerosene, MM bbl	+ 0.943		+ 0.707							
8. Diesel oil MM bbl	+ 1.414		+ 0.896							
9. Gas oil MM bbl										
10. Cycle oil MM bbl	+ 1.320		+ 1.980							
11. Heavy residual MM bbl	+ 0.943									
12. Coke and carbon 10XMM lb			+ 4.033							
13. L.P.G. 10XMM lb	+ 6.860		+ 15.000		+ .0508					
14. Hydrogen MM lb	+ 0.950		+ 8.900						− .2000	
15. Methane MM lb	+ 12.780		+ 34.860							− .5500
16. Ethylene (mixed) MM lb	+ 6.510		+ 17.410		−1.6100					
17. Ethane (mixed) MM lb.	+ 9.930		+ 32.250		−3.0190					
18. Propylene MM lb	+ 3.630		+ 7.580		− .7580					
19. Propane MM lb	+ 2.150		+ 5.080		− .5080					
20. Butylenes MM lb										
21. Butanes MM lb										
22. Pure ethylene MM lb					+1.6100		− .8300			
23. Pure ethane MM lb					+3.0190					
24. Steam MMM lb	− 0.801		− 1.402		− .0148		− .0103			− .0023
25. Power MM kw-hr	− 2.511		− 3.999		− .0194		− .0800		− .4640	− .5600
26. Fuel 10XMMM BTU	−139.000		−242.000				− .2010			− .0450
34. Nitrogen MM lb							+6.8000			
35. Ethylene Glycol MM lb							+1.0000			
39. Ammonia MM lb									+1.0000	+1.0000
40. HCN MM lb										
41. Acrylonitrile MM lb										
42. Methanol MM lb										
43. Sulphur MM lb										
44. Sulphuric acid MM lb										
45. Nitric acid MM lb										
46. Paraxylene MM lb										
47. Dimethyl terephthalate MM lb										
48. Dacron polymer MM lb										
49. Dacron Staple MM lb										
59. Ammonium nitrate MM lb										
60. Urea MM lb										
61. Carbon dioxide MM lb										
74. Nylon salt MM lb										
76. Nylon filament MM lb										

Ammonia from Ethylene (33)	Ammonia from Ethane (34)	...	Nitric Acid from Ammonia (43)	Dimethyl Terephthalate (air oxidation) (44)	...	Dacron Polymer (46)	Dacron Staple (47)	...	Ammonium Nitrate from Ammonia (55)	Urea from Ammonia (56)	...	Nylon Filament (73)
− .6290												
	− .5780											
− .0023	− .0023			− .0030		− .0060	− .0500		− .0007	− .0028		− .0555
− .5600	.5600		− .1200	− .5200		− .2500	−1.2000		− .0170	− .0340		−1.6000
− .0450	− .0450			− .2800		− .1000				− .2250		
												− .2200
						− .3230						
+1.0000	+1.0000		− .2860						− .2380	− .5800		
				− .4000		+ .3350						
			+1.0000						− .7630			
				− .6800								
				+1.0000		−1.0100						
						+1.0000	−1.0000					
							+1.0000					
									+1.0000			
										+1.0000		
										− .7500		
												−1.0000
												+1.0000

Source: W. Isard et al., Industrial Complex Analysis and Regional Development, pp. 40–49.

inputs of the fertilizer operation, is to be operated. For each column of Table 17A.1, whose (column) number appears inside a box in Figure 17.3, we multiply the inputs and outputs in that column by the number on top of that box. This gives us the totals for that activity. Next, over all activities in Figure 17.3 we sum the totals for each type of input and output to obtain the overall total of each commodity input or each commodity output associated with the Dacron A complex (except for the nonlinear inputs of labor and capital). These totals are recorded on column 1 of Table 17.1. Because labor and capital inputs vary non-linearly with the level of most of the activities considered, it was necessary to make side computations to estimate these inputs for each activity included in the Dacron A complex. Over all activities in this complex, the totals of the labor and capital inputs are recorded at the bottom of Table 17.1.

In similar manner we calculated total requirements and yield for each of the complexes listed at the head of a column of Table 17.1, as well as for many others that were examined in the analysis.

Concluding Remarks and Synthesis: Some Elements Critical for World Organization

INTRODUCTION

It is now time to sit back, to seek some overview of the ground we have covered. In particular, we want to evaluate the different elements of analysis covered in looking at social problems—those with us and those in prospect. Of course, we need not pursue an evaluation; we could claim that an evaluation is too much to ask of an introductory textbook. Yet this should not be so for an introductory textbook in regional science, because we claim that the justification for regional science as a distinct social science field lies in its ability to effectively attack an important set of social problems with its unique, multidisciplinary focus. Further, we want to look ahead. We want to ask: Where do we go from here? Is there some path open for making a more concerted effort to deepen our understanding and increase our ability to come to grips with social problems? What are the prospects for new knowledge and wisdom along the path?

Recall that in this text we have tried to introduce the student to many of the important areas of regional science. We could not cover all areas or the text would have been a survey at the expense of analytical depth. Rather, we tried to cover the basic tools of regional science and related areas, but in such a way that we were better able to see a range of significant problems that confront society and our potential for doing something about them.

475

We could at this point go over the chapters, one by one, indicating the basic contents of each and putting everything together in a final, balanced synthesis for general use. We prefer not to do this, because it is something the reader can do for himself. Instead, we seek a summary or synthesis along a fresh direction. At the moment it seems best to confront squarely a problem that will be increasingly with us in the next century, namely that of world organization. The rapid spread of communication channels and facilities over the entire globe and major advances in transport technology will bring everybody within a few hours of each other. They will literally shrink the world. The problem then becomes one of orderly rearrangement and patterning, over both space and time, of the billions of people involved.

THE RATIONALE FOR WORLD ORGANIZATION

The need for world organization is not a new one. It has existed for a long time. Certainly there is and has been a need for it as a means to curb major warfare among nations. Technological advance has made this need still more forceful, because of the tremendous new potentialities for destruction that have emerged in recent decades. At the same time, the great strides taken in communications and transport technology facilitate the task.

The need becomes still more intense because of the great problems of environmental management. At one time, outputs of pollutants and inputs of ecologic goods could be ignored because they involved what were considered to be zero costs. Then, a case could be made for nonintervention by world authorities, especially where all economic goods used as inputs were locally supplied and all economic goods produced as output were locally consumed. However, today pollutants can no longer be considered zero cost goods, and dangerous exposure to their output (in a sense, forced and nonrejectable consumption) too often extends far beyond any local area—as, for example, with mercury pollution and strontium fallout. There are major spread effects and externalities in the sense that nonlocal populations may be adversely affected by activities in a local area. Hence there is a need for an authority that goes well beyond local areas, as indicated in Chapter 13. In fact, it appears that the environmental problems may be severe enough to require, as with control of modern warfare, a drastic revision in world organization. Incremental change, such as that associated with the processing and analysis of data on a systematic and comprehensive basis by a United Nations that is granted some additional powers, may not be in order. Rather, a qualitative jump in world organization may be required, such as the jump implied in Chapter 12 when we speculated on the emergence of an eighth-order node. Such a node might be endowed with strong taxing and redistributive powers. It might have full control of all extraterrestrial activity, as well as major control of military activities and those which use scarce resources or are highly polluting.

Let us set forth some of the arguments for resource-use control. We will do so boldly, recognizing that we may be intruding on the traditional fields of political science and international relations. But we will do so with the hope that the multidisciplinary focus of regional science on space, spatial interdependence, and interregional linkages will bring new light to the age-old problem of world organization, and thereby allow us to make some contribution to world welfare.

What is the basic argument for a qualitative jump in world organization from the standpoint of resource-use control? At one level, the argument starts with a very general thesis. The earth has limited resources. Broadly speaking, demands for these resources come from at least two sources. First, for a given standard of living, there are the demands by numbers of population, designated by P. According to some scientists, the prospect of at least a doubling of global population is almost assured, particularly because 38 to 48 percent of the population in the poor nations are fifteen years old or less (and thus entering child-bearing age), and because a significant decrease in the mortality rate in these nations is to be expected. Others, less optimistic, see the population expanding many more times. In any case, large increases in P, population numbers, imply large increases in demand for scarce resources.

Coupled with large increases in P are demands for an increase in living standards, designated by S, the per capita income required to achieve any given living standard. These demands are at all levels. By the year 2000, we can expect more than a doubling of the standard of living of the rich—perhaps even a tripling, such as seems to have occurred in the last twenty five years. For the poor, who aspire to the standards of the rich, we may expect at least a tripling—even though this would not bring to a halt the increase in the absolute per capita income differences between the rich and the poor. Hence, according to one broad-gauged, expert social scientist, we may expect that the inertial tendency of the rich to consume more and more (which would take some time to change, if change were possible), coupled with the urge of the poor to catch up, will lead to at least a trebling of S. For the world, this corresponds to an increase in per capita income from \$600 to \$1,800 (in constant dollar terms).[1] An income of \$1,800 per capita corresponds to half the 1972 U.S.-Western European level. In sum, this argument implies perhaps a twelvefold increase in the product $P \times S$, in demands for goods and thus in the pressure upon our limited resources.

Countering this pessimistic type of reasoning is the view that maintains that technological advance will make this increase in demand possible without increasing the pressure on resources. Has it not done so in the past? Have not our estimates of resource reserves constantly increased, partly as a result of technological advance and further exploration, and kept pace with our consumption levels? This is questionable. But even if it is true, we must keep in mind several counterbalancing factors. One is the increasing fraction of research and development expenditures that seems to be going to military research. A second is that we have passed the stage where only negligible technology and capital resources need be devoted to the control of pollution emissions. Rather we confront a need, mounting perhaps exponentially with increase in GWP (gross world product), to combat pollution, as we have repeatedly stated. We can no longer fall back on natural production processes to take care of our pollutants. This exponentially mounting need will require, generally speaking, an exponentially mounting stock of capital to handle the output of pollutants. This, too, will constitute a major challenge for technology.

[1] See Gunnar Adler-Karlsson, "Some Roads to Humanicide," *Instant Research on Peace,* Vol 3, No. 4, 1973, pp 198–210.

Suppose that potential technological advance can make strides to meet demands. It still may be necessary to establish maximum standards of living, parallel to minimum standards. Basic institutional changes will be required to guide and shape such technological advance and the allocation of its fruits. A world unit such as the United Nations is hopelessly inadequate for the task. A unit that is largely dependent on financial contributions of those member nations —such as the United States, Soviet Union, China, France, Japan, and other major nations—whose production, consumption, and military activities must be most severely regulated, cannot function effectively, as the last decades have demonstrated. Nor does it seem possible to increase incrementally the power of the ill-constituted United Nations to that level that is essential, given the structure and functioning of the United Nations and nations in the international arena. What is required, and is inevitable if mankind is to survive on this planet, is a new world organization — a strong unit with major taxing power, power of enforcement and regulation, and powers to effect a world redistribution of goods, capital, and other mobile resources. In short, a well-defined node is required, one effectively above and dominant to each of the lower-order nodes with respect to clearly determined policy areas.

SOME SPECIFIC FUNCTIONS OF A NEW WORLD UNIT

The Taxing Power and Social Welfare Functions

We can be more specific. We must give to the new world unit the taxing power to effect progressive taxation—even to the point where, at some high enough level of annual income (say $1 million or $10 million), 100 percent of any increment of income is taxed away. At this point in time, few people have such a high income. Thus, a grant of taxing power of this order, which in effect sets a maximum allowable income, may be considered politically feasible. Not many persons would be affected. Also, in the first five years of the new organization's life, tax rates might be set very low for all incomes up to, say, $100,000 per annum, making the tax burden negligible for people with these incomes; and low enough for incomes in the range of $100,000 to $999,999 to cause a *small* tax burden for persons with these incomes. Such a tax scheme might raise revenues more than sufficient for a new unit in the throes of organization and early operation.

Of course, with time, as both the forces of technological development and inflation are at play, money incomes of all individuals would rise substantially (real incomes would rise at a smaller rate). Hence money (as well as real) tax revenues of the new world unit would also increase substantially, and should certainly be adequate for operations if coupled with a gradual increase in tax rates across the board for incomes less than the maximum.

Another specific function of the world unit would be to specify and where possible enforce minimum standards of living for all people of the world, recognizing that the content of that standard would need to vary significantly among regions. Such variations would be required because of different cultural heritages, different needs imposed by the environment, and numerous other factors. In theory, such minimum standards could be achieved *if* it were possible to stimulate sufficient economic activity (of the right kind) in all regions and local areas, making an adequate per capita income available everywhere. In practice, as we will discuss later, it will not be possible without intervention and assistance by the world unit; and even with intervention and assistance, some form of redistribution of income, productive forces, and goods will be necessary to insure that everywhere the minimum standard is realized. In effect there will be a need for worldwide social welfare and poverty programs—not only of the sort we are and have been exploring in the United States and in other nations but also of new scope and dimensions. Such programs imply new forms of public administration, new channels of communications, and new structures for decision-making authority. The new world unit will need to be experimental in these matters, and continue being experimental, for a minimum standard of life should be a sine qua non of world society. In one way, the achievement of it would constitute a real movement in the direction of economic democracy. The one-dollar–one -vote principle of the free market, capitalist system would thus be partially replaced by a one-man–one-vote system.

Beyond having the power to tax and redistribute, the world unit must be in a position to take vigorous leadership in bringing about major social, political, and economic changes. It must mount more effective programs to curb world population growth, because this will become the concern of all populations subject to taxation for the support of social welfare and poverty programs. Programs to reduce birth rates will of course be aided by tendencies to reduce family size as family income rises, which also tend to make the child-bearing population more receptive to family planning efforts. The world unit must take the initiative in educating people to lower their material aspirations, and to transform to other ends their urge to catch up in material levels of living. The world unit might even encourage certain people to accept a level below the high absolute levels they may already have achieved.

At the same time, the world unit must guide technological development into the right channels. Research and development efforts to build up military capability must be brought to a halt. Such efforts must be concentrated in areas that can lead directly or indirectly (via spinoffs) to significant increases in the productivity of enterprises producing food, housing, clothing, and other items essential for a healthy life. Research and development efforts must also be channeled to the control of pollution generation, to maintaining and even raising the quality of the environment where it has been allowed to deteriorate, and to building up institutions and providing facilities to advance the cultural, social, and political welfare of people. These institutions might strengthen the cohesiveness of mankind and eliminate discrimination, caste systems, and other institutions that deprive individuals of basic freedoms.

With regard to the attainment of political democracy, the world unit must encourage all individuals to participate in the political process and in decision-making at the right levels, and make such participation possible. This will be aided by a rise in per capita income and higher educational attainment of people. It must be recognized also that the introduction of still another level of government in world political organization signifies both a more elaborate and a more specialized communications and decision-making structure.

In one sense, decision-making power and influence tend to be directly and indirectly lodged at the peak of the pyramid. The pyramid, however, is becoming more extensive and inclusive at its base. So there must be a wider, albeit indirect, contribution to decision-making at the top via more extensive and efficient communication channels with the base. We must avoid the undesirable situation in which too many decisions are made at the top, leaving too little time available for the consideration of each decision which in turn leads to the making of poorer decisions. The structure of decision-making and organization must be changed to allow for more and more delegation of authority and decision-making so that the decisions to be reached at the top can be judiciously and properly made. In brief, there should be greater centralization with regard to the making of certain types of decisions and exercise of certain types of power, while there should be greater decentralization with regard to the making of other types of decision and exercise of other types of power. In this way, the overall concentration of decision-making and exercise of power is not increased—and perhaps is significantly reduced to that which is optimal from the standpoint of social welfare, taking into account economic efficiency and the value of c-participation, c-solidarity, and other noneconomic commodities that can be produced (generated) by this process.

The Police Power and the Military Function

Other duties of a world unit can be fruitfully considered in terms of the framework of public sector activities discussed in Chapter 13. There we indicated that one of the more traditional functions of the public sector is to provide services (commodities) that are nonmarketable. One of the main services to be produced by a world unit is c-security, which by and large refers to defense (military) and police and fire protection. Clearly the world unit must have an effective police force, supported by revenues raised through its own taxing powers. But how large should this police force be? The answer to this question depends in large part on the size of the police force of other units in the world organization structure. We must discuss this point in some detail.

If there is an eighth-order node representable by a strong effective world unit, there are also a number of seventh-order nodes. One might constitute the power elite concentrated along the Washington–New York–Boston axis. Others might constitute the power elite in greater metropolitan agglomerates such as Moscow, Peking, Tokyo, and Paris. Perhaps in the future the power elite in New Delhi and other key areas may qualify. Each seventh-order node may in turn be conceived as "lording" it over a series of sixth-order nodes, and so forth, until we come to the grass-roots level. Now, because of the need for prompt action, the presence of only small scale economies and other factors, we can see that it becomes an exceedingly complex problem to provide c-security in the sense of protection against aggression by other major nodes and people inclined to use force or violence. One line of thinking that is current among international analysts and peace scientists is the notion of a balance of power among *blocs* of nations. This notion—which may well be out of date one or two years hence—visualizes that blocs of nations exist, each with overkill capacity. So size no longer matters, but speed of action and reaction does. More important, a universal recognition arises that, because of built-in reaction systems, all lose everything if a major conflict materializes. Because everyone has everything to lose by such a conflict, and nothing to gain, no one is motivated to initiate a major conflict.

The recognition of this point by all Big Powers suggests that these powers might be motivated to disarm in balanced fashion, by large or small steps. Such a process is very difficult to achieve, as history testifies. Actually, history records that by and large the Big Powers have moved in the opposite direction. In recent decades, they have armed more and more in a rather balanced manner, thereby increasing still more their overkill capacity. (In specific directions, though, they may reduce armaments in a balanced fashion, by small steps.) Thus the question of the size of a police force in a new world unit relative to the police force of a major power is a thorny one. Nonetheless, it must be confronted.

Ideally, the military-police power of each of the seventh-order nodes should be reduced considerably, to well below that of the world unit. In turn, the police force of each of the sixth-order nodes should be considerably below that of its respective seventh-order node; and so forth. This is very unlikely in the foreseeable future. On the other hand, even though the Big Powers are armed well and above the threshold of overkill, some analysts argue that this type of situation is stable, provided the Big Powers recognize (as they do) that all lose in any major conflict. More specifically, they argue that a node, if it is a major power, may maintain its strength in order to preserve relative position among Big Powers, and also to control all the smaller nodes over which it "lords." In this way, internal conflict within the domain of each major power may be minimized. (When a seventh-order node does not constitute a major power, we may imagine that the world unit steps in and effectively achieves order whenever conflict arises in the domain of that node.) In this sense, stability may be achievable, though it is a stability that has several undesirable features. One is the fact that large amounts of resources are devoted to armaments that could be devoted to peaceful uses. A second is the possibility that a madman might "push the button" that initiates and simultaneously effects universal destruction. A third is the fact that the seventh-order node of each bloc, when it is a major power, may more easily and is more likely to repress sixth, fifth, fourth, and other lower order nodes without intervention by other major powers, because these other powers may consider intervention equivalent to meddling in the internal affairs of the first major power. In effect, each major bloc—the seventh-order node and its hinterland—is a world of its own and all non-seventh-order nodes within a bloc are thus potentially subject, perhaps more than ever, to exploitation and domination by the seventh-order major power.

Of course, we must keep in mind the sharply contrasting point of view, which can be forcefully and convincingly put, that no effective and stable balance of military power is achievable among blocs headed by major powers except a balance of zero or near-zero military power.

Another desirable feature of a bloc arrangement that has been suggested is the increased likelihood that each major power might take on the responsibility to foster and nurture the economic development of all underdeveloped regions within its bloc. That is, it might assume, in a paternalistic fashion, the role of benign dictator, either directly or indirectly. In one sense, this might be construed as economic colonialism. In another sense, it does suggest the responsibility of a seventh-order node to look after the welfare of its "constituents"—or at least to assist the effort of and contribute to the programs of the world unit in this regard. Such, of course, would diminish the level of taxation required by the world unit and also its powers. On certain counts this is desirable, because it would represent decentralization. On other counts it may be undesirable, because it makes the underdeveloped regions still more economically dependent on that Big Power which is its seventh-order node. Of course, where the seventh-order node is not sufficiently industrialized and lacks the necessary capital, personnel, and other resources to assist the underdeveloped regions, we may envisage that the world unit would step in and provide these resources from some stocks which it may build up for these purposes.

Thus we may visualize that the function of providing police protection against aggression by nations through use of force and violence might be assigned to a world unit, as an eighth-order node, and a set of Big Powers, each heading a bloc, as the seventh-order nodes. There may also be at this level one or two blocs headed by nations not yet having attained the status of Big Power, but aspiring to it, though desirably in nonmilitary ways.

Beyond police protection (at all levels), there are other security-type functions which fall within the jurisdiction of the public sector. These relate to fire protection, disease control, and emergency services needed as a result of earthquakes, floods, and other acts of nature. Some of these functions could be partially or largely taken over by a world unit.

Regulation of Multinationals and the Environment

In addition, the world unit should take on a number of regulatory functions. It is not necessary here to go over the several traditional regulatory functions of the public sector. One new one, however, is very clear—it is the regulation of multinational enterprises. Multinational enterprises may be defined as those having substantial productive investments, as well as marketing and sales operations, in more than one country. Some of these enterprises are globally oriented and sensitive to the needs of the people in the several regions where they produce and market their goods, whether developed or underdeveloped. Most are not. Some are egocentric. Some are profit-mad. Some are highly materialistic, and so forth. Clearly their activities can involve exploitation, as when they are able to evade taxation by various devices (as a number notoriously do), and when they otherwise fail to support financially the services and programs provided by both governmental and nongovernmental units in the several nations in which they operate. Multinational enterprises should be required to contribute financially to these units. They should be regulated so that they cannot exploit the people of a region or profit from manipulation and dealings on international money markets, thereby interfering with sound monetary and fiscal policies of nations. They must not be permitted to use their economic power to interfere with the political freedom and rights of a population (as ITT attempted to do in Chile), or to influence the operation of political parties within national units (as they did with regard to the Republican party in the United States in 1972). Their operations, like the operations of local enterprises in a region, should be required to be consistent with local, regional, and national plans, and in time, global plans. But to do this requires a governmental unit or organization that is multinational in character, not just national, because agreement on the manner of their regulation must be reached among two or more nations. Here, then, is another major function of a new world unit endowed with effective regulatory authority.

For example, when the regulated activity concerns the operations of international monopolies, such as found in the communications sector, the world unit may need to consider regulating the price that is charged to the consumer. As with intranational regulation of monopolies, discussed in Chapter 13, marginal cost pricing may be required if the communications activity is subject to decreasing unit costs because of scale economies. The case for this would be even stronger if marginal cost pricing permitted profits for an enterprise engaged in the activity. Or, if marginal cost pricing would involve losses for the enterprise, the world unit might assent to average cost pricing, even though this would mean higher prices and lower output, and thus less consumption. Or the world unit might insist on marginal cost pricing to effect lower prices and more consumption, but provide a subsidy to cover the losses of an enterprise.

As emphatically stated several times, a major, and perhaps the most important, regulatory function of the world unit would center around environmental management. This regulatory function must also be viewed in terms of the broader framework of externalities control and management, as discussed in Chapter 13. The world unit might require, on a worldwide basis, that all emitting activities pay to appropriate governmental authorities an amount equal to the social costs caused by the pollutants they emit. For each enterprise, this would entail an upward shift in its average and marginal cost curves, and thus a shift of the relevant industry's supply curve upward and to the left, as suggested in Figure 13.7. Or the world unit might require each enterprise to use pollution-control equipment, say the very best in terms of state-of-the-art technology. This would lead to the same kinds of shifts in average and marginal costs curves and in the industry supply curve. Further, the world unit might require each consumer who generates pollution in his consumption activity to pay the resulting social cost. This would have the effect of lowering his effective demand curve for the product he consumes, and thus the market demand curve for the commodity consumed would shift downward and to the right, as indicated in Figure 13.8.

Taking into account externalities also means taking into account social benefits. Here the world unit plays a major role in its various social welfare programs designed to achieve social justice. In Chapter 13, we indicated how the notion of social benefits can be conceptually incorporated in the effective demand curve for a product. But in many other chapters also, we have been concerned with properly constraining social justice objectives so as to achieve a certain amount of efficiency. This has been so whether we were discussing the problems of ghettos and other subareas in a metropolitan region or of the many regions in the United States, or of India and the many other regions of the world.

Looked at in one way, this book concerns the attainment of a balance between social justice and efficiency within a multiregion framework. This also must be a basic concern of the world unit. Hence, we can now proceed to summarize the contents of each chapter from the viewpoint of the operation of a world unit. As we do so, we also keep in mind the traditional public sector function to supply basic information useful to citizens. For example, individuals need information on the employment market, or on the types and quality of goods being produced. Businesses need information on new technological developments, prices in different markets, and labor conditions in different regions. Farmers need information on new kinds of crops, new ways of cultivation, and prices in various markets. Because of scale economies in the collection and processing of such information, it would be highly inefficient and in most cases too costly for each behaving unit to collect and process information on its own. So the world unit or other governmental and nongovernmental units must do this. But also, as we shall see, the world unit will need to collect and process information for achieving its own social justice and efficiency objectives.

SUMMARY OF THE BOOK FROM A WORLD ORGANIZATION VIEW

Each of the chapters of this book directly pertains to some problem of world organization, or to some elements of the analytical framework that will be required in the pursuit of a balance of social justice and efficiency. In Chapter 2, we addressed ourselves to the question of relevant properties of cities and regions, identifying jobs and adequate income as two key properties. We then viewed the job- and income-creating sectors of a region's economy, as they are interconnected, with the use of the input-output framework.

Of course, from the standpoint of world organization, the concern with gainful economic employment and adequate income for all peoples is of utmost importance. We shall certainly need to have some centralized collection and processing of data in input-output format, to know what is going on at any point in time—not only in the world as a whole but also in each one of its major regions and in each national or other regional unit. We want to be in a position to evaluate how well the world economy and the economies of its different regions are performing, especially problem regions (including those in the process of development). Hence, we will constantly need data in regional input-output form, as was made clear in the discussion of social problems in Chapters 2 and 3. Within the world unit a central statistical agency, collecting, compiling, and processing data in input-output and many other ways, will be essential.

The need for such work may be less pressing for the development of input-output tables at the local and metropolitan region level, though such tabulations are as important as those at the world region level. Yet the work of the world unit in developing standard procedures and how-to-do-it manuals, together with the development of quality data, can be extremely useful both in cutting costs of all input-output work and in improving its quality.

Moreover, as we noted, the centralized collection and processing of data must go beyond the economic realm and embrace the ecologic. The rapid industrialization and urbanization of the world threatens to disrupt the physical environment. This threat is extremely serious, necessitating action by the world and other behaving units to set proper constraints on the economic and other activities in which we engage. So an essential task will be to describe with data what is currently happening, and constantly update the data. Here we find an input-output format, with additional rows for ecologic commodities and additional columns for strategic ecologic production processes, exceedingly useful.

People, resources, economic activities, and organizations are spatially distributed in different patterns and densities, as indicated in Chapter 3. Our concern with the balance between social justice and efficiency, then, must relate to the real-life spatial distributions of all of these. But to understand these distributions the world and other governmental units must collect and process data relating to all kinds of commodity shipments, migration, capital movements, and other spatial flows. The world unit should develop an interregional input-output flows table for the different world regions, as well as a separate, and perhaps more detailed, input-output table for each region. It will want to give particular attention to the exports and imports between pairs of regions, and must be alert to any undesirable trends or developments.

We must constantly bear in mind that the advantages stemming from geographic specialization—due to different resource endowments in different parts of the world, and exploitation of scale-localization-urbanization economies—also mean increasing interdependence of regional economies. As more and more regional economies become tied to their export activities, they are increasingly vulnerable to any forces of depression in the world economy. We need to watch carefully the growth of the world economy over time, and we can only do this effectively through a world organization with a high-quality statistical and analytical competence. With standard procedures developed (such as those noted above), reliable comparisons can be made. We need sound comparative data on per capita incomes, industrial employment, and productivity by sectors and by regions. In this way we can have more accurate estimates of the discrepancies among regions.

However, other governmental units need to construct interregional input-output tables as well. National units, like the central governments of Japan and Yugoslavia, should do so to help in developing appropriate regional policies within their political boundaries. These tables must also be developed to provide basic information on the export markets of any region, industrial linkages, relative composition of employment opportunities, and other items to the various metropolitan, state, local, and other intranational units.

Both regional scientists and those involved in planning and development agencies at local, metropolitan, national, world region, and world levels must have some knowledge of the workings of the economic market. For this purpose, the analysis of a purely competitive market is extremely useful—both because important sectors of the regional economies of the world still operate under or close to conditions of pure competition, and because in regulating monopolies and other exploitative organizations, it is useful to refer to what an equilibrium price and equilibrium output would be under pure competition. These notions are often useful for thinking about social welfare and social justice. Accordingly, the materials in Chapter 4 which discuss demand and supply schedules and curves, and the determination of an equilibrium market price, are essential. Equally basic for the analysis of social problems in the real world are the different kinds of costs discussed in Chapter 5 that arise in the production of various goods and services, whether they be economic or noneconomic. Most individuals are associated with behaving units that are concerned with maximizing profits from production, gains from trade, or gains from noneconomic activity. Accordingly, these units must be directly concerned with the costs of their operation, because the difference between their costs and the revenues, satisfactions, or other benefits they acquire determines profits and gains. But individual behaving units and private organizations are not the only ones concerned with costs.

In particular, if we think of our world unit, it must look at not only its own costs of operation but also the costs of private sector enterprises. In articulating plans to achieve social justice it must be able to estimate how these costs change with scale of output. To realize scale economies means that production and public facilities cannot be uniformly distributed over space, and that people cannot have equal access to every commodity and service produced. This in turn implies a certain amount of social injustice because of important cost and efficiency considerations.

Once cost analysis (for both new facilities, and the expansion and contraction of existing facilities) is incorporated into the thinking underlying decisions of local, urban, regional, national, world regional, and world authorities, it must be extended to consider the differences in costs that arise at different locations on the earth's surface. That is, it must be extended to incorporate locational cost differentials—for example, labor, transport, and energy cost differentials. These differences among locations and regions must be taken into account by any governmental authority concerned with industrialization to spark economic development. It cannot expect development to be sparked by establishing an industry at a location if that industry were to be forced to operate at high costs, say because of high transport costs to the market and high fuel costs. For a given location, it must consider those industries which can operate most efficiently there. Or, if it must subsidize industries, it should subsidize those which are least inefficient and most likely to become efficient after an infant-industry stage. In essence, the research analyst in the governmental unit must be aware of differentials arising from the use of ubiquities in production, weight losses, transport rates less than proportional to distance, number of loadings and unloadings of materials required, and underemployment in an immobile labor force. Locational analysis, then, is necessary—whether we think of a metropolitan or regional planning authority considering the promotion of new industries in an industrial district to provide jobs for its unemployed, or a nation concerned with the redistribution of industries to rejuvenate depressed areas, or a world unit concerned with introducing a few small factories in a poverty-stricken rural area.

But it is insufficient just to consider the locational cost differentials with respect to a specific industry, in isolation from other industries. Economic as well as other activities agglomerate because of scale, localization, and diverse economies that are possible by spatial juxtaposition. Because of these agglomeration factors, we must consider urbanization phenomena along with industrialization. In fact, a certain amount of urbanization is essential if industrialization is to be healthy and have a sound economic base. Yet we must recognize also that beyond a certain urban mass, agglomeration diseconomies begin to appear. Hence, governmental development or planning agencies must be concerned with the various factors that determine an efficient pattern of cities by city size and spatial distribution. To conduct research on these factors is no easy matter, as noted in Chapter 7. Historically, the question of an optimal size for cities has teased social scientists, city planners, architects, and engineers for centuries. But it is one that has never been, nor is likely to be, satisfactorily answered.

Another approach to the analysis of spatial and other linkages of industries within metropolitan areas and regions of various types is that which is possible with the use of input-output tables. As we know, these tables *depict* interindustry structures in terms of the inputs of each industry to every other industry. The input-output framework can be extremely useful also for *projecting* the nature and type of urban and regional development that might occur as the result of the introduction of a basic new industry or facility. That is, it can be a useful tool for impact analysis. The approach involves many strong assumptions, some of which can be relaxed when a study is being done by a sophisticated input-output analyst in conjunction with those who fully know the region being studied. Together they can determine where and when constant production coefficients and linear relations must be replaced with nonlinear relations and with side computations to effect the appropriate adjustments. Also, they can take into account the limits to expansion and growth, given the available resources for capacity additions, local resistances to change, localization and urbanization economies that might crop up, environmental costs and gains, and labor supply conditions. In addition to use in development planning for both backward and advanced regions, the input-output technique can be a very effective tool for new town planning, particularly when looking at the question of whether a sound economic base exists for a new town.

Although we do not expect policy formulators and decision makers to be familiar with the algebra of input-output (which we presented in Chapter 7), they should be aware of the ways in which input-output computations can be programmed for examining alternative plans for new towns, regional development, industrial districts, and industrial complexes. The computer turns out to be an extremely efficient tool for testing the feasibility and consistency of alternatives. The input-output technique itself is a very flexible tool because sectors can be organized, and aggregated and disaggregated in various ways in order to throw light on the particular problems of a particular region or city, and the various ways of attacking them.

Of course, history is not just the record of the occurrence of a basic new industry development at a location and the subsequent impact as may be spelled out in input-output terms. Much more complex phenomena are involved, as is clear when one studies historical materials on cities throughout the world. Notwithstanding this, the location type of analysis that we can do with the comparative cost approach as developed in Chapter 6, complemented with the agglomeration economies and input-output approaches of Chapter 7, does provide a great deal of understanding of past urban and regional development. The synthesis of these approaches enables a development authority, whether it be local, urban, regional, world regional, or world, to do more effective planning. This synthesis must represent one of its key tools for analysis and evaluation of different development policies.

But if we just use the synthesis—which basically relates to the unrestricted operation of behaving units, and emphasizes efficiency and profit motives—we will be indicating how to make more efficient a system that is highly unjust. We must be directly concerned with the injustice reflected in the increasing discrepancies over time in per capita income and ownership of wealth among areas of the world. It then becomes essential for us in planning and development work to use input-output and comparative costs not only for projecting what might happen at a particular location, particularly when it is positively affected, but also for projecting what happens at other locations where no new industries are located. Sometimes they are favorably affected, other times adversely affected. In any case, we must study these extraregional effects. Thus, we need to obtain a comprehensive interregional input-output snapshot and develop a comprehensive interregional impact analysis. We turned to this problem in Chapter 8.

By focusing on the interrelations of economies through trade, the interregional table is useful for examining the impacts of basic new industries in a given region upon all sectors in all regions. A governmental authority interested in regional or world development will find the analysis of Chapter 8 a necessity in evaluating alternative social welfare programs. It will also find relevant the analysis on the equilibrium price conditions regarding interregional trade as they suggest how the volume of trade may be affected when the authority regulates international monopolies that exploit labor in underdeveloped regions or discriminate among consumers in different world regions. Other interregional aspects that must be examined include the effects of absentee ownership, and particularly obstacles to human migration. We saw that market imperfections have led to increasing per capita income discrepancies. The need for assistance and intervention by a world unit and national and regional governments is still intense—perhaps even more intense as the percentage of those living at the subsistence level continues to increase. This situation is, of course, a challenge to a world government as well as urban and regional planning authorities.

There are a number of other important flows that must be analyzed. We look at population flows with the use of the gravity model. This model enables us to dig more deeply into some of the social problems within metropolitan regions by exposing different perceptions and socioeconomic obstacles and resistances. Also, we examined the flow of capital from one region to another, largely to exploit opportunities for profit in the latter. From an efficiency standpoint this is desirable, in the sense that it permits production of commodities at a lower cost than otherwise. And in general it would appear that consumers gain from lower prices and investors gain from greater returns. Nonetheless, numerous problems and qualifications arise. Investments in an underdeveloped region by foreign capitalists may forestall local initiative, drain profits from the region, lead to insensitivity to the needs and working conditions of the local population, and contribute to instability in international money markets. Further, when capital flows represent foreign assistance provided by one national government to another, they can induce undesirable economic dependence (benign colonialism). So the control of capital flows and their use is a very complex problem, whether viewed from the standpoint of development of world regions or of regions within a nation. Finally, we indicated the importance of noneconomic flows like the flow of ideas and the flow of noneconomic commodities such as c-power. We noted that these flows are quite critical in decision-making among the elite of a nation or world region.

Having considered the economic forces that determine prices and costs, the economic activities that arise at different locations and their impacts, and the trade, migration, and spatial flows that occur in a multiregion society, we confronted another critical aspect of real life. This aspect concerns the way information and actions are perceived, strategies constructed, and decisions made in risky or uncertain situations in which only incomplete knowledge is available. We illustrated this in Chapter 9 with regard to a basic location-investment decision by a Greek industrialist and the decision of a mayor regarding the level of social welfare programs that he will support. We were interested in identifying different methods, and the associated costs, of influencing the decision of an investor or political leader. We saw how different attitudes on his part as well as ours can lead to different estimates of these costs. Further, we saw how related psychological elements enter into the picture and affect perceived payoffs and utilities. That is, we recognized that decision-making by key leaders, investors, and other behaving units in the urban as well as the world scene involves much more than simply sitting down and making clear-cut, objective estimates of the revenues, costs, and profits associated with each action alternative. Rather, several estimates of revenues, costs, and profits can be made for each alternative, each estimate relating to a different state of affairs that might emerge. Then the decision maker may choose one of them as relevant; the one chosen often depends on his attitude. It is in this setting that citizens, concerned groups, and governmental authorities—from the local level up to the world unit—must operate and try to influence or change decisions dealing with everything from the local environment to the direction of world development.

This problem of fuzziness, unpredictability, and indeterminacy concerning decisions that a key leader might make—because we do not know what his attitude is today or might be tomorrow, or what the attitude of his peer group is today or might be tomorrow—is compounded because many important decisions are what we have characterized as *interdependent* decisions. We analyzed these decisions in Chapter 10. Because a behaving unit is not likely to know beforehand what the actions of other behaving units will be, it again confronts elements of uncertainty. All kinds of new elements, many psychological, become involved in any decision. Yet a world unit or a local governmental authority must deal with this and other individuals, trying to constrain or influence their behavior. And this is what we must confront. This happens at the local, metropolitan, regional, multiregional, world regional, and world planning levels.

In Chapter 10, we began to analyze interdependent decision-making situations, often designated *games*. This is an extremely important area for study, for it is here that most major and minor conflicts arise—whether, at the one extreme, they are the typical husband-wife conflicts or, at the other, Big Power conflicts. We paid particular attention to the problems of forestalling deterioration of residential neighborhoods, degradation of the environment by its many users (whether it be litter, noise, carbon monoxide, BOD, or visual degradation), and exhaustion of resource potentials (such as fishing or ocean resources). This type of analysis is also appropriate for analyzing the escalation of military activities and expenditures. Clearly, all these matters must be the concerns of the world unit. But they are also important to the many different kinds of governmental units, organizations, citizen groups, and others motivated to improve social welfare at all levels.

Against the background of Chapter 10, we attempted some analysis and specification of desirable features of cooperative procedures. We immediately recognized in Chapter 11 that though it is possible to point out to participants in a game that there are joint actions that will improve the outcome for each of them (when compared with their current position), it is difficult to induce or persuade them to agree on a specific superior joint action. The participants may have different preferences for the several joint actions that can lead to their mutual improvement. One participant most prefers one joint action—which would improve the lot of both and which may be efficient—and chooses to hold out for it. Another participant most prefers another joint action, which also involves mutual improvement and which may be efficient. Hence, we may have a new conflict—a conflict over which efficient joint action to take.

Obviously some compromise must be suggested to, and adopted by, the participants. In Chapter 11 we looked at some simple (for example, split-the-difference) and some sophisticated (for example, veto incremax) cooperative procedures whereby effective compromises can be reached. We considered desirable properties of cooperative procedures. But we found our current list of desirable properties far from complete. For example, we have no good definition of strategic potential that would allow us to include a property in our list that would recognize this factor for each participant. But we must realize, whatever the conflict that we confront, that it is important to work on the development of a wide variety of cooperative procedures, each based on a set of desirable properties. No one procedure will be successful in all conflict situations. It is essential to have a variety of cooperative procedures to draw upon for effective development work at the small-community as well as at the world level.

Conflict and the resolution of conflict will always be with us. Clearly, one step in achieving resolution is understanding the inner workings of the behaving unit better. When the behaving unit is an individual, we must then become steeped in the traditional field of psychology, which is beyond the jurisdiction of the field of regional science. We have, though, presented relevant materials from psychology relating to utility as a payoff concept, and in relation to attitudes, objectives, and motivations. On the other hand, when the behaving unit is an organization, it is relevant for regional science (as well as many other disciplines) to be involved in the study of its internal workings. It is quite proper for the regional scientist to be concerned with organization theory and to be concerned with how organizations behave, whether they be economic, political, social, or cultural. Admittedly, however, the set of urban and regional problems that have concerned the regional scientist in the past, present, and probably the future are related more directly to the behavior of economic and political organizations than to that of social and cultural organizations. Hence the regional scientist tends to concentrate on the behavior of the former.

We need not repeat how economic and political organizations of all sorts are intimately involved in urban and regional problems—by the actions they take, by the way they constrain the action spaces of individuals and other organizations, and by the way they exercise their power. They are frequently acting in mutually dependent decision-making situations, usually situations of conflict. In any case, whether we wish to understand better what evolves in the urban and regional system or affect what evolves by influencing the actions taken by organizations, we must know how organizations behave. If we wish to do something about urban and regional problems, we will generally need to do something about organizations as well.

In Chapter 12, we saw the difficulty of specifying the why, how, who, when, and where of organizations at any point in time. When we look at organizations we must admit that they can be extremely complex systems of interacting individuals, often reaching inconsistent decisions. This is especially so with big organizations like ITT, the Catholic Church, Mitsubishi, and other entities that wield tremendous economic and political power in the world system. However, because these organizations are huge, powerful, and frequently incomprehensible —to us as well as to their top officials who supposedly know, but actually do not know, all that goes on—it is essential for us to try to comprehend their behavior and ways to influence it. We have already indicated how the multinational corporation requires regulation. This must be done by a new world unit. Perhaps the research staff, analysts, and decision makers in the world unit will never understand more than a fraction of the ways these organizations behave. Nonetheless it is essential to understand as much as we can, both of multinational organizations and the numerous other organizations that operate primarily within national, regional, state, and local boundaries.

But we must recognize that as individuals concerned with social welfare, we must work through organizations. These are frequently the governmental agencies that are, in effect, political organizations, and that we often designate the public sector. Hence, although we may be concerned with ITT and General Motors, their objectives, action spaces, internal structures, and communication channels, we must also be concerned with the same elements of political organizations. Recall our view of world society as a hierarchical organization of nodes and central places. We questioned the rationale behind this view in order to suggest that a different structure might be more efficient in achieving the objectives we think important for world society. In this chapter, we have suggested that a new world unit be added to this hierarchy as an eighth-order node. But now we must be sensitive to various questions. What should be the communications structure in this new hierarchy? How much decentralization should there be in the pattern of decision-making? Who should set goals, and which ones? In determining goals at any specific node, what procedure for representation should be used? How should we resolve the conflicting goals set forth by the different nodes? How should we define membership and the tasks to which each member will be assigned?

Further, we must recognize that the public sector consists of many subsectors, the world unit being one. As a public subsector it will have its own problem of internal organization and communication; its own problem of procedure in defining its goals; its own problem of collecting and processing information, and defining what is relevant; its own problem of maintaining morale, cohesiveness, and productivity; and its own problem of incorporating flexibility into its operations. In short, it will be a complex organization that will need to get started, evolve, and change in structure, function, and character to meet the objectives that are set for it as the node at the top of the world spatial hierarchy.

The world unit as a public subsector will have many functions. In the beginning of this chapter we discussed a number of them, such as control and regulation of multinational enterprises, control of military activities and expenditures, and increasingly, the management and regulation of the environment. Turning to this last function, recall that in Chapter 14 we again posed the problem of conflict in the context of environmental management. We indicated that we need to have systematic and comprehensive data on how the ecologic system operates and how it interacts with other systems, in particular the economic system. We suggested the input-output framework as one effective way of organizing the data on relevant ecological commodities. Clearly, because the information for such a table must be obtained on a worldwide as well as a regional basis in a consistent and systematic fashion, much of the data work and processing must be done and/or coordinated by the world unit. There is no getting around this job. Further, it must take on the tremendously difficult job of defining environmental quality regions for purposes of administration, regulation, and watchdog operations. This job is exceedingly difficult because airsheds, watersheds, and other environmental sheds know no political boundaries. They cut across nations, states, provinces, and world regions. Moreover, they also cut across each other so that no simple pattern for administrative and other purposes is attainable. On the other hand, the strong interrelationship among water, land, air, sonic, visual, and other pollution requires a single, coordinated attack on all pollution.

These, however, will not be the most difficult tasks of the world unit regarding environmental management. The most difficult tasks will be associated with conflict resolution. In Chapter 14, we illustrated some conflicts with respect to recreational development and preservation of coastal wetlands. We characterized these as relatively simple conflicts. And when they arise and are confined within the boundaries of a national unit, they are likely to be by and large manageable. Many conflicts of this type are assignable to the national political unit. But when we get to broader problems such as mercury pollution, ocean pollution, and pollution of airsheds that extend well beyond national boundaries, the world unit certainly will need to intervene to resolve conflicts and to develop proper regulation. In its environmental management work, it will need to consider all indirect and diffusion effects, inclusive of health effects, and estimate as best it can ecological cost differentials among locations. It will need to weigh the demands of the developed nations against those of the developing nations. It will need to take into account the different perceptions of nations, their different notions of equity, their different consumption levels and needs for new industry, their different capabilities to invest in pollution-control equipment, the different degrees to which they have exploited the environment in the past, and so forth. It will be no easy task to evolve policy in this hornet's nest of conflicts.

The conflict problem was extended when we proceeded to discuss development theory and social welfare analysis in Chapter 15. We saw that the concept of development and its measurement can at most be fuzzy, because there are so many key *nonmaterial* dimensions of development that cannot be measured and evaluated. Likewise with the concept of social welfare. Clearly, however, the amount of social welfare obtainable by a regional society is closely linked to the level of its economic development. Such development affects the amount of resources potentially available for educational, health, and many other social welfare programs, particularly those concerned with the nonmaterial dimensions of life. In turn, the level of economic development in a region is related to its export base, which by definition is oriented to demands outside the region, the backward and forward linkages of this base, the agglomeration economies realizable, the extent to which the region has realized and continues to realize growth from import substitution, the extent to which it contains centers that have been and continue to be growth poles with significant spread effects, and so forth. This view of factors conditioning development is one that emphasizes the demand side.

Another equally significant view emphasizes the supply side, with regard to which linear and other mathematical programming techniques can be particularly enlightening. They identify feasible and efficient combinations of output-supplying activities, given resource constraints, and then determine an optimal combination for a stated objective such as maximizing GNP or total employment. Hence, they are exceedingly useful in social welfare planning. But how useful, and the extent to which they should be employed, depends upon the basic values of a society. In the United States and other industrialized nations, where emphasis is placed on the individual's freedom (qualified to preclude him from exploiting others as well as certain community resources and values), the role for social welfare planning and thus development programming is rather small. In the context of the United Nations, where emphasis is placed on cooperative solutions (joint actions), subject to certain guarantees of individual freedom, the role for social welfare and development programming is correspondingly large. But it is only a potential role at the moment, because of the UN's small command of resources.

At this point, we clearly see one of the conflict dimensions that is likely to emerge concerning the establishment of a world unit. The "have-not" nations are likely to press for the establishment of such a unit having substantial taxing powers, broad social planning powers, and control over a major program of development assistance. The "have" nations are likely to want a world unit having minimal taxing powers, limited social planning powers, and little ability to support development assistance. From the practical standpoint, it is the individuals of the "have" nations who are likely to be most curtailed in their economic activities and promotion schemes. Moreover, the "have" nations are the ones likely to be subject to the largest amount of taxation for social welfare planning.

In Chapter 16, we broadened the framework of mathematical programming to encompass a multiregion system and showed specifically how programming techniques are useful. We can specify constraints and the objective function in terms of magnitudes that are considered significant as social welfare indices. We can observe the cost of setting a constraint, and how this cost varies for different alternatives involving different levels for the constraint. Further, we can state constraints in terms of goals of regions, or levels of specific programs that might be reasonable.

However, whether we do specify goals, programs, or both as constraints, all kinds of conflicts will be generated. There will be a tremendous number and variety of differences among individuals and interest groups as to their preferences for these goals and programs. These innumerable conflicts will need to be resolved by a central planning authority within a world unit, just as they are by central planning authorities within existing national units.

In achieving reconciliation of conflicts among regions relating to differences in basic values, desired goals, and desired levels and composition of specific programs, a central planning agency may want to fall back as much as possible on the political process as a "natural" resolution mechanism, and one that is likely to reflect the underlying or implicit social welfare function of the multiregion system. But where it cannot rely on the political process, it must look at possible cooperative procedures, particularly those for breaking deadlocks, such as the ones we discussed in Chapter 16 in the context of a three-region conflict situation over goals.

Finally, in Chapter 17 we presented the tale of Puerto Rico, an experience in economic development. From the standpoint of a regional scientist at the midpoint of the twentieth century, this experience was very successful. The strong elements of existing analytical techniques were combined and formulated in new ways to meet the particular problems and situation of Puerto Rico. An industrial complex technique was forged, and the findings of a study employing this technique were utilized to help spark a significant industrial development. By 1970, the pot-bellies and other evidence of grinding poverty, at least that which was visible, had disappeared.

From the standpoint of a regional scientist going into the last quarter of the twentieth century, the experience of Puerto Rico was at best only somewhat successful. Though all the criteria of success as set down by him in 1950 were achieved, negative scores must be set down on criteria that had been ignored in 1950, but cannot be ignored in 1975. We do not need to repeat the importance of the noneconomic dimensions associated with the identity and cohesiveness of a society, the preservation of cultural and social institutions, and the maintenance of the physical environment. The Puerto Rican experience clearly points up the need to utilize the broader definitions of development as discussed in Chapter 15. It indicates that along with changes in economic indices, we must carefully watch changes in social and environmental indices as development proceeds. It also suggests, as we move into a future world of increasing affluence and industrialization, that positive social and political development for many regions, Puerto Rico included, may require preclusion of economic growth. In fact, we may need to conduct industrial complex analysis in reverse.

One challenge for the regional scientist of 1975 is the evolution of an overall or "total" index of development, which we now lack. It should synthesize appropriately and effectively the numerous indices we have been using, as well as others that need to be developed to take into account dimensions thus far not made precise and recorded.

This problem will also challenge, strain, and vex the key decision makers and leaders of any effective world unit that may evolve as an eighth-order node. This problem will be very taxing because, as already noted, social development processes in different world regions are not isolated. They are complexly, and too often subtly, interdependent. It is difficult to relate the level of the cohesiveness of the culture in one world region with that in another, something that needs to be done to take into account security and other values. For this reason, analysts of the world unit may justify their not attacking directly this phase of the problem. On the other hand, the interconnectedness of economic and industrial development in the different world regions, because of their impact on the physical environment, cannot be ignored. Concretely, the world unit cannot ignore the contribution of each world region to the total pollution load and in turn the feedback impact upon the welfare of other world regions. Hence, this interconnectedness, as it directly impinges on the physical environment, will compel the world unit to evolve a total index of development, which is much more than a refined concept of GNP or GWP. This index will need to cover basic noneconomic dimensions, however inadequately it may be possible to do so.

CONCLUDING REMARKS

We now bring this chapter and book to a close. We see that the work of a regional scientist must be directed at all levels of regions—from the small community at one end of the scale to the world region at the other.

His concern may be for a single region or a multiregion system. His problem may be to obtain and process data in developing an essential and accurate description of the current state and trends of a region or multiregion system. He may be conducting partial analyses such as a single industry (fertilizer) or a single sector (housing) study. At a more complicated level, he may want to plan new complexes (industrial districts, activity complexes, new towns, urban complexes), or invigorate depressed regions, or revitalize metropolitan subareas (ghetto rehabilitation). Or, at a still more complicated level, he may be developing a transportation network for a multiregion system (such as for Japan), or evolving an environmental management policy for a multinational region (such as the Baltic Sea and the surrounding lands), or studying an optimal pattern of cities for a continent (like North America or Africa). Or, at the most complicated level, he may propose the structure and functions of a new node within the hierarchical structure of the world order, capable of evolving and administering a world environmental-management policy and a multiregion development program, as well as a program for curtailment of military expenditures and control of multinationals.

A tremendous variety of studies can be undertaken by regional scientists. In such studies, they will need to apply today, and evolve and apply tomorrow, a variety of *theories* ranging from partial to general equilibrium, and from static to dynamic—in the areas of location, consumption and production, transportation and spatial flows, land and other resource utilization, city systems and population distributions, organizations and interest groups, interdependent decision-making and conflict resolution, and development and social welfare in general. At the same time, they will need to use and develop a variety of *techniques* and *operational models* that go well beyond those currently used: comparative cost, industrial complex. input-output, linear programming, integer programming, simulation models, and multivariate and other techniques. In all this, they must be concerned with diverse problems. At the one extreme, they must provide subsistence for a local population; at the other, they must be concerned with broad issues of world social welfare.

We must end the book, recalling that it is an introduction only—an introduction to a multidisciplinary way of thinking about a number of critical social problem areas, and of orienting new concepts, theories, and techniques. One thing is clear. A number of fruitful paths for research, both theoretical and applied, now emanate from regional science.

Index